Contents

CD-ROM

These chapters can be found on the ActiveBook CD-ROM in the back of this student book under the 'Additional chapters' menu. Click on the PDF on the first page of the chapter to print or use the ActiveBook pages in class.

T129S4A

Welcome to OCR GCSE History B Modern World History

This book has been written specifically to support you during your OCR History B GCSE Modern World History.

The course includes a student book with ActiveBook, a teacher guide and an ActiveTeach CD-ROM.

HOW TO USE THIS BOOK

The OCR GCSE History B (Modern World) student book covers all of the content in the OCR J417 specification. Chapters match the sections in the specification and the information is divided into key questions to directly match the specification. The following studies in depth can be found on the ActiveBook CD-ROM:

- Mao's China, c.1930–76
- Causes and events of the First World War, 1890–1918
- End of Empire, 1919–69
- The USA, 1945–75: Land of freedom?

Click on the PDF of the first page of each chapter to print or use the ActiveBook pages in class.

Lots of the lessons begin with a 'Getting Started' activity to encourage you to really think about the content right from the beginning of the lesson.

Each lesson has objectives so you know what you will learn and which skills you will be developing in each lesson.

Definitions of new words can be found in the margin next to where the word appears in the text to help put the word in context. All key words can also be found in the Glossary (pp. 377–378).

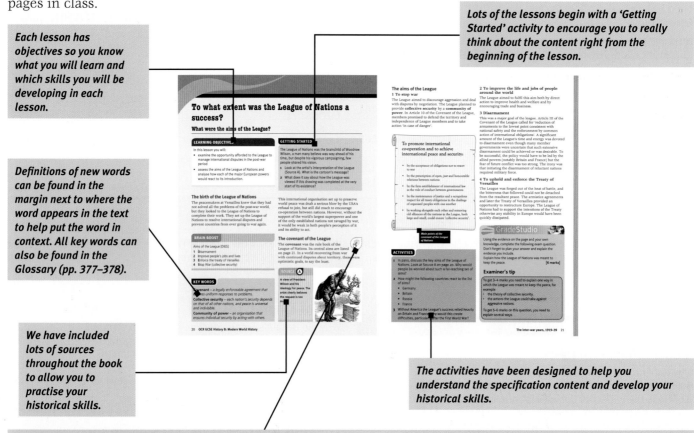

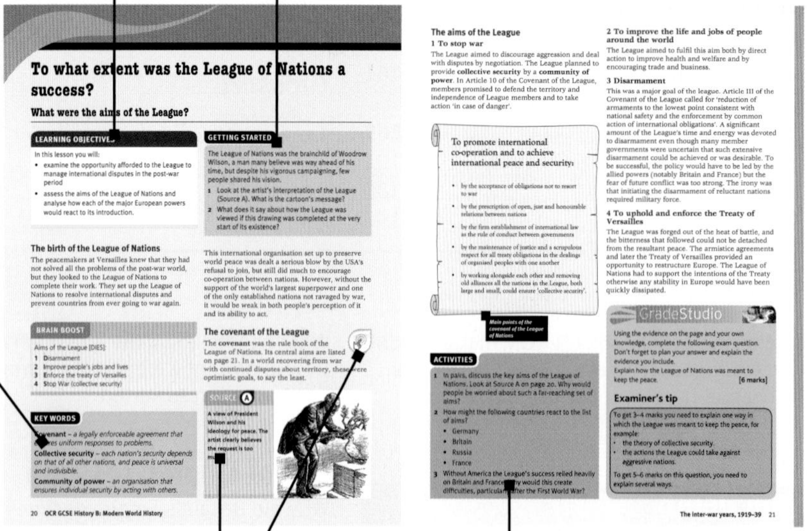

We have included lots of sources throughout the book to allow you to practise your historical skills.

The activities have been designed to help you understand the specification content and develop your historical skills.

The logos represent the following additional resources which are available on the teachers' copy of the ActiveTeach CD-ROM:

Here you will find interactive activities that can be used as a whole-class teaching tool. Activities range from review triangles to interactive maps and decision-making activities. All activities are also accompanied by teacher notes with learning objectives and AfL opportunities.

From here you can launch video clips to support the student book and specification content. All video clips are accompanied by activity notes.

OCR GCSE History B

Mo[...]orld

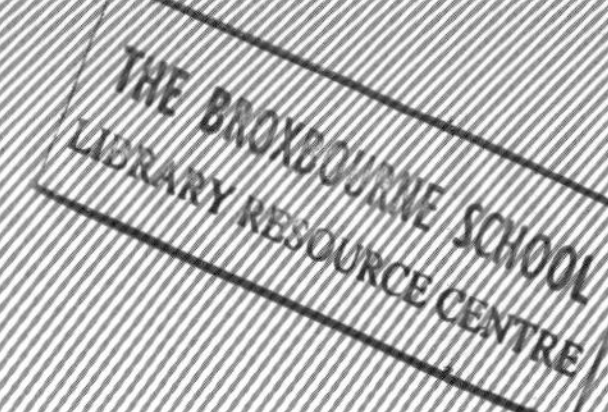

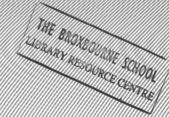

THE BROXBOURNE SCHOOL
LIBRARY RESOURCE CENTRE

THE BROXBOURNE SCHOOL
LIBRARY TEXTBOOK LOAN

This book is loaned by the Library on behalf of the HISTORY DEPT. Please return the book to the library on or before the last date shown below.

~~11 JUL 2016~~ ICA
~~10 JUL 2017 Jodie Ferdenzi~~

-9 JUL 2018

Alex Brodkin Ellen Carringt[...]
Richard Kerridge Greg Lace[...]

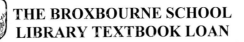

www.heinemann.co.uk

✓ Free online support
✓ Useful weblinks
✓ 24 hour online ordering

01865 888080

CD ROM ISSUED WITH BOOK

OCR AND HEINEMANN ARE WORKING TOGETHER TO PROVIDE BETTER SUPPORT FOR YOU

BROXBOURNE SCHOOL LIBRARY
T12954A0281

Heinemann is an imprint of Pearson Education Limited, a company incorporated in England and Wales, having its registered office at Edinburgh Gate, Harlow, Essex, CM20 2JE. Registered company number: 872828

www.heinemann.co.uk

Heinemann is a registered trademark of Pearson Education Limited

Text © Pearson Education 2009

First published 2009

13 12
10 9 8 7 6 5 4 3

British Library Cataloguing in Publication Data
A catalogue record for this book is available from the British Library

ISBN 978 0 435510 22 0

Copyright notice
All rights reserved. No part of this publication may be reproduced in any form or by any means (including photocopying or storing it in any medium by electronic means and whether or not transiently or incidentally to some other use of this publication) without the written permission of the copyright owner, except in accordance with the provisions of the Copyright, Designs and Patents Act 1988 or under the terms of a licence issued by the Copyright Licensing Agency, Saffron House, 6–10 Kirby Street, London EC1N 8TS (www.cla.co.uk). Applications for the copyright owner's written permission should be addressed to the publisher.

Edited by Caroline Low, Virgo Editorial and Robin Haig
Designed by Pearson Education
Project managed and typeset by Wearset Ltd, Boldon, Tyne and Wear
Original illustrations © Pearson Education, 2009
Illustrated by Tek-Art, Crawley Down, West Sussex and Wearset Ltd, Boldon, Tyne and Wear
Cover design by Pearson Education
Picture research by Q2AMedia
Cover photo/illustration © Getty Images/US Air Force
Printed in China (SWTC/03)

Acknowledgements

The authors and publisher would like to thank the following individuals and organisations for permission to reproduce copyright material:

p9 Source B John Maynard Keynes, *The Economic Consequences of Peace* (1920), Harcourt, Brace and Howe, New York, reproduced with permission of Palgrave Macmillan. **p11 Source B** R, Henig, 'Versailles and After 1919-1933', in Chris Cook, John Stevenson (eds), *The Routledge Companion to World History Since 1914* (2005), Routledge. **p19 Source D** David Kennedy, 'Freedom From Fear' (1999) in David M. Kennedy and C. Vann Woodward (eds), *The Oxford History of the United States: The American People in Depression and War, 1929-45*, Oxford University Press US, by permission of Oxford University Press. **p35 Source F** Penguin. **p81 Source C** Joseph Buttinger, *A Dragon Defiant: A Short History of Vietnam* (1972), published by Praeger, reproduced with permission of Greenwood Publishing Group, Inc., Westport, CT. **p110 Source B** International Publishers. **p119 Source B** Lutterworth. **p164 Source C** Thomas Childers, *Formation of the Nazi Constituency* (1986), Routledge. **p173 Source A (top quotation)** from *The Nazis: A Warning from History* by Laurence Rees, published by BBC Books. Reprinted by permission of The Random House Group Ltd. **p173 Source A (middle quotation)** Penguin. **p173 Source A (bottom quotation)** Michael Burleigh, *The Third Reich: A New History* (2000), Macmillan. **p231 Source A** Michael Lynch, *Stalin and Krushchev: The USSR, 1924-64* (1990), reproduced by permission of Hodder & Stoughton Ltd. **p318 Source C** Flora Thompson and H.J. Massingham, *Lark Rise to Candleford: A Trilogy* (1973), by permission of Oxford University Press. **p347 Source B** McGraw Hill. **p353 Source B** Robert Pearce, *Contemporary Britain 1914-1979* (1997), Pearson Education Ltd.

The authors and publisher would like to thank the following individuals and organisations for permission to reproduce photographs:

p2 Private Collection/Archives Charmet/The Bridgeman Art Library. **p3** Illingworth, Leslie Gilbert/National Library of Wales, Aberystwyth/British Cartoon Archive. **p6T** Rex Features. **p6B** Bettmann/CORBIS. **p7** Mary Evans Picture Library. **p8** Fotolibra. **p9** Punch Ltd. **p12** Mary Evans Picture Library. **p19** Mary Evans Picture Library. **p20** Punch Ltd. **p29** Topham/TopFoto. **p32** David Low/Evening Standard on 19 January 193/British Cartoon Archive. **p35** David Low/Evening Standard on 3 April 193/British Cartoon Archive. **p36** Punch Ltd. **p40** Punch Ltd. **p42** Punch Ltd. **p44** Popperfoto/Getty Images. **p46** David Low/Evening Standard on 15 March 1937/British Cartoon Archive. **p47** Imperial War Museum IWM PST 3140. **p48** David Low/Evening Standard on 20 September 193/British Cartoon Archive. **p55** David Low/Evening Standard on 24 October 194/British Cartoon Archive. **p57** Bettmann/Corbis. **p58** Bettmann/Corbis. **p60** Illingworth, Leslie Gilbert/National Library of Wales, Aberystwyth/British Cartoon Archive. **p65T** Punch Ltd. **p65B** David Low/Evening Standard on 1 April 194/British Cartoon Archive. **p66** Punch Ltd. **p71** Bettmann/Corbis. **p73** Bettmann/Corbis. **p74** Bettmann/Corbis. **p75** Associated Press. **p84** Malcolm Browne/Associated Press. **p85** Bettmann/Corbis. **p90** Private Collection/Peter Newark American Pictures/The Bridgeman Art Library. **p91** Time Life Pictures/Contributor/Getty Images. **p92** Nicholas Garland/Daily Telegraph on 8 May 197/British Cartoon Archive. **p94** Illingworth, Leslie Gilbert/National Library of Wales, Aberystwyth/Daily Mail on 29 October 1962. **p97** Lionel Cironneau/Associated Press. **p99** Michael Rougier/Stringer/Time & Life Pictures/Getty Images. **p101** Bettmann/Corbis. **p102** The Herb Block Foundation. **p104** Josef Koudelka/Magnum Photos. **p105** Nicholas Garland/Daily Telegraph on 5 December 198/British Cartoon Archive. **p107** Bettmann/Corbis. **p108** J.L. Atlan/Sygma/Corbis. **p112** Bettmann/Corbis. **p113** Patrick Robert/Sygma/Corbis. **p115** Associated Press. **p117** Ho New/Reuters. **p118** Alex Wong/Staff/Getty Images News/Getty Images. **p121** Michel Philippot/Sygma/Corbis. **p123** Kurt Strumpf/Associated Press. **p126** Keystone/Getty Images. **p129** Gary Hershorn/Reuters. **p135** Kevin Lamarque/Reuters. **p136** Scott Barbour/Getty Images. **p140** Goran Tomasevic/Reuters. **p141** Olivier Coret/In Visu/Corbis. **p143** Khalid Mohammed/Associated Press. **p145** Rex Features. **p146** Guardian. **p151** German Photographer (20th Century)/Private Collection/Peter Newark Pictures/The Bridgeman Art Library. **p153** Fotolibra. **p154** Three Lions/Stringer/Hulton Archive/Getty Images. **p155** Bettmann/Corbis. **p157** Austrian Archives/Corbis. **p159** Heckscher Museum of Art, Huntington, NY, USA/© DACS /The Bridgeman Art Library. **p161** Hugo Jaeger/Stringer/Time & Life Pictures/Getty Images. **p162** Historical Standard/Corbis. **p167** Bettmann/Corbis. **p169** David Low/Evening Standard on 3 July 193/British Cartoon Archive. **p173** Bettmann/Corbis. **p174** Sidney 'George' Strube/Daily Express on 24 July 193/British Cartoon Archive. **p175** Private Collection/Peter Newark Military Pictures/The Bridgeman Art Library. **p176** Associated Press. **p178** Hulton-Deutsch Collection/Corbis. **p181** Bettmann/Corbis. **p182** A Krause/The Guardian. **p184** Deutsches Historisches Museum, Berlin, Germany/© DHM/The Bridgeman Art Library. **p186L** Bundesarchiv Bild. **p186R** BPK/Nationalgalerie, SMB. **p188T** Hulton-Deutsch Collection/Corbis. **p188B** Bettmann/Corbis. **p189** Deutsches Historisches Museum, Berlin, Germany/© DHM/The Bridgeman Art Library. **p194L** RIA Novosti/TopFoto. **p194R** David King Collection, London. **p197** David King Collection, London. **p198** Hulton Archive/Stringer/Getty Images. **p199** The Print Collector/Alamy. **p204T** INTERFOTO Pressebildagentur/Alamy. **p204B** Popperfoto/Contributor/Getty Images. **p205** Popperfoto/Contributor/Getty Images. **p207** The Print Collector/Alamy. **p209** Keystone Archives/HIP/TopFoto. **p213** INTERFOTO Pressebildagentur/Alamy. **p215** Bettmann/Corbis. **p217** Museum of the Revolution, Moscow, Russia/The Bridgeman Art Library. **p220** Hulton-Deutsch Collection/Corbis. **p226** 1946 (colour litho), Russian School, (20th century)/Private Collection /The Bridgeman Art Library. **p227** Deni, Viktor N. "Vragi piatiletki" 1929. Political poster collection, RU/SU 1072, Hoover Institution Archives. **p228** Margaret Bourke-White/Stringer/Time & Life Pictures/Getty Images. **p229** Austrian Archives/Corbis. **p234** Ian Goodrick/Alamy. **p235** The Illustrated London News Picture Library, London, UK/The Bridgeman Art Library. **p236L** David King Collection, London. **p241** Private Collection/Peter Newark American Pictures/The Bridgeman Art Library. **p244** Bettmann/Corbis. **p245** Private Collection/Peter Newark American Pictures/The Bridgeman Art Library. **p247** FPG/Staff/Hulton Archive/Getty Images. **p248** Hulton Archive/Staff/Hulton Archive/Getty Images. **p249** Hulton Archive/Staff/Hulton Archive/Getty Images. **p252** The Granger Collection/TopFoto. **p253** Jack Benton/Staff/Hulton Archive/Getty Images. **p254** American School, (20th century)/Private Collection/Peter Newark American Pictures/The Bridgeman Art Library. **p257** Bettmann/Corbis. **p258** John Kobal Foundation/Contributor/Hulton Archive/Getty Images. **p262** Bettmann/Corbis. **p263** Bettmann/Corbis. **p265** FPG/Staff/Hulton Archive/Getty Images. **p266** Dorothea Lange/Stringer/Hulton Archive/Getty Images. **p279** 1933 (print), American School, (20th century)/Private Collection/Peter Newark American Pictures/The Bridgeman Art Library. **p281** Private Collection/Peter Newark American Pictures/The Bridgeman Art Library. **p286** Historical Picture Library/Corbis. **p289** Mary Evans Picture Library. **p293** Punch Ltd. **p294** Punch Ltd. **p297L** Punch Ltd. **p297R** Punch Ltd. **p298** Suffrage Atelier/Museum of London. **p301** Mary Evans Picture Library. **p302** Hulton-Deutsch Collection/Corbis. **p303** Private Collection /The Bridgeman Art Library. **p305** Mary Evans Picture Library. **p307** Imperial War Museum, London, UK /The Bridgeman Art Library. **p310** Lordprice Collection/Alamy. **p311** English School, (20th century)/Private Collection/Barbara Singer/The Bridgeman Art Library. **p313** Punch Ltd. **p314** Imperial War Museum. **p316** Imperial War Museum. **p317** The Art Archive/Imperial War Museum. **p318** Mary Evans Picture Library. **p319L** Punch Ltd. **p319R** Hulton/Archive/Getty Images. **p320L** Mary Evans Picture Library. **p320R** Mary Evans Picture Library. **p322** 1909 (colour litho), Walker, Jack (fl.1909)/Private Collection / The Bridgeman Art Library. **p324** Punch Ltd. **p325** Imperial War Museum. **p329** Sidney 'George' Strube/Daily Express on 14 October 194/British Cartoon Archive. **p331** Keystone/Stringer/Getty Images. **p333** Keystone/Stringer/Hulton Archive/Getty Images. **p334** Topham/AP/TopFoto. **p335** Peter Kemp/Associated Press. **p338** Chris Batson/Alamy. **p341L** Hulton-Deutsch Collection/Corbis. **p341R** Michael Cummings. **p346** PA Photos/Topfoto. **p348** Michael Cummings. **p350** Shepard Sherbell/Corbis. **p351** Carl Giles/Sunday Express on 4 February 1973//British Cartoon Archive. **p352** Bettmann/Corbis. **p353** Emmwood (John Musgrave-Wood). **p355** Stanley Franklin/Daily Mirror on 9 June 1964/British Cartoon Archive. **p357** Emmwood [John Musgrave-Wood]/Daily Mail on 3 March 1966/British Cartoon Archive. **p358** Michael Cummings/Daily Express on 1 April 1964/British Cartoon Archive. **p360** Leslie Illingworth/National Library of Wales, Aberystwyth/Daily Mail on 3 November 1961/British Cartoon Archive. **p362** Keith Waite/Daily Mirror on 10 November 1971 /British Cartoon Archive. **p367L** Mary Evans Picture Library. **p367M** Illingworth, Leslie Gilbert/National Library of Wales, Aberystwyth/British Cartoon Archive. **p367R** Nicholas Garland/British Cartoon Archive. **p372L** Mary Evans Picture Library. **p372R** Associated Press. **p374** Mary Evans Picture Library. **p375** Shepard Sherbell/Corbis.

Every effort has been made to contact copyright holders of material reproduced in this book. Any omissions will be rectified in subsequent printings if notice is given to the publishers.

Websites
There are links to relevant websites in this book. In order to ensure that the links are up to date, that the links work, and that the sites are not inadvertently linked to sites that could be considered offensive, we have made the links available on the Heinemann website at www.heinemann.co.uk/hotlinks. When you access the site, the express code is 0220P.

VOICE YOUR OPINION!

There are many important historical debates that you need to be familiar with for your GCSE. We have flagged up some examples throughout the text for you to discuss and form an opinion on.

HISTORY DETECTIVE

There just isn't enough room to include all of the facts in this book so you are going to have to be a detective and find out some for yourself!

FACT FILE

Fact file boxes contain a list of facts important to the historical context and will help you to develop your knowledge.

BRAIN BOOST

Brain Boost sections have been designed to help with your revision and can be re-visited at any time during your course.

GRADE STUDIO

Grade Studio is designed for you to improve your chances of achieving the best possible grades. You will find Grade Studio activities throughout the student book on the CD-ROM. Look for this logo to see where activities will be on the CD-ROM.

VOICE YOUR OPINION!

Wilson's Fourteen Points still stand today as a revolutionary concept. They look as if they could have been written in any decade of the 20th century. Examine the list.

- How many of these points have been agreed today?
- How far would you agree that Wilson's greatest asset was also his weakness?

HISTORY DETECTIVE

Both Lloyd George and Clemenceau were forced to be more hardline because of pressures at home. Can you find out why?

Fact file

- Total troops dead – 8 million
- Total troops wounded – 21 million
- France lost around 250,000 buildings and 8000 sq miles of farmland

BRAIN BOOST

Territory
Reparations
Army
Blame
Blocked from Anschluss

The acrostic above is a useful way of remembering the key impacts the treaty had on Germany. The key word is **blame** (article 231) – it is the link word that justified the allies imposing all the terms.

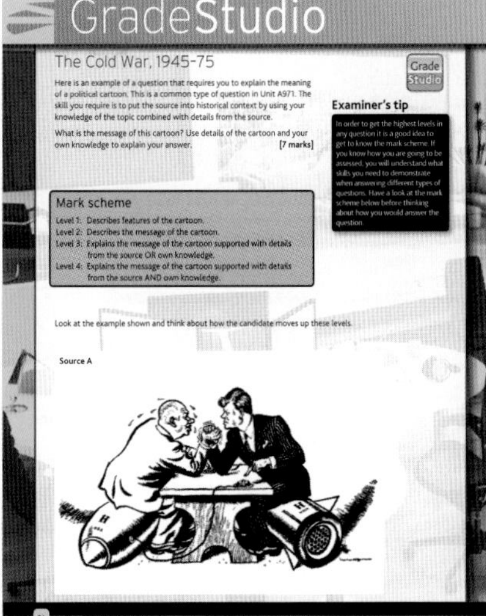

GradeStudio

The Cold War, 1945-75

Here is an example of a question that requires you to explain the meaning of a political cartoon. This is a common type of question in Unit A971. The skill you require is to put the source into historical context by using your knowledge of the topic combined with details from the source.

What is the message of this cartoon? Use details of the cartoon and your own knowledge to explain your answer. **[7 marks]**

Examiner's tip

In order to get the highest levels in any question it is a good idea to get to know the mark scheme. If you know how you are going to be assessed, you will understand what skills you need to demonstrate when answering different types of questions. Have a look at the mark scheme below before thinking about how you would answer the question.

Mark scheme

Level 1: Describes features of the cartoon.
Level 2: Describes the message of the cartoon.
Level 3: Explains the message of the cartoon supported with details from the source OR own knowledge.
Level 4: Explains the message of the cartoon supported with details from the source AND own knowledge.

Look at the example shown and think about how the candidate moves up these levels.

Source A

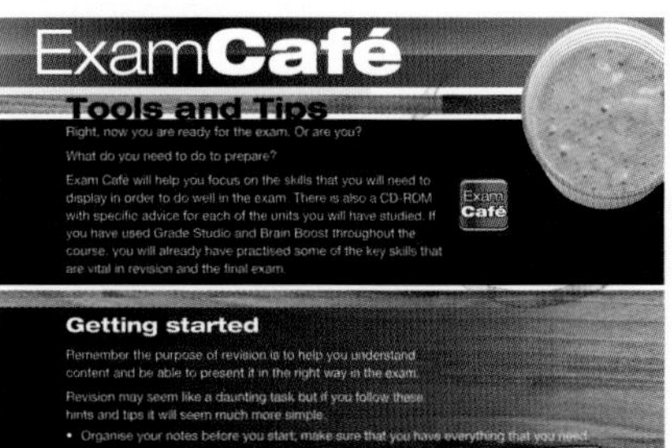

ExamCafé

Tools and Tips

Right, now you are ready for the exam. Or are you?

What do you need to do to prepare?

Exam Café will help you focus on the skills that you will need to display in order to do well in the exam. There is also a CD-ROM with specific advice for each of the units you will have studied. If you have used Grade Studio and Brain Boost throughout the course, you will already have practised some of the key skills that are vital in revision and the final exam.

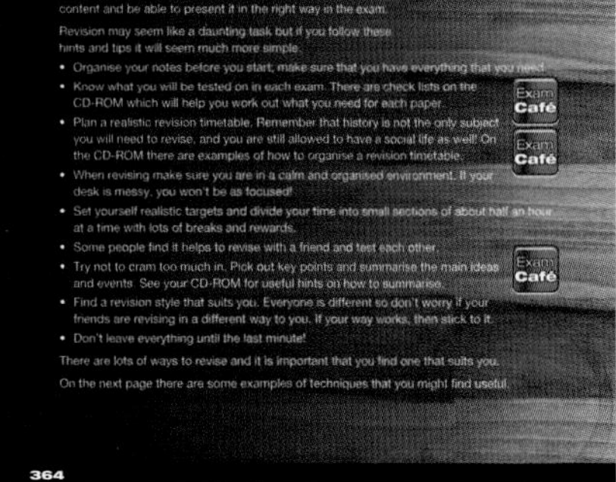

Getting started

Remember the purpose of revision is to help you understand content and be able to present it in the right way in the exam.

Revision may seem like a daunting task but if you follow these hints and tips it will seem much more simple.

- Organise your notes before you start; make sure that you have everything that you need.
- Know what you will be tested on in each exam. There are check lists on the CD-ROM which will help you work out what you need for each paper.
- Plan a realistic revision timetable. Remember that history is not the only subject you will need to revise, and you are still allowed to have a social life as well! On the CD-ROM there are examples of how to organise a revision timetable.
- When revising make sure you are in a calm and organised environment. If your desk is messy, you won't be as focused!
- Set yourself realistic targets and divide your time into small sections of about half an hour at a time with lots of breaks and rewards.
- Some people find it helps to revise with a friend and test each other.
- Try not to cram too much in. Pick out key points and summarise the main ideas and events. See your CD-ROM for useful hints on how to summarise.
- Find a revision style that suits you. Everyone is different so don't worry if your friends are revising in a different way to you. If your way works, then stick to it.
- Don't leave everything until the last minute!

There are lots of ways to revise and it is important that you find one that suits you.

On the next page there are some examples of techniques that you might find useful.

364

EXAM CAFÉ

Exam Café is to be used when revising and preparing for exams. Exam Café could be used in revision classes after school or in revision lessons.

Exam Café will help you prepare for the final exam. Like Grade Studio, Exam Café is in the student book with additional resources on the CD-ROM. From the ActiveBook CD-ROM you will be able to access a number of useful resources which will help you to organise your revision, practise exam questions, access sample mark schemes and locate extra resources to stretch yourself. Look for this logo to see where activities will be on the CD-ROM.

Exam
Café

How to use this ActiveBook CD-ROM

In the back of your copy of the student book you will find an ActiveBook CD-ROM. This is for individual use and includes a copy of the book on-screen, some Grade Studio activities that have been designed for individual student use and the whole Exam Café resource.

ACTIVETEACH CD-ROM FOR TEACHERS

To use the OCR GCSE B Modern World History ActiveBook CD-ROM in a whole-class environment your school needs to purchase the ActiveTeach CD-ROM. The ActiveTeach CD-ROM provides the book on-screen to be used for whole-class teaching and allows you to add your own resources into the Resource Bank and use annotation tools. The Zoom feature helps to examine sources and focus the class. The CD-ROM also includes interactive activities to be used on the whiteboard to engage your class as well as additional video resources.

You will see logos throughout the student book lessons to indicate where additional teaching resources appear on the ActiveTeach CD-ROM. There are over 100 interactive activities and video clips, plus activity notes for all of these resources and all of the teaching notes and worksheets from the teacher guide on the ActiveTeach CD-ROM which are all helpfully divided into lessons to ease your planning. In addition to these interactive activities, there are 16 Grade Studio activities and Exam Café resources for every chapter and specification point.

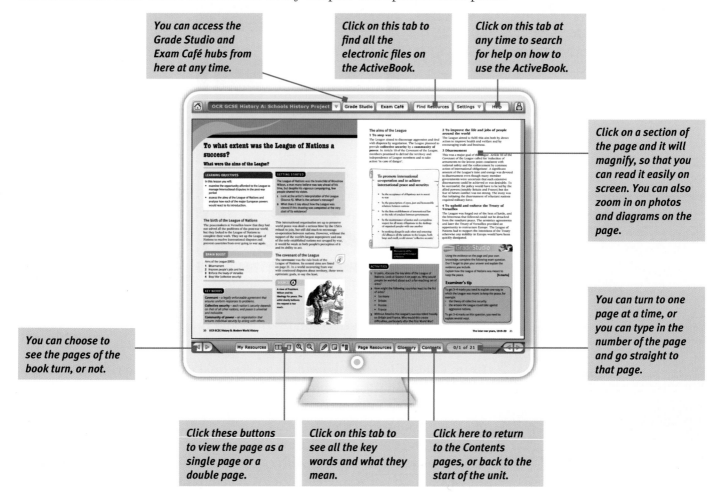

You can access the Grade Studio and Exam Café hubs from here at any time.

Click on this tab to find all the electronic files on the ActiveBook.

Click on this tab at any time to search for help on how to use the ActiveBook.

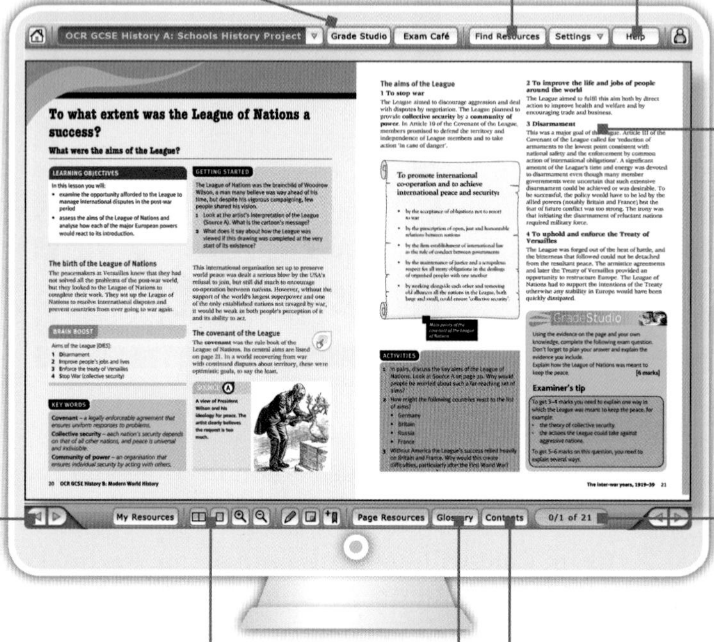

Click on a section of the page and it will magnify, so that you can read it easily on screen. You can also zoom in on photos and diagrams on the page.

You can choose to see the pages of the book turn, or not.

You can turn to one page at a time, or you can type in the number of the page and go straight to that page.

Click these buttons to view the page as a single page or a double page.

Click on this tab to see all the key words and what they mean.

Click here to return to the Contents pages, or back to the start of the unit.

The OCR GCSE History B Modern World History course

The tables below will show you the different options that your teacher will have chosen for you.

FULL COURSE:

Unit A971:		
International Relations: You will study *one* of the following:		
The inter-war years, 1919–39	The Cold War, 1945–75	A new world? 1945–2005
Depth Study: You will study *one* of the following:		
Germany, 1918–45	Russia, 1905–41	
The USA, 1919–41	Causes and events of the First World War, 1890–1918	
The USA, 1945–75: Land of freedom?	Mao's China, c.1930–76	
End of Empire, 1919–69		
Unit A971 is worth 45 per cent of your final mark		

Unit A971 tests what you know about the topics you have studied and how you can apply this knowledge.

Unit A972:	
You will study *one* of the following:	
How was British society changed, 1890–1918?	How far did British society change between 1939 and the mid-1970s?
Unit A972 is worth 30 per cent of your final mark	

Unit A972 tests your ability to analyse and evaluate sources, using your own knowledge to put the sources into historical context.

In the full course you will also complete a single Controlled Assessment unit. You will study a topic and then be given a question to answer. The question changes every year and your answer should be around 2000 words long. Remember that this word limit is only a guideline and some students might do more or less than this.

Controlled Assessment:
You will study *one* of the following:
The role of the individual in history
A thematic study in 20th-century history
A Modern World study 1850–2005
A study in-depth
This unit will be worth 25 per cent of your final mark

UNIT A973: HISTORICAL ENQUIRY

The Controlled Assessment task tests your ability to conduct a historical enquiry. This allows you to form your own opinions and conclusions about the events that you will study.

The focus will depend on which option you complete:

The role of the individual in history:	A thematic study in 20th-century history:	A modern world study:	A study in-depth (1850–2005):
You should consider: • The significance of the individual. • The impact of the individual on other people, both within and beyond their lifetime. • NB: The individual must be from the 20th or 21st century.	You should consider: • The changing nature of the theme over a period of at least 40 years and what led to these changes. • What remained unchanged.	You should consider: • What is happening today and the different ways it is reported. • Why the issue matters today. • How the past and present are connected. • How current issues can only be understood by studying the past.	You should consider: • Different features of society and its diversity. • The values and beliefs of different groups. • Important individuals. • Change and continuity and their causes.
Examples: Rasputin; Hitler; Rosa Parks; Martin Luther King.	**Examples:** Warfare; the role of women; technology and the environment.	**Examples:** International terrorism; the Middle East; the environment; Iraq and Afghanistan.	**Examples:** Germany, 1918–45; Russia, 1905–41; the USA, 1919–41.

You will not be allowed to study anything that you will be assessed on in your options for Unit A971 or A972.

During the assessment you will be allowed to use any notes you have already completed in class as well as other resources such as books, photographs, primary sources and the internet.

You will be assessed on your ability to use historical sources as evidence to support your arguments and conclusions.

HOW SHOULD YOU ORGANISE YOUR NOTES?

It is important to remember that everyone learns in a different way. What might work for the person sitting next to you might not work for you. It is important that you find a style that suits you.

Research has shown that people learn in one of the following ways:

Visual learners	
What is a visual learner?	How do I know if I'm a visual learner?
Visual learners like to learn by looking and seeing.	You may be a visual learner if you: • have neat and organised work • are good at spelling and reading • imagine tasks • follow rules carefully • see things that others miss • remember information by using pictures • like to see instructions • like to use colours in your work.

Auditory learners	
What is an auditory learner?	How do I know if I'm an auditory learner?
Auditory learners like to learn by listening.	You may be an auditory learner if you: • can repeat word for word what has already been said • are easily distracted by noise • prefer to discuss ideas rather than writing them down • move your lips when reading • often sit with your head to one side when listening.

Kinaesthetic learners	
What is a kinaesthetic learner?	How do I know if I'm a kinaesthetic learner?
Kinaesthetic learners like to learn by doing things.	You may be a kinaesthetic learner if you: • use lots of hand movements when you talk • are tactile • need to use your hands when you are learning • move around the room a lot.

- What type of learner are you?
- How could you adapt your notes to make sure that you make the best use of the strengths of your personal learning style?
- Try to keep this in mind whenever you are making notes.

The inter-war years, 1919–39

Introduction

In early 1919, representatives of the victorious powers in the First World War met in Paris to draw up the peace treaties to end the war. The failure of these treaties to create a stable and fair peace settlement made it certain that Europe would face further international problems and disputes. The Treaty of Versailles imposed on an unwilling and embittered Germany was particularly controversial and left the Germans determined to reverse its terms at the first opportunity.

Yet the peacemakers of 1919 sincerely believed that they had given the chance of a peaceful future. They set up the League of Nations to resolve international disputes and prevent countries from ever going to war again. This international organisation set up to preserve world peace was dealt a serious blow by the USA's refusal to join, but still did much to encourage co-operation between nations. Without the world's largest superpower and one of the only established nations not ravaged by war, it would be weak in both people's perception of it and its ability to act. However, the League made a number of useful attempts in the 1920s to reach international agreements to prevent future conflict leading to war. It had some successes, particularly in Greece, in persuading nations to resolve conflicts peacefully.

SOURCE A

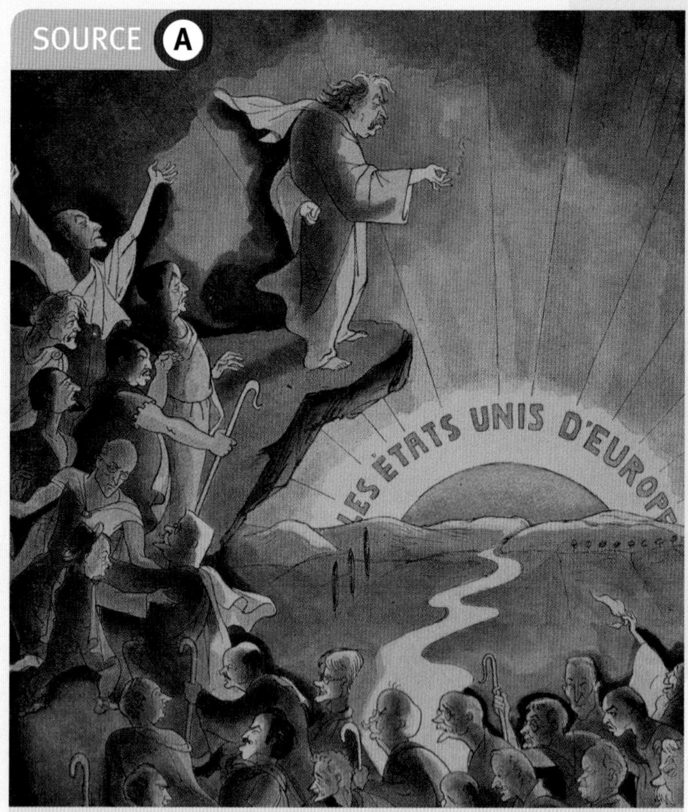

An optimistic French view of the opportunity afforded by the League of Nations.

TIMELINE

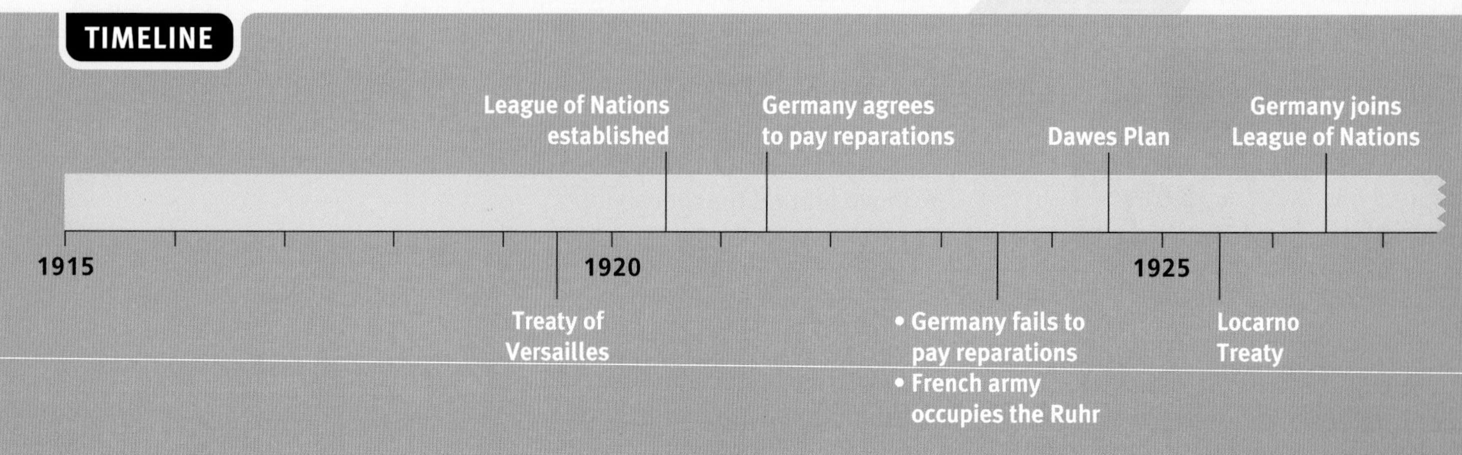

However, the Great Depression, starting in 1929, created a more unstable international climate, in which aggressive nations, prepared to use war to achieve their aims, challenged the principles of international peace and co-operation on which the League was based. The League proved too weak to stand up to Japanese aggression in Manchuria, and could not prevent the Italian invasion of Abyssinia. By the mid-1930s it had lost its authority and had ceased to play an effective part in international affairs.

During the 1930s, the greatest threat to international peace was Hitler's desire to rebuild the military might of Germany and to reverse the territorial losses incurred in the Treaty of Versailles. Ignoring limits placed on Germany by the treaty, he built up the armed forces and followed an aggressive foreign policy which saw Austria, Czechoslovakia and finally Poland fall under Nazi control. Britain and France had followed a policy of appeasement during the 1930s, hoping that differences between them and Hitler could be resolved by negotiation. By September 1939 it was apparent that this policy had failed.

SOURCE B

A prophetic cartoon that illustrates the dangers of managing world affairs in such a way.

ACTIVITIES

The League of Nations was set up after the most destructive war in world history; if successful it would be nothing short of miraculous. Discuss or write a short answer for the following questions.

1 Look at the artist's interpretations of the League in Source A. Why do you think it was not able to carry out its optimistic targets?

2 What does it say about how the League was viewed if this drawing was completed at the very start of its existence?

3 Does it matter that the leading powers in the Peace Conference made up the central backbone of the League?

4 Consider the timeline and the introductory text.

5 a Why do you think the League did not last a generation?

b What was the difference between the 1920s and 1930s?

c Was the League of Nations doomed from the start?

6 Look at the modern cartoon of the UN, the League's successor, in Source B. Do you think that the international community is now able to work collaboratively for peace? Explain your answer.

Were the Peace Treaties of 1919–23 fair?

What were the motives and aims of the 'Big Three' at Versailles?

The terms of the armistice

When nations make peace at the end of a war, they first agree the terms on which they will stop fighting (the armistice), before they meet to discuss and agree the terms of the peace treaty that formally ends the war. The First World War was exceptionally damaging and bitterly fought. As it came to an end, the defeated powers sought an armistice, but the victors were determined that its terms should be so severe that there would be no chance of hostilities breaking out again. The armistice terms came to have an important effect on the terms of the peace treaties themselves. For example, in the armistice agreed with Germany, the principle of **reparations** was accepted. Germany also agreed to leave Alsace-Lorraine, and that its armies would evacuate all areas on the left bank of the Rhine. Each of these found its way into the final peace **treaty**, as did other military restrictions placed on Germany by the armistice. Thus terms that were intended primarily to bring the fighting to an end actually became part of the treaty that punished Germany.

In January 1919 representatives from 32 countries met in Paris for a conference that would make the peace settlement at the end of the First World War. The tasks they faced were huge. The Europe of 1914 had been swept away by the impact of war. Nobody knows how many died in the war – at least eight million fighting men and a further eight million civilians is a reasonable guess.

The Russian and Austro-Hungarian empires had collapsed, the former replaced by an unpredictable communist dictatorship pledged to destroy capitalism throughout the world. Large areas were left devastated by the fighting, and the European economy was shattered by the costs of war.

KEY WORDS

Reparations – *payments made by Germany to compensate other countries for damage caused during the First World War.*

Treaty – *a formal, written agreement between two or more states stating objectives for peace, trade and security.*

KEY PEOPLE

Woodrow Wilson – *President of the USA 1913–21.*

David Lloyd George – *Prime Minister of Britain 1916–22.*

Georges Clemenceau – *Prime Minister of France 1917–20.*

LEARNING OBJECTIVES

In this lesson you will:

- examine the key motives and aims of the 'Big Three' at the peace conference
- evaluate the impact of the different aims and motives in shaping the Treaty of Versailles.

Fact file

- Total troops dead – eight million
- Total troops wounded – 21 million
- France lost around 250,000 buildings and 8000 sq miles of farmland
- Britain spent the modern equivalent of £9 billion on the war (most of this was loaned from the USA)
- Major European countries – Germany, Russia and Austria – collapsed in revolution
- Bad harvests and poor weather led to flu outbreaks across Europe that killed twice as many people as the war.

In these circumstances, to agree a peace settlement that everyone, victors and defeated, found fair and acceptable would have been an impossible task. What is remarkable is that the peacemakers achieved as much as they did.

All the politicians at the Paris Peace Conference were under pressure to meet the expectations of public opinion. The problem was that people in different countries wanted different outcomes.

The Italians were determined to gain the territory that they thought would make them a great power. The French wanted to make Germany pay, and so did the British, although they had a leader who increasingly doubted the wisdom of doing this. The Americans were not really enthusiastic about being involved in European affairs at all. **Wilson**, **Clemenceau**, **Lloyd George** and the Italian Prime Minister, Orlando, all found that they were not free to make the peace they wanted, as public opinion at home would not let them.

Europe before 1919.

Europe after 1919.

ACTIVITIES

Balancing activity

Answer the following questions by placing the countries or their respective leaders on an opinion line.

- Who was to blame for the war?
- Who caused the most damage?
- Who joined the latest?
- Who lost the most men?
- Who was in a position to fix things?
- Who could gain the most from the peace settlement?

VOICE YOUR OPINION!

The peace treaties made with the defeated nations in 1919–20 redrew the map of Europe, set up the League of Nations – the first international organisation for maintaining world peace – and brought freedom to many ethnic groups previously under foreign rule.

- Do you think there are any reasons why this view might be too ambitious?
- How would the nations of Europe devastated by war be able to uphold their promises?

The 'Big Three'

Of the nations that assembled in Paris to make peace, three possessed the power to make decisions which, more often than not, the others would have to accept. These were the great powers that had won the war: the USA, France and Britain. They were represented at the peace conference by President Wilson and prime ministers Clemenceau and Lloyd George, known collectively as the 'Big Three'. Italy and Japan were the other members of the Council of Ten (there were two members from each of the five powers), which met daily at the conference to take all the important decisions.

Great Britain

Lloyd George became leader of Britain's coalition government in 1916. In December 1918 his government won a massive election victory by promising to 'squeeze the German lemon till the pips squeak'. The British blamed the Germans for the war and wanted to make them pay; some even suggested that the Kaiser should be hanged. Lloyd George probably knew early on that a harsh peace would store up trouble, but he was constrained by British public opinion and election promises.

Lloyd George was determined to preserve Britain's interests as the greatest naval power. He also wanted the German fleet sunk – a matter that the Germans resolved by sinking all their ships, held captive at Scapa Flow. By the completion of the treaty, however, British public opinion was shifting. As a trading nation, Britain knew that German recovery was essential to the European economy, and that large reparations payments would make this impossible. The British were not prepared to help France keep Germany weak.

France

Clemenceau became French prime minister in 1917 when defeat in the war seemed a real possibility. He rallied the country, and led it to victory. As chairman of the peace conference, he was personally willing to compromise in order to find a settlement, but he knew what his countrymen expected. France had borne the brunt of the fighting on the Western Front. Much of north-east France was devastated. The French expected Germany to pay for this destruction, and wanted to ensure that Germany would never invade France again.

Clemenceau found it hard to achieve his aims. Neither Britain nor the USA shared France's enthusiasm for punishing Germany, nor did they want to provide guarantees for French security in future. Clemenceau's demand for the German frontier to be pushed back to the Rhine was bluntly rejected. When the terms of the Treaty of Versailles became known, it was condemned throughout France. Within a few months, Clemenceau's government was overthrown and his political career ended.

HISTORY DETECTIVE

Both Lloyd George and Clemenceau were forced to be more hardline because of pressures at home. Can you find out why?

The USA

Woodrow Wilson was a leading democrat in the American government when the war began and became president in 1916. He was a man of strong principles, who found it hard to accept other people's views. At first, he kept the USA out of the war, until by 1917 he had become convinced that 'to make the world safe for democracy' the USA would have to fight the Germans. However, once the war was won, Wilson wanted a fair settlement that would guarantee future world peace. In January 1918 he outlined his 'Fourteen Points', the principles that he believed should guide peacemaking when the war ended (see below). The most important thing was **self-determination** – people of different national groups had the right to rule themselves.

At Paris, Wilson tried to have every decision debated by all 32 nations. But this was too slow, and most nations were interested only in their own problems. Wilson was increasingly forced to compromise on his Fourteen Points, and had to place his hopes in the new League of Nations to put right any problems with the peace treaties.

The Fourteen Points

1. No secret treaties.
2. Freedom of the seas.
3. The removal of economic barriers.
4. The reduction of armaments.
5. Settlement of all colonial claims.
6. Germans to leave Russian territory and a settlement of all questions affecting Russia.
7. Germans to leave Belgium.
8. French territory freed and Alsace-Lorraine returned to France.
9. Italian frontiers adjusted to take into account the nationality of the population.
10. The peoples of the Austro-Hungarian Empire to be given self-determination.
11. Germans to leave Romania, Serbia and Montenegro and international guarantees of their **independence** to be given.
12. The people of the Ottoman Empire to be given self-determination, and the Dardanelles to be permanently opened to international shipping.
13. An independent Polish state to be created with access to the sea.
14. A general association of nations to be formed to give guarantees of political independence to great and small states alike.

VOICE YOUR OPINION!

Wilson's Fourteen Points still stand today as a revolutionary concept. They look as if they could have been written in any decade of the 20th century. Examine the list.

- How many of these points have been agreed today?
- How far would you agree that Wilson's greatest asset was also his weakness?

GradeStudio

Explain why France wanted a harsh peace to be imposed on Germany. **[6 marks]**

ACTIVITIES

1. Why was it so difficult to make a peace settlement which would please everyone?
2. How were the important decisions made during the peace conference?
3. What were the main differences in the aims of the 'Big Three'?

KEY CONCEPTS

Independence – *the condition of being politically free. Essential aspects are liberty to make one's own decisions and free will.*

Self-determination – *freedom of the people of a given area to determine their own political status; independence.*

Get your sources sorted

Essential knowledge:

- Germany had just been defeated in the First World War.
- The peace treaty was imposed on Germany.
- Clemenceau wanted to ruin Germany.
- The treaty blamed Germany for the war and made her pay for ALL the damage.
- Germany lost land, her armed forces, raw materials, colonies and industry.
- The Germans hated the treaty.

Assess the source

What is the message of this cartoon?

SOURCE A

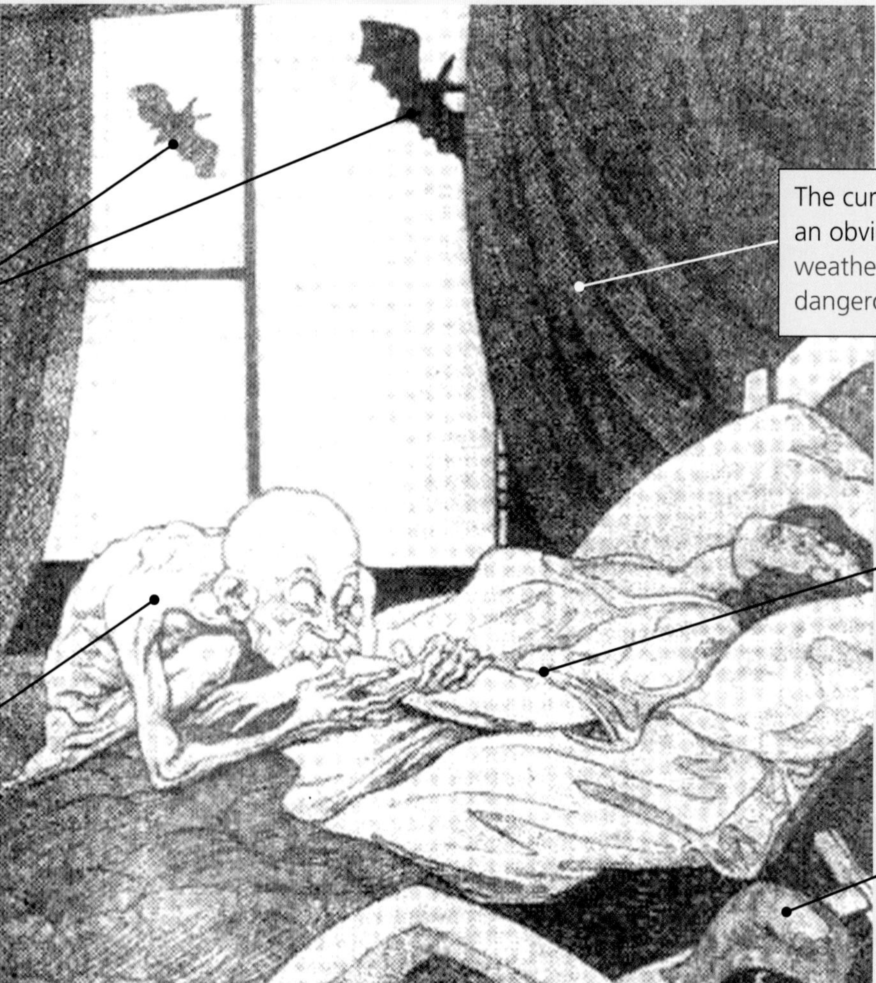

Two bats outside the open window – more vampires? This could mean Britain and America or perhaps even Russia.

The curtains are blowing in an obvious wind. Unstable weather represents the dangerous new Europe.

A young girl, beautiful but sick. The fragile new Germany.

A vampire which is sucking the girl's blood. This quite clearly represents Clemenceau sucking the blood (reparations) from Germany.

Weapons laid aside. Germany is helpless to defend herself because she has lost her army.

A cartoon from a German newspaper, July 1919, called 'Clemenceau the Vampire'. Clemenceau was the prime minister of France. He wanted a treaty that would cripple Germany.

The 3 Cs and a J

Look at the following questions and fill your answer into the frame around the cartoon.

- **Context** – What was happening at the time?
- **Content** – What is happening in the cartoon?
- **Comment** – What is the meaning of the cartoon?
- **Judgement** – Use your own knowledge to put it into context.

SOURCE B

The Treaty includes no provision for the economic rehabilitation of Europe – nothing to make the defeated Central Powers into good neighbours, nothing to stabilise the new States of Europe, nothing to reclaim Russia; nor does it promote in any way a compact of economic solidarity or to adjust the systems of the Old World and the New ... Reparation was their main excursion into the economic field, and they settled it from every point of view except that of the economic future of the States whose destiny they were handling.

John Maynard Keynes, *The Economic Consequences of Peace* (1920).

This means that nobody really thought about how each country would rebuild its economy.

Europe was at a crisis point before the war because some countries had been greedy capturing land and resources. There was an imbalance of power. Versailles, dominated by Britain, France and the USA, did nothing to change this.

According to Maynard Keynes the biggest concern of the Big Three was to help themselves.

This source is an excellent example of contemporary opinion because it was produced one year after the treaty was signed.

SOURCE C

We hoped to establish justice, fair-dealing between nations, and the honest keeping of promises; we thought to establish a good and lasting peace which would, of necessity, have been established on good will. The Peace Treaty has done nothing of the kind.

General Hubert Gough, speech at a Union of Democratic Control (11 November 1920).

GIVING HIM ROPE?
German Criminal (to Allied Police). "Here, I say, stop! You're hurting me! [Aside] If I only whine enough I may be able to wriggle out of this yet."

***This cartoon by a British artist appeared in* Punch *on 19 February 1919. The caption reads:* German Criminal to Allied Police: *Here, I say, stop! You're hurting me!* (Aside: *If I only whine enough I may be able to wriggle out of this yet.*)**

ACTIVITIES

- Examine the visual sources and apply the methodology to analyse them.
- Evaluate your ability to use the method and the purpose of each element.

Study how Sources A and B have been analysed, then with the help of your teacher try the remaining examples. The 3 Cs frame is a good way to get you started. Applying the 3 Cs and then adding judgement is a very good way of accessing the top levels of the mark scheme because it encourages you to link your thoughts together.

Why did the victors not get everything they wanted?

LEARNING OBJECTIVES

In this lesson you will:

- examine the difficulties of the discussions at Versailles and why it was hard to satisfy such a diverse range of people
- evaluate the concerns shared by the Big Three and assess the ambitions of the peacemakers in context.

GETTING STARTED

Look at Source A. If this is a fair illustration of Wilson in the post-war period, can you suggest a reason why

a he may not be in tune with his fellow peacemakers?

b the peace treaty could be very prone to failure?

KEY WORDS

Armistice – *agreement to stop fighting so that peace terms can be discussed.*

Concession – *a part of an agreement that acknowledges one group's right to a request. Concessions are often traded to broker an overall agreement.*

KEY CONCEPTS

Pragmatism – *a practical, matter-of-fact way of approaching or assessing situations or of solving problems.*

Obligation – *a social, legal or moral requirement, such as a duty or promise that compels one to follow or avoid a particular course of action.*

SOURCE A

A cartoon from an American newspaper in 1919 that depicts Wilson as admirable but ultimately misguided.

Concession with contempt

Once the conference met, the Big Three came to realise that compromises would be necessary. They frequently and strongly disagreed. The British and French would not accept Wilson's vision of a new international order based on the Fourteen Points, and the British and the Americans would not back up France in making a peace that would keep Germany weak.

However, all leaders got their way on some issues, and failed to do so on others.

- Although he championed the rights of different nationalities to rule themselves, in dealing with Italy's and Japan's territorial demands Wilson was prepared to give way and to ignore this principle of self-determination. Had he not done so, they would have refused to sign the treaties.
- Lloyd George fought hard to keep German territorial losses to a minimum, and argued for more German border areas to be given plebiscites (a vote on which country to join), but he was also capable of insisting on increases in reparation payments to suit British interests.
- When Clemenceau insisted on the German frontier being pushed back to the Rhine, Wilson threatened to quit the conference and return home. The French had to be satisfied with the demilitarisation of the Rhineland.

To make matters worse, the British very quickly came to see the Treaty of Versailles as a mistake. Quite clearly, none of the victors got the peace they wanted, not least because they all wanted a different kind of peace. However, even when the nations first assembled in Paris, they were not free to shape the peace as they wished. Four important factors limited their freedom of action.

1 Wartime commitments and secret treaties

While the war was going on, a number of promises of territory were made to certain countries to encourage them to fight. Now that the war was over, these nations would expect the promises to be kept.

- Italy had joined the war on the Allies' side after the secret Treaty of London (1915) was signed, promising it a share in any partition of the Ottoman Empire or of German colonies, as well as significant areas of the Austro-Hungarian Empire.
- Japan's claims on China and parts of the German Pacific Empire had also been supported by the British in 1917.

Wilson was horrified to hear of the extent of these commitments, most of which went against his principle of self-determination. Britain and France were much less enthusiastic about keeping their side of these bargains once the fighting stopped, but sometimes they could not avoid it.

Although the more extreme of the Italian demands for territory were resisted by the Allies at the peace conference, Italy still made substantial gains from Austria in South Tyrol, Trentino and Istria (but not the port of Fiume, which was given to Yugoslavia).

2 The collapse of the Russian and Austro-Hungarian empires

In early 1917 the Russian monarchy had collapsed under the pressures of fighting a losing war against Germany and Austria-Hungary. By the end of the year, Russia was defeated. In March 1918 Russia's new Bolshevik government signed the Treaty of Brest-Litovsk with the Germans. Under the harsh terms of this treaty, Russia gave up huge areas on its western borders: Finland, the Baltic States, its Polish provinces and the Ukraine. Although the treaty was annulled by Germany's defeat, most of the lost territory (the exception was the Ukraine) was not recovered by Russia, which was embroiled in civil war until 1920. The populations of these areas were quite distinct national groups. As neither Germany nor Russia would rule them, they would rule themselves. The peacemakers might discuss or adjust the frontiers of these states, but Germany's defeat and Russia's collapse brought them into existence.

Similarly, in Austria-Hungary the war brought the end of the monarchy. This sprawling central European empire contained dozens of different national groups. Some, such as the Czechs and Slovaks, declared their independence while the war still continued. As the empire fell apart, new countries emerged in its place. When the peace conference met, the new states of Austria, Hungary, Czechoslovakia and Yugoslavia already existed. True, their boundaries had not been finally decided, but the peacemakers did not make extensive changes to them.

3 The terms of the armistice

When nations make peace at the end of a war, they must first agree the terms on which they will stop fighting (the **armistice**) before they meet to discuss and agree the terms of the peace treaty that formally ends the war. The armistice terms were particularly severe after the destruction and brutality of the First World War, and these came to have an important effect on the peace treaties themselves. For example, in the armistice agreed with Germany, the principle of reparations was accepted. Germany also agreed to leave Alsace-Lorraine and that its armies would evacuate all areas on the left bank of the Rhine. Each of these found its way into the final peace treaty.

SOURCE B

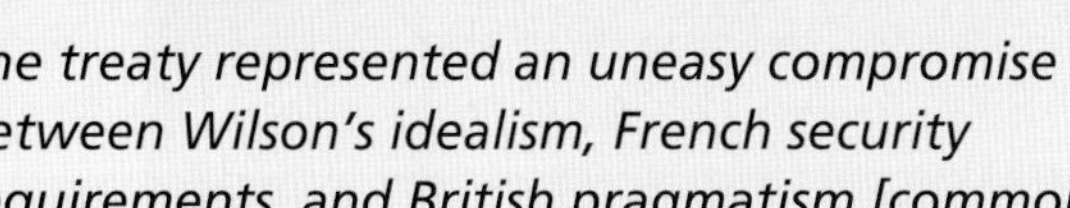

The treaty represented an uneasy compromise between Wilson's idealism, French security requirements, and British pragmatism [common sense].

The British historian R. Henig, speaking in 1995.

4 Public opinion

All the politicians at the Paris Peace Conference were under pressure to meet the expectations of public opinion. The problem was that people in different countries wanted different outcomes. For example, the Italians were determined to gain the territory that they thought would make them a great power. Wilson, Clemenceau, Lloyd George and the Italian Prime Minister, Orlando, all found that they were not free to agree the peace terms they wanted, as public opinion at home would not let them.

VOICE YOUR OPINION!

- What do you think they got right at Versailles?
- What were the dangers of the decisions?
- How accurate are the following historical equation statements for Europe after 1919?

  Too independent = too weak
  Weak Germany = weak Europe

  Now try one of your own.

The terms of the treaty

War guilt	Germany had to accept the blame for the war.
Article 231 of the treaty	'Germany accepts responsibility for causing all the loss and damage to which the Allied governments have been subjected as a consequence of the war imposed upon them by the aggression of Germany.'
Military restrictions	Tight restrictions were placed on Germany's armed forces. • No air force. • Army limited to 100,000 men. No conscription. • No tanks. • Navy limited to 15,000 men. • No submarines. • Size and number of naval ships limited.
Reparations	As Germany accepted the blame for the war, the Allies could demand payment for all the damage caused. Germany was required to pay compensation – reparations – to the Allies. A Reparations Commission was set up to fix the amount. It reported in 1921. Germany was presented with a demand for £6600 million.
German territory	Germany lost all of its colonies overseas. Alsace-Lorraine and the Saar coal region in western Germany were also lost. A union or 'Anschluss' with Austria was forbidden. Western Prussia and Upper Silesia went to a new Poland. Danzig became a free city protected by the League of Nations.
The League of Nations	The first item in all the peace treaties with the defeated nations was the 'Covenant' (the rules) setting up the League of Nations.

SOURCE C

A German cartoon from 1919 about the Treaty of Versailles. It shows the figure of Germany about to be guillotined. The other three figures (left to right) are Wilson, Clemenceau and Lloyd George.

Germany's colonial losses

Germany's colonies were given to the victorious powers as mandates. This means they were governed by one of the victorious powers until they were ready for independence.

- Togoland and Cameroons – to Britain and France.
- German South West Africa – to South Africa.
- German East Africa – to Britain.
- New Guinea – to Australia.
- Samoa – to New Zealand.
- Pacific islands north of the equator – the Marshalls, Marianas and Carolines – to Japan.

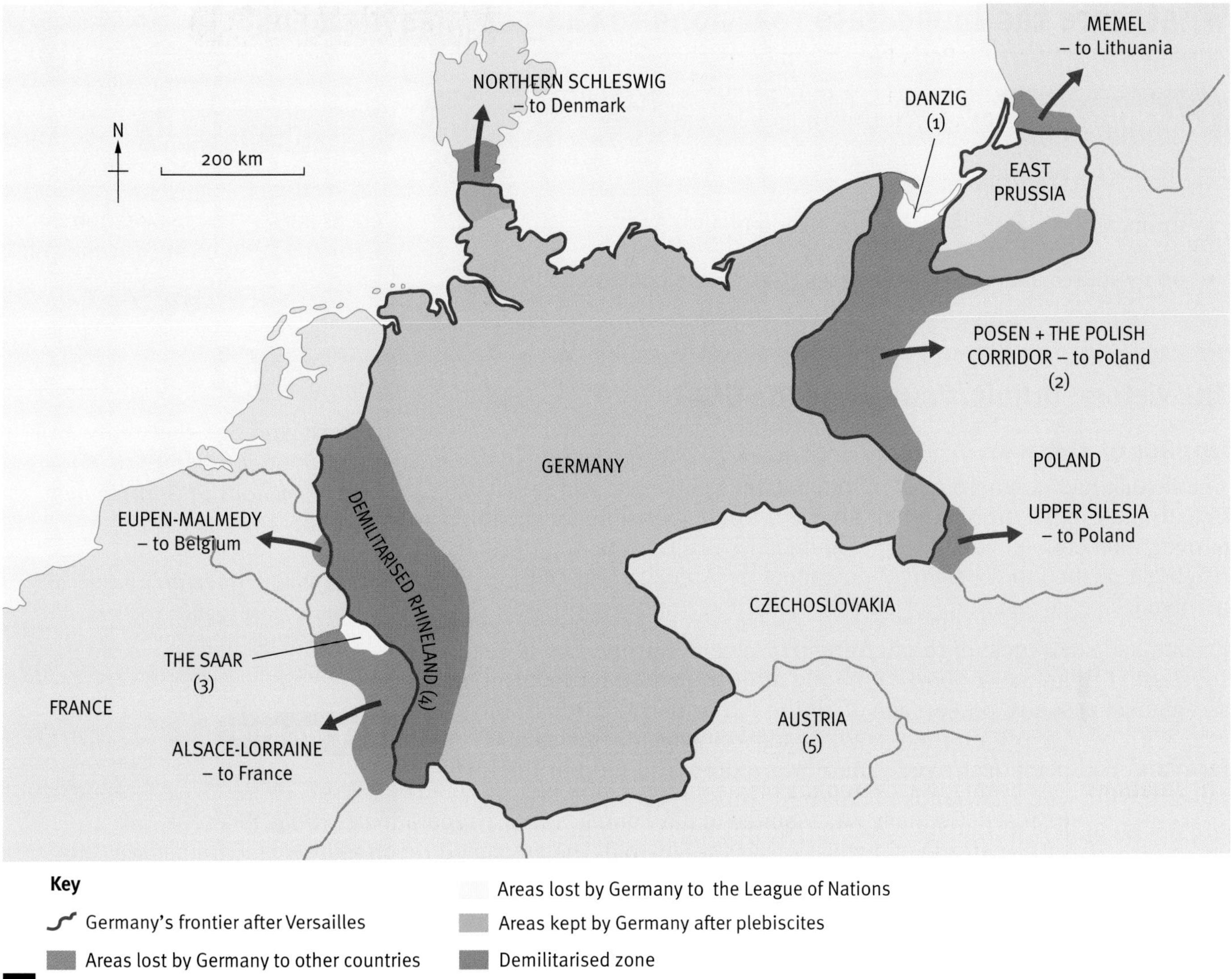

MEMEL
– to Lithuania
NORTHERN SCHLESWIG
– to Denmark
DANZIG
(1)
N
200 km
EAST
PRUSSIA
POSEN + THE POLISH
CORRIDOR – to Poland
(2)
GERMANY
POLAND
DEMILITARISED RHINELAND (4)
EUPEN-MALMEDY
– to Belgium
UPPER SILESIA
– to Poland
CZECHOSLOVAKIA
THE SAAR
(3)
FRANCE
AUSTRIA
(5)
ALSACE-LORRAINE
– to France

Key

- Germany's frontier after Versailles
- Areas lost by Germany to other countries
- Areas lost by Germany to the League of Nations
- Areas kept by Germany after plebiscites
- Demilitarised zone

Territorial terms of the Versailles settlement.

1. DANZIG was made a free city under League of Nations authority. Poland could use the port for its external trade.
2. THE POLISH CORRIDOR gave Poland access to the sea. It also split East Prussia from the rest of Germany.
3. THE SAAR was put under League of Nations authority for 15 years. France was given the production of the Saar coalfields as part of the reparations payments.
4. THE RHINELAND was to be permanently demilitarised by Germany. It would be occupied by the Allies for 15 years.
5. ANSCHLUSS (union) between Germany and Austria was forbidden.

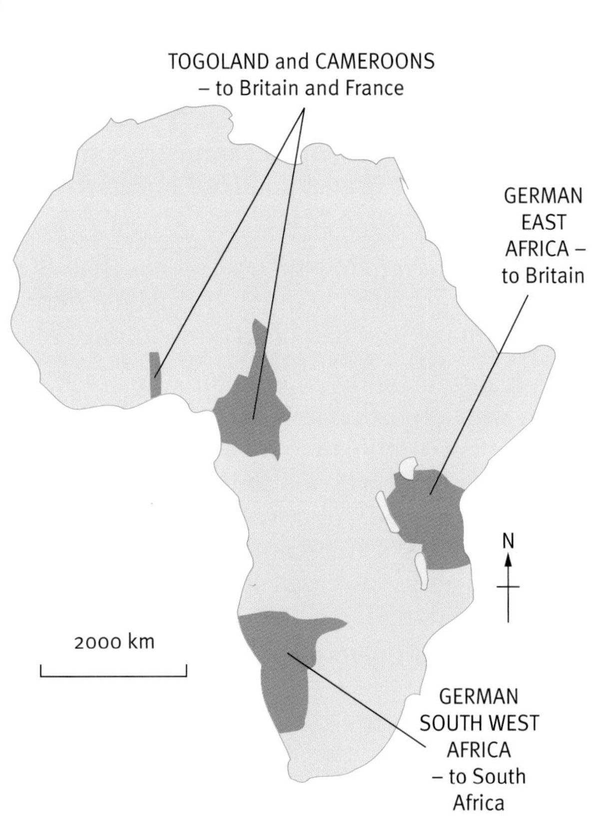

Germany's colonies in the Pacific were also allocated as mandates.

- New Guinea – to Australia
- Samoa – to New Zealand
- Pacific islands north of the Equator – the Marshalls, Marianas and Carolines – to Japan.

What were the immediate reactions to the peace settlement?

LEARNING OBJECTIVES

In this lesson you will:

- examine the reactions to the peace settlement
- apply source analysis skills to assess Germany's position up to 1923.

GETTING STARTED

Do you feel that any government could survive the humiliation that Germany suffered in 1919 and still keep the support of its people?

The victors: Britain, France and the USA

Impact of the war

The British had nowhere near as much damage at home as France or Belgium, though a number of air attacks were responsible for the deaths of over 1000 people. However, economically, Britain was in tatters. It had been pushed to the point of defeat before America became involved. The government owed over £1 billion to the Americans.

France had seen most of the fighting in Western Europe and it needed substantial financial support to rebuild after the war. Moreover, it had the highest casualty percentage of all the major participants in the war, with over a million men dead. Roads, railways, factories and farmland had been destroyed. There was a dramatic drop in the birth rate after the war, thousands of children were orphans, and the state spent a great deal of money in caring for millions of wounded people. The loss of nearly 750,000 homes meant more than two million people became homeless.

Political response

In Britain the expansion of governmental powers and responsibilities in dominions of the British Empire had grown dramatically. Britain turned to the colonies for help in obtaining essential war materials that had become difficult to source. The British political system had also changed: new government ministries and powers were created, and new taxes were levied and laws enacted. Once commissioned, many of these stayed in place.

France was desperate to gain assurances that its borders would remain intact. The government wanted to crush Germany, because of the appalling damage that had been done to the French people.

The USA had reluctantly entered the war in 1917. Repeated attacks on American ships (most notably the *Lusitania*) and the loss of Russia to the allied war effort combined to force America's hand. Wilson had said the 'world must be made safe for democracy'. However, according to the majority of the Senate, America's role was one of cautionary support and then retreat. Wilson's grand ambitions for a unified, democratic and co-operative world showcased at Versailles were not shared by his government, and in March 1920 the Senate rejected the treaty and vetoed America's proposed lead role in the League of Nations.

SOURCE 

Those who sign this treaty, will sign the death sentence of many millions of German men, women and children.

Count Brockdorff-Rantzau, leader of the German delegation to Versailles (15 May 1919).

KEY WORDS

Diktat – *a harsh, unilaterally imposed settlement with a defeated party.*

Republic – *state which does not have a monarch.*

Propaganda – *the spreading of ideas, information or rumour for the purpose of helping or injuring an institution, a cause, a person or a nation.*

KEY CONCEPTS

Betrayal – *the act of violating trust; an exhibition of disloyality.*

Hypocrisy – *being insincere by pretending to have qualities or beliefs not really held.*

Vengeance – *punishment in return for harm done.*

Instability – *the quality or condition of being erratic and undependable.*

America's rejection of the Treaty of Versailles was a complex issue but the policy of isolationism that followed led to further indirect support of the League's agenda without political obligation.

ACTIVITIES

To fully appreciate the effects felt by the average German in 1919 you are going to write a short newspaper article. You must be sympathetic to the shock of the peace and the needs of the people. Most importantly you should acknowledge the efforts Germany went to before the conference to show that the country was willing to avoid another war, and pick out the most damaging parts of the treaty in German eyes.

Public response

In Britain, people's expectations of the government were transformed. Average citizens had never been more involved in the nation's destiny. They felt Britain had to maintain its global status and that the Empire was a crucial extension of that. Women found that their arguments for equality had found a firmer platform thanks to their efforts in the war.

In France, the population wanted a return to normality as soon as possible. People had lost their livelihoods and felt that the government had to respond in a definitive way to restore the losses. Clemenceau felt significant public pressure to respond swiftly and decisively towards Germany.

For the American population there was a general feeling that the USA had been fighting someone else's war. Many Americans had lost friends and relatives in a war over 3000 miles away.

- German-Americans felt a strong sense of **betrayal**.
- Irish-Americans were bitter that Irish independence had not been addressed at Versailles.
- Right-wing Republicans were anxious to obstruct the peace for fear that Wilson would be re-elected. Even members of Wilson's own party felt he was out of touch and arrogant and had endangered future prospects of peace by being too aggressive with Germany.
- All of the political fears fed the population's rejection of Wilson's agenda. American people felt that they would be called upon to defend a country anywhere in the world.
- The remit of the League went too far – it was like signing a 'blank cheque'.

The vanquished: Germany and the unbearable diktat

While the armistice of 1918 marked an end to hostilities, the political and social turmoil within Germany meant the reality of defeat took some time to hit the German people. Until the last days of war, the German people, soldiers and civilians had been led to believe victory was only a few steps away. The shame of defeat on this fledgling nation was a cruel blow to their pre-war ambitions.

When it came to the settlement, the Germans had good reason to believe that the Allies would treat them mercifully. They assumed that peace would be based on the principles of Wilson's Fourteen Points. The Kaiser, whom many blamed for the war, surrendered his throne in the German Revolution of November 1918 and was replaced by a new democratic, republican government. It was thought this would be satisfactory for a respectable resolution among 'equals'.

However, German confidence was misplaced. The harsh terms of the armistice clearly indicated the kind of peace that would eventually be made. More ominously, none of the defeated nations were allowed representatives at the Paris Peace Conference. The final terms of the Treaty of Versailles were presented to the Germans with no negotiation – a '**diktat**' (dictated peace), as they called it.

Why was the Treaty of Versailles signed?

The new German government knew it had no choice but to sign the Treaty, and was promptly blamed by the entire German nation when it did so. Extremist opponents of the government blamed the 'November Criminals' (those who had asked for peace in November 1918) and claimed that they had 'stabbed Germany in the back'. Many Germans were only too ready to believe the myth that their country had not really lost the war, but had been betrayed by disloyal Jews and socialists. From the very start, the German people did not accept the treaty as a just peace, and many were prepared to do everything they could to make sure the Treaty did not work.

How did the German people react?

The Germans were stunned by the severity of the treaty and considered rejecting it outright, but the alternative was a resumption of the war. For Germans of all political orientations, the reparation payments were the most hated and distressing feature of the Weimar government's responsibilities. Worse still, they were not capable of paying the annual requests because they had lost many of their most productive areas of natural resources and industry. Germany paid the first year and then defaulted on the next two.

The remaining peace treaties, 1919–23

LEARNING OBJECTIVES

In this lesson you will:

- examine the methods of settlement used to deal with the other members of the Triple Alliance
- analyse, with reference to Wilson's Fourteen Points, how far a workable peace was achieved elsewhere in Europe.

The Treaty of St Germain, September 1919

This was the treaty signed by the Allies with Austria. Austria accepted the break-up of the Austro-Hungarian Empire. Austria and Hungary were left as small independent states.

Reparations

Austria agreed to pay reparations, but the collapse of the Bank of Vienna in 1922 meant nothing was paid.

Military restrictions

Austria was permitted an army of no more than 30,000 men.

1 South Tyrol and Trentino to Italy.
2 Istria and Trieste to Italy.
3 Croatia, Bosnia and Herzegovina to Serbia, creating Yugoslavia.
4 Transylvania to Romania.
5 Galicia to Poland. The new state of Poland also received territory from Germany and Russia.
6 The new state of Czechoslovakia was created.

The impact of defeat

- It was impossible to give every national group self-determination. Most of the new states contained defeated minorities who continued to create problems.
- Splitting up the empire created economic problems. Roads and railways had not been built to suit the new states, and the new nations had their own taxes on trade, where previously trade had been free.
- Several small, weak states now existed where there had previously been one large state.

The Treaty of Neuilly, November 1919

This was the treaty signed by the Allies with Bulgaria.

Reparations

Bulgaria had to pay £100 million in reparations.

Military restrictions

Bulgaria's army was limited to 20,000 men.

The Treaty of Trianon, June 1920

This was the treaty signed by the Allies with Hungary. With the Treaty of St Germain, it marked the break-up of the Austro-Hungarian Empire.

Reparations

Hungary agreed to pay reparations, but the collapse of Hungary's economy in the early 1920s meant nothing was ever paid.

Military restrictions

Hungary was permitted an army of no more than 35,000 men.

The impact of the defeat

- A communist state under Bela Kun was established in 1919. He was overthrown later in the year and a military dictatorship set up under Admiral Horthy.
- The Hungarians continued to resent a settlement that left up to 3 million Magyars (Hungarians) under foreign rule.

The Treaty of Sèvres, August 1920, amended by the Treaty of Lausanne, July 1923

These treaties were signed by the Allies with Turkey.

Impact of the Treaty of Sèvres

- The Turks were so outraged by the terms of the Treaty of Sèvres that the Sultan's government was overthrown in an uprising led by Mustapha Kemal.
- Rather than fight Kemal, the Allies agreed to amend the Treaty of Sèvres. This led to the signing of the Treaty of Lausanne in July 1923.

The Treaty of Lausanne

- Turkey recovered Smyrna and Eastern Thrace from Greece.
- All foreign troops left Turkey.
- Turkey regained control over the Straits.
- Turkey did not have to pay reparations.
- No limits were placed on Turkey's armed forces.

BULGARIA
(2)
Black Sea
500 km
Constantinople (3)
GREECE
N
Smyrna (1)
TURKEY
Rhodes and the Dodecanese Is. to Italy
SYRIA
LEBANON
Mediterranean Sea
IRAQ
Persian Gulf
PALESTINE
ARABIA (made independent)
TRANSJORDAN

The Treaty of Sèvres

1 Smyrna and **2** Eastern Thrace were lost to Greece. In Europe Turkey was left with only the small area around Constantinople.
3 The Straits of the Dardanelles and the Bosphorus were opened to ships of all nations.
The Ottoman Empire was split up. Arabia was made independent. Turkey's other possessions in the Middle East were made League of Nations mandates and allocated to Britain and France.
4 An independent Armenian State was to be created. The Allies could keep troops in Turkey to ensure the treaty was obeyed.

ACTIVITIES

Look at the terms of the other peace treaties.

a How do they compare to the Treaty of Versailles?
b In what way did they improve the countries?
c What other impacts did they have?

Could the treaties be justified at the time?

LEARNING OBJECTIVES

In this lesson you will:

- analyse whether the treaties could be justified at the time
- practise your skills in answering exam questions about the meaning of sources.

Glory in the spoils

There is no doubt that the treaties which established the peace settlement at the end of the First World War imposed very strict terms upon the defeated countries.

- Germany lost all its colonies and, in total, 13 per cent of its land. Nearly six million German citizens now found themselves living outside Germany's borders. The Germans were also forced to agree to pay huge reparations and carry out massive reductions in their armed forces.
- Austria saw its empire disbanded and was also forced to pay reparations to the Allies. It too had its armed forces reduced. Similar penalties were also imposed on Bulgaria and Hungary.
- The Turks were so angered by their territorial losses that they rose up and overthrew their own government. The Allies then agreed to less severe terms in the Treaty of Lausanne in 1923.

The terms of the treaty were strict, but they were not entirely unexpected. When the armistice was signed in November 1918 the Germans knew they would have to pay reparations, surrender territory and reduce their armed forces. These were the usual consequences of defeat in war. Indeed, some historians think that the Germans might have imposed even harsher terms on the Allies if they had won the war.

Although the strict terms of the Treaty of Versailles aroused much criticism, this did not mean that the treaty-makers had simply acted foolishly or were not aware of what they were doing.

The 'Big Three' met after the most terrible war in history. They were determined to make sure that war would not happen again. Some of the decisions the peacemakers had to make were extremely difficult. The Austro-Hungarian Empire was breaking up, large areas of Europe had been devastated, communism was spreading and Europe's economy was in tatters. There was a need to restore stability – and quickly.

Perhaps, therefore, those historians who have condemned the Treaty of Versailles have been over-critical. Perhaps the peacemakers did a reasonable job considering the problems they faced. However, the view held by most historians since 1919 is that the treaties were too harsh and were likely to lead to future war. It would only be a matter of time before the Germans, in particular, set about seeking revenge.

SOURCE 

It was a peace of revenge. It sowed a thousand seeds from which new wars might spring. It was as though the Devil had sat beside Clemenceau and whispered madness into the ear of Wilson and grinned across the table at Lloyd George.

An extract from a book written by a British historian in 1929.

SOURCE 

Lloyd George told one of his officials that the treaty was
'... all a great pity. We shall have to do the same thing all over again in twenty-five years at three times the cost'.

An extract from a book on the Treaty of Versailles, written in 1969.

ACTIVITIES

Look back through the chapter and your notes and try to identify the impacts of the decisions.

The purpose of this task is to show the importance of assessing situations in balance.

Use your task to plan the essay on the next page.

SOURCE C

PEACE AND FUTURE CANNON FODDER
1940 CLASS
PEACE TREATY
The Tiger: "Curious! I seem to hear a child weeping!"

This cartoon by Will Dyson was published in a British newspaper in 1919. The 'Big Four' are seen leaving Versailles. Dyson shows Orlando, the Italian prime minister, as well as Lloyd George (at the back), and Wilson (far right), while Clemenceau, the prime minister of France (in front) stops as he hears a child weeping. The child represents 'the class of 1940'. Dyson thought that the terms of Versailles would lead to further war in 1940. He was wrong by only four months!

SOURCE E

This is not peace. It is an armistice for fifteen years.

The judgement of Marshall Foch on the Treaty of Versailles. Foch was the French commander-in-chief of the Allied armies in the final year of the war.

GradeStudio

Study Source C. What is the meaning of this cartoon? Use the source and your own knowledge to explain your answer. **[6 marks]**

Examiner's tip

Remember in this type of question you have to do three things:

- Explain what the message of the cartoon is.
- Support your ideas with evidence from the source.
- Explain your ideas using your own knowledge of the event that the cartoon is about.

ACTIVITIES

Put the following words in order of their damage to Germany. You could use a thinking skills triangle to help order them.

- Reparations
- War guilt
- Loss of economic power
- Loss of empire
- Loss of army
- Failure to recognise pre-war tension.

SOURCE D

To be sure, the First World War had shattered the Austro-Hungarian Empire and left Germany defeated. But the treaty signed in the Hall of Mirrors at Versailles on 28th June 1919 neither extinguished the ambitions that had ignited the war nor quieted the anxieties it had spawned. Victors and vanquished agreed only that the conflict had been a dreadful catastrophe, a blood spilling man killing, nation eating nightmare of unprecedented horror. All were determined to avoid its re-occurrence, more precisely each nation was determined to avoid the repetition of its own role in it.

David Kennedy, *Freedom From Fear* (1999).

To what extent was the League of Nations a success?

What were the aims of the League?

LEARNING OBJECTIVES

In this lesson you will:

- examine the opportunity afforded to the League to manage international disputes in the post-war period
- assess the aims of the League of Nations and analyse how each of the major European powers would react to its introduction.

GETTING STARTED

The League of Nations was the brainchild of Woodrow Wilson, a man many believe was way ahead of his time, but despite his vigorous campaigning, few people shared his vision.

1 Look at the artist's interpretation of the League (Source A). What is the cartoon's message?
2 What does it say about how the League was viewed if this drawing was completed at the very start of its existence?

The birth of the League of Nations

The peacemakers at Versailles knew that they had not solved all the problems of the post-war world, but they looked to the League of Nations to complete their work. They set up the League of Nations to resolve international disputes and prevent countries from ever going to war again.

This international organisation set up to preserve world peace was dealt a serious blow by the USA's refusal to join, but still did much to encourage co-operation between nations. However, without the support of the world's largest superpower and one of the only established nations not ravaged by war, it would be weak in both people's perception of it and its ability to act.

BRAIN BOOST

Aims of the League [DIES]:

1 **D**isarmament
2 **I**mprove people's jobs and lives
3 **E**nforce the treaty of Versailles
4 **S**top War (collective security)

The covenant of the League

The **covenant** was the rule book of the League of Nations. Its central aims are listed on page 21. In a world recovering from war with continued disputes about territory, these were optimistic goals, to say the least.

KEY WORDS

Covenant – *a legally enforceable agreement that ensures uniform responses to problems.*

Collective security – *each nation's security depends on that of all other nations, and peace is universal and indivisible.*

Community of power – *an organisation that ensures individual security by acting with others.*

SOURCE A

A view of President Wilson and his ideology for peace. The artist clearly believes the request is too much.

The aims of the League

1 To stop war

The League aimed to discourage aggression and deal with disputes by negotiation. The League planned to provide **collective security** by a **community of power**. In Article 10 of the Covenant of the League, members promised to defend the territory and independence of League members and to take action 'in case of danger'.

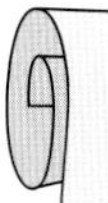

To promote international co-operation and to achieve international peace and security:

- by the acceptance of obligations not to resort to war
- by the prescription of open, just and honourable relations between nations
- by the firm establishment of international law as the rule of conduct between governments
- by the maintenance of justice and a scrupulous respect for all treaty obligations in the dealings of organised peoples with one another
- by working alongside each other and removing old alliances all the nations in the League, both large and small, could ensure 'collective security'.

Main points of the covenant of the League of Nations

ACTIVITIES

1 In pairs, discuss the key aims of the League of Nations. Look at Source A on page 20. Why would people be worried about such a far-reaching set of aims?

2 How might the following countries react to the list of aims?
- Germany
- Britain
- Russia
- France

3 Without America the League's success relied heavily on Britain and France. Why would this create difficulties, particularly after the First World War?

2 To improve the life and jobs of people around the world

The League aimed to fulfil this aim both by direct action to improve health and welfare and by encouraging trade and business.

3 Disarmament

This was a major goal of the league. Article III of the Covenant of the League called for 'reduction of armaments to the lowest point consistent with national safety and the enforcement by common action of international obligations'. A significant amount of the League's time and energy was devoted to disarmament even though many member governments were uncertain that such extensive disarmament could be achieved or was desirable. To be successful, the policy would have to be led by the allied powers (notably Britain and France) but the fear of future conflict was too strong. The irony was that initiating the disarmament of reluctant nations required military force.

4 To uphold and enforce the Treaty of Versailles

The League was forged out of the heat of battle, and the bitterness that followed could not be detached from the resultant peace. The armistice agreements and later the Treaty of Versailles provided an opportunity to restructure Europe. The League of Nations had to support the intentions of the Treaty otherwise any stability in Europe would have been quickly dissipated.

GradeStudio

Using the evidence on the page and your own knowledge, complete the following exam question. Don't forget to plan your answer and explain the evidence you include.

Explain how the League of Nations was meant to keep the peace. **[6 marks]**

Examiner's tip

To get 3–4 marks you need to explain one way in which the League was meant to keep the peace, for example:
- the theory of collective security.
- the actions the League could take against aggressive nations.

To get 5–6 marks on this question, you need to explain several ways.

How successful was the League in the 1920s?

LEARNING OBJECTIVES

In this lesson you will:

- examine the successes of the League in international diplomacy throughout the 1920s
- develop your ability to categorise and prioritise evidence to form a judgement.

Successes and failures in peacekeeping

The peace treaties of 1919–20 did not resolve all the territorial disputes caused by the war.

- The Turks were so outraged by the peace settlement that they refused to accept it. They went on fighting, mainly against the Greeks, until the Allies were ready to agree to the Treaty of Lausanne in 1923.
- The Italians were dissatisfied with their gains, and managed to hold on to Fiume after D'Annunzio's occupation of 1919–20.
- The Poles were especially active, grabbing much of the area of Teschen from Czechoslovakia in early 1919 (the League finally fixed this border between the two countries in 1920). More importantly, the Poles were at war with Russia until 1921, gaining much of the Ukraine and Belorussia.

In the face of continuing violence and uncertainty, the League only gradually established a role for itself in dealing with international crises. Even when it did become involved, its record in resolving crises was mixed.

Vilna, 1920

This area was claimed by both Poland and Lithuania. In 1920, during the Russo–Polish War, Vilna was occupied by Polish forces, which later refused to leave. The League was very reluctant to become involved. Taking action against Poland would have required armed forces, but League members were not willing to supply them. In addition, Britain and France saw Poland as a strong barrier against Germany and communist Russia and did not wish to upset it. The League tried to negotiate a deal, but in 1923 it confirmed Poland's occupation of Vilna. Sporadic fighting between the two sides continued until 1927.

Successes and failures of the League in the 1920s.

Date	Place/event	Action taken by League
1920	Vilna	The League ordered the Poles to leave, but was ignored
1921	Silesia	The League settled a dispute between Germany and Poland in 1921 by holding a plebiscite
	Aaland Islands	A League investigation settled a dispute between Sweden and Finland
1922–23	Austria-Hungary	The League helped prevent economic collapse by arranging loans and sending economic experts
1923	Corfu	The League tried to stop a war in Corfu, but Italy refused a League order to leave
	Memel	The League tried unsuccessfully to make the Lithuanians leave in 1923
	Ruhr	The League was unable to stop the French invasion of the Ruhr in Germany
1924	Mosul	The League arbitrated in favour of British Iraq and against Turkey
1925	Bulgaria	Greece stopped its invasion when condemned by the League

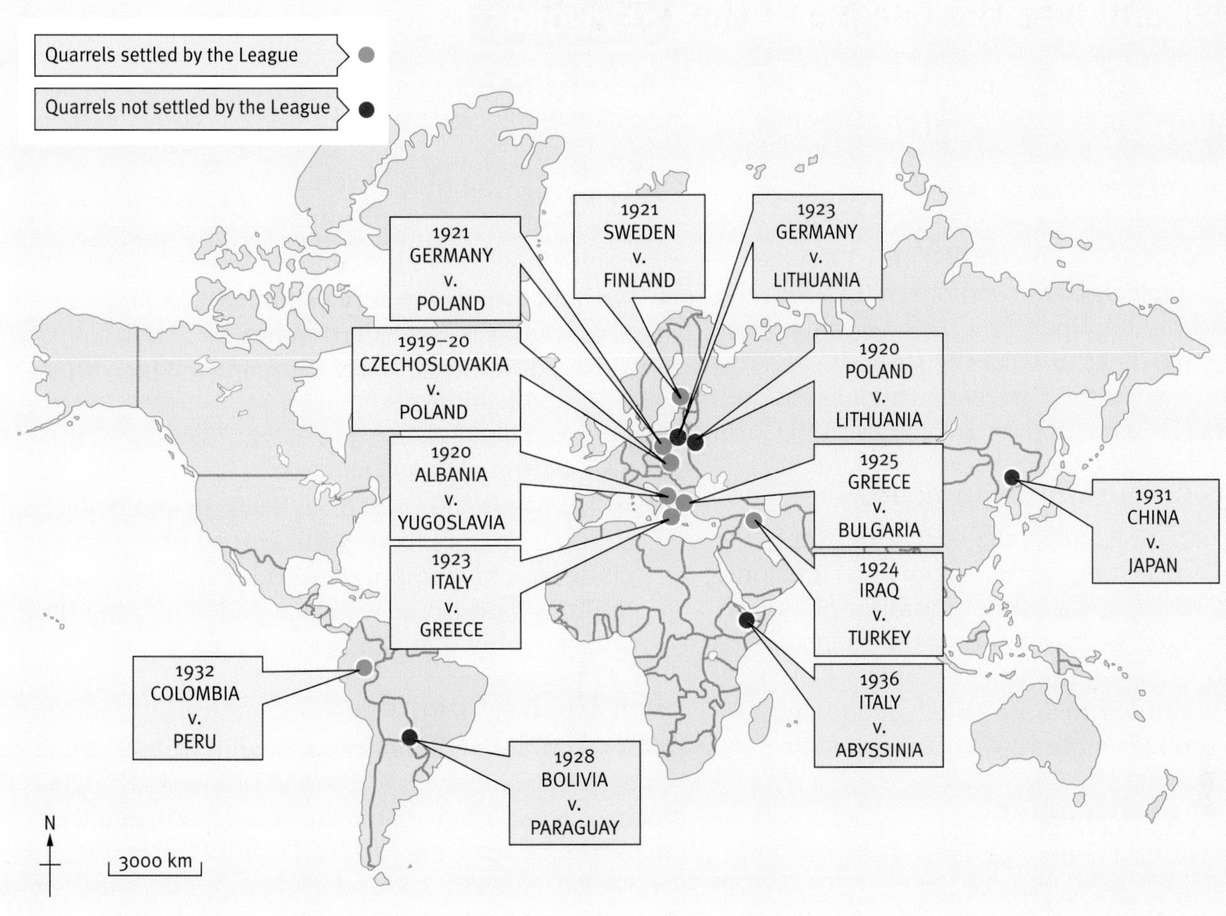

Upper Silesia, 1921

Upper Silesia was one of several plebiscite areas defined in the Treaty of Versailles. Upper Silesia contained large numbers of Poles and Germans, and since the areas was particularly important for its industry, both Poland and Germany were determined to acquire the territory. In the **plebiscite** held by the League in March 1921, the people voted in favour of Germany by 700,000 votes to 480,000. The League decided to **partition** the area. Germany received over half the land and population, while the Poles had most of the industry. This caused great bitterness in Germany, but both countries accepted the decision.

KEY WORDS

Plebiscite – *a referendum, when all electors can vote on an important issue.*

Partition – *an attempt to resolve political disputes through the drawing of territorial boundaries.*

Economic collapse in Austria and Hungary, 1922–23

In 1922–23, Austria and Hungary faced bankruptcy. Their economies had not recovered after the war, and now, burdened with reparations payments, it seemed that they would simply collapse. The League arranged international loans for the two countries, sending commissioners to supervise how the money was spent. In effect, the League temporarily took over the economic management of the two countries. With this help, both Austria and Hungary were able to begin economic recovery.

Corfu, 1923

In August 1923, five Italian surveyors who were working for the League of Nations in mapping the Greek–Albanian frontier were killed on the Greek side of the border. Mussolini, the new Italian dictator, took advantage of the situation, demanding compensation from the Greek government. When this was not forthcoming, he bombarded and occupied Corfu. The Council wanted to condemn Italy, but the great powers would not permit it. Instead, they put pressure on the Greeks to accept Mussolini's demands. Only when the Greeks had apologised and paid up did Mussolini withdraw his forces from Corfu.

The Greek–Bulgarian dispute, 1925

After the Treaty of Neuilly, the border between Greece and Bulgaria remained a source of tension between the two nations. After a number of violent incidents, the Greeks invaded Bulgaria in October 1925. On this occasion the League intervened effectively. It condemned the Greek action and pressurised them to withdraw, which they did.

Attempts at disarmament

The League's attempts to organise a disarmament conference were less successful:

- the disarmament conference of 1923 failed because Britain objected.
- the disarmament conference of 1931 was wrecked by Germany.

However, the League did endorse the Kellogg–Briand Pact of 1928, a pact agreed by the French and US governments to outlaw war, which was signed by 23 nations and supported by 65.

Humanitarian successes of the League

The League was the first international organisation to suggest that the world community should take collective action to tackle problems such as starvation, disease and child slave labour. In the 1920s the League:

- **repatriated** 400,000 First World War prisoners of war.
- worked to prevent **leprosy**, and took steps to kill mosquitoes to prevent malaria.
- closed down four Swiss companies which were selling illegal drugs.
- attacked slave owners in Sierra Leone and Burma and set free 200,000 slaves.
- in 1922 helped refugees in Turkish camps by sending doctors to stop the spread of typhoid and cholera, and spending around £10 million on building homes for refugees and supplying them with farming tools and equipment.

KEY WORDS

Repatriated – *the process of return of refugees or soldiers to their homes, most notably following a war.*

Leprosy – *a disease characterised by patches of altered skin and nerve tissue (lesions) that gradually spread to cause muscle weakness, deformaties and paralysis.*

The Health Committee

Vast resources and scientific research were channelled into ending leprosy, malaria and yellow fever. This focused on starting an international campaign to exterminate mosquitoes. The Health Committee also worked successfully with the government of the Soviet Union to prevent typhus epidemics, including organising a large education campaign about the disease. The Health Committee was an essential and relatively successful branch of the League.

International Labour Organisation

In 1919, the International Labour Organisation (ILO) was created as part of the Versailles Treaty and became part of the League's operations.

- The ILO successfully restricted the addition of lead to paint.
- It convinced several countries to adopt an eight-hour work day and 48-hour working week.
- It worked to end child labour, increase the rights of women in the workplace, and make shipowners liable for accidents involving seamen.
- It continued to exist after the end of the League, becoming an agency of the United Nations in 1946.

BRAIN BOOST **SUCCESSES OF THE LEAGUE IN THE 1920s [KABAMS]**

Kellogg–Briand Pact – 1928, signed by 23 nations and supported by a further 65 to outlaw war
Austrian/Hungarian support – the League's economic support helped their economies to recover
Bulgaria – 1925, Greece invaded Bulgaria, but withdrew when Bulgaria appealed to the League
Aaland Islands – 1921, the League said the islands should belong to Finland, Sweden reluctantly agreed
Mosul – 1924, the Turks demanded Mosul from Iraq, the League refused and Iraq retained its independence
Silesia – 1921, Germany and Poland agreed to the partition after a plebiscite

Slavery Commission

The Slavery Commission sought to eradicate slavery and slave trading across the world, and fought against forced prostitution. Its main success was through pressing the governments who administered mandated countries to end slavery in those countries.

- The League secured a commitment from Ethiopia to end slavery as a condition of membership in 1926.
- It worked with Liberia to abolish forced labour and inter-tribal slavery.
- It gained the emancipation of 200,000 slaves in Sierra Leone.
- It fought against organised raids against slave traders in its efforts to stop the practice of forced labour in Africa.
- It reduced the death rate of workers constructing the Tanganyika railway from 55 per cent to 4 per cent.
- Records were kept to control slavery, prostitution, and the trafficking of women and children.

Commission for Refugees

Led by Fridtjof Nansen, the Commission for Refugees looked after the interests of refugees including overseeing their repatriation and, when necessary, resettlement.

- At the end of the First World War there were two to three million ex-prisoners of war dispersed throughout Russia. Within two years of the commission's foundation, in 1920, it had helped 425,000 of them to return home.
- It established camps in Turkey in 1922 to deal with a refugee crisis in that country and to help prevent disease and hunger.

It also established the Nansen passport as a means of identification for stateless peoples.

Limitations of the special commissions

While the special commissions were very effective in some areas and had many positive results, they did have some limitations. Some of these are outlined for each agency below:

- Health Committee – disease would always be a problem. Each area and each community presented its own problems which only time and a great deal of money could solve.
- International Labour Organisation – it was difficult to ensure all countries and companies complied with the new rules and regulations. Big business was not always pleased with government interference, and the economic instability in Europe and isolation of the USA meant that far-reaching changes were restricted.
- Slavery Commission – approaching slavery as an open issue forced it 'underground' as people increasingly began to be traded on the black market.
- Commission for Refugees – racism and animosity remained a problem in many countries, and success in this area was dependent on success in all the other areas of the League; this made lasting progress difficult.

GradeStudio

'The League of Nations had its greatest successes in the work of the special commissions.'

How far do you agree with this statement?

[10 marks]

Examiner's tip

When a question asks you 'how far you agree', you are being assessed on your ability to present, support and explain two sides of an argument. It is important that before you tackle questions like this one, you plan your answer.

In this question you need to explain how some of the League's special commissions were successful, but you also need to explain either some of the League's other successes, or the limitations of the special commissions. To do this you will need to think about what you learnt on pages 22–24.

Copy out and complete the table below, to help you plan your response to this question:

Successes of the special commissions	Counter-argument:
Conclusion:	

How far did weaknesses in the League's organisation make failure inevitable?

LEARNING OBJECTIVES

In this lesson you will:

- examine the strengths and weaknesses of the structure of the League of Nations and the roles of its members
- assess the potential problems that would occur due to the nature of the League's organisation and members.

The covenant of the League of Nations

The covenant of the League of Nations (the document that outlined its aims) was written into each of the peace treaties signed in 1919–23. Wilson hoped this would ensure that the League was accepted by all nations. However, from the start, the League shared many of the weaknesses of the treaties themselves. The defeated powers were not consulted about the League and were not invited to join. The victorious powers did not really agree among themselves about the League. Wilson's idealism and belief in co-operation between nations were not shared by the cynical and worldly wise Europeans. Lloyd George went along with the idea to keep Wilson happy, and the French agreed on the basis that anything which might give them additional security against Germany was worth trying.

Most important of all, Wilson's failure to persuade the US Congress to accept the treaties meant that the USA never joined the League. The absence of the world's most powerful nation seriously undermined the League's authority to deal with international problems.

The structure and organisation of the League

To carry out its work, the League needed a structure that would enable nations to meet, discuss and resolve international problems. It was decided that the League would be based in Geneva, Switzerland. All the member states could send representatives to the Assembly. This was the League's parliament. It met every year and had ultimate authority over the League's actions. In the Assembly, all nations were equal and had one vote. The Assembly was too large to react quickly to international crises, so a smaller group called the Council was set up; this met more frequently.

The great powers attempted to control the Council. Britain, France, Italy and Japan were permanent members and were originally matched by representatives from four other states. The number of additional states represented increased to nine over the years.

Finally, to ensure that the League's operations functioned smoothly, it had its own administrative staff – the Secretariat. This was the League's civil service, which arranged the work of the Council and Assembly.

Membership

The League had 42 members when it was set up, and this number increased over the years. However, it was not just the USA that was not a member. At first, all the defeated nations were excluded. They were all later allowed in – Germany joined in 1926, although it left again when Hitler came to power in 1933. Russia was also excluded because other nations refused to recognise its communist government. It was finally admitted to the League only in 1934. Other founder members of the League, such as Japan and Italy, subsequently left it. So the League was never an organisation of all states, or even of all the most important states.

The League was dominated by Britain and France, who disagreed significantly over the role that the League should play in international affairs. Britain regarded the League as a harmless talking shop, but did not want to give it real authority or power. France, on the other hand, wanted the League to enforce the terms of the peace treaties. This difference in attitude between the two powers most involved in the League's work inevitably weakened it.

Security issues

The real test for the League came when it had to deal with aggression. In theory, the Council could raise armed forces from member states, but in practice countries were very reluctant to agree to this. The Covenant said the League should use sanctions to deter aggressors – all members would refuse to trade with them until the aggression ceased. However, the League was only as strong and determined as its members, and nations often looked to the League to solve problems that they would not deal with themselves. Although the League could sometimes pressurise small nations into obedience, it was too weak to deal with great powers like Japan and Italy.

Idealism

The creation of the League was an idealistic attempt to make sure nations did not have to live through the horrors of the First World War again. It was the first organisation in which governments worked together for world peace. Its agencies also carried out much successful humanitarian work. Its campaigns for better health and working conditions, to help refugees return to their homes and to free slaves, did much to improve people's lives across the world. The International Labour Organisation (ILO) encouraged governments to recognise trade unions and to improve workers' pay and pensions. Even when governments did not accept everything proposed by the League's agencies, public awareness of a whole range of social issues was increased.

However, the idealism of the League was also a weakness. All the member states, large and small, had equal voting rights, and all decisions (in both the Assembly and the Council) had to be unanimous. This was fine when members agreed with each other, but not when they disagreed.

The work of the commissions illustrates how the League was powerless to make progress against the wishes of individual states. The Covenant committed all members to reducing armaments, yet the disarmament commission found this impossible to achieve. The French regarded disarmament as giving away their security, while the Germans, who had been disarmed under the terms of the Treaty of Versailles, thought they had a right to re-arm, at least to the level of the other powers. Not until 1932 was the commission finally able to set up a Disarmament Conference. By then, much of the spirit of co-operation and trust the League originally enjoyed had disappeared. The conference could agree nothing, and France's refusal to disarm was the perfect excuse for Hitler to walk out of the conference (and the League) in 1933.

The Mandates Commission was only slightly more successful. The mandated powers were supposed to administer the mandates on behalf of the League and to prepare them for eventual independence. In practice, they treated them more or less as colonies. Iraq's independence in 1932 was the only example of a mandate being freed in the interwar period.

Conclusion

The circumstances in which the League was set up, and in particular the refusal of the USA to join, left it with serious weaknesses. It was not well equipped to deal with cases of aggression, and had no armed forces of its own. It worked well when members wished to co-operate, and through its agencies had many worthwhile achievements. However, its creators were too optimistic and idealistic in expecting all nations to accept its authority.

The structure of the League of Nations.

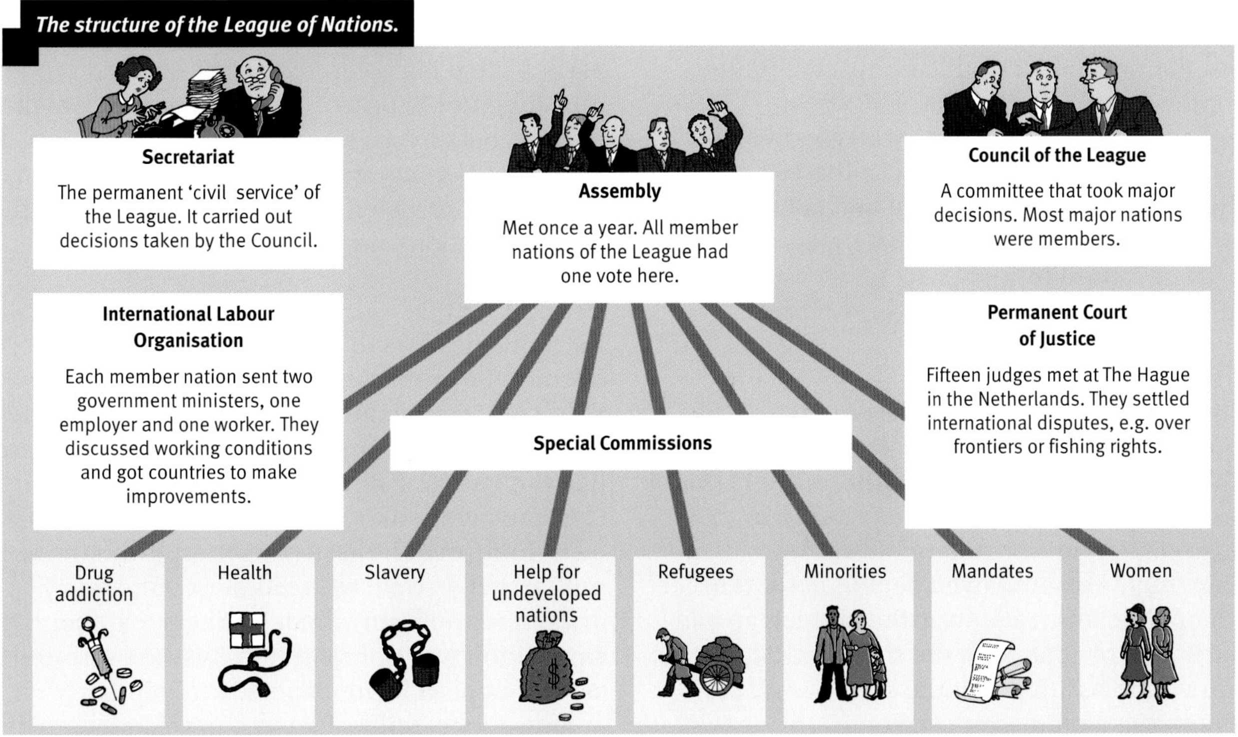

Secretariat
The permanent 'civil service' of the League. It carried out decisions taken by the Council.
Assembly
Met once a year. All member nations of the League had one vote here.
Council of the League
A committee that took major decisions. Most major nations were members.
International Labour Organisation
Each member nation sent two government ministers, one employer and one worker. They discussed working conditions and got countries to make improvements.
Special Commissions
Permanent Court of Justice
Fifteen judges met at The Hague in the Netherlands. They settled international disputes, e.g. over frontiers or fishing rights.
Drug addiction
Health
Slavery
Help for undeveloped nations
Refugees
Minorities
Mandates
Women

How far did the Depression make the work of the League more difficult?

LEARNING OBJECTIVES

In this lesson you will:

- examine the consequences of the American Wall Street Crash on the economies of Europe
- assess the long- and short-term effects of the crash on the effectiveness of international diplomacy and the League of Nations in the 1930s.

GETTING STARTED

'In 1929 America paid the price of ignoring their political destiny in Europe in favour of an economic one. A lackluster League had required far more financial support than would have been necessary if America had only joined the League. Subsequently America's economic collapse had a far deeper impact on an already fragile Europe.'

How far is this a fair assessment that America damaged the League's opportunity for success?

Global economic crisis

The Great Depression was sparked off by the Wall Street Crash – the collapse of the US stock market – in October 1929. The slump in American share prices was a disaster not just for America, but for the world economy. The wave of bankruptcies that followed the crash sent the US economy into a downward spiral that had a deep impact on world trade. Hardly a country in the world remained unaffected. The only exception was the Soviet Union, whose economy was not dependent on trade with other nations. The slump in world trade made all other nations poorer, and unemployment soared as industries ground to a halt.

Although this was an economic crisis, it soon had harmful political effects, which impacted on the work of the League of Nations. The Great Depression did much to destroy the goodwill on which the League had depended in the 1920s. The 1930s brought increasing tension and conflict, as nations struggled to cope with the effects of the crash. Their failure to find peaceful ways of doing this culminated in the Second World War.

Unemployment

Millions of workers lost their jobs because of the crash. Across the industrialised states, unemployment was five times higher in 1932 than it had been in 1929. In the USA, 30 per cent of the working population was unemployed. Not surprisingly, the unemployed demanded action from the politicians. However, the politicians had little idea how to cope with the situation. Their first reaction was to assume that the slump was temporary and would soon correct itself.

Meanwhile, the unemployed became ever more desperate. The effects of unemployment were different from country to country, but everywhere governments became uncertain, unstable and preoccupied more with solving their own problems than with tackling international difficulties.

Extremism

In some countries, notably Germany, the Depression helped extremist political parties come to power. Voters were tempted to follow any politician who offered a solution to unemployment. They felt they had nothing to lose, as democracy had failed them. These extremist parties were often nationalist – they had a hatred of other nations, and were concerned only with their own national interests. Where such parties came to power, they often showed an unwillingness to accept international agreements and a willingness to use force to achieve their aims. The League of Nations found it almost impossible to deal with the more violent international climate of the 1930s, as nations simply ignored its authority.

Militarism

Extremist leaders looked to foreign policy success to distract the attention of their people from troubles at home. Dictatorships re-armed their countries and prepared their populations for war. Political parties like the Fascist Party in Italy and the Nazis in Germany were like armies – they even had their own uniforms. In these countries, ordinary life was militarised. People who did not accept party discipline were punished. Workers lost their rights. Opposition was not tolerated. Women and children, as well as men, were expected to join party organisations. Militarism in a powerful country like

Germany posed a great threat to other countries. Sooner or later the dictatorships would use their power. The consequences of increasing militarism in Germany are described later. Two other powers whose militarism did much to destroy international peace in the 1930s were Japan and Italy.

How the Depression affected the League

- **Britain and France** no longer wished to sort out international disputes that would cost them money and could further damage their trade.
- Desperate people suffering terrible economic hardship increasingly turned to leaders offering radical solutions. This led to the rise of **militaristic fascist governments**.
- There was **less international co-operation**. The USA and other nations looked to take care of themselves instead of worrying about world peace and humanitarian issues.

SOURCE A

A member of the Italian Fascist Youth organisation receives his rifle from Mussolini.

ACTIVITIES

1 Complete the table below by placing the sentences in the correct column.

American isolationism	Rise of extremist governments	Weakening of Britain and France

- Increasing challenges to peace treaties
- Reduced the League's ability to take military action
- Reduced the League's ability to threaten aggressive nations
- Countries sought to fix economic problems by conquering new lands
- The main powers of the League became less committed
- America took no interest in international affairs
- No American loans available
- Increasing challenges to the League

2 **a** Using the evidence you have gathered in the lesson, decide what you think was the biggest area of difficulty the League faced after 1929. Decide on a format to display this judgement; you may want to use a pie chart, a priority pyramid or a PEE paragraph, for example.

b Share your answers with a partner and consider their opinion.

c Challenge your partner to explain their judgement with reference to at least three other factors that they didn't choose.

d Using the information you have gathered from the diagrams and your discussions, now place the areas of difficulty in a priority pyramid in order of importance.

VOICE YOUR OPINION!

There is a saying in international affairs that 'when America sneezes, the world catches a cold'.

- What does this suggest about the American influence on other countries' economies?
- What does this reveal about the Wall Street Crash?
- How far do you think this saying still applies today?

Why did the League fail over Manchuria and Abyssinia?

LEARNING OBJECTIVES

In this lesson you will:

- investigate the League's inability to control events in Manchuria and Abssyinia
- compare and contrast the treatment of Japan and Italy as Council Members against other League members.

GETTING STARTED

Italy and Japan were ambitious nations when they joined the League of Nations. They were respected as such with their positions on the Council.

1 List with a partner five reasons why that may have been misguided.

  You may want to look back at previous notes to help you.

2 Was the League able to satisfy their needs after 1929?

Increasing militarism in Japan

Japan was already established on the Asian mainland: its victory over Russia in the war of 1905 had given Japan control over much of Manchuria, and in 1910 it had annexed Korea. Moreover, Japan emerged from the First World War as the most important power in Asia, acquiring colonies in the Pacific and control over German territories leased from China. Yet Japan was not satisfied by these gains for several reasons:

- Rapid population growth and industrial development meant that Japan had to import food and raw materials.
- The Allies' refusal to refer to racial equality in the peace treaties of 1919–20 was deeply offensive to the Japanese.
- The Japanese government had accepted an inferior position in the Washington Naval Agreements (1922), which permitted Japan only three ships to every five built by Britain and the USA. The Japanese military took this as a sign that they could not trust their politicians to protect Japan's interests.

Tension between the military, who wanted a policy of aggressive expansion in Asia, and the politicians, who were much more cautious, grew worse during the 1920s. The army began to act without government approval. In 1928 it had the local warlord in Manchuria, Chang Tso Lin, assassinated because it thought the government's policy of friendship towards Chang was wrong. The army simply wanted to annex Manchuria.

There were also increasing economic difficulties towards the end of the 1920s. The price of rice began to collapse because of over-production, and Japan's farmers saw their incomes fall sharply. Moreover, the export of silk, mostly to the USA, was seriously affected by the Depression. By 1932 the price was only one-fifth of what it had been a decade earlier. Japanese industry was also in a dire

Japan had gained control of much of Manchuria following war with Russia in 1905; it had annexed Korea in 1910.

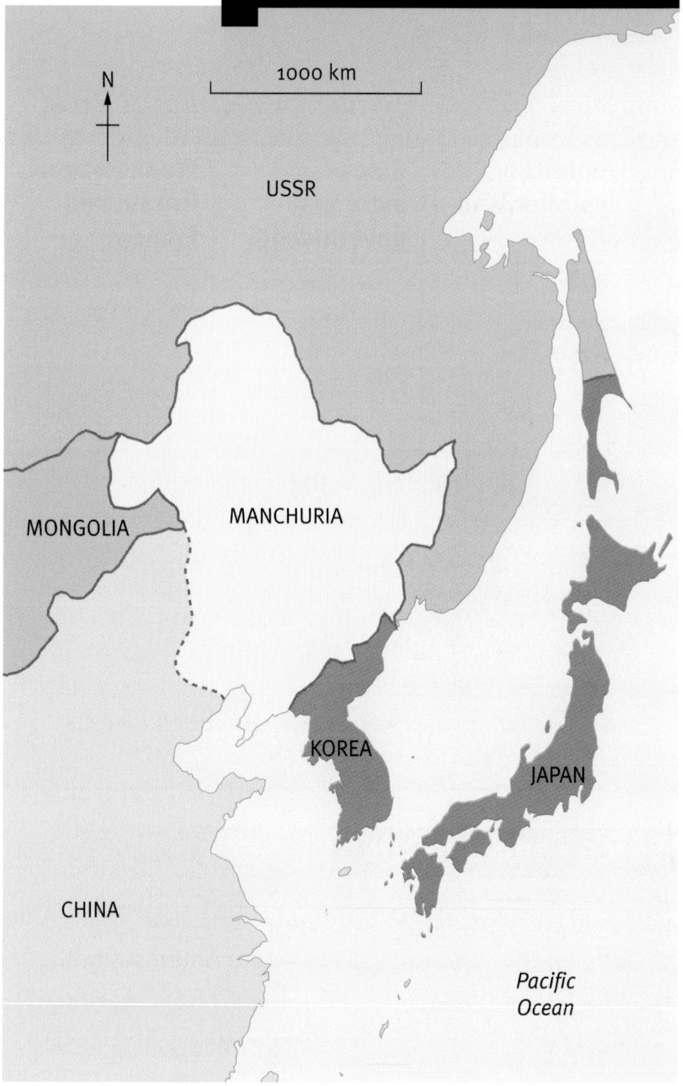

state – production and employment fell 30 per cent between 1929 and 1931. While the government seemed unable to cope with these developments, the army's policy of territorial conquest and expansion seemed to offer the people some hope.

The Mukden incident

In September 1931, the army staged the so-called Mukden incident, which led to the seizure of Manchuria and the establishment of the Japanese puppet state of Manchukuo. The government in Tokyo had advance warning of these plans, but did not intervene. Politicians needed great courage to stand up to the army, since assassinations were common. In May 1932 a group of soldiers murdered the prime minister, Inukai Tsuyoshi, in his own house. In February 1936 a full-scale military revolt in Tokyo was crushed only after many politicians and government officials had been murdered. Such events undermined normal political life. After 1932 Japan's governments were dominated by military men, and followed ever more aggressive policies, culminating in the invasion of China in 1937.

The League's failure in Manchuria, 1931–33

Manchuria is a part of northern China that is fertile and rich in natural resources such as coal and iron ore. In the 1920s China was weak, and in many areas local leaders, or **warlords**, were more important than the national government. Japan took advantage of this weakness to expand its interests in Manchuria.

KEY WORDS

Warlord – *a military commander exercising civil power in a region, whether in nominal allegiance to the national government or in defiance of it.*

The Japanese already had an army (known as the Kwantung army) stationed in southern Manchuria to protect the territory gained from Russia in 1905. They also owned the South Manchurian Railway. The Chinese regarded the area as theirs, and claimed that they had been forced, first by Russia and later by Japan, to accept foreign domination of Manchuria. By the late 1920s many Chinese were moving into Manchuria to settle, attracted by the availability of land and work. At the same time, the Chinese government was beginning to stand up to the warlords, and the Japanese feared that the Chinese might soon be strong enough to challenge them in Manchuria.

Exasperated by what they believed was their own government's weakness in dealing with China, in September 1931 officers of the Kwantung army staged the Mukden incident. The exact sequence of events remains unclear; however, on the night of 18 September, there was an explosion on the South Manchurian Railway just outside the city of Mukden. The Japanese claimed that this was sabotage by the Chinese, who subsequently opened fire on the Japanese railway guards. The Chinese denied this, claiming that all their soldiers were back in their barracks at the time. Whatever the truth of the matter, the incident was very convenient for the Kwantung army, giving it an excuse to begin the takeover of Manchuria.

SOURCE A

The Sleeping Giant Begins to Feel It

An American cartoon of 1937 commenting on the Japanese invasion of China.

VOICE YOUR OPINION!

Study the map of Asia.

- How easy would it have been for the Mukden incident to be staged by either side?
- The benefit for Japan is quite obvious, but how would the event benefit China?

There is no doubt that the Japanese government was appalled by the invasion, but as it progressed successfully an outburst of nationalism swept Japan, leaving the government no choice but to accept what had occurred. In 1932 Manchuria was renamed Manchukuo, and the last Chinese emperor, **Pu Yi**, removed from power in his own country in 1911, was installed by the Japanese as a puppet ruler.

How did the League of Nations react?

At first, the occupation of Manchuria looked like an obvious case of aggression by Japan. However, the Japanese had long-standing economic rights there, agreed by treaty with the Chinese. Most nations were inclined to regard Manchuria as a Japanese sphere of interest, and were not keen to get involved. In addition, the Japanese had successfully sown confusion about the true circumstances of the Mukden incident, and insisted that they were just defending themselves from Chinese attacks. Nevertheless, when China appealed for the League's help, it could not ignore what was going on. The League instructed Japanese forces to withdraw, but it was ignored, and the further advance of the Japanese into Manchuria left little doubt of their intentions.

In truth, there was little that the League could do if Japan remained determined to ignore its authority. For most League members, events in East Asia seemed very distant. China's internal turmoil was well known, and many League members secretly sympathised with Japan's attempts to impose 'order' on the region. The League decided to set up a Commission of Inquiry under **Lord Lytton**, which was sent to the area to gather information and report on what happened. When the report was published in late 1932, it condemned Japan's actions. The members of the League accepted Lytton's conclusions. The Japanese response was simple: they ignored the report and left the League.

The occupation of Manchuria did not end Japanese aggression in China. Early in 1932 Japanese and Chinese troops clashed in Shanghai, and during four weeks of fighting the Japanese bombed parts of the city. In February 1933 the Japanese occupied Jehol province, which bordered Manchuria. These actions were just a prelude to the full-scale invasion of the Chinese mainland that commenced in July 1937. In the months that followed, fighting spread through much of China, and by 1938 many of China's most important cities were under Japanese occupation. Many historians regard July 1937 as the true starting date of the Second World War.

The League had been exposed as powerless to deal with Japanese aggression in Manchuria. However, because these events took place in East Asia and not in Europe, they were not too damaging to the League's authority. It was easy for the League's supporters to continue to believe that, if a similar crisis occurred in Europe, where vital interests of the great powers were at stake, the League would be able to cope with it.

SOURCE B

This cartoon by David Low in 1932 attacks the weakness of the League in bowing to Japanese military aggression.

Increasing militarism in Italy

Italy, like Japan, emerged from the First World War dissatisfied with the gains it had made. The years immediately after the war were marked by great instability as the country tried to cope with its economic problems. Unemployment rose rapidly, and extremists on left and right struggled to take control.

By 1922, **Mussolini**'s Fascist Party, or Blackshirts, had emerged as the dominant group. After staging his 'March on Rome' in October that year, Mussolini was invited by the king to become prime minister. It took some time for him to take complete control of the country, but by 1926 he was firmly established as dictator – he preferred the title 'Il Duce'.

ACTIVITIES

1 Examine the two cartoons of events in Manchuria (Sources A and B).

   a How far do they fit with the conclusions you have drawn from the text?

   b Were Britain and America justified in criticising other countries for their expansionist policies?

   c What does this event reveal about the effectiveness of the League of Nations sanctions when faced with a large threat?

   d What was the damage caused by Japan leaving the League?

2 Imagine that you are one of Lord Lytton's advisors sent out to Asia to try to resolve the dispute between China and Japan. Compile a report that considers the following:

- China's right to call on the League for support
- a recognition of Japan's need to expand
- a re-affirmation of the aims and intentions of the League
- specific discussion points about the dispute
- a judgement to be presented to the League advising the best course of action. You can feel free to select alternative options to the League in the face of this crisis.

Once in power, Mussolini put into practice the extreme right-wing policies of his Fascist Party. Opposition was crushed and other political parties were banned. He took command of the economy, controlling working conditions, pay and prices by law. His achievements seemed impressive. New roads were built, marshes were drained, dams were constructed for hydroelectric power, and railways were electrified. In foreign affairs, Mussolini quickly made a name for himself. He built up Italy's armed forces and was not afraid to use the threat of violence. The Corfu incident of 1923 showed that Mussolini would follow an aggressive, nationalistic foreign policy.

KEY PEOPLE

Lord Lytton – *ageing politician who led a British enquiry after a lengthy visit to the Far East, including Manchuria, reported in October 1932.*

Pu Yi – *the last emperor (1908–12) of China, who, in 1934, became the emperor of the Japanese puppet state of Manchukuo, or Manchuria.*

Benito Mussolini – *Italian Fascist dictator and prime minister (1922–43) who conducted an expansionist foreign policy, and who was an ally of Hitler.*

The invasion of Abyssinia

Like other nations, Italy was hit badly by the Great Depression. When unemployment rose, Mussolini turned to foreign adventures to distract the Italian people from the troubles at home. The first victim was the African state of Abyssinia, a poor, undeveloped state in north-east Africa. Most historians believe that the resulting crisis was a death-blow to the League, which found it impossible to take effective action to stop Italian aggression.

Abyssinia was almost the only part of Africa not under European control and, being located next to the Italian colonies of Eritrea and Somaliland, it was an obvious target for Mussolini's colonial ambitions. Italy had attempted to conquer Abyssinia before, and one of Mussolini's aims was to avenge the humiliation suffered by the Italians at the Battle of Adowa (1896). Despite the Treaty of Friendship that Italy had signed with Abyssinia in 1928, it was clear by 1934 that Mussolini was planning war. In December 1934 a clash between Italian and Abyssinian troops at the oasis of Wal Wal gave Mussolini the excuse he needed. Although the League attempted to intervene in the dispute, tension increased and by September 1935 war seemed near.

The League's failure in Abyssinia, 1935–36

The League was in an impossible situation. Both Italy and Abyssinia were member states, bound in theory to accept the League's authority in settling their dispute. But it was obvious that Mussolini wanted war. If he invaded Abyssinia, the League would have to take action; but what action? Everything would depend on the attitude of Britain and France, the two great powers of the League. If they were determined enough, Mussolini might be forced to back down. However, they needed Mussolini's friendship because they saw him as a potential ally against Germany.

In January 1935, the French foreign minister, Laval, met Mussolini in Rome. A number of secret agreements were made, some of which concerned Abyssinia. Laval thought he was making economic concessions in North Africa so as to win Mussolini's friendship. But Mussolini interpreted France's approach as an indication that he could do as he liked in Abyssinia. In any case, Mussolini assumed that Britain and France, both major colonial powers themselves, would not object to Italy acquiring another African colony of its own. There was some surprise, then, when Britain tried to warn Mussolini off from invading Abyssinia. In September 1935, Sir Samuel Hoare, the British foreign secretary, made a vigorous speech to the Assembly of the League, calling for collective resistance to any Italian aggression.

In spite of the warnings, Italy's invasion of Abyssinia commenced on 3 October 1935. The Abyssinian forces stood little chance against the modern Italian army, but the country was huge and the roads poor, so the Italian troops were not able to advance quickly. At first, it seemed the League would take the strong action that Hoare had demanded. Within a week the League had condemned Italy as an aggressor, and soon afterwards it imposed sanctions, by which the League members were forbidden to trade with Italy. Crucially, however, the sanctions were not extended to basic war materials such as coal, iron and oil. Even Mussolini later admitted that this would have stopped the invasion within a week. But Britain and France were unwilling to risk provoking Mussolini more than necessary. As a result, they kept the Suez Canal open to the Italians, allowing Mussolini to supply his armies in Abyssinia.

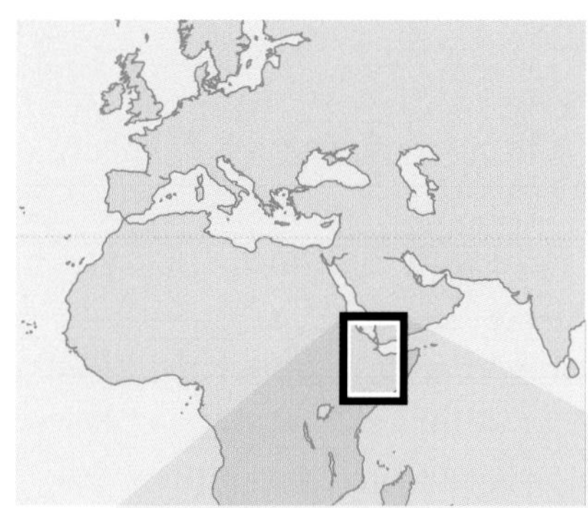

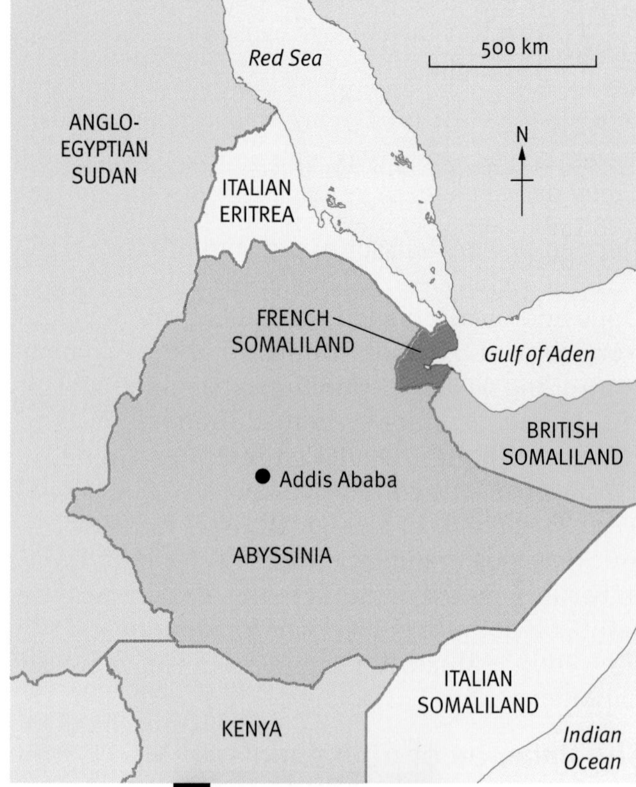

Location of Abyssinia and surrounding European colonies in Africa, c.1935.

The Hoare–Laval plan

Behind the scenes, Britain and France undermined the apparently tough actions of the League. Desperate for a settlement with Italy, Hoare and Laval met in December and agreed a plan that was designed to bring the invasion to an end. Abyssinia would be split up, with Italy gaining much of the fertile lands in the north and the south of the country. Another huge area in the south would be reserved for Italian economic expansion and settlement. Abyssinia would be reduced to half its original size, and limited to the barren, mountainous region. The only compensation for Abyssinia would be a narrow strip of land providing access to the Red Sea – the so-called 'corridor for camels'.

The Hoare–Laval Plan was never put to Abyssinia or Italy. Almost immediately, details of it were leaked to the press, causing a public outcry. Hoare and Laval were forced to resign. However, the damage had been done. Everyone now knew that the British and French had been talking tough, but were not prepared to back up their threats with action. Just the opposite – they seemed willing to reward Mussolini for his aggression.

SOURCE C

The bombing was magnificent sport. One group of Abyssinian horsemen gave the impression of a budding rose unfolding as the bomb fell in their midst and blew them up.

Description by Mussolini's 19-year-old pilot son of one attack in Abyssinia by the Italian air force.

The end of the League of Nations

The League was, of course, completely powerless when its most important members would take no effective action. Abyssinia was left helpless against the Italians, who now pressed home the invasion with greater determination. Only the difficulty of the terrain could slow the advance of the Italian troops, who were using modern weapons such as bombers, tanks and poison gas, against Abyssinian troops often armed only with spears. On 5 May 1936 Italian troops entered the Abyssinian capital, Addis Ababa, in triumph.

SOURCE D

POISON
POISON GAS
POISON GAS
"PAH! THEY WERE UNCIVILIZED SAVAGES, WITHOUT IDEALS."
(Copyright in All Countries)

Cartoon from the *Evening Standard*, April 1936, commenting on Mussolini's invasion of Abyssinia.

Three days earlier the Abyssinian emperor, Haile Selassie, had fled the country. He travelled to Geneva, where on 30 June he addressed the Assembly of the League of Nations. He spoke for three-quarters of an hour, summarising the events of the war and protesting against the failure of the League to deal with the invasion. His speech marked the end of the League's existence as an important international organisation. Nobody took it seriously in future, and it played no significant part in the events which, from 1936, rushed its members towards another war.

Mussolini's invasion of 1935–36 went unchecked by other nations. From 1936 Italy sent troops to support the Nationalist side in the **Spanish Civil War**. At first, Mussolini was suspicious and jealous of the German dictator **Adolf Hitler**, but the signing of the agreement which became known as the Rome–Berlin Axis in 1936 marked the first move towards the alliance of Italy and Germany in the Second World War.

SOURCE E

I, Haile Selaisse, Emperor of Abyssinia, am here today to claim that justice which is due to my people, and the assistance promised to it eight months ago, when fifty nations asserted that aggression had been committed in violation of international treaties.

Haile Selaisse addressing the Assembly of the League of Nations, 30 June 1936.

KEY PEOPLE

Adolf Hitler – *Austrian-born German dictator who led the Nazi Party, elected to restore Germany to its former status in Europe.*

KEY CONCEPTS

Spanish Civil War – *a war fought in Spain in the late 1930s. It was between loyalists (those loyal to a recently elected government) and fascists, led by General Francisco Franco. The fascists won the war and set up Franco's long rule of Spain as a dictator.*

SOURCE F

The real death of the League was in December 1935, not 1939 or 1945. One day it was a powerful body imposing sanctions, seeming more effective than ever before; the next day it was an empty sham, everyone scuttling from it as quickly as possible. What killed the League was the publication of the Hoare–Laval Plan.

The judgement of the British historian A.J.P. Taylor on the impact of the Abyssinian crisis on the League of Nations, written in 1966.

SOURCE G

THE AWFUL WARNING.

FRANCE AND ENGLAND (*together?*). "WE DON'T WANT YOU TO FIGHT, BUT, BY JINGO, IF YOU DO, WE SHALL PROBABLY ISSUE A JOINT MEMORANDUM SUGGESTING A MILD DISAPPROVAL OF YOU."

This British cartoon of 1935 presents international politics as a stage musical. Britain and France are shown singing to Mussolini, 'We don't want you to fight, but by jingo if you do, We will probably issue a joint memorandum, Suggesting a mild disapproval of you.'

Conclusion

The failures of the League over Manchuria and Abyssinia left weak nations defenceless against aggression by powerful neighbours. Manchuria and Abyssinia were occupied by foreign powers and abandoned by the League. Other nations realised that they could no longer look to the League for security. Furthermore, violence and aggression had been shown to pay. Although Italy and Japan left the League, they continued to play an active part in international affairs. They kept the territory they had gained and suffered no penalty. They were encouraged to take further aggressive actions. Japan persisted in its attacks on China. Italy intervened in the Spanish Civil War and later occupied Albania (in April 1939).

The weakness of Britain and France in dealing with the Abyssinian crisis mirrored the weakness of the League itself. Up to 1936 they could pretend that collective security was the way to deal with international aggression. From 1936 onwards they had to find different ways of dealing with the dictators. Above all, they had to accept that nobody would do this for them. Although they continued to appease Hitler, re-armament began in earnest as the democracies faced up to the fact that, in the end, they might have to fight another war.

The Manchurian and Abyssinian crises destroyed the idea of collective security by demonstrating that League members would not act together firmly in the face of determined aggression. This also destroyed the credibility of the League as a peacekeeping organisation.

ACTIVITIES

1 Consider Source D in the context of your own knowledge.
   - a Does Mussolini appear to be acting fairly?
   - b What impact do you think his desire to capture Abyssinia would have on the League?
   - c How far do you think Mussolini's desires are led by examples elsewhere, for example Hitler and the Japanese invasion of Manchuria?

2 Examine the two cartoons of events in Abyssinia (Sources D and G).
   - a How far do they fit with the conclusions you have drawn from the text?
   - b What was the grave mistake made by Hoare and Laval?
   - c What is the damage of Italy leaving the League?
   - d What does this event reveal about the effectiveness of the League of Nations sanctions when faced with a large threat?

Explain why the League failed in Abyssinia. **[6 marks]**

Why had international peace collapsed by 1939?

What were the long-term consequences of the peace treaties of 1919–23?

LEARNING OBJECTIVES

In this lesson you will:

- consider the decisions made at Versailles and focus specifically on the long-term impact on Germany
- assess the most damaging decisions at Versailles from the German perspective.

GETTING STARTED

1 After studying the League of Nations and European difficulties since 1918, speculate on the causes of the Second World War.

2 How would the following countries conduct their foreign policy?
- Britain
- France
- Germany
- America
- Russia.

The Second World War started barely 20 years after the first had finished. Hopes of establishing permanent peace were destroyed by the Great Depression and the rise to power of aggressive, militaristic regimes in Germany, Italy and Japan. Hitler's takeover in Germany in 1933 was a major turning point. His foreign policy challenged the Treaty of Versailles directly and put Europe on the path to war.

The legacy of the First World War peace settlements

The peace settlement after the First World War left many nations, both victors and losers, dissatisfied. Some of the problems caused by this were resolved, more or less peacefully, during the 1920s. But in Germany resentment of the Treaty of Versailles persisted. As early as 1920, Hitler stated in the Nazi Party Programme that he would get rid of the Treaty of Versailles, gain *Lebensraum* (living space) for the Germans by conquering land to the east, and unite all Germans in a new German Empire (*Reich*). Since other nations could be expected to resist these aims, Hitler's policies would mean that Germany would have to become a great military power again – something forbidden in the Treaty of Versailles.

However, it was not just extremists like Hitler who wanted to overturn the terms of the peace settlement. The aims of **Stresemann**, German foreign minister between 1923 and 1929, were in some respects similar to those of Hitler. However, whereas Stresemann was willing to work co-operatively with other nations to achieve his aims peacefully, Hitler was prepared to use force. Nonetheless, it was clear that many Germans did not accept the settlement of 1919–23 and this left Germany's future unresolved.

KEY PEOPLE

Neville Chamberlain – *British prime minister between 1937 and 1940, closely associated with the policy of appeasement to Nazi Germany.*

Gustav Stresemann – *chancellor (1923) and foreign minister of the Weimar Republic, who tried to reconcile former enemy nations to Germany, to remove the harsh clauses of the Treaty of Versailles, and to regain for Germany a respected place in the world.*

SOURCE A

The historian, with every justification, will come to the conclusion that we were very stupid men ... We arrived determined that a Peace of wisdom and justice should be negotiated; we left the conference conscious that the treaties imposed upon our enemies were neither just nor wise.

Harold Nicholson, British diplomat, speaking in 1919. He was one of the leading British officials at the Paris Peace Conference.

SOURCE B

Three great tasks confront German policy in the near future. In the first place the solution of the reparations problem in a way tolerable to Germany. Secondly, the protection of Germans abroad – those 10 to 12 million who now live under a foreign yoke ... The third great task is the readjustment of our eastern frontiers: the recovery of Danzig and the Polish corridor and correction of the frontier in Upper Silesia.

From a letter written in 1925 by Stresemann, the German foreign minister.

SOURCE C

If only we could sit down at a table with the Germans and run through all their complaints and claims with a pencil, this would greatly relieve all tension.

Neville Chamberlain speaking in 1938.

Once the international system of collective security began to crumble under the impact of the Great Depression, the way was open for Hitler to make Germany a great power again. He was helped by the weakness of the system set up to enforce the peace settlement. The League of Nations had no armed forces. The idea of collective security was fine as long as nations wanted peace, but it gave no security against determined aggressors.

Moreover, Britain and France found it hard to agree about how to treat Germany. The British felt that Germany had been harshly treated at Versailles and saw nothing wrong in making concessions. The French were fearful of Germany becoming strong again. Desperate to avoid another war, Britain and France responded to Hitler's demands with a policy of appeasement – making concessions to him in the hope that he would be satisfied.

SOURCE D

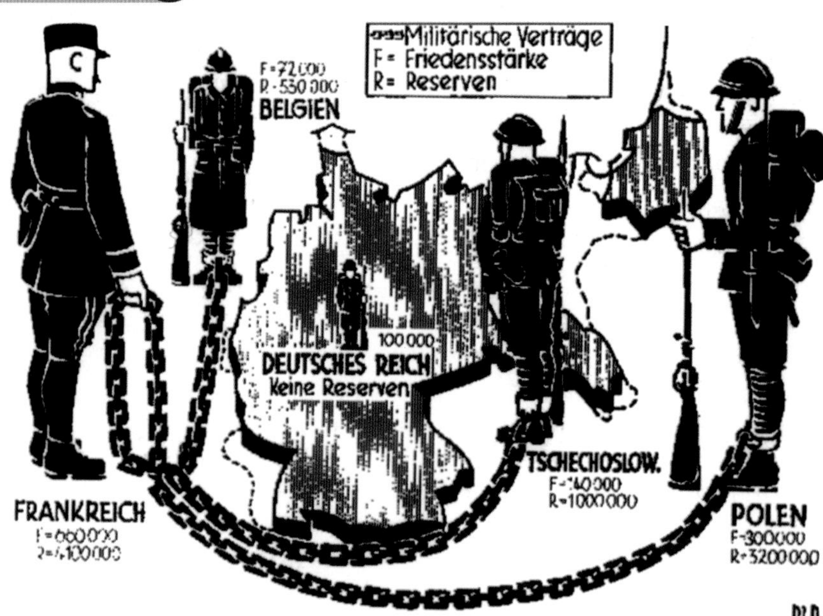

A Nazi propaganda cartoon commenting on the Treaty of Versailles. It shows Germany, its army limited by the treaty, surrounded by hostile neighbours.

Fact file

The British policy of appeasement

Appeasement is most closely associated with **Neville Chamberlain** (British prime minister 1937–40), but the policy was followed by Britain almost from the time Hitler came to power in 1933. By the 1930s most British politicians did not believe that all the terms of the Versailles settlement could be maintained; it was vital to reach an agreement with Germany that would settle its grievances once and for all. Appeasement assumed that Hitler would keep his side of a bargain, but Chamberlain himself doubted whether appeasement would finally work, although like most politicians in Britain and France, he would try almost anything to avoid war.

ACTIVITIES

1. Read Sources A, B and C and remind yourself of the aims of Clemenceau, Lloyd George and Wilson during the Treaty of Versailles. To what extent were they 'stupid men'?
2. Consider Source D and discuss your interpretation with a partner.
   - **a** List three things that the cartoon suggests about the legacy of the Treaty of Versailles.
   - **b** Given that this was a contemporary image, what consequences do you think it might have had on how Britain and France treated Germany?

What were the consequences of the failures of the League in the 1930s?

LEARNING OBJECTIVES

In this lesson you will:

- examine the way in which Hitler viewed the League of Nations and the steps he took to overcome it
- explore the continuity and significance of the failure of the League of Nations in allowing Hitler to expand according to his plans.

GETTING STARTED

As you read through this lesson, note down the failures of the League of Nations to stop Hitler.

- How was Hitler able to take advantage of the weaknesses of the League?
- To what extent was the League involved in key events?
- What could the League have done differently?

How did Hitler destroy the Treaty of Versailles?

One of the central aims of the League of Nations was to uphold the Treaty of Versailles. Between 1933 and 1936, Hitler destroyed the Treaty of Versailles, finding this surprisingly easy to do. One reason was his determination and willingness to take risks. Another was the weakness of other nations and their unwillingness to stop him.

Germany leaves the League of Nations and the Disarmament Conference, October 1933

The League of Nations Disarmament Conference started in 1932 and dragged on unsuccessfully into 1933. The Germans said they would be happy to accept disarmament if every nation disarmed; if not, they wanted to increase their armaments to French levels. The French would neither disarm nor allow German re-armament. This gave Hitler an excuse to leave the conference while pretending that Germany wanted peace. In fact, almost from the moment Hitler came to power, Germany had been re-arming. On the same day he withdrew Germany from the League of Nations. Many in Britain blamed France for the failure of the Disarmament Conference.

SOURCE 

I think it would be a mistake to seem to be on the side of France about the secret re-arming of Germany. To do that means that we appear to re-endorse that wicked Versailles Treaty and to justify the evil policies of France towards reconciliation over the past ten years.

From a letter written in 1934 by a British Labour Party politician.

The population of the Saar votes to rejoin Germany, January 1935

The Treaty of Versailles had placed the Saar, an important coal-mining area on the Franco–German border, under League of Nations administration for 15 years. In January 1935, the people of the Saar voted by 477,000 to 48,000 to return to Germany. This overwhelming vote was a tremendous propaganda success for Hitler, who increased its international impact by promising to make no further claims on French territory, thereby giving up German claims to Alsace and Lorraine, which had also been lost in the Treaty of Versailles.

German air force and army, March 1935

In March 1935, Hitler announced that Germany had a military air force (the Luftwaffe), and that he was introducing conscription (compulsory military service) to expand the army to half a million men. It was an open secret that Germany had been re-arming for some time, but this announcement was a clear rejection of the military restrictions in the Treaty of Versailles. Britain, France and Italy formed the so-called Stresa Front, condemning German re-armament and agreeing to work together to preserve existing treaties. But as Hitler expected, they were not prepared to take any action.

Anglo-German Naval Treaty, June 1935

This treaty allowed the Germans to build a navy 35 per cent of the size of Britain's. It seemed to guarantee Britain permanent naval superiority over Germany, and was consistent with Britain's policy of trying to control and satisfy legitimate German demands. In fact, it merely permitted Germany to ignore the naval restrictions in the Treaty of Versailles, including those on the possession of submarines and battleships, and to build up a navy as quickly as possible. By signing this treaty, Britain officially recognised that the military terms of the Treaty of Versailles were dead. Britain had consulted neither France nor Italy before signing – the Stresa Front had collapsed.

German re-occupation of the Rhineland, March 1936

While the Rhineland remained demilitarised, Germany was vulnerable to attack from the west. Pursuing a more aggressive policy in the east meant that the Rhineland would first have to be made secure. On 7 March 1936, Hitler took a big gamble by marching his troops into the demilitarised zone. His armies were not prepared for war, and he could not know how Britain and France would react. But the French would not act alone and the British saw no reason to risk war in order to stop Hitler 'marching into his own backyard'. Hitler had used force and nobody had tried to stop him. In future, the threat of war would lie behind all of Hitler's demands.

The Rome–Berlin Axis and the Anti-Comintern Pact

Hitler's successes made it easier for him to develop closer relationships with possible allies such as Italy and Japan. The Rome–Berlin Axis (1936) was not a formal alliance but an informal agreement between Hitler and Mussolini to work more closely together. Thus both Italy and Germany gave support to the nationalists in the Spanish Civil War. This war, which broke out in 1936, gave Hitler an opportunity to test much of his new military equipment. The Anti-Comintern Pact (1936) committed Germany and Japan to hostility towards the Soviet Union, and Italy joined the pact in 1937. A full military alliance between Germany and Italy (the Pact of Steel) was signed in 1939, and expanded in 1940 to include Japan.

SOURCE B

THE GOOSE-STEP

"GOOSEY GOOSEY GANDER,
WHITHER DOST THOU WANDER?"
"ONLY THROUGH THE RHINELAND—
PRAY EXCUSE MY BLUNDER!"

A British cartoon of 1936 about the remilitarisation of the Rhineland. The 'goose-step' was the style of marching used by the German army.

GradeStudio

How far do you agree that the League failed miserably to achieve its aims? Explain your answer.

[10 marks]

How far was Hitler's foreign policy to blame for the outbreak of war in 1939?

LEARNING OBJECTIVES

In this lesson you will:

- examine the nature of Hitler's foreign policy and the reaction of other countries to it
- investigate and evaluate the concept of appeasement and where it failed in its objective to pacify Hitler.

KEY PEOPLE

Neville Chamberlain – *British prime minister between 1937 and 1940, closely associated with the policy of appeasement to Nazi Germany.*

Anschluss, March 1938: Why did Hitler bother to invade Austria?

Austria is a German country both by language and by culture. Hitler had been born and raised in Austria, and his desire to unite all Germans was well known. Although the Treaty of Versailles forbade the union of Germany and Austria (Anschluss), it seemed obvious that he would try to bring it about.

A strong Nazi Party already existed in Austria. In 1934, Nazis murdered the Austrian Chancellor, Dollfuss, during an attempted takeover which failed only when Mussolini, the Italian dictator, threatened to intervene. At this time, Mussolini was suspicious of Hitler, and regarded Austria as being in Italy's sphere of interest.

In 1936, Dollfuss's replacement, Schuschnigg, agreed to appoint Nazis to the government. In return, Germany promised to respect Austria's independence. But in January 1938, Austrian police raided Nazi headquarters in Vienna and found plans to take over the government. On 12 February, Schuschnigg met Hitler at Berchtesgaden and agreed to appoint Seyss-Inquart, a Nazi supporter, as Minister of the Interior, and to lift all restrictions on Nazi Party activities.

By making concessions to Hitler, Schuschnigg hoped to preserve Austria's independence. However, Schuschnigg also announced that a plebiscite would be held for the Austrians to decide whether or not Austria would remain an independent nation. If the vote went in Schuschnigg's favour, Hitler's plans for the gradual takeover of Austria would be undermined.

On 11 March, Hitler demanded that the plebiscite be postponed. When the Austrians agreed, he demanded the replacement of Schuschnigg by Seyss-Inquart. The plan was for Seyss-Inquart to become chancellor and then request German help to restore order in Austria. At 8pm, Seyss-Inquart was appointed chancellor, and the Germans invaded Austria the following day.

The German invasion of Austria was one of the worst-planned invasions in history. German tanks had to refuel at petrol stations along the road to Vienna, and German commanders had to use tourist guides to plan their routes. But there was no resistance from the Austrians and the invasion was completed without bloodshed. Austria was absorbed into Germany; the Anschluss had occurred.

This time, Mussolini did not object. Since the creation of the Rome–Berlin Axis in 1936, Hitler and Mussolini had worked together more closely. Without Italy's protection, Austria was doomed; Britain and France would not intervene. Although many people in those countries were worried by Hitler's methods, most were reassured by a plebiscite held on 10 April, in which over 90 per cent of Austrians approved the Anschluss.

The Czechoslovakian crisis, 1938

After the Anschluss, it was clear that Czechoslovakia would be the next country to attract Hitler's attention. A free and hostile Czechoslovakia would make it impossible for Germany to fight a war in the west. Czechoslovakia's geographical position, with its land thrusting deep into German territory, would be a direct threat to Germany. Although not a large nation, Czechoslovakia was well defended and had a modern and well-equipped army.

However, it had one crucial weakness which Hitler planned to exploit. Its population included several ethnic minorities, among them 3.5 million ethnic Germans living in the Sudetenland, a part of Czechoslovakia along the German–Czech border. The Sudeten Germans could be used to stir up trouble against the Czech government.

A Czech–German war?

The Czechs knew that to surrender the Sudetenland would make them defenceless against Germany, since all Czechoslovakia's frontier defences against Germany were in the Sudetenland. Handing these over would mean that Hitler could easily take over the rest of Czechoslovakia whenever he wanted. It began to look as though war between Germany and Czechoslovakia might break out. If so, then France and probably Britain would go to Czechoslovakia's aid. However, neither Britain nor France wanted to fight against Germany.

Chamberlain was sure that a peaceful solution could be found to the Czech crisis. On 15 September 1938 he met Hitler at Berchtesgaden in Germany to discuss the crisis. Hitler made it clear that the crisis could be solved only by the transfer of the Sudetenland to Germany. Chamberlain indicated that he had no objection to this as long as the transfer was done peacefully.

A week later on 22 September, having in the meantime forced the Czechs to agree to the loss of the Sudetenland, Chamberlain returned to Germany to meet Hitler at Bad Godesberg. But Hitler now demanded that the Sudetenland be handed over by 1 October, and that claims on Czech territory by Hungary and Poland be met. If his demands were not met by 1 October 1938, Germany would invade Czechoslovakia. Europe was on the brink of war.

SOURCE A

GOOD HUNTING

Mussolini. "All right, Adolf—I never heard a shot"

A British cartoon of February 1938. Mussolini (on the left) is saying to Hitler, 'All right, Adolf, I never heard a shot.' In 1934 Mussolini had defended Austrian independence, but by 1938 the relationship between Italy and Germany had become much closer.

The Munich Conference

Chamberlain was desperate for any solution that would avoid war. When Mussolini proposed a four-power conference, both Chamberlain and Hitler, who now saw the prospect of achieving his aims without having to fight, agreed to attend. On 29 September 1938, Chamberlain, Hitler, Daladier (the French prime minister) and Mussolini met in Munich and signed an agreement that gave Hitler the terms he had demanded at Bad Godesberg. It was also agreed that Czechoslovakia's new frontiers would be guaranteed by the four powers. This enabled the British and French to claim that Czechoslovakia had been saved.

In fact, the guarantee was meaningless. Hitler had no intention of keeping to it and soon both Poland and Hungary grabbed the territory that they wanted while the traditional rivalry and dislike between Slovaks and the more prosperous Czechs within what was left of the country further threatened the Czechoslovakian government.

SOURCE B

The final settlement forced Czechoslovakia to cede to Germany 11,000 square miles of territory in which dwelt 2,800,000 Germans and 800,000 Czechs. Within this area lay all the vast Czech fortifications. Czechoslovakia's entire system of rail, road, telephone and telegraph communications was disrupted. [It] lost 66 per cent of its coal, 80 per cent of its lignite, 86 per cent of its chemicals, 80 per cent of its cement, 80 per cent of its textiles, 70 per cent of its electrical power and 40 per cent of its timber. A prosperous industrial nation was split up and bankrupted overnight.

An American historian, William Shirer, writing in 1959, summarised the damage that the Munich Agreement did to Czechoslovakia.

'Peace for Our Time'

The Soviets were not invited to the Munich Conference. Everyone knew they would never agree to Hitler's terms. The Czechs were not even consulted and had no choice but to agree. The day after the conference, Chamberlain met Hitler alone and they agreed an Anglo-German Declaration. The two countries promised never to go to war with each other again, and that they would settle all disputes between the two countries by consultation. It was a copy of this agreement that Chamberlain waved to the cheering crowds on his return to Britain. He announced to the British public, 'I believe it is peace for our time.'

By 10 October 1938 German troops had completed the occupation of the Sudetenland. Czechoslovakia was now defenceless against its enemies.

VOICE YOUR OPINION!

Place these factors in order of importance for the outbreak of war in 1939.

- Hitler's policies
- Peace treaties
- Appeasement
- Failure of the League
- Anti-war feeling in Britain and France
- The Depression.

Czechoslovak territorial losses from the Munich Agreement, 1938.

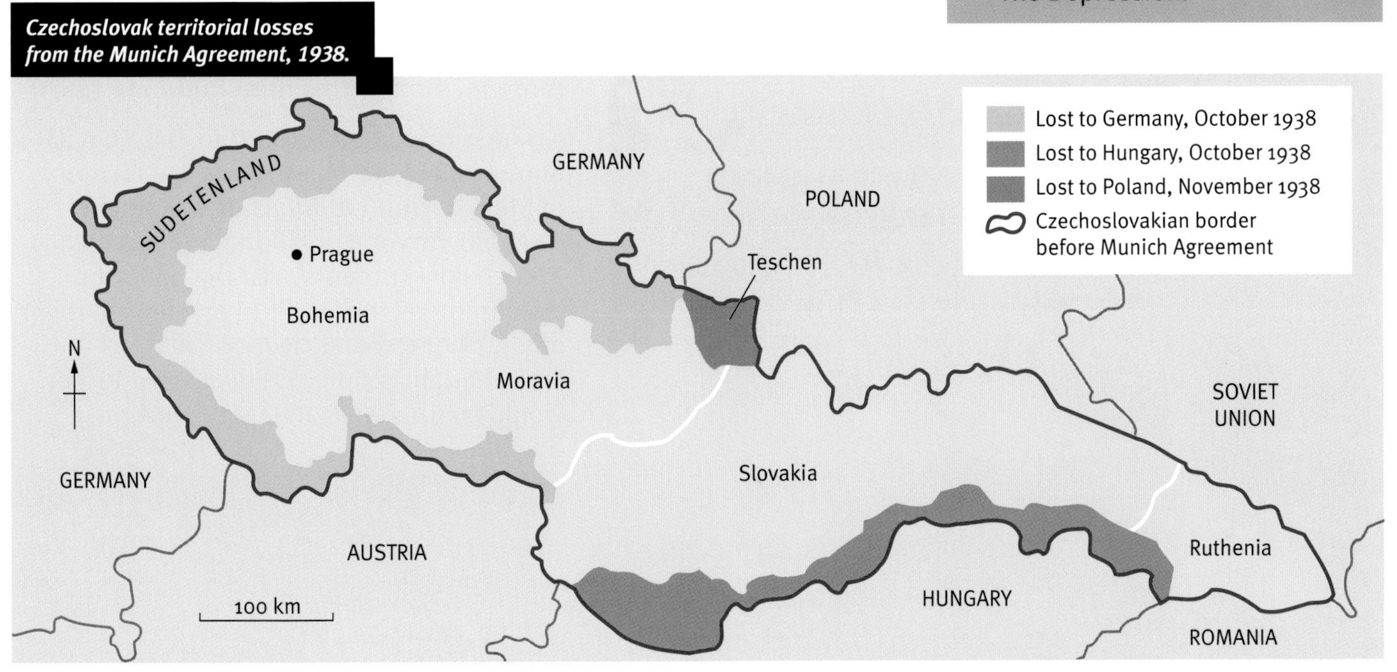

SOURCE C

Chamberlain's return from Munich. He is waving a copy of the agreement to the crowd.

GradeStudio

'The Second World War started because of the inability of Britain and France to challenge Hitler's aggression.'

How far do you agree with this statement? **[10 marks]**

SOURCE D

At the airport Daladier turned up his coat collar to protect his face from the rotten eggs he expected from the crowd. To his astonishment there were no eggs or shouts of 'We are betrayed.' Instead they were actually cheering him – shouting 'Vive Daladier', 'Vive la Paix', 'Vive la France!' Daladier turned to a colleague and whispered, 'The fools!'

From Daladier's own account of his return to France from the Munich Conference.

Hitler destroys Czechoslovakia, March 1939

At Munich, Hitler had given Chamberlain meaningless promises about the future of Czechoslovakia. Chamberlain thought that the Munich Agreement had secured 'peace for our time'. He was wrong. Within six months Hitler's armies were on the march again. Czechoslovakia could not survive in its weakened state. Internally torn apart by the hostility between the Czechs and the Slovaks, and with much of its territory already seized by Germany, Poland and Hungary, it was incapable of defending itself. In March 1939, Hitler ordered his armies to occupy Bohemia and Moravia, two parts of Czechoslovakia that had been protected by the Munich Agreement. Slovakia then became nothing more than a puppet-state under German domination. Hungary took the opportunity to grab yet more territory – this time Ruthenia.

Czechoslovakia had ceased to exist. On 23 March 1939 Hitler also seized the territory of Memel from Lithuania. It was finally clear to everyone, including the British and French governments, that the policy of appeasement was dead. In an effort to deter any further German aggression, Chamberlain promised Poland that Britain would guarantee its independence.

Was the policy of appeasement justified?

LEARNING OBJECTIVES

In this lesson you will:

- examine the nature and need for appeasement
- examine critically the policy of appeasement and identify where it failed in its objectives.

GETTING STARTED

Discuss with a partner the positives and negatives of letting people get what they want.

What kind of a situation does that create?

List the reasons you think that Britain would feel it necessary to let Hitler and Germany get what they wanted.

Why appease?

There are strong differences of opinion between historians about appeasement. After the Second World War, many British historians shared the feeling of shame that Britain had not stood up to Hitler earlier, particularly as Chamberlain's claim to have brought back 'peace with honour' from Munich rested on the betrayal of Czechoslovakia. These historians portrayed Chamberlain as a weak man who was taken in by Hitler. More recently, though, some historians have begun to restore Chamberlain's reputation by explaining why he acted as he did and how restricted his options were. Consider the arguments given for and against appeasement below, and decide whether you think appeasement was justified.

The arguments for appeasement

1 Sympathy for Germany

At first, many people felt that there was some justice in Hitler's claims. The British accepted that the Treaty of Versailles was too harsh and Germany had a right to be treated more fairly and to be accepted as a great power. So in 1935 they were happy to sign the Anglo-German Naval Agreement, which ignored the terms of the Treaty of Versailles. When Hitler remilitarised the Rhineland in 1936, there was a feeling that he was just 'marching into his own backyard', and when Anschluss occurred in 1938, the Austrians were simply achieving the self-determination denied them at Versailles. Each single step that Hitler took could be justified, and it was always possible to believe that, with just one more concession, he would be satisfied and demand no more.

2 The desire for peace

It was perfectly understandable that Britain and France would want to find peaceful solutions to Germany's problems, and so avoid another war. Memories of the horrors of the First World War were still strong. Most Europeans placed their trust in the League of Nations and the idea of collective security. Decent, democratic politicians in Britain and France at first simply found it hard to accept that the rise of brutal, militaristic regimes in Germany, Italy and Japan would make it necessary again to prepare for war. To make matters worse, they were still coping with the impact of the Great Depression, and were concerned that their economies were just not strong enough to bear the costs of re-armament.

3 The threat of Communism

In dealing with the aggressive nature of German policies in central and eastern Europe, Britain and France faced a serious problem. They could not actually protect countries like Czechoslovakia and Poland from attack, as they were too far away. The only great power that could protect these countries was the Soviet Union. But with good reason, Britain and France, and more so, Czechoslovakia and Poland, hated and feared Stalin's communist tyranny just as much as they hated Nazi Germany. Most western politicians could not make up their minds which of Germany and the Soviet Union was the greater threat.

4 Time to re-arm

The strongest argument for appeasement was that Britain was just not ready to fight. A re-armament programme to prepare Britain for war began only in 1936, and was not planned for completion until 1940. When the crises of 1938 occurred, Britain desperately needed more time to build up its strength. By giving in to Hitler's demands at Munich, war was postponed for a year, and when it did eventually come, Britain had made just enough preparations to survive.

The arguments against appeasement

1 The appeasers misjudged Hitler

The appeasers made the crucial mistake of treating Hitler as they would treat each other – as a rational politician who was open to reasoned argument. They did not realise until too late that they were dealing with a determined, unscrupulous tyrant, who would interpret any concession as a sign of weakness. The more they gave him the more he demanded.

SOURCE A

The cartoon clearly identifies the double standard that typified foreign policy. War was always an objective.

2 Appeasement was morally wrong

Britain and France were so afraid of another war that they allowed Germany to break international agreements without punishment, and finally abandoned Czechoslovakia to its fate in return for meaningless promises. Appeasement was simply another word for weakness and cowardice.

3 The appeasers missed excellent chances to stop Hitler

The appeasers were so busy looking for chances to give Hitler what he wanted that they missed good opportunities to resist him. After the remilitarisation of the Rhineland in 1936, Hitler admitted that any sign of military action by the French would have led him to withdraw his troops immediately. At Munich in 1938, Britain and France abandoned Czechoslovakia, a well-defended and well-armed country which could have put up significant resistance to German attack.

ACTIVITIES

1. Arrange the following statements in order of importance to answer the question Why did nobody confront Hitler?
   - Memory of the horror of 1914–18
   - Economic weakness caused by the Depression
   - Hitler seemed reasonable
   - The feeling that Versailles was unfair
   - French unwillingness to act without Britain
   - British preoccupation with their Empire
2. Discuss your ideas with your classmates and create a whole-class diagram. How far does it compare with your own?

GradeStudio

How far do you agree that following the policy of appeasement was a mistake? **[10 marks]**

How important was the Nazi–Soviet Pact?

LEARNING OBJECTIVES

In this lesson you will:

- find out about the Nazi–Soviet Pact and understand its role in the origins of the Second World War
- assess the reasons why the pact was signed, who it benefited and how it changed the situation.

GETTING STARTED

Consider Sources A and B. Discuss with a partner what you think they reveal about the way the Russian and the German leaders felt:

a about each other
b about their pact
c about their future as allies.

Hitler turns to Poland

After the destruction of Czechoslovakia, it was clear that Poland would be Hitler's next target. Germany had obvious claims on some Polish territory. The 'Polish Corridor', which split East Prussia from the rest of Germany, had been taken from Germany by the Treaty of Versailles, as had the city of Danzig, which was now a 'free city' under League of Nations control. Hitler wanted these areas back. He also wanted Polish territory as *Lebensraum* (living space).

Despite this, the Poles enjoyed a friendly relationship with Hitler's Germany until 1939. The Polish government sympathised with the Nazis' authoritarian and anti-Semitic (anti-Jewish) policies. They had even taken part in the destruction of Czechoslovakia after the Munich Conference by grabbing Teschen. At first, the Poles found it hard to take seriously Hitler's demands and increasing threats against them. They even thought their best hope of survival was to try to avoid making commitments to either of their two powerful neighbours, Germany and the Soviet Union.

Britain's promise

Britain's guarantee to preserve the independence of Poland made the Poles feel safer than they really were. There was little that Britain and France could do to stop a German invasion of Poland – it was too far away from them. So the attitude of Poland's other powerful neighbour, the Soviet Union, would be crucial. Would it help Poland against a German attack?

Discussions between Britain, France and the Soviet Union took place through early August 1939, but collapsed because of distrust between the two sides, and also because the Poles refused to let Soviet troops enter their territory in advance of an attack by Germany. The Soviets thought that Britain and France would be happy to see the Soviet Union doing all the fighting if war broke out with Germany.

SOURCE A

A Soviet viewpoint on the Pact.

The Nazi–Soviet Pact

On 23 August 1939 the sensational news broke of an agreement signed in Moscow by the foreign ministers of the Soviet Union and Germany, Molotov and Ribbentrop. They had agreed to a non-aggression pact – a promise not to fight each other. Secretly, they had also decided to split up Poland between them. Fascist Germany and the communist Soviet Union gave every appearance of being bitter political enemies. Nobody really believed that the pact made any difference to their mutual hatred. So why did they make an agreement not to fight each other?

Why was the Nazi–Soviet Pact important?

The pact left Britain and France to fight Germany alone. Hitler did not really believe they would go to war over Poland, but almost had second thoughts when Britain's reaction to the pact was the signing of a formal alliance with Poland on 25 August 1939. This time Britain and France would not be able to back down in the face of Nazi aggression. If they did, it would signal to the world that they could no longer be regarded as great powers, and unlike in 1938, re-armament meant that they were now more ready for war. But the Anglo-Polish alliance did not really change anything. It took only a few days for Hitler to recover his nerve and order that Poland be invaded on 1 September. When Hitler ignored Britain and France's ultimatum to call off the attack, they declared war on 3 September. Nevertheless, within three weeks Poland had been defeated, its armies completely powerless against the *Blitzkrieg* (lightning war) launched by Germany. Two weeks into the fighting, Soviet armies invaded Poland from the east, at the same time occupying the Baltic states (Estonia, Latvia and Lithuania).

SOURCE B

THE SCUM OF THE EARTH, I BELIEVE ?
THE BLOODY ASSASSIN OF THE WORKERS, I PRESUME ?
RENDEZVOUS

The great dictators unite: a cartoon from September 1939.

The pact made war inevitable

The pact was the single most important short-term cause of the Second World War. This means that it explains how and why the war broke out at the time it did. Hitler had planned to invade Poland, and now he knew that he could do so without direct interference from any other great power. Once he attacked, Britain would be forced to honour its guarantee to Poland. Of course, this could not save Poland because there was nothing that Britain and France could do to stop the German invasion, but it would mean war.

ACTIVITIES

1 a Using the information on the page, create a spider diagram that charts the signing of the Nazi–Soviet Pact. Possible headings could include:
- Aims of Russia
- Aims of Germany
- Role of Britain
- Terms of the pact
- Impact of the pact

b Share your diagram with a partner.

2 'Britain's indecision forced Stalin's hand; the pact was an investment in Russian security and not an alliance of friends.'

a How far do you think this an accurate interpretation of the Nazi–Soviet Pact?

b How far do you think this was a common opinion at the time?

Why did Britain and France declare war on Germany in September 1939?

LEARNING OBJECTIVES

In this lesson you will:

- examine the long- and short-term factors that prompted the decision to go to war in 1939
- consider the implications of declaring war and assess the difficulties faced by political leaders in such a context.

War is declared, September 1939

Neither Britain nor France wanted to go to war with Germany in 1939. They would have preferred a peaceful solution to the Polish crisis and did their best to persuade the Poles to negotiate with Hitler over the disputed areas, Danzig and the Polish Corridor. The problem was that the Poles did not want to negotiate – they knew from the example of Czechoslovakia that negotiating with Hitler could be fatal. Anyway, once the Nazi–Soviet Pact was signed, negotiations would have been meaningless as Germany and the Soviet Union had secretly resolved to split Poland between them.

A state of war

When Germany invaded Poland on 1 September 1939, Britain and France did not declare war immediately. They delayed, still hoping that there might be a chance to make Hitler changes his plans. They both knew they could not save Poland. However, they were both allied to Poland and had to take some action. On 3 September the British government sent Hitler an ultimatum (Source B). The French sent a similar ultimatum. When no replay was received by 11 a.m., Britain declared war on Germany.

Britain and France went to war because they were forced to. Hitler had finally pushed them to the point at which they had to resist. The alternative was national humiliation and acceptance of German domination of Europe.

How far do you agree that the Nazi–Soviet Pact was the most important cause of war in September 1939? Explain your answer. **[10 marks]**

BRAIN BOOST

Why 1939?

- Hitler's refusal to comply
- New complications with Nazi–Soviet Pact
- Britain's re-armament programme
- Ten years since Depression
- Invasion of Poland
- Disdain for other nations and members of British government

GETTING STARTED

Arrange the events in the correct chronological order.

- German invasion of Poland
- Abyssinian crisis
- Treaty of Versailles
- German invasion of Czechoslovakia
- Nazi–Soviet Pact
- Occupation of Sudetenland and Munich Conference
- Anschluss
- Crisis in Manchuria
- German troops enter the Rhineland.

SOURCE 

It is not Danzig that is at stake. For us it is a matter of expanding our living space to the east. There is therefore no question of sparing Poland and we are left with the decision: to attack Poland at the earliest opportunity. We cannot expect a repeat of Czechoslovakia. There will be war.

Hitler speaking at a conference of his generals, May 1939.

SOURCE 

Unless not later than 11 a.m., British summer time, today September 3rd, satisfactory assurances have been given by the German government and have reached His Majesty's Government in London, a state of war will exist between the two countries from that hour.

The ultimatum from the British to the German government, 3 September 1939.

The inter-war years, 1919–39

If you have chosen to answer the source-based question on this topic, you will be given a single source, and asked one question which will require you to interpret the source (AO3, though you will also need to use your knowledge and understanding, AO1 and AO2, to help you answer). Here is an example.

Source A

Study the source carefully, and then answer the question which follows.

A cartoon published in a German newspaper in June 1919.

1 a Study Source A. What is the message of this cartoon? Use details of the cartoon and your own knowledge to explain your answer. **[7 marks]**

Examiner's tip

The message of the cartoon is what the cartoonist wants to tell the person looking at the cartoon. Usually cartoons have more than one message, but there will always be one main message that is more important than the others. Your task is to work out this main message, and to do so successfully you will need to use your knowledge of what was going on at the time.

Mark scheme

Level 1: Describes features of the cartoon.
Level 2: Describes the message of the cartoon.
Level 3: Explains the message of the cartoon supported with details from the source OR own knowledge.
Level 4: Explains the message of the cartoon supported with details from the source AND own knowledge.

Answering the question

STEP 1: What does the cartoon show? There is no need for you to describe the cartoon, but you do need to notice and understand its details. The people are sad, held behind the barbed wire and controlled by the rifles with fixed bayonets.

STEP 2: What does the cartoon mean in relation to what was happening at this time? Germany had just been defeated in the First World War, which helps to explain the people's sadness. In fact, you could say that one message of the cartoon is that the Germans were depressed at losing the war, but this is not the main message. Isn't there something more specific about the events of June 1919?

STEP 3: What does the cartoonist want to say to us? In June 1919 the Treaty of Versailles was signed. The cartoonist wanted to comment on the Treaty. His main message was to denounce the Treaty for its harmful effects on Germany.

STEP 4: How does the cartoonist get the message across to the audience? The question tells you to use details of the cartoon and your knowledge to explain your answer. The cartoon shows the German people as crushed and imprisoned by the military power of the Allies. This is a way of saying that the Treaty is unfair, does not treat the Germans as equals and will give them no hope for the future. The cartoon helps us to understand why the Germans regarded the Treaty as a Diktat, and why they never really accepted it.

Student's response

Here is one student's response to the question. Read it and decide how you could improve it.

In the cartoon you can see people walking behind barbed wire. They look very sad. I think it shows that Germany has been beaten in the war and that now they will be like prisoners. The Allies want to make sure that Germany can never attack them again so they are going to keep them prisoners.

Examiner's comment

This answer gives us a reasonable interpretation of the cartoon which includes the message that Germans will be like prisoners from now on. However, it fails to use the specific context of the cartoon – that it is a comment on the signing of the Treaty of Versailles – and therefore it cannot be identifying the main message that the cartoonist had in mind. An answer like this would receive some marks, but to achieve a top-level answer you would first have to identify what the cartoonist wanted to say about the treaty, and then use details of the cartoon to explain the message.

The inter-war years, 1919-39

The source-based question will always be followed by a single question asking you to explain why an event or development occurred. This question will not use a source, and will test AO1 and AO2. Here is an example.

1 b Explain why Germany's armed forces were limited by the Treaty of Versailles. **[8 marks]**

Answering the Question

STEP 1: Although knowing how Germany's armed forces were limited by the Treaty will help you answer (by giving you ideas about a range of possible reasons), this is not really what the question is asking. Answers which simply describe the restrictions in the Treaty will only get low marks.

STEP 2: Think of the reasons you will be writing about. One decision you have to make is how many reasons will be needed. It is possible to earn full marks by explaining only two reasons, but perhaps the best advice is to think of three, just in case one of your explanations is not as good as the others.

STEP 3: Work out the explanations for each of your reasons. Try to make sure all of the reasons with their explanations are clearly different and separate from each other.

Mark scheme

Level 1: General answer lacking specific content and knowledge. [1–2 marks]

Level 2: Identifies and/or describes how Germany's armed forces were limited by the Treaty of Versailles. [3–4 marks]

Level 3: Explains why Germany's armed forces were limited by the Treaty of Versailles. [5–8 marks]
One explained reason are worth 5–6 marks.
Two or more explained reasons worth 6–8 marks.
E.g. 'Germany's forces were limited to avoid war in the future. Many people believed that German aggression had led to the war. The theory was that if she was disarmed, the world would be a more peaceful place because Germany would not be able to launch military strikes'. [6 marks]

Examiner's tip

Make sure you understand the difference between giving a reason and explaining it. This question asks for explanation, and how well you do this will determine the mark you earn. For example, you could say that Germany's forces were limited *to make sure there would not be another war.* This is giving a reason, but on its own it is not enough. You need to go on to explain **why** the Allies wished to avoid future wars with Germany – perhaps by pointing out how costly the First World War had been, both financially and in terms of lives lost.

Student's response

Read the following answer. How many reasons have been given, and how many are explained?

There is more than one reason why Germany's forces were limited by the Treaty of Versailles. France wanted Germany to be weak so that it could never attack again. The fighting on the Western Front had been mainly in France and the country had suffered a lot of damage so the French wanted a guarantee this would not happen again. Another reason was that the British wanted to make sure that Germany could never challenge Britain's naval power again.

Examiner's comment

This answer gives us two reasons, one for France and the other for Britain. For the first it also tells us **why** the French wanted Germany to be weak, so this reason is explained. Giving one explained reason is enough to get the answer into the top level, but not to earn the highest mark. To do this you would need to explain at least two reasons. Here, the second reason is not developed. If an explanation had been provided, for example by adding that the reason why the British wanted to destroy Germany's naval power was to safeguard its trade with its colonies around the world, then this answer could have scored a top mark.

The Cold War, 1945–75

Introduction

As the Second World War drew to a close, the fragile alliance between the Soviet Union and the Western Allies (Britain, France and the USA) began to break up as a result of the deep-rooted suspicion which East and West felt for each other. By 1949 relationships had deteriorated to the point where a 'Cold War' had begun, as the two sides sought to extend their influence and win diplomatic victories over their opponents. This was not a military war, but instead a war of words and of propaganda. The communist Soviet Union and its allies sought to discredit the capitalist USA and its allies.

By the end of 1948 Europe had became divided by an 'iron curtain' separating the democratic, capitalist West from the communist East. The history of the next 30 years is the history of conflict between East and West, as each side sought to score diplomatic and tactical victories over the other. Although the United Nations had been formed to help maintain peace in the world, it was powerless to prevent increasingly sour relations between the USA and the Soviet Union.

After the Second World War, the USA poured huge sums into western Europe to help bring about economic recovery and prevent the spread of communism. The Soviet Union resented American interference and took steps to assert its authority, for example in the Berlin Blockade and the building of the Berlin Wall. It also ensured that those countries which were communist remained so – as Hungary and Czechoslovakia found to their cost. It would be wrong, however, to see the Cold War as a purely European conflict. The Americans were equally keen to stop the spread of communism outside Europe. Indeed, they went to war in both Korea and Vietnam to do so. In 1962 their determination to prevent the Soviet Union stationing nuclear missiles in Cuba almost brought about the world's first nuclear war.

The charismatic American President John F. Kennedy was keen that the USA stood firm against Soviet influence in neighbouring Cuba. After intense diplomacy both sides claimed a victory and closer relations between Kennedy and the Soviet leader, Nikita Khrushchev, was one positive outcome, albeit short-lived.

In Vietnam, American military might came up against an extremely determined opposition and found out that superior spending power and weapons did not guarantee victory. The horrors of the Vietnam War were beamed into the homes of Americans and this led to a massive wave of anti-war feeling that eventually dragged the USA out of Vietnam by 1975.

By 1975 the Cold War was still freezing, and it would get colder in the 1980s before it thawed at the end of that decade. This chapter is focused on the reasons for the Cold War and the conflicts under its umbrella until 1975.

TIMELINE
Communists seize power in Czechoslovakia
Berlin Blockade
1944
1946
1948
1950
Communist regime established in Bulgaria by USSR
• Communist regimes established in Romania and Hungary by USSR
• USSR annexes Baltic States
• Yalta Conference
• Potsdam Conference
• Atomic bombs dropped on Japan
• Communists dominate the government in Poland
• Truman Doctrine announced
• Marshall Plan announced
• USSR forms the Communist Information Bureau (Cominform)
• Soviet scientists develop atomic bomb
• Communist People's Republi
of China founded
• USSR found Comecon in response to the Marshall Plan
• NATO founded
• Communist German Democrat
Republic (East Germany) founde

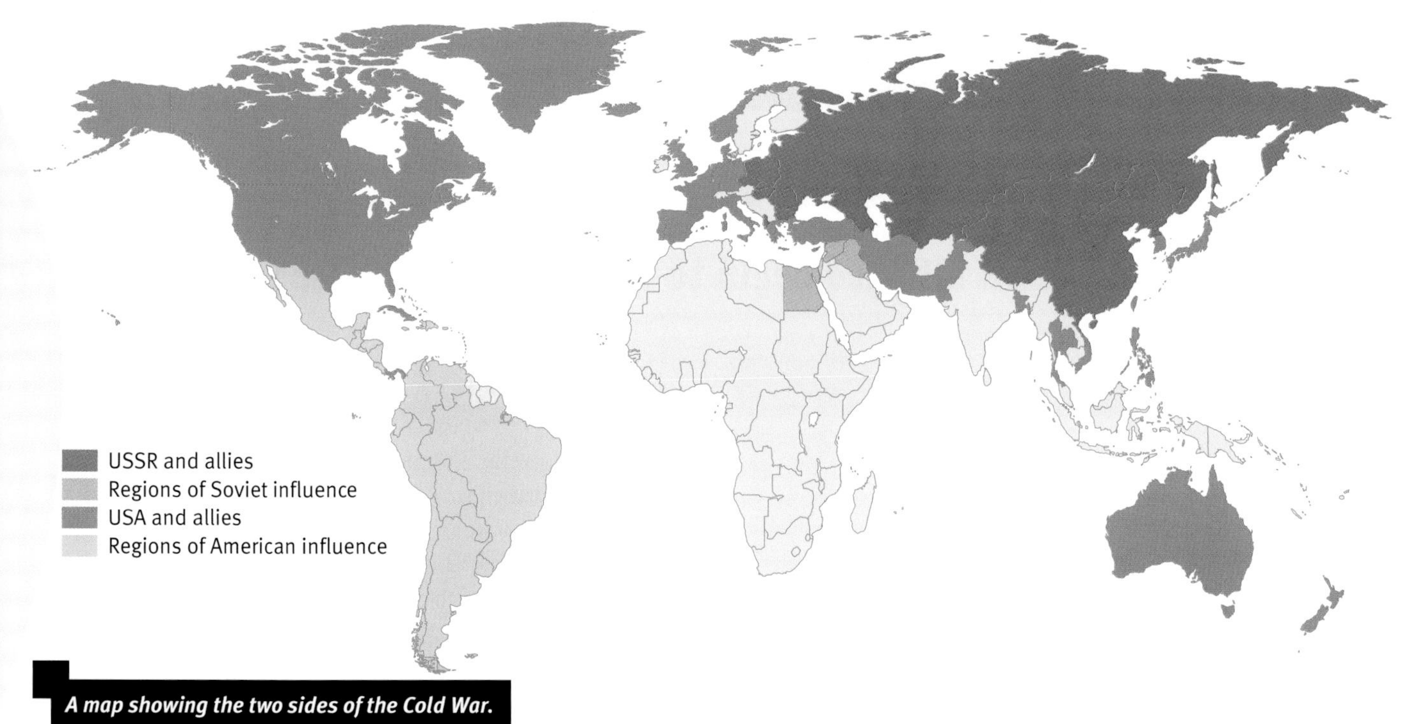

A map showing the two sides of the Cold War.

David Low's cartoon 'Look things in the face', which highlights the differences in ideology between East and West.

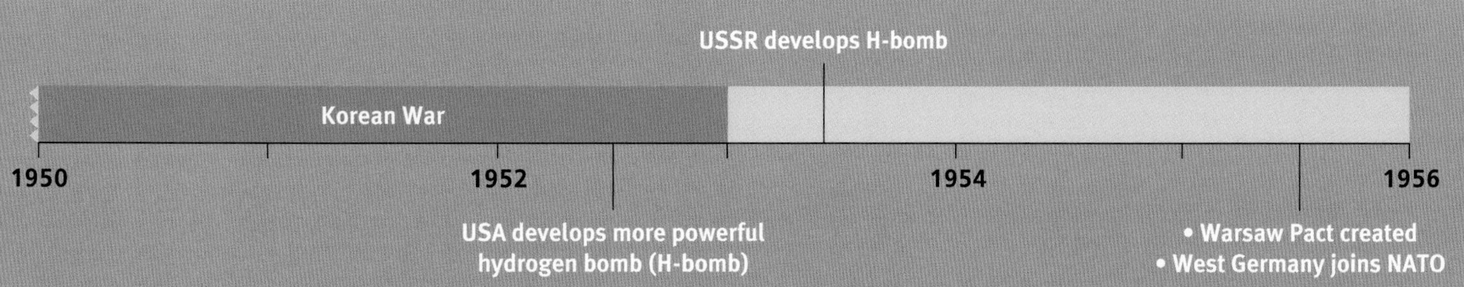

Who was to blame for the Cold War?

Why did the USA–USSR alliance begin to break down in 1945?

LEARNING OBJECTIVES

In this lesson you will:

- learn about the reasons for the Cold War
- make judgements on who was to blame for the start of the Cold War.

GETTING STARTED

Look at the cartoon on page 55. Under one arm the man has either a ballot box or a book. Write down what is written on each of them and work out what each phrase means. Is one 'better' than the other?

Opposing ideologies

As the cartoon shows, underlying the tension between East and West were differences of opinion on how countries should be governed. Britain and America gave **democracy** a political emphasis, involving universal voting, free speech (including criticism of the government), a two-or-more-party system and governments responsible to parliament (representative government). To the Soviets the emphasis was economic, concerning the ownership and operation of industry for the people; and politically it meant a one-party system restricting inappropriate criticism and opposition in the interests of national solidarity.

KEY WORDS

Capitalist – *somone who believes that the private ownership of trade and industry for profit is the best way to organise the economy.*

Communist – *someone who believes that the state should own all property.*

Democracy – *a political system in which the people exercise power through elected representatives.*

CAPITALISM

Wealthy people (**capitalists**) invest their money in land and industry. They employ the workers and keep all the profits that are made. There is a democratic system, with a number of political parties.

COMMUNISM

There is a classless society with no individual profit-making. Land and industry are owned by the state and profits are used for the good of all. There is only one political party.

KEY PEOPLE

Winston Churchill – *British politician, Prime Minister from 1941 to 1945, and again in 1951–55.*

Franklin D. Roosevelt – *President of the USA 1933–45.*

Joseph Stalin – *Leader of the Soviet Union 1922–53.*

KEY CONCEPTS

United Nations – *an organisation set up in 1945 with the aim of preventing future wars.*

The Yalta Conference

In February 1945, **Franklin D. Roosevelt** of the USA, **Joseph Stalin** of the Soviet Union and **Winston Churchill** of Britain met at Yalta in the Soviet Union. The war in Europe was drawing to a conclusion and decisions had to be made about how Europe was to be organised after the war. It was decided that:

- Germany should be divided into 'zones of occupation', one controlled by the USA, one by the Soviet Union, one by Britain and one by France. Since the German capital, Berlin, would be in the Soviet zone, it would also be divided into four similar sections.
- Once Germany was defeated, the Soviet Union would join the war against Japan.
- A **United Nations** organisation would be set up to keep peace after the war.
- As east European countries were liberated from Nazi occupation, they would hold free elections to set up democratic governments.

SOURCE A

Churchill, Roosevelt and Stalin in discussion at Yalta, February 1945.

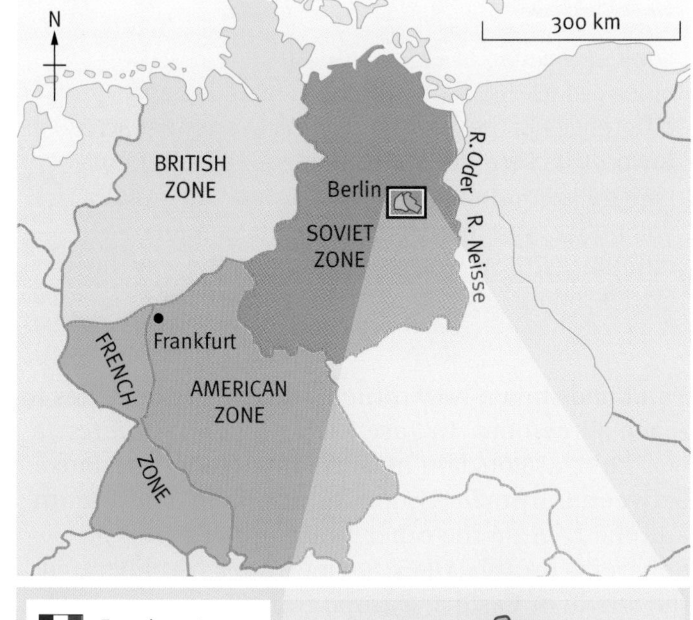

The division of Germany in 1945.

The struggle for control of Poland in 1945

Stalin wanted to keep the parts of Poland that he had won in the Nazi–Soviet Pact of 1939. He also wanted Poland expanded westwards by giving it parts of Germany. That would make Germany weaker and put a **buffer zone** between Germany and the Soviet Union. Germany had invaded the Soviet Union twice in 30 years, and Stalin wanted to make sure it did not happen again. He also wanted to make sure that Poland had a pro-Soviet government.

ACTIVITIES

In groups of three, each of you will take on the role of one of the leaders at the Yalta Conference. Read the information about Poland then make an argument for what you think your leader would want. Try to set out your case calmly. When all three of you have stated your case, compare your arguments with those of other groups. How are they similar and how are they different?

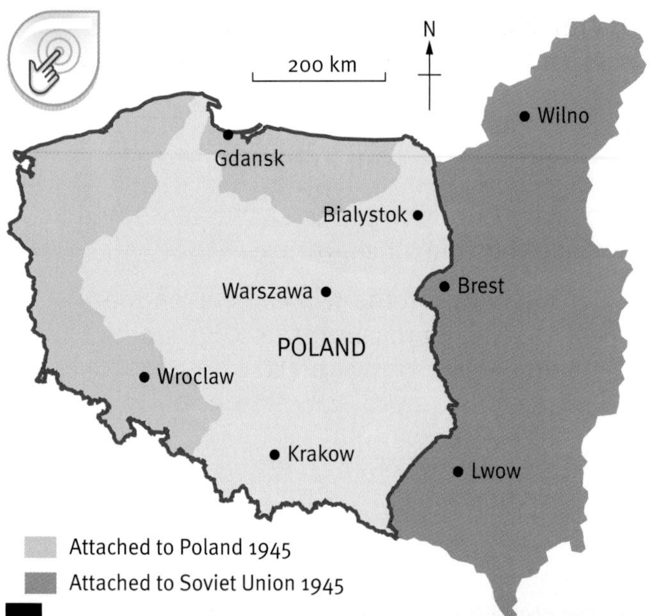

Eastern Europe in 1945 showing Poland and Russia.

Stalin already had a government in exile (the Lublin Poles) ready to take over. But Roosevelt and Churchill supported another group, the strongly anti-communist 'London Poles'. These Poles had helped organise the Warsaw Uprising in August 1944, aiming to gain part of Poland before Stalin's Red Army took full control of the country. The uprising was defeated by the Nazis and nearly 300,000 Poles were killed. The Red Army was ordered not to help in the uprising. Stalin wanted to make sure that when his army cleared the Germans out of Poland, the Lublin Poles would have complete control. By January 1945 this had happened.

ACTIVITIES

Think back to the previous activity. Did you decide on a course of action because of the strength of the argument you heard or because of the person arguing it? Do you think this would have had an effect on the actual proceedings in Yalta?

KEY WORDS

Atomic bomb – *a devastating new type of bomb developed in the USA in 1945.*

Buffer zone – *an area of land between two hostile countries.*

KEY PEOPLE

Clement Attlee – *British politician and leader of the Labour Party, Prime Minister 1945–51.*

Harry S. Truman – *President of the USA 1945–53.*

The Potsdam Conference

Attlee, Truman and Stalin at the Potsdam Conference, July 1945.

ACTIVITIES

Look at the map of Eastern Europe and read the text on pages 62–63. Highlight the similarities and differences in the way the Soviet government acted towards its **satellite states** immediately after (and sometimes during) the Second World War. What do you notice? Are there more similarities than differences? How would you describe the way the Soviet Union took control of Eastern Europe?

Yalta had shown how difficult it was for the Allies to reach agreement. In July 1945 a second conference was held, at Potsdam in Germany. Here, divisions between the Soviet Union on one hand, and Britain and the USA on the other, were much more apparent. By July 1945, Soviet troops had liberated the whole of Eastern Europe from Nazi control. The USA and Britain had hoped that there would be free elections to set up democratic governments. Instead Soviet troops remained in the liberated countries.

By the time the conference got under way on 17 July 1945, the Americans had successfully tested an **atomic bomb**. One of **Truman**'s first actions at Potsdam was to inform Stalin and Attlee that his country now had the bomb. He was confident that it would be years before the Soviet Union had one, so the USA could get tough with the Soviet Union.

The Potsdam Conference showed that Truman was not prepared to let Stalin have things all his own way. In July, Churchill lost a general election in Britain and was replaced by the Labour leader, **Clement Attlee**. Since Attlee was new and inexperienced, the conference was really a personal duel between Truman and Stalin.

The following points were agreed:

- Germany would be divided as agreed at Yalta, and the Allies would receive reparations.
- Poland's eastern border would be moved west to the rivers Oder and Neisse.
- The Nazi Party was banned and its leaders were to be tried as war criminals.
- Germans living in Poland, Hungary and Czechoslovakia would be sent back to Germany.

However, there were several major disagreements:

- The Soviet Union wanted to impose severe reparations on Germany to cripple it for years to come. Truman blocked this.
- The Soviet Union wanted to share in the occupation of Japan once it was defeated. Truman refused.
- Britain and the USA wanted a greater say in Eastern Europe. They did not accept that Stalin had the right to set up pro-Soviet governments in these countries. Stalin said that this was what they had agreed at Yalta.

The Potsdam Conference had shown how divided the former wartime allies were.

The division between them became even more apparent in the months after the conference. The development of the atomic bomb in the USA was a major source of worry to Stalin, who feared that the USA might use the threat of the bomb to prevent the spread of communism. He ordered his scientists to work flat out to develop a Soviet atomic bomb.

ACTIVITIES

Look through the decisions made at each of the conferences. Make a list of the decisions that benefited the West (largely the USA but nominally still Britain as well) and a separate list of the decisions that benefited the USSR (the East). Then answer the question below.

GradeStudio

Which side gained the most from the Yalta and Potsdam conferences? Give reasons for your answer.

[10 marks]

Mark scheme

Level 1:	1–2 marks	General answer lacking specific contextual knowledge. e.g. Asserts one or the other side won but offers no real evidence to support claim.
Level 2:	2–4 marks	Identifies that one or other may be the winner and may identify a reason to support claim. Higher level for more basic identification and reasons.
Level 3:	3–6 marks	Explains answer. e.g. 'The Soviet leader, Stalin, can claim to have gained the most from the two conferences because he achieved the negotiation of the extension of the Polish borders in his favour. He also…' This level of detail needed and more than once for top end of mark.
Level 4:	6–9 marks	Balanced argument. Level 3 answer with good level of explanation on both sides. e.g. Above with… 'However, Truman did gain some concessions from Stalin with the block on crippling German reparations. Furthermore…'
Level 5:	9–10 marks	Explains with evaluation. Balanced argument with a detailed evaluation. e.g. Levels 3 and 4 answer with own opinion on who gained the most.

How had the USSR gained control of Eastern Europe by 1948?

LEARNING OBJECTIVES

In this lesson you will:

- learn about the continuities in Soviet policy towards its satellite states.

KEY WORDS

Expansionist – *seeking to expand your country's power or territory.*

Iron curtain – *a metaphor used by Churchill to describe the post-war division of Europe.*

Satellite states – *smaller countries that look to a bigger one for protection and trade.*

GETTING STARTED

Cover up the cartoon in Source B and read the Churchill speech in Source A. What images does he conjure up? Could you draw a cartoon to sum up this short extract?

SOURCE 

From Stettin in the Baltic to Trieste in the Adriatic, an ***iron curtain*** *has descended across the continent. Behind that line lie all the capitals of the ancient states of central and eastern Europe – Warsaw, Berlin, Prague, Vienna, Budapest, Bucharest and Sofia. All these famous cities and the populations around them lie in the Soviet sphere and all are subject to a very high and increasing measure of control from Moscow.*

An extract from Churchill's speech at Fulton, Missouri, on 5 March 1946.

SOURCE B

Cartoon showing Churchill peeping under the Iron Curtain, 1946.

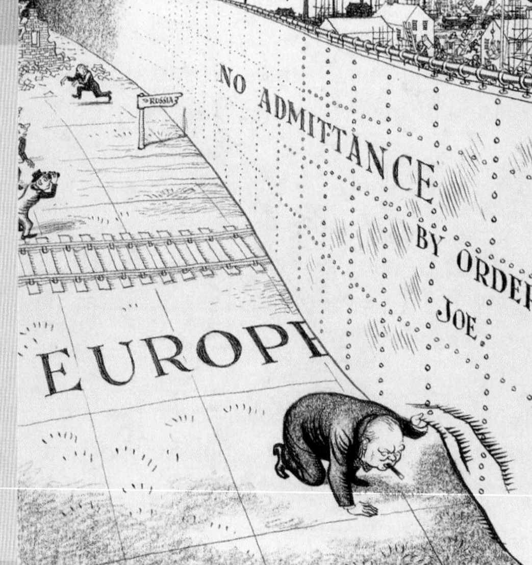

SOURCE 

Mr Churchill now takes the stand of the warmongers and he is not alone. He has friends not only in Britain, but in the United States ... As a result of the German invasion, the Soviet Union's loss of life has been several times greater than that of Britain and the USA put together. And so what can be surprising about the fact that the Soviet Union, anxious for its future safety, is trying to see to it that governments loyal to the Soviet Union should exist in the countries through which the Germans made their invasion? How can anyone who has not taken leave of his senses describe these peaceful hopes of the Soviet Union as ***expansionist****?*

Stalin's response to Churchill's speech, 1946.

The fall of the 'iron curtain' across Europe

After the UK General Election of 1945, Churchill was no longer the British prime minister. Free from the chains of office, he went on a tour of America where he was treated as a hero. In Fulton, Missouri, on 5 March 1946, he coined a phrase that would be used for the next 40 years when the East/West divide was mentioned (see Source A). The speech declared that Europe was being divided into two separate halves by Soviet policy. In the West were free, democratic states, but in the East, behind an 'iron curtain' were countries under the domination of communist parties subject to the Soviet Union. However, Stalin did not agree with Churchill's reading of the way events had unfolded (Source C).

Why did the USSR seek to dominate Eastern Europe?

Between 1945 and 1948 the Soviet Union made sure that every country in Eastern Europe had a government that was both communist and sympathetic to the Soviet Union. As far as Stalin was concerned, this was a defensive measure aimed at creating a buffer zone between the Soviet Union and the West. The Soviet Union had been invaded from the west twice in the past 30 years; the establishment of communist governments in Eastern Europe would make such an invasion more difficult.

Of course, as far as the West was concerned, and the USA in particular, the Soviet Union was not acting defensively. It was taking the first steps towards world domination. Here was clear proof that the Western way of life was under threat. The spread of communism had to be stopped.

We are concerned that the USSR is not taking defensive action. We think that she is taking the first steps towards world domination and our western way of life is under threat. We must stop the spread of communism.
We are taking defensive measures to create a 'buffer zone' between the Soviet Union and the West. We have been invaded twice in the last 30 years, by creating sympathetic governments in Eastern Europe another invasion would be much more difficult.

GradeStudio

What is the message of the cartoon in Source B? Use details of the cartoon and your own knowledge to explain your answer **[7 marks]**

Mark scheme

Level 1:	1–2 marks	Using surface features only. 'The cartoonist is showing a big iron curtain separating Europe.'
Level 2:	2–3 marks	Interpretation only. 'The Soviets have built an iron curtain.'
Level 3:	4 marks	Main message. 'There is a division between East and West Europe.' 'Churchill, a major European statesman, has noticed there is a barrier between East and West Europe.'
Level 4:	5–6 marks	Main message supported by details of the cartoon OR by contextual knowledge. 'Churchill has called this an *iron curtain* because he sees the barrier between East and West Europe as a very real one, it has been drawn as one draws a curtain.' OR 'The Second World War is over and the final meetings between the American president, British prime minister and Soviet leader had not gone well. No agreement could be found on several issues and once out of power in the UK Churchill felt that he could talk freely about what he saw happening in Europe.'
Level 5:	7 marks	Main message supported by details of the cartoon AND by contextual knowledge. Both sides of level 4.

Examiner's tip

Cartoons are a fun way of summarising big historical events. Remember, in order to do well in exams you must go beyond 'saying what you see'. Use your historical knowledge to add some detail.

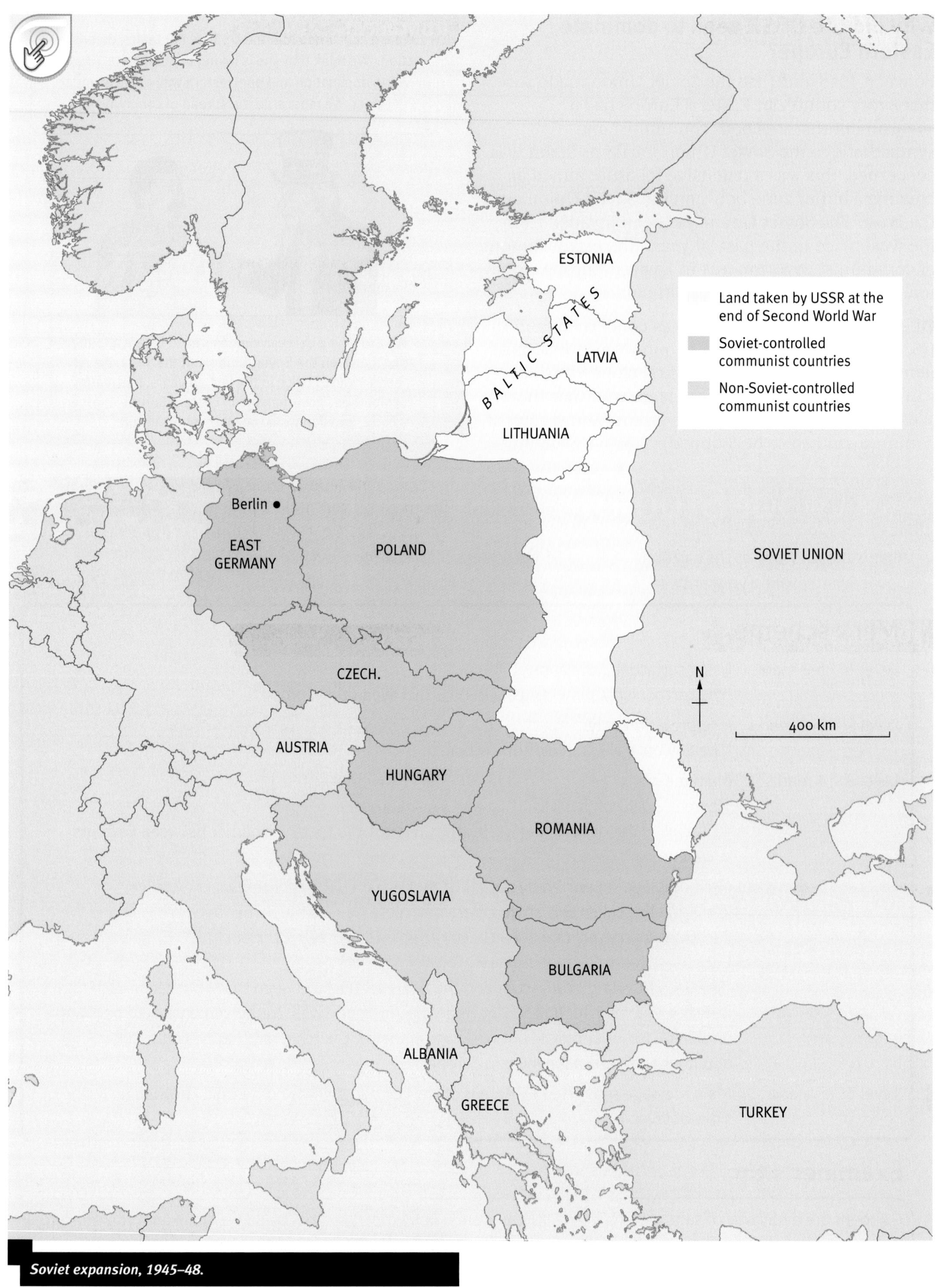

Soviet expansion, 1945–48.

THE BALTIC STATES

At the end of the war, the Soviet Union extended its border some 500 kilometres west. It did this by formally **annexing** Latvia, Lithuania and Estonia, which it had occupied during the war with Finland in 1939–40. It also kept control of the eastern half of Poland, which it had occupied under the terms of the Nazi–Soviet Pact in 1939 (although the Germans had occupied this area from 1941 to 1945).

CZECHOSLOVAKIA

Following the war, a **coalition** government ruled Czechoslovakia. From 1946 the Communists were the largest party in the coalition. In 1948 the Communists used the army to seize control. Many non-communists were arrested and the non-communist foreign secretary, Jan Masaryk, was murdered. Rigged elections were held in which the Communists won a landslide victory. Other political parties were then banned.

POLAND

At the request of Britain and the USA at the end of June 1945, Stalin included a few London Poles in the new Polish government. In January 1947, however, fresh (rigged) elections saw the return of a totally communist government. The leader of the London Poles, Mikolaczyk, fled from Poland, fearing for his life.

EAST GERMANY

The Soviet Union controlled the eastern section of Germany after the war. In 1949 it became a separate communist state, the German Democratic Republic (East Germany).

ROMANIA

After the expulsion of the Nazis, a coalition government dominated by communists was set up in Romania. In February 1945 the Soviet Union forced the king to appoint a communist prime minister. By the middle of the year, communists were in control, and in 1947 the monarchy was abolished.

HUNGARY

In November 1945 free elections were held, and the non-communist Smallholders' Party won the most seats. In August 1947 fresh (rigged) elections were held and the Communists won total control. All other political parties were then banned.

YUGOSLAVIA

In Yugoslavia the communist resistance had fought bravely against the Germans, and in 1945 its leader, Marshal Tito, was elected president. At first, Tito and Stalin got on well, but relations deteriorated as it became clear that Tito did not intend to follow orders from Moscow. Yugoslavia was expelled from the Communist Information Bureau (Cominform), and economic **sanctions** were applied against it by other communist countries. Tito countered this by taking aid from the West – much to the annoyance of Stalin.

GREECE

Here the communists were not successful. They fought a civil war against the government supported by Britain and the USA. Stalin stuck by his promise to the Western allies not to provide support for the Greek communists, who were finally defeated in 1949.

BULGARIA

In late 1944 a communist-dominated coalition government was set up. In November 1945 the communists won rigged elections, and in 1946 they abolished the monarchy.

KEY WORDS

Annex – *add to a country's territory.*

Coalition – *a temporary alliance of political parties made in order to form a government .*

Sanctions – *impositions placed on a state in order to coerce it.*

How did the USA react to Soviet expansionism?

LEARNING OBJECTIVES

In this lesson you will:

- learn about the consequences of Soviet action in Eastern Europe
- explain what the American reaction to Soviet action was.

GETTING STARTED

Imagine you are President Truman in 1947. How would you react to the Soviet Union annexing neighbouring countries or installing puppet governments in them? What would you do?

SOURCE A

The free peoples of the world look to us for support in maintaining their freedoms ... I believe that it must be the policy of the United States to support people who are resisting attempted subjugation by armed minorities or by any outside pressures. I believe that we must help free peoples to work out their own destiny in their own way.

Extracts from President Truman's speech on 12 March 1947.

The Truman Doctrine

As the USSR established dominance over Eastern Europe following the Second World War, President Truman felt there was little he could do because the Soviet Union had liberated the countries in question from Nazi occupation. Then, in February 1947, Truman was informed by the British that they could no longer afford to station troops in Greece and Turkey. Truman knew that the withdrawal of British troops would almost certainly lead to the Soviet Union taking control of these two countries. He therefore paid for British troops to stay in the area and gave financial support to the two governments. This was the beginning of the American policy of 'containment' – preventing the further spread of communism. The policy was officially announced in a speech made by Truman on 12 March 1947.

The views put forward in the speech have since become known as the 'Truman Doctrine'.

In this speech, Truman let it be known that the USA was prepared to give help to any country under threat from communism. What form of help would there be for countries under threat from communism? Would Truman send troops into trouble-spots? This would be an act of hostility and would certainly lead to a war with the Soviet Union. Instead Truman would use America's wealth to shore up the crumbling economies of Europe; he believed that communism flourished wherever there was misery and want – if you take away the misery and want, you take away the need for communism. Europe already owed the USA $12 billion and between 1948 and 1952, through this new plan, the Marshall Plan, Europe would get another $13 billion.

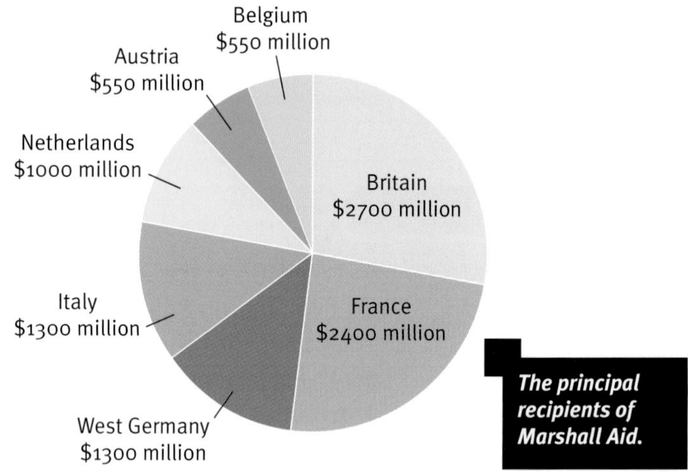

The principal recipients of Marshall Aid.

Fact file

The Marshall Plan was named after General George Marshall, the US Secretary of State. He made a speech in June 1947 claiming that the aid was aimed at ending hunger and poverty. Any country could apply for the money (Poland and Czechoslovakia were keen to apply but were not allowed to do so).

ACTIVITIES

As you have seen, the European countries were keen to have the money, but did everyone view the plan in a positive way? Look at Sources B and C on page 65. Do the two cartoons agree in their appraisal of the Marshall Plan?

SOURCE B

A cartoonist's view of the Marshall Plan, drawn in 1947.

SOURCE D

The Marshall Plan was seen in the Soviet Union as the Americans wanting to impose their influence over the countries to which they gave Marshall Aid. It was seen as an aggressive act on behalf of the Americans. This is why it was never accepted by our country.

Dimitri Sukhanov, a senior Soviet politician in 1947, commenting in 1988 on the Marshall Plan.

Soviet reactions to the Marshall Plan

Truman wanted to end hunger and want in Europe so there would be no collapse into communism, and also so American companies would have greater trading opportunities. Stalin did not see things in quite the same way!

In September 1947 the Soviet Union formed the Communist Information Bureau (Cominform) to strengthen ties between communist countries. The Communist parties in Western Europe (those in Italy and France were particularly strong) were ordered to try to wreck their countries' use of American aid by strikes, but they were unsuccessful. In January 1949, Stalin announced the formation of the Council for Mutual Economic Aid (Comecon) to rival the Marshall Plan. The communist countries, however, did not have surplus funds to provide financial assistance to each other.

SOURCE C

David Low's 'Gnashing teeth' cartoon, first published in the *Evening Standard*, April 1949.

What were the consequences of the Berlin Blockade?

Background

- It had been agreed at Yalta that Germany would be split into four parts. This led to a split between East and West. This caused a special problem for the capital, Berlin, because it was in East Germany and the Allies did not want to give it up. Therefore, Berlin was also split in half.
- The post-war economy of the whole of Germany was in ruins.
- The Americans introduced the Marshall Plan and West Germany (and West Berlin) benefited; unsurprisingly East Germany (and East Berlin) did not.

ACTIVITIES

Historians seldom agree on anything – they write different histories because of their background and opinions. Working in pairs, one of you should write a brief history of this period from an American point of view, the other from a Soviet one. Compare your paragraphs.

You need to have an opinion – it doesn't matter whether you feel sympathy towards America or the Soviet Union, as long as you can back it up.

SOURCE E

THE BIRD WATCHER

A cartoon published in July 1948. The birds are carrying supplies into Berlin.

Developing problem

- Britain and America combined their parts of West Germany into 'Bizonia'.
- They introduced a new currency: the Deutschmark.
- Stalin was worried that a prosperous West Germany would pose a threat to Soviet security (Germany had invaded Russia twice in the past 30 years) and he did not want to see a wealthy West Germany next to a poor East Germany.

Soviet reaction

- Stalin decided to test the strength of the Allies and slow down the economic growth of the country by placing a blockade on West Berlin.
- Two million people lived in the Soviet zone but not under Soviet rule.
- All road and rail links were blockaded on 24 June 1948.

Crisis

- The Americans and British could not smash through the blockades, as this would be seen as an act of war.
- Stalin hoped the Allies would abandon their zone and leave the whole of Berlin in his hands.
- The Allies could not back down as this might encourage Stalin to make other demands elsewhere in Europe.

Decision

- The Americans and British took the decision to send supplies to West Berlin by air from their bases in West Germany.
- This was a massive task as West Berlin would need over 5000 tons of food and other necessities a day to survive.
- Non-stop flights were needed.
- B-29 bombers were stationed in Britain: this meant that the Soviet Union was in range of atomic weapons.
- Now the ball was back in Stalin's court. If he shot the planes down, he would be seen as the aggressor.

ACTIVITIES

In Source E, Stalin is shown leaning out of a chimney, about to take pot-shots at storks.

- What is the impression of Stalin given by the cartoon?
- Does this seem a likely action for a world leader?

Detail

- For the best part of a year planes flew in and out of West Berlin: over two million tons of supplies were delivered and approximately 275,000 trips were made.
- Stalin called the blockade off on 12 May 1949; his gamble had failed.

Consequences

- The blockade strengthened Allied resolve to stand up to Stalin whatever the cost.
- West Germany was formally united and free elections were held in August 1949. Konrad Adenauer's Christian Democrats won; he was a committed opponent of communism.
- The North Atlantic Treaty Organisation (NATO) was formed in April 1949 This was a military alliance that promised to help if any of the members were attacked. This was significant because it was the first time America had signed up to a peacetime military alliance; it showed the determination of its members to stand up to communism.
- Stalin's response was to form the Warsaw Pact, a similar military alliance comprising of Eastern European countries under Soviet influence.

Fact file

The two alliances

NATO: USA, Britain, Belgium, Canada, Denmark, France, Iceland, Italy, Luxembourg, Netherlands, Norway and Portugal. Greece and Turkey joined in 1952 and West Germany in 1955.

The Warsaw Pact: Soviet Union, Albania (expelled 1968), Bulgaria, Czechoslovakia, East Germany, Hungary, Poland and Romania.

Fact file

In 1949 the Soviet Union's scientists successfully developed an atomic bomb.

ACTIVITIES

Use the sub-title headings on pages 66–67 and make a flow diagram that shows how each of them is related to the other. Think carefully how you will place each one.

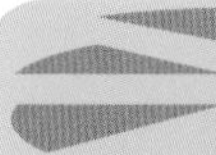

GradeStudio

Look at Source E. What is the message of this cartoon? Use details of the cartoon and your knowledge to explain your answer. **[7 marks]**

Mark scheme

Level 1:	1–2 marks	Using surface features only. 'Stalin is shooting storks carrying food and supplies out of the sky.' 'It shows Stalin in the ruins of Berlin.'
Level 2:	2–3 marks	Interpretation only. 'Stalin is responsible for ruining Berlin.' 'People in Berlin need food and supplies.'
Level 3:	4 marks	Main message. 'Stalin is not happy that supplies are getting into Berlin so he is shooting them down.'
Level 4:	5–6 marks	'Main message supported by details of the cartoon OR by contextual knowledge. 'The cartoonist sees Stalin as the opposite of a Santa popping out of the chimney shooting the storks, who are usually carrying babies, to the people of Berlin. Stalin is effectively killing the babies, the food and supplies, of Berlin that is keeping the city alive.' OR 'Stalin's blockade of Berlin was followed by an attempt by the USA and Britain, represented by the storks, to deliver supplies. The world waited to see if Stalin would shoot down the planes: he didn't but the cartoonist must have thought he might.'
Level 5:	7 marks	Main message supported by details of the cartoon AND by contextual knowledge. Both sides of level 4.

Who was more to blame for the start of the Cold War, the USA or the USSR?

LEARNING OBJECTIVES

In this lesson you will:

- evaluate historical factors in order to make a judgement on significant events.

USA-controlled factors:

1. President Truman was much more suspicious and less trusting of the USSR than Roosevelt.
2. The USA dropped atomic bombs on Japan to end the Second World War in that region.
3. The Truman Doctrine and Marshall Plan promised aid to countries willing to stand up to the communist threat.
4. The North Atlantic Treaty Organisation (NATO) was set up as a military alliance between European and North American countries.
5. America, Britain and France formally united their zones of occupied Germany to create the new Federal Republic of Germany.
6. The Federal Republic of Germany joined NATO.

USSR-controlled factors:

1. The Baltic States were under Soviet occupation at the end of the war.
2. Bulgaria, Romania and Hungary were under Soviet occupation.
3. Poland gained a communist-dominated government supported by the USSR.
4. The Communist Information Bureau (Cominform) was formed.
5. The Berlin Blockade.
6. Council for Mutual Economic Aid (Comecon) was formed.
7. The Soviet part of Germany became the German Democratic Republic.
8. Soviet scientists developed the atomic bomb.
9. The Warsaw Pact was formed as a military alliance of communist states.

Other factors:

1. The conferences between the Allied leaders at the end of the Second World War.
2. The death of Roosevelt in the USA and the election of Attlee in the UK.

All these factors need to be given more detail if they are to be of help to you in answering this question. The formulaic response would be to expand on all the American factors then offer the Soviet factors as a contrast before adding the 'other' factors and a conclusion. However, your work will be more interesting to read if you have an opinion at the beginning, then go about proving it.

Step 1:
Go through your notes and add detail to the above points. Complete extra research if necessary.

↓

Step 2:
Each factor has a different level of importance; decide on the appropriate level of importance for each factor. At this stage you may begin to leave the less important factors out.

↓

Step 3:
Decide your answer to the question: who was to blame for the Cold War?

↓

Step 4:
Divide your reasons into two: one side is your argument for who was most to blame for the Cold War, the other is recognising that there is an alternative opinion but arguing that it is not as accurate as yours.

↓

Step 5:
Look again at your points to support your argument and see if you can put any together to make better statements.

↓

Step 6:
Do the same to the other side of the argument, although here you should aim to group together factors that are similar.

↓

Step 7:
Write up your answer. Start with who you think was to blame and support your argument with the evidence you have collected. Then acknowledge the other opinion, also with supporting evidence. Make sure your conclusion matches your introduction.

GradeStudio

Who was to blame for the Cold War? **[10 marks]**

Examiner's tip

This question is asking for you to make an argument and come up with a decision. It is always easier to avoid committing yourself to one side of the argument, but when you have an opinion you work harder to explain it and therefore get higher marks.

Start by making two lists: one for all the things the USA and the West may have done to encourage hostility between the two sides and one for the things the USSR was responsible for. Make sure you have some details about each one, for example how their activities may have been to blame for prolonging the Cold War. When you have your detailed lists you will be able to make an informed decision, and you can then begin writing your answer.

Who won the Cuban Missile Crisis?

How did the USA react to the Cuban Revolution?

LEARNING OBJECTIVES

In this lesson you will:

- learn about the consequences of America's reaction to the Cuban Revolution
- investigate interpretations of the Cuban Missile Crisis.

GETTING STARTED

You are about to investigate the Cuban Missile Crisis. Most historians would agree that this is the closest the world has come to a nuclear war. To get you thinking about the events leading up to the crisis, do the following:

- Draw a graph in your book. Label the x-axis 'level of tension' and divide the axis into 'low', 'moderate' and 'high'.
- The y-axis will be your timeline, so you should plot the relevant years (1949–62) onto it. Try and make it to scale so you get a sense of the passing of time.
- Write the events onto your graph, deciding whether they cause low, moderate or high levels of tension between the USA and the USSR.
- Your teacher may want to discuss these with you or the class, so be ready to explain your reactions.

Post-war events in Europe had led to bitter tension between the USA and the Soviet Union, but the hostility between them was not confined to Europe. The Americans believed that it was their duty, and necessary to American security, to resist the expansion of communism wherever it occurred. During the 1960s this led them to the brink of nuclear war over the stationing of Soviet missiles on Cuba. A timeline of the events of the Cold War from 1949 to the Cuban Missile Crisis of 1962 is shown below.

The USA's role in Cuban affairs up to 1959

In 1898 the Americans had helped the Cubans to win independence from Spain. From that time, the USA had played a major part in Cuban affairs. The Americans built a huge naval base at Guantanamo and American companies invested heavily in Cuban industry. American companies had large stakes in most Cuban companies, particularly in mining and agriculture. In 1934 the Americans helped the Cuban military officer Fulgencio Batista to establish himself in power. His government became increasingly **corrupt** and **repressive**, and many Cubans saw him as a symbol of the American control of Cuba.

The Cuban Revolution, 1959

In 1959 Batista was over thrown by **Fidel Castro**. The new leader proposed **reforms** to improve the economy of Cuba and in particular to end corruption in government and the exploitation of Cuban peasants and sugar mill workers. Castro began appointing communists to his government

TIMELINE

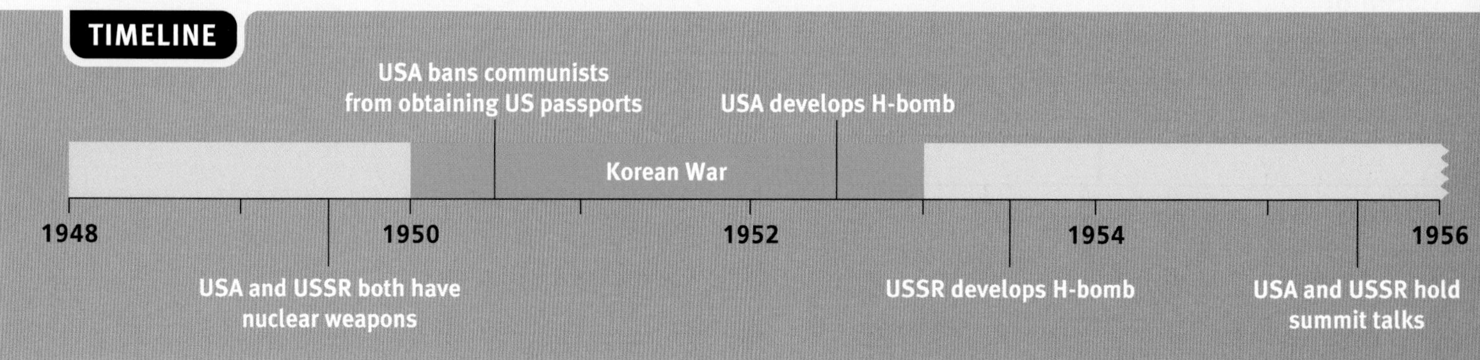
USA bans communists from obtaining US passports
USA develops H-bomb
Korean War
1948
1950
1952
1954
1956
USA and USSR both have nuclear weapons
USSR develops H-bomb
USA and USSR hold summit talks

and signed a trade agreement with the Soviet Union, in which Cuban sugar would be swapped for machinery, oil and economic aid.

The USA reacts to the Cuban Revolution

Not surprisingly, the USA was extremely concerned to see an island that was only about 150 kilometres away from its southern coast adopting what looked like communist policies and establishing such friendly relations with the Soviet Union. It decided to take action to bring Castro into line. In the summer of 1960, the USA stopped buying Cuban sugar, and later in the year it banned all trade with Cuba. Then, in January 1961, it broke off diplomatic relations.

The Americans hoped that these measures would starve Castro into submission. But they seem to have pushed him closer to the Soviet Union. The Americans were aware that among the 'aid' that Castro was receiving from the Soviet Union were weapons. America tried to 'encourage' Castro with economic sanctions, but when this failed something more drastic had to be done.

The Bay of Pigs

In April 1961 the new American president, **J.F. Kennedy**, decided to support an invasion by the 'Cuban exiles'. These were a group of Cubans who had fled the country when Castro took over. They wanted a return to the days of Batista.

The exiles received military training, weapons and transport from the American Central Intelligence Agency (**CIA**), and aimed to launch an attack on the coast of Cuba at the Bay of Pigs. They intended to establish a base for guerrilla activities against Castro

KEY CONCEPTS

CIA – *(Central Intelligence Agency) the USA's secret intelligence agency.*

Superpower – *term used to describe the USA and the USSR in the decades after the Second World War.*

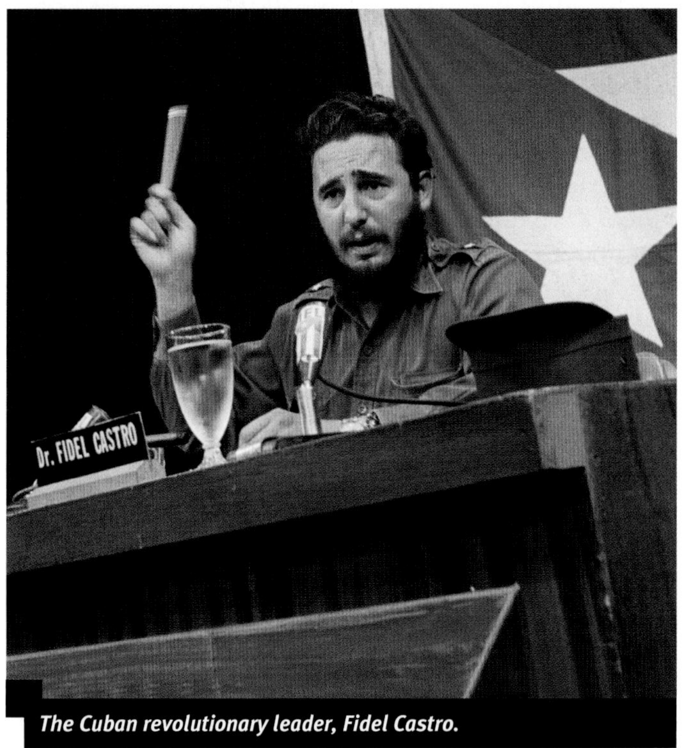
Dr. FIDEL CASTRO

The Cuban revolutionary leader, Fidel Castro.

KEY WORDS

Corrupt – *acting dishonestly, usually in return for money.*

Nationalise – *place a private business under government control.*

Repressive – *restraining personal freedom.*

Reform – *make changes in order to improve things.*

KEY PEOPLE

John F. Kennedy – *President of the USA 1961–63.*

Fidel Castro – *Cuban revolutionary leader and prime minister of Cuba, 1952–76.*

Nikita Khrushchev – *Leader of the Soviet Union 1953–64.*

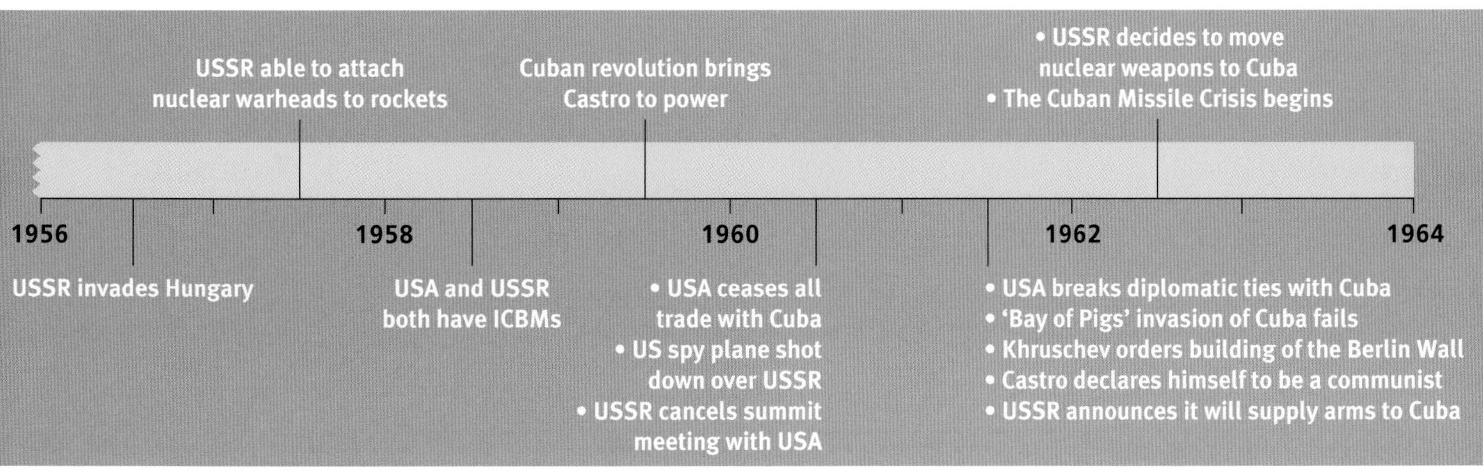
USSR able to attach nuclear warheads to rockets
Cuban revolution brings Castro to power
• USSR decides to move nuclear weapons to Cuba
• The Cuban Missile Crisis begins
1956
1958
1960
1962
1964
USSR invades Hungary
USA and USSR both have ICBMs
• USA ceases all trade with Cuba
• US spy plane shot down over USSR
• USSR cancels summit meeting with USA
• USA breaks diplomatic ties with Cuba
• 'Bay of Pigs' invasion of Cuba fails
• Khruschev orders building of the Berlin Wall
• Castro declares himself to be a communist
• USSR announces it will supply arms to Cuba

and were confident that the Cuban people would support them. However, the Bay of Pigs invasion was a disaster. A force of 1400 exiles landed in Cuba, but found themselves facing over 20,000 Cuban troops. There was no popular uprising to support the invasion, and those exiles who were not killed were quickly taken captive. Even though Kennedy was able to claim that there was no direct American government involvement in the invasion, Castro and Khrushchev knew that it had been planned by the CIA. Kennedy had been humiliated.

Consequences of the invasion

The Bay of Pigs invasion convinced Castro that he needed more support from the Soviet Union to defend himself against possible American attacks. In September 1961, Krushchev publicly announced that he would provide arms to Cuba. Within months Castro had an army with the latest military equipment, such as tanks and missiles, and large numbers of 'technicians' to help train his troops.

The USA was alarmed at what was happening in Cuba. In July 1961 Castro had **nationalised** all American industries, and in December he had announced that he himself was a communist. Now he had a well-trained army with many of the most up-to-date modern weapons.

ACTIVITIES

Imagine you are an advisor to the president of the USA. It is 1959 and you have just received intelligence reports informing you that Fidel Castro has taken over Cuba and is making major changes to the way the country is run. You have three choices:

1 go straight in with American troops and get rid of Castro
2 show Castro who's boss by not buying from him
3 wait and see what develops.

Think of the good and bad points of each course of action and make a note of your answer. Be ready to justify your answer to the rest of the class. For example, 'go straight in with American troops because the USSR hasn't really got involved in a major way yet, and if we do nothing things could get worse.'

Fact file

Operation Mongoose

After the failure of the Bay of Pigs attack, the American president J.F. Kennedy authorised a series of secret operations against Cuba. It was called the Cuban Project but codenamed Operation Mongoose, and its aim was to remove Fidel Castro from power and replace him with a new government which would be no threat to the USA.

VOICE YOUR OPINION!

Revisit the three options you were given for how the USA could respond to the Cuban Revolution in 1959.

- It is now July 1961. In hindsight, would the first option have been the USA's best course of action in dealing with Castro? Explain your thinking.
- How critical do you think the situation in Cuba has become for the Americans?

HISTORY DETECTIVE

Find out more about Operation Mongoose. Why was the operation given this code name?

GradeStudio

Explain why the USA attacked at the Bay of Pigs. **[6 marks]**

Mark scheme

Level 1:	1 mark	General answer, lacking specific contextual knowledge e.g. 'They did this because they were worried about what was happening in Cuba.'
Level 2:	2 marks	Identifies or describes reasons e.g. 'They did this to get rid of the USSR.' 'The Americans wanted control of Cuba back.'
Level 3:	3–6 marks	Explains reasons e.g. 'The Americans wanted control of Cuba back for several reasons; firstly America had supported the Cubans win independence from the Spanish and felt that they had a right to make money from the island. Secondly…'

Examiner's tip

Always remember to have an opinion and back it up with facts.

Why did Khrushchev put missiles into Cuba?

LEARNING OBJECTIVES

In this lesson you will:

- learn about the significance of the Cuban Missile Crisis
- examine the attributes of the two leaders.

GETTING STARTED

Look at the Fact file on Khrushchev. With him now in charge of the Soviet Union, do you think things will be any different? What evidence is there to support your answer?

Fact file

Nikita Khrushchev.

- Khrushchev became leader of the Soviet Union in 1953 following the death of Stalin.
- He 'de-Stalinized' the USSR; he was responsible for changing the way Stalin was seen by many Soviets at the time.
- He reformed agriculture by reducing taxes on farming profits and provided incentives to farm on unused, or 'virgin', land. Production between 1952 and 1958 more than doubled.
- To improve industrial production he promised material rewards, in contrast to Stalin's use of coercion.
- In foreign policy he was seen on the world stage as a truly international statesman. He travelled the globe, taking part in many summits.
- The Cuban Missile Crisis was seen in the USSR as a failure and was attributed to Khrushchev's weakness as a leader.
- He was forced out in 1964.

Increasing tension

After the Bay of Pigs fiasco, what the Americans were most concerned about was nuclear weapons. Khrushchev did not give Castro nuclear weapons, but his friendship with the Cuban leader meant that there was every chance that he might try to station nuclear weapons on the island. In September 1962, President Kennedy warned the Soviet Union that he would not allow Cuba to become a base for Soviet nuclear missiles. Khrushchev assured Kennedy that he had no intentions of doing so. However, he had decided as early as May that if weapons could be stationed on Cuba without detection, that was what he would do.

American cities that could be reached by missiles fired from Cuba.

ACTIVITIES

Looking at the map above, note down the benefits to the Soviet Union of placing missiles on Cuba. (Think about the relationship between the USA and the USSR at this time – use your chart from an earlier lesson to place the events in context.)

Missiles or no missiles?

On 14 October 1962, an American U-2 spy plane flew over Cuba and took pictures of what looked like missile sites being built. Some were near completion and would be ready to fire missiles in just seven days. Even more worrying was the news that a fleet of Soviet ships was sailing to Cuba – presumably carrying more missiles for the new sites.

Kennedy was now in a very difficult position. He could not allow the Soviet Union to station nuclear weapons on Cuba, as that would place virtually the whole of the USA within range of nuclear missiles. But how could he stop it? Since Khrushchev denied that there were nuclear missiles on Cuba and thought that Kennedy was a weak leader, he would hardly respond to American demands to remove them. Other measures, such as invading Cuba or bombing the missile sites, would have dire consequences. At the very least, the Soviet Union would be likely to invade West Berlin. Much more likely would be the outbreak of a general war between the USA and the Soviet Union, with the chance of nuclear weapons being used.

Fact file

The Korean War

In 1950 troops from communist North Korea invaded South Korea, which was anti-communist. President Truman was convinced that the Soviet Union had told North Korea to invade, and he persuaded the United Nations to send a force under General MacArthur to help the South Koreans.

The American policy had stopped the spread of communism into South Korea, but at the cost of worsening relations between the USA and both China and the Soviet Union, and at the cost of thousands of American soldiers' lives.

VOICE YOUR OPINION!

Who now has the upper hand? Be sure to back up your judgement with facts.

A photograph of the missiles sites in Cuba with labels added by the American government.

Why did Kennedy react as he did?

LEARNING OBJECTIVES

In this lesson you will:

- learn about the chronology of the Cuban Missile Crisis
- examine the role of the individual in shaping the course of history.

GETTING STARTED

Look at the Fact file on Kennedy. Does his personality seem to be different from that of earlier presidents? Would you expect him to be more or less sympathetic to the Soviet Union? What evidence do you have for your answer?

The American naval blockade of Cuba

Kennedy and his advisers meet for 13 days and nights from 16 October. By 22 October, Kennedy had decided to place a blockade around Cuba to stop the Soviet fleet landing its missiles. The USA would also prepare troops ready for an invasion of the island if necessary. That day, Kennedy broadcast the news of his planned blockade on American television and called on Khrushchev to remove the missiles from Cuba.

The next day (23 October), Khrushchev replied that there were no nuclear missiles on Cuba and that the Soviet Union would ignore the blockade, which it called an act of piracy. The world now held its breath. Soviet ships were sailing towards an American blockade. If they ignored it, they would be fired on and war would be certain to follow.

On 24 October 1962, a group of Soviet ships reached the American blockade. One oil tanker was allowed through without being searched. The other ships turned back. President Kennedy's brother, Robert, said that in the eyeball-to-eyeball confrontation 'Khrushchev just blinked'. Nuclear warfare had been avoided.

Kennedy had stood his ground and it seemed that the crisis had been averted. However, it was not over, even though the Soviet ships had turned around. The Soviet Union still had missiles on the island which had to be moved.

Letters from Khrushchev

Then, on 26 October, Khrushchev sent Kennedy a letter suggesting that, if the Americans lifted the blockade and promised not to invade Cuba, the nuclear weapons would be removed. This was excellent news for Kennedy and was the first time that the Soviet Union had admitted that it had nuclear weapons on Cuba. But before the USA could reply, things took a turn for the worse.

Fact file

- Kennedy was in power for only two years. He took up office in 1961 after a close-run contest with Richard Nixon, but he was assassinated in 1963.
- He served in the Second World War and became the youngest ever US president at the age of 43.
- He is remembered largely because of the controversy over his assassination, but in the USA he always ranks highly in public opinion polls.
- During his short term in office he sent troops to Vietnam, saw the start of the American Civil Rights Movement, presided over the early years of the 'space race' and saw the construction of the Berlin Wall.

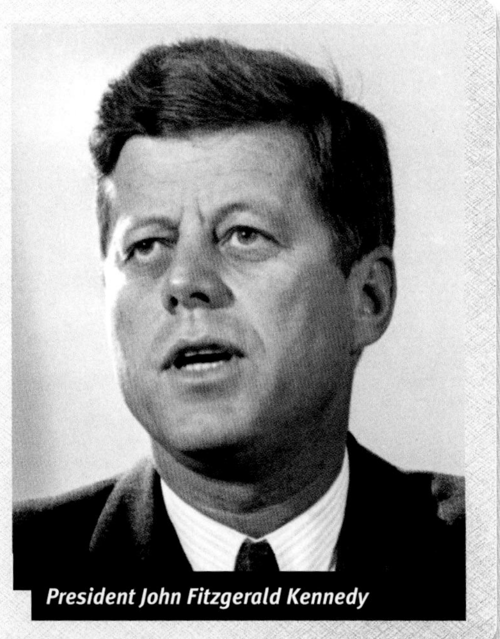

President John Fitzgerald Kennedy

On 27 October, a second letter arrived from Khrushchev. It said that Soviet missiles on Cuba were no more of a threat to the USA than American missiles in Turkey were to the Soviet Union. Khrushchev said that he would remove the Cuban missiles if the USA removed its missiles in Turkey.

The Americans had considered removing the missiles in Turkey, but felt strongly that they could not be seen to do so because the Soviet Union had demanded it. Then on the same day a U-2 spy plane was shot down over Cuba. Some of Kennedy's advisers wanted him to take military action. Instead he decided to ignore Khrushchev's second letter and respond to the first. Kennedy sent a letter saying that he agreed to the terms set out in the letter of 26 October, but that if the missiles were not removed, an attack would follow.

On the same day, Robert Kennedy went to visit the Soviet ambassador in Washington and told him that the Americans would consider removing missiles in Turkey 'within a short time'. On 28 October, Khrushchev sent a message saying that the missiles on Cuba would be dismantled. The crisis was over.

ACTIVITIES

1 Read over the information on the Cuban Missile Crisis in this and the previous lesson. To show that you can be selective, draw a timeline that covers the October crisis (from 14 to 28 October). On the timeline be sure to include the relevant events, but explain why the event you have included deserves its place on your line. In other words, you are explaining the significance of the event.

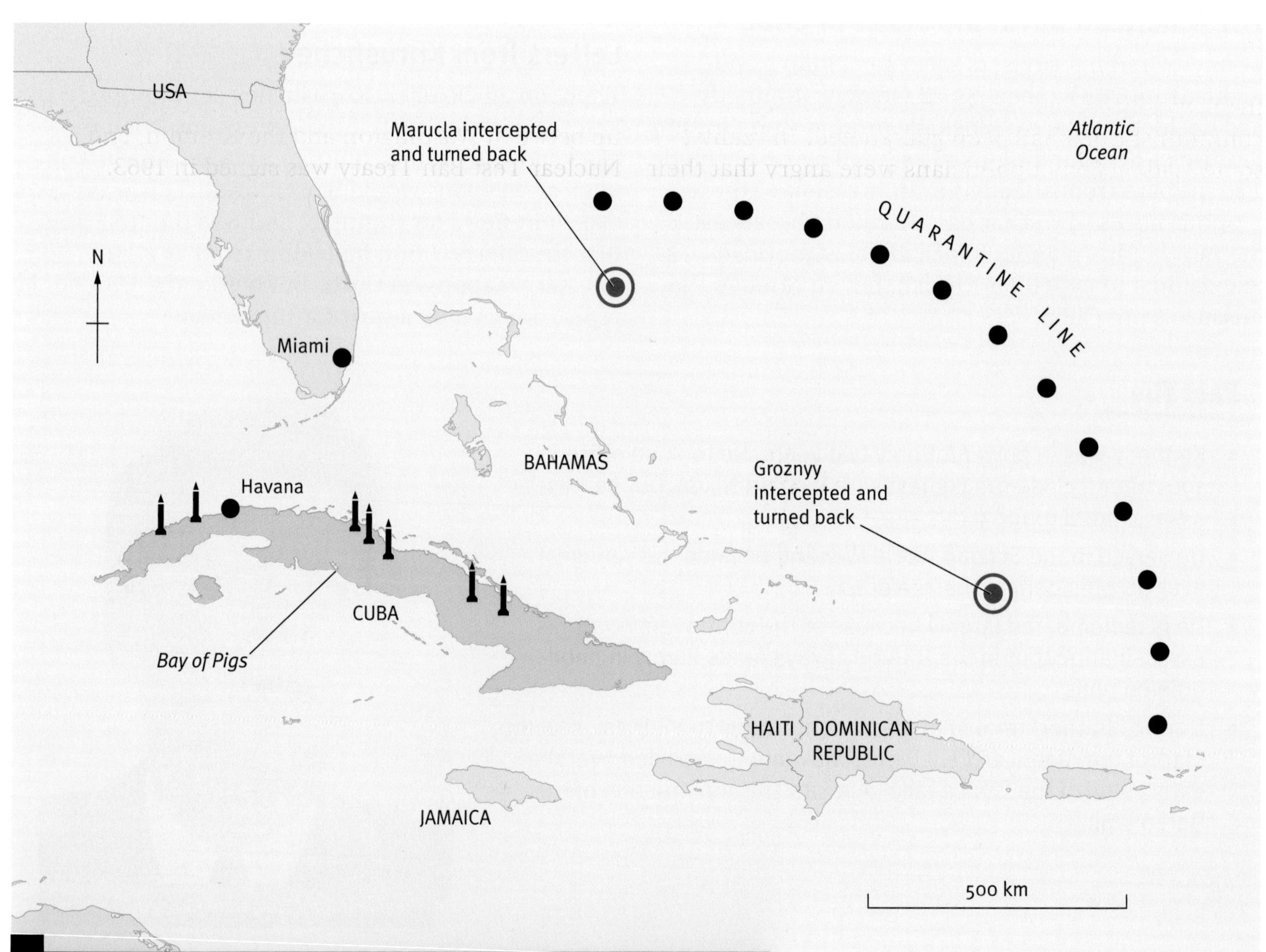

A map showing the naval blockade of Cuba, the position where Soviet ships were turned back, and the location of missile sites on Cuba.

Who won the Cuban Missile Crisis?

LEARNING OBJECTIVES

In this lesson you will:

- make judgements on the consequences of historical events.

GETTING STARTED

In pairs, take on the roles of Kennedy and Khrushchev. Look back at your recent work on each of them and make a case for your leader having the best claim to be the winner of this crisis.

The aftermath of the crisis

Although Khrushchev had thought that Kennedy was a weak president, the American leader had emerged from the crisis as the victor – especially as the deal on the missiles in Turkey was kept quiet. Khrushchev claimed that the crisis was a victory for the Soviet Union and that the independence of communist Cuba had been guaranteed. In reality, some leading Soviet politicians were angry that their country had been forced to back down. This played a significant part in Khrushchev's dismissal in 1964.

ACTIVITIES

1. a Make a list of the positive (good for the USA) decisions Kennedy made during the Cuban Missile Crisis.
   b Now do the same for Khrushchev (good decisions for the USSR).
   c Make a list for both men of the negative decisions they made.
2. Which of the two leaders showed themselves to be most capable during the Cuban Missile Crisis? This is called making a hypothesis.
3. Source A contains some extracts that shed light on Kennedy's thinking during the Cuban Missile Crisis. Read through the extracts and add to your list. Has you hypothesis changed?
4. Now answer the question, 'Who was the winner of the Cuban Missile Crisis?'

The two sides had learned from the crisis that confrontation between them threatened world peace. So steps were taken to reduce the threat of nuclear war. A direct 'hot-line' phone link was set up between Washington and the Kremlin, and a Nuclear Test Ban Treaty was signed in 1963. Although the two sides had nearly gone to war, the crisis had helped to thaw the Cold War just a little.

GradeStudio

Who was the winner in the Cuban Missile Crisis, the USA or the USSR? **[10 marks]**

Mark scheme

Level 1:	1–2 marks	General answer lacking specific contextual knowledge. e.g. Asserts one or the other side won but offers no real evidence to support claim.
Level 2:	2–4 marks	Identifies that one or other may be the winner and may identify a reason to support claim. Higher level for more basic identification and reasons.
Level 3:	3–6 marks	Explains answer. e.g. 'The Americans can claim to have won the Cuban Missile Crisis because not only were missiles removed from Cuba in a very public way, the deal struck between the leaders about the American missiles coming out of turkey was kept quiet.' This level of detail needed and more than once for top end of mark.
Level 4:	6–9 marks	Balanced argument. Level 3 answer with good level of explanation on both sides. e.g. Above with… 'However, Khrushchev could also claim victory because Cuba maintained her independence…'
Level 5:	9–10 marks	Explains with evaluation. Balanced argument with a detailed evaluation. e.g. Levels 3 and 4 with own opinion on who won.

SOURCE A

Tuesday 16 October

The group discusses whether the USA could be under threat from Cuba. President Kennedy seems to think that the threat is not really increased.

General Maxwell Taylor:	I'd like to stress this last point, Mr President. We are very vulnerable to a conventional bombing attack in the Florida area.
Douglas Dillon:	What if the planes carry a nuclear weapon?
The president:	Well if they carry a nuclear weapon...
Rusk:	We could just be utterly wrong – but we've never really believed that Khrushchev would start a nuclear war over Cuba.
Bundy:	What is the impact on the balance of power of these missiles?
The president:	What difference does it make? They've got enough to blow us up now anyway. This is a political struggle as much as military.

On the Thursday and Friday of the same week, the president and his advisors met to continue their discussions of the crisis. In a private chat with his brother on Thursday, the president said he could not imagine how they could justify ever starting a nuclear war. On Friday the military met with him and talked tough by comparing backing down now with the appeasement of Hitler in the 1930s.

Discussions between President Kennedy and aides concerning the crisis.

How did America view the result of the Cuban Missile Crisis?

President Kennedy was a new, young president and he had shown himself to be a capable negotiator. The Soviets had backed down in the face of a determined leader who refused to lift the naval blockade, and this did much for Kennedy's prestige. However, not everybody saw it like this; General LeMay had told the president to invade and that the affair was the 'greatest defeat in our history'. American missiles in Turkey were removed but this was kept quiet from the American people and so a potentially difficult piece of military planning was kept under wraps.

How did the Cubans view the result of the Cuban Missile Crisis?

The Cubans felt a little put out by the fact that the whole episode was played out by the USA and the USSR and certain strictly Cuban concerns were overlooked (for example, Guantanamo Bay). This soured relations between Moscow and Havana for a while, but Cuba continued to look to the USSR for protection.

How did the Soviets view the result of the Cuban Missile Crisis?

Khrushchev came off worse in the aftermath and, although this crisis cannot be blamed solely for his demise, he was out of a job within two years. The deal to remove American missiles from Turkey was kept secret. This could have been used by a more able leader for some political kudos at home; instead, he was accused by his enemies of not being able to handle international crises. Furthermore, the Soviets had sent ships to Cuba and retreated.

Conclusion

Whoever you decide won or lost in this crisis, the main point is that Cuba remained a communist country right on America's doorstep. This has continued to be a sore point right up to the present day. In addition, the leaders of the USA and the USSR were gone within two years. Kennedy and Khrushchev felt they could do business with each other but any advancements made in East–West relationships were cut short.

KEY PEOPLE

Robert Kennedy – *the president's brother.*

Robert McNamara – *Secretary of State for Defense.*

Paul Nitze – *Assistant Secretary of State for Defense.*

Douglas Dillon – *Treasury Secretary.*

Dean Rusk – *Secretary of State.*

George Ball – *Under Secretary of State.*

McGeorge Bundy – *President's aide.*

General Maxwell Taylor – *Chairman, Joint Chiefs of Staff.*

General Curtis Le May – *Air Force Chief of Staff.*

Why did the USA fail in Vietnam?

Why did the USA get increasingly involved in Vietnam?

LEARNING OBJECTIVES

In this lesson you will:

- learn about the reasons for American involvement in the Vietnam War
- investigate the importance of political leaders during the Vietnam War.

GETTING STARTED

Study the lyrics to the protest song in Source A. Why did the Vietnam War become so unpopular?

Bruce Springsteen updated the lyrics and sang the same song to get the American troops out of Iraq. Was either man successful in their aims?

SOURCE A

If you love your Uncle Sam,
Bring them home, bring them home.
Support our boys in Vietnam,
Bring them home, bring them home.

It'll make our generals sad, I know,
Bring them home, bring them home.
They want to tangle with the foe,
Bring them home, bring them home.

They want to test their weaponry,
Bring them home, bring them home.
But here is their big fallacy,
Bring them home, bring them home.

I may be right, I may be wrong,
Bring them home, bring them home.
But I got a right to sing this song,
Bring them home, bring them home.

Bring 'Em Home **by Pete Seeger © 1966 Storm King Music, Inc.**

HISTORY DETECTIVE

Research different anti-war songs of the 1960s. Compare them with protest songs for today.

- Are there similarities between the content?
- Are they an effective way of getting a message across?
- Who listens to these songs?
- Do they work?

The war the USA could not win

As the Cuban Missile Crisis deepened, another conflict began that would dominate American news for over a decade: the Vietnam War. This war was fought thousands of miles away against an enemy that was vastly inferior, but somehow it proved a disaster for the USA. Why did America decide to get involved in a dispute halfway across the world?

Background to the Vietnam War

Vietnam had been a French colony until it was captured by the Japanese in 1941. After the Japanese defeat in the Second World War, the French tried to regain their old territory, but they were defeated by the Viet Minh, the armed forces of the Vietnamese independence movement. Vietnam was freed from French rule in 1954, but was divided into two separate countries. North Vietnam was run as a communist country and led by **Ho Chi Minh**. South Vietnam was anti-communist and led by **Ngo Dinh Diem**.

Diem's government in the south was hated by many of its people. He was a Catholic who ruled a largely Buddhist population in a corrupt and repressive way. Many Vietnamese peasants gave their support to the Vietcong, a group of communist guerrillas in South Vietnam who wanted to overthrow Diem. The Vietcong received supplies from the government in North Vietnam.

Diem's government, however, received aid from the Americans. They based their policy on the 'domino theory'. They believed that the Vietcong were trying

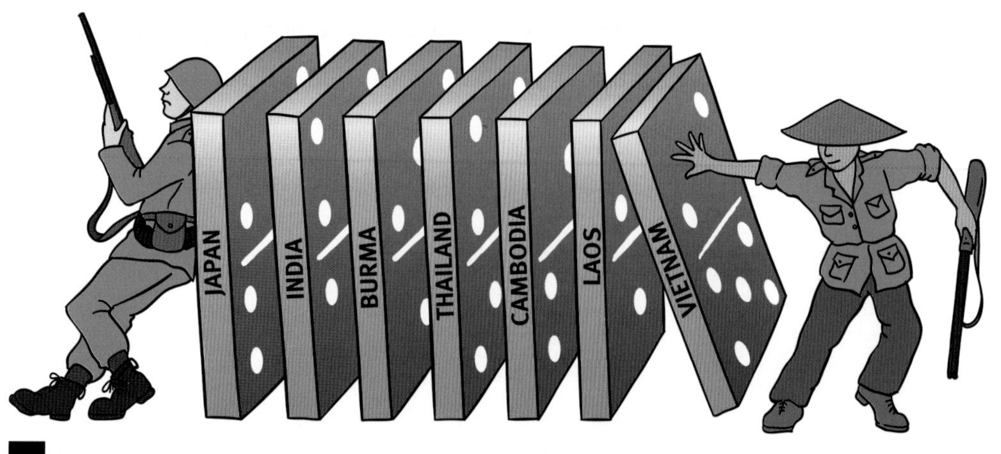

According to the domino theory, the Americans thought that if one country in Asia fell to communism, neighbouring countries would follow.

KEY PEOPLE

Ho Chi Minh – *communist leader of North Vietnam.*

Ngo Dinh Diem – *anti-communist leader of South Vietnam.*

Senator Joe McCarthy – *anti-communist American senator who conducted a witch-hunt of government departments looking for communist sympathisers to 'out'.*

to spread communism into South Vietnam. If the Vietcong were successful, the Americans believed that other countries in Asia would fall to communism like a row of dominoes. It was vital that the South Vietnamese government was supported, so Vietnam became part of the USA's Cold War containment policy.

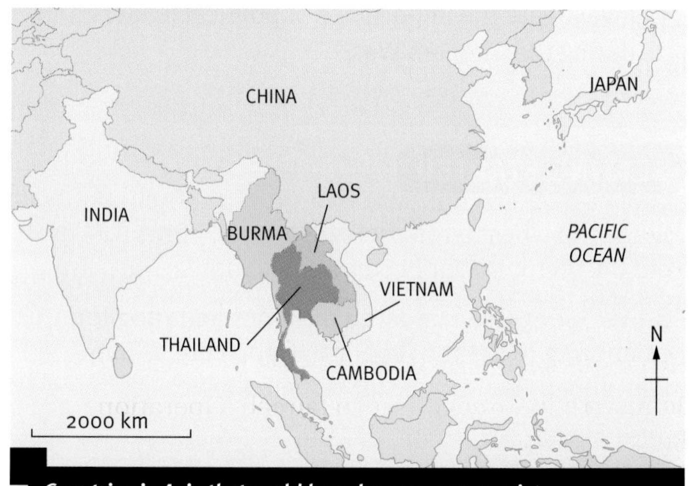

Countries in Asia that could have become communist.

Should the USA get involved in Vietnam?

There was a strong case for American involvement in Vietnam, but what else was happening at the time?

- America, under President Truman, had launched the Marshall Plan, the aim of which was to support countries against communist aggression by supplying economic aid and so reducing the chances of communism taking root.
- The USA was supporting a war in Korea and thousands of Americans were being killed there.
- **Senator Joe McCarthy** was fuelling anti-communist feeling with his 'Red Scare' (see Fact file).

VOICE YOUR OPINION!

Given the events in America during the period, should the USA have become involved in the Vietnam War? You must be prepared to support your argument with historical facts.

Fact file

McCarthyism

Post-war America was intensely anti-communist. In 1947, ten Hollywood film producers were sent to jail for refusing to tell the 'Un-American Activities Committee' whether they had ever been members of the Communist Party. In 1950 a law was passed banning communists from obtaining American passports.

A leading figure in the 'Red Scare' was Senator Joe McCarthy, who whipped up anti-communist feeling by claiming that he had a list of over 200 communists working in government departments. Although this was unlikely, anti-communist feeling was running so high that few politicians were prepared to stand up to him. Between 1950 and 1954 hundreds of Americans had their careers ruined as a result of accusations made in the communist 'witch hunt'.

Finally, in 1954 McCarthy's 'evidence' was exposed as nothing more than rumour and his influence came to an abrupt end.

Increasing US involvement in Vietnam

Between 1954 and 1960, the USA sent equipment and 'military advisers' into South Vietnam. Meanwhile, the Vietcong and North Vietnam were being supplied by China and the Soviet Union. From 1961 President Kennedy began increasing the number of advisers in South Vietnam until there were more than 11,000 Americans in the country.

By 1963 the Americans had decided that Diem was too corrupt to support, and he was deposed and replaced by anti-communist army generals. Despite American aid, the Vietcong had managed to take over about 40 per cent of the countryside of South Vietnam by 1963.

After Kennedy's assassination in 1963, **President Johnson** decided to increase American involvement in Vietnam. When North Vietnamese torpedo boats attacked American torpedo boats in the Gulf of Tonkin in 1964, it gave Johnson the excuse he wanted to take direct military action. As a result of the 'Tonkin incident' (in which no serious damage was done), Congress gave Johnson the authority to 'take all necessary steps, including the use of force' to defend South Vietnam.

Johnson and Vietnam

Johnson's first move was to launch 'Operation Rolling Thunder' against North Vietnam, to stop it supplying the Vietcong. The USA bombed factories, supply lines, ports and military bases. The idea was for the bombing to be so heavy that troops would not be needed. However, the bombing was unsuccessful, so in July 1965 180,000 American troops were sent to Vietnam. Soon the number had risen to over half a million. The bombing of North Vietnam continued until more bombs had been dropped on it than had been dropped in the whole of the Second World War.

SOURCE B

We fight this war because we must fight if we are to live in a world where every country can shape its own future. And only in such a world will a future be safe. We are in Vietnam because we have a promise to keep. Since 1954 every American president has offered support to the people of South Vietnam. We have helped to build and we have helped to defend. Over many years we have made a national pledge to help South Vietnam defend its independence. To dishonour that pledge, to abandon this small and brave nation to its enemies, and to the terror that must follow, would be an unforgivable wrong.

President Johnson speaking in 1965.

SOURCE C

The total tonnage of bombs dropped between 1964 and the end of 1971 was 6.2 million. This means that the US has dropped 300 pounds of bombs for every man, woman, and child in Indochina, and 22 tons of bombs for every square mile. Enormous craters dot the landscape in many regions, covering dozens of square miles. Hundreds of villages were totally destroyed by bombs and ***napalm****, forests over vast areas* ***defoliated****, making the land infertile for years, and crops destroyed, with little or no consideration for the needs of the people, merely on suspicion that some of the crop might benefit the enemy.*

Joseph Buttinger attempted to document the effect that the war had on the people of Vietnam in his book *A Dragon Defiant* (1972).

ACTIVITIES

1. Look through the above text and note what you think were the major causes of American involvement in Vietnam.
2. Look again at what American involvement in Vietnam meant. Did the level of involvement increase or decrease? What is the evidence for your answer?

KEY WORDS

Defoliate – *strip all foliage from trees.*

Napalm – *a jelly-like substance consisting of petrol thickened by special soaps.*

KEY PEOPLE

Lyndon B. Johnson – *President of the USA 1963–69.*

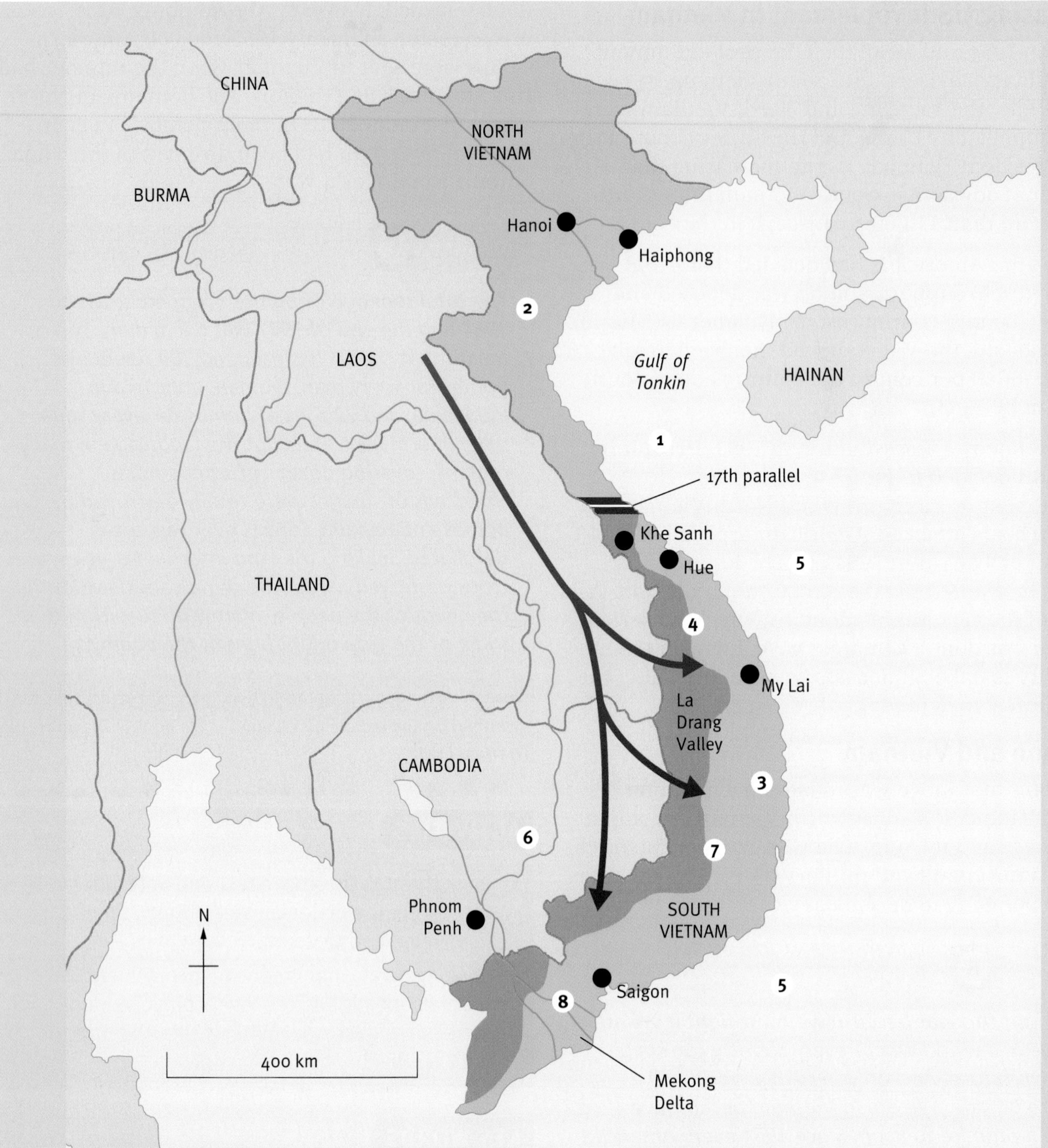

War in Vietnam

1. 2 August 1964. North Vietnamese ships attack a US destroyer in the Gulf of Tonkin. US Congress passes the Tonkin Resolution giving President Johnson wide military powers.
2. 7 February 1965. Operation Rolling Thunder – bombing of targets in North Vietnam.
3. 14 November 1965. US Army fights North Vietnamese in La Drang Valley.
4. 22 January–7 April 1968. Siege of Khe Sanh: 6000 American troops evacuated after 77 days.
5. Tet Offensive, 30 January–26 February 1968. Vietcong attack Hue, Saigon and other towns.
6. 1 May–29 June 1970. USA invades Cambodia.
7. 30 March 1972. North Vietnamese begin conventional invasion of the south.
8. 30 April 1975. North Vietnamese troops take Saigon. South Vietnam surrenders. (The last US troops had left Vietnam on 29 March 1973.)

→ Ho Chi Minh Trails – a network of tracks for bicycles, trucks and tanks. It was the supply route from the north to the south

■ Demilitarised zone

■ Areas controlled by the Vietcong in 1973

TIMELINE

Truman *1945–53*

Truman had already had to deal with the Berlin Blockade and had instigated the Marshall Plan. In 1950 he had to get tough with North Korea and send in troops to the south to ensure the whole of Korea did not become communist. His response to the growing tension in Vietnam was to help finance the French fight to reclaim Vietnam.

Eisenhower *1953–61*

Against a back-drop of McCarthyism and success in Korea, 'Ike' increased financial support to the French to pay for 80 per cent of the cost of their fight. Eisenhower saw Vietnam divided at the 17th parallel and financially supported Diem as prime minister of South Vietnam. He also sent military advisors to the area.

Kennedy *1961–63*

Kennedy increased the number of military advisors to 800, allowed US pilots to fly combat missions whilst pretending to be instructors and overthrew the unpopular Diem and replaced him with Vietnamese generals. The amount of US money, materials and support all increased under JFK.

Johnson *1963–69*

LBJ's ambassador in Vietnam gave him a stark choice upon entering office: either increase US involvement in Vietnam or face a communist victory. Johnson did not want to be the first American president to lose a war so he massively increased US involvement. The Tonkin incident allowed him to introduce ground forces and air power.

Nixon *1969–74*

The war was becoming increasingly unpopular, and Nixon promised to end America's involvement in it. He ended the 'draft' of young Americans into the forces and gradually withdrew his forces under a policy of Vietnamisation. He oversaw the ceasefire in 1973.

Ford *1974–77*

The war seemed to be over for Ford but it started again in 1974. This time no American troops were sent over, only supplies. The communists overran much of South Vietnam and took Saigon in 1975. Laos and Cambodia fell to communists in 1976.

Timeline of American presidents during the Vietnam War

The timeline on page 83 shows the role of the six different American presidents in Vietnam, spanning three decades.

ACTIVITIES

1. Hold a class debate on the involvement of the different US presidents in the Vietnam War. Students could take on the roles of the six presidents for a 'hot seat' session. Pupils can ask each president in turn questions about their involvement in the war – the reasons for what they did.
2. Using the information in this lesson, from the map and the timeline of American presidents, work out under whose leadership the events (1 to 8 on the map) took place. Decide which president was most responsible for American involvement in the Vietnam War.

VOICE YOUR OPINION!

You have already investigated music as one form of peaceful protest. The Buddhist (see opposite) monks came up with another peaceful, albeit lethal, method. Do you think this was any more effective than music? Explain your answer.

GradeStudio

Explain why some Vietnamese monks resorted to setting fire to themselves. **[6 marks]**

Mark scheme

Level 1:	1 mark	General answer, lacking specific contextual knowledge e.g. 'They did this because they were worried about what was happening in Vietnam.'
Level 2:	2 marks	Identifies or describes reasons e.g. 'They were setting fire to themselves as a protest.' 'The monks wanted fairer treatment at the hands of the Diem government.'
Level 3:	3–6 marks	Explains reasons e.g. 'Firstly, the monks noticed that Buddhists in Vietnam were being treated unfairly by the Catholic government despite Buddhists representing about 70% of the population and Catholics only 10%. Secondly...'

CASE STUDY

Buddhism in Vietnam

Most people in Vietnam were Buddhists (approximately 70 per cent of the population). However, some had become Catholic because they wanted to please their colonial masters, the French. Catholics were rewarded with the top jobs and became the largest land owners in Vietnam, despite constituting only 10 per cent of the population.

When Vietnam was split in two at the 17th parallel, the Americans placed Ngo Dinh Diem, a devout Catholic, in power. This angered Buddhists.

On 8 May 1963 Buddhists met in Hue to celebrate the birth of the Buddha (his 2527th birthday). The police opened fire in an attempt to disperse the crowd, and in the ensuing panic one woman and eight children were killed. The Buddhists wanted to show their anger at this and show the world how much they hated the Diem government. To do this they asked for monks to volunteer to commit suicide. Thich Quang Due, a 66-year-old monk, was the first to volunteer. On 11 June 1963 he sat down in the middle of a busy Saigon street, had petrol poured over him and then was set alight. He sat very still while all around him people screamed and other Buddhists handed out leaflets calling for Diem's government to show charity and compassion to all religions.

Diem's response was to arrest thousands of Buddhists monks; many were never seen again. Over the next three months five more monks committed suicide in the same way. Some members of the government offered to buy the petrol.

The Buddhist monk Thich Quang Due burning to death in Saigon, June 1963.

What were the different ways that the USA and the Communists fought the Vietnam War?

LEARNING OBJECTIVES

In this lesson you will:

- learn about the key differences in the way the two sides fought the Vietnam War.

GETTING STARTED

What does Source A below tell you about the tactics used by the American troops in Vietnam? Would you expect this particular tactic to be successful?

US firepower versus Vietcong guerrilla tactics

The American troops in Vietnam had vastly superior weapons to those used by the Vietcong. American soldiers had mortars, machine guns and rocket launchers and were supported by tanks, armoured vehicles and helicopters. Yet they could not win the war. Why was this?

The main reason for the American failure is that the way the war was fought gave an advantage to the Vietcong. The Americans could easily win any pitched battle, but the Vietcong avoided this strategy and instead fought a guerrilla war. They came out of the jungle to carry out acts of sabotage and sudden ambushes, and then quickly returned into the jungle. As they had the support of most of the local population, they could easily be absorbed back into village life, and the Americans could not tell the difference between ordinary peasants and Vietcong members.

The American soldiers in Vietnam, who had an average age of just 19, found the war extremely frustrating. They might be victims of an ambush or a booby trap in which their comrades were killed or maimed. Yet when they went off in pursuit of the Vietcong who had attacked them, they were met by a wall of silence from villagers. Under these

SOURCE A

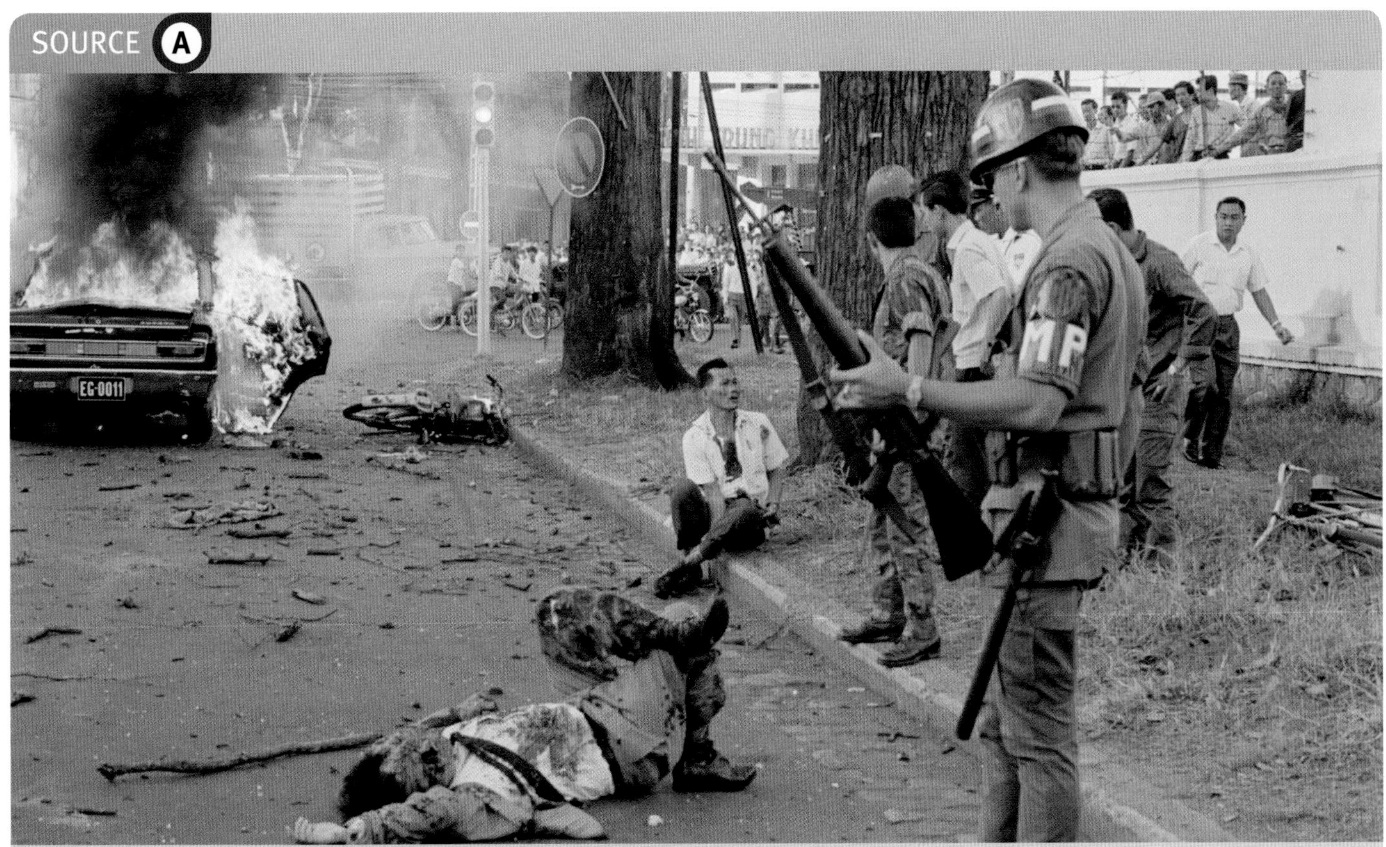

US soldiers looking at injured and dead Vietnamese people.

circumstances, soldiers sometimes lost control and carried out terrible atrocities. One of the most infamous of these occurred at My Lai in March 1968. A group of American soldiers landed by helicopter to search for Vietcong; when they could not find any, they rounded up the inhabitants of the village and massacred them all. The officer in charge, Lieutenant William Calley, was tried for the murder of 109 civilians. He was found guilty and sentenced to life imprisonment. But he was released to house arrest on the instructions of President Nixon after serving only three days.

New tactics

The Americans adopted a variety of tactics to try to defeat the Vietcong guerrilla warfare.

- Strategic villages were set up. Whole villages were moved to new sites behind barbed wire. Careful control was kept over who entered and left the villages. Special aid was given to villagers to try to win their support.
- As the Vietcong could hide easily in the jungle, the Americans carried out a policy of defoliation. The leaves were removed from the trees by dropping Agent Orange (a strong chemical) from the air. The jungle was destroyed, and even today some areas are unfit for human habitation.
- Napalm, a type of petroleum jelly that burns fiercely and sticks to the skin, was dropped from aircraft to burn jungle or set fire to villages. Thousands of innocent villagers received terrible burns.

However, the new tactics did not work. The Vietcong continued to receive supplies from North Vietnam down a series of jungle tracks called the Ho Chi Minh trail. Lorries, bikes and human backs carried millions of tons of supplies provided by North Vietnam and China. In the jungle, the Vietcong built an extensive network of tunnels where they had storehouses, workshops, kitchens and even hospitals. No amount of Agent Orange would destroy such a system.

The cost of the war in civilian lives was enormous. It has been estimated that 300,000 South Vietnamese civilians were killed in 1968. These deaths occurred in a war that the Americans were fighting to 'save the people from the evils of communism'. No wonder so many South Vietnamese hated the Americans and so many American soldiers began to wonder what they were doing in Vietnam.

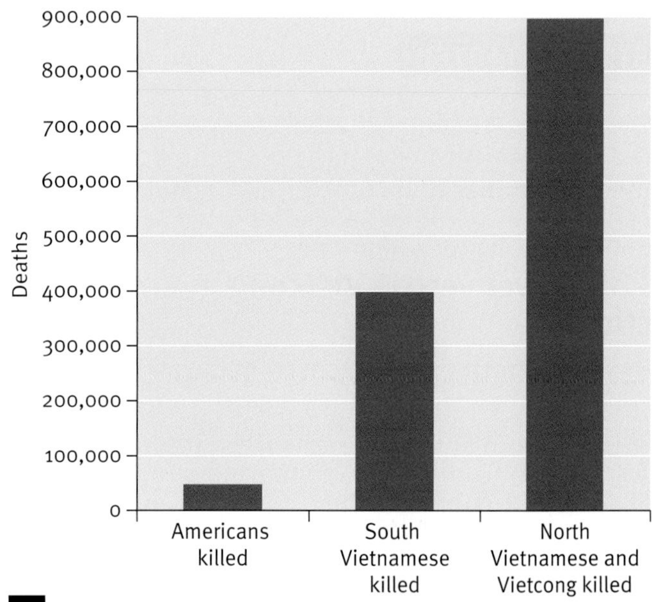

Deaths in the Vietnam War.

The Tet Offensive

Although the Vietcong largely stuck to guerrilla warfare, they did carry out some major offensives. One of these was the Tet Offensive of 1968, when communist troops attacked major South Vietnamese towns and American bases. They even carried out an attack on the American embassy in Saigon. At first the Americans were pushed into retreat, but they soon hit back and regained all the towns and bases that had been captured. By the end of the offensive, 50,000 communist troops had been killed. The Vietcong had hoped that the offensive would result in a revolution in South Vietnam, but it did not.

GradeStudio

What were the tactics used by the Americans to try to win the Vietnam War. **[4 marks]**

The examiner would award one mark for each relevant point and one additional mark for supporting detail.

e.g. 'The Americans used a weapon called Napalm (a jelly that burns everything it touches) to try to clear the jungle so they could see where the Vietcong were hiding.' (This would be two marks – one relevant point with supporting detail).

ACTIVITIES

List the different strategies used by the American forces and the Vietcong in fighting the war. Then match the sources from this Key Question to the comments in your list.

Get your sources sorted

What are the messages of the following sources?

The author of Source A develops two reasons why the Americans did not win the Vietnam War. The key parts of the text that allow you to pinpoint the two reasons have been highlighted. Using the text, now write down what the message of the source is.

SOURCE A

The problem with the American strategy was that, though the suffering of the enemy was great, it was not enough to make them concede. Throughout the war, the capacity of the North Vietnamese to absorb pain outstripped that of the Americans to inflict it. For the Americans, the war was a 'limited one' far from home. For the North Vietnamese it was total: they were fighting to defend their homeland.

A modern historian's view of the reasons why the Americans did not win the Vietnam War.

Source B is a different source. It is different for several reasons. Read the source and work out at least two reasons why Sources A and B are different. The answers are given below so cover them up now!

Differences:

- Source B is written by a soldier whereas Source A is written by a historian.
- The purpose of each source is different: Source A is written to explain why the Americans failed in Vietnam, Source B isn't trying to explain anything. The soldier is recounting his experiences; you as the historian have to use his experience as evidence.
- Source A gives two clear reasons for the failure of US troops, whereas Source B is just a piece of evidence that you have to use.

Typically you are asked to compare two sources for information. When you analyse sources as we have done here the comparison becomes easier. Start with the big theme of the two sources (reasons for American failure in Vietnam), then mention how each source informs us of something different about the same big theme.

SOURCE B

The most feared mine was the Bouncing Betty. It was conical shaped, three prongs jutting out of the soil. When your foot hit the prong, a charge went off that shot the mine into the air, a yard high, showering shrapnel everywhere. It's a mine that goes after the lower torso: a terrible mine… On one occasion after my company had encamped and sent out patrols there was a large explosion only 200 yards away… We raced out there and only two men were living out of a patrol of eight or so. Just a mess. It was like a stew, full of meat and flesh and red tissue and white bone.

Tim O'Brien served in the Vietnam War as an infantryman. In this passage he describes the dangers of going out on patrol. Over 10,000 US soldiers lost limbs during the war; a considerable number of these injuries were caused by Vietcong mines.

Whose tactics were the most effective – the USA's or the communists'?

LEARNING OBJECTIVES

In this lesson you will:

- learn about the different tactics used by the two sides
- make a judgement on the effectiveness of the tactics used by either side.

GETTING STARTED

Return to the map of Vietnam on page 82 and look at the Ho Chi Minh trail. What might have been the purpose of such a trail?

Expensive American weapons

The Americans threw everything at this war; a huge amount of money was spent equipping their soldiers with the latest weapons. By 1968 the cost had risen to $30,000 million a year. Money spent pursuing victory was money that could not be spent on issues at home (crime, education etc.). Far from delivering victory, the new weapons like napalm (see page 86) and Agent Orange meant that Vietnamese citizens were indirectly targeted, leading to huge numbers of civilian casualties. Increasing numbers of them began to side with the Vietcong who were, of course, trying to force the Americans to leave Vietnam.

The War at home

There was no chance of a Vietnamese retaliatory strike against the American homeland, but Americans were still deeply affected by the war. News broadcasts bringing home the tragedy of the war for both the Americans (as they saw troops being delivered home in coffins) and the Vietnamese (pictures of children running through the streets suffering the effects of napalm) appeared on tea-time news programmes. Many Americans began questioning the tactics being used.

My Lai

One tactic that shocked many was the massacre of over 300 women and children of the village of My Lai in March 1968. The slaughtered women and children were thought to be hiding members of the Vietcong and whilst they huddled together US troops shot them. Lieutenant William Calley served three years of house arrest for the atrocities after being charged with having been responsible for the crime.

Vietcong tactics

The Vietcong did not have the vast resources of the US army; they could not buy expensive weapons, so instead they had to rely on what we call guerrilla tactics. This involved hiding in the jungle and making surprise attacks as soldiers went past or planting bombs to blow up unsuspecting soldiers. This led the American soldiers to be very wary of anybody and any place. As Captain E.J. Banks said,

ACTIVITIES

Using the above information draw a table with two columns: one column for American tactics and one for the Vietcong's. On the American side make a list (with a little detail) about the type of tactics the Americans used. You may wish to use information from elsewhere in this chapter or do extra research to find more examples of atrocities. While reading the following information on the Vietcong complete the other column.

SOURCE A

(1) Not to do what is likely to damage the land and crops or spoil the houses and belongings of the people.

(2) Not to insist on buying or borrowing what the people are not willing to sell or lend.

(3) Never to break our word.

(4) Not to do or speak what is likely to make people believe that we hold them in contempt.

(5) To help them in their daily work (harvesting, fetching firewood, carrying water, sewing, etc.)

(6) In spare time, to tell amusing, simple, and short stories useful to the Resistance, but not to betray secrets.

(7) Whenever possible to buy commodities for those who live far from the market.

(8) To teach the population the national script and elementary hygiene.

Viet Minh (Vietnamese Independence Movement Armed Forces) Directive, 1960.

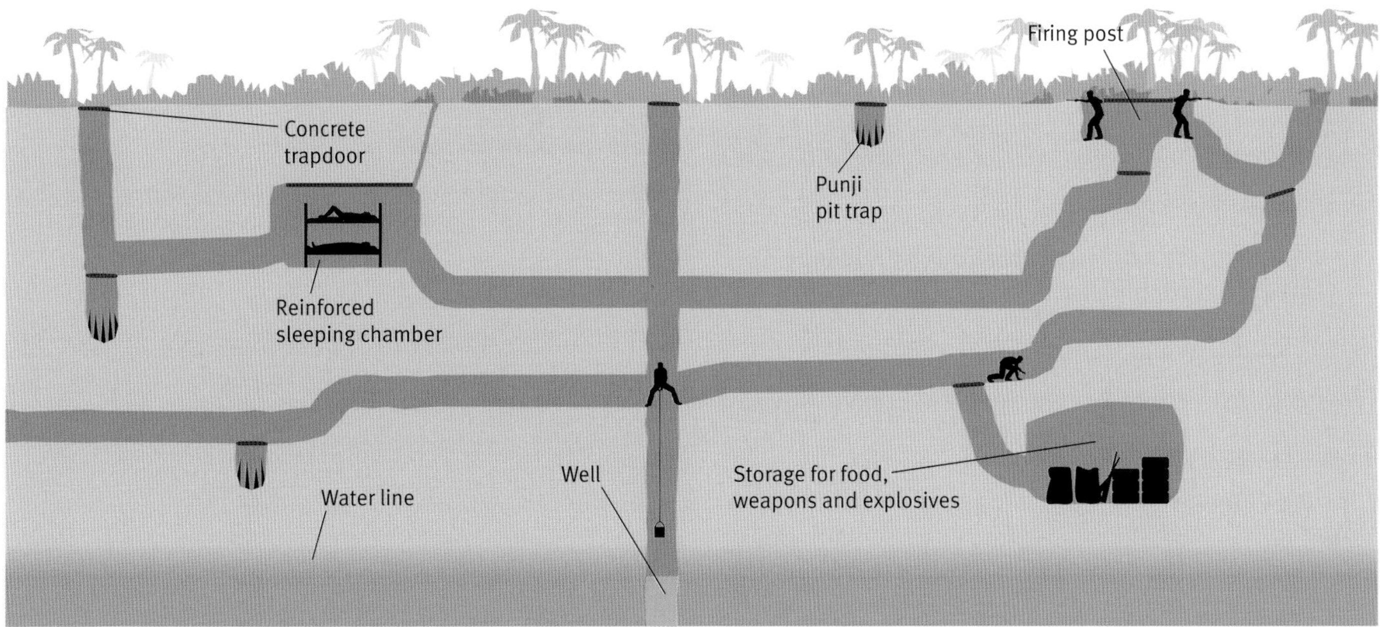

'You never knew who was the enemy and who was a friend. They all looked alike. They were all Vietnamese. Some of them were Vietcong... The enemy was all around you.'

Foreign aid

The Vietcong were also driven by a passionate belief in the justice of their cause, whereas the American soldiers never felt certain about the justice of theirs. The Vietcong were reinforced by supplies from China and the Soviet Union, so they had replacements when vehicles and other equipment were destroyed. The total aid from China and the Soviet Union has been estimated at over $2billion.

Underground bunkers

The Vietcong built an extensive network of underground tunnels and bunkers so they could keep well hidden from American soldiers. Tunnels would include workshops to make and store weapons, hospitals to treat the injured, kitchens to prepare food for the Vietcong and the villagers, and booby-traps in case they were discovered.

SOURCE B

I saw the terrible destruction that was done to our country. I saw the villages and fields destroyed. Every time the Americans increased their destruction of our land, more and more young men and women would rally to our side to join us in our fight for freedom.

A member of the Vietcong explains the effects of the American tactics in Vietnam.

The Vietcong may not have been able to wipe out the American army by force, but they could certainly make life difficult for them.

GradeStudio

'The main reasons American troops were withdrawn from Vietnam was the success of the Vietcong.' How far do you agree with this statement? **[10 marks]**

Examiner's tip

This question is asking you to compare the tactics used by the Vietcong with other reasons for American withdrawal from the country. Make sure you know what the other reasons are before you start answering this question, and that you have an opinion.

Mark scheme

Level 1:	1–2 marks	General answer lacking specific contextual knowledge.
Level 2:	2–4 marks	Identifies or describes methods.
Level 3:	3–6 marks	Explains similarities or differences.
Level 4:	6–9 marks	Explains similarities and differences.
Level 5:	9–10 marks	Explains with evaluation of 'how far'.

Why did the USA withdraw from Vietnam?

LEARNING OBJECTIVES

In this lesson you will:

- explore a range of reasons for the American withdrawal from Vietnam
- hypothesise and challenge that hypothesis.

GETTING STARTED

From your reading you will already have formed an opinion on why the US army should withdraw from Vietnam. Note down your reasons and when completing the following pages find evidence to support your point of view.

Look back at Pete Seeger's protest song about the Vietnam War (Source A on page 79). Hopefully, you will have researched more protest songs; now is the time to see if they worked.

Time to get out

The Tet Offensive did have a major effect on America. By 1968, 300 Americans a week were being killed in a war that was costing $30,000 million a year. In 1967, *Life* magazine calculated that the war was costing $400,000 for each Vietcong guerrilla killed. Many Americans now realised that their politicians and generals were wrong when they said that victory was near. After all the cost in both money and lives, the Vietcong could still attack South Vietnam's capital, Saigon. The time had come to withdraw.

Protest at home

Most Americans supported their government's decision to send troops to Vietnam. They genuinely believed that there was a communist threat and that it was in the USA's interests to fight it. But as the war went on, attitudes changed. Vietnam was the first 'televised war'. Night after night, pictures could be seen of villages being napalmed, of civilian casualties and of American soldiers killed before

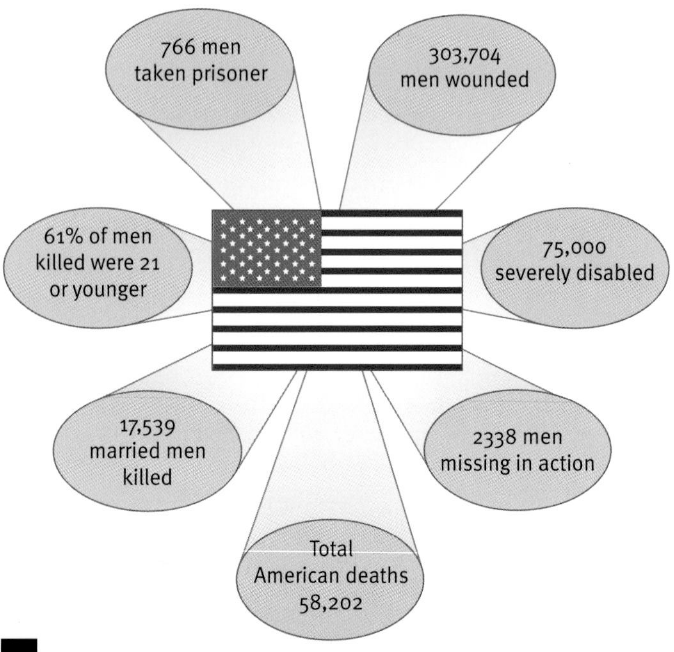

The human costs of the Vietnam War in America.

SOURCE A

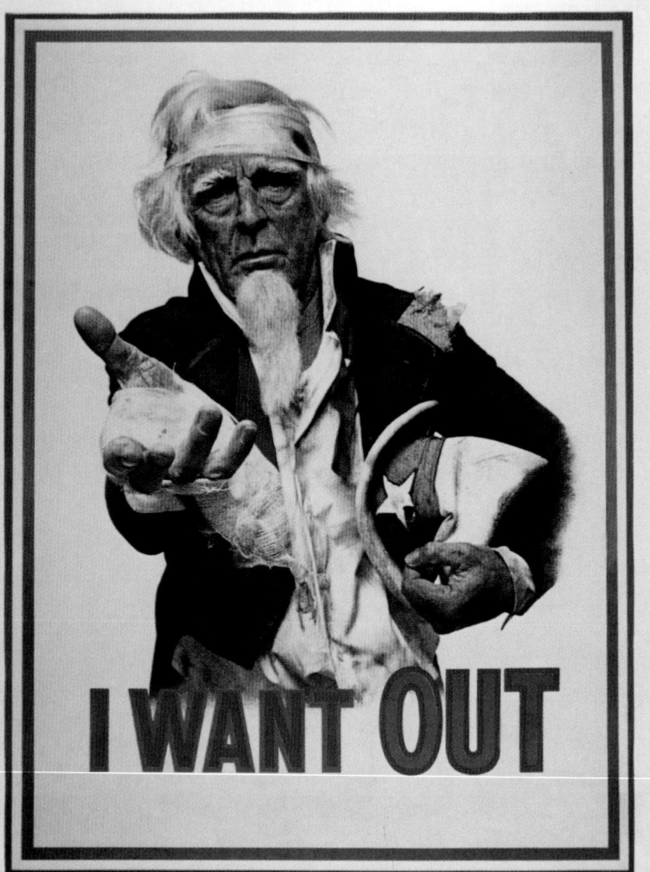

An American anti-war poster. It is based on a recruiting poster from the First World War, but on this occasion Uncle Sam is wounded and wants to get out of the war.

SOURCE B

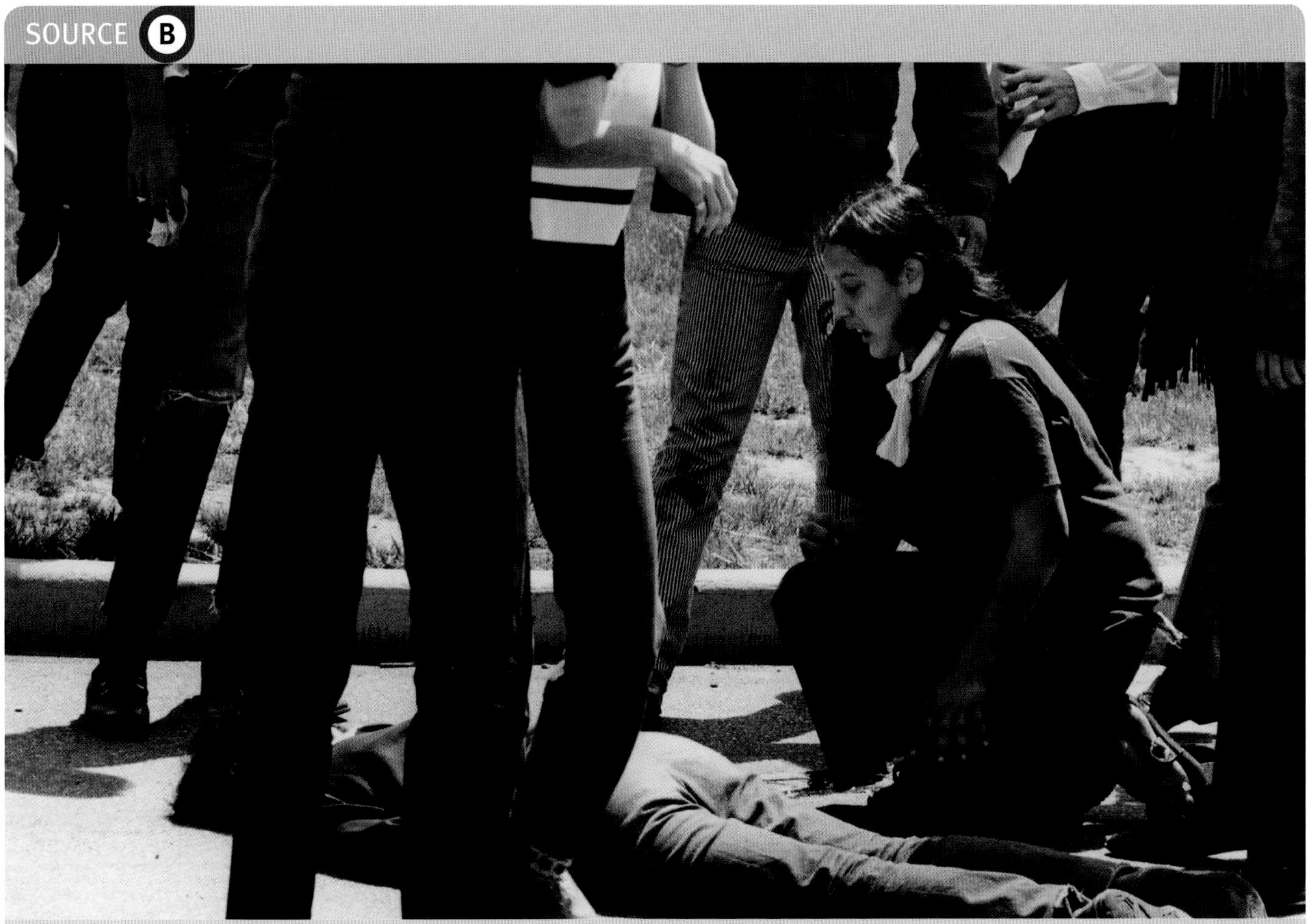

On 4 May 1970, 3000 students gathered at Kent State University to protest against the Vietnam War. At midday, National Guardsmen fired tear gas to break up the demonstration. Some students threw the tear gas canisters back and hurled stones at the troops, who opened fire. Four students, none of whom were involved in the demonstration, were killed. President Nixon later called the student protestors 'bums'.

they were out of their teens. Stories soon reached home of widespread drug addiction and indiscipline in the army. When the My Lai atrocity was reported in 1969 (see page 88), many Americans were shocked that their own troops could do such a thing.

As more and more sons and brothers returned either in body bags or maimed for life, public opinion began to turn against the war. There were increasing numbers of demonstrations in American cities, and thousands of young men burned the 'draft cards' that called them up to fight in Vietnam. Some fled abroad to avoid having to fight in a war of which they disapproved so much. President Johnson came under enormous criticism and across the USA students taunted him with chants of 'Hey, hey, LBJ, how many kids did you kill today?' Johnson decided to end the bombing of North Vietnam and not to stand for re-election in 1968. It was left to the next president, **Richard Nixon**, to find a way to get American troops out of Vietnam.

SOURCE C

I don't give a damn
For Uncle Sam
I ain't going
To Vietnam

An anti-war protest chant from the late 1960s.

KEY PEOPLE

Richard Nixon – *President of the USA 1969–74.*

KEY CONCEPTS

Vietnamisation – *the process of training the Vietnamese army to fight the Vietcong.*

Vietnamisation

President Nixon had a difficult task in taking the USA out of the Vietnam War. He could not just say that the Americans had decided that it was all too much trouble and they were going to leave. Since 1965 American governments had been persuading people at home and abroad that the war was both just and vital to American interests. Thousands of Americans had died fighting for their country and it would be an insult to their memory merely to withdraw the troops and admit defeat. But the American people had turned against the war and Nixon had promised that he would bring it to an end. His solution was to introduce a policy of '**Vietnamisation**'. The Americans would give the war back to the South Vietnamese.

Obviously the South Vietnamese army was not strong enough to fight the war on its own, so the Americans would help build it up and would train and equip it. Then American troops could withdraw. While this policy was being put in place, peace talks would be held with North Vietnam to try to end the war.

The communists triumph

The Americans slowly withdrew, and at first the new policy appeared to be working well. Soon half the male population of South Vietnam was in the army, and a major offensive by the North Vietnamese was successfully resisted. Then, in February 1973, a ceasefire was agreed with North Vietnam and the Vietcong. By the end of the year, all American troops had left Vietnam and the war appeared to be over.

ACTIVITIES

Use Source D to explain the problems facing the American president in 1969.

You must:

- Say who the president is.
- Explain the significance of the date (1969).
- Explain what Vietnamisation was.

SOURCE D

A British cartoon showing the problems faced by President Nixon in 1969.

The reality was something different, however. The Americans had suspected that the ceasefire might not last and had promised South Vietnam further support if fighting broke out again. They did not keep this promise. When the war restarted in 1974, the Americans sent supplies, but no troops.

During 1975 communist troops over-ran much of South Vietnam, and Saigon fell in April. Neighbouring Laos and Cambodia were also captured by communist forces. In 1976 North and South Vietnam were united in a single communist country under the rule of Ho Chi Minh. The American policy of containment in south-east Asia had failed.

ACTIVITIES

Make a spider diagram with the title 'Reasons the Americans withdrew from Vietnam'. Around it place the reasons you can deduce from the above text. Try to expand the reasons beyond just a title. When you have done this, number them in order of importance and write a reason next to your top three reasons (be ready to justify these in class). You may want to make changes to your order.

Use your diagram to plan the essay below.

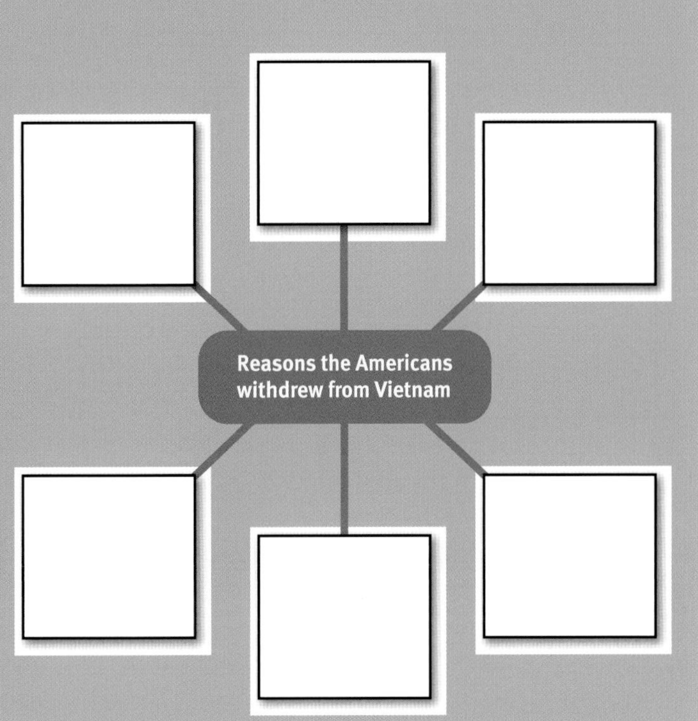

GradeStudio

Why did the Americans withdraw from Vietnam in 1973? **[6 marks]**

Examiner's tip

The mention of a specific year makes the question much broader. It is not enough just to write a list of all the factors that made the USA pull out; you have to work hard to explain each factor and why it contributed to the withdrawal in 1973. You will have to explain why some events didn't lead to a withdrawal at the time but contributed to one later on.

Look back at the two earlier sections of this chapter. The American government was engaged in many different parts of the world in trying to contain communism. The Cuban Missile Crisis never drew US troops into action, but the Vietnam War did. Look through the next few pages and draw up another timeline, placing events on it that are significant to the Vietnam War. You could add to the timeline with your own research.

GradeStudio

The Cold War, 1945-75

Here is an example of a question that requires you to explain the meaning of a political cartoon. This is a common type of question in Unit A971. The skill you require is to put the source into historical context by using your knowledge of the topic combined with details from the source.

What is the message of this cartoon? Use details of the cartoon and your own knowledge to explain your answer. **[7 marks]**

Examiner's tip

In order to get the highest levels in any question it is a good idea to get to know the mark scheme. If you know how you are going to be assessed, you will understand what skills you need to demonstrate when answering different types of questions. Have a look at the mark scheme below before thinking about how you would answer the question.

Mark scheme

Level 1: Describes features of the cartoon.
Level 2: Describes the message of the cartoon.
Level 3: Explains the message of the cartoon supported with details from the source OR own knowledge.
Level 4: Explains the message of the cartoon supported with details from the source AND own knowledge.

Look at the example shown and think about how the candidate moves up these levels.

Source A

Examiner's tip

When using a source like the one shown it is tempting to give the examiner a list of things you can see. These kinds of answers are only using the source for information and rarely get beyond Level one.
The trick is to try to use the source to make judgements or give opinions about what it means. This is called making inferences and is a skill that you need to apply in Units A971 and A972.

Examiner's comment

In the source I can see two men arm-wrestling whilst sitting on bombs. The message of this source is that Khrushchev and Kennedy are locked in a power struggle over the Cuban Missile Crisis. Sooner or later one of them will have to give in, and when they do it could result in nuclear war.	This answer is at Level two. To develop it you need to support your ideas with either details from the source or your own knowledge on this topic.
The message of this source is that Khrushchev and Kennedy are locked in a power struggle over the Cuban Missile Crisis, which could result in nuclear war. This is represented in the source by the image of the two men having an arm-wrestling match. Sooner or later one of them will have to give in and when they do it could mean big trouble, as both men are ready to press the button that *will* set off the bombs they are sitting on.	This is a good Level three answer. To develop it to Level four you should also put the source into its historical context using your own knowledge. Try to write your own Level four answer using the mark scheme to help you.

A new world? 1948–2005

This chapter will address three fundamental questions relating to the post-war period:

1 How secure was the USSR's control over Eastern Europe?
2 How effective has terrorism been since 1969?
3 What is the significance of the Iraq War?

The first question will address the degree to which the Soviet Union controlled Eastern Europe. It will be particularly concerned with the impact and significance of the uprisings in Hungary and Czechoslovakia, the construction of the Berlin Wall, and the impact of the Solidarity Movement on the USSR's control. Finally, it will assess the responsibility of Mikhail Gorbachev against other factors in the USSR's eventual demise.

The second part of this chapter will look at the history, workings and significance of three terrorist groups (Provisional Irish Republican Army, Palestine Liberation Organisation and Al-Qaeda) and the differences between them. It will be concerned with their effectiveness particularly in relation to securing their goals. It will also address the features of terrorism such as their motives, methods, aims and organisation, the role of religion, and the importance of leaders. Finally, it will look at the reaction to these terrorist groups, especially from particular governments and society in general. Throughout this enquiry, these three groups will be compared with each other.

The final part of this chapter will touch upon the significance of the Iraq War. It will concentrate on the reasons for, results of and opposition to the invasion. It will then assess the impact of the invasion both inside Iraq and in the wider world.

Overall, therefore, this chapter's history of the 'New World' begins with the Soviet Union's control of Eastern Europe and concludes with the aftermath of the invasion of Iraq. During this time, international terrorism began to be more widespread in both Europe and the wider world. Whilst these historical events and developments are undoubtedly significant in their own right, it would be wrong to assume that they are only linked by chronology.

Moreover, the connections and links between these three key questions of history are legion. Firstly, the history of all three is intertwined to some extent. The Soviet Union's control of Eastern Europe symbolised the conflict between the USA and the USSR. However, this period witnessed a steady decline in Soviet control, and consequently the Soviet Union became less of a threat to world peace and security. In its place, terrorism emerged as the most dangerous threat to states. It was because of this growing phenomenon that the Iraq War occurred, since America in particular was very concerned about the former president of Iraq Saddam Hussein's suspected links to terrorism.

SOURCE 

The Wall will remain as long as the conditions that had led to its construction are not changed. It will still exist in 50 and even in 100 years.

Erich Honecker, East German Communist Party chief, speaking about the Berlin Wall, 19 January 1989.

Secondly, there are some even more direct links between the collapse of the Soviet Union, which was brought about in part by its failure in Afghanistan, and the rise of the terrorist organisation Al-Qaeda, which had its origins in the battle against the Soviet Union in Afghanistan. In addition, the situation in post-war Iraq has had many implications for the effectiveness of terrorist groups, notably Al-Qaeda. In short, there are plenty of links between these three key questions.

Finally, these separate questions are also linked in terms of the opportunities they provide for historical investigation. As an example, when looking at the role of key individuals, it will be possible to look separately, yet comparatively, at Mikhail Gorbachev, George W. Bush and Osama bin-Laden. Next, the skill of comparison will be tested by the study of the differences and similarities between the Hungarian Uprising and the Prague Spring, along with the differences between the Provisional Irish Republican Army, the Palestine Liberation Organisation and Al-Qaeda. Another key area of investigation will be the reaction to key events such as the USSR's reaction to unrest in its satellite republics, and the reaction of the Iraqi population to the country's invasion. Finally, these key questions will shed light on the power of different agencies to have influence in international relations, such as the USSR, the USA, and certain terrorist organisations.

The uncertainty in Iraq is an appropriate way for this chapter opener on the 'new world' to end. It is clear that the world has become more unpredictable over the course of the last six decades, and yet although international conflict might have changed in terms of its location, nature and participants, it nevertheless still occurs. The situation in 1948 was in many ways determined by events in international relations during the first half of the twentieth century, and it is highly likely that the fate of future generations will be heavily influenced by the events that have taken place between the years 1948 and 2005.

SOURCE B

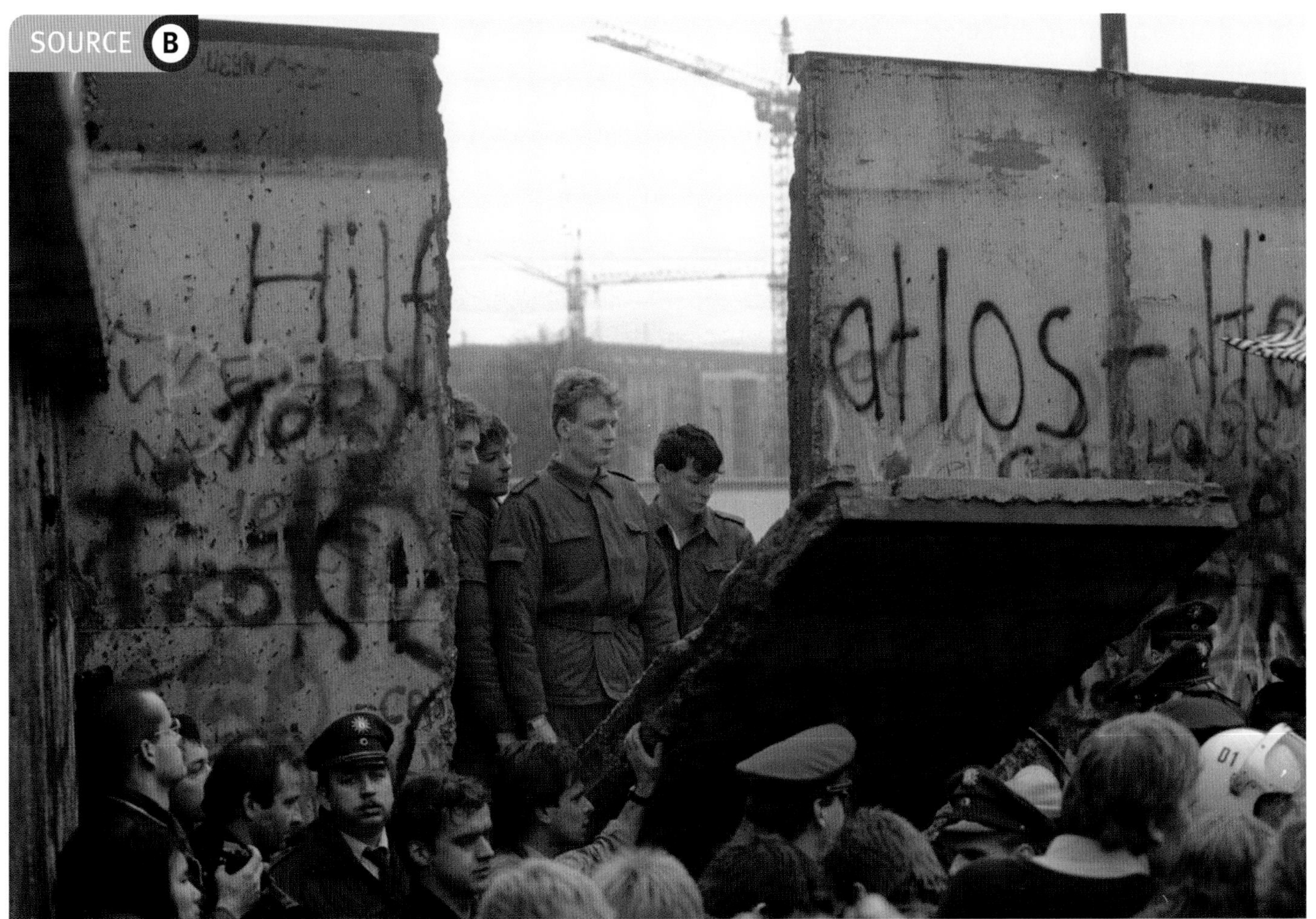

On 9 November 1989 the wall came down. This image depicts an East German soldier walking through a segment of the wall, as West Berliners can be seen celebrating the historic occasion.

How secure was the USSR's control over Eastern Europe, 1948–c.1989?

Why was there opposition to Soviet control in Hungary in 1956 and Czechoslovakia in 1968, and how did the USSR react to this opposition?

LEARNING OBJECTIVES

In this lesson you will:

- examine the events of 1956 in Hungary and of 1968 in Czechoslovakia
- learn to analyse the causes and consequences of the Hungarian Uprising and the Prague Spring.

Background knowledge

The previous chapter related to the origin and nature of the Cold War, but this key question is concerned with how secure Soviet control was in Eastern Europe during this period. It will look at the nature of Soviet control at different times and in four different areas: Hungary, Czechoslovakia, Berlin and Poland. The key point for students to investigate is what patterns these events reveal about Soviet Union control of Eastern Europe during this time. The final lesson will analyse the role of Gorbachev in bringing about the relaxation of Soviet control in Eastern Europe by 1989.

Essential knowledge

The period 1955–68 was a time of great tension in the Cold War. The Soviet Union had signed the Warsaw Pact and the space race had begun. Although Nikita Khrushchev had already started to criticise Stalin, who had died in 1953, he showed no signs of slowing down in the arms race.

Khrushchev and Poland

However, it was also a time when the Soviet Union faced opposition from within Eastern Europe, beginning in Poland in June 1956, where after a rebellion against government officials had begun in Poznań, Khrushchev sent in Soviet troops to restore order. Afterwards, Poland remained loyal to the Soviet Union and the Warsaw Pact.

In October 1956, Hungarian students rioted and smashed statues of Stalin. They were angry with the Stalinist government of Hungary and the Soviet-imposed policies. Their protests began a chain of events which led to the **liberal communist**, **Imre Nagy**, succeeding the unpopular **Mátyás Rákosi** as Prime Minister of Hungary.

GETTING STARTED

This key question involves Eastern Europe, so before you begin, test your geographical knowledge on which countries are actually in Eastern Europe. Six of the twelve below are.

- Bulgaria
- Albania
- France
- Italy
- Czechoslovakia
- Austria
- Hungary
- Poland
- Romania
- Belgium
- Spain
- Finland.

Now look at these six Eastern European countries on the map on page 62. Can you spot the large country which is very close to all of them?

BRAIN BOOST

K – Khrushchev – policy of **de-Stalinisation** gave Hungarians hope
H – Hungarian Patriotism – particularly in the face of Soviet control
R – Religious Identity – rallied around to support **Cardinal Mindszenty**
U – USA – the Hungarians hoped that the USA would support an uprising
S – Student Protests – in support of Poland's demands for similar reforms

Causes of the Hungarian Uprising

- Khrushchev's policy of 'de-Stalinisation' unintentionally caused problems in Hungary since it gave those who hated the hard-line Stalinist regime of Mátyás Rákosi the encouragement to free themselves of the Stalinist influences in their country.
- Hungarian patriots hated Russia's excessive control. In particular, the Hungarians disliked the Hungarian Secret Police (AVH), Russian control of the economy, and the lack of basic freedoms such as a free press.
- The Hungarians were devout Catholics yet the Communist Party had practically banned religion. They had also imprisoned and tortured Cardinal Mindszenty for opposing communism.
- Hungarians thought that the United Nations or the US president, Dwight D. Eisenhower, would help them if they began to rebel against the Soviet Union.
- Students in Hungary rioted against the Soviet Union in support of **Władysław Gomułka**, the Polish Communist leader who had stood up to Khrushchev weeks earlier. They wanted similar reforms in Hungary.

KEY PEOPLE

Władysław Gomułka – *Communist leader of Poland, 1956–70.*

János Kádár – *Communist leader of Hungary, 1956–88.*

Cardinal Joseph Mindszenty – *Polish churchman who was a cardinal from 1946 until his death in 1975.*

Imre Nagy – *Leader of Hungary, 1953–55, 1956.*

Mátyás Rákosi – *Stalinist ruler of Hungary, 1952–53.*

Nagy in power

The Hungarian uprising succeeded in getting Nagy into power. Hungary's new leader removed state control of the mass media and encouraged public discussion on political and economic reform. This led to democracy, and included freedom of speech and freedom of religion. As such, Nagy announced that he was freeing Mindszenty and other political prisoners. Even more controversially, Nagy announced that Hungary was going to leave the Warsaw Pact and appealed through the United Nations for powerful states, such as the USA and the UK, to recognise Hungary's existence as a neutral state.

Soviet response to the Hungarian Uprising

The Soviet response was unsurprisingly very brutal. On 25 October, Soviet tanks opened fire on protesters in Parliament Square. They faced resistance from the Hungarian people – even children – who fought the Russian troops with machine guns. At dawn on 4 November, 1000 Russian tanks rolled into Budapest, where it took just six days to crush the Hungarian resistance. It is thought that approximately 4000 Hungarians were killed during the fighting. Thousands more Hungarians were arrested, imprisoned and executed. Khrushchev installed a pro-Russian politician, **János Kádár**, as prime minister instead of Nagy. Nagy himself was secretly tried, sentenced to death, and executed in June 1958.

SOURCE A

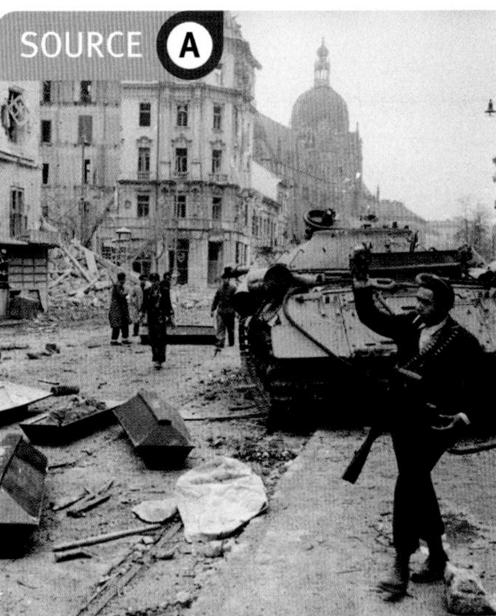

A photo of the aftermath of the Soviet army's invasion of Hungary in 1956.

KEY CONCEPTS

Censorship – *excluding information from the public.*

De-Stalinisation – *undoing the work of Stalin.*

Liberal communist – *someone who believes in the aims of communism but does not want to remove basic individual freedoms.*

Socialism – *a theory situated somewhere between capitalism and communism.*

VOICE YOUR OPINION!

Imagine you lived in an Eastern European country. You have just witnessed the Soviet Union's response to the Hungarian uprising.

- How does that make you feel?
- Are you going to be more likely to start a rebellion against the Soviet Union in your own country?
- Or are you likely to just accept it as you are scared of the Soviet response?

Causes of the Prague Spring

The response of the Soviet Union to the Hungarian uprising was so strong that no other country in Eastern Europe dared to rise up against the Soviet Union. However, all this changed in the spring of 1968, when Czechoslovakia attempted to break away from Soviet influence. This happened for several reasons:

- **Antonín Novotný**, president of Czechoslovakia, had begun to lose control the previous year with declining government popularity and the clumsy handling of a student protest. The Czechoslovaks were particularly unhappy with Novotný because of the bad state of the Czechoslovakian economy along with the large amount of censorship and the lack of other freedoms. This led to his fall from power in March 1968.
- **Alexander Dubček**, a more liberal communist, became the new First Secretary of the Communist Party of Czechoslovakia on 5 January 1968. In April 1968, Dubček's government announced an Action Plan for what it called a 'new model of **socialism**'. It removed state controls over industry, allowed freedom of speech and showed greater tolerance towards political and social organisations which were not under Communist control.
- Finally, it was thought by some Czechoslovaks that the USA would help them if they challenged Soviet influence in their country.

KEY WORDS

Brezhnev Doctrine – *the idea that if one communist country moves towards capitalism, it threatens all communist countries.*

Détente – *a cooling down period in international relations.*

Prague Spring – *period between January and August 1968 when the Czechoslovak government gave its citizens more political rights.*

The Prague Spring

The period in 1968 between Dubček's accession to power in January and the Soviet military response in August is known as the **Prague Spring** because Dubček tried to increase individual liberty in Czechoslovakia during this period. Dubček announced that he was still committed to democratic communism, but other political parties were set up. Although Dubček cleverly stressed that Czechoslovakia would stay in the Warsaw Pact, he still received a visit from President **Josip Tito** of Yugoslavia, a country not in the Warsaw Pact. This was enough for the Soviet Union leader, **Leonid Brezhnev**, to take action.

Soviet response to the Prague Spring

At a meeting in Bratislava on 3 August 1968, Brezhnev read out a letter from some Czechoslovak Communists asking for help. He publicly criticised the Czech leadership as 'revisionist' and 'anti-Soviet', and announced the **Brezhnev Doctrine**, which meant that the USSR would not allow any Eastern European country to reject Communism.

On 20 August 1968, 500,000 Warsaw Pact troops invaded Czechoslovakia. The occupying armies quickly seized control of Prague and the Central Committee's building, taking Dubček and other reformers into Soviet custody. Before they were arrested, Dubček urged the people not to resist. The Czechoslovaks listened, and instead they stood in front of the tanks, and put flowers in the soldiers' hair. However, there were still casualties, with over 70 civilians being killed as a result of the Soviet Union's invasion. Famously, **Jan Palach**, a Czech student, burned himself to death in January 1969 in protest at the actions of the Soviet government.

BRAIN BOOST

AN – Antonín Novotný – unpopular leader who turned people against the Soviet regime
AD – Alexander Dubček – liberal communist leader who had a new plan of action
USA – United States of America – which the Czechoslovaks thought would help them

Dubček and most of the reformers were returned to Prague on 27 August, and Dubček retained his post as the party's first secretary for a while. However, within the space of a few months, Brezhnev installed **Gustáv Husák**, an opponent of Dubček's reforms, as leader of the Czechoslovakian Communist Party. Gradually, the achievements of the Prague Spring were phased out over a period of several months.

SOURCE B

Alexander Dubček addressing East Germans in 1968. East Germans were generally very supportive of the Czech reformist leader.

Reaction to the Soviet response

Just as before, people in the West were horrified by this latest Soviet response to any unrest within its own sphere of influence. In spite of this, however, the decade after the Prague Spring saw a period of **détente**, a reduction in tension in international relations during the Cold War. This would last throughout most of the 1970s.

KEY PEOPLE

Leonid Brezhnev – *Leader of the Soviet Union, 1964–82.*

Alexander Dubček – *Briefly Prime Minister of Czechoslovakia, 1968–69.*

Gustáv Husák – *President of Czechoslovakia, 1975–89.*

Nikita Khrushchev – *Leader of the Soviet Union, 1953–64.*

Antonín Novotný – *President of Czechoslovakia, 1957–68.*

Jan Palach – *Czech student who committed suicide in 1969 in protest against the Soviet Union's invasion.*

Joseph Stalin – *Leader of the Soviet Union, 1920s–53.*

Josip Tito – *President of the Socialist Republic of Yugoslavia, 1953–80.*

GradeStudio

Why did the Soviet Union react in such an aggressive way in both Hungary and Czechoslovakia? **[6 marks]**

How similar were events in Hungary in 1956 and in Czechoslovakia in 1968?

LEARNING OBJECTIVES

In this lesson you will:

- examine the similarities and differences between 1956 and 1968
- learn to identify and explain the continuity and change between these two periods.

What were the similarities between the uprisings in Hungary and Czechoslovakia?

Similar causes

- In both cases there was hostility to Russian control over too many aspects of life and anger at the country's poor economic performance.
- There was also a shared hope that the United Nations or the USA would help once the resistance got under way.
- Both events were triggered by intellectuals from universities who launched protests against the Soviet-backed regimes in their country.
- Both the events started when the Soviet Union refused to support the existing government. Rákosi of Hungary wanted Soviet help to make 400 arrests, while Novotný wanted assistance in dealing with student protests.

Similar key personalities

- Both Rákosi and Novotný were unpopular leaders at the time of the event in their own countries, but both stayed loyal to the Soviet Union.
- Both Nagy and Dubček were communists yet they believed in a more liberal version of communism.
- The replacements for Nagy and Dubček, Kádár and Husák respectively, were both sympathetic to the Soviet regime.
- Both the leaders of the Soviet Union at the time, Khrushchev and Brezhnev, were keen to use the events as opportunities to prove their leadership credentials.

Similar events

- In both Hungary and Czechoslovakia, there were brief periods when the new government introduced reforms such as the extension of free speech.

VOICE YOUR OPINION!

Why were Khrushchev and Brezhnev both so concerned about the Warsaw Pact?

SOURCE A

'She might have invaded Russia', the title of a cartoon published in the *Washington Post*, 3 September 1968.

- The Soviet Union was alarmed when Hungary announced plans in 1956 to leave the Warsaw Pact, and in 1968 alarm bells began to ring when Josip Tito, whose country, Yugoslavia, was not part of the Warsaw Pact, visited Czechoslovakia.

Similar Soviet response

- The actual strength of the Russian invasion force was overwhelming in both cases.
- The West failed to help either Nagy or Dubček once the Soviet Union had invaded.

What were the differences between the uprisings of 1956 and 1968?

Different causes

- The 1956 uprising started with riots in Hungary, but this was not the case in Czechoslovakia.
- Nagy announced he was going to leave the Warsaw Pact whereas Dubček stressed that he would stay.

Different events

- The uprising was better planned in Czechoslovakia than in Hungary, since Dubček's government had a proper socialist Action Plan.
- The Hungarians attempted to introduce genuine democracy, while Dubček stressed that he wanted communism, albeit 'democratic communism'.
- The period of time when there was a breakaway from Soviet rule was longer in Czechoslovakia. There were four months of freedom in Czechoslovakia, as opposed to just five days of freedom in Hungary.
- The Catholic Church took a lead in events in Hungary, but not in Czechoslovakia.

Different responses from the Soviet Union

- When the Red Army invaded, the Hungarians fought back whereas the Czechoslovaks made only **passive resistance**.
- The punishment from the Soviet Union was also different. Some 4000 Hungarians were executed, whereas only 47 Czechoslovaks were arrested.
- This is also true of the leaders, as Dubček was arrested and briefly detained whereas Nagy was executed in 1958.

Conclusion

Overall, it appears that the causes of each event, along with the personalities involved, were fairly similar. This was because the Soviet Union's control of Eastern Europe did not vary a great deal from country to country and therefore was likely to arouse the same type of resistance within the different countries of Eastern Europe. The main differences are found in both the nature of the anti-Soviet resistance and the Soviet response. The reasons for these differences were mainly because of the timing of each event. The 1956 uprising occurred just after the establishment of the Warsaw Pact, when the Cold War was escalating, while 1968 took place during the Vietnam War and in an era of international caution. This is likely to have made Brezhnev exercise a little more restraint in his response than Khrushchev.

KEY CONCEPTS

Passive resistance – *resistance using non-violent methods.*

GradeStudio

'The Hungarian Uprising and the Prague Spring were similar.' How far do you agree with this statement? Explain your answer. **[10 marks]**

Examiner's tip

The purpose of this task is to enable you to understand that to get eight marks, you need to explain both the similarities and the differences. To get a further two marks, you need to come to a judgement, based on the information already gathered, about *how far* you agree with the statement.

Get your sources sorted

Essential knowledge

- The Prague Spring was a period when the authority of a Communist-led regime was challenged.
- It took place in Czechoslovakia between the months of January and August 1968.
- During this period the Czechoslovak government, headed by Dubček, implemented many reforms which the Soviet Union found unacceptable.
- Eventually, the Soviet Union's response was to invade Czechoslovakia.
- There was little resistance by the Czechoslovaks and the work of the Dubček government was gradually undone.

What is the message of the source? (Prague Spring)

Before you begin to answer this question, remember what is meant by the 'message' of the source. It is not simply a quote from a source, nor a description of what it shows, but rather the overall impression that the source conveys about one or more particular things. For instance, it is wrong to say in the source below that the message is a young girl being knocked down by a Soviet solider. Instead, the message is that the Soviet Union is a bully to its weaker neighbours and shows no regret or remorse for its actions. It is best to begin your answer with 'The message of this source is…' Once you have worked out the message, ensure that you support your argument using information from both the source and your own knowledge. If you do this, you can get the full seven marks.

Flowers are being given by the girl to the soldier in 1945. This represents the gratitude which Czechoslovakia had for the Soviet Union in 1945 but the flowers are conspicuous by their absence in 1968.

The cartoonist is trying to compare the different stages in Czechoslovakia's history – liberated by the Soviet Army in 1945 yet invaded by the same army in 1968.

SOURCE A

A drawing on the wall of a Prague Street in 1968.

The soldier is standing in front of the girl with a weapon in both pictures without much facial expression. This highlights the military strength of the Soviet army and could also show that the Soviet army did not seem to have much moral concern when using this strength.

Holding out flowers in 1945 but lying dead in 1968. This clearly represents the recently established and militarily weak Czechoslovakia. The girl could also represent Czechoslovakia's innocence in this affair. Her lying dead in 1968 represents the casualties that were suffered as a result of the Soviet army's invasion.

What is the message of the source? (Prague Spring)

This shows that by August the Soviet Union felt that the situation in Czechoslovakia had to be dealt with by force.

This shows that the Soviet Union viewed a free press and the revival of non-communist political parties as counter-revolutionary forces.

SOURCE B

The party and government leaders of the Czechoslovak Socialist Republic have asked the Soviet Union and other allies to give the Czechoslovak people urgent assistance with armed forces. This request was brought about ... by the threat from counter revolutionary forces ... working with foreign forces hostile to socialism.

A Soviet news agency report, 21 August 1968.

This source is unlikely to be an accurate reflection on what the leaders of the Czechoslovak Socialist Republic wanted as it is taken from a Soviet news agency report, which would not have had the freedom to criticise the Soviet Union. This source is a very good example of the arguments at the time, because Czechoslovakia was occupied on the very day the report was made.

This highlights arguably the main reason why Brezhnev decided to pursue military action, namely the meeting between Dubček and Tito of Yugoslavia, whose country was not a member of the Warsaw Pact.

What is the message of the cartoon?

Study Source C. What is the message of this cartoon? Use details of the cartoon and your own knowledge to explain your answer.

Remember to think about how this particular source links in with the question. Think about the following questions:

- What is the meaning of the cartoon?
- What is happening in the cartoon?
- What was happening at the time?

SOURCE C

A cartoon published in an English newspaper, December 1980. The caption reads: *Soviet Union soldier to Polish Government:* 'Excuse me sir – is this lady bothering you?'

Why was the Berlin Wall built in 1961?

LEARNING OBJECTIVES

In this lesson you will:

- examine the reasons why the wall was built
- learn to understand the links and connections between the different causes.

GETTING STARTED

You have learnt a little about Berlin in the previous chapter. Use that information, along with the clues in brackets, to describe what happened during these key years.

- 1945 (suicide, four zones)
- 1948 (blockade)
- 1948–49 (airlift)
- 1949 (end of blockade)

Why was the Berlin Wall built?

The construction of the Berlin Wall in 1961 was perhaps the most concrete symbol of the divisions between the 'communist world' and the 'free world'. The building of the Berlin Wall came about as a result of a four-stage process:

1 Germany became formally divided

The unification of the three zones controlled by the Western allies occurred in 1949, after the Berlin Airlift. Together they formed the Federal Republic of Germany, better known as West Germany. Stalin responded by renaming the Russian-controlled eastern section of Germany the German Democratic Republic, better known as East Germany. Germany was now officially divided into two separate states. This meant that Berlin became the focus of attention in the Cold War.

2 West Germany became more prosperous than East Germany

West Germany was always the more prosperous of the two newly created states. Stalin had forbidden Eastern Europe access to Marshall Aid, whereas the new West Germany did have access to it. As a result, East Germans suffered from poor housing, food shortages and low wages, and with 25 per cent of industrial output going to the Soviet Union, there was no evidence that the situation would improve as the 1960s approached.

3 East Germans left to go to West Germany

Many East Germans simply left and went to West Germany to share in the growing prosperity of that state. The East German government had tried to stop the flow westwards in 1952 by building a fortified border. But there remained one place where any East German could go to and move to the west – Berlin, which was situated in the heart of East Germany itself. By 1961, around three million people had done this, including highly qualified workers who East Germany could not afford to lose. This was a major coup for the West, while West Berlin was now a worry and embarrassment for the Soviet Union.

4 The Vienna Summit (4 June 1961)

At the Vienna Summit of June 1961, Khrushchev demanded that the USA leave West Berlin within six months. As well as being angry at the number of 'defectors', Khrushchev also believed that West Berlin was a centre for US **espionage**. Kennedy refused to accept this and Khrushchev's next move, little over a month later, was to build the Berlin Wall.

VOICE YOUR OPINION!

What does the building of the Berlin Wall reveal about the Soviet Union?

BRAIN BOOST

D – Division – Germany was split into two, which put the focus on Berlin
P – Prosperity – West Germany became richer, which meant that more people would want to come there from East Germany
D – Defections – from East Germany to West Germany
V – Vienna Summit – no compromise led to construction of Berlin Wall

Construction of the Berlin Wall

On 13 August 1961, Khrushchev closed the border between East and West Berlin using barbed wire and ordered the building of the Berlin Wall. By 16 August, the barbed wire was being removed and replaced with a wall of concrete blocks. Within days, West Berlin was surrounded by a wall which, by the end of August, seemed all but impossible to cross.

SOURCE A

Peter Fechter, aged 18, became one of the first victims of the East German border guards when he tried to climb over the wall into West Berlin.

Fact file

- Total length of the wall – 155 km
- Length through the city – 43 km
- Watch towers – 302
- Bunkers – 20
- People who successfully crossed the Berlin Wall to freedom – more than 5000
- People arrested in the border area – 3200
- People killed in the death area – almost 200

Look back through this lesson and your notes and write an answer to the following question.

Explain why the Berlin Wall was built. **[8 marks]**

Consequences of the Berlin Wall

At first, the Soviet Union regarded it as a propaganda success, but as time went on, it became a propaganda disaster – a symbol of all that was bad about Soviet rule. People from East Germany still tried to cross into West Berlin, and almost 200 people were shot dead on the eastern side of the wall. The West called the Berlin Wall the 'Wall of Shame' and it served to remind those who lived in Berlin that those in Soviet-controlled East Berlin lived far inferior lives to those who lived in West Berlin.

KEY CONCEPTS

Espionage – *the use of spies by governments to discover the secrets of other nations.*

How important was 'Solidarity'?

LEARNING OBJECTIVES

In this lesson you will:

- examine the importance of Solidarity
- assess the links and connections between the different causes of the collapse of the Soviet Union.

Immediate impact of Solidarity

In 1980, **Lech Wałęsa**, along with some of his trade union friends, founded Solidarność (**Solidarity**). Solidarity was the first non-communist **trade union** in a communist country. It was originally led by Wałęsa in response to long-running concerns about low wages and food shortages that the Polish Communist government could not solve. It was not long before the organisation had ten million members, and Wałęsa was its undisputed leader. In August 1980, Wałęsa led the Gdańsk shipyard strike which gave rise to a wave of strikes over much of the country. Wałęsa, a devout Catholic, developed a loyal following and the Communist authorities were forced to capitulate. The Gdańsk Agreement, signed on 31 August 1980, gave Polish workers the right to strike and to organise their own independent trade union.

SOURCE A

1980 strike at Gdańsk shipyard, birthplace of Solidarity.

Solidarity restricted in the short term

In the short term, Solidarity did not seem to have a significant impact. In 1981, General **Wojciech Jaruzelski**, who had replaced **Edward Gierek** as leader of the Communist Party in Poland, introduced martial law, imprisoned Lech Wałęsa and 10,000 others, and declared Solidarity to be an

KEY CONCEPTS

Civil liberties – *freedoms that protect the individual from the government.*

Martial law – *a system of rules during times when the military is in charge.*

Trade union – *an organisation of workers with common goals such as securing higher wages and fairer working conditions.*

KEY WORDS

Solidarity – *a non-communist Polish trade union federation.*

Eastern Bloc – *a term used during the Cold War to describe the Soviet Union and the countries it controlled.*

KEY PEOPLE

Edward Gierek – *Leader of Poland, 1970–80.*

Mikhail Gorbachev – *Leader of the Soviet Union, 1985–91.*

Wojciech Jaruzelski – *Prime Minister of Poland, 1981–86, President of Poland, 1989–90.*

Tadeusz Mazowiecki – *Prime Minister of Poland, 1989–91.*

Lech Wałęsa – *Chairman of Solidarity, 1980–90.*

HISTORY DETECTIVE

Can you find out which demands were actually agreed at the Gdańsk Agreement?

illegal organisation. Even after **martial law** was lifted in July 1983, a number of restrictions remained in place for several years that drastically reduced **civil liberties** and economic activity in Poland.

Solidarity's importance in Poland

Although Jaruzelski's actions had significantly reduced the potential impact of Solidarity, they could not stop a growing movement of resistance to communism from within Poland. In the long term, reformers in Poland were helped by the fact that **Mikhail Gorbachev** had gained power in the Soviet Union. In 1986 Gorbachev made it clear he would no longer interfere in the domestic policies of other countries in Eastern Europe. Jaruzelski was now forced to negotiate with Wałęsa and the trade union movement. This happened in early 1989 with the Roundtable Talks between the weakened government of Jaruzelski and the Solidarity-led opposition. This led to Solidarity becoming a legitimate political party and the holding of semi-free elections in 1989. In these elections, the Solidarity movement gained 99 out of 100 freely contested seats in the Polish Senate. The Iron Curtain was being lifted. By the end of August a Solidarity-led coalition government was formed, and in December **Tadeusz Mazowiecki** was elected Prime Minister. He was the first non-communist prime minister in Central and Eastern Europe since the Second World War. Less than a year later, Lech Wałęsa had become the first non-communist president of Poland.

Solidarity's importance to the collapse of the Soviet Union

The 1989 elections in Poland, in which anti-communist candidates won a striking victory, sparked off a succession of peaceful anti-communist revolutions in East Germany, Hungary, Czechoslovakia and Bulgaria. Solidarity's example was instrumental, therefore, in the fall of the Berlin Wall in 1989, the **Eastern Bloc**'s effective dismantling, and the subsequent collapse of the Soviet Union in the early 1990s.

ACTIVITIES

'Solidarity' was the name of a trade union federation set up in the Gdańsk shipyard, Poland, in September 1980. Within ten years, it had played a significant role in bringing about an end to Communist rule in Poland along with the collapse of the Soviet Union in the early 1990s.

Before we attempt to analyse the importance of Solidarity, it is vital to think about what 'important' actually means. Did it alter the history of the Cold War or were there other factors involved? Was it only important to Poland or elsewhere in Eastern Europe as well? Other factors to consider are whether it is best to divide the answer into what was important about it and what was not important. Alternatively, is it better to think about the importance in the short term followed by the long term?

SOURCE B

More pay

End to censorship

The establishment of free trade unions

The same welfare benefits as party workers

The broadcasting of Church services

Election of factory managers

Some of the 21 demands of the Gdańsk shipyard workers, put forward by Lech Wałęsa, the leader of Solidarity, to the Polish government in August 1980.

HISTORY DETECTIVE

There were several peaceful revolutions in 1989, but the anti-communist revolution in Romania was the only one in which the leaders were executed and the communist regime was violently overthrown. Can you find out why?

Why was the Soviet Union unable to stop the Solidarity movement? **[6 marks]**

How far was Gorbachev responsible for the collapse of the Soviet Empire?

LEARNING OBJECTIVES

In this lesson you will:

- examine the role of Gorbachev and other factors in bringing about the collapse of the Soviet Empire
- assess how Gorbachev's actions and other factors helped to cause this event.

The Soviet Union and the Soviet Empire

The Soviet Union comprised 15 Communist republics. It was officially established in 1922 and was governed by a system of one-party rule by the Communist Party. These republics were member states of the Soviet Union. In addition, the Soviet Union exercised a great deal of influence in certain Eastern European states, namely Poland, Hungary, Romania, Bulgaria, Czechoslovakia and East Germany. These states were not part of the Soviet Union but they were members of the Warsaw Pact and Comecon which meant that their foreign and economic policy was heavily influenced by the Soviet Union. As such, these states were considered part of the Soviet Empire and this meant that the Communist Party of the Soviet Union had direct control over an enormous population and geographical area.

The collapse of Soviet control in Eastern Europe

In December 1991, just a few months short of its 70th birthday, the Soviet Empire dissolved itself and soon ceased to exist. Its collapse was sudden and dramatic, though not easy to explain. The final nail in the coffin of the Soviet Empire arguably came with the holding of free elections in Poland in 1989 and the ousting of the Communist government. This led to revolutions in other Eastern European states. By 1990, Soviet Socialist Republics such as Lativa, Estonia and Lithuania had declared themselves independent of the Soviet Union. It was only a matter of time before the USSR would cease to exist and this duly came in December 1991 with the establishment of the Commonwealth of Independent States. Gorbachev resigned as President of the USSR and all Soviet institutions ceased operations as individual republics became sovereign. The speed of this collapse was due to the way in which the momentum generated from key events, such as the Solidarity Movement's triumph in the 1989 elections and the fall of the Berlin Wall soon after, combined with the sense of opportunism felt amongst Eastern European states due to the rare absence of Soviet control.

GETTING STARTED

Can one person ultimately be responsible for such a major political event as the collapse of the Soviet Empire? Look at the quotes below in pairs and decide where you would stand on the opinion line.

SOURCE 

We cannot make great historical events, but must adapt ourselves to the natural course of things and limit ourselves to securing what is already ripe.

Otto von Bismarck (1815–98) speaking to the North German Reichstag in 1869.

SOURCE 

At any given moment by the sudden decision of his will, a man may introduce into the course of events a new, unexpected and changeable force, which may alter that course.

Views of Sainte-Beuve, a historian of the French Revolution (quoted in *The Role of the Individual in History*, Plekhanov, 1940).

SOURCE 

Men make their own history, but they do not make it just as they please; they do not make it under circumstances chosen by themselves, but under circumstances directly found, given and transmitted from the past.

Karl Marx (quoted in *The Eighteenth Brumaire of Louis Bonaparte*, Karl Marx, 1852).

KEY CONCEPTS

Glasnost – *Russian term for greater openness and transparency in Soviet government.*

Perestroika – *Russian term for the restructuring of the Soviet economy.*

Republic – *a state that is not ruled by a monarch.*

KEY PEOPLE

Boris Yeltsin – *first President of the Russian Federation, 1991–99.*

SOURCE D

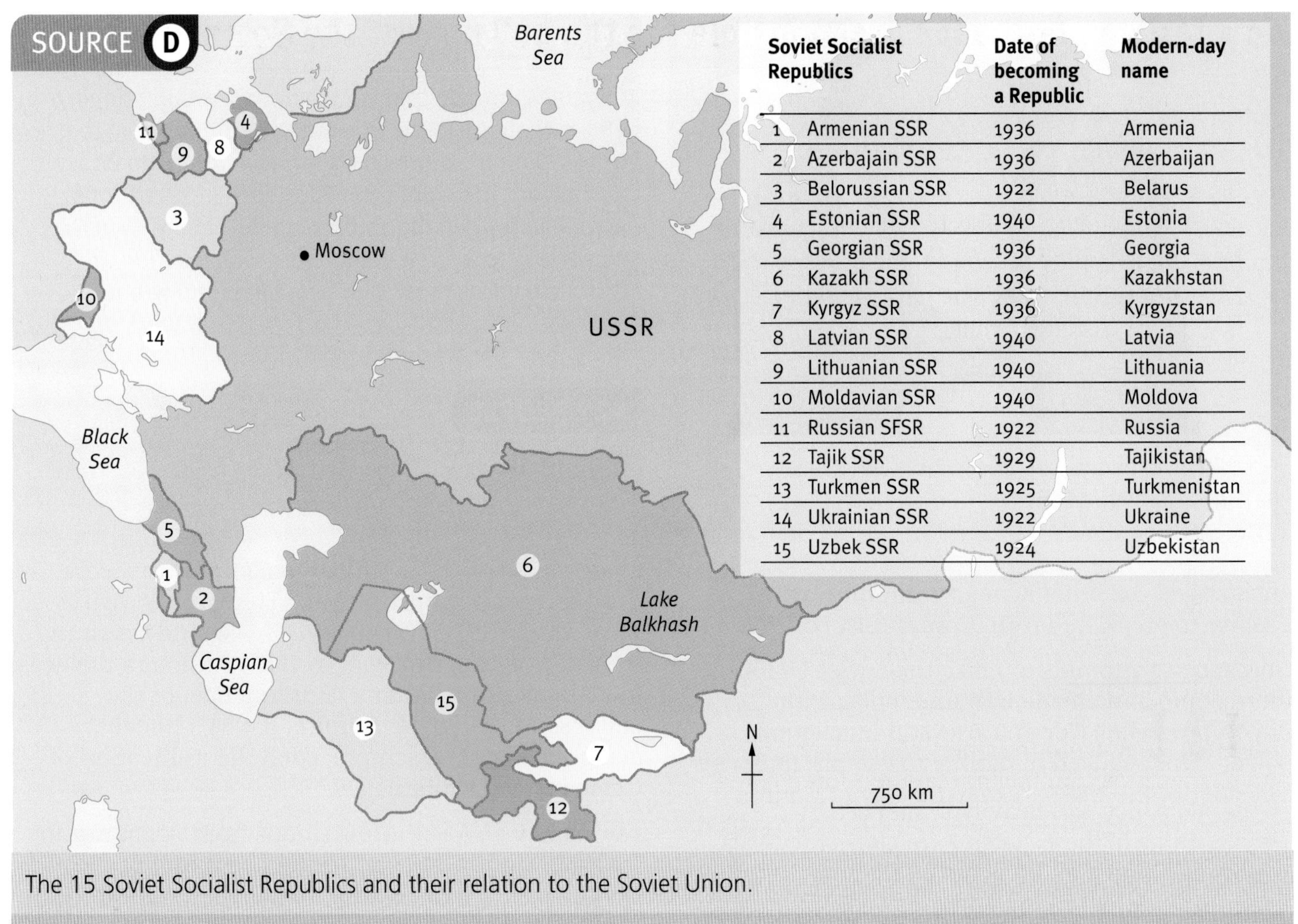

	Soviet Socialist Republics	Date of becoming a Republic	Modern-day name
1	Armenian SSR	1936	Armenia
2	Azerbajain SSR	1936	Azerbaijan
3	Belorussian SSR	1922	Belarus
4	Estonian SSR	1940	Estonia
5	Georgian SSR	1936	Georgia
6	Kazakh SSR	1936	Kazakhstan
7	Kyrgyz SSR	1936	Kyrgyzstan
8	Latvian SSR	1940	Latvia
9	Lithuanian SSR	1940	Lithuania
10	Moldavian SSR	1940	Moldova
11	Russian SFSR	1922	Russia
12	Tajik SSR	1929	Tajikistan
13	Turkmen SSR	1925	Turkmenistan
14	Ukrainian SSR	1922	Ukraine
15	Uzbek SSR	1924	Uzbekistan

The 15 Soviet Socialist Republics and their relation to the Soviet Union.

Gorbachev's responsibility for the collapse of the Soviet Empire

The president of the Soviet Union during this time was Mikhail Gorbachev. There are many reasons to argue that he was responsible for the collapse of the Soviet Empire.

Gorbachev's domestic reforms

These had the effect of destabilising the Soviet Union. First, his policy of **Glasnost** – which allowed for greater openness and transparency about government policy – meant that the Communist Party lost its grip on the media, resulting in them exposing some extremely embarrassing truths about the communist regime. For instance, in the spirit of *Glasnost*, Gorbachev revealed to the world that in March 1940, Joseph Stalin had given the orders for the execution of 25,700 Polish soldiers in Soviet prison camps.

Secondly, he introduced a policy of **Perestroika** – restructuring of the Soviet economy by for example encouraging private ownership – which, although well-intentioned, had the effect of reducing Soviet control of the economy, since the existing Soviet structures could not allow these reforms to take place. This increased the layers of bureaucracy and corruption within the Soviet economy, which led to shortages of goods and high inflation, and a resulting decrease in the quality of life for Russians. The Soviet Union had experienced periods of economic difficulty before but the situation was different now owing to the fact that Gorbachev's reforms meant that dissent and freedom were allowed.

Gorbachev underestimated the impact of his ideas on different parts of the Soviet Empire, and his reforms undeniably put the position of Communist governments within the Soviet Empire in jeopardy since they encouraged greater freedom across the Communist world. This sparked a widespread demand for change in states such as Poland, East Germany and Hungary but, unlike previously, Gorbachev was not prepared to commit the Red Army to prop up these Communist governments. This was a crucial decision since the Red Army's threat of force had previously been a key factor in holding the Empire together. Even though some of the anti-Communist rebellions would witness Soviet military or KGB pressure, such as the Baltic Republics in 1990, it was too little too late as, by this point, many Soviet-dominated governments had suddenly collapsed between 1989 and 1990. Arguably, if the Soviet Union had acted militarily in response to the unrest in Poland, it would not have

SOURCE E

Gorbachev in one-to-one discussions with Reagan, Reykjavik Summit, 1986.

encouraged the other states within the Soviet Empire to break free from Communist control.

Gorbachev's attempts to make the Soviet Union more democratic made him unpopular with uncompromising Communists still in positions of power. This reduced his ability to use his authority as leader of the USSR to keep the Soviet Empire together. In August 1991 he survived a coup staged by hard-liners in the Communist Party. His actions caused bitter divisions within the Soviet Union. Even though he survived the coup, his authority was undermined and he was replaced by Boris Yeltsin, who became president of the Russian Federation.

Foreign policy

Gorbachev realised that the USSR could not afford the arms race – the continuation of the Cold War was significantly harming the country's economy – and in 1987 he signed the Intermediate-Range Nuclear Forces Treaty with the USA, eliminating both nuclear and conventional cruise and ballistic missiles with intermediate ranges. This meant the Cold War was all but over.

Gorbachev's decision in 1988 to signal an end to the Brezhnev Doctrine was a momentous decision. Many groups within the Eastern European countries realised that Gorbachev would not send in Soviet tanks, which led to demonstrations against communist governments throughout Eastern Europe.

ACTIVITIES

The table on page 111 lists the 15 different Soviet Socialist Republics. Use the internet to find out the different dates that each of them withdrew from the Soviet Union and create your own timeline of when they became independent from the Soviet Union.

ACTIVITIES

Consider the role that Gorbachev played in bringing about changes to the Soviet Union. It may help to think about his domestic reforms and foreign policy and assess the extent to which each of his actions actually brought about this change. Finally, conclude by coming to a judgement about which action of Gorbachev was most significant in bringing about change.

KEY PEOPLE

Ronald Reagan – *President of the USA, 1981–89.*

Over the next few months the communists were ousted from power in Poland, Hungary, Bulgaria, Romania and East Germany. This would result in the fall of the Berlin Wall in 1989. Although this was not a cause, but rather a consequence, of the collapse of the Soviet Empire, it was a hugely symbolic event which preceded the unification of Germany in October 1990.

Gorbachev also withdrew troops from Afghanistan by 1989. In this way, he was conceding that the USSR was not in a position to use force to interfere in the affairs of other countries.

Other reasons for the collapse of the Soviet Empire

On the other hand, there were several other reasons why the Soviet Empire collapsed, which were outside the control of Gorbachev.

War in Afghanistan

Six years before Gorbachev came to power, in 1979, the Soviet Union invaded Afghanistan to try to prop up the communist government there, which was being attacked by Muslim **Mujahideen** fighters. This was a war which angered the Muslim world (approximately one million Afghan civilians are thought to have died during the Soviet Union's ten years of occupation) and was a problem for the Soviet Union as there were large Muslim populations living within its borders. Over 10,000 Soviet soldiers had been killed. Therefore, the negative effect of this war can hardly be blamed on Gorbachev and might have even been worse had he not withdrawn the troops.

KEY WORDS

Mujahideen – *armed fighters who subscribe to militant Islamic ideology.*

SOURCE F

Soviet troops withdrawing from Afghanistan in 1988.

Cost of arms race

Russia could not afford the arms race. In 1980, **Ronald Reagan** became president of the USA. As a strong anti-communist, he denounced the Soviet Union as an 'evil empire' and increased spending on arms. There was no way that the Soviet economy was in a position to compete with this.
Compared with the USA, the Soviet economy was backward, its factories and mines decrepit and out of date. In addition, decrepit industry was causing increasing environmental problems such as the Chernobyl nuclear power plant explosion of 1986, the drying up of the Aral Sea and widespread pollution. Gorbachev had no choice but to reform the Soviet economy.

Poverty and social unrest

The majority of people in Eastern Europe were much poorer than even the poorest people in the capitalist West. In addition to the unrest over food shortages, crime, alcoholism and drugs were out of control in Soviet towns. At the same time awareness of the disparities in living standards grew with, for example, the increasing availability of television. Poverty was nothing new for the Soviet Union, but such developments ensured a far more intense reaction. Gorbachev, unlike his predecessors, did not have the ability to shield the public from these uncomfortable facts.

Conclusion

Overall, Gorbachev was responsible for the fact that the Soviet Empire disintegrated when it did. Had he done nothing, however, the result could well have been just the same, but with more bloodshed and chaos. Gorbachev was responsible only up to a point for the collapse of the Soviet Empire. In 1985 when he came to power, he realised that the Soviet economy was devastated, to a large extent as a result of communist policy. Gorbachev recognised that economic reforms and new foreign policy approaches were needed to stabilise the situation. He was forced to act because of factors outside his control. It is hard to imagine that Gorbachev could have prevented the collapse of the Soviet Empire, but at the same time it is very difficult to deny that his actions played a large part in this process.

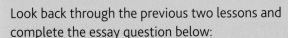

GradeStudio

Look back through the previous two lessons and complete the essay question below:

'Gorbachev was the most important reason why the Soviet Empire collapsed.' How far do you agree with this statement? Explain your answer. **[10 marks]**

ACTIVITIES

One of the hardest things to remember from this chapter will be the different names of the various key figures during this period. Try to fill in the blanks below by recalling the names you have learned on the previous pages.

Five non-Russian rulers:

L___ _A___A
E_____ __E_E_
G_____ __SA_
R_____ __A_A_
I___ N_ __

Five significant Russian rulers:

B____ __L____
J_____ ____I_
N_____ ________E_
L_____ _R______
M______ ___B_____

VOICE YOUR OPINION!

Put the following factors in order of their importance to the collapse of the Soviet Empire.

- Empire
- Afghanistan
- Cost of the arms race
- Information about Western success
- Gorbachev.

How effective has terrorism been since 1969?

What is terrorism, why do people become terrorists and why do people/organisations resort to terrorism?

LEARNING OBJECTIVES

In this lesson you will:

- examine what is meant by terrorism
- learn how to make links between the different causes of terrorism.

GETTING STARTED

What do you think is meant by terrorism?

What is terrorism?

There are often disagreements about who is a 'terrorist', since there is no single definition which is accepted internationally. Usually, this disagreement comes about because a terrorist organisation might see itself as an army which is at war with a particular government or an international organisation. However, on the evidence of the three definitions given on this page, it is possible to pick out some common ground about what is meant by terrorism. The three groups that will be looked at in this section, namely the **Provisional IRA** (PIRA), **Palestine Liberation Organisation** (PLO) and **Al-Qaeda**, have fulfilled all these criteria at one time or another throughout their history.

Common features of the different definitions of terrorism	
Tactics	Carries out serious violence including mass murder or uses the threat of violence
Agents	Consists of non-governmental groups or individuals
Targets	Targets the civilian population in peacetime
Aims	Two main aims are to intimidate a population and to put pressure on a government or organisation in order that the terrorist group get their own way

SOURCE A

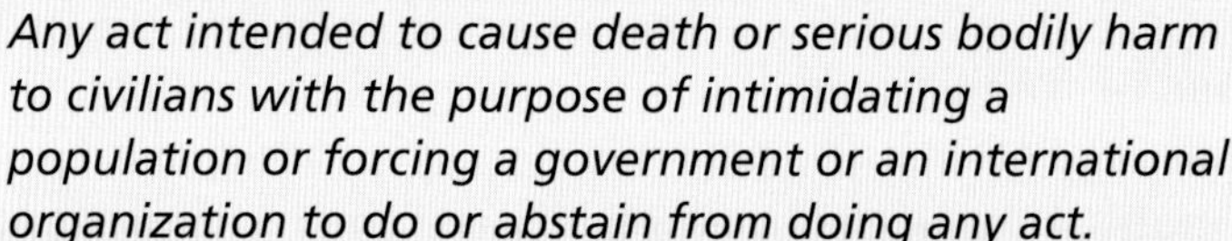

Any act intended to cause death or serious bodily harm to civilians with the purpose of intimidating a population or forcing a government or an international organization to do or abstain from doing any act.

United Nations' definition of terrorism.

SOURCE B

Activities that involve violent ... or life-threatening acts ... to intimidate or coerce a civilian population; to influence the policy of a government by intimidation or coercion.

Terrorism as defined by the US Federal Criminal Code.

SOURCE C

Terrorist offences are certain criminal offences ... which may seriously damage a country or an international organisation where committed with the aim of: seriously intimidating a population; or unduly forcing a Government or international organisation to perform or abstain from performing any act.

Definition of terrorism given by the European Union.

KEY PEOPLE

Osama bin Laden – *the most recognisable name associated with Al-Qaeda since it began operations in 1988.*

Causes of terrorism

There are four main causes of terrorism which are fairly common:

- desire for land
- existence of poverty
- fundamentalist religious beliefs
- individual factors.

Poverty

Over-populated countries with low growth rates are likely to have high unemployment and a significant amount of poverty. In these areas of deprivation, people are more likely to feel that they have fewer options and might consider the possibility of uprooting a government if it meant they could, for example, feed their families. Many Palestinians after the Second World War became refugees living in refugee camps, which made them more willing to support or join the PLO. However, poverty is not a motivation in all cases since **Osama bin Laden** (see Source D) is a multi-millionaire and yet he is still a terrorist.

SOURCE D

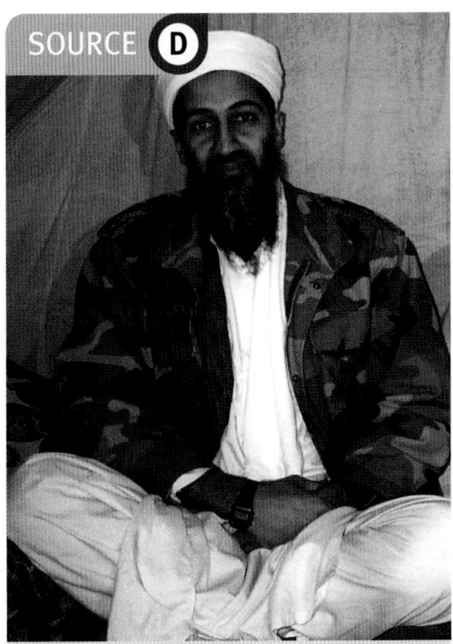

Osama bin Laden, one of the world's most wanted terrorists, and leader of the terrorist group Al-Qaeda.

Desire for land

Terrorist acts have frequently occured because a minority group wants to gain control of a territory from a government, which most likely represents a larger group. The government is to some extent perceived as foreign, and its treatment of minority groups is seen as unfair. The Provisional IRA, the PLO, the Tamil Tigers, and lately, Iraqi **insurgents**, have all used violence against civilians in pursuit of their political goals, which have been the self-determination of their people from a government that is in control of land which they feel should be occupied by them. However, an international organisation like Al-Qaeda has attacked a whole range of targets, such as Kenya (2002), Istanbul (2003), Madrid (2004) and Jordan (2005), demonstrating that their concerns are not merely about borders and territories.

Religious beliefs

In recent years, some terrorist groups have used their interpretation of a religion to justify their actions. For instance, despite Islamic teachings against **suicide** and killing innocent people in battle, terrorist groups like Al-Qaeda have used a **fundamentalist** form of **Islam** to justify an unholy war of terrorism. (The role of religion in terrorism is considered in greater depth in the next section.)

Individual factors

Whether or not one is a religious fundamentalist or lives in poverty, it takes a particular type of person to decide to become a terrorist. It is possible that to become a terrorist, you need to be addicted to power, or feel insecure and threatened by the bigger powers, or be envious of the material benefits of the wealth and excesses of the West, or be angry at perceived oppression and injustice in the world.

KEY WORDS

Al-Qaeda – *terrorist group which aims for an end to foreign influence in Muslim countries (active since 1988).*

Islam – *a religion which originated with the teachings of the prophet Muhammad in the 7th century.*

Palestine Liberation Organisation – *terrorist group which originally aimed for the annihilation of Israel and a right of return and self-determination for Palestinians (active since 1964).*

Provisional IRA – *terrorist group which aimed to end Northern Ireland's status in the UK and bring about a United Ireland (officially active: 1969–1997).*

KEY CONCEPTS

Fundamentalist – *someone who strictly adheres to a set of basic religious principles in reaction to the teachings and workings of modern life.*

Insurgent – *someone who is involved in a violent uprising, lacking the organisation of a revolution, against a sovereign government.*

Suicide bomber – *someone who attacks a target, with an intent to kill others and cause great damage, knowing that he or she will probably die in the process.*

What roles do religion, ideology and nationalism play in terrorism?

LEARNING OBJECTIVES

In this lesson you will:

- examine the role of religion in the three terrorist organisations
- analyse the importance of religion to terrorism compared with other factors.

KEY CONCEPTS

Holy scriptures – *texts which various religions consider to be sacred.*

KEY WORDS

Qur'an – *central religious text of Islam.*

What is the role of religion, nationalism and ideology in terrorism?

One of the most controversial issues surrounding terrorist groups is the extent to which religion plays a role in terrorist activity. Religious fundamentalism refers to a total commitment to the belief in **Holy scriptures** and absolute religious authority, in contrast to the modern-day trends of social and political life. Fundamentalism is certainly one of the drivers of terrorism. In a world dominated by change and uncertainty, some individuals find certainty by dedicating themselves to an ideology or religion, to define the way they live their lives in the present day. In exceptional instances this can lead to suicide attacks – a tactic that has been used by both the PLO and Al-Qaeda. However, there is much crossover between the roles of religion, nationalism and ideology in terrorism. In the case of the PIRA, for example, their unambiguous ideology calls for the creation of an all-Irish state. However, this ideology is clearly nationalist since it amounts to the creation of an Irish nation at the expense of an independent Northern Ireland. Moreover, this nationalist ideology cannot be separated from religion since the creation of such a state was perceived as being pivotal to protecting the interests of the Catholic community in Northern Ireland from the Protestant-dominated Unionists.

GETTING STARTED

In groups, discuss the following question. Is religion a cause of terrorism or is it used by terrorists as a way of getting younger volunteers to act on behalf of them?

KEY WORDS

Allah – *name used by Muslims to refer to God.*

To further understand the role played by these three forces in terrorism, it is necessary to look at two different aspects of each terrorist group: the essence of the conflict they are fighting, and how the three forces of religion, ideology and nationalism are used to motivate the terrorists.

What is the essence of the conflict?

In the case of the PIRA and the PLO, the motivation for their terrorism arises out of a nationalist grievance (a border dispute, rather than a religious conflict). However, the PIRA have seen themselves as the defenders of the Northern Ireland Catholic community who have been denied civil rights, and Arab nations have frequently presented the Arab–Israeli conflict as a confrontation between Muslims of the Arab nations and the Jews of Israel. Despite this, it is important to avoid the generalisation that all Catholics feel represented by the PIRA or that all Muslims feel represented by the PLO. Some Catholics, particularly those living in Britain, have actually been victims of PIRA violence. In addition, the Jordanian government (like the PLO, comprised mainly of Muslims) expelled the PLO from Jordan in 1970.

The ideology of Al-Qaeda is Islamic fundamentalist because it perceives itself as being the defender of Muslims in the face of threats from Christian and Jewish influences. As there is no border dispute, religious differences feature far more prominently than with the other two terrorist organisations. However, some of its attacks have been on Muslims, such as the Istanbul bombings in 2003 which left several Muslims dead. Overall, therefore, there is a religious element to the conflict in all three cases, but this is true to a greater extent in the case of Al-Qaeda.

However, although religion, nationalism and ideology might represent elements of the conflict, it is another thing to say that they are the most vital part of the conflict. Would religion have been an element of the PIRA conflict were it not for the economic disparities between Catholics and Protestants? Was the PLO really a nationalist organisation when it desired closer unity amongst all Arab peoples from different countries? Is the ideology of Al-Qaeda based on a coherent set of principles or is the essence of its conflict based on maximising opportunities that are presented to them, such as infiltrating the sectarian conflict in the aftermath of the Iraq War?

What is used to motivate the terrorists?

Both Al-Qaeda and the PLO have argued that dying while fighting for the cause of **Allah** reserves a special place and honour in Paradise. This type of argument has played a part in recruiting terrorists and persuading some to turn themselves into suicide bombers. However, there are other factors to consider in assessing the role of religion in motivating the suicide bomber, namely the financial security given to a suicide bomber's family, and the influence of a religious book such as the **Qu'ran** when it is misinterpreted to influence vulnerable and impressionable minds.

The biggest argument against religion being a motivating factor for terrorists is the fact that some of the loudest criticism of terrorist organisations like Al-Qaeda comes from Muslims who are angry that their religion has been distorted by the terrorists. In the case of the PIRA, it would be wrong to dismiss religion as a motivating factor. It is worth noting that the PIRA got most of its membership after events such as Bloody Sunday in 1972 where the Catholic population felt under threat from the British government. However, we cannot dismiss the impact of nationalism and ideology as a way of motivating the terrorists. Both have the potential to unify large groups of people behind a cause. Arguably, in the case of the PLO, nationalism was a bigger motivating influence than ideology since it consisted of communist factions such as the Palestinian People's Party and the more nationalist Fatah. However, on the other hand, Al-Qaeda can hardly claim to use nationalism as a motivating force since it has supposedly influenced many people to commit atrocities in their own countries. The people responsible for the London bombings on 7 July 2005 were all raised in England. Overall, therefore, these three forces can be a motivating factor when it comes to recruiting terrorists, but the motivation of the terrorist is often linked to other factors such as financial advantages.

Explain the role of religion in terrorism. **[6 marks]**

This image is taken from a video released on 14 January 2004, the day of a suicide attack in Israel. It shows the 22-year-old Palestinian suicide bomber and mother of two, Reem al-Reyashi, posing with a weapon before the attack.

Why is terrorism generally condemned? Is terrorism ever justified?

LEARNING OBJECTIVES

In this lesson you will:

- examine the main reasons why terrorism is generally condemned
- assess the differences and similarities between these condemnations.

SOURCE 

Every nation, in every region, now has a decision to make. Either you are with us, or you are with the terrorists. From this day forward, any nation that continues to harbour or support terrorism will be regarded by the United States as a hostile regime.

Extract from a speech which US President George W. Bush gave on 21 September 2001.

The vast majority of people would automatically condemn terrorism. In countries such as Britain and the USA, terrorism is consistently condemned by politicians and the media. Source A reveals the extent to which the recent US President **George W. Bush** viewed terrorism as a threat. Terrorism is generally condemned because of the threat it poses to civilian populations, and because the consequences are so awful.

Why does terrorism threaten us?

The PIRA, PLO and Al-Qaeda, as with other terrorist organisations, have all been condemned by numerous groups around the world. There are several reasons for this:

1 Obscene number of casualties

The most obviously shocking feature about terrorism is the large number of casualties. Appalling natural disasters such as earthquakes and flooding can cause devastating destruction of human life, but whereas tragedies such as these cannot be prevented, acts of terrorism are carried out deliberately. Few people therefore allow themselves to feel much sympathy with the cause of the terrorist, because of the fact that the terrorist act leaves behind so many victims. Al-Qaeda's attacks on 11 September 2001 caused the deaths of 2974 people, in addition to the 19 hijackers.

2 Civilian casualties

It is extremely easy to condemn any preventable loss of life, whatever the circumstances. However, it is especially difficult to justify the fact that the most common victim of a terrorist attack is a civilian. A civilian, almost by definition, will not have put themselves in harm's way but they are still not safe from the terrorists. This was the case for the civilians on the Avivim school bus in Israel (1970), those in the crowded shopping centre in Omagh (1998) or those on the busy train in Madrid (2004), who suffered at the hands of the PLO, PIRA, and Al-Qaeda respectively. The PIRA was responsible for the deaths of 1821 people during the **Troubles** up to 2001, with civilians making up 621 of these casualties.

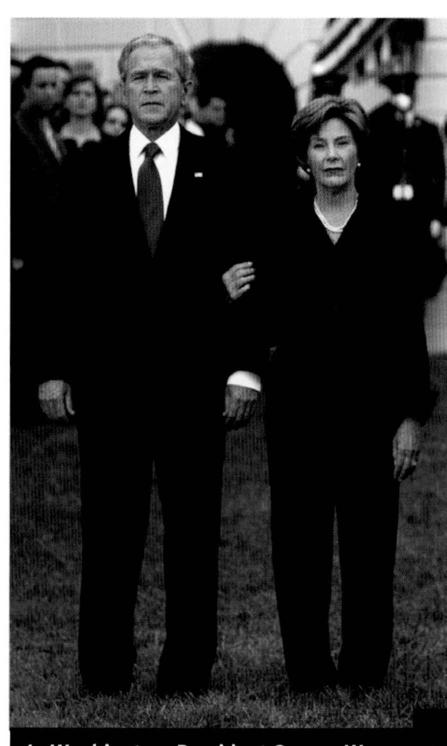

In Washington, President George W. Bush and his wife Laura observed a minute's silence on the lawn of the White House on the seventh anniversary of the terrorist attacks in New York and Washington on 11 September 2008.

KEY PEOPLE

George W. Bush – *President of the USA, 2001–09.*

KEY WORDS

Troubles – *a period of activity involving violence between the PIRA and its adversaries which lasted from the late 1960s until the late 1990s.*

3 Spreads fear and intolerance

Terrorists aim to cause as much loss of life as is possible through their actions. In addition to this, they also want to destabilise government and society and are fully aware that their actions can serve to make people more fearful and less tolerant of others around them. Al-Qaeda's recent terrorist activities have led to many tensions between different religious communities, and they preceded the US decision to detain terrorist suspects without trial in a detention centre in Guantánamo Bay, Cuba. Consequently, many have condemned terrorists for their attacks on the values and processes of democracy.

4 Gives religion a bad name

A major criticism of terrorism is the way in which it uses and abuses religion for the sake of its narrow and merciless causes. In particular, there has been widespread outrage from many parts of the Islamic community at the way in which Al-Qaeda has identified its struggle with Islam, causing many people to erroneously associate their actions with the teachings of the Qur'an.

Overall condemnation of terrorism

Together the above reasons show why terrorism is generally condemned. This criticism emerges as a result of feeling both outraged and threatened by their direct (casualties) and indirect (attitudes) impact. Many people are united in their condemnation of terrorism but are often divided about their proposals to deal with the problem.

SOURCE B

As far as Islam is concerned ... it does not provide any cover or justification for any act of violence, be it committed by an individual, a group or a government. ... I most strongly condemn all acts and forms of terrorism because it is my deeply rooted belief that not only Islam but also no true religion, whatever its name, can sanction violence and bloodshed of innocent men, women and children in the name of God.

Extract from *Murder in the Name of Allah* by Mirza Tahir Ahmad, 1989.

SOURCE C

Q: When did you turn to offensive action?

A: After internment. Before, anything else was a retaliation, because the British army was bad to the people. So we thought retaliatory action and sabotage. But after internment we went to all offensive, all offensive action.

Q: But wasn't the killing of Gunner Curtis, the first soldier to die, an offensive action?

A: No. It was on retaliation for the bad treatment of British troops in Belfast.

Taken from an interview with Seán Mac Stíofáin some time after the Troubles had begun.

CASE STUDY

Is terrorism ever justified?

It is common practice for terrorist groups to attempt to justify their actions to the rest of the world. Two of the most common justifications used by terrorist groups are:

- it is the only course of action that could achieve a specific aim
- the acts of violence are retaliation to a similar action perpetrated against the terrorists or the people they claim to represent.

The PIRA would argue that an increase in terrorist activity throughout the Troubles gradually forced the British to the negotiating table which led to the Anglo-Irish Agreement of 1985. More recently, Sinn Féin has been part of the historic power-sharing arrangement in Northern Ireland, with Martin McGuinness, a one-time leading figure of the PIRA, being elected to the position of deputy First-Minister in 2007. However, this was not simply a result of their terrorist activity since the PIRA had to decommission their weapons and renounce the armed struggle. Moreover, Sinn Féin's key position at the negotiating table was arguably more a result of the political success of the hunger strikes than the terrorist attacks of the PIRA.

Source C shows a second justification offered for terrorism, namely that the PIRA saw themselves as reacting to violence from the British Army in events such as internment and Bloody Sunday. As such, the PIRA maintained that the only way to defend Catholics in Northern Ireland was by taking the fight to the British. However, many of the targets of their terrorist activities were civilians who had no responsibility for those events, and the PIRA's actions sometimes had the opposite effect of encouraging Unionist violence against the people they were trying to protect. This was demonstrated by the UVF attacks in Dublin and Monaghan in May 1974.

Overall, it is clear that terrorist groups have enjoyed different levels of success but if one takes the view that the end does not justify the means, this alone does not justify the actions of terrorist groups.

How different are terrorist groups in their membership, aims, motives and methods?

LEARNING OBJECTIVES

In this lesson you will:

- examine the membership, aims, motives and methods of three terrorist organisations
- learn to make effective comparisons.

N
NORTHERN IRELAND
Londonderry
Atlantic Ocean
Belfast
Portadown
Dublin
REPUBLIC OF IRELAND
Celtic Sea
200 km

The division of Northern Ireland from the Republic of Ireland.

The Provisional IRA

On 6 December 1921, most of the island of Ireland was granted independence from the UK, leading to the creation of the Republic of Ireland (an independent state) and Northern Ireland (part of the United Kingdom).

The Irish Republican Army (IRA) was a paramilitary organisation who wanted to put pressure on the British government to unite Northern Ireland with the Republic of Ireland. They were composed of **radical**, mostly **left-wing**, Catholics. They were all Irish **nationalists**. In 1968, the situation in Ireland became more tense and some within the IRA felt that the organisation's tactics were not strong enough to put pressure on the British government and so they broke away to form the PIRA.

HISTORY DETECTIVE

What effect do you think the events of Bloody Sunday had on the membership levels of the PIRA?

Aims and motives of the PIRA

Since its emergence in 1969, the PIRA has sought an end to British influence in Northern Ireland and the creation of an all-island Irish state. They have also aimed to defend the Catholic community from attack and support it in its desire for further civil rights.

Methods of the PIRA

There have been five main stages in the methods used by the PIRA.

1 Use of as much force as possible (1969–75)

Throughout this period, the PIRA aimed to inflict a level of casualties on the British forces to such an extent that the British government would be forced by public opinion to withdraw from Ireland. They used methods such as landmines, bombs and numerous shooting incidents to apply this pressure. They took their terrorist activities to mainland

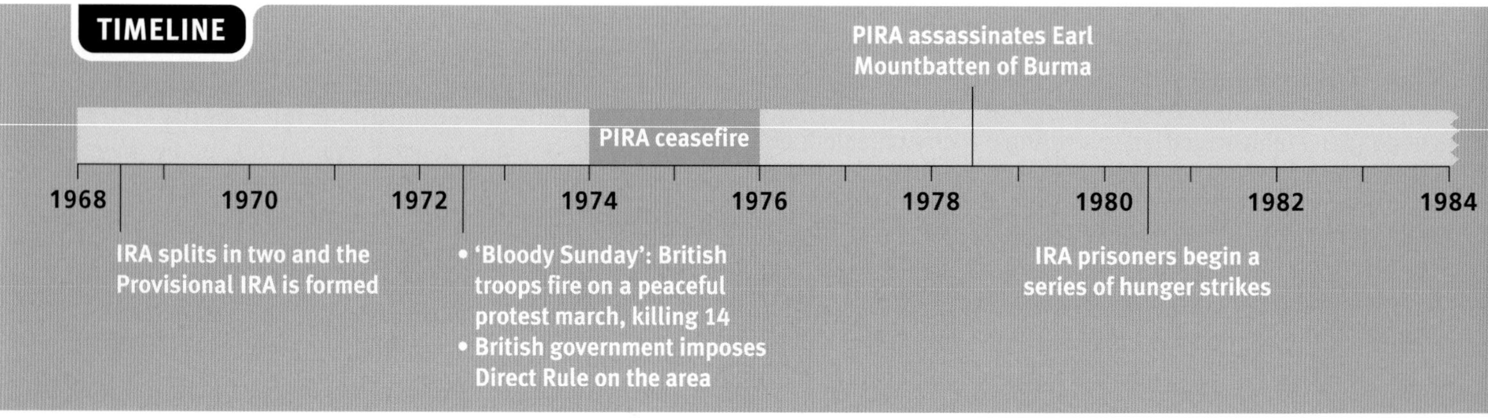
TIMELINE
PIRA assassinates Earl Mountbatten of Burma
PIRA ceasefire
1968
1970
1972
1974
1976
1978
1980
1982
1984
IRA splits in two and the Provisional IRA is formed
• 'Bloody Sunday': British troops fire on a peaceful protest march, killing 14
• British government imposes Direct Rule on the area
IRA prisoners begin a series of hunger strikes

Britain, where they were responsible for numerous attacks including the M62 coach bombing (February 1974) and the Guildford pub bombing (October 1974). By the mid-1970s, it became clear, however, that any hopes held by the PIRA leadership of a quick military victory were evaporating.

2 Ceasefire (1975–76)

In 1975, following secret meetings between PIRA leaders and Merlyn Rees, the PIRA began a ceasefire in February 1975. The PIRA initially believed that this was the start of a long-term process of British withdrawal, but later came to the conclusion that Rees was trying to bring them into peaceful politics without offering them any of the guarantees they wanted. Consequently, the ceasefire broke down in January 1976.

3 The 'Long War' (late 1970s–late 1990s)

Under new leadership, allegedly including Gerry Adams (future president of Sinn Féin), the PIRA evolved a new strategy termed the 'Long War', which involved a reorganisation of the PIRA into small cells with a focus on more selective operations against specified targets. As part of this strategy, they attempted to assassinate high-profile figures such as Margaret Thatcher in 1984. Alongside this approach, they increasingly recognised the propaganda value of some of their actions and began to pursue a dual political strategy.

4 Political strategy (1980s–)

Sinn Féin was the political party most closely associated with the PIRA. The political appeal of Sinn Féin was immensely helped when seven members of the IRA and three other Irish nationalists starved themselves to death in prison in protest against the British government's refusal to grant them special prisoner status, as they argued that they were political prisoners. Sinn Féin had some success with the passing of the Anglo-Irish Agreement in 1985, which aimed to bring an end to the Troubles. This started to convince the PIRA that it was possible to make gains without violence.

5 Peace strategy (1998)

After numerous false starts, the IRA eventually called a ceasefire which brought Sinn Féin into the peace process, leading to the Good Friday Agreement of 1998. This came about as a result of a great deal of goodwill on both sides of the conflict and intervention on the part of the British, Irish and American governments.

SOURCE A

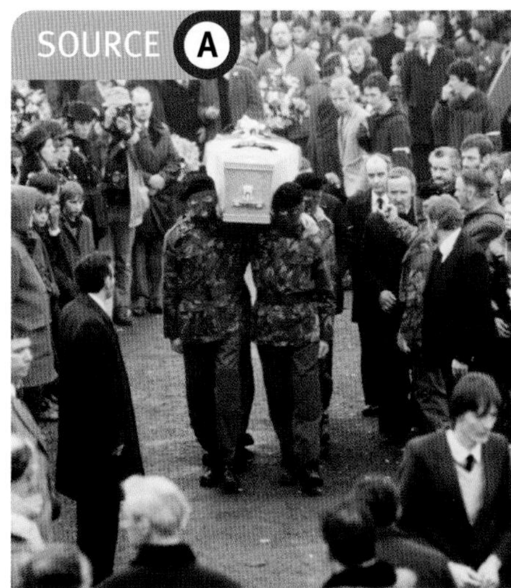

A casualty of the Troubles is carried through the streets of Northern Ireland.

ACTIVITIES

Was Gerry Adams really a member of the PIRA? Why might there be more than one interpretation about this?

KEY WORDS

Left wing – *a body of political thought which generally criticises the existing social order and argues in favour of a society where all people have equal opportunities.*

Nationalists – *people who hold views focusing on the importance of the nation.*

Radical – *someone who holds an extreme viewpoint.*

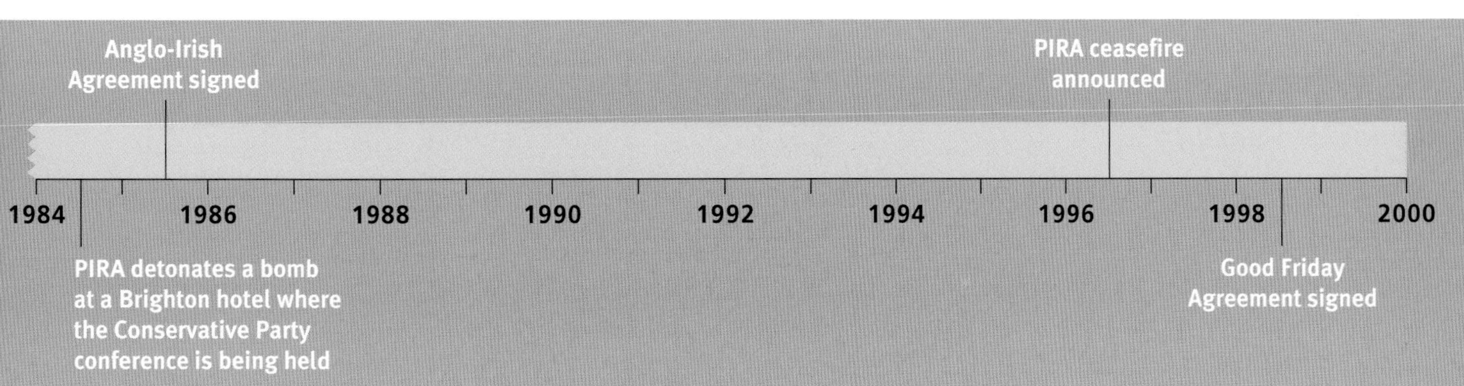
Anglo-Irish Agreement signed
PIRA ceasefire announced
1984
1986
1988
1990
1992
1994
1996
1998
2000
PIRA detonates a bomb at a Brighton hotel where the Conservative Party conference is being held
Good Friday Agreement signed

The Palestine Liberation Organisation

On 14 May 1948, the state of Israel was created by dividing the existing area of Palestine into separate Jewish and Arab states.

The Palestine Liberation Organisation (PLO) was a paramilitary organisation composed of radical Arabs and Palestinian nationalists, whose original aim was the destruction of the state of Israel and self-determination for the Palestinian Arabs. The PLO was founded by the Arab League in 1964, but it did not become an independent organisation until February 1969. Yasser Arafat was Chairman of the PLO from 1969 to 2004, followed by Mahmoud Abbas (since October 2004).

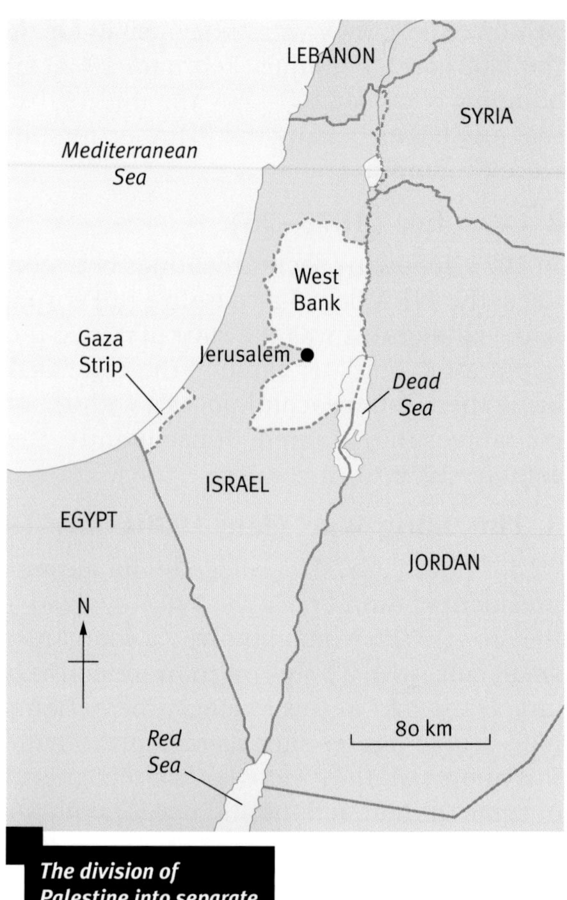
LEBANON
SYRIA
Mediterranean Sea
West Bank
Gaza Strip
Jerusalem
Dead Sea
ISRAEL
EGYPT
JORDAN
N
Red Sea
80 km

The division of Palestine into separate Jewish and Arab states.

Aims of the PLO

The basic aim of the PLO was to provide Palestinian Arabs with a country of their own in Palestine. In the early part of its history, it pledged to destroy the state of Israel as part of this aim, though it later recognised Israel's right to exist. In addition, the PLO also aimed for closer Arab unity.

Methods of the PLO

The PLO's strategy changed considerably from the time when it first started until the signing of the Oslo Accords in 1993.

1 War of Attrition (1969–70)

This was a military tactic in which the PLO attempted to win a war by wearing down Israel to the point of collapse through repeated attacks on its people. During this period, the PLO launched artillery attacks on Israeli settlements and **kibbutzim**, while **fedayeen** launched attacks on Israeli civilians. Although the PLO launched many attacks of this sort, they saw that, given the power of the Israeli military, there was a need for a new strategy

2 Targeted terrorism (1972)

In 1972, Black September, a group with ties to **Yasser Arafat**'s Fatah organisation, took members of the Israeli Olympic team hostage. They killed 11 Israeli athletes and coaches and one German police officer. The fact that this took place during the Olympic Games raised international awareness of their cause.

HISTORY DETECTIVE

Find out why the PLO left the Arab League in 1969 and became an independent organisation.

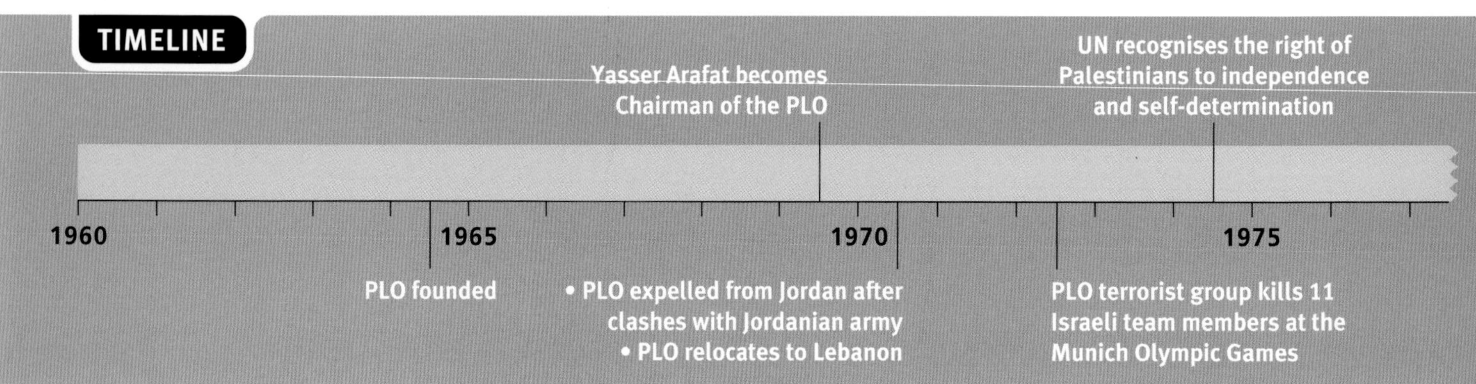
TIMELINE
Yasser Arafat becomes Chairman of the PLO
UN recognises the right of Palestinians to independence and self-determination
1960
1965
1970
1975
PLO founded
• PLO expelled from Jordan after clashes with Jordanian army
• PLO relocates to Lebanon
PLO terrorist group kills 11 Israeli team members at the Munich Olympic Games

SOURCE B

Image of one of the masked terrorists overlooking the balcony of the Israeli team quarters during the Israeli Olympic team hostage crisis, 1972.

3 First Intifada (1987–93)

In the aftermath of the PLO's involvement in the Lebanese Civil War, which seriously destabilised the organisation, there were some murmurings of a peaceful approach, but these came to nothing. In 1987, tension escalated with a mass Palestinian uprising against Israeli rule which spread throughout **Gaza**, the **West Bank** and East Jerusalem. The actions of the protestors ranged from civil disobedience to violence, along with general strikes and boycotts of Israeli products. They were keen to raise international attention, and several Palestinian demonstrations included stone-throwing by Palestinian youths against the heavily-armed Israeli Defence Forces. Following the **Intifada**, Arafat effectively recognised Israel's right to exist in return for an understanding that the Palestinians would be allowed to set up their own state in the West Bank and Gaza. This paved the way for the USA to enter into diplomatic negotiations with the Palestinians.

VOICE YOUR OPINION!

Why would the PLO want the world to see pictures of young Palestinians throwing stones at Israeli tanks?

4 Negotiating a settlement (1993)

The Oslo Accords of 1993, agreed by Israeli Prime Minister **Yitzhak Rabin** and PLO Chairman Yasser Arafat, granted the Palestinians the right to self-government in the Gaza Strip and the city of Jericho in the West Bank, through the creation of the **Palestinian Authority**. The PLO had used negotiating tools to get as close to their stated aims as was realistically possible, but this by no means marked the end of the conflict, as a Second Intifada, with repeated suicide bombings, took place in 2000–04.

KEY CONCEPTS

Fedayeen – *a term used to describe militant groups formed from within the Palestinian refugee population.*

Intifada – *a Palestinian uprising against Israeli rule.*

KEY PEOPLE

Yasser Arafat – *Chairman of the Palestine Liberation Organisation, 1969–2004.*

Yitzhak Rabin – *Prime Minister of Israel, 1992–95.*

KEY WORDS

Gaza – *the largest city in the Gaza Strip and the Palestinian territories.*

Kibbutzim – *collective communities in Israel that were traditionally based on agriculture.*

Palestinian Authority – *an organisation created in 1994 and linked to the PLO, formed to provide a limited form of self-governance for the Palestinian people.*

West Bank – *a landlocked territory on the west bank of the River Jordan.*

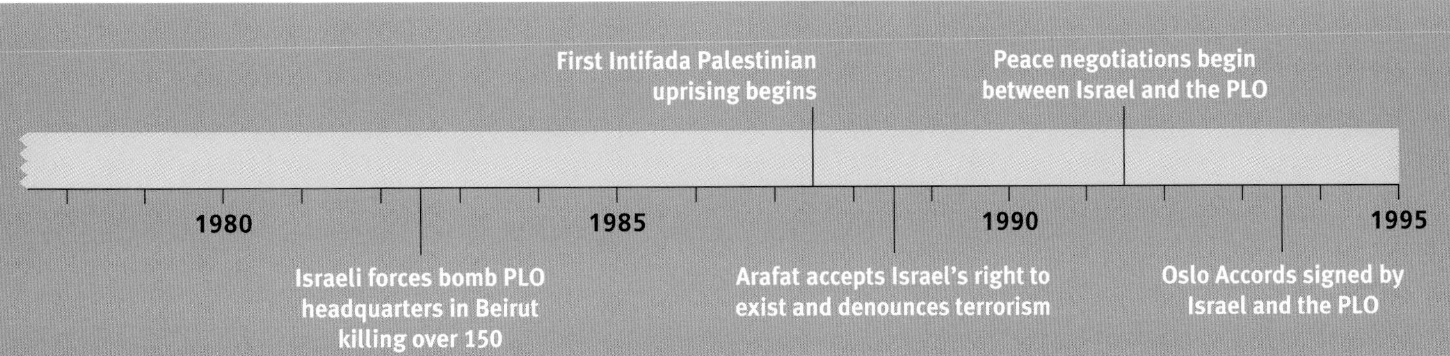
First Intifada Palestinian uprising begins
Peace negotiations begin between Israel and the PLO
1980
1985
1990
1995
Israeli forces bomb PLO headquarters in Beirut killing over 150
Arafat accepts Israel's right to exist and denounces terrorism
Oslo Accords signed by Israel and the PLO

Al-Qaeda

In December 1979, the Soviet Union invaded Afghanistan to support the communist government in its fight against the Mujahideen resistance. Thousands of Muslim volunteers from around the Middle East came to Afghanistan to defend the Mujahideen.

Al-Qaeda was officially founded in August 1988, as an international organisation whose aim was to build on the operation in Afghanistan to assist Islamist struggles in other parts of the world. Al-Qaeda is composed of Islamic fundamentalists, and it is currently led by Osama bin Laden and **Ayman al-Zawahiri**.

Aims of Al-Qaeda

The primary aim of Al-Qaeda has always been to end foreign influence in Muslim countries such as Iraq and Saudi Arabia. It has also stated its intention to destroy Israel, topple pro-Western dictatorships around the Middle East, and unite all Muslims behind the principle of an Islamic nation which would follow the rule of the first **Caliphs**, who succeeded the Prophet **Muhammad** in the 7th century.

Methods of Al-Qaeda

Al-Qaeda is an example of an organisation which, unlike the other two organisations, has considerably expanded its operations over time.

1 Fighting the Soviet Union (1988–89)

The conflict in Afghanistan had almost ended by the time Al-Qaeda was formed. Their involvement consisted of recruiting thousands of foreign Mujahideen to help in the fight against the Soviet Union.

2 International terrorism (1992–)

Bin Laden wished to establish operations in other parts of the world, and over the course of the last 15 years Al-Qaeda has done this. Their attacks have included the detonating of two bombs in Yemen aimed at American soldiers on their way to Somalia (1992), the bombing of the US naval vessel, USS *Cole* (2000) and the transport bombings in Madrid (2004) and London (2005). Many of these attacks involved the use of bombs, and some were suicide attacks.

Grade
Studio

Describe the origins of Al-Qaeda. **[4 marks]**

KEY WORDS

Taliban – *the organisation which ruled most of Afghanistan during 1996–2001.*

Caliphs – *the previous name for heads of state of Islamic communities which were ruled by Islamic religious law.*

KEY PEOPLE

Muhammad – *a man revered by Muslims as the messenger and prophet of God.*

Ayman al-Zawahiri – *a prominent leader of Al-Qaeda.*

VOICE YOUR OPINION!

In groups, consider what rights the terrorists are taking away from citizens by pursuing these aims.

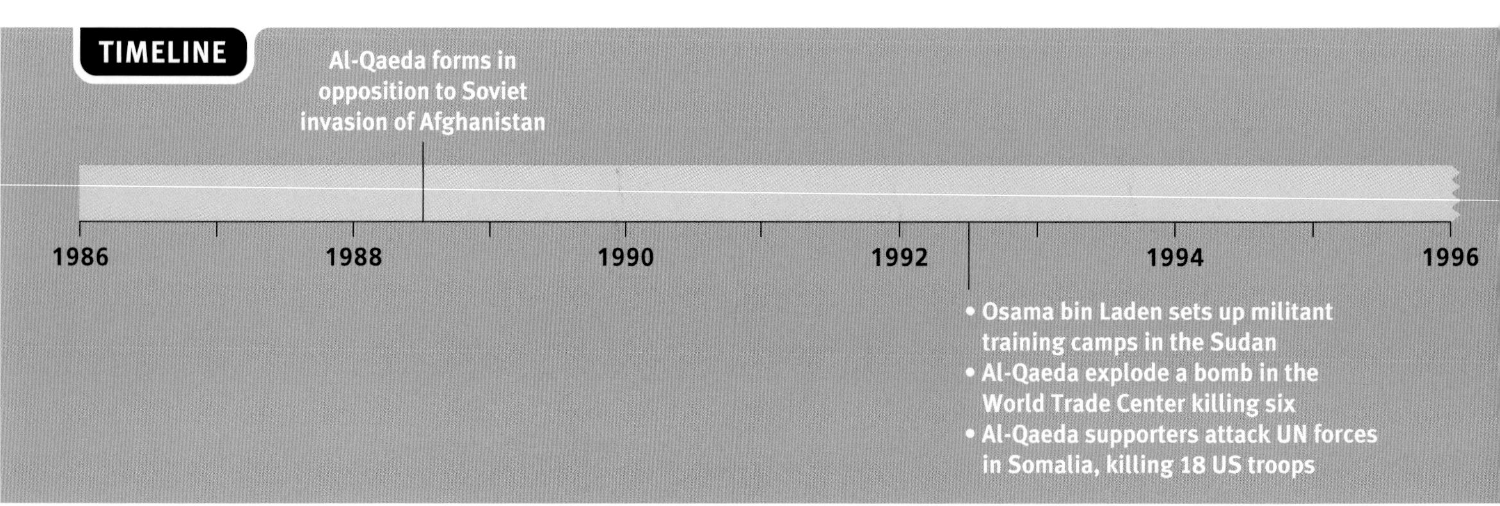
TIMELINE
Al-Qaeda forms in opposition to Soviet invasion of Afghanistan
1986
1988
1990
1992
1994
1996
• Osama bin Laden sets up militant training camps in the Sudan
• Al-Qaeda explode a bomb in the World Trade Center killing six
• Al-Qaeda supporters attack UN forces in Somalia, killing 18 US troops

3 Terrorism in Iraq (2003–)

Although they have clearly not ceased their international terrorist activities, the Iraq War and the ensuing instability and chaos has provided Al-Qaeda with an opportunity to use terrorism against Western forces. Suspected Al-Qaeda terrorists are likely to have been responsible for kidnappings and a string of suicide-bomb attacks in the region.

Comparing the different aims

A closer look at the aims of these three terrorist organisations can reveal several important differences.

- The PLO and the PIRA are aiming for a change in geographical borders so that the people they represent (Palestinian Arabs and the Irish respectively) can govern themselves, whereas Al-Qaeda does not have such a specific territorial issue. Instead, it has far more global aims than either the PIRA or the PLO.
- Whereas the PLO and Al-Qaeda have aimed at destroying a particular state (Israel), the PIRA have called for the removal of British influence from one particular territory rather than its destruction.

GradeStudio

'Different terrorist groups have similar aims.' How far do you agree with this statement? Explain your answer. **[10 marks]**

There are also some key similarities between the aims of these three organisations.

- They have all aimed at removing the influence of a particular government from a particular territory.
- The PIRA, PLO and Al-Qaeda all aim for some type of unity. The PIRA want to unite the two different Irish states, the PLO want Arab unity in the Middle East, and Al-Qaeda want Islamic unity.

Comparing the different methods

The interesting thing to note is how the methods of terrorist groups have changed according to their effectiveness. All three terrorist organisations have expanded and modified their operations to varying degrees. In addition, they have sought not only to cause loss of life but also to raise awareness of their stated aims.

GradeStudio

'Different terrorist groups use similar methods.' How far do you agree with this statement? Explain your answer. **[10 marks]**

Examiner's tip

In order to get full marks, it is important to demonstrate three things: knowledge of all three terrorist organisations; evidence of both similarities and differences in the methods of terrorist groups; and an overall judgement.

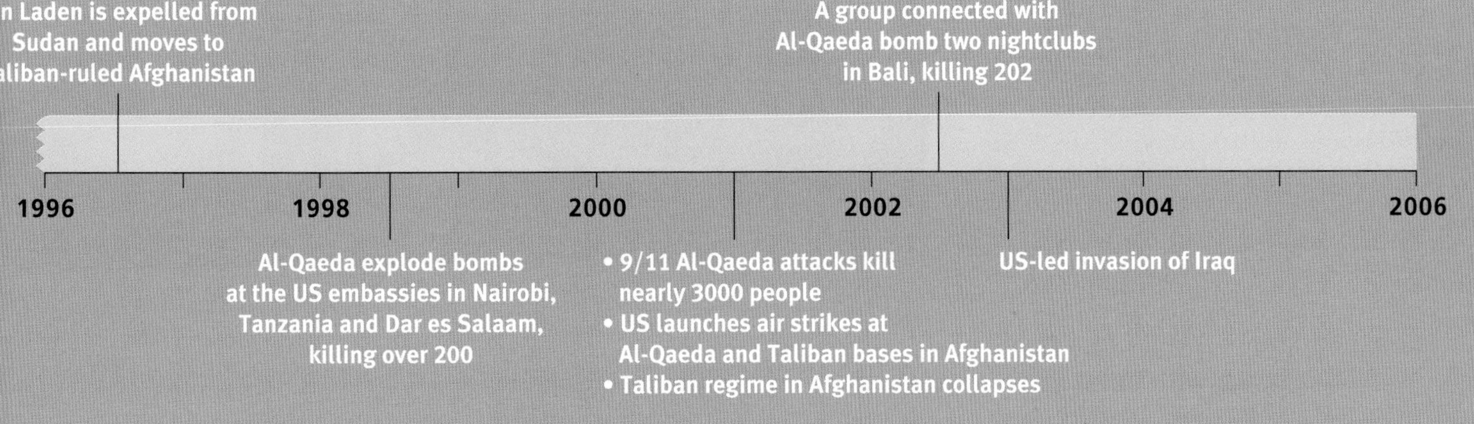
in Laden is expelled from Sudan and moves to aliban-ruled Afghanistan
A group connected with Al-Qaeda bomb two nightclubs in Bali, killing 202
1996
1998
2000
2002
2004
2006
Al-Qaeda explode bombs at the US embassies in Nairobi, Tanzania and Dar es Salaam, killing over 200
• 9/11 Al-Qaeda attacks kill nearly 3000 people
• US launches air strikes at Al-Qaeda and Taliban bases in Afghanistan
• Taliban regime in Afghanistan collapses
US-led invasion of Iraq

How important are the leaders of terrorist groups?

LEARNING OBJECTIVES

In this lesson you will:

- examine characteristics of the leadership of each of the three terrorist organisations
- learn how to analyse the different factors which determine the importance of strong leadership.

KEY PEOPLE

Martin McGuinness – *involved in the leadership of the IRA during the 1970s. Deputy First Minister of Northern Ireland, 2007–.*

Seán Mac Stíofáin – *first Chief of Staff of the PIRA.*

Importance of leadership

Most active terrorist groups will have a clear and identifiable leader. Often, a leader of a terrorist organisation lasts longer in their role than a leader of a government in a democracy. However, their position is rarely secure, often depending upon the nature of their control, authority and the structure of the terrorist organisation.

Leadership of the PIRA

The PIRA was organised into small, tightly knit cells under the leadership of the Army Council. Some former Chiefs of Staff include **Seán Mac Stíofáin** and **Martin McGuinness**. Apart from a few isolated incidents, the leadership of the PIRA generally commanded a strong degree of loyalty. After it re-organised its structures after the 1975 ceasefire, its numbers diminished to only a few thousand members, but their ability to organise themselves for attacks on specific targets led the British and Irish government to consider them a potent and capable terrorist organisation. Since the 1970s, the IRA has frequently been infiltrated by the British government, leading to the execution of some 63 people as informers during the Troubles.

SOURCE A

A photo taken of PIRA peace talks in 1972 when leaders of the PIRA held a press conference in Derry. From left to right: Martin McGuinness, David O'Connell, Seán Mac Stíofáin, and Seamus Tuomey.

Leadership of the PLO

Yasser Arafat, as Chairman of the PLO, relied on the support of the Fatah Party, which was the largest faction of the PLO. The PLO has a legislative body, the Palestinian National Council, yet most power and decisions were controlled by the PLO Executive Committee, in which Fatah was dominant. However, Arafat could not directly control its different factions, and this led to disagreement in the aftermath of the Ten Point Program in 1974. Several radical PLO factions broke away to form the Rejectionist Front, which would act independently of the PLO over the course of the following years. Arafat was not able to carry everyone in the PLO movement with him when he entered into a series of negotiations with the government of Israel in the Madrid Conference (1991), which led to the Oslo Accords. Following on from this, **Hamas** and other militant organisations rose to power and shook the foundations of the authority which Fatah under Arafat had established. However, Arafat remained in his position until a month before his death in 2004.

Leadership of Al-Qaeda

Although Al-Qaeda and Osama bin Laden have become virtually synonymous, bin Laden does not run the organisation single-handedly, relying heavily on a close-knit group of advisers such as Dr Ayman al-Zawahiri. Al-Qaeda's leadership oversees a loosely organised network of cells. It can recruit members from thousands of Muslim radicals around the world. Its infrastructure is small, mobile and **decentralised**, with each cell operating independently and its members not knowing the identity of other cells. Local operatives rarely know anyone higher up in the organisation's hierarchy. Although Al-Qaeda has a reputation as a vast global network, many experts believe that Al-Qaeda itself has just a small core of adherents, but serves as the inspiration to countless violent Islamic extremists. In this way, it can claim credit for any terrorist attack that any loosely affiliated organisation might carry out, but at the same time it can distance itself from these groups in order to avoid infiltration. Osama Bin Laden has released numerous videos which make him an increasingly recognisable figure to the whole world, and he is consequently still seen as the leader of the movement, despite his followers not even knowing for sure whether he is still alive.

Importance of leadership

The leadership of a terrorist group is extremely important and is often vital to its longevity. It is clear that leaders of terrorist groups operate in different ways. Bin Laden makes himself frequently visible through videos, thereby ensuring that his message is spread, whereas the PIRA have been a little more secretive about who was actually in charge of PIRA operations. One similarity that is very noticeable is that both the PIRA and Al-Qaeda have organised themselves into small cells rather than having big organisations, due to the constant fear of infiltration. There have been several cases of infiltration, particularly in the PIRA, and leaders have inevitably chosen to surround themselves with as few people as possible.

Explain why the leadership of a terrorist group is so important. **[6 marks]**

KEY WORDS

Hamas – *organisation created in 1987 as an Islamic paramilitary organisation and political party.*

KEY CONCEPTS

Decentralised – *when decision-making is closer to the citizens or members of the organisation and away from a central decision-making body.*

ACTIVITIES

Read the information above and use it to complete the following table:

	PIRA	**PLO**	**Al-Qaeda**
Do their leaders lead on their own or with others?			
How do their leaders organise the movement?			
How do their leaders convince others to follow?			

How have governments reacted to terrorism?

LEARNING OBJECTIVES

In this lesson you will:

- examine the different ways in which governments have reacted to terrorism
- learn how to compare the reaction of different governments.

Government reaction to terrorism

Governments have responded to terrorism in a variety of ways, ranging from pre-emptive or reactive military action to negotiation to increased intelligence and surveillance activities. Often, governments have tried more than one tactic in their efforts to combat terrorism. Some have resorted to the detention of suspects for a given period of time without trial, the freezing of financial assets and the enhancement of police powers. The different governments concerned have responded to the PIRA, PLO and Al-Qaeda in many different ways, though this chapter will focus on one particular approach that a government has taken for each one.

Reaction to the PIRA: increased intelligence and surveillance activities

It is very difficult to defeat an enemy that you cannot see. This was the problem facing the British government as, unlike in conventional warfare, they never knew when and where the next PIRA bomb would come. Infiltration of the IRA, therefore, was a key component of the British government's war against the PIRA. It gave the government valuable information, which it could then use to arrest high-profile PIRA figures. This was undoubtedly a factor which led to the arrest of so many PIRA volunteers in the aftermath of the ceasefire in 1975 and which, in turn, forced the terrorist organisation to operate in small cells which would be harder to infiltrate.

Reaction to the PLO: attempts at negotiation

Throughout the First Intifada, the Israeli government had become increasingly tired of the constant violence. They therefore became far more open to the possibility of entering into negotiations with the PLO, who themselves were suffering a little by 1991 as their funding from the Arab Gulf States had been cut off due to their pro-Iraqi stance during the first Gulf War. This led to the signing of the Oslo Accords in August 1993, in which the PLO would acknowledge the state of Israel and pledge to reject violence, and Israel would recognise the PLO as the official Palestinian Authority, allowing Yasser Arafat to return to the West Bank. These Accords were the first direct, face-to-face agreement between Israel and political representatives of the Palestinians.

GETTING STARTED

As terrorism has become an increasing problem for governments, several anti-terrorist measures have been issued. For example, there is now increased security at airports. Can you think of any other measures that governments have taken in recent years in response to terrorism? As an extension, think of other things that you would do which have not already been done by governments.

KEY WORDS

Northern Alliance – *an Afghan military-political grouping which took part in the fight against the Taliban regime.*

KEY PEOPLE

Mullah Omar – *head of the Taliban regime, 1996–2001.*

KEY CONCEPTS

Pre-emptive strike – *a strike that has happened not in response to anything but taking place before an expected invasion or offensive.*

SOURCE A

Yitzhak Rabin, Bill Clinton and Yasser Arafat during the official signing of the Oslo Accords on 13 September 1993 in Washington DC.

Reaction to Al-Qaeda: military action

The action of the US government to Al-Qaeda terrorist activity has been one of military action. In response to the embassy bombings in East Africa, the US military launched cruise missiles on targets in Sudan and Afghanistan. After the attacks of 11 September 2001, the USA offered the Taliban leader, **Mullah Omar**, a chance to surrender bin Laden and his top associates. When this failed to happen, the USA and its allies invaded Afghanistan, and together with the Afghan **Northern Alliance** removed the Taliban government. This led to the destruction of Al-Qaeda training camps in Afghanistan, which clearly had a de-stabilising effect on the operating structure of Al-Qaeda. However, Al-Qaeda's top two leaders, bin Laden and al-Zawahiri, both evaded capture, and Al-Qaeda operations have continued.

Consequences of government reaction

In some cases, the reaction of the government to terrorism has actually benefited the terrorists. If the government reacts to terrorist activity in an aggressive way, as was the case with the policy of internment following the events of Bloody Sunday, this can serve to boost the membership and popularity of the terrorist organisation.

ACTIVITIES

In groups, study carefully the reaction of the three governments to the three terrorist organisations and make an argument for which reaction you think was the most justified. Make sure that you explain not only the positives of one but also the negatives of the other two.

GradeStudio

'Governments always react in the same way when dealing with terrorist organisations.' How far do you agree with this statement? Explain your answer. **[10 marks]**

How effective have terrorist groups been?

LEARNING OBJECTIVES

In this lesson you will:

- examine the different ways in which terrorist organisations have been effective
- learn how to analyse an appropriate way to measure the effectiveness of a terrorist group.

GETTING STARTED

Do you remember the stated aims of the three terrorist organisations? Try to write down as much as you can remember about their aims. As a clue, two of the terrorist groups' aims were connected with borders and one was about foreign influences.

How to measure the effectiveness of a terrorist group

It is difficult to know the best way to measure the effectiveness of a terrorist group. Measures could include their impact on civilian life and governments, and their ability to attract membership and support. For example, the PIRA were responsible for the deaths of 1821 people in 1969–2001, the Al-Qaeda-inspired bombs in Madrid (March 2004) played a part in the collapse of José María Aznar's Spanish government (which had supported the Iraq War), and the PLO were considered to be one of the richest of all terrorist organisations, with billions of dollars in assets and secret investments around the world. However, on its own this does not answer the question of whether or not the terrorist groups were effective. To do this, it is important to see whether or not each terrorist group actually achieved its stated aims, and over what period of time.

Effectiveness of the PIRA by the time of the Good Friday Agreement

It is clear that the central aim of the PIRA, namely a united Ireland instead of a division between Northern Ireland and the Republic of Ireland, has not been realised. The Good Friday Agreement, however, has not ruled out indefinitely the possibility of a united Ireland, since one of its main provisions was that the constitutional status of Northern Ireland could be changed following a majority vote of its citizens. In addition, it has dramatically reduced British influence in Northern Ireland and has led to some measures, concerned with human rights and equality, that have undoubtedly helped the Catholic community. Overall, the PIRA has achieved some of its aims but has not managed to achieve its ultimate goal of a united Ireland.

Effectiveness of the PLO by the time of the Oslo Accords

The PLO's fundamental aim was to provide Palestinian Arabs with a country of their own in Palestine, and the Oslo Accords provided that only to some extent. It gave the Palestinians self-rule in the Gaza Strip and the Jericho area, and a withdrawal of Israeli forces from those areas. In other words, the Palestinians got part of a country of their own. However, the PLO certainly had not achieved its original stated aim of destroying the state of Israel, as by this time it had formally recognised the right of the state of Israel to exist in peace and security. One of the problems of the Oslo Accords was that many issues, such as the fate of Jerusalem, security arrangements and settlements, were postponed for future discussion, which delayed any agreement on these important issues. Overall, the PLO achieved some of its aims but, as with the PIRA, did not manage to achieve its ultimate goal.

Effectiveness of Al-Qaeda by the time of the Iraq War

Although Al-Qaeda's main aim has been to end foreign influence in Muslim countries, the consequence of its actions has been an increasing amount of foreign influence in Muslim countries such as Afghanistan and Iraq. It has also failed in its intention to destroy the state of Israel, though it has caused a great amount of instability in the world. Overall, therefore, Al-Qaeda has been almost totally unsuccessful in achieving its stated aims.

KEY CONCEPTS

Disarmament – *the act of reducing, limiting, or abolishing weapons.*

Overall effectiveness of terrorist organisations

The overall conclusion about the effectiveness of these terrorist organisations is that none of them has been totally effective in achieving its aims, but that the PLO and the PIRA did partially achieve their aims in 1993 and 1998 respectively. They achieved this through certain sacrifices on their part, namely the commitment to **disarming** (PIRA) and a recognition that the state of Israel has a right to exist (PLO). It is of little surprise that the one organisation which has been the least successful in achieving its stated aims, Al-Qaeda, has been the one which has been the most unwilling to compromise.

VOICE YOUR OPINION!

Do you think that there are other ways of measuring the effectiveness of a terrorist organisation besides whether or not it has achieved its stated aims?

ACTIVITIES

In groups, organise and deliver a presentation about the overall effectiveness of one of these terrorist organisations. You should present this to the rest of the class using PowerPoint. Your presentation should include your rationale for determining whether or not the terrorist organisation is actually effective.

GradeStudio

Explain whether the PIRA has been successful. **[6 marks]**

Student's response

The clearest way to judge the success of the PIRA is through an analysis of what they had achieved by 1998. It is clear that the Good Friday Agreement of 1998 can be considered both a success and a failure for the PIRA.

On the one hand, it can be considered a success given that the Good Friday Agreement of 1998 led to a reduction of British influence in Northern Ireland, which was a key aim of the PIRA. Furthermore, the PIRA saw themselves as protectors of the Catholic community in Northern Ireland and the fact that this Agreement led to measures which benefited that community, such as the recognition of the Irish language and the establishment of the Northern Ireland Human Rights Commission, is also evidence of their success. Finally, the terms of the Agreement meant that some former members of the PIRA would be released from prison.

On the other hand, the fundamental aim of the PIRA, namely the creation of a united island of Ireland, was not recognised by this Agreement since it allowed Northern Ireland to maintain its independence until decided otherwise by a majority vote of its citizens. This is unlikely to happen given the considerable degree of support for Unionism in Northern Ireland.

Overall, it is clear that the PIRA had some success with the Good Friday Agreement owing to the fact that it represented an improvement upon the situation which they were confronted with upon their formation in 1969. However, the Agreement did not satisfy all of their stated aims and can therefore not be considered totally successful.

What is the significance of the Iraq War?

Why did the multinational force invade Iraq in 2003?

LEARNING OBJECTIVES

In this lesson you will:

- examine the key factors involved in the invasion of Iraq
- learn how to explain the strength of the multinational force's case and the most important causes of the invasion of Iraq.

GETTING STARTED

Look carefully at Colin Powell's speech below.

- What is his stated reason for the USA going to war in Iraq?
- What other reason is implied in his speech? *(Tip – Look carefully at the last couple of sentences)*

SOURCE A

We know that Saddam Hussein is determined to keep his weapons of mass destruction; he's determined to make more. Given Saddam Hussein's history of aggression...should we take the risk that he will not some day use these weapons...The United States will not and cannot run that risk to the American people. Leaving Saddam Hussein in possession of weapons of mass destruction for a few more months or years is not an option, not in a post-September 11th world.

Extract from a speech which US Secretary of State, Colin Powell, gave in February 2003 to the United Nations.

Background knowledge

On 20 March 2003, Iraq was invaded by a multinational force, which was largely dominated by the militaries of the USA and the UK. This is testament to the significant role played by both President Bush and Prime Minister **Blair** in bringing about the invasion. In the months preceding the invasion, they spelt out their case to the United Nations, and to their own **legislatures** and populations. But although the USA and UK played a central part, it is important to remember that the eventual invasion was carried out by a **multinational force**, with significant contributions from countries such as Poland, South Korea, Romania, Australia, El Salvador, Albania and Bulgaria, along with several others.

Weapons of mass destruction and terrorist links

Colin Powell's speech (Source A) makes the point that **Saddam Hussein**'s possession and continued pursuit of **Weapons of Mass Destruction** (WMDs) posed an immediate threat to the world. Despite the fact that the United Nations Weapons' Inspection Team had not finally concluded that there were WMDs in Iraq, the USA and UK were convinced that Saddam Hussein had them and were worried that he might use them.

One of the reasons why the USA believed that Saddam Hussein was capable of using these weapons was because of a strong belief that his regime had links with terrorist associations, including Al-Qaeda. Inevitably, the possibility was mentioned that Saddam Hussein might have had connections with the suicide attacks on the USA on September 11 2001. Although this is difficult to confirm or deny, it is certainly true that any link which was made between Saddam Hussein and the September 11 attacks served to strengthen the case for war.

One of the reasons why the legitimacy of the war in Iraq has been questioned to such an extent stems from the fact that, even after six years from the date of the invasion, it would seem that there were never any WMDs in Iraq and there is still no evidence to link Saddam Hussein with the 9/11 attacks.

KEY PEOPLE

Tony Blair – *Prime Minister of the United Kingdom, 1997–2007.*

Saddam Hussein – *President of Iraq, 1979–2003.*

VOICE YOUR OPINION!

You have just learned the reasons why the USA and the UK declared war on Iraq. Discuss in groups whether you think that this constitutes a justifiable reason to go to war with another country.

GradeStudio

Look back through this lesson and complete the question below:

'The multinational force had a strong case for going to war.' How far do you agree with this statement? Explain your answer. **[10 marks]**

Examiner's tip

The purpose of this task is to enable you to understand that any exam question such as this requires you to show both points of view using an appropriate amount of your own knowledge in order to get eight marks. To get a further two marks, you need to come to a judgement, based on the information already gathered, about *how far* you agree with the statement.

Other causes of the Iraq war

In the period following the invasion of Iraq, it turned out that no WMDs were found in Iraq, and no direct evidence came to light that Saddam Hussein had been directly involved with the suicide attacks of September 11. Naturally, this played a big part in the opposition to the Iraq War (see pages 136–137). There were, however, other factors which, though not stated at the time, might have had an influence on why the multinational force chose to invade Iraq.

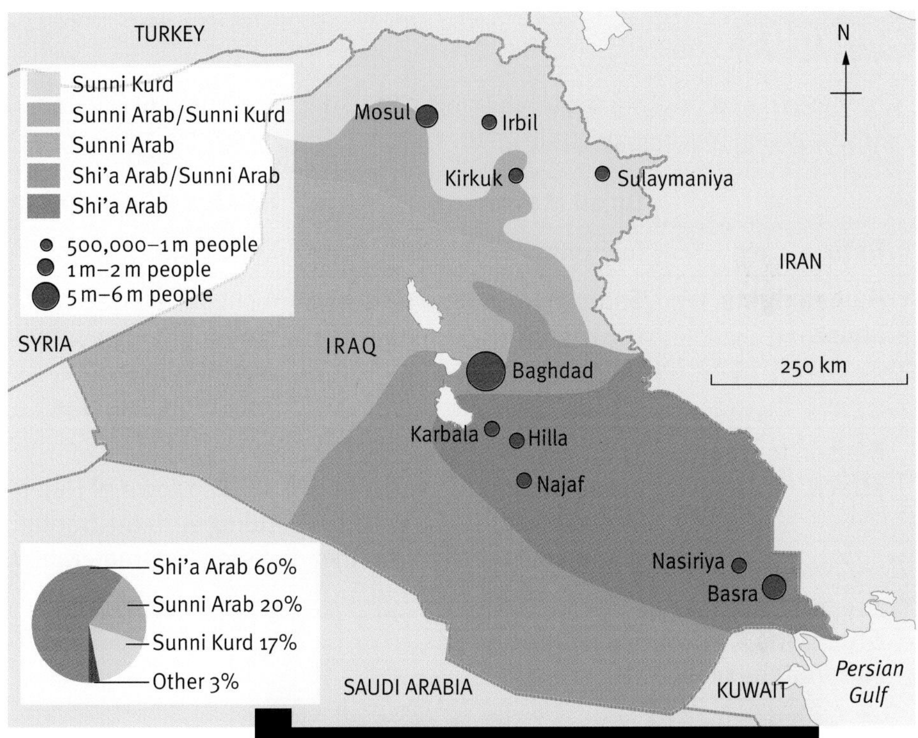

This map shows how the Shi'a Arabs, Sunni Arabs and Sunni Kurds mostly live separate from each other.

The role of religion and the divisions within Iraqi society

The major religion in Iraq is Islam. Out of the Muslims in Iraq, there are two main groups:

- **Shi'a Arabs** and **Sunni** Arabs inhabit two distinct regions in Iraq (see map). Both groups can be classified as Iraqi Arab Muslims.
- **Kurds** are mostly Sunni Muslims. They are not Arabs and are therefore different to Sunni Arabs. This group can be classified as Sunni Kurds.

Tensions have long existed between Shi'a Arab Muslims, Sunni Arab Muslims and Sunni Kurds. Saddam Hussein was a Sunni Arab Muslim. This contributed to the human rights abuses which took place in Iraq under Saddam Hussein against the Shi'a Arabs and the Kurds (see overleaf).

KEY WORDS

Arab – *an Arabic-speaking person who can trace his roots to the tribes of Arabia.*

Kurd – *a member of an Iranian-speaking ethnic group in Kurdistan. Most Kurds are Muslims.*

Legislature – *a representative assembly with the power to create, amend, reject and confirm laws.*

Multinational force – *a force composed of military elements of nations who have formed an alliance for some specific purpose.*

Shi'a – *second largest denomination of Islam*

Sunni – *largest denomination of Islam.*

Saddam Hussein's human rights record

During the reign of Saddam Hussein, there were many human rights abuses by the Iraqi government. There was mass murder, including the use of chemical weapons, high levels of torture, severe punishments such as the death penalty and amputations for criminal offences like theft and corruption. In addition, full political participation at the national level was restricted only to members of the Arab **Ba'ath Party**, which was loyal to Saddam Hussein. This meant that it was impossible for Iraqi citizens to change their government or establish new political parties unless they expressed support for the government. The main groups who suffered most from Saddam Hussein's regime were the Kurds and the Shi'a Muslims.

VOICE YOUR OPINION!

People in Iraq did not have any political rights. This meant that many could neither vote nor stand in elections. How important is it to live in a society which has political rights for its citizens?

KEY WORDS

Ba'ath Party – *the political party of Saddam Hussein which held power in Iraq from 1968 until the invasion of Iraq in 2003.*

ACTIVITIES

Compare the political rights which Iraqis had under the regime of Saddam Hussein with the political rights of citizens in a modern democratic state.

	Dujail Massacre	**Halabja Poison Gas Attack**	**Al-Anfal Campaign**
Date	July 1982	March 1988	1986–89
Human rights abuse	Saddam Hussein ordered the killing of 148 people of the town of Dujail	A chemical attack left around 5000 people dead and 7000 people with long-term illnesses	A campaign of extermination against the Kurds which left over 50,000 civilians dead
Reason for the attack	There was an attempted assassination of Saddam Hussein near Dujail which was blamed on those in the town	Saddam believed that the Kurdish town of Halabja was siding with the Iranians during the Iraq–Iran War	Saddam wanted to rid Iraq of the Kurds. This was an act of **genocide**
Group who suffered the most	Shi'a Arabs	Kurds	Kurds

HISTORY DETECTIVE

What is the link between the Dujail Massacre and 30 December 2006?

Iraq's oil reserves

Another possible factor is that the invasion of Iraq enabled the USA to have greater access to and control over Iraqi oil. It is certainly true that the more control Saddam Hussein had over **Middle East** oil, the more damage he could do to the economies of Western countries, especially since Iraq has one of the largest reserves of petroleum in the world. However, others have rejected this as a cause of war, arguing that if the USA were simply concerned about oil they could have made a deal with Saddam Hussein rather than go to war with him.

VOICE YOUR OPINION!

Would it ever be right to go to war for the sake of oil? Discuss this question in pairs.

Spreading democracy

Since the invasion, Iraq has become a **democracy** and therefore stands out as one of the few democracies in the Middle East. One stated reason for the invasion of Iraq was that the USA and the UK wanted to make that region of the world more democratic. Some of the reasons for this include the fact that democracies are less likely to go to war with each other and more likely to trade with each other.

Sources B and C clearly suggest that George W. Bush and Tony Blair were firm believers in the benefits of democracy. Some, however, will argue that there are many other countries that are not democracies but do not get invaded by the USA or the UK. Nevertheless, Iraq has indeed since become a democracy (see page 143), although whether or not the desire to spread democracy was a genuine cause of the invasion is a matter for debate.

SOURCE 

The establishment of a free Iraq at the heart of the Middle East will be a watershed event in the global democratic revolution.

An extract from a speech which US President, George W. Bush, gave on 6 November 2003 to the US Chamber of Commerce.

SOURCE 

And let the future government of Iraq be given the chance to begin the process of uniting the nation's disparate groups, on a democratic basis, respecting human rights.

An extract from a speech given by Tony Blair on 18 March 2003 to the House of Commons.

SOURCE D

A smiling Prime Minister Blair and President Bush hold a joint press conference prior to the Iraq War.

ACTIVITIES

1. Why do the different dates of Sources B and C matter so much when analysing how far the desire to spread democracy was a cause of the Iraq invasion?
2. The argument of spreading democracy has been mentioned far more since the invasion than it was before. What might the reasons for this be?

KEY CONCEPTS

Democracy – *a form of government where supreme power is held by the people under a free electoral system.*

Genocide – *deliberate and systematic destruction of an ethnic, racial, religious, or national group.*

Middle East – *a loose term to describe countries in Western Asia and parts of North Africa.*

GradeStudio

Look back through the previous two lessons and complete the essay question below:

'The most important reason why the multinational force invaded was the oil in Iraq.' Do you agree? Explain your answer. **[10 marks]**

Was the invasion legal? Why was there opposition in many countries to the invasion?

LEARNING OBJECTIVES

In this lesson you will:

- examine the different reasons why there was such opposition to the war
- learn how the reasons for the opposition to the war have changed over time.

Opposition to the Iraq War

Before the war had even begun, anti-war groups organised public protests across the world. On 15 February 2003, approximately eight million people protested against the war, with some three million people demonstrating in Rome and around two million in London. In some Arab countries, demonstrations were organised by the government. Since the invasion, there have continued to be anti-war protests in both Britain and the rest of the world, particularly on the anniversary of the Iraq War.

Was the Iraq War legal or not?

The Iraq War has many supporters and detractors. The question of whether the war was legal has often been a huge factor in determining whether people have supported the invasion. The US and UK governments were aware of this and strenuously put forward their different legal justifications for war.

The USA's legal justification: preemptive self-defence

The USA's justification was based on preemptive self-defence. This is a slight variation to the established rule in international law which allows a state to go to war to defend itself from attack, as President Bush argued that Iraq's actions, together with the growth of weapons of mass destruction, posed a threat to the USA which warranted justification. In short, Bush argued that the USA would be under threat unless Iraq was invaded, even though Iraq had not physically attacked the USA. This so-called Bush doctrine has its detractors, among them Kofi Annan, who has argued that it would inevitably lead to a breakdown in international order because any country could see a potential attack from another country and use this as a basis for war. Some also questioned how much of a threat Iraq posed to the USA given that there was little evidence it possessed weapons of mass destruction.

GETTING STARTED

Do you think it is justified for one country to go to war with another based on the fear that it might one day attack them or one of their allies?

SOURCE A

An anti-war protest in London, 15 February 2003, just a few weeks before the invasion of Iraq in 2003.

The UK's legal justification: authorised by United Nations Resolution 1441

The UK argument was slightly more complex and relied on previous United Nations Resolutions. In Resolution 687, agreed in 1991, the United Nations Security Council imposed obligations on Iraq to eliminate its weapons of mass destruction to restore international peace and security in the region: any breach of this resolution by Iraq would warrant the use of force. Resolution 1441, agreed 11 years later in 2002, witnessed the Security Council unanimously agree that Iraq had failed to comply with Resolution 687 and must therefore face severe consequences. Therefore, the UK government argued that since Iraq was in breach of 687 it warranted the use of force under Resolution 1441.

However, many have argued that the UK government should have sought another UN Security Council resolution after 1441 which specifically authorised war against Iraq, rather than assume that criticism of Iraq's current position in Resolution 1441 amounted to a legal basis for war. This formed the basis of several countries' opposition to the war. Lord Bingham, a former senior UK Law Lord, argued that there was not enough evidence to suggest that Iraq was failing to comply with Resolution 687, given the progress and findings of Hans Blix's team of weapons inspectors.

Conclusion

Any judgement of the legality of the war depends on the interpretation of the law. It might depend on something like whether or not military force was the obvious implication of Resolution 1441, or whether an undeniably evil dictator with a history of aggression and a poor record of honesty should be considered a threat in an age of increasingly available weapons of mass destruction. These answers are not straightforward. The legal basis for war from both the USA and the UK has faced a great deal of criticism but it is something that both countries have always considered very important as a rationale for the invasion.

Other reasons for opposition to the Iraq War before the invasion

There was an immense feeling of opposition to the war from millions of people. Apart from doubts about the war's legality, there were two other main reasons for opposition to the Iraq War before the invasion.

No WMDs had yet been found

On the eve of the invasion, Hans Blix reported that he had so far been unable to find any WMDs in Iraq. Although he refused to rule out the possibility that some might one day be found, it was clear that many countries, such as France, China and Russia, felt that he should have been given more time to finish his report. Some went even further and claimed that Bush and Blair had deliberately inflated intelligence about Iraq's weapons in order to justify an invasion of the country.

Concern for Iraqi civilians

Opponents of the invasion also claimed that it would lead to the deaths of thousands of coalition soldiers as well as Iraqi soldiers and civilians, and that it would damage peace and stability throughout the region and the wider world.

Reasons for opposition to the Iraq War after the invasion

Opponents of the 2003 Iraq War remain unhappy with the invasion for the three reasons stated above. However, there have been more recent criticisms of the Iraq War after the invasion.

The war diverted attention away from the real threat of terrorism

Since the invasion of Iraq, the world has witnessed bombings in Istanbul, Madrid, London, Jordan and Algiers, the bombing of the Danish Embassy in Pakistan and the attacks in Mumbai. Al-Qaeda was suspected of being involved in most of these attacks. Some intelligence reports have argued that the problem of terrorism is not going away and that the preoccupation with Iraq is only giving the terrorists more freedom and motivation to act.

Inadequate planning from the USA

Although the invasion of Iraq was completed with relative ease, there has been a great deal of criticism of the lack of adequate planning for a post-war Iraq. Only 130,000 US troops were committed, together with 45,000 UK troops. The multinational force has not always had sufficient backing to cope with the demands placed on it. There have also been more serious charges of strategic miscalculations by senior figures in the Pentagon, along with inadequate equipment for the troops. **Paul Wolfowitz**, the former US Deputy Secretary of Defence, has even acknowledged that mistakes have been made.

HISTORY DETECTIVE

Use the internet to check how the following four actions and people are linked together:

1. The UK government's claim that Saddam Hussein could deploy WMDs within 45 minutes of an order to use them
2. Andrew Gilligan
3. The death of Dr David Kelly
4. Hutton Inquiry.

KEY CONCEPTS

Legitimate – *in accordance with the law or the expressed will of the people.*

KEY PEOPLE

Paul Wolfowitz – *US Deputy Secretary of Defence, 2001–05.*

Explain why there was opposition to the Iraq War. **[6 marks]**

Examiner's tip

The most important thing to remember in any six-mark question is to ensure that you do not just describe a factor but also explain it in sufficient detail.

How was the invasion completed so quickly?

LEARNING OBJECTIVES

In this lesson you will:

- examine the different reasons why the invasion of Iraq was completed so quickly
- learn how to explain which reason was the most important.

GETTING STARTED

The **United Nations Security Council** (UNSC) has the power to declare war. It has 15 members, of whom five (France, China, Russia, the UK and the USA) are permanent while the ten other member states are elected for two-year terms.

Any resolution brought before the UNSC needs a majority vote to be passed, but if any of the permanent powers use their veto, this can terminate the resolution.

Identify whether each of the following statements are true or false:

- A UN resolution would fail if China vetoed it.
- A UN resolution would pass if 12 members of the UNSC, including the five permanent members, supported it.
- A resolution would definitely pass if it was approved by all five permanent members.
- A resolution would pass if everyone supported it except France.

VOICE YOUR OPINION!

The UK prime minister, Tony Blair, did not need Parliament's approval to declare war, but on 18 March 2003 the House of Commons voted by 412 to 149 to allow the UK government to ensure Iraq's disarmament using 'all means necessary'. Why do you think Blair allowed Parliament to vote on this issue when he did not need to?

The role of the United Nations

The United Nations played an extremely significant role in the background to the 2003 invasion of Iraq but ultimately played no role in the invasion itself. This dramatic set of circumstances came about as a result of a four-step process.

Step 1: Bush approaches the UNSC

In October 2002, the US Congress passed a law which allowed President Bush to use military force against Iraq. This paved the way for the US president to approach the United Nations Security Council.

Step 2: The USA and UK draft UNSC resolution

The USA and the UK jointly drafted UNSC Resolution 1441 which offered Iraq a final opportunity to comply with its disarmament obligations. On 8 November 2002, the resolution was passed unanimously by the UNSC with a 15–0 vote. Even Iraq agreed to this resolution and, in November 2002, it allowed the United Nations weapons inspectors, led by **Hans Blix**, to visit sites where WMD production was suspected.

TIMELINE
The war officially begins. The first missiles and air strikes target Baghdad. They are aimed at high-level Iraqi government officials though civilian buildings are also hit.
US forces take control of Saddam International Airport
Mar 2003
Apr 2003
The first 'friendly fire' incidents by the US military on allied British personnel occurred when a British Tornado fighter plane was hit by an American Patriot missile. Less than two weeks into the war, seven British soldiers had died from 'friendly fire'.
US forces reach the outskirts of Baghdad
Baghdad falls to US forces, ending Saddam Hussein's 24-year rule in Iraq. This is famously symbolised when a huge iron statue of Saddam Hussein is brought down (see page 140).

Step 3: UNSC refuses second resolution

The UNSC refused to agree to a second resolution which would allow for an invasion of Iraq. This was because most of the countries which voted in favour of Resolution 1441 thought that if there was any further Iraqi breach of its disarmament obligations, the matter would return to the UNSC. Furthermore, Hans Blix and his inspection team had failed to find any WMDs in Iraq. This prompted the president of France, **Jacques Chirac**, to declare on 10 March that France would veto any resolution which would automatically lead to war. This meant that the argument for a second resolution, which would have authorised an invasion of Iraq, was effectively abandoned – the United Nations would have no part in any invasion of Iraq.

Step 4: The USA and UK decide to go it alone

The USA and UK were still convinced of the need to invade Iraq. Although Hans Blix and his team had failed to find any WMDs, it was proving difficult to work out what Iraq had done with known chemical and biological stockpiles. However, Bush and Blair were not going to let the United Nations prevent them from applying what they believed was the necessary pressure on Saddam Hussein. Their role, therefore, was crucial in pursuing military action against Iraq after the Blix report had failed to yield anything concrete. On 16 March, Bush, Blair and the Spanish Prime Minister, **José María Aznar**, gave the Iraqi government a day to provide evidence that they had disarmed. A few days later, all three countries, along with several others who made up the multinational force, were at war with Iraq.

KEY CONCEPTS

Friendly fire – *fire during wartime from one's own side or allied forces.*

United Nations Security Council – *the part of the United Nations which is in charge of maintaining international peace and security.*

KEY PEOPLE

José María Aznar – *Prime Minister of Spain, 1996–2004.*

Hans Blix – *Chairman of the United Nations Monitoring, Verification and Inspection Commission, 2000–03.*

Jacques Chirac – *President of France, 1995–2007.*

ACTIVITIES

Was it right for the USA and the UK to bypass the UN? In your groups, discuss whether or not the USA and the UK were right to go ahead with the war without authority from the United Nations.

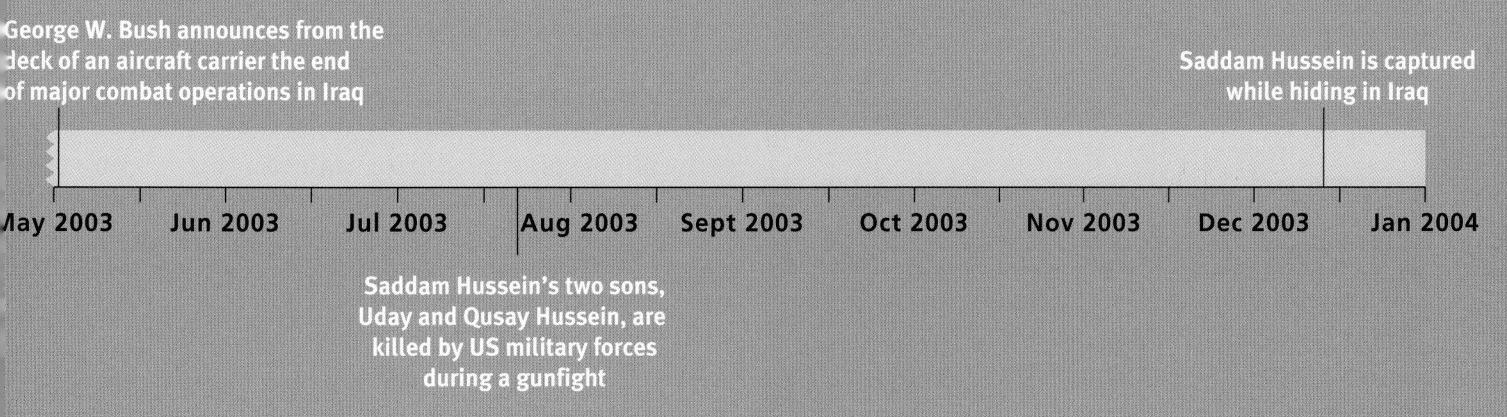

George W. Bush announces from the deck of an aircraft carrier the end of major combat operations in Iraq
Saddam Hussein is captured while hiding in Iraq
May 2003
Jun 2003
Jul 2003
Aug 2003
Sept 2003
Oct 2003
Nov 2003
Dec 2003
Jan 2004
Saddam Hussein's two sons, Uday and Qusay Hussein, are killed by US military forces during a gunfight

SOURCE A

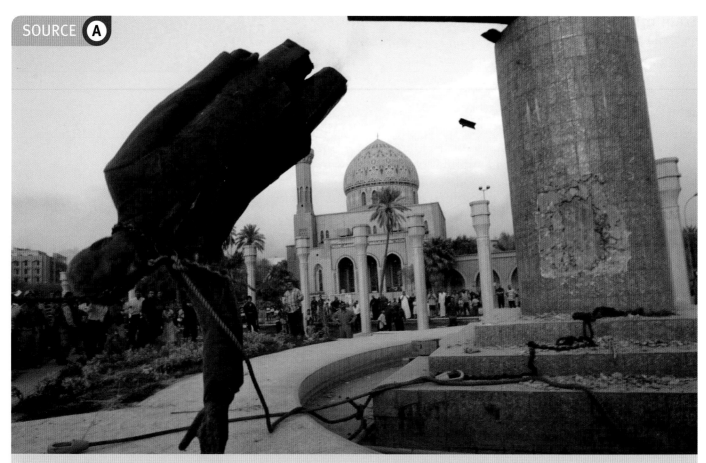

The pulling down of a statue of Saddam Hussein by US troops in Baghdad on 9 April 2003 marked the symbolic overthrow of the Iraqi leader.

Describe the main events in the invasion of Iraq in 2003. **[4 marks]**

Examiner's tip

In order to get the four marks, you need to ensure that you make at least two points backed up by some detail. A point which is supported by some detail ought to read like this: *On 9 April, Baghdad fell to US forces. This was symbolised when US troops pulled down a statue of Saddam Hussein.*

ACTIVITIES

As with many invasions, the first major part of the campaign was an aerial attack. Make a list of all the advantages and disadvantages of beginning an invasion by dropping bombs over a target rather than committing ground troops.

Why the Iraq invasion was completed so quickly

Baghdad was under the control of the USA less than a month after the invasion first began. This reflected the strength of the USA and the weakness of Iraq. Some of the factors behind the swift victory were expected, such as the strength of the US military, but there were other factors too, such as the poor leadership of the Iraqi military.

Strength of the US and UK military

The most obvious reason for the speed of victory was the strength of the US and UK military. Crucially, they had supreme control of the air during the early stages of the conflict. They pinpointed targets and destroyed them before Iraqi ground troops even arrived. This prevented Iraqi **mobilisation** of their air force, which might have held up the progress of the multinational force. In addition, the main battle tanks of the UK and US proved more than able to counter the Iraqi opposition.

Iraqi military weakness

Throughout the 1990s, Iraq suffered as a result of severe **economic sanctions** which were placed on it. This harmed its economy which meant that it could not develop its military power as it would have liked. Unsurprisingly, therefore, the Iraqi army was extremely ill-equipped in comparison to the US and UK forces. For instance, it was unable to mobilise its air force to attempt a defence of its territory. On the ground, it possessed tanks which were outdated. It was clearly not in a strong enough position to withstand the military might of the US- and UK-dominated multinational force.

SOURCE B

The bombing of Baghdad in March 2003. This formed part of the six-week 'Shock and Awe' phase of the invasion (19 March–1 May 2003).

Poor morale among Iraqi forces

The previous two paragraphs show how far the odds were stacked against Iraq even before the invasion began. It proved an extremely difficult task to lift the spirits of the Iraqi forces, and throughout the conflict they suffered from poor morale. There were numerous reports of entire Iraqi army units disappearing into the crowds upon the approach of invading troops, or even surrendering to the US and UK forces. This was to a large extent due to their obvious fear of defeat but the low morale was sometimes brought about as a result of pressure from the US **Central Intelligence Agency (CIA)**.

Poor leadership of the Iraqi military

The final reason why the Iraqi invasion was completed so quickly was the inadequate leadership of the Iraqi military. Saddam Hussein refused to believe that the USA would invade a **sovereign** country, and he was therefore not as prepared to deal with the invasion as he could have been. In addition, the Iraqi army was hampered by incompetent leadership throughout the invasion. For example, Qusay Hussein's irregular movement of troops made it difficult to defend Baghdad, which fell soon after the invasion had begun.

GradeStudio

'The most important reason why the invasion of Iraq was completed so quickly was the weak leadership of the Iraqi military?' Do you agree? Explain your answer. **[10 marks]**

Examiner's tip

One approach which you can take with this answer is to try to link together the different reasons. For instance, there are obvious links to be made between the poor morale of the Iraqi soldiers and the strength of the US military. Also, do not forget to come to a judgement at the end of your answer which is supported by clear explanation.

VOICE YOUR OPINION!

The Iraqis suffered as a result of not having adequate leadership. In pairs, discuss how you could be a good leader in time of war. What types of things would you have to consider? What issues would you be likely to face?

KEY CONCEPTS

Economic sanctions – *measures applied by one or more countries to another country, including tariffs, trade barriers and import or export quotas.*

Mobilisation – *act of assembling troops and supplies and making them ready for war.*

Sovereign – *independent of any outside authority.*

KEY WORDS

Central Intelligence Agency – *a US organisation which collects and analyses information about foreign governments, corporations and persons.*

What were the consequences of the invasion inside Iraq and internationally, and was the invasion of Iraq a success?

LEARNING OBJECTIVES

In this lesson you will:

- examine the consequences of the Iraq War for those living in Iraq, the multinational force and internationally
- learn to make links between the different consequences of the Iraq War, to be able to explain the overall consequences of the Iraq War in a structured and organised way.

GETTING STARTED

The Iraqi government has estimated that by the summer of 2008 over 150,000 Iraqis had been killed as a result of the Iraq War. In pairs, consider the following questions: Does that figure come as a shock to you? Does that change your mind about anything connected with the war? Why is that number so high?

The post-invasion condition of Iraq

Breakdown in law and order

While the headline-grabbing message soon after the invasion was that Iraq had been liberated, the reality was that law and order had quickly broken down. There was a significant amount of looting accompanied by a great deal of violence, which rendered areas such as Baghdad and Basra extremely unsafe. Hospitals were being targeted and stripped of supplies and there were numerous reports of rape and murder in the city. This led to a humanitarian crisis since it became too dangerous for United Nations Relief Agencies to provide the essential humanitarian aid. The resulting conditions in Iraq meant that Iraqis were more likely to direct their anger at the Coalition forces.

The Iraqi insurgency

Although the fall of Saddam Hussein was met with a great deal of celebration in Iraq, many groups, such as the Sunni Arabs, remained loyal to the old regime and were uncertain of their future in a new, largely Shi'a-dominated Iraq. Shortly after the invasion had begun, these groups began to attack the US-led multinational force in Iraq and the new Iraqi government. This type of violence became known as the Iraqi **insurgency**.

The aims of the insurgents were to get the Americans and British out of their country and to disrupt any efforts by the new Iraqi government to establish itself. The insurgency has been helped by foreign Islamist volunteers, some of whom might be connected to Al-Qaeda, and by the fact that both the Iraqi army and the police force were disbanded. The insurgents' method of attack has usually been through the bombing of market places and other locations by suicide attacks and roadside car bombs. They have increasingly targeted the civilian population of Iraq, particularly the Shi'a community. The 2007 Qahtaniya and Jazeera bombings were the deadliest of the insurgency, with 796 people killed in one day.

KEY CONCEPTS

Boycott – *abstention from using, buying, or dealing with someone or some organisation as a means of protest.*

Constitution – *rules and principles which are used as a basis for governing.*

Insurgency – *violent internal uprising against a sovereign government which lacks the organisation of a revolution.*

Interim government – *a government which is set up to hold power until a permanent government can be established.*

Referendum – *direct vote in which the people are asked to either accept or reject a particular proposal.*

Transitional government – *an elected government which acts as a bridge between the interim and the permanent government.*

The methods used by the Americans and British against the insurgency

The most direct consequence of the invasion for the multinational force has been the number of casualties. In 2008, the total stood at around 4500 soldiers of the multinational force killed in action since March 2003, and this includes over 4000 US soldiers. The large majority of these soldiers were

SOURCE A

The scene of a car bomb in Baghdad, 14 June 2004.

killed not during the invasion but during the insurgency, which has led to counter-insurgency operations of immense proportions. The aim of these operations has been to capture the weapons, materials and people who pose a threat to the multinational forces as well as the Iraqi security forces. There has also been a focus on hunting down the remaining leaders of the former regime. On 22 July 2003, US troops killed Saddam's two sons, Uday Hussein and Qusay Hussein, during a raid. Saddam Hussein himself was captured on 14 December 2003, tried by the Iraqi **interim government**, and executed on 30 December 2006.

Human rights abuses of the multinational force

The occupation of Iraq has lasted for over five years and has seen some of the heaviest fighting since Vietnam, which has had a devastating impact on the multinational force. To make matters even worse, it has also brought shame on certain parts of the US and UK military because of alleged human rights abuses. The most infamous example was the reports of torture and prisoner abuse of Iraqi prisoners in Abu Ghraib prison. In 2004, accusations of abuse, torture and homicide were directed at certain members of the US army. The US Department of Defense responded by removing 17 soldiers and officers from duty. Seven soldiers were charged with dereliction of duty, maltreatment, aggravated assault and battery and were convicted by a military court, sentenced to prison, and dishonourably discharged from military service.

The exposure of the actions of a small minority of soldiers has made the task of the multinational force far more difficult. It has helped to turn public opinion in Iraq and other countries even more against the war and the occupation.

Was the invasion of Iraq a success?

In military terms, the invasion was successful because it took President Bush just over 40 days to declare an end to major combat operations in Iraq. However, the overwhelming majority of the Coalition Forces' casualties came after the completion of the initial invasion. Also, the unexpected momentum of the Iraqi insurgency increased the strain on US and UK resources, which has hindered progress in Afghanistan. Newly-elected American President Barack Obama has led calls for a shift in focus towards the war in Afghanistan.

In terms of uniting the international community, there were numerous countries that comprised the multinational force, and the USA and the UK now have another potential ally in the Middle East, which could be of vital strategic importance. However, many key countries (namely France, Russia and China) did not support the war, and America's actions have strained its relations with the EU and the United Nations. However, this might change under President Obama since he opposed the war in 2003.

Finally, the invasion can also be categorised as a success because it removed the dictatorship of Saddam Hussein's Ba'ath Party and paved the way for democratic government in Iraq. However, many Sunni Muslims have felt alienated from the new regime and this has been one of the main factors behind the insurgency. In addition, the new democratic government of Iraq has not met certain expectations, particularly with women's rights.

	Date	Purpose
Operation Phantom Fury	8 November 2004	Joint US–Iraqi offensive against the Iraqi insurgency stronghold in the city of Fallujah
Operation New Market	25 May 2005	Sweep of an area near Haditha to rid the Euphrates river bank of Iraqi insurgents
Operation Phantom Strike	15 August 2007	A major offensive launched by the multinational force to disrupt Al-Qaeda and Shi'a extremist operations in Iraq

The issue of how far the invasion of Iraq was a success depends on how one judges the success of an invasion. It is clear the invasion was more successful in battle than in victory.

Everyday life for the Iraqi people

It is certainly true to say that everyday life for the Iraqi people has changed dramatically since the invasion. In many respects, this has been a negative change, with machine-gun fire and roadside bombs affecting them on a near-daily basis. The six-figure death toll of Iraqi civilians makes it likely that practically every single person in Iraq will know someone who has died in this conflict. However, there have been some positive changes in the lives of Iraqi people. It is now a more pluralist society, which in the fullness of time will allow Iraqis to gain exposure to different ideas and opportunities. There have been some modest changes in granting more freedom and independence to Iraqi women. For instance, in the December 2005 elections to the Council of Representatives, 68 women were elected.

VOICE YOUR OPINION!

Although most people would agree that the human rights abuses committed by some members of the multinational force were inexcusable, not everyone is so convinced that it was right to publicise the abuses. Discuss in groups the advantages and disadvantages of this publicity.

GradeStudio

Explain why the invasion of Iraq has proved so devastating for the multinational force. **[6 marks]**

The international consequences of the Iraq War

The effects of the Iraq War outside Iraq can be divided into three main categories:

- Loss of influence for the USA and the UK.
- A decline in security for people in certain parts of the world.
- A positive effect on certain countries in the Middle East.

Loss of influence for the USA and UK

Many people both in Iraq and in the wider world believe that the American-led occupation of Iraq has done more harm than good. As a result of this, the governments of the USA and the UK have lost popular support at home, and their traditional alliances with and influences among other states have also been damaged. For instance, their standing has been decreased in the United Nations, a factor that is likely to seriously affect their ability to exert international pressure in the future should similar situations arise.

Decline in security

The Iraq War has inevitably diverted attention and resources from the threat posed by Al-Qaeda. The major bombings in Madrid (11 March 2004) and London (7 July 2005), as well as the attempted London bombing (21 July 2005), arguably suggest that the Iraq War has played a role in motivating and reinforcing extremism. Although the links between these terrorist cells and Al-Qaeda are inconclusive, it is clear that most participants had only recently been converted to extremism, having no previous record of terrorist activity. In group or individual statements, those responsible directly associated their actions with the recent wars and the target nations' involvement in them. Some have suggested that the Iraq War has increased the membership of Al-Qaeda and the passions of radical Muslims, whereas others argue that the

HISTORY DETECTIVE

Investigate the effect of the Madrid bombings on the Spanish government of José María Aznar. Think about the timing of the bombings and the different interpretations of who was to blame and why that might be significant.

SOURCE B

This double-decker bus was ripped apart during a suicide attack in London on 7 July 2005. The suicide bomber was an 18-year-old English Muslim. He killed 13 passengers.

Iraq War is not the reason for this terrorist activity but simply used as an excuse by terrorists to spread fear and unrest.

Change in the Middle East

The transition to democracy in Iraq has had an impact on neighbouring countries like Saudi Arabia which, in 2005, held its first **municipal** elections to choose half of the new council members in Riyadh. The war in Iraq also caused the USA to withdraw its troops stationed in Saudi Arabia in August 2003; their presence in the country for the past decade had caused a great deal of anger there.

The Iraq War also caused a significant amount of damage to Iraqi oil production. This is one of the factors that led to a shortage in the supply of oil, resulting in higher global prices for oil. This has dramatically increased the importance of the Middle East, given that five out of the six countries with the largest oil reserves are Saudi Arabia, Iran, Iraq, Kuwait and the United Arab Emirates.

KEY WORDS

Municipal – *relating to the local government of a small geographical area, usually a town.*

'The most important consequence of the invasion of Iraq was the Iraqi insurgency.' How far do you agree with this statement? Explain your answer. **[10 marks]**

Examiner's tip

In your answer, try to organise the consequences into the three different categories of Iraq, the USA and internationally. In addition, try to link together the different consequences of the invasion, such as the fact that the Iraqi insurgency has caused large numbers of casualties for multinational troops.

A new world? 1948–2005

Here is an example of a question that requires you to explain the meaning of a political cartoon. This is a common type of question in Unit A971. The skill you require is to put the source into historical context by using your knowledge of the topic combined with details from the source.

What is the message of this cartoon? Use details of the cartoon and your own knowledge to explain your answer. **[7 marks]**

Examiner's tip

In order to get the highest levels in any question it is a good idea to get to know the mark scheme. If you know how you are going to be assessed, you will understand what skills you need to demonstrate when answering different types of questions. Have a look at the mark scheme before thinking about how you would answer the question.

Source A

A cartoon from a British newspaper in January 1990 showing the communist hammer and sickle in tears.

Look at the example below and think about how the candidate moves up these levels:

	Examiner's comment
In the source I can see a hammer and a sickle in tears.	When using a source like the one shown it is tempting to give the examiner a list of things you can see. These kinds of answers are only using the source for information and rarely get beyond level one.
The message of this source is that the communist ideas within the Soviet Union are being destroyed. The Soviet Union is beginning to break up.	This answer is at level two. To develop it you need to support your ideas with either details from the source or your own knowledge on this topic. The trick is to try to use the source to make judgements or give opinions about what it means. This is called making inferences and is a skill that you need to apply in both papers. Here is an answer that does this. The inferences have been highlighted.
The message of this source is that the Soviet Union is being destroyed. This is represented in the source by the fact that the hammer and sickle are no long entwined, but have been separated and are now showed back to back, weeping.	This is a good level three answer. To develop it to level four you should also put the source into its historical context using your own knowledge.

Try to write your own level four answer using the mark scheme to help you.

Mark scheme

Level 1: Describes features of the cartoon.
Level 2: Describes the message of the cartoon.
Level 3: Explains the message of the cartoon supported with details from the source **OR** own knowledge.
Level 4: Explains the message of the cartoon supported with details from the source **AND** own knowledge.

Germany, 1918–45

Overview of 1918–45

This study is in four parts, the first of which deals with the Germany that emerged from the First World War. It was a much weaker country than the one that had entered the war in 1914. The army was defeated, the economy was in ruins, and law and order was coming under serious threat as a number of extremist groups tried to seize power.

The first of the four parts deals with the Weimar Republic. This is the name given to the period of German history between 1918 and 1933. The would-be leaders of the new Germany got together in the small German town of Weimar in 1918 and put together a constitution that made the country one of the most democratic of its time. However, the republic soon ran into difficulties. It was highly unpopular because of its association with the hated Treaty of Versailles, and it soon faced uprisings in Berlin and Munich. In 1923 the failure to keep up reparations payments led to the French occupation of the Ruhr and the rapid spiralling of prices into hyperinflation.

GETTING STARTED

In groups of three, categorise the timeline covering the period 1918–45 into three themes: social, political and economic. Make sure you understand the meaning of these before you start the activity. When you have decided which events are which, use the text of the chapter to add more detail and events. You should end up with a thorough timeline right at the beginning of your work.

The work of Gustav Stresemann helped restore the German economy and improve relationships with foreign countries. Loans negotiated by Stresemann with the USA helped pay the continuing war reparations demanded by the French government. Matters improved further in 1925 when Germany, France and Belgium signed the Locarno Pact, in which the three countries agreed to respect their common borders – this represented a big step forward for Germany. An even greater step came

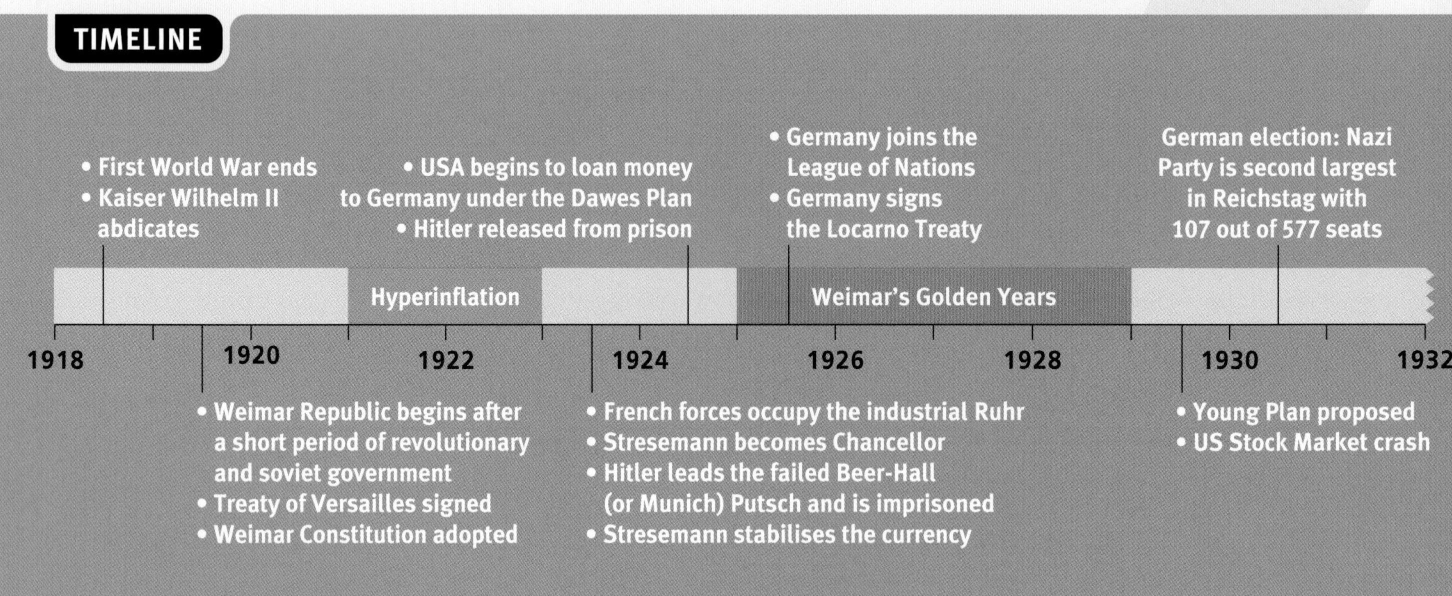

TIMELINE
• First World War ends
• Kaiser Wilhelm II abdicates
• USA begins to loan money to Germany under the Dawes Plan
• Hitler released from prison
• Germany joins the League of Nations
• Germany signs the Locarno Treaty
German election: Nazi Party is second largest in Reichstag with 107 out of 577 seats
Hyperinflation
Weimar's Golden Years
1918
1920
1922
1924
1926
1928
1930
1932
• Weimar Republic begins after a short period of revolutionary and soviet government
• Treaty of Versailles signed
• Weimar Constitution adopted
• French forces occupy the industrial Ruhr
• Stresemann becomes Chancellor
• Hitler leads the failed Beer-Hall (or Munich) Putsch and is imprisoned
• Stresemann stabilises the currency
• Young Plan proposed
• US Stock Market crash

the following year when Germany was accepted into the League of Nations, and in 1928 Germany was one of 60 countries to sign the Kellogg–Briand Pact formally renouncing war as an instrument of foreign policy.

At last Germany's international standing was repaired, and the country entered a period of prosperity reflected in notable achievements in art and culture, with painters such as George Grosz and Hannah Hoech, and the Bauhaus movement in architecture and style. However, the prosperity was based on loans from the USA, and once these were withdrawn the German economy collapsed. You will be asked to make judgements on the strength of the republic and whether it was doomed from the start.

The focus of the second section begins with the consequences of the Wall Street Crash that brought economic ruin to Germany and increased support for extremist parties such as the Nazis. You will be asked to explain how a small right-wing political party with its roots in the beer halls of Munich was able to rise to power in only 15 years. Analysis of Hitler's role in the rise of the Nazi Party will be key to this investigation. You will explore to what extent his extreme ideas reflected the wishes of the German people, and how he was able to take full advantage of any event that might lend itself to heaping blame on the Jews. Despite spending nine months in prison, Hitler was able to dominate Germany by 1933 and rule as dictator until 1945.

The third and fourth sections investigate the Nazi regime in detail. In 1933 Adolf Hitler became chancellor and set about restoring Germany's greatness. Unemployment was virtually eliminated; roads, schools and hospitals were built; people saved in national savings schemes to buy cars or go on foreign holidays; and conditions at work were improved. Under Nazi rule the economy improved and stability was restored, as behind the propaganda machine of the Nazi Party Hitler was able to do as he liked. Success came and Hitler regained many of the territories Germany had lost at the Treaty of Versailles; he was regarded by many as a great statesman. But these successes came at a high price. Hitler's totalitarian regime limited personal freedom and dealt harshly with any opposition, potential or real. It also carried out policies based on the Nazi belief in the supremacy of the Aryan race, with horrific consequences for Slavs, gypsies and, especially, the Jews. Membership of the Nazi Party was necessary in practice for anyone who wanted to get on in life, while the Nazis instituted medals for mothers with large families, clubs for boys and girls to practise their skills and a school curriculum rewritten to reflect Nazi ideology. You will be asked to evaluate whether the German people were better off under Nazi rule and how the approaching war affected their lives.

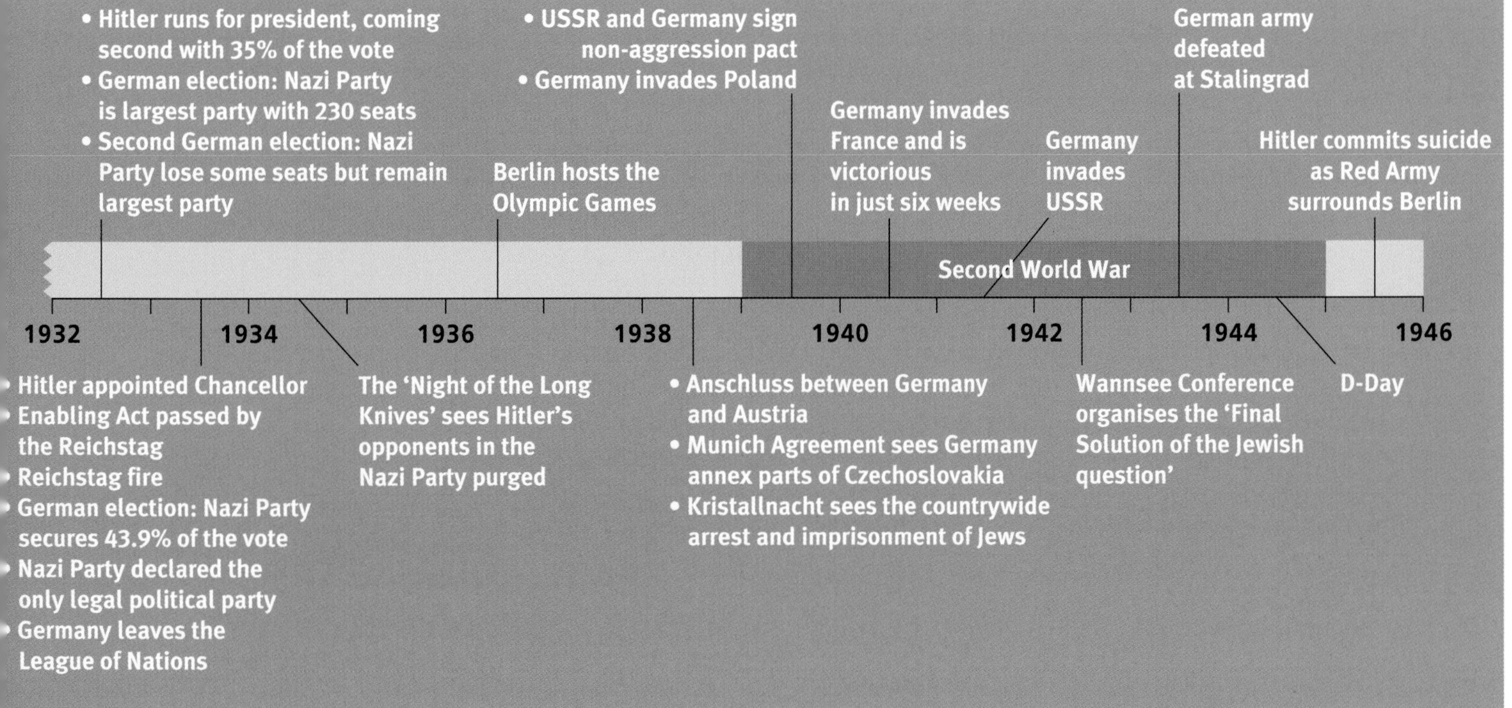

• Hitler runs for president, coming second with 35% of the vote
• German election: Nazi Party is largest party with 230 seats
• Second German election: Nazi Party lose some seats but remain largest party
Berlin hosts the Olympic Games
• USSR and Germany sign non-aggression pact
• Germany invades Poland
Germany invades France and is victorious in just six weeks
Germany invades USSR
German army defeated at Stalingrad
Hitler commits suicide as Red Army surrounds Berlin
Second World War
1932
1934
1936
1938
1940
1942
1944
1946
• Hitler appointed Chancellor
• Enabling Act passed by the Reichstag
• Reichstag fire
• German election: Nazi Party secures 43.9% of the vote
• Nazi Party declared the only legal political party
• Germany leaves the League of Nations
The 'Night of the Long Knives' sees Hitler's opponents in the Nazi Party purged
• Anschluss between Germany and Austria
• Munich Agreement sees Germany annex parts of Czechoslovakia
• Kristallnacht sees the countrywide arrest and imprisonment of Jews
Wannsee Conference organises the 'Final Solution of the Jewish question'
D-Day

Was the Weimar Republic doomed from the start?

How did Germany emerge from defeat in the First World War?

LEARNING OBJECTIVES

In this lesson you will:

- examine the immediate aftermath of the First World War and its effects on Germany
- assess whether Germany coped well with the transition to peace by explaining the significance of post-war events.

GETTING STARTED

Look back over your work on the Treaty of Versailles. In pairs, look at the various articles and discuss whether Germany would have been happy with them. Rank them, with the most unacceptable at the top. Share your list with others and explain how you decided on the order.

The end of the war

In September 1918, Allied troops broke through the German Hindenburg line on the Western Front. Defeat in the war now looked inevitable for Germany. The British blockade of German ports had produced serious food shortages in Germany, and there were many calls for the country to make peace. In October, sailors at the naval base at Wilhelmshaven mutinied, and there was a further mutiny at Kiel when the order was given for one last attack on the British navy. On 7 November, Kurt Eisner declared Bavaria to be a **socialist republic**, and all over Germany workers and soldiers formed councils similar to the soviets in Russia.

This 'German Revolution' so frightened Germany's leaders that they persuaded **Kaiser Wilhelm** to **abdicate**. President Wilson had already made it clear that there could be no peace if the Kaiser remained in office – and Germany desperately needed peace.

So on 9 November, Kaiser Wilhelm stood down and Friedrich Ebert, one of the leaders of the Social Democratic Party (SPD), announced that Germany was now a republic. Ebert himself was to be **president** and his colleague, Philipp Scheidemann, became **chancellor**.

SOURCE 

We sat in our bunkers and heard about the mess behind the lines, about the dry rot setting in back home. We felt that the Frenchmen and Tommies were no longer our enemies, that there was worse to come. Real poison was being brewed in the witches' cauldron at home

A German lieutenant describing his thoughts on hearing of the unrest in Germany in November 1918.

Problems for the new government

To restore order in Germany, the new government without delay signed an armistice with the Allies on 11 November 1918. Many Germans were shocked by the German surrender, even though there was really little choice. The decision to sign the armistice soon gave rise to the 'stab in the back' theory – the idea that Germany had been betrayed by its politicians and should have fought on. **Nationalists** called Ebert's government 'The November Criminals'. The new republic had got off to a very unpopular start.

KEY PEOPLE

Kaiser Wilhelm II – *emperor of Germany 1888–1918.*

A major problem for Ebert was establishing how Germany should be governed. Some Germans wanted a system of government based on **communism**, as had recently been established in Russia. In January 1919 the Spartacus League, Germany's Communist Party, staged a revolt in Berlin in an attempt to seize power and make Germany a communist country. Ebert's government had few troops, as the army had been disbanded after the war. So the government formed units of volunteer soldiers. These 'Freikorps' (Free Corps) soldiers were bitter opponents of communism and crushed the revolt. On 15 January the leaders of the revolt, Karl Liebknecht and Rosa Luxemburg, were executed by the Freikorps. (Later, in 1920, when a Soviet republic was proclaimed in Munich, the Freikorps crushed that too.) The actions of the Freikorps led to bitter hostility between the SPD and the German Communist Party (KPD), which lasted throughout the time of the Weimar Republic.

Democracy established

Just four days after the execution of Liebknecht and Luxemburg, elections were held for a National Assembly, which would draw up a new **constitution** for Germany. The SPD won the most seats, but it did not have a majority. However, after joining in **coalition** with the Centre Party (Z) and Democratic Party (DDP), it had the support of more than three-quarters of the 423 deputies.

As there was unrest in Berlin, the National Assembly held its first meeting in the town of Weimar. So the constitution that it drew up was called the Weimar Republic.

The Weimar Republic

- Germany was to be a democracy. The Reichstag (Parliament) was to make laws and control the government.
- Men and women aged 21 and over could vote in elections for deputies to the Reichstag. Voting was by proportional representation (PR), so a party receiving 10 per cent of the votes had 10 per cent of the deputies.
- The head of the government was the chancellor.
- The head of state was the president, who was to be elected every seven years. The president could dissolve the Reichstag, order fresh elections and, in times of emergency, suspend the Reichstag and rule by himself (Article 48).

This new constitution had several weaknesses. Between 1919 and 1933, no party won more than half the votes cast in elections for the Reichstag. As a result, the system of proportional representation

SOURCE B

The Freikorps on parade.

KEY WORDS

Abdicate – *(of a monarch) to renounce the throne.*

Chancellor – *the senior government official, similar to our prime minister.*

Coalition – *a temporary alliance between political parties, usually made in order to form a government.*

Communism – *a political belief that everything should be shared out equally depending upon need.*

Constitution – *set of principles according to which a country is governed.*

Nationalists – *people who hold views focusing on the importance of the nation.*

President – *the head of state of a country.*

Republic – *a country without a monarchy.*

Socialism – *a political belief that the means of production should be owned by the state and not in the hands of private investors.*

ACTIVITIES

There are a lot of difficult words to learn here, but you must know their meaning if you are to be successful with this chapter. Create a word puzzle for a member of your class. Swap with them to see if you can do their puzzle.

meant that no party won more than half the seats. Consequently, all governments were coalitions between two or more parties. When faced with serious political problems, the various members of the coalitions often fell out. In addition, many people, such as the aristocratic families (Junkers), industrialists and members of the army, did not like the new democracy. They wanted Germany to have one strong leader, as it had before the war.

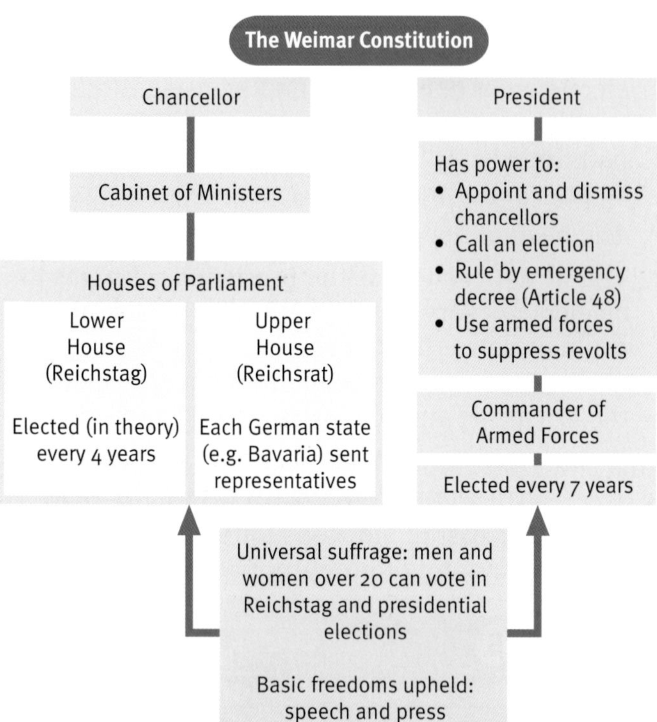

But whatever problems there were in the constitution of the Weimar Republic were nothing compared to the series of crises that the government had to face in the period 1919–24. The first of these, and in some ways the cause of all of them, was the peace settlement at the end of the First World War.

SOURCE C

We trusted the suggestion that the peace would be based on Wilson's Fourteen Points. What is now given us is a contradiction of that promise. Such a dictated peace will provoke fresh hatred between the nations and, in the course of time, fresh killing.

President Ebert condemning the proposed Treaty of Versailles in May 1919.

GradeStudio

'Explain how Germany emerged from the First World War in a very bad state.' **[6 marks]**

Mark scheme

Level 1:	1 mark	General answer, lacking specific contextual knowledge e.g. 'Germany emerged badly.'
Level 2:	2 marks	Identifies or describes reasons e.g. 'Germany emerged badly because their Kaiser had abdicated which meant they had to go from a monarchy to a republic in a very short space of time.'
Level 3:	3–6 marks	Explains reasons e.g. 'Firstly, Germany emerged badly because the transition from monarchy to republic was achieved very quickly but not to everybody's agreement as the actions of the Sparticists and Freikorps demonstrated. Secondly…'

Examiner's tip

Don't forget **PEEL**.

Start your paragraph by making a **P**oint.

Explain your point by using your lists.

Make your answer better by supporting your explaination with **E**vidence.

Finally ensure you answer the question by making a **L**ink back to it.

What was the economic and political impact of the Treaty of Versailles on the Weimar Republic?

LEARNING OBJECTIVES

In this lesson you will:

- analyse the impact of the Treaty of Versailles and make connections between aspects of the treaty and some of the reactions to it.

GETTING STARTED

You are about to investigate the impact of the Treaty of Versailles on the Weimar Republic. Look at the cartoon: it is very clear what the cartoonist thinks of the treaty and the French prime minister. Cartoons sometimes have a caption underneath them to help explain their message; write a caption for this one.

KEY WORDS

Friekorps – *paramilitary, or military-style, organisations independent of the state.*

General strike – *a widespread refusal to work, as a form of protest.*

Putsch – *an attempt to overthrow the government.*

Reparations – *compensation for war damage paid by a defeated state.*

Spartacists – *communist group led by Luxemburg and Liebknecht, which took part in a failed uprising in 1919.*

Vindictive – *having a strong desire for revenge.*

A cartoon from a German magazine in July 1919. The vampire-like man is Georges Clemenceau, the French prime minister.

The impact of the Treaty of Versailles on Germany

The Treaty of Versailles was a **vindictive** treaty which punished Germany for its part in the war. Germany was split in two. It lost 13 per cent of its territory, including Alsace-Lorraine and West Prussia, and 10 per cent of its population, and restrictions were placed on the size of its armed forces and the weapons those forces could have. Article 231 of the treaty (the 'War Guilt' clause) stated that Germany had to take full responsibility for starting the war and causing any damage that had occurred. This clause was the basis for the **reparations** payments that it was decided Germany should pay. No figure was set until 1921, when it was decided that Germany should pay £6600 million.

The Germans were furious at the terms of the treaty. They claimed that they had agreed to the armistice because they believed that the peace treaty would be based on Wilson's Fourteen Points. These had been published in January 1918 and were much less severe than the final treaty. The Germans also complained that they had been given no say in negotiating the treaty. They said it was a 'Diktat' (a dictated peace). Later opponents of the treaty were to argue that, if the German people had no say in drawing up the treaty, then they had no obligation to abide by its terms.

The new chancellor, Philipp Scheidemann, at first suggested that Germany should not sign the treaty. However, there was little choice as the Allies would probably have invaded if the Germans had refused to sign. So the treaty was signed – and the Weimar Republic became even more unpopular.

The Kapp Putsch

SOURCE A

The Munich Putsch – the scene in Munich on the morning of 9 November 1923.

The Spartacist uprising of January 1919 was only one example of political problems faced by the Weimar Republic. The Spartacists had been defeated with the help of the **Freikorps**, but this group itself caused the government great difficulties. Among its members were a group of extreme nationalists who opposed democracy and believed that the only way to prevent the spread of communism was through strong leadership and a strong army.

The Treaty of Versailles said that Germany's army must number no more than 100,000, including the volunteer Freikorps units. But in 1920 when Ebert tried to disband the Freikorps, there was rebellion. The Freikorps marched on Berlin and proclaimed Dr Wolfgang Kapp as Germany's new leader. Since the army refused to fire on the Freikorps, the government fled. But Kapp was not popular with the people, who obeyed a government request for a **general strike**. Soon gas, water and electricity were cut off and Berlin came to a halt. Kapp was forced to flee to Sweden, the government returned and the Freikorps were disbanded.

Even so, ex-members of the Freikorps continued to cause difficulties. They formed a group called 'Organisation Consul', which in 1921 murdered Matthias Erzberger, a leading politician who had agreed to the signing of the Treaty of Versailles. In 1922 the group murdered Walther Rathenau, Germany's foreign minister.

The Munich Putsch

In 1923 the Weimar Republic faced another attempt to overthrow it. By 1923 the German economy had been reduced to ruins by hyperinflation and the French occupation of the Ruhr (see page 155). The leader of the Nazi Party, **Adolf Hitler**, believed that the Republic was on the verge of collapse and decided to try to seize power. On 8 November 1923, Hitler and his supporters broke up a meeting in a Munich beer-hall at which leaders of the Bavarian state government were speaking. He forced the leaders to agree to take part in a **putsch** (rebellion) against the government. However, they were allowed to leave the meeting and, once free, they quickly changed their minds.

On 9 November, 3000 Nazis, led by Hitler and **General Ludendorff**, the First World War army hero, marched on Munich. Hitler thought the police and army would join his revolution. Instead the police opened fire on the marchers, and 16 Nazis were killed. Hitler and Ludendorff were arrested for conspiracy. Hitler used his trial to make long speeches criticising the government and setting out his plans for the future of Germany. The publicity he received turned him into a national figure.

At the end of the trial, Hitler was sentenced to just five years in prison and he was released after nine months. Ludendorff was found not guilty. There were two other important outcomes of the trial. First, Hitler now realised that power could best be achieved in Germany through the ballot box rather than an armed uprising. Second, during Hitler's time in prison he began work on his book *Mein Kampf* (My Struggle). This book set out his main beliefs, although few people at the time can have thought that he would ever get the chance to put them into practice.

KEY PEOPLE

Adolf Hitler – *Chancellor of Germany 1933–45.*

General Ludendorff – *hero of the First World War who became an early supporter of the Nazi Party.*

The economic crisis of 1923

During the First World War, the German government paid its bills by printing more banknotes. This sounds like a good solution, but in reality having more money in circulation means that prices rise. As prices rise, so workers demand more wages. This makes goods dearer to produce and so more expensive to buy. Workers therefore demand more wages and so it goes on. This is known as **inflation**.

When a country suffers high inflation, its currency is worth less to foreign countries, which expect more of it in exchange for their goods. This is what happened in Germany from 1914 onwards, but particularly during 1923.

In 1921 the Allies fixed the reparations that Germany had to pay at £6600 million. The Germans, like all the major powers in Europe, had spent huge sums on the war. After the war, valuable raw materials in Germany, such as coal and iron, were taken away as the Allies tried to make sure that Germany remained weak. Towards the end of 1922, Germany failed to make a reparations payment. When Germany asked for more time to pay reparations Britain agreed but France did not.

The French and Belgians responded by occupying the industrial heartland of Germany, the Ruhr. This area of Germany was the centre of Germany's coal, iron and steel production. Without the materials from this area, Germany was in severe trouble. It damaged production in other industries which could not run without coal. The collapse of industrial production actually cost Germany more than it would have done if the government had simply paid the reparations.

The French were only concerned about getting the money they were owed under the terms of the Treaty of Versailles and certainly did not care if Germany's economy suffered. Initially, the British supported France's actions but came to realise that they would suffer if Germany suffered. The two countries traded with each other to a large degree and, although not dependent on this trade, the loss of Germany as a market for goods would be felt by British business. On 11 January 1923 the French army occupied the Ruhr valley with the intention of taking the value of the missing payments in goods. The German government ordered a policy of **passive resistance** and German workers went on strike. Production fell and the French and Belgians could not take the goods they wanted. This action was completely legal because of the terms of the Treaty of Versailles; however, many countries felt sympathy for Germany. Eventually, the French withdrew from the area in 1925 as Germany negotiated the Dawes Plan.

KEY WORDS

Bartering – *using goods or services as a means of exchange instead of money.*

Hyperinflation – *a very extreme increase in prices.*

Inflation – *a general increase in prices.*

Passive resistance – *resistance using non-violent methods.*

SOURCE B

As soon as I received my salary, I rushed out to buy the daily necessities. My daily salary was just enough to buy a loaf of bread and one small piece of cheese or oatmeal. A friend of mine, a clergyman, came to Berlin with his monthly salary to buy a pair of shoes for his baby. He could only afford a cup of coffee.

A German journalist describes the effects of hyperinflation in Germany.

SOURCE C

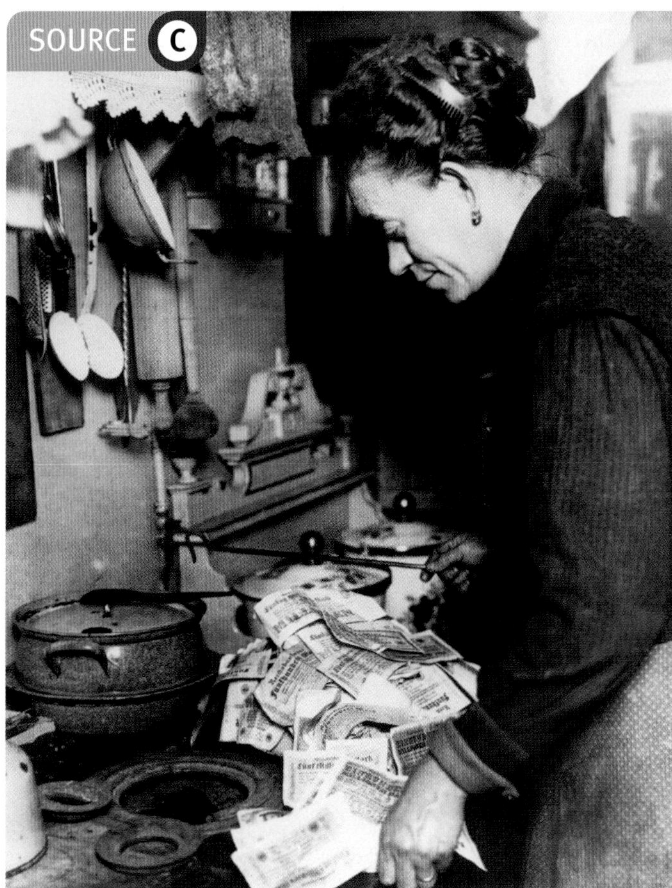

A housewife using paper money to cook with because it is cheaper than buying fuel.

Although it seemed that the Germans had won this particular battle, they still had to pay their workers and meet their other bills. So they printed more and more banknotes. This led to a particularly severe type of inflation known as **hyperinflation**. In December 1921 a loaf of bread cost just under four marks. In September 1923 it cost 1.5 million marks. People's wages went up too, but not by as much. Banknotes were collected in and re-stamped with different values. But it made little difference.

Paper money became practically worthless and **bartering** became common as people settled their bills by paying in eggs or bread. Foreign goods were also so expensive that few Germans could afford them. Hardest hit were people who had saved carefully for their old age, expecting to have enough money to live in comfort in their retirement. Suddenly their savings would not buy a week's groceries. At first, many people in work found that their wages went up too, but as wages failed to keep pace with the dramatic price rises, so people's living standards fell. Many people could not afford to eat properly and hunger was common.

Of course, there were those who gained from the hyperinflation. People who had borrowed large sums of money suddenly found that they could pay it back out of a week's wages – and foreigners visiting Germany discovered that small amounts of their own currency could be traded for millions of marks.

The situation was extremely serious. Thousands of Germans had become destitute and there was a real danger that law and order might break down. It was no coincidence that Hitler chose just this time to try to mount the Munich Putsch.

GradeStudio

What was the impact of the Treaty of Versailles on the Weimar Republic up to 1923? **[4 marks]**

Examiner's tip

The question is asking you to describe how the Weimar Republic was affected by the Treaty of Versailles. You should start with a brief description of the key points of the treaty and then move on to describe its impact.

One mark for each relevant point: additional mark for supporting detail.

ACTIVITIES

You need to be able to recall this information quickly in an exam, so this activity is designed to help you make notes on it. The impact of the Treaty of Versailles can be broken down into five major areas:

- the initial reaction
- the Kapp Putsch
- the Munich Putsch
- the occupation of the Ruhr
- the economic crisis of 1923.

Use the title 'What was the impact of the Treaty of Versailles on the Republic?' as the centre for a spider diagram and place the five major areas around the edge. Each of the five areas should be split into: background detail, causes of event and consequences of event. Then join any similarities between events together.

To what extent did the Republic recover after 1923?

LEARNING OBJECTIVES

In this lesson you will:

- learn about the extent of the German recovery between 1923 and 1929
- analyse the contribution of one key person during a key period.

GETTING STARTED

Read Source B. What sort of man do you think Gustav Stresemann was? What clues are there in what he says that lead you to your conclusions?

The Stresemann era

By mid-1923 the German economy was in ruins and the Weimar Republic close to collapse. Yet within a few years it had returned to prosperity and stability. How did this happen? Much of the credit for the transformation must go to Gustav Stresemann, who became chancellor in August 1923. He was a committed nationalist, but he believed that Germany's problems could be solved only by moderation and by working with other countries.

One of Stresemann's first acts was to introduce a new currency, the Rentenmark. At the same time, government spending was reduced (700,000 government employees lost their jobs). These measures helped end the hyperinflation and brought confidence back.

Stresemann also put down left-wing uprisings in Thuringia and Saxony, and dealt with the attempted putsch by the Nazis in Munich. For the rest of the 1920s, there was political stability in Germany and extreme parties, such as the Communists and Nazis, found it difficult to win large numbers of seats in the Reichstag.

Stresemann was chancellor for just four months, but he was foreign minister for five years. It was in this office that he had his greatest success. In 1924 he negotiated the Dawes Plan with the Allies. Under the terms of this plan, the USA agreed to loan Germany 800 million gold marks. It was also decided that the annual reparations payments should be reduced and Germany given longer to pay. In 1929 the Young Plan further extended the time that Germany had to pay reparations until 1988 (though payments actually ceased in 1930).

SOURCE A

Gustav Stresemann became chancellor of Germany in 1923.

To what extent did the Republic recover after 1923?

These economic measures, together with further loans from the USA, helped the German economy to recover. Between 1924 and 1929 Germany received over 25 billion marks in loans, which enabled German industry to be rebuilt. Stresemann also had great success in improving relations with other countries. In 1925 he signed the Locarno Pact with France and Belgium, in which the countries agreed to respect their common borders. Then in 1926 Germany joined the League of Nations.

SOURCE B

A nation must not adopt the attitude of a child who writes a list of his wants on Christmas Eve, which contains everything that the child will need for the next fifteen years. The parents would not be in a position to give all this. In foreign policy, I often have the feeling that I am confronted with such a list.

Gustav Stresemann explains why he signed the Locarno Pact when it appeared to accept the Treaty of Versailles.

Fact file

Gustav Stresemann (1878–1929)

- He was a businessman and politician.
- His political beliefs are not easy to define as they do not conform to the usual 'left/right' classifications.
- He had business links with the USA before the First World War.
- After the war he set up the German Peoples' Party (DVP) supported by mainly middle- and upper-class Protestants. The DVP stood for Christian family values, secular education, lower tariffs, opposition to welfare spending and agrarian subsides and hostility to Marxism. The DVP gradually began co-operating with centre and left-wing parties.
- Stresemann spent a brief period as chancellor but failed to deal firmly enough with the culprits of the Munich putsch, and this led the Social Democrats to leave the coalition that he led.
- For the next 8 years (the remainder of his life) he continued as Foreign Minister, whatever the make-up of the government.
- He was friendly with many foreign leaders and won the Nobel Peace prize in 1926 (shared with his French counterpart Aristide Briand).
- He died of a stroke aged 51 in 1929.

ACTIVITIES

Complete the following table:

Stresemann's success	How this helped Germany
1924 The Dawes Plan	
1925 Locarno Pact	
1926 Germany joined the League of Nations	
1928 Germany signed the Kellogg–Briand Pact	
1929 The Young Plan	

This international acceptance of Germany was reinforced in 1928 when it was one of 60 countries to sign the Kellogg–Briand Pact, which renounced war as an instrument of foreign policy. Finally, the introduction of the Young Plan meant that German reparations were reduced by over 67 per cent and the country was given a timetable for making payments. The Allied powers adopted this in 1930, although the Wall Street Crash of 1929 had a major impact on its implementation.

Stresemann was strongly criticised for being too willing to co-operate with Germany's former enemies. But he firmly believed that revision of the Treaty of Versailles could not happen overnight and had to be done by co-operation with foreign countries. Others, particularly Adolf Hitler, disagreed.

GradeStudio

To what extent did the Weimar Republic recover after 1923?

[10 marks]

Examiner's tip

Use the table you have just completed to help you, but also try to include extra detail from the sources above.

What were the achievements of the Weimar period?

LEARNING OBJECTIVES

In this lesson you will:

- examine the achievements of the Weimar Republic
- use sources to investigate attitudes towards the achievements of the Weimar Republic.

GETTING STARTED

In this section you will be investigating the culture of the Weimar Republic. Historians use the word 'culture' to describe activities like art, literature and music. Before you look at the Weimar artists, can you think of any current artists whose work is controversial? Tracey Emin put her unmade bed on display, Damien Hurst puts dead animals in formaldehyde and Banksy draws on walls. Why do you think some people might not like their work?

Art and culture under the Weimar Republic

The economic recovery experienced in Germany after 1924 was reflected in a cultural revival that could be seen in a variety of fields from architecture to opera. Under the Kaiser, there had been censorship in Germany. Now there was a new spirit of freedom, in which criticism of the government and even songs and books mentioning sex were allowed! Berlin became a thriving centre of the arts, with over 120 newspapers and 40 theatres. German literature flourished, with Erich Remarque's *All Quiet on the Western Front* selling over half a million copies. German playwrights such as Bertolt Brecht won international fame too. Painters such as George Grosz and Hannah Hoech became well known for their original style, and Walter Gropius founded the Bauhaus group, which brought in new ideas in architecture and sculpture.

KEY WORDS

Capitalist – *a person who makes money by employing people.*

Decadent – *reflecting a state of moral or cultural decline.*

ACTIVITIES

What did George Grosz think of the Weimar politicians?

The painter George Grosz lived during the Weimar period, and his paintings are very useful to historians. They cannot necessarily be relied on to give us an accurate picture of the period, but they do give us an insight into the thinking of certain groups of people. George Grosz was a member of the Neue Sachlichkeit movement (New Objectivity), a group of artists who believed art should comment on society and should be understood by ordinary people. Let's see if we can understand one of his paintings!

There are four groups of people in this picture. See if you can identify them all.

- Politicians (Grosz thinks the politicians do not know what they are doing and has drawn them accordingly).
- The Army (telling the politicians what to do).
- **Capitalists** (telling the politicians what to do).
- The mass of people (doing what they are told, blinded by who is making the decisions).

SOURCE A

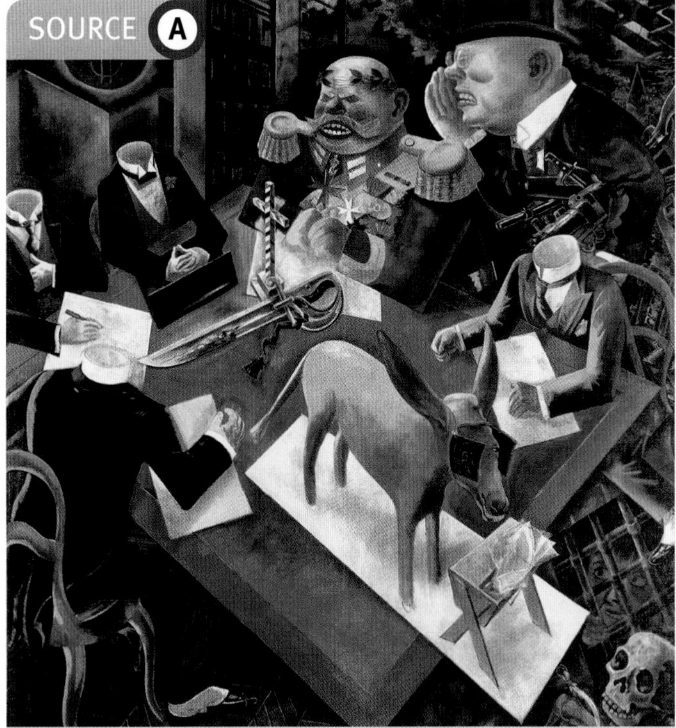

Eclipse of the Sun, painted by George Grosz in 1926.

HISTORY DETECTIVE

There are many Grosz paintings on the internet. Investigate more of them and work out their meanings. You could also investigate other members of the Neue Sachlichkeit movement (for example, Otto Dix or Bertolt Brecht) to see if their work is critical of the Weimar Republic.

Some Germans hated the new ideas in art and considered them **decadent** and unpatriotic. They wanted art to celebrate the traditional values of German society. They argued that the new artistic styles, popular music, jazz and clubs showed how Germany was going into moral decline.

What were the achievements of the Weimar period?

As you have read, the Weimar Republic inherited serious political and economic problems in 1919 and then faced even more difficult ones in the years up to 1923. Under these circumstances, it was a major success to maintain political stability in Germany and prevent a revolution from leading to more extreme government. By the mid-1920s, the German people seemed to have accepted the Weimar Republic, and there was less demand for a return to the 'good old days' of the Kaiser.

After 1924 the successes of the Republic are much easier to see. Stresemann's work brought economic recovery and international acceptance for Germany. There was also significant achievement in the arts, with Gropius, Brecht and Grosz winning international fame.

However, this 'golden age' was to some extent an illusion. Economic prosperity was based largely on foreign loans. At the same time, exports were falling and the government was spending huge sums on welfare and health care. Could it last? Already by 1928 there were serious disputes between unions and employers. Meanwhile, the farmers had never shared in the apparent prosperity. Prices for farm produce fell during the 1920s and many farmers were in debt.

The political stability was also wafer-thin. In 1925 Hindenburg was elected president, and he was a strong supporter of the Kaiser. Many Germans resented the fact that the Treaty of Versailles had not been reversed and blamed the government for it.

While things were going well, the Weimar Republic's achievements looked impressive. Once things went wrong, they looked much less so.

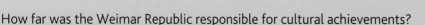

GradeStudio

How far was the Weimar Republic responsible for cultural achievements? **[10 marks]**

Mark scheme

Level 1:	1–2 marks	General answer lacking specific contextual knowledge e.g. Says that there were achievements but gives no real explanation of what they were.
Level 2:	2–4 marks	Identifies achievements and may list one or two of them but only gives a basic response. Higher level for more identification and reasons.
Level 3:	3–6 marks	Explains answer. e.g. 'One of the major cultural achievements of the Weimar Republic was the new spirit of freedom in art. Artists like George Grosz painted political life as they saw it without fear of punishment. Grosz was able to satirise the politicians in his paintings like *Eclipse of the Sun* where he showed the politicians as 'headless' and led by the army and the capitalists.' This level of detail needed and more than once for top end of mark.
Level 4:	6–9 marks	Balanced argument. Level 3 answer with good level of explanation on both sides. e.g. Above with… 'However, not everyone would approve of the cultural changes and some saw the changes as decadent and not at all German. Furthermore…'
Level 5:	9–10 marks	Explains with evaluation. Balanced argument with a detailed evaluation. e.g. Levels 3 and 4 with own opinion on whether there were any real achievements.

Why was Hitler able to dominate Germany by 1933?

What did the Nazi Party stand for in the 1920s?

LEARNING OBJECTIVES

In this lesson you will:

- examine how Hitler managed to impose his views on the party he joined
- use historical sources to explain the appeal of the early Nazi Party.

GETTING STARTED

Look at the photo of Hitler's membership card in Source A. Hitler was not membership number 555, but, historians think, number 55. Why would an extra 5 be placed on the card?

The birth of the German Workers' Party

In January 1919, three Germans formed a small party called the German Workers' Party (DAP). Adolf Hitler joined the party in September 1919. He quickly showed a talent for public speaking, was invited to join the party's executive committee and was put in charge of propaganda. In 1920 he played a major part in writing the party's 25-point programme, setting out its beliefs. This programme showed the early **anti-Semitism** of the party, but it also contained many socialist ideas. The socialist ideas were not thought to have been Hitler's suggestions.

SOURCE A

Deutsche Arbeiter-Partei (D. A. P.)
Ortsgruppe München Abteilung:

Mitgliedskarte

für Herrn Adolf Hitler

München, den 1. Jan. 1920

Nr. 555

Für den Arbeitsausschuß:

Schriftwart

Drexler

Diese Karte gilt als Ausweis bei geschlossenen Versammlungen

Adolf Hitler's membership card of the DAP.

In April the DAP was renamed the National Socialist German Workers' Party (Nazi Party for short) and later in the year it bought a Munich newspaper, the *Volkischer Beobachter*. This paper was well known for its anti-Semitic views – it had once had a headline reading 'Clean out the Jews once and for all'. The newspaper was used to spread Nazi views, and support for the party began to grow.

SOURCE B

Goodness! He's got a big gob. We could use him.

A comment made by Anton Drexler on first hearing Hitler speak in public.

SOURCE C

1 *We demand the union of all Germany in a Greater Germany on the basis of the right of national self-determination.*

2 *We demand equality of rights for the German people in its dealings with other nations, and the revocation of the peace treaties of Versailles and Saint-Germain.*

3 *We demand land and territory (colonies) to feed our people and to settle our surplus population.*

4 *Only members of the nation may be citizens of the State. Only those of German blood, whatever be their creed, may be members of the nation. Accordingly, no Jew may be a member of the nation.*

The leaders of the Party promise to work ruthlessly – if need be to sacrifice their very lives – to translate this programme into action.

The first four points of the 25 points of the German Workers' Party and its concluding statement.

ACTIVITIES

Look at the four points in Source C. Which of them might appeal to the following people? There may be more than one point for each person.

- Herr Schmidt: a German-born citizen who fought bravely in the First World War.
- Herr Meyer: a poor, illiterate German-born citizen with four children.
- Frau Müller: a teacher with liberal political leanings.
- Frau Brun: a retired housewife and small shop-owner.

What other sections of society might have gained or lost from the four points?

SOURCE D

Nazi stormtrooopers at an early rally, c.1923.

Hitler becomes party leader

In 1921 Hitler became party leader and in the same year founded the Sturmabteilung ('Stormtroopers' or 'Brownshirts'). The SA was a paramilitary organisation that paraded in full military uniform, wearing the Nazi swastika. Its main task was to protect Nazi meetings and disrupt those of its opponents. The military style of the organisation attracted many unemployed soldiers, and the Stormtroopers soon developed a reputation for brutality against Nazi opponents.

The Munich Putsch and its consequences

By 1923 the Nazi Party had grown to 35,000 members, although support was based largely in Bavaria. Hitler was convinced that the Weimar Republic's problems gave him the opportunity to seize power, but his Munich Putsch was unsuccessful and Hitler was imprisoned (see page 154). The failed putsch had an important impact on the Nazi Party. Its leader was jailed, its newspaper in Munich was banned, and so was the party itself.

KEY CONCEPTS

Anti-Semitism – *hostility to Jewish people.*

VOICE YOUR OPINION!

Were there factors in place at this stage that might point towards Hitler becoming the dictator he did?

Why did the Nazis have little success before 1930?

LEARNING OBJECTIVES

In this lesson you will:

- learn about the political, social and economic reasons for the Nazis' lack of success between 1923 and 1930
- investigate the range of political options available to the Germans during the 1920s.

GETTING STARTED

Before looking at the relative lack of success of the Nazi Party you should revisit your work on the recovery of the Weimar Republic. How stable do you think the Weimar government was at this point?

The change of tactics after the Munich Putsch

While Hitler was in prison, some of his supporters formed the National Socialist Freedom Party, but in December 1924 (when Hitler came out of prison) the party won only 14 seats in the Reichstag. Hitler was determined to try to win power by legal means, but the success of Stresemann's policies meant that there was very little support for **extremists** such as Hitler.

In 1925, however, Hitler persuaded the authorities to lift the ban on the Nazi Party and set about reorganising it. He made a bad start in February when he made a speech that was so critical of the government that he was banned from public speaking for two years.

Hitler then divided Germany into 34 districts and put a leading Nazi in charge of increasing support in each area. He also founded the Hitler Youth as well as a personal bodyguard, the Schutzstaffel (SS). In 1926 he called a party conference and persuaded the members of his party to re-adopt the original 25-point programme.

By the end of 1926 the Nazi Party had 50,000 members, and in 1927 it held its first Nuremberg **rally**. It had become a nationally known party with a strong leader and effective propaganda. But despite all the hard work, the party was not making gains in terms of the number of deputies elected to the Reichstag. In the 1928 election, the Nazis won just 12 seats and were only the eighth largest party.

SOURCE 

	Left	Centre	Right
Parties in the Weimar Republic	KPD USPD SPD	DDP	DVP DNVP
		(Centre Party Z, had support from all three classes	
Supported by:	Working class	Middle class	Upper class

A political spectrum of parties in Germany, c.1920.

KPD = Communists

USPD = Independent Social Democratic Party

SDP = Social Democratic Party

DDP = German Democratic Party

Z = Catholic Centre Party

DVP = German People's Party

DNVP = German National People's Party

SOURCE B

1921	1922	1923	1924	1925	1926	1927	1928	1929	1930	1931	1932	1933
2	1.5	4	5	3.5	10	6	6	8	14	24	30	26

Percentage of labour force unemployed 1921–33.

Political stability in Germany in the 1920s

Despite the constitution's use of **proportional representation** as the method for electing deputies to the Reichstag, the years following the Munich Putsch were a period of stability. Politically, the public were voting for the '**moderate**' parties; the SPD consistently attracted between 20–30% of the votes in the 1920s. There was conflict within the SPD over whether to adopt socialist policies to benefit the working class, or to adopt more moderate policies and push for slower change. Ultimately a compromise was found, and the SPD usually helped maintain the government in office.

- The Left: parties on this side of the spectrum generally want greater change and more power for ordinary people.
- The Right: parties on the right tend to want little change; we call this conservative because they want to conserve the country as it is. In Germany this meant the restoration of the Kaiser and power in the hands of the few (or just one person), not the many.
- The Centre: parties here tend to want moderate change. The 'Z' party was set up to protect the interests of the Catholic Church, so appealed to all three classes.

SOURCE C

Government report on the National Socialists:

'In spite of their very well prepared and thoroughly organised propaganda, this is a party that isn't going anywhere. It is a numerically insignificant, radical, revolutionary splinter group that is incapable of exerting any noticeable influence on the great mass of the population or on the course of political developments.'

Quoted in Thomas Childers, *The Foundation of the Nazi Constituency*, Croom Helm, 1986 (taken from Philip Sauvain, *Germany in the Twentieth Century*, Stanley Thornes Ltd, 1997).

Economic prosperity

Economically, the period saw a gradual rise in the standard of living of most of the German people. There were, however, certain sections of society that did not like the classes beneath them (the urban middle class of state employees and tradesmen) becoming richer, and bankruptcies grew from the farming sector.

As long as Germany kept receiving loans from the USA the economy would survive.

Social factors

Socially, people had more freedom than under the autocratic Kaiser; the theatre put on plays that criticised the German way of life, paintings commented on society and were accessible to the general public, literature had a social message and music also reflected modern issues.

ACTIVITIES

There are several reasons – political, social and economic – why the Nazis made very little impression on politics between 1923 and 1930. With reference to the material on pages 161–64, create a spider diagram with the question 'Why did the Nazis have little success before 1930?' at the centre and with three legs (political, social and economic) coming from it. Now write at least two points for each leg.

KEY WORDS

Extremist – *a person who holds extreme political views. In Germany the extreme parties were the Nazis on the right and the Communists on the left.*

Moderate – *neither right-wing nor left-wing.*

Proportional representation – *an electoral system that elects political parties according to the proportion of the votes they receive.*

Rally – *a mass meeting with parades and speeches.*

Why was Hitler able to become Chancellor in 1933?

LEARNING OBJECTIVES

In this lesson you will:

- examine the main reasons why Hitler was able to become Chancellor in 1933
- identify, analyse and comment on the main features that allowed Hitler to become Chancellor.

Key events in Hitler's rise to power

Hitler's rise to power was in no way predetermined; in 1929 few people would have predicted he would be Chancellor in 1933. However, economic and political events took a turn for the worse, and Hitler was able to capitalise on them to maximum advantage.

The impact of the Depression on Germany

In October 1929, two significant events had a dramatic effect on Germany. On 3 October, Gustav Stresemann died; Germany had lost one of its most able politicians. Then on 29 October, the Wall Street Crash began in the USA. As a result of the dramatic fall in share prices, many American businesses went bankrupt. American banks called in the loans they had made to Germany. Without these loans, German industry could not operate, especially as the American markets for their goods had now collapsed. Factories closed and millions of workers lost their jobs. Those in work had to take wage cuts and go on to short-time working.

SOURCE A

Germany has lost her ablest politician. Gustav Stresemann lived and worked without stint for the internal reconstruction of his shattered country. As for peace and co-operation abroad, he laboured with immense energy. The task he took up when he became Chancellor would have frightened a smaller man. The domestic recovery of Germany and her new standing in Europe give measure to his achievement.

The obituary of Gustav Stresemann from *The Times*, 4 October 1929.

SOURCE B

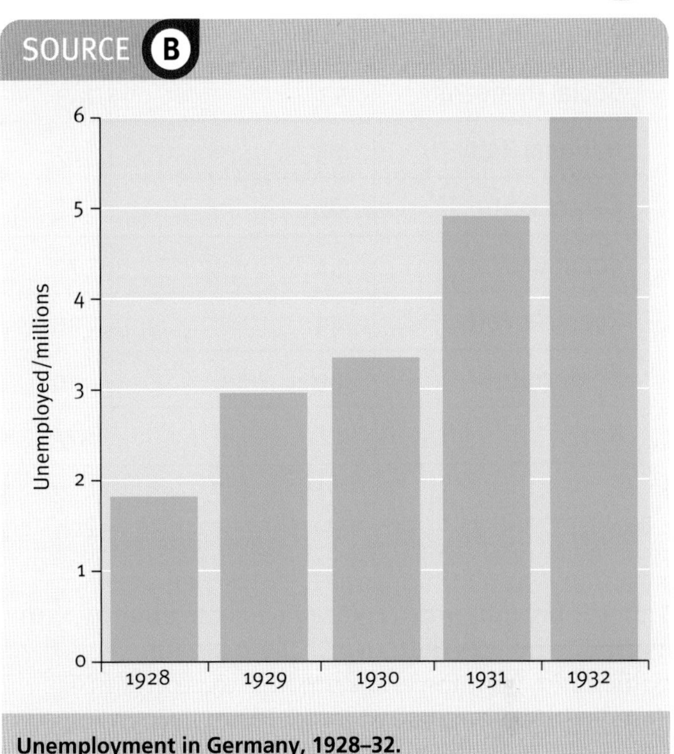

Unemployment in Germany, 1928–32.

The political, economic and social crisis of 1930–33

In 1929 the government was a coalition led by Hermann Müller of the Social Democratic Party. His coalition could not agree on how to deal with the effects of the Depression and in March 1930 he resigned as Chancellor. Müller was succeeded by Heinrich Brüning of the Centre Party. Brüning did not have a majority in the Reichstag and so had to rely on **President Hindenburg**, using Article 48 of the constitution to get his measures adopted. Between 1930 and 1932 the Reichstag met less and less frequently, and Hindenburg issued over 100 **presidential decrees**.

During this time, Hitler exploited the government's problems by holding huge rallies and touring Germany, promising to restore the country's economy. The socialist elements of the party's programme were forgotten as Hitler tried to win support from the German middle classes and industrialists. In the elections of September 1930, the Nazis won 107 seats. In the next election, in July 1932, they won 230 seats (although they dropped back to 196 in November 1932).

SOURCE C

Party	1928	1930	July 1932	November 1932
Social Democrats	153	143	133	121
National Party	73	41	37	52
Centre Party	62	68	75	70
Communists	54	77	89	100
People's Party	45	30	7	11
Democrats	25	20	4	2
Nazis	12	107	230	196

Results of elections to the German Reichstag, 1928–32 (main parties only).

In 1932 Bruning was replaced as chancellor by **von Papen**, who was then overthrown by von Schleicher. Von Papen plotted revenge and in January 1933 persuaded Hindenburg to replace von Schleicher with Adolf Hitler. Von Papen was to be vice-chancellor. He thought that support for the Nazi Party was now in decline and that Hitler could be manipulated to do what he wanted. On 30 January 1933, Hitler became Chancellor. But he was not a man to be manipulated.

Reasons for Nazi support

- The Nazi Party was anti-communist. It therefore appealed to all those who feared what communism might bring, and particularly to industrialists, who feared that a communist government would take over their businesses. Hitler conveniently dropped the socialist elements of the Nazi programme and in return won the support of the industrialists. One leading industrialist gave the party one million marks.
- The Nazi promise to reverse the Treaty of Versailles and restore Germany's military strength appealed to nationalists and to those who believed the 'stab in the back' theory about the end of the war. Most importantly, it won the support of Germany's armed forces.
- The promise to tackle unemployment obviously appealed to the millions who were out of work or feared losing their jobs as a result of the Depression. The promise of strong government also attracted the support of many middle-class Germans who remembered the difficulties of 1923.
- Many women were attracted to the party by its emphasis on family life and self-discipline. This message was reinforced by heavy propaganda campaigns.
- Hitler's anti-Jewish campaign may seem strange to us today, but it was highly effective. He knew that many people were having a hard time and wanted someone to blame. He told them that their difficulties were caused by the Weimar Republic, the communists and especially the Jews (though no credible reason for blaming the Jews ever emerged). So Hitler provided a scapegoat and this helped increase his support.
- Hitler was a skilled public speaker, and his colleague, **Joseph Goebbels**, made effective use of propaganda. Those who would have spoken up against the Nazis were often persuaded not to do so by a visit from the Stormtroopers.

KEY PEOPLE

Joseph Goebbels – *an able Nazi politician who was in charge of propaganda.*

President Hindenberg – *President of Germany 1925–34.*

Von Papen – *Chancellor between May and November 1932.*

KEY WORDS

Presidential decree – *an order made by the president that has the force of law although it has not been approved by parliament.*

How did Hitler consolidate his power in 1933?

LEARNING OBJECTIVES

In this lesson you will:

- examine the events of 1933 which resulted in Hitler achieving total power
- assess the significance of the Reichstag fire and the Enabling Law for the Nazi rise to power.

KEY CONCEPTS

Dictatorship – *government by a ruler who has absolute power.*

Totalitarian state – *a state in which the government has total control over every aspect of its citizens' lives.*

The election of March 1933

Hitler had become chancellor, but he did not have full power. He headed a coalition government in which only three of the 12 Cabinet ministers were Nazis. He therefore needed to hold a new election in which the Nazis would win sufficient seats to govern on their own.

An election was called for March 1933 and the Nazis set about persuading the German people to support them. Their main tactic was to emphasise the threat to Germany from the communists. Hitler fully exploited the advantages he had as chancellor by banning communist election meetings and shutting down communist newspapers. Thousands of Stormtroopers were enrolled as special constables. These men often 'overlooked' Stormtrooper brutality towards opponents of the Nazis which they saw in the streets.

The Reichstag fire

On 27 February 1933 the Reichstag building in Berlin was burned to the ground, and a Dutch communist, Marinus van der Lubbe, was caught in the building with matches and firelighters. He confessed to starting the fire, was put on trial and was later executed.

SOURCE A

The Reichstag building on fire, 27 February 1933.

Hitler was delighted by what had happened. Here was the evidence for what he had been saying for years. The communists were trying to seize power by violent revolution, and they had to be stopped. He had 4000 leading communists arrested and persuaded President Hindenburg to sign a 'Decree for the Protection of the People and the State'. Hitler used these emergency powers to prevent the Nazis' political opponents from holding public meetings, and to arrest more communists.

The Reichstag fire was extremely convenient for the Nazis, and some historians have suggested that they started the fire themselves. There is no objective evidence to suggest this, but it remains extremely doubtful that van der Lubbe was part of a communist conspiracy and he always denied this. The fire was probably started by one communist, but it gave Hitler the opportunity to take action against his opponents.

The steps taken by the Nazis helped to increase the number of Nazi deputies in the Reichstag to 288 out of 647. This was not the 50 per cent that Hitler wanted, but two things gave him a majority in the Reichstag. First, he banned the 81 communist deputies from taking their seats; and secondly, he won the support of the Centre Party by saying that he would not pass any measures that would harm the Catholic Church. Germany now had a fully Nazi government.

SOURCE B

I decided to go to Germany to see for myself. Since the workers would do nothing, I had to do something by myself. I considered arson a suitable method. I did not wish to harm private people, but something that belonged to the state. I acted alone, no one helped me, nor did I meet a single person in the Reichstag.

A statement made by van der Lubbe to the police in March 1933.

The Enabling Act of 1933

Hitler was not a supporter of parliamentary democracy and wanted to make changes to the German constitution to give him greater power. He needed a two-thirds majority in the Reichstag to make such changes, and his banning of the Communist Party and support from the Centre Party gave him this majority.

On 23 March 1933 the Reichstag met to discuss the passing of the Enabling Law. This would give Hitler the power to make laws without the Reichstag for a period of four years. In effect, it would make him a dictator in Germany. Hitler had the majority he needed, but to make sure he got his way he surrounded the building with Stormtroopers to intimidate those who wanted to vote against the measure. The Reichstag passed the law by 441 votes to 84 and effectively voted itself out existence. The Reichstag met only 12 times between 1933 and 1939, and passed just four laws – all without a vote. The only speeches made were by Hitler.

The establishment of the Nazi dictatorship

After March 1933, Hitler used his new powers to turn Germany into a **totalitarian state** – that is, one where the state has control over all aspects of its citizens' lives. In July, the Law Against the Establishment of Parties stated that the Nazi Party was the only political party in Germany. Democracy in Germany was dead.

SOURCE C

I was told that a young Dutchman had turned up in Berlin of whom we could make use. This Dutch communist, van der Lubbe, would climb into the Reichstag and blunder about conspicuously. Meanwhile, I and my men would set fire to the building...

We prepared a number of fires by smearing chairs and tables and by soaking carpets and curtains in paraffin. At exactly 9.05 we finished and left.

I am writing this confession because the SA has been betrayed by the evil plans of Goering and Goebbels. I shall destroy it the moment these traitors have been removed.

This account is part of the evidence published against the Nazis by communists in 1934. It is said to be a confession written by Karl Ernst, a senior member of the SA, in June 1934. He ordered that the document should be published only if he met a violent death. He died in the Night of the Long Knives (see page 169).

VOICE YOUR OPINION!

Do you think Hitler would have been able to pass the Enabling Law without the Reichstag fire?

GradeStudio

Why was Hitler able to dominate Germany by 1933? **[6 marks]**

Mark scheme

Level 1:	1 mark	General answer, lacking specific contextual knowledge e.g. 'Hitler was able to dominate Germany because he was put in charge and had lots of power.'
Level 2:	2 marks	Identifies or describes reasons e.g. 'Hitler was able to dominate Germany because once in power he strengthened his control by putting in place new laws.' More reasons for more marks.
Level 3:	3–6 marks	Explains reasons e.g. 'Firstly, Hitler was able to dominate Germany because once in power he strengthened his control by putting in place new laws. He was able to pass the Enabling Act of 1933 which gave him power to make laws without parliament for four years. Secondly...'

Examiner's tip

This is not an opportunity to tell the story of how Hitler came to power; you must be much more focused. Did Hitler dominate Germany in any way before 1933? What was he doing during the 1920s? Were he and his colleagues improving party organisation and his public speaking abilities during this period? What steps did he take once in power to strengthen his position?

The Nazi regime: how effectively did the Nazis control Germany, 1933–45?

How much opposition was there to the Nazi regime?

LEARNING OBJECTIVES

In this lesson you will:

- examine the extent of opposition to the Nazi regime
- assess the success or otherwise of opposition to the Nazi regime.

GETTING STARTED

You have a decision to make: you are well on the way to becoming the dictator of your country and rule your party completely, but there are still some who might challenge you. What will you do? Will you try to talk the challengers round to your way of thinking or deal with them ruthlessly? Read on to find out what Hitler did.

The 'Night of the Long Knives'

Hitler was concerned not just with opposition from outside the Nazi Party but with opposition from within it as well. The Stormtroopers (SA) had been loyal servants of the Nazi Party since their formation in 1921, but once Hitler was in power they became a problem. The SA expected to be given well-paid jobs in the government as a reward for their loyalty. Their leaders also wanted Hitler to merge them with the German army and put the combined force under the command of Ernst Röhm, the SA leader. Under no circumstances would Hitler allow this because he saw the independence of the SA as a problem: their hunger for street violence was a direct threat to his power and something had to be done about it. Furthermore, a move to unite the SA with the army would alienate the leaders of the Reichswehr (the official German army). This was something Hitler would not allow to happen because he needed the army commanders on his side. There were further reasons why Hitler wanted to do something about the SA leaders, particularly Ernst Röhm. Many of them had left-wing views which would offend the big businesses that had helped fund Hitler in the period up to 1933. Röhm might even emerge as a rival to Hitler's leadership of the party.

SOURCE A

THEY SALUTE WITH BOTH HANDS NOW.

A cartoon published in an English newspaper on 3 July 1934.

ACTIVITIES

Examine Source A. Which event is this cartoon commenting on? (Consider the date it was published.) Now identify the main characters and explain its meaning.

As well as problems within the party, Hitler wanted to silence critics of his regime. If supporters of von Papen and old enemies could be brought into line, Hitler's work would be easier. On the night of 30 June 1934, Hitler ordered his elite bodyguard (the SS) to arrest and execute the leaders of the SA. Röhm and hundreds of other Stormtroopers were executed. Hitler had manufactured a dossier accusing Röhm of plotting to overthrow him; perfect justification for dealing with him harshly. Hitler also took the opportunity to settle a few old scores – he had von Schleicher, his predecessor as chancellor, put to death, as well as old Nazi member Gregor Strasser whose actions in resigning from the party in 1932 had angered Hitler. The former state commissioner, Gustav Ritter von Kahr, who had crushed the Beer Hall Putsch in 1923 also suffered a gruesome fate: his body was discovered hacked to death in a wood outside Munich. People inside Germany and around the world were shocked by what had happened, but Hitler's propaganda convinced many of them that Röhm and the other leaders were a genuine threat to the country. President Hindenburg even went as far as thanking Hitler for saving Germany from possible revolution.

Hitler justified the actions by saying '… I was responsible for the fate of the German people, and thereby I became the supreme judge of the German people.' The actions were legally sanctioned with the 'Law Regarding Measures of State Self-Defence', which legalised the murders that took place a few days earlier. The army warmly welcomed the events and Hitler showed that no law could contain him.

The death of Hindenburg and the oath of allegiance

A few weeks after the Night of the Long Knives, the ageing Hindenburg died. Hitler decided that the country no longer needed a president. Instead the office would be combined with that of chancellor, and Hitler would be known as 'Führer' (leader) of Germany. From 1934 the army swore an **oath of allegiance** to Hitler, not to Germany as it had previously. It seemed that, as far as the Nazis were concerned, Hitler *was* Germany.

SOURCE B

I swear by almighty God this sacred oath that I shall render unconditional obedience to Adolf Hitler, the Führer of the German Reich and people, supreme commander of the armed forces, and that I shall, as a brave soldier, be ready at all times to give my life for this oath.

The oath of allegiance for Wehrmacht officers. There was a separate oath for civil servants.

ACTIVITIES

As you read this section, make notes under the following headings:

- Enabling law
- Artists and authors
- Religion
- The army
- Young people
- Upper classes.

Once you have identified the parts of the text that relate to each of the bullet points, consider where the opposition to Nazism came from and consider how successful it was.

Opposition to Nazi rule

It is very difficult to judge the amount of opposition to the Nazis because officially no opposition was recognised. The Nazi propaganda machine gave the impression that everyone loved the Führer and that the German people were all grateful to him for restoring Germany's greatness. In reality, many people objected to the personal restrictions placed upon them and to the treatment of the Jews. But there was a big difference between objecting to some of Hitler's policies and active opposition. And, of course, the Nazis made sure that opposition to their rule was extremely dangerous. Consequently there was little effective opposition, and it was only during the strains of the Second World War that German opposition to the Nazis became apparent to the outside world.

In 1933 Hitler had used the Enabling Law to ban all political parties other than the Nazis. His two main opponents, the Social Democratic Party (SPD) and the Communist Party (KPD), went underground and published anti-Nazi propaganda, but little of it reached the German people.

KEY CONCEPTS

Oath of allegiance – *an oath of loyalty sworn to a head of state.*

Opposition from artists and authors was more common, but here the opposition was largely concerned with the restrictions on artistic freedom. Some spoke out against the restrictions, but most chose either to suffer in silence or to emigrate. One of the most famous emigrants was the physicist Albert Einstein.

Opposition within the Church

The Nazis were aware of the importance of maintaining good relationships with the Church in Germany. Many Germans were committed Christians and opposition from the Church would prove very difficult to counter.

At first the Christian churches seemed to be keen to work with the Nazis. The government's encouragement of family values and its campaign against immorality in Germany was very much in keeping with Christian beliefs. In 1933 the Catholic Church and the Nazis signed an agreement called the Concordat. The Church agreed not to make comments on political matters if the Nazis did not interfere in religion. Hitler failed, however, to keep his promise. He interfered more and more in Church matters, for example closing down Catholic Youth movements because they rivalled his own Hitler Youth. In 1937 Pope Pius XI denounced Nazism as anti-Christian, and in 1941 a letter from the Pope criticising the Nazis for their abuse of human rights was read out in Catholic churches. Hitler responded by sending nuns and priests to labour camps.

Relations with Protestant churches also deteriorated sharply under the Nazis when Hitler set up the Reich Church. Some 800 Protestant churchmen, such as **Pastor Martin Niemöller**, were sent to labour camps for speaking out against the Nazis. Co-operation with the churches had turned to confrontation.

SOURCE C

In Germany, they came first for the Communists,

And I didn't speak up because I wasn't a Communist;

And then they came for the trade unionists,

And I didn't speak up because I wasn't a trade unionist;

And then they came for the Jews,

And I didn't speak up because I wasn't a Jew;

And then ... they came for me ...

And by that time there was no one left to speak up.

Poem attributed to Pastor Martin Niemöller, who was imprisoned in Nazi concentration camps for his opposition to Nazi rule.

Opposition within the army

Some army generals were highly suspicious of the Nazis. One of the most prominent was **General Ludwig Beck**, who disagreed with Hitler's expansionist foreign policy. Hitler's reaction was to sack large numbers of generals in 1938, including General Beck.

Opposition among youth groups

Although the Hitler Youth movement was very popular with many German youngsters, some objected to the restrictions it placed on them. Around one million young people refused to join the Hitler Youth Movements. They did not want regimentation and training for the army or motherhood. Instead they were more interested in dancing to American

Fact file

The Edelweiss Pirates

Young people are often at the forefront of resistance to oppressive regimes and this was certainly the case in Nazi Germany. Typically, the age of membership of youth organisations like the Edelweiss Pirates and its subgroups (the Navajos, Kittelbach Pirates and Roving Dudes) was 14–18 years of age. The groups were a reaction against the hard discipline and strict gender segregation in the official Hitler Youth movement. The groups were mainly male but some girls did attend the casual meetings and this offered the chance of sexual experimentation. Members would dress in a different way to 'normal' young people as an expression of their freedom; they would sing songs and listen to American Jazz which the Nazis found abhorrent. The groups rebelled against the regimented activities of the Hitler Youth and would pick fights with its members or disrupt the organised activities if possible.

This sort of behaviour, despite not threatening to bring the Nazi regime tumbling down, did act as a rejection of the norms of Nazi society. The regime dealt with any suspected or proven 'pirates' harshly. In extreme cases, young people were sent to concentration camps or prison; some were even hanged. Often, the pirates would be taken into custody and have their heads shaved so everyone knew who they were.

Groups like the Edelweiss Pirates helped army deserters and those hiding from the Nazi regime and should be recognised as a resistance movement.

and English songs and listening to jazz music. They listened to overseas radio stations, which meant that they heard anti-Nazi ideas. The Helmuth Hubener Group handed out leaflets which protested against the Nazi regime and provided translated BBC broadcasts and anti-government leaflets. Its leader, Helmuth Hubener, was arrested by the Gestapo and executed by guillotine in 1942. The Nazis condemned these members of the 'Swing' movement as degenerate and issued pictures to help identify them.

Other problems came from gangs such as the Navajos Gang or Edelweiss Pirates. These groups were usually made up of 14–17-year-olds (between leaving school and signing up for the army). They often fought members of the Hitler Youth, and in some cities, such as Cologne, they became a genuine problem for the authorities.

Opposition among the upper classes

There was increasing opposition to the Nazis from within the German upper classes. Although they had originally approved of the way that the Nazis brought stability back to Germany, by 1940 they were tired of Nazi brutality and feared that Hitler's aggressive foreign policy might lead to Germany's ruin.

Two main upper-class organisations opposed the Nazis.

- The Kreisau Circle was led by Helmuth von Moltke, from one of Germany's most famous aristocratic families. They wanted to see the Nazis overthrown, but were not men of violence. In 1944 their group was discovered and the leaders were executed.
- A second group was the Beck–Goerdeler Group, named after Ludwig Beck and Carl Goerdeler. The two leaders of this group realised that the only way to rid Germany of Hitler was to assassinate him (see notes on the July Plot opposite).

Growing opposition during the war

When the Second World War began to go badly for the Germans, some of the opposition to the Nazis turned to open resistance.

KEY PEOPLE

General Beck – *former German Chief of the General Staff 1935–38, shot for his involvement in a plot to assassinate Hitler in 1944.*

Pastor Martin Niemöller – *an outspoken opponent of Nazi control of the churches.*

Field Marshal Rommel – *German general who commanded troops in Africa in the Second World War and temporarily halted the Allied advance.*

A group of university students in Munich led by Hans and Sophie Scholl formed the White Rose movement. They handed out pamphlets appealing for people to oppose the policies of the Nazi regime. In 1943 the government arrested and executed the Scholls and other leading members of the organisation.

The activities of gangs such as the Navajos Gang or Edelweiss Pirates also became more serious as they helped spread Allied propaganda and sometimes helped Allied airmen to escape. In 1944 a group of Edelweiss Pirates took part in an attack on the Gestapo in which a senior officer was killed. As a result, 12 pirates were publicly hanged.

In July 1944 one of the supporters of the Beck–Goerdeler Group, Count Claus von Stauffenberg, placed a briefcase with a bomb in it under a table at a meeting attended by Hitler. The bomb went off, but Hitler was not seriously injured. Those responsible for the 'July Plot', including Beck and Goerdeler, were executed. **Field Marshal Rommel**, one of Germany's greatest generals, committed suicide to avoid the disgrace of a trial.

HISTORY DETECTIVE

Here are some other people who resisted the Nazi regime. Find out a little about why they resisted and what fate awaited them:

Colonel Claus Schenk Graf von Stauffenberg
General Hans Oster
Carl Friedrich Goerdeler
Pastor Dietrich Bonhöffer
Joachim Gottschalk
Carl von Ossietzky
Adolf Reichwein
Julius Leber

GradeStudio

How much opposition was there to the Nazi regime? **[10 marks]**

Examiner's tip

A 'how much' question is asking you to quantify your answer. How much compared to the rest of the population? When you answer you must decide how typical these acts of resistance were.

How effectively did the Nazis deal with their political opponents?

LEARNING OBJECTIVES

In this lesson you will:

- examine the range of organisations which the Nazis used to control the German people
- analyse the effectiveness of the way the Nazis dealt with political opponents.

GETTING STARTED

Ten per cent of political crime in Germany was discovered by the Gestapo, 10 per cent by the normal police, and the other 80 per cent by the public at large. What does this statistic tell you about the ability of the Gestapo?

SOURCE A

The idea that the Gestapo itself was constantly spying on the population is demonstrably a myth.

From Laurence Rees, *The Nazis: A Warning from History*.

SOURCE B

While much information flowed from the judicial system to the Gestapo, an operation swathed in secrecy offered nothing in return.

From Michael Burleigh, *The Third Reich*.

SOURCE C

Those who fell into the clutches of the Gestapo had to reckon with fearsome torture.

From Ian Kershaw, *Hitler 1936–45*.

ACTIVITIES

The above quotes are from respected historians. What are they saying about the role of the Gestapo?

SOURCE D

Himmler with SS men in 1933.

ACTIVITIES

To be a member of the SS in its early days you had to be able to prove your German ancestry back to 1750, and if you wanted to marry you had to get a special SS marriage certificate. Using the sources above, consider what sort of men would have been recruited to the SS.

Methods of control and repression

Although the Nazis' main weapons for enforcing compliance with their rule were persuasion and propaganda, behind the flags, displays and radio broadcasts was a ruthless system for dealing with their opponents.

The role of the SS

The main organisation was the Schutzstaffel (SS). It was formed in 1925 as an elite bodyguard and from 1929 came under the leadership of **Heinrich Himmler**. After the **purge** of the SA in 1934, it was the Nazis' main security force. Gradually the SS split into three main sections:

- A section responsible for national security.
- The Waffen SS, a group of highly skilled and dependable soldiers who fought alongside the regular army.
- The Death's Head Units, who ran the concentration camps and later the death camps.

ACTIVITIES

How did the Nazis exercise control? Look again at the notes in this section, and using the headings below work out what each of the organisations did and how effective they were.

Organisation	What they did	Effectiveness
Schutzstaffel (SS)		
Geheime Staatspolizei (Gestapo)		
The People's Court		
Concentration camps		

The Gestapo

The Geheime Staatspolizei (Gestapo) was a state police force set up by **Hermann Goering** in 1933. It was led by **Reinhard Heydrich** and was ruthless in dealing with opposition to the Nazis. Its task was to 'discover the enemies of the state, watch them and render them harmless'. The Gestapo had the power to arrest and detain suspects without trial. An extensive web of informers ensured that the authorities quickly learned of anyone plotting against them.

Nazi control of the German courts

From 1933 the German courts were 'Nazified'. Hitler set up a 'People's Court' to try people who opposed the Nazi regime. Judges had to be loyal Nazis and could be depended on to give the 'right' verdict. Under this system, the number of political prisoners increased dramatically. Between 1930 and 1932 just eight people were found guilty and executed. Between 1934 and 1939, 534 people were executed. By 1939 there were 162,734 people under 'protective arrest'.

The Nazis also made use of concentration camps – labour camps where 'enemies of the state' could be sent. Discipline was very harsh and food very poor. Few people survived a stay in the camps. At first, most prisoners were communists or trade union leaders. Later other 'undesirable' groups were also sent to the camps (e.g. Eastern Europeans, Jews, homosexuals and religious fundamentalists). In 1942, when the Nazis came up with their 'Final Solution' to the 'Jewish problem', many of these concentration camps became death camps.

SOURCE E

A cartoon from a British newspaper in February 1936.

KEY PEOPLE

Hermann Goering – *leading member of the Nazi Party who was Hitler's designated successor.*

Heinrich Himmler – *head of the Gestapo and Waffen SS and Minister of the Interior. Himmler was largely responsible for the Final Solution.*

Reinhard Heydrich – *architect of the Final Solution and Himmler's right-hand man. He was assassinated by Czechs in 1942.*

KEY WORDS

Purge – *the removal from an organisation of people who are considered undesirable.*

How did the Nazis use culture, propaganda and the mass media to control the people?

LEARNING OBJECTIVES

In this lesson you will:

- examine the use of culture, propaganda and the mass media under Nazi rule
- analyse sources to show the effectiveness of Nazi propaganda.

Use of propaganda in Nazi Germany

An essential part of Nazi control in Germany was the use of propaganda. The German people were bombarded with the party message to ensure that Hitler's regime had popular support.

In 1933 the Ministry for People's Enlightenment and Propaganda was set up under Joseph Goebbels. He saw his duty as twofold. He had to get the Nazi message across and at the same time ensure that any views hostile to Nazism were suppressed. So, Goebbels' ministry controlled the radio, the press and all areas of culture, such as films, literature, art and the theatre. Journalists were given detailed instructions about what to write in their newspapers and what could be broadcast on radio. The Nazis made sure that the radio was easily available to all Germans. Radios were so cheap that the German people had more of them per head of the population than even the wealthy Americans.

In addition, all films, plays and literature had to conform to Nazi beliefs or they could not be performed or published. In this way, 'undesirable' influences, such as jazz or Black American music, could be kept from the German people.

SOURCE A

In the next issue there must be a lead article featured as prominently as possible, in which a decision of the Führer, no matter what it may be, will be discussed as the only correct one for Germany.

Instructions issued to the press by the Ministry of Propaganda and Enlightenment in 1939.

GETTING STARTED

Look at Source A below. What propaganda method is being used here? How many more can you think of?

Book burning

In May 1933 there was a public book burning in Berlin. Goebbels watched Berlin students set fire to a collection of books that had been looted from libraries in the city. Altogether the writings of over 2500 writers were banned. Many of these writers were famous authors from the Weimar Republic. Similar restrictions were placed on musicians, poets and playwrights. In contrast, those who the Nazis approved of, like Wagner, were positively encouraged.

There were also great public displays of Nazism to promote support. Posters and photographs of Hitler, together with swastika flags, were to be found all over Germany. Hitler was always portrayed as a strong and confident leader (Source B).

SOURCE B

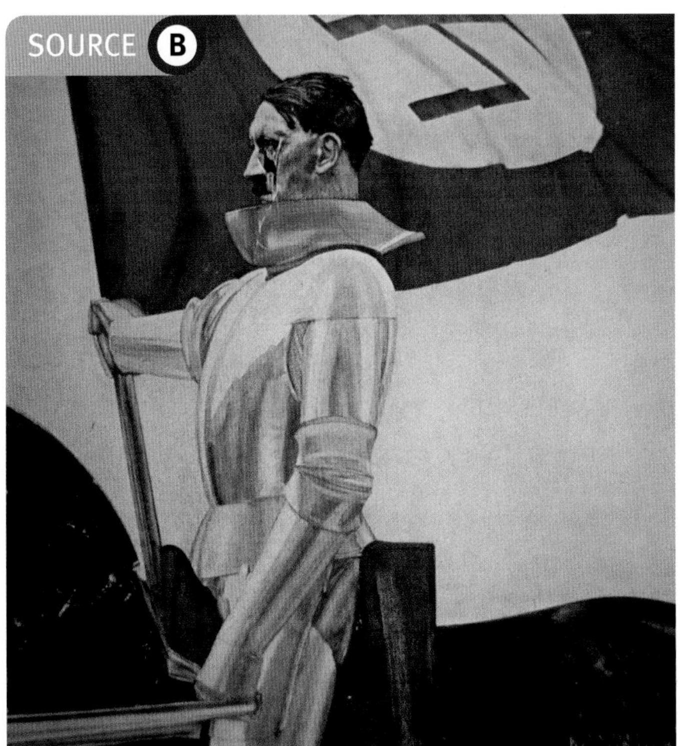

1938 portrait of Hitler by Hubert Lanzinger, entitled *Hitler the Standard Bearer*. Here, Hitler is portrayed as a medieval knight on a noble crusade to save humanity by making it purer.

SOURCE C

Jesse Owens in action at the 1936 Berlin Olympic Games.

ACTIVITIES

How effective is Source B as a piece of propaganda? Does the image in Source C change your answer?

Perhaps the most famous of these public displays were the Nuremberg rallies. Each year an enormous rally of soldiers and party officials took place in a stadium especially designed for the occasion. Other processions and rallies were held throughout the year to celebrate special events, such as the Führer's birthday in April.

The 1936 Olympic Games

The greatest propaganda coup for Hitler came in 1936 when the Olympic Games were held in Berlin. The games were used to promote German technical efficiency and the supremacy of the **Aryan race**. A brand new stadium was built holding 100,000 spectators, and it was the first Olympics to be broadcast on television. Foreign visitors were highly impressed with the excellence of the facilities and the efficiency of the organisation. Of course, Hitler ensured that the negative sides of Nazism, such as the restrictions on personal freedom and the mistreatment of the Jews, were kept in the background.

To Hitler's great joy the German team won 33 gold medals, 26 silver and 30 bronze – far more than any other team. However, he was less pleased about the performance of American athlete Jesse Owens. Owens was black, and according to Nazi racial theories inferior. Yet he was the star of the games, winning four gold medals and breaking 11 world records. Not surprisingly, Hitler refused to shake hands with the man who single-handedly showed Nazi racial theory to be nonsense.

KEY CONCEPTS

Aryan race – *according to Nazi racial theories, Germans and other 'Nordic' types – tall, lean, athletic, blond and blue-eyed – belonged to a separate and superior race known as the Aryan race.*

GradeStudio

Study Source B. What is the message of this source?

[6 marks]

Jewish persecution in Nazi Germany, 1933–38

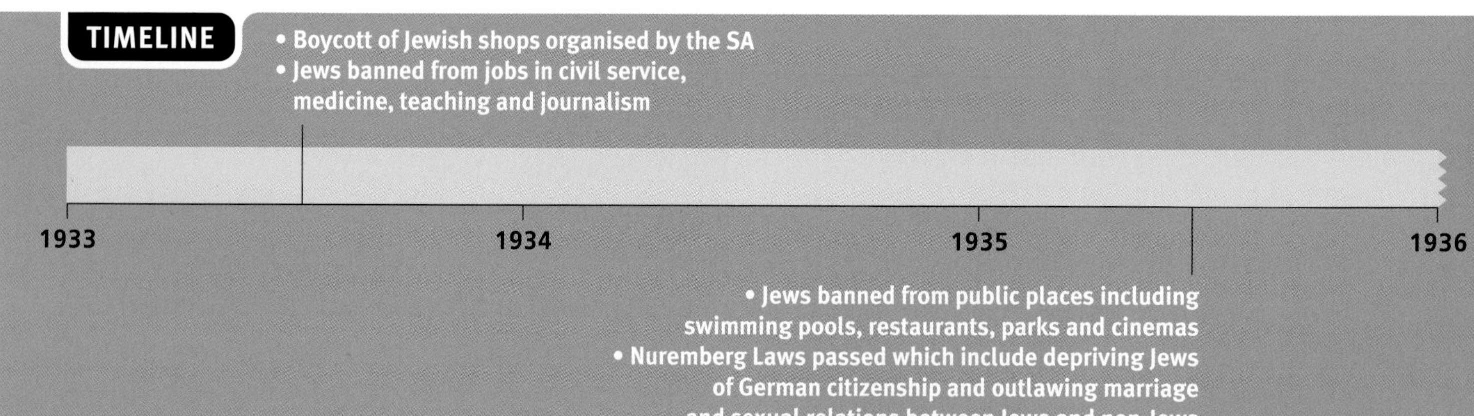

TIMELINE
• Boycott of Jewish shops organised by the SA
• Jews banned from jobs in civil service, medicine, teaching and journalism
1933
1934
1935
1936
• Jews banned from public places including swimming pools, restaurants, parks and cinemas
• Nuremberg Laws passed which include depriving Jews of German citizenship and outlawing marriage and sexual relations between Jews and non-Jews
• Hundreds of Jews arrested and sent to concentration camps

Why did the Nazis persecute many groups in German society?

LEARNING OBJECTIVES

In this lesson you will:

- examine the main groups persecuted by the Nazis and the methods of persecution used
- analyse why these groups were persecuted and examine the similarities between their persecutions.

Belief in the superiority of the Aryan race

Hitler and the Nazis believed that the German people were a 'master race' – that the Germanic racial group (the Aryans) was superior to all other groups. The ideal Aryan was tall with blond hair and blue eyes, and Hitler was frequently photographed with men and women who fitted this model.

Pride in one's racial background is a natural and common phenomenon, but the Nazis took this belief to extreme lengths. Race farms were set up, where carefully selected women were mated with ideal males in a form of selective breeding to produce children of the approved racial type. Not only did they believe that their race was best, but they believed that others were inferior. Jews, Eastern Europeans and blacks were classed as *Untermenschen* (inferior people) who were not worthy of respect.

KEY WORDS

Civil service – *the administrative branch of government.*

Scapegoat – *someone who is blamed (often unfairly) for bad things that have happened.*

GETTING STARTED

Look back at the 25-point programme of the Nazi Party from the early 1920s. How many of them would make life difficult for Jewish people to survive in Germany if they were ever enacted? Explain your answer.

Hitler's anti-Semitism

Even before Hitler came to power, he had set out his racial views in *Mein Kampf* and in speeches and Nazi literature. In Hitler's opinion, the Jews were not only an inferior race, but they had also joined with the communists to undermine Germany's efforts in the First World War. Since 1918, according to Hitler, the Jews had continued trying to ruin the German economy. At first, few people accepted Hitler's views on race. After all, many German Jews had fought with great bravery for their country in the war. But as Nazi propaganda continually reinforced the message, more and more people seemed prepared to accept the Jews as **scapegoats** for all that had gone wrong in Germany between 1918 and 1933.

Discrimination against and persecution of the Jews

Once in power, Hitler wasted little time in putting his anti-Semitic policies into action. On 1 April 1933 the SA organised a boycott of Jewish shops

KEY CONCEPTS

Concentration camp – *a camp for political prisoners and other undesirables.*

Ghetto – *part of a town or city, usually very poor, occupied by a minority group such as the Jews.*

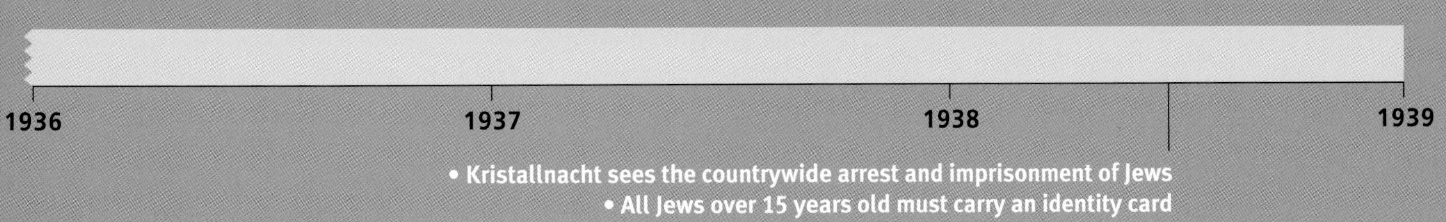

- Kristallnacht sees the countrywide arrest and imprisonment of Jews
- All Jews over 15 years old must carry an identity card
- Jewish men must add 'Israel' to their name, Jewish women 'Sara' to theirs
- Jews banned from attending university and practising law or medicine

SOURCE A

My grandmother was 90 years old. She went to a shop to buy some butter. In the door of the shop was a Stormtrooper with a gun. He said, 'You don't want to buy from a Jew.' My grandmother shook her stick and said, 'I will buy my butter where I buy it every day.' But she was the only customer that day. No one else dared. They were too scared of the man with the gun.

A Berlin woman remembers an incident in 1933.

throughout Germany. Sometimes Stormtroopers stood outside shops and physically prevented people entering (Source A). By 1934, all Jewish shops had been marked with the yellow Star of David or had the word 'Juden' written on the shop front.

Kristallnacht

Large numbers of Jews decided to emigrate from Germany – in the 1930s, half the German Jewish population left the country. Many others felt that they could not leave their homeland and hoped that things would not get worse. But in 1938 they did. A Jewish student shot dead a German diplomat in the embassy in Paris. The authorities in Germany reacted by ordering widespread attacks on Jewish homes, businesses and synagogues. In this *Kristallnacht* (Night of Broken Glass), 8000 Jewish homes and shops were attacked and synagogues were burned to the ground. Over 100 Jews were killed and thousands were sent to concentration camps.

Kristallnacht was followed by a new set of anti-Semitic laws. The Jewish community had to pay a fine of one billion marks for the murder of the diplomat in Paris. Jews were no longer allowed to run businesses and had to sell them to non-Jews at artificially low prices, and Jewish children were banned from school.

ACTIVITIES

Using the information in this lesson, describe how the Nazis made everyday life unpleasant for Jewish people.

The Final Solution

When the Second World War broke out in 1939, the Nazis gained control of much of Europe and millions of Jews came under their control. Many of them were herded into **ghettos** in the cities, where conditions were so bad that thousands starved to death. Others were sent to **concentration camps** to join other victims of the Nazi regime.

In 1941 the Germans invaded the Soviet Union. As the German army advanced, it was followed by 3000 men in the *Einsatzgruppen*. This was a group of four death squads whose job it was to kill communist officials and Jews in the occupied territories. By the end of 1941 some half a million Jews had been shot or poisoned by exhaust fumes from specially built vans.

SOURCE B

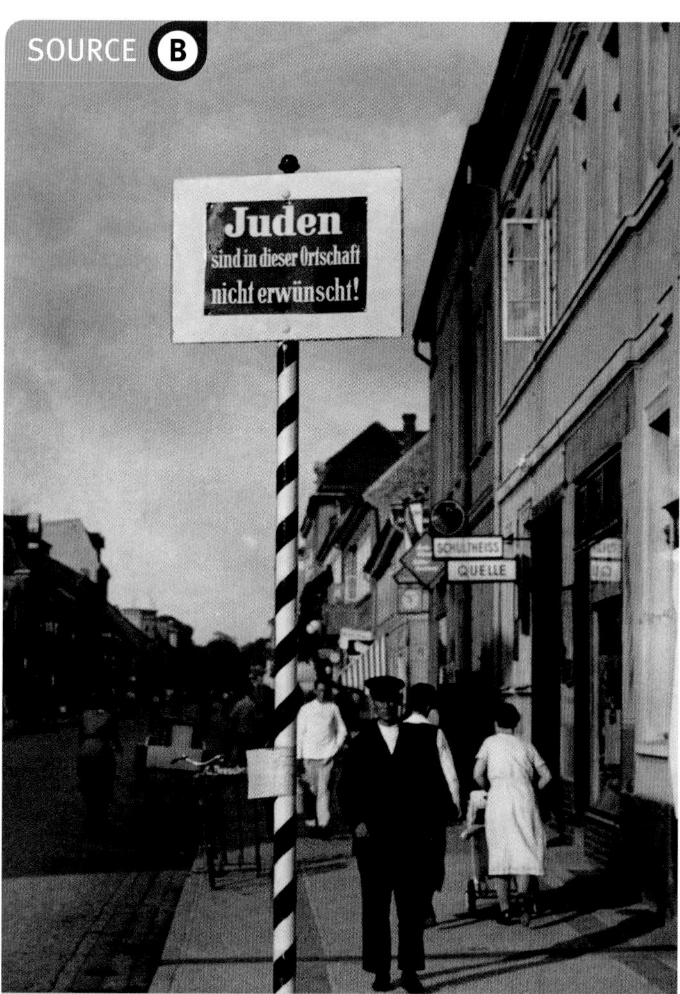

Anti-Semitic sign, stating 'Jews not wanted in this place!'

The setting up of the extermination camps

In January 1942 at the Wannsee Conference in Berlin, the Nazi authorities decided on a 'Final Solution' to the 'Jewish problem'. The Jewish people of Europe were to be rounded up and sent to extermination camps where they would be put to death. By the summer of 1942 six concentration camps had been converted into extermination camps, and in the next four years almost six million Jews were slaughtered in what has become known as the Holocaust.

Various methods were used to carry out the killing. At first, shooting was common, but it proved too slow. So instead huge chambers were built, disguised as showers. Up to 2000 Jews at a time were led into the showers, supposedly for 'delousing'. Then gas was released and within three minutes everyone was dead. Useful by-products such as gold teeth, hair and glasses were removed from the bodies which were then burned in huge ovens. In some of the camps, medical experiments were carried out on Jews to find out the limits of human endurance. For example, some Jews had major surgery performed on them without anaesthetics.

The need for secrecy

The Germans did not publicise what they were doing and Himmler, the leader of the SS in charge of the camps, ordered that the work should be kept secret. Propaganda films showing good conditions in the camps and talk of 'resettlement' of the Jews gave the impression that they were being treated well. This helped the round-up of Jews run more smoothly and minimised opposition. But word spread amongst the Jewish community about what was really happening. Soon Jewish people reacted with horror to names such as Auschwitz, Dachau and Bergen-Belsen.

The Allied governments were in a very difficult position. They were aware that something terrible was happening, but not the scale of it. And in any case, there was little that they could do. At the time, many Jews hoped that the Allies would bomb the extermination camps, but the Allies did not consider this a practical, or humane, thing to do.

As defeat loomed for Germany, an attempt was made to cover up what had happened. To speed the process of killing, the Germans had built railway lines running directly into the camps. These were pulled up, but there was no disguising what had been done – especially as the Allied soldiers found thousands of Jews in the camps, abandoned to die of starvation or diseases such as **tuberculosis**.

Number of Jews killed in death camps and by the Einsatzgruppen, shown by country

Poland	3,000,000
Soviet Union	1,252,000
Hungary	450,000
Romania	300,000
Baltic States	228,000
Germany/Austria	210,000
Netherlands	105,000
France	90,000
Bohemia/Moravia	80,000
Slovakia	75,000
Greece	54,000
Belgium	40,000
Yugoslavia	26,000
Bulgaria	14,000
Italy	8000
Luxembourg	1000
Norway	900
Total	**5,933,900**

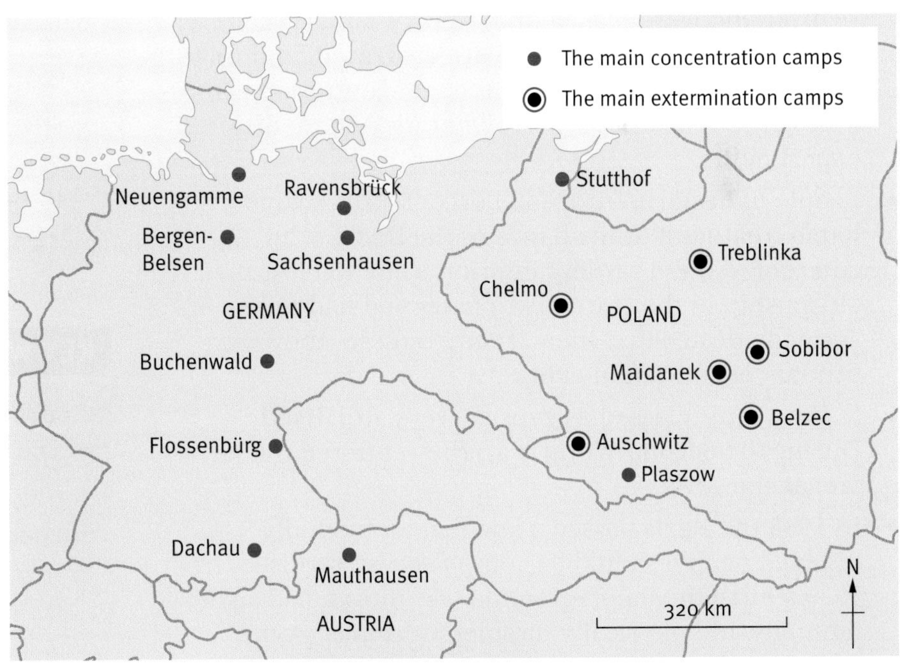

HISTORY DETECTIVE

After the Second World War, many senior Nazis were put on trial for crimes against humanity. Carry out research into these Nuremberg trials. What can you find out about the trial of Rudolf Hoess?

ACTIVITIES

1 Complete the table for the persecuted groups under Nazi rule.

Group	Persecution	Development	Numbers involved
Jews			
Homosexuals			
Eastern Europeans			
Gypsies			
Mentally disabled			
Physically disabled			
Tramps and beggars			

2 Answer the following questions:
  a What similarities do the persecutions of the different groups have in common?
  b Why were these groups persecuted?

The persecution of other minorities in Nazi Germany

- Homosexuality was despised by the Nazis as it was not in keeping with their ideal of Aryan masculinity. From 1936 all homosexuals were included in a national register and were placed under police supervision with a night **curfew**. Many were **castrated**, and up to 15,000 homosexuals were sent to concentration camps during the 1930s. Some were later used in medical experiments.
- People of Eastern European descent also received harsh treatment at the hands of the Nazis, who considered them racially inferior. They too lost their citizenship in the Nuremberg Laws and had to live on specially designated sites. If they refused, they were sent to concentration camps.
- Many people classed as gypsies were **sterilised**. During the Second World War, they suffered the same fate as the Jews.
- In 1933 the Nazis passed a law that all mentally disabled people should be compulsorily sterilised. In 1939 a **euthanasia** programme was introduced against mentally and physically disabled Germans. Some 70,000 adults and 5000 children were put to death by lethal injection, gassing or starvation. The master race, it was considered, should not include disabled people. Nazi propaganda was used to persuade people that euthanasia for the disabled was a good thing.
- Even tramps and beggars were dealt with severely. Up to half a million of them were rounded up and put into labour camps, and many were sterilised.

Describe the methods the Nazis used to deal with the 'Jewish problem'. **[4 marks]**

Examiner's tip

With a question like this, just take each step chronologically, explaining how one step grew to the next. Be very careful with the language you use to describe events.

KEY WORDS

Castration – *removal of testicles.*

Curfew – *a time set for when you have to be in your home.*

Euthanasia – *painless killing of someone usually because they have an incurable disease, or, in the case of the Nazis, because they were considered unfit to live.*

Sterilise – *deprive of the ability to have children.*

Tuberculosis – *a respiratory disease that kills. It can be rapidly passed on through close confinement, for example in a concentration camp.*

The Nazi regime: what was it like to live in Nazi Germany?

What was the purpose of the Hitler Youth?

LEARNING OBJECTIVES

In this lesson you will:

- investigate the reasons for the success of the Hitler Youth
- use sources to make judgements as part of a historical enquiry.

GETTING STARTED

One of the main aims of the Nazi Party was to indoctrinate the young in Nazi propaganda. Judging by Source A, how successful do you think they were?

The Hitler Youth and the League of German Maidens

The Nazis were particularly anxious to win the hearts and minds of the young in Germany. They knew that, no matter how much propaganda they used, there would always be some adults who rejected their ideas. But if the young could be **indoctrinated** into the Nazi way of thinking, then those views were likely to stay with them for the rest of their lives. This was the major purpose of the Hitler Youth, which had been founded in 1926. By the time the Nazis took power in 1933, it had 100,000 members.

- Boys aged between 6 and 10 years joined the Little Fellows; then from 10 to 14 years they went on to the Young Folk; finally, from 14 to 18 years they became members of the Hitler Youth.
- Girls joined the Young Girls between 10 and 14 years, and from 14 to 17 years they joined the League of German Maidens.

These youth organisations provided ideal opportunities for the leaders to put across Nazi beliefs, and members were encouraged to report their parents or teachers if they criticised the Nazi regime. But they had another purpose too. The Hitler Youth was also a training ground for the army, and great emphasis was placed on physical activity and military training. Girls did not join the army, but they were still encouraged to keep fit in preparation for motherhood – the opportunity to give birth to future soldiers.

At first, membership of the Hitler Youth was not **compulsory**, but it proved attractive to many young people with its regime of camps, sporting activities and marches. By 1936 there were over five million members and competition from other organisations was limited. Youth clubs connected with other political parties or with churches were shut down. In 1936 the Hitler Youth Law made membership compulsory, although some young people were still reluctant to join. By 1939, as the table shows, the vast majority of young Germans were part of the organisation.

SOURCE A

Hitler addresses the Hitler Youth at a Nuremberg rally, c.1938.

Membership of Nazi youth organisations, 1933–39

Year	Membership	Percentage of German population aged 10–18 years in Nazi youth organisations
1933	2,292,041	30
1934	3,577,565	47
1935	3,394,303	42
1936	5,437,601	63
1937	5,879,955	65
1938	7,031,266	77
1939	7,287,470	82

SOURCE B

KOMM ZU UNS!
O.S.
DEUTSCHES JUNGVOLK
IN DER HITLER-JUGEND

A recruiting poster for the Hitler Youth.

Members of these organisations were attracted by a variety of reasons until 1936 when membership became compulsory. Initially uniforms were smart and treasured by members in a time when children would not have had many clothes. Activities were organised such as camps and sporting activities that appealed to young boys. Girls would go to hostels and take part in stereotypically female activities such as household chores. The boys' movement became more militaristic as the focus was placed on marching and fighting. Many surviving members of these organisations talk of their experiences of membership in glowing terms and of how people (many Jewish children) who could not be members felt like outsiders.

KEY WORDS

Compulsory – *required by law.*

Indoctrinated – *persuaded to accept a set of beliefs uncritically.*

ACTIVITIES

1. Analyse Source B. How is the Nazi propaganda machine trying to appeal to young people to join the Hitler Youth?
2. How successful was the Nazi propaganda machine at appealing to young people? Explain your answer by using the table above.

VOICE YOUR OPINION!

The Nazis gained a lot from their youth organisations. Working in pairs, make a list of all the benefits to the Nazis of the Hitler Youth. Share your list with others in the class. Discuss whether you think that young people were willing participants in these organisations.

How successful were Nazi policies towards women and the family?

LEARNING OBJECTIVES

In this lesson you will:

- examine a school timetable for evidence of Nazi ideology
- analyse a source for information on Nazi ideology.

GETTING STARTED

Before you start your investigation into Nazi education make sure you have your school timetable to hand. What is taught in subjects like Maths, Geography and History? Be ready to compare it with a Nazi school's timetable.

Education under the Nazi regime

The youth movements were not the only way the Nazis were able to persuade young people to accept Nazi beliefs. Education also played a major part in winning the hearts and minds of the young. They directed what was to be taught in schools and placed special emphasis on the subjects that they considered suitable. So subjects like History (to show how successful the Nazis had been) and Biology (to explain Nazi racial beliefs) became much more important. The amount of time given to physical education trebled in the 1930s. Other subjects, such as Race Studies and Ideology, also appeared on the timetable, as Nazi beliefs were taught as accepted facts.

Education for boys and girls was different. A greater emphasis was placed on domestic science and other subjects suitable for motherhood in girls' schools, whereas the importance of military training was emphasised in boys' schools.

In the classroom, Nazi ideas were promoted by using textbooks that had been rewritten to conform to Nazi beliefs, and by ensuring that lessons were taught by teachers who supported the party. A mixture of propaganda and intimidation led to 97 per cent of teachers becoming members of the National Socialist Teachers' League, founded to encourage teachers into the 'correct' way of thinking.

Examples used in class exercises further encouraged support for Nazi views. Geography lessons emphasised the harshness of the Treaty of Versailles, Physics lessons concentrated on weapon making, and even Maths lessons for young children were sometimes about bombing Jewish ghettos. Of course, a major message that was continually repeated in schools was the supremacy of the Aryan race and the inferiority of blacks, Eastern Europeans and, in particular, Jews.

ACTIVITIES

Look at the timetable below. What evidence is there to illustrate that this is a timetable for a girls' school? What would you expect to be on it if it were for a boys' school?

SOURCE A

Periods	Mon	Tues	Weds	Thu	Fri	Sat
8.0–8.45	German	German	German	German	German	German
8.50–9.35	Geography	History	Singing	Geography	History	Singing
9.40–10.25	Race Study	Race Study	Race Study	Race Study	Race Study	Race Study
10.25–11.0	Break – with sports and special announcements					
11.0–12.05	Domestic Science with Mathematics					
12.10–12.55	The Science of breeding (Eugenics) – Health Biology					
2.0–6.0	Sport each day					

A 1935 school timetable for a girls' school.

SOURCE B

We do not consider it correct for the woman to interfere in the world of a man. We consider it natural that these two worlds remain distinct. What the man gives in courage on the battlefield, the woman gives in self-sacrifice. Every child that a woman brings into the world is a battle; a battle waged for the existence of her people.

From Hitler's Address to Women at the Nuremberg rally in 1934.

The role of women in Nazi society

As you will have realised from the way girls were treated, the Nazis had very strong views about the place of women in society. It was their duty to remain at home as child-bearers and as supporters of their husbands. They were not considered equal. Employment opportunities for women declined, and under the Nazis there were fewer women teachers, doctors and civil servants. They were banned from being judges and removed from jury service because they were said to be incapable of thinking without emotion. As a shortage of workers developed, particularly in the war years, more women were encouraged to work, but they were never allowed to join the armed forces, as women did with such distinction in Britain.

As far as the Nazis were concerned, women should be encouraged to have as many children as possible. Hitler was alarmed at the falling birth rate in Germany, so contraception was discouraged and mothers with eight children or more were awarded a golden Mother Cross (with silver for six children and bronze for four). Motherhood and family life were also prominent in Nazi propaganda. Posters and broadcasts emphasised the qualities of 'traditional' German women. In some cities, women were banned from smoking because it was 'unladylike', and make-up and the latest fashions were discouraged. Ideal German women had flat heels, plaited hair and no make-up.

Of course, many German women objected to their role as second-class citizens, and some joined illegal opposition political parties to campaign for better status. But in most countries in the 1930s women were not considered to be the equal of men. Nazi beliefs about women were not necessarily unusual, just more extreme than elsewhere.

HISTORY DETECTIVE

There is no shortage of Nazi material on the internet. Find another poster that appeals to one of the family members mentioned above and say how it is successful.

ACTIVITIES

In what way does the poster in Source C reflect the Nazi view of the family?

SOURCE C

A Nazi poster showing an ideal German family.

GradeStudio

Study Source C. Why do you think this poster was published in Germany? **[7 marks]**

Examiner's tip

This is a reasonably straightforward question; it is asking you to consider the purpose of the source. It is asking you to explain its meaning and tie it in to Nazi family policy.

Were most people better off under Nazi rule?

LEARNING OBJECTIVES

In this lesson you will:

- examine Nazi policy on reducing unemployment in the 1930s
- investigate how successful the Nazis were in making Germans better off.

The effectiveness of Nazi economic policies

When Hitler came to power, the German economy was in ruins as a result of the world Depression that set in after the Wall Street Crash. Unemployment stood at six million, and Hitler took steps to bring this figure down. After all, he had promised in 1933 to beat unemployment within four years.

Re-armament and public works programmes

A number of methods were used to win the battle against unemployment. Hitler's re-armament policy led to increased production in the iron and steel industry, and in companies making weapons. Obviously more workers were needed for this. Hitler also reduced the number of unemployed men by putting them into the army. It was estimated that Germany's army had 750,000 more soldiers in 1938 than in 1933. The Nazis also helped create jobs by spending money on public works. For example, a network of motorways (autobahns) across Germany was begun. Between 1933 and 1938, over 3000 kilometres of autobahns were constructed. Help was also given to private firms to build houses. These measures helped reduce unemployment to only 218,000 by July 1938.

Employment rises but wages fall

But things were not quite as rosy as they looked. Unemployment fell in all European countries as the Depression came to an end, so perhaps the achievements of the Nazis were not so great. Also there was no improvement in the level of wages. People's average working week rose from 45 hours in 1928 to 50 in 1939 and over 60 towards the end of the war. Yet wages were lower in 1938 than they had been in 1928.

GETTING STARTED

Revisit the terms of the Treaty of Versailles. Which of them did Hitler break in order to bring prosperity back to Germany?

ACTIVITIES

Clearly the Nazi Party reduced unemployment, but at what cost? Write down all the positive things done in this area. Then make a list of all the negative points. What do you think? Were the German people better off under the Nazis?

Conditions for workers

German workers also lost the right to have their own trade unions. Instead the government set up the German Labour Front. Two other organisations, 'Beauty of Labour' and 'Strength Through Joy', were set up to promote better working conditions and to give rewards for good work, but there is no doubt that under the Nazis German workers worked harder and for less reward. There was also a shortage of consumer goods for Germans to buy as the German economy became increasingly linked to preparing for war.

By 1939 the Nazis had reduced unemployment and brought political stability to Germany. But this was achieved at a very heavy cost. Hitler's totalitarian regime had abolished many of the rights that citizens in other countries took for granted. In Nazi Germany there were no opposition political parties and no free trade unions. The media were censored, workers had longer hours for less pay and freedom of speech was stifled. Education, the churches, the courts, local government and even youth clubs were rigorously controlled by the Nazi regime. Yet none of this compares with the treatment handed out to minority groups in Germany, particularly the Jews.

Beauty of Labour

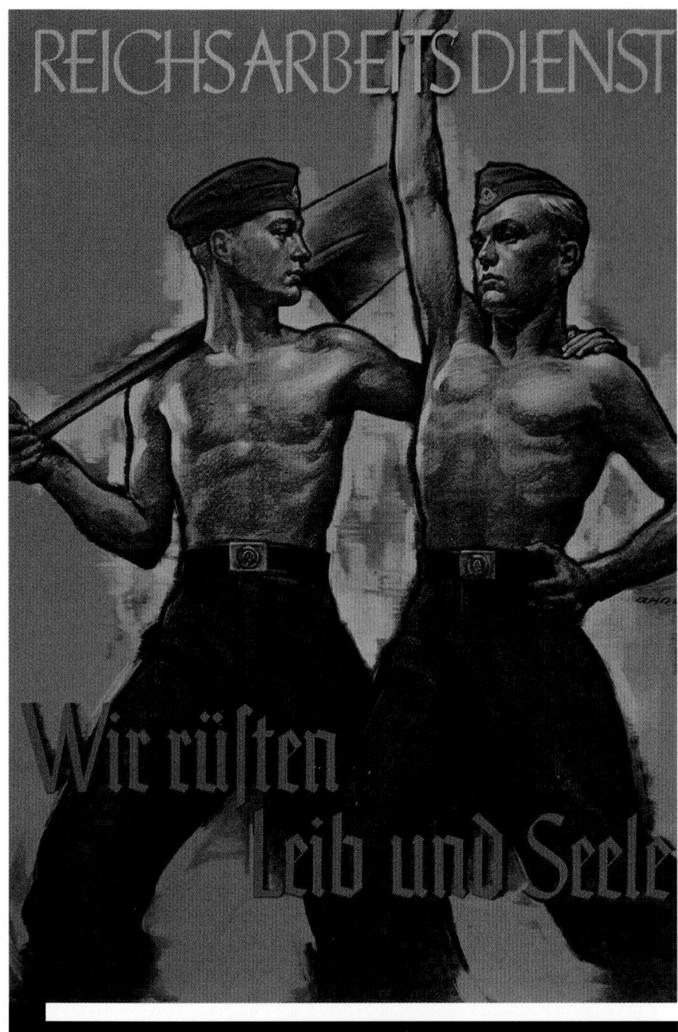

'We Build Body and Soul.' c.1935.

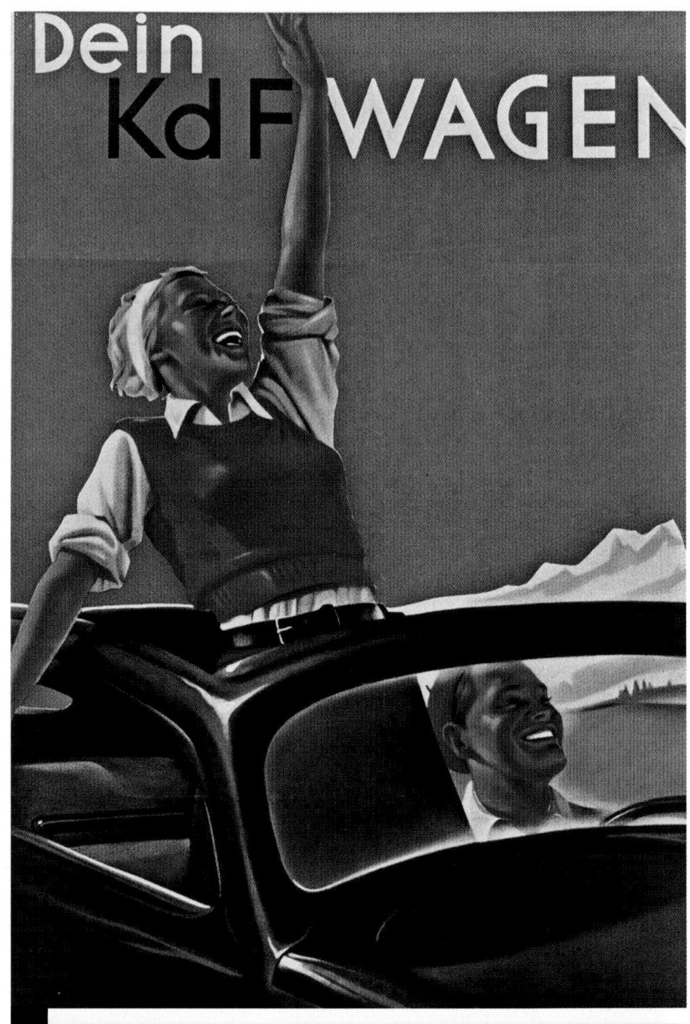

'Your own KdF car', 1939.

The two posters are typical Nazi propaganda; they are both part of the Beauty of Labour campaign that aimed to make people enjoy their work more. The first is trying to recruit volunteers to the Nazi Labour Service, the second is a tourist poster showing the wonderful new roads, roads created by the Beauty of Labour programme.

Explain how the first uses typical Nazi images to appeal to its target audience. How would the second appeal to travellers from outside Germany?

You may recognise this car as the icon of sixties' popular culture: the Volkswagen Beetle. However, it had its start in life as part of the Nazi 'Strength through Joy' programme, a programme enabling people to save for foreign holidays and even cars.

Does the second picture show you how people saved for these cars?

Not everyone who saved for a car or holiday got one. What do you think the government did with the money collected from the savers?

How did the coming of war change life in Germany?

LEARNING OBJECTIVES

In this lesson you will:

- examine the effects of the Second World War on the German people
- investigate the effects of Nazi policy during the Second World War.

GETTING STARTED

In order to more fully understand the impact of the Second World War on the German people you must have some understanding of the course of the war. Using any resources that come to hand, construct a basic timeline of the main military events of the war: be sure to include all battles/events that include the Germans.

A war on two fronts

In the first few years of the Second World War, the German **blitzkrieg** tactics brought outstanding victories and western Europe was quickly overrun. At home, Nazi propaganda films celebrated victory over the French, and the German people rejoiced at the revenge they had gained for their harsh treatment in the Treaty of Versailles. Victory had been won with such ease that there had been little cost to Germany. In fact the spoils of war – raw materials, captured land, slave labourers – opened up the prospect of Germany becoming a very rich and powerful country. It was true that food and clothes rationing had been introduced at the end of 1939, but this seemed a small price to pay.

In 1941, Hitler launched his attack on Soviet Russia. At first, the Germans made rapid advances and drove deep into the Soviet Union. By the end of 1941, however, the advance had ground to a halt in the Russian winter. Soon the campaign became a bleeding sore in which the Germans lost nearly 200,000 men. Setbacks soon occurred elsewhere, too, as the German army suffered defeats in North Africa.

The impact of the Second World War on the lives of the German people

Conversion to a war economy

After 1941, the German people began to realise how difficult war was when you were not winning. Supplies were needed for the armed forces and sacrifices had to be made at home. Goebbels stepped up his propaganda campaign to raise morale and ask for sacrifices. When a call went out for warm clothing for the troops in the Soviet Union, the German people donated 1.5 million fur coats. In 1942 Albert Speer was made armaments minister and told to organise the country for 'total war'. German factories were forced to work longer hours and food rations were cut. More and more women were drafted into the factories to keep production up.

The bombing of German cities

While these sacrifices were being made, another factor entered the equation. From 1942 the Allies began bombing raids on German cities. They intended to destroy important factories and disrupt production of goods for the war. However, they were quite prepared to cause civilian casualties too, since this was considered an acceptable way to break the morale of the German people and force surrender.

'Thousand bomber' raids poured bombs on to German cities and killed more than half a million civilians. In one raid alone, on Dresden in February 1945, 135,000 Germans died. By April 1945 Berlin was in ruins and its people were starving.

These raids were often followed by pamphlet drops, which encouraged the German people to give in. By the beginning of 1945, with the German armies in retreat, shortages of basic foods, more than three million civilians dead and many major cities reduced to rubble, most Germans were happy to end the war. The problem was that the Führer, who was seen less and less frequently, was determined to fight on. So the German people had to endure four more months of fighting. It was no wonder that opposition to Nazi rule grew dramatically in the last year of the war.

Fact file

Effects of the Allied air raids on Hamburg:

Factories destroyed	600
People killed	40,000
People badly injured	40,000
Homes destroyed/uninhabitable	60%

SOURCE A

An Allied plane dropping bombs on a German city.

SOURCE B

Hitler and Goebbels enjoying Eintopf at Hitler's headquarters.

ACTIVITIES

One-dish day (Eintopftag) was introduced in order to cut down on the amount of food eaten once a week. Eintopftag was every Sunday.

Use Source B to explain how Eintopftag would help the war effort. Do you think it would be welcomed by many Germans?

VOICE YOUR OPINION!

At what point in the war do you think it started going wrong for the Nazis?

GradeStudio

'Most German people benefited from living inder the Nazi regime.' How far do you agree with this statement? Explain your answer. **[10 marks]**

Examiner's tip

This is the big question that summarises your knowledge of the last section. It is clearly contentious and you must look at both positive and negative aspects of life in Nazi Germany. Start by writing a list of the positives and negatives. Ensure you say who benefited and who lost out. You will be able to see the shape of your answer clearly now; one side will have more evidence to back it up than the other. Write your two sections including evidence and finish with a statement that incorporates a direct answer to the question.

Get your sources sorted

Essential knowledge

- Hitler wanted to create a master-race and eliminate undesirables.
- This race was called the Aryan race and the perfect specimens were athletic, blonde and blue-eyed.
- Members of the SS had to have a special licence before they could marry.
- Mothers were encouraged to have large families by medals awarded according to the number of children they had.

What is the message of the source?

Look back at earlier 'Get your sources sorted' sections to remind yourself what is meant by the 'message' of the cartoon. Use your contextual knowledge (knowledge of what is happening in this period) to help inform your answer. The clear message here is that you must stay healthy in order to have lots of children. This message is quite straightforward so you will need to support your answer with information from both the source and your own knowledge.

SOURCE 

The artist is showing the father as an idealistic Nazi father figure – he is athletic, blonde and healthy; an ideal father.

The mother is standing next to her husband cradling a small child. This depiction of the mother shows an idealised version of what the Nazis wished all their mothers to be like. She has her hair tied up, showing that she is ready for the day-to-day business of running a family and doing all the chores you would expect. She is protective of the small child but also proud and showing him off to the viewer (this is what you could have if you were healthy).

He has his father's protective hand on his shoulder. The son is a copy of the father – an example of a good Nazi child. His fist is clenched in determination to be like his father.

Both are pretty girls with neat and tidy hair. They are carrying toys and a basket. Both girls are copies of their mother and are depicted ready to do women's work: the doll representing childcare and the basket shopping.

'Healthy Parents Have Healthy Children'.

GradeStudio

Germany, 1918-45

Grade Studio

Here is an example of a question that requires you to consider two sides of an argument. This is a common type of question in Unit A971. The skill you require is to use your knowledge of the topic to give evidence in supporting a two-sided argument.

'Hitler controlled the German people only through terror and coercion.'

To what extent do you agree with this statement?
Explain your answer. **[10 marks]**

Examiner's tip

Think about everything you have learnt about how Hitler controlled Germany and decide which bits are relevant to this question. It's always a good idea to plan what specific evidence you are going to use to support each side of the argument. Look at this mark scheme before thinking about what you would need to do to answer this question

Mark scheme

Level 1: General and vague assertions
Level 2: Identifies or describes factors from at least one side of the argument
Level 3: Explains evidence supporting one side of the argument
Level 4: Explains evidence supporting both sides of the argument
Level 5: As level four, but also reaches and supports a final judgement in answer to the question.

Look at the example below and think about how the candidate moves up these levels.

People living in Nazi Germany were often too scared to speak out against Hitler and the Nazis. Hitler used force to terrorise people into submission. Anyone who disagreed with Nazi policies ran the risk of imprisonment, torture and even death at the hands of the Gestapo and so many people were too scared to question Hitler's authority.

Examiner's comment

This is a good start. The candidate is using the principle of a three part paragraph: They have made a clear **point**, supported it with specific **evidence** and then linked the evidence to the question in order to **explain** their ideas.

By giving examples of how Hitler controlled the German people the candidate has achieved level two: identification.

In the example above the candidate explains their evidence and so the answer moves up to level three. This will earn approximately half marks.

To go up to level four you need to explain the other side of the argument.
Now look at this example:

Examiner's comment

People living in Nazi Germany were often too scared to speak out against Hitler and the Nazis. Hitler used force to terrorise people into submission. Anyone who disagreed with Nazi policies ran the risk of imprisonment, torture and even death at the hands of the Gestapo and so many people were too scared to question Hitler's authority.

However, this was not the only method Hitler used to control the people of Germany. He also developed policies that were popular in order to win public support. In the 1920s Germany had faced many economic hardships, such as having to pay back heavy reparations to the victors of the First World War. Then, in the 1930s the worldwide Depression caused massive unemployment. In an economic climate that saw people struggling to make ends meet, Hitler provided people with jobs on public works such as building autobahns. This made Hitler popular with the German people and demonstrates that his control was based on more than just terror and coercion.

By explaining evidence from both sides of the argument the candidate moves up to level four. To strengthen this still further the candidate could explain more than one piece of evidence for each argument.

To attain level five the candidate needs to reach an overall judgement about the original question: was terror and coercion the only way that Hitler controlled Germany? It is important to save something new for this conclusion, rather than just summarising what has already been said.

Have a go at writing your own conclusion in which you reach and explain a clear judgement in answer to this question.

Russia, 1905–41

Introduction

In 1905 Russia was a backward country with a mainly rural economy run by an absolute monarch, Tsar Nicholas II. By 1941 the country had experienced the Second World War, two revolutions, a civil war and the assassination of the ruling family. The leader who had emerged, Stalin, was a feared and ruthless dictator who crushed all opposition, even turning against his colleagues in the Communist Party. What follows is an attempt to explain these traumatic changes.

At the beginning of the 20th century, industry in Russia was growing fast, creating new cities and an industrial working class. In the poor conditions and social misery of these cities, revolutionary groups, committed to overthrowing the Tsar's regime, could flourish.

In 1905 the growth of opposition, combined with a Russian defeat in the war against Japan, led to a revolution against the Tsar's rule. Nicholas was forced to introduce reforms, including the creation of a Duma (parliament).

But the Tsar soon regained his authority. His secret police broke up the revolutionary groups, and many of their leaders were forced to flee into exile.

Although Nicholas appeared to have restored his control, the impact of the First World War showed that this was only a temporary state of affairs. After early successes the Russian armies suffered terrible defeats. Back home there was rapid inflation and shortages of basic necessities, such as food. In March 1917 the Tsar was forced to accept that he had lost the support of his people. He abdicated and was replaced by a Provisional Government. This government lasted only a few months before it too was overthrown. The first section will address the question why the Tsarist regime collapsed.

ACTIVITIES

Look at the events that happened in Russia between 1905 and 1941. Using just the information above, make a graph to chart the fortunes of the country over the course of the 36-year period. On the x-axis plot the extent of the country's fortunes and on the y-axis the dates and events, with a brief explanation of why you think something was good or bad for Russia. What do you think is the overall 'feel' of what happened to Russia between 1905 and 1941?

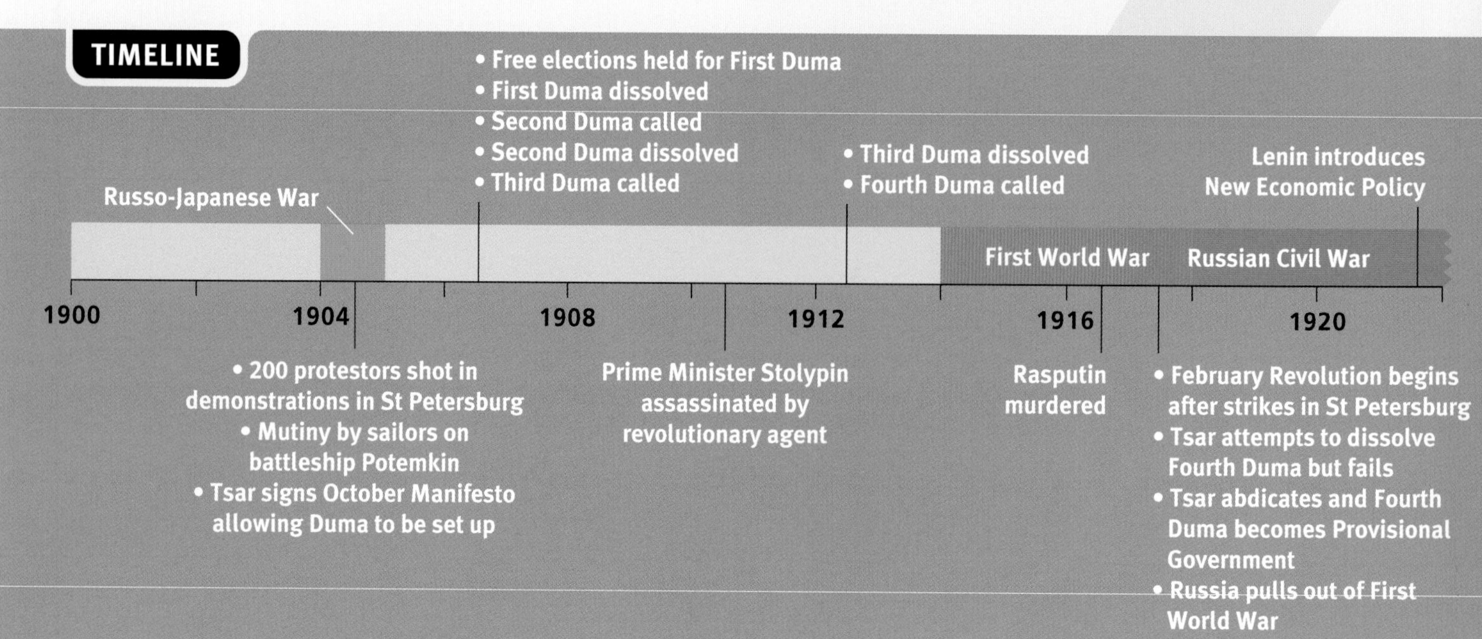
TIMELINE
Russo-Japanese War
• Free elections held for First Duma
• First Duma dissolved
• Second Duma called
• Second Duma dissolved
• Third Duma called
• Third Duma dissolved
• Fourth Duma called
Lenin introduces New Economic Policy
First World War
Russian Civil War
1900
1904
1908
1912
1916
1920
• 200 protestors shot in demonstrations in St Petersburg
• Mutiny by sailors on battleship Potemkin
• Tsar signs October Manifesto allowing Duma to be set up
Prime Minister Stolypin assassinated by revolutionary agent
Rasputin murdered
• February Revolution begins after strikes in St Petersburg
• Tsar attempts to dissolve Fourth Duma but fails
• Tsar abdicates and Fourth Duma becomes Provisional Government
• Russia pulls out of First World War

From November 1917 the Bolsheviks (later called Communists) governed Russia. Under Lenin the Bolsheviks defeated their opponents in the civil war and began building a new communist Soviet Union. A detailed explanation of this will form the second section.

On Lenin's death in 1924, Stalin emerged as the new leader. The focus of the third section is how Stalin was able to gain and hold onto power.

The fourth and final section concentrates on Stalin's determination to modernise the Soviet Union, and the impact of his policies. He gained control of the countryside and brutally enforced collectivisation of agriculture, and his Five-Year Plans saw massive government investment in heavy industry. By the time of the Second World War, the Soviet Union had been transformed into one of the world's great industrial powers, but at great cost.

A map of the Russian Empire.

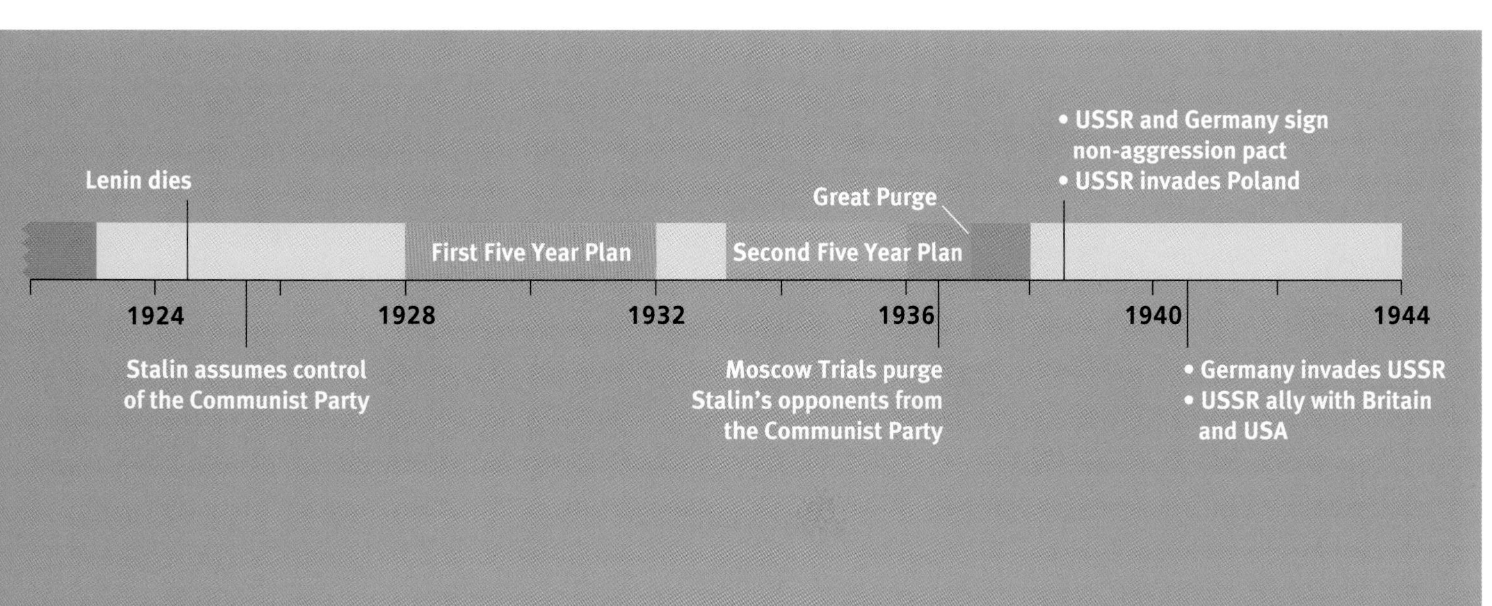

Why did the Tsarist regime collapse in 1917?

How well did the Tsarist regime deal with the difficulties of ruling Russia up to 1914?

LEARNING OBJECTIVES

In this lesson you will:

- examine the key features of Russian society c.1905
- analyse the key features and characteristics of Russian society c.1905.

KEY WORDS

Anarchy – *a state of chaos and disorder due to lack of government control.*

Dissent – *opposition to official rules.*

Provincial governors – *rulers of provinces.*

Russian Orthodox Church – *the national church of Russia.*

GETTING STARTED

Compare Sources A and B. Most Russians were peasants (Source A) who worked on the land. Others were industrial workers (Source B) who worked in the growing towns and cities.

In pairs, discuss what the two groups might have in common and what differences they might have.

HISTORY DETECTIVE

You may have already studied how the Industrial Revolution affected living standards in Britain. If you can picture the problems that this process brought to Britain, it may help you to visualise what it was like living in Russia at the start of the twentieth century.

KEY PEOPLE

Tsar Nicholas II – *Tsar of Russia, 1894–1918.*

SOURCE A

Russian peasants in their village, mid-1890s.

SOURCE B

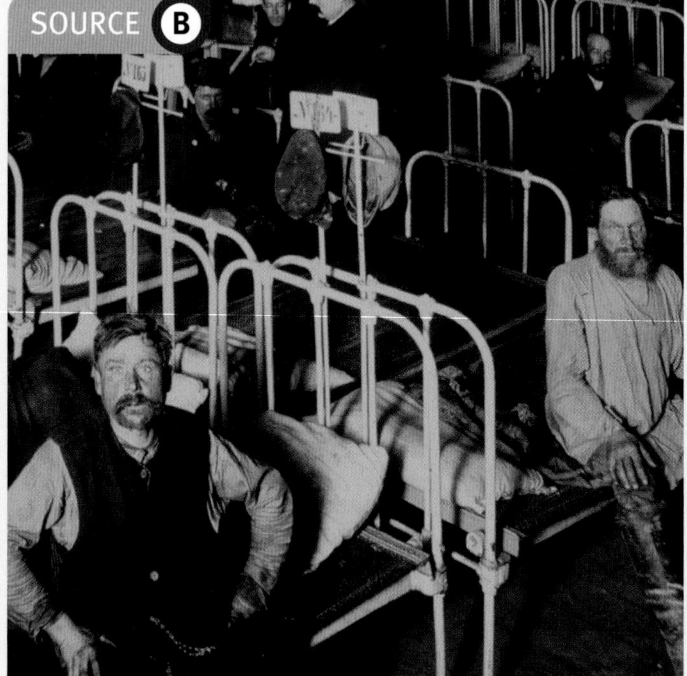

Boarding house for industrial workers, Moscow, 1911.

Background

In March 1917, **Tsar Nicholas II** was forced from power by a revolution, and Russia ceased to be a monarchy. The revolution was sparked off by the pressures of war, but it had its roots in the failure of the Tsarist regime to modernise itself. Nicholas ruled over the most backward of all the great powers – a country in which the people enjoyed very little political freedom, and in which industrialisation was only just getting under way. Most Russians were poor peasants living in the countryside. Despite only just surviving a first revolution in 1905, the Tsar was still the absolute ruler of his country, and his reluctance to share power eventually lost him the support of almost every group in Russian society.

Main features of Russian society and Tsarist rule in the early 20th century

Imperial Russia

Russian rulers were known as Tsars, or emperors. Unlike the rulers of the other great powers, in 1900 the Tsar still ruled the country himself from his capital, St Petersburg, with the help of ministers he chose, who were answerable only to him. Russia had no parliament, and the people had no right to vote in elections. Local government was in the hands of **provincial governors** appointed by the Tsar. This was a very personal system, where a lot depended on the ability of the Tsar. If he were strong and talented, Russia's government might work well, despite the size of the country. But if the Tsar was weak, Russia might slip back into **anarchy**. Most Tsars therefore ruled in a harsh and repressive manner, crushing any sign of **dissent** from their people. In many ways, Russia in 1900 was still stuck in the Middle Ages, rather than a modern state on the threshold of the 20th century.

Fact file

In this book we will spell Tsar T-S-A-R, but when you read other books you may find it spelt Tzar, Csar or Czar. It is still the same word, but because of difficulties translating the Russian language into English there are a number of ways of spelling some words; Tsar is one of them.

VOICE YOUR OPINION!

Study Source C. What problems can you see of ruling over such a diverse mix of people?

SOURCE C

Great Russian	55.6	
Ukrainian	22.4	
Polish	7.9	
White Russian	5.8	
Jewish	5	(defined by faith not language)
Kirgiz	4	
Tartar	3.4	
Finnish	3.1	
German	1.8	
Latvian	1.4	
Bashkir	1.3	
Lithuanian	1.2	
Armenian	1.2	
Romanian/Moldavian	1.1	
Estonian	1	
Mordvinian	1	
Georgian	0.8	
Tadzhik	0.3	
Turkmeian	0.3	
Greek	0.2	
Bulgarian	0.2	

The major nationalities of the Russian Empire (in millions) according to the 1897 census.

Russia was a deeply religious, Christian country. The link between the **Russian Orthodox Church** and the Tsar was close. The Church did much to uphold the authority of the Tsar, and in return had considerable political influence. However, Russia's size and diversity meant that many Russians were not members of the Orthodox Church. There were countless religious sects, not to mention other Christian churches and the different religions of the many nationalities that lived within the Russian Empire.

When Tsar Nicholas II came to the throne in 1894, he seemed to have much to offer. He was hard working, sincere and devoted to his family. However, he also had significant weaknesses. He was indecisive and found it hard to concentrate on governing the country. Worst of all, he was not able to respond to the great pressures for change that were building up in Russian society. Instead, he wanted to turn the clock back to an imaginary golden age when the Tsar's power was unchallenged. Just when Russia needed a flexible and imaginative leader, it got a Tsar who saw any modernisation as a threat to his own position.

KEY WORDS

Okhrana – *the Tsar's secret police.*
Zemstvo – *local council.*

KEY PEOPLE

Karl Marx – *influential German political theorist, author of the Communist Manifesto.*

The countryside

Russia was a rural society in which most people were poor. Most of the population were peasants who lived off the land. Until the mid-19th century, most peasants lived under a form of slavery known as serfdom. They had to work for the landowner whose land they lived on, and in return they had the right to work on their leased fields. In 1861 Tsar Alexander II abolished serfdom and allowed the former serfs to buy their land, although it was often not enough to make a decent living. The village elders retained control over the lives of individual peasants, who were not free to leave the village without permission. Peasants were allocated strips of land in fields, in accordance with traditional farming practice. This was very inefficient and made it difficult for new methods to be introduced.

Although Russia could usually produce enough food for its people, bad harvests sometimes brought famine. By the end of the 19th century, there was a growing realisation that agriculture needed modernising. The population was growing fast and there was not enough land to go round.

Landowners

Although there was poverty in the Russian countryside, there was also great wealth. The great landowners held on to large estates when the serfs were freed, and they were the most important and influential members of rural society. They provided local government in the villages, and acted as a link between the common people and the wishes of the Tsar. However, their position was becoming less secure. Tensions were increasing between them and the peasants, who wanted the land for themselves. Many landowners ran their estates inefficiently and frittered away their wealth. But the better landowners realised that they had to run agriculture more efficiently. These landowners dominated the local councils, called **zemstvos**, which began to press the Tsar for reforms.

The cities

By 1900 the process of industrialisation had begun. Towns and cities grew as people moved from the countryside to look for work in the factories. Russia now had an industrial working class – people who would previously have been peasants, but who now lived and worked in the cities. After Witte became Minister of Finance in 1892, the government encouraged the development of industry, and during the 1890s the Russian economy grew faster than that of any other country in Europe. This growth continued, more slowly, right up to the outbreak of war in 1914. A whole range of industries – mining, iron and steel, textiles, oil, food processing, railways – came into being. Foreign investment flooded in to take advantage of the boom. Within a single generation, Russia became a significant industrial power.

However, the pace of development created problems. Living and working conditions in the industrial cities were appalling. The government did little to protect workers from exploitation. There were few controls on child labour, industrial injuries were common, and employers paid starvation wages. In these circumstances, dissatisfaction and unrest increased among the workers. The cities turned into breeding grounds for revolutionary ideas.

Opposition to the Tsar

Russia had a tradition of revolutionary violence against the monarchy. This was not surprising in a country where opposition to Tsarist rule was illegal. In 1881 revolutionaries had assassinated Tsar Alexander II. The rapid social and economic changes of the late 19th century gave great opportunities for revolutionary groups to spread their ideas among the working people.

ACTIVITIES

Look at the diagram of Russian society c.1905.

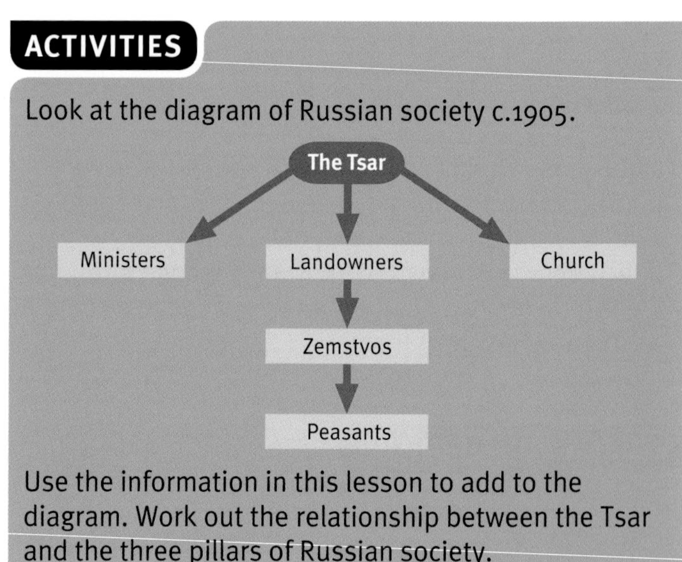

Use the information in this lesson to add to the diagram. Work out the relationship between the Tsar and the three pillars of Russian society.

Marxists

The most important of Russia's revolutionaries were the **Marxists**. These were followers of **Karl Marx** (1818–83), the German socialist, who in his book *Das Kapital* had described how capitalism would collapse and be replaced by communism. Although they claimed to be struggling to bring about a workers' revolution, these revolutionaries came mainly from Russia's emerging middle classes. They were constantly harassed by the Tsar's secret police, and many spent years in exile, either in Siberia or abroad.

The revolutionaries argued a lot among themselves. At a conference in London in 1903, the most important of the revolutionary groups, the Social Democratic Party, split into two factions. These were known as the **Bolsheviks** and the **Mensheviks**.

Other revolutionary groups had their own distinctive ideas. Unlike the **Social Democrats**, who believed that the revolution would happen through the struggles of the industrial workers, the **Social Revolutionaries (SRs)** believed that revolution in Russia would have to be based on the peasants and their struggle for land.

Repression

By the early years of the 20th century, it was clear to many Russians that change was needed to deal with the country's problems. But the Tsar's response to this was more repression. The **Okhrana**, the secret police, were extremely effective in dealing with opposition groups. An extensive network of informers made sure the authorities knew about the revolutionaries' plans. Many opponents of the regime were tortured, imprisoned or even executed. Disturbances in the countryside were crushed by troops. However, Tsarist repression was not just a matter of violence towards the opposition. Newspapers were heavily censored, and even the activities of moderate organisations like the zemstvos were strictly controlled so that there was no criticism of the Tsar.

KEY CONCEPTS

Bolsheviks – *a party led by Lenin which took its name from the Russian word for 'majority'. They believed in seizing power at the first opportunity.*

Marxists – *followers of Karl Marx's theory that social change could only happen after a violent struggle between the ruling capitalist class and the workers.*

Mensheviks – *a party that took its name from the Russian word for 'minority', although its support increased in later years. The Mensheviks believed in co-operating with other groups to improve the lives of working people.*

Social Democrats – *a party that wanted change. The Social Democrats were prepared to make this happen through the industrial workforce.*

Social Revolutionaries (SRs) – *a party that wanted change, but expected it would happen through the struggles of the peasants and their desire for land.*

SOURCE D

A picture from the early 20th century showing the structure of Russia's society before 1917. The workers at the bottom are commenting on each of the classes above them, from top to bottom. 'We work for them while they dispose of our money, pray on our behalf, eat on our behalf and shoot at us.'

VOICE YOUR OPINION!

How fair is the cartoon's description of Russian society before 1917?

How did the Tsar survive the 1905 revolution?

LEARNING OBJECTIVES

In this lesson you will:

- examine the key events of the 1905 revolution in chronological order
- analyse the causes of the 1905 revolution and make judgements on their importance.

GETTING STARTED

Look at Source B. It shows Russian troops attacking Russian people. With a partner, discuss what you think could make this happen.

SOURCE A

Russia's comprehensive defeat at the hands of a small, supposedly inferior, Asian country was an undeniable humiliation ... Within Russia, the incompetence of the government, which the war glaringly revealed, excited the social unrest which it had been specifically designed to dampen.

Michael Lynch writing in *Reaction and Revolutions: Russia 1881–1924.*

VOICE YOUR OPINION!

Look back at the sections on Opposition to the Tsar and Repression. Do you agree with Source A that the war with Japan 'excited the social unrest' that caused the 1905 revolution, or were there deeper forces at play?

SOURCE B

Russian soldiers killing peaceful demonstrators outside the Winter Palace.

Background: The Russo-Japanese War, 1904–05

In February 1904, war broke out between Russia and Japan over Manchuria, an area of northern China. Russia had built an important extension of the Trans-Siberian railway in the area. When war came, most people thought that Russia would have little difficulty in beating Japan, which was regarded as a second-class power. But the war showed the weaknesses of the Tsar's regime. Fighting in the Far East placed Russia at a severe disadvantage, and the Japanese quickly gained the upper hand. The Russian Baltic Fleet was ordered to sail halfway round the world to take part in the fighting. During their eight-month journey the Russian commanders opened fire on the British fishing fleet by mistake; this cost them £65,000 in compensation. When they finally faced the Japanese fleet at the battle of Tsushima in May 1905, the Russians were decisively defeated. It was the first time a major European power had been beaten by an Asian nation in a war in modern times. The Tsar was forced to ask the Japanese for peace.

SOURCE C

Tsar Nicholas II in one of his finest uniforms.

The 1905 Revolution

Defeat in the war helped to spark off revolution in Russia. The Tsar was so shaken by events in Manchuria that he relaxed control at home. In November 1904 a national congress of zemstvo representatives met in St Petersburg and demanded political reform. Strikes broke out in several industries, with the workers demanding better conditions. The growing wave of discontent was finally turned into a revolution by the events of Bloody Sunday (9 January 1905).

ACTIVITIES

Using the timeline on page 192, take the events of 1904–12 and create your own timeline but with more detail. You must explain why each event deserves a place on your timeline.

Bloody Sunday

A mass demonstration had been organised in St Petersburg. The plan was to march to the Winter Palace to present a petition to the Tsar, asking for better wages and working conditions. Father Gapon, a priest well known for his work with trade unions in the city, led the procession. The marchers were orderly and unarmed, but when they reached the palace they were fired on by troops. Soldiers also attacked marchers elsewhere in the city. Around 200 people were killed.

Bloody Sunday did great damage to the relationship between the Tsar and his people. The respect that he had previously enjoyed was lost. There were riots and strikes in towns throughout the country, and peasants turned against the landowners in the countryside. At first, the disturbances lacked leadership and co-ordination. Even so, the authorities found it impossible to restore control. In an attempt to calm the situation, the Tsar promised to allow a parliament (the Duma) to meet, but refused to give it any real power. The offer was ignored.

Strikes and mutiny

As the strikes grew worse, it became clear that the Tsar might be overthrown. In June, there was a mutiny on board the Russian battleship *Potemkin*. Two thousand people were massacred as troops opened fire on crowds supporting the mutineers in the port of Odessa. The mutiny showed that the Tsar was in danger of losing the support of his armed forces.

As the months passed, the opposition began to organise more effectively. Even middle-class professionals like doctors and teachers formed unions to demand reforms. Later, a political party, the Constitutional Democrats, or Kadets, was set up to pursue these aims. By August 1905 a Peasants' Union had been formed, which organised strikes of agricultural workers. Most important of all, however, was the emergence of organisations representing the industrial working classes.

KEY WORDS

Soviet – *an elected workers' council.*

Fact file

The reforms of Petr Stolypin

Stolypin was the Russian Prime Minister between 1906 and his death in 1911. He had a privileged childhood but as an adult concerned himself with the problems of Russian peasant farmers. He was marshall of Kovno (in the west of Russia) and here the farmers owned the land they worked on. This meant they were more efficient than peasants in the communal system of central Russia.

Stolypin become Minister of the Interior in April 1906, then Prime Minister in July 1906. His task was to restore order. This meant working with politicians on the royalist right and socialist left – an impossible task and one that would isolate him in the middle. Stolypin wanted to give all peasants property rights and full civil equality, modernise local government to include those who owned property or were citizens, protect Jews, introduce schooling for all and improve the conditions of factory workers. However, this would go too far for the right and not far enough for the left. Stolypin dissolved the second Duma when it would not do as he wanted and changed the electoral law so that the third Duma was more amenable to his aims. Over the next few years the third Duma proved unwilling to implement much of what Stolypin wanted. This led to a showdown between Stolypin and the Tsar over who should dominate in the west of Russia: the Polish nobility (as the State Council wanted) or the Russian land-owning peasants (as Stolypin wanted). Stolypin's 'back me or sack me' threat to the Tsar resulted in his victory but at a huge cost: his tactics alienated everyone and he was assassinated at the theatre in full view of the Tsar in 1911.

Stolypin had tried to do the impossible by creating a bigger land-owning class that would want to tie itself to the good of Russia. This would ensure peace and the maintenance of the status quo because the new land-owning peasants throughout Russia would not want to rock the boat if they became more prosperous. Stolypin's 'gamble on the strong' had failed and by 1917 the Tsar had been overthrown.

The St Petersburg Soviet

Throughout the year, workers had been setting up councils, or **soviets**, in their workplaces. Then, in October, the St Petersburg Soviet was set up. This was like an alternative city council, to which all the workplace soviets sent representatives. Similar soviets were organised in other cities. The St Petersburg Soviet was deeply influenced by revolutionary ideas and quickly organised a general strike, which brought the whole economy to a standstill. For a while, it seemed as if the soviet was the only organisation in the country with any authority. It published its own newspaper, organised food supplies, set up law courts and established an armed force.

The Tsar's survival

The Tsar realised that he would have to make **concessions**. He issued the October Manifesto, promising to turn Russia into a **constitutional monarchy** and give people more freedom. An elected parliament (Duma) would have the power to make laws. In this way, the **manifesto** promised the middle classes what they had been demanding. They now became alarmed by the extremism of the workers and peasants, which threatened to undermine social order completely. By issuing the manifesto, the Tsar had succeeded in splitting the opposition.

In fact, the Tsar had acted in bad faith. As soon as circumstances permitted, he was determined to recover as much power as he could. First, he moved against the St Petersburg Soviet and arrested its leaders. Then, in December, an uprising organised by the Moscow Soviet was bloodily **repressed**. In little more than a month, the 1905 revolution had collapsed. Now the country waited to see what would become of Nicholas's promised **reforms**.

KEY WORDS

Concession – *something that is given away in order to reach agreement.*

Constitutional Monarchy – *a monarchy where the monarch is head of state but power resides in a parliament.*

Dissolved – *closed down and disbanded.*

Manifesto – *a set of aims or promises which political parties make (generally before an election).*

Reforms – *changes to the way things are done.*

Repressed – *subdued by force.*

Attempts at reform

The Tsar had survived, but only by making concessions. It was not possible to go back on all of these, however much the Tsar wanted to. Russia had changed and the Tsar's power was no longer absolute. Russia was now to have an elected parliament. What remained uncertain was how much power Nicholas would allow it.

- The first Duma met in 1906. Most of the revolutionaries refused to take part in the elections, so the assembly was dominated by the Kadets. There were also around 200 peasant representatives. The Duma demanded further concessions from the Tsar, including the confiscation of all large estates (so the land could be distributed to the peasants), making government ministers responsible to the Duma, and the abolition of the Tsar's emergency powers, including use of the death penalty. The Tsar simply **dissolved** the Duma. When some Duma members called on people to refuse to pay their taxes, they were arrested.
- A second Duma, which met in 1907, ended the same way. This time the revolutionaries did stand for election, which meant that the Duma was even less acceptable to Nicholas, so again was dissolved.

ACTIVITY

Stolypin remains a controversial figure for modern historians: some say that had he stayed alive his reforms would have saved Russia from the future revolution and bloody civil war that followed. Others claim that he had no support base at the time, and without this his reforms could never have taken hold. Research more about Petr Stolypin and his attempts at reform, in particular find out about 'Stolypin's neckties' and 'Stolypin's carriages'. Then decide for yourself whether Stolypin could have saved the Tsar.

KEY CONCEPTS

The Duma and the State Council – *the Duma was intended to be a legislative parliament filled with representatives of political parties. However, it could not enact its own laws. The State Council had equal power to the Duma. It was half appointed by the Tsar and half by the zemstvos. The Duma's proposals had to be approved by both the Tsar and the State Council.*

- By the time the third Duma met, later in 1907, the government had changed the rules so that more of its supporters, such as rich landowners, were elected. This produced a Duma more to the Tsar's liking. It was dominated by Octobrists – moderates who thought that the concessions in the October Manifesto were sufficient. Any opposition in the Duma was kept within limits acceptable to the Tsar.

Conclusion

It would be easy to conclude that Russia's experiment with parliamentary democracy was a sham. However, the existence of the Duma was evidence that the Tsar's position had changed. For the first time, people could share in Russia's political life. The Duma could debate important issues, people could read about them in the newspapers, the Tsar's ministers went to the Duma to answer questions – in short, there was more freedom and openness than before. Russia had begun to evolve towards a more modern, democratic system of government. Who knows where this might have led had it not been for the interruption of the First World War?

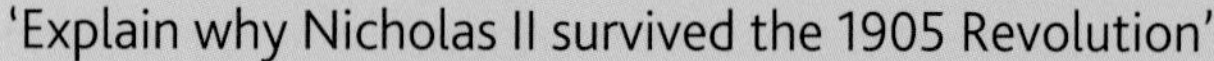

GradeStudio

'Explain why Nicholas II survived the 1905 Revolution' **[6 marks]**

Examiner's tip

There are really two levels of response to this question:

The first may give reasons (such as the revolution led to the formation of the Duma) but it will not explain them. The second level will clearly explain the reasons and link them back to the question (with the formation of the Duma, the Russian people now had the opportunity to participate in the political life of their country. This movement towards a more modern and open Russia was a clear reason why Tsar Nicholas II survived the 1905 Revolution).

Now you have one reason. See if you can find and explain two more; do not forget to link each reason directly back to the question, as the example above has done.

How far was the Tsar weakened by the First World War?

LEARNING OBJECTIVES

In this lesson you will:

- examine the problems facing the Tsar during the First World War and their relative importance
- investigate the relationship between Rasputin and the royal family and use sources to explain his significance.

GETTING STARTED

Think back to Russia's last major international conflict: the war with Japan in 1905. If you were the Tsar what would you be thinking about this new conflict?

Germany declares war on Russia

When Germany declared war on Russia, on 1 August 1914, everybody expected the war to be short. Russia, like the other nations dragged into the war, was totally unprepared for lengthy hostilities. Once it became clear that the war would last months or even years, the Tsar's government soon proved incapable of responding to the challenge.

Like the war on the Western Front, fighting on the Eastern Front quickly became bogged down, with neither side capable of striking a decisive blow. A Russian advance into East Prussia in autumn 1914 was halted by the Germans at Tannenberg, where 100,000 Russians were killed. An offensive in 1916, organised by General Brusilov, made significant advances against the Austrians. However, with German help, the Austrians halted the Russian advance. This was the Russians' last success. Their armies eventually collapsed in 1917, but this was due more to poor leadership, inadequate supplies and political developments at home, than to defeat in the field.

Problems in the agricultural sector

Around 15 million peasants were drafted into the Russian army, but their removal from agricultural production had surprisingly little effect. Throughout the war, Russia produced ample food. As with other supplies, the problem was not so much production as transport. Russia's railway system was unable to keep the country and its armies supplied, and the incompetence of the Tsarist administration made matters worse. Almost from the start of the war, Russia's cities experienced food shortages. These became severe as the war continued, and were an important factor in the outbreak of revolution in 1917.

Problems in the economic sector

Russia was a poor country and could not afford a long war. The government was forced to borrow from other countries, and to print money. At the same time, its income from taxes was falling. In August 1914 the government prohibited the sale and manufacture of alcohol. Previously around a quarter of all its revenues had been raised from alcohol sales. The result was inflation – Russia's money lost value. As wages failed to keep up with price rises, workers became worse off.

Problems in the industrial sector

Meanwhile, industry geared production to the war effort. The output of heavy industries, such as iron and steel, increased, as did that of armaments and clothing manufacturers with government contracts. Other industries suffered badly – many factories closed as consumers could not afford their goods. Job losses, higher prices and food shortages began to have an impact on the urban population. Among the working class, enthusiasm for the war quickly disappeared, to be replaced by discontent and waves of strikes. The strikers were disillusioned with the Tsar and wanted the war to end.

Problems in the middle classes

The discontent of the working classes was matched among the middle classes. When the Duma met in August 1915, a 'Progressive Bloc' of moderate politicians was formed to press the Tsar for a representative government that could unite the country and fight the war more effectively. The Tsar rejected the idea and dissolved the Duma after a month. Just as in 1905, war was creating a situation in which more and more of the Tsar's subjects were losing faith in his ability to rule the country.

VOICE YOUR OPINION!

With a partner, look through the problems facing the Tsar because of the First World War. Which of the reasons do you think was the most important in undermining the Tsar's power?

Conclusion

By 1916, the Tsar was **alienated** from almost all Russians apart from his immediate advisers. In 1915 he had taken over personal command of Russia's armies. In reality he was no more than a **figurehead**, but the task took him away from Petrograd (as St Petersburg had been renamed at the start of the war) and left government in the hands of **Tsarina Alexandra** and her favourite, **Rasputin**. It would be hard to imagine a more disastrous situation.

The role of Rasputin in the Tsar's downfall

Rasputin was a Siberian peasant who had a reputation as a mystic or holy man. He also claimed to be a healer, and it was in this capacity that he was introduced to the royal family in 1905. The Tsar's only son, Alexis, suffered from haemophilia – a condition that prevented his blood from clotting. The slightest accident could therefore be fatal to him. Rasputin seemed able to control the condition, and thereby gained the friendship of the Tsar and Tsarina. Despite stories of Rasputin's sexual adventures among the female nobility, the royal family stayed loyal to him.

Until the Tsar's departure for the front in 1915, Rasputin was not allowed any political influence. Once the Tsar was away, however, the Tsarina came increasingly to rely on Rasputin's advice. Ministers were appointed and sacked according to his whims. There were rumours that Rasputin was the Tsarina's lover, and that they were plotting to make peace with the Germans. The story sounded all the more plausible given the Tsarina's German background.

Eventually, a group of noblemen decided to kill Rasputin. One night in December 1916, Rasputin went to the home of Prince Yusupov for dinner. An initial attempt to poison him failed, and Rasputin was finally shot and killed. His body was dumped in one of the city's canals. The identity of the conspirators was common knowledge, but none received serious punishment. Too many people, including many close to the royal family, were involved in the plot. The murderers had killed Rasputin not because they wished to harm the Tsar, but because they were his friends. And by December 1916 the Tsar did not have many friends left.

SOURCE A

A Russian cartoon showing Rasputin with the Tsar and Tsarina.

SOURCE B

Rasputin with his admirers, c.1915.

KEY WORDS

Alienated – *having lost the sympathy of other people.*

Figurehead – *someone who is in nominal charge but in fact has no power.*

ACTIVITIES

1. Do Sources A and B agree with the information about Rasputin?
2. Based on the information you have, are they useful pieces of evidence for the historian wishing to research the role of Rasputin during the First World War?

KEY PEOPLE

Rasputin – *a supposed mystic and healer who gained great influence over the Tsar's family during the First World War.*

Tsarina Alexandra – *wife of Tsar Nicholas II and mother to their son, the Tsarevich Alexis.*

Why was the revolution of March 1917 successful?

LEARNING OBJECTIVES

In this lesson you will:

- examine the factors that led to the March 1917 revolution
- compare the 1905 and March 1917 revolutions in order to distinguish what made the March 1917 revolution successful.

GETTING STARTED

While reading through the following information, make notes on the role of the following factors:

- lack of food and pay
- the weather
- the army
- the Tsar
- the Duma
- the Petrograd Soviet.

Background to the revolution

By early 1917 all the ingredients for revolution existed in Russia. The Tsar had lost all support, the government was incompetent, the army faced defeat and its loyalty was suspect. Perhaps most important of all, workers in the capital, Petrograd, were struggling to survive on insufficient food and pay. Strikes were common. Yet when the revolution did take place, it came as a surprise and was unplanned.

The events of March 1917

In early March 1917 a particularly severe wave of strikes hit factories in Petrograd. By 10 March, industry had almost come to a halt. Unusually mild weather encouraged demonstrators on to the streets. At first the authorities were able to control the crowds peacefully, but finally the soldiers were ordered to fire on the demonstrators. They were reluctant to do this because many shared the grievances of the workers. The men of the Petrograd garrison had only recently been drafted into the army. Most were peasants. They, too, were hungry and cold, but they also deeply resented the harsh discipline of military life. By 12 March, many in the garrison had begun to **mutiny**. Government buildings were attacked and **ransacked**. Within a few hours, Petrograd was in the hands of rioting mobs.

Tsar Nicholas was unaware of how serious the situation had become. He was at his country estate outside Petrograd,

SOURCE A

Soldiers in Petrograd supporting the revolution of March 1917.

ACTIVITIES

Make a diary for the month of March 1917. Ensure you include the following key dates: 10, 12, 14 and 15 March.

receiving over-optimistic reports from his ministers. He made matters worse by ordering the dissolution of the Duma. This served only to persuade the middle classes to join the revolution. As the disorder continued, it seemed that only a Duma government could bring the disturbances to an end. Delegates of workers and soldiers began to pledge their support for a Duma government. Although the Duma had refused the Tsar's order to dissolve, its leaders were reluctant revolutionaries. Whether they liked it or not, however, they were emerging as Russia's new rulers.

The Petrograd Soviet re-emerged on 12 March. From the start, the soviet asserted its authority over the armed forces. Many of its members were soldiers who had mutinied against their officers. They wanted to make sure that they would not suffer **reprisals**. The soviet's famous Order Number One stated that soldiers did not need to obey any orders from the Duma that went against orders of the soviet. It set up soldiers' committees throughout the armed forces, which did much to undermine the authority of officers, and abolished the harsher aspects of military discipline. The government had lost command of its own armed forces.

The Tsar's reaction

On 15 March, Nicholas finally decided to **abdicate**. His generals advised him that the situation was hopeless and that any attempt to put down the revolution using troops from outside the capital would only make matters worse. As his son Alexis was so young, he chose to give the throne to his brother, Michael. But the time for monarchy was past. The people had decided that Nicholas would be the last Tsar. When moderates in the Duma spoke in favour of a constitutional monarchy, they were openly jeered.

So, on 14 March, the Duma announced the formation of a Provisional Government, which would rule until elections could be held for a new Assembly. The first Prime Minister was Prince Lvov, and the government had members from several parties, including a Social Revolutionary, **Kerensky**, as Minister of Justice. It immediately announced a series of reforms, which transformed Russia overnight into one of the freest countries in the world. There was freedom of the press, the vote for all adults over 21, abolition of the death penalty and full civil rights for all regardless of religion.

Conclusion

The revolution seemed to have triumphed, but worries remained. How would the new government cope with the real problems of Russian society – the war, the land question, food supplies? And how would it deal with the power of the Petrograd Soviet, which had better claims to represent those who had really made the revolution – the workers and soldiers of Petrograd?

Explain why the Tsarist regime collapsed in 1917.

[6 marks]

Examiner's tip

The first stage to planning your answer is to identify two or three reasons why the Tsar was removed from power in 1917. When you have done this, you need to explain each of these reasons. Remember, to access the higher levels in the mark scheme, you must explain two or three reasons.

VOICE YOUR OPINION!

The Tsar had been in trouble before (in the 1905 Revolution). Why do you think he decided to abdicate this time?

KEY WORDS

Abdicate – *renounce the throne.*

Mutiny – *rebellion by the armed forces.*

Ransack – *go through a place stealing and causing damage.*

Reprisals – *attacks on other people in retaliaiton for attacks they have made on you.*

KEY PEOPLE

Alexander Kerensky – *Prime Minister of Russia July–October 1917.*

How did the Bolsheviks gain power, and how did they consolidate their rule?

How effectively did the Provisional Government rule Russia in 1917?

LEARNING OBJECTIVES

In this lesson you will:

- examine the problems facing the Provisional Government of 1917
- assess how events affected the fortunes of the Bolsheviks.

GETTING STARTED

The Provisional Government was only ever meant to be temporary – its job was to hold power until proper elections could take place. However, there were a number of decisions that could not wait.

- You have just overthrown your Tsar (his family have been ruling Russia for over 300 years).
- Your country is still at war.
- Peasants are seizing landowners' estates and killing any who resist.
- There is not enough food to go round.
- And now your soldiers are deserting the front line (Source A).

What would you do?

Background

In the four years after the overthrow of the Tsar in March 1917, Russia suffered further revolution, civil war and widespread devastation. The result was the emergence of the world's first communist state. Under the leadership of **Lenin**, the **Bolsheviks** overthrew the Provisional Government in the revolution of November 1917. They then defeated their enemies in a bloody civil war that lasted until 1920. How did a small revolutionary **socialist** party manage to seize and hold on to power, when the great majority of the Russian people did not support it?

The problems facing the Provisional Government

The Provisional Government failed to deal with almost all the challenges it faced. It was a divided government, made up of members from several different parties. The middle-class Kadets wanted to restore order and create a parliamentary democracy. The socialists wanted to push the revolution further and transfer more land to the peasants. During its short life the government split several times as ministers quarrelled among themselves. In July, Kerensky replaced Lvov as Prime Minister. There were many other ministerial resignations and changes, which showed the government's divisions and weakened its authority.

The one major decision that the government did take was disastrous. It decided to continue the war. When Russia's armies were ordered to take the offensive in June, the soldiers' response was wholesale desertion and mutiny. Henceforth it was clear that Russia had lost the war against Germany. In many areas, the army ceased to offer any resistance to the German advance.

SOURCE A

A Russian soldier trying to stop colleagues from deserting in 1917.

ACTIVITIES

Complete the table below, taking care when thinking what the outcomes of the government's actions were.

Problems faced	Provisional Government action	Outcome
The Provisional Government was made up of members from several different parties		
Shortage of food		
The re-establishment of the Petrograd Soviet		

Attempts were made to improve food supplies to the cities. Rationing was introduced, and the government established a **monopoly** over grain trading. But transport problems continued, and the peasants were reluctant to sell their grain for increasingly worthless money. As the winter of 1917 approached, Russia's cities faced food shortages again. Meanwhile, the government lacked the political will to deal with the land issue. Its policy was simply to leave the problem for the new Assembly.

The soviets

The re-establishment of the Petrograd Soviet was followed by the setting up of workers' and soldiers' soviets across Russia. The Petrograd Soviet co-ordinated the activities of the national soviet movement, and it soon became obvious that its authority over the working classes, coupled with the military force it possessed through its Order Number One, made it an alternative national government. Although at first it was prepared to work with the Provisional Government, it became increasingly hostile as it fell under the influence of revolutionary groups, particularly the Bolsheviks.

Proceedings of the Petrograd Soviet, to which there were often over a thousand delegates, were noisy, chaotic and unproductive. Its power was exercised through a small executive committee, which the Bolsheviks targeted for takeover. As the power of the Provisional Government ebbed away during 1917, so control of the soviet became more important. Whoever controlled the soviet could also control Russia.

SOURCE B

The Provisional Government has no real power of any kind and its orders are carried out only to the extent that the soviet of workers' and soldiers' deputies permits it. The soviet controls the essential levers of power, insofar as the troops, the railways, and the postal and telegraph services are in its hands. One can assert bluntly that the Provisional Government exists only as long as it is permitted to do so by the soviet.

From a letter written by a minister in the Provisional Government, March 1917.

KEY WORDS

Monopoly – *exclusive control of trade in a commodity, such as grain, or a service.*

KEY PEOPLE

Vladimir Ilyich Lenin – *Bolshevik leader who became the first leader of the Soviet Union.*

KEY CONCEPTS

Bolshevik – *the larger of the two groups which split from the Social Democrats in 1903, and the main instigators of the Russian Revolution.*

Communism – *a political belief that everything should be shared out equally depending upon need.*

Socialism – *a belief that the means of production should be owned by the state and not in the hands of private investors.*

Fact file

Lenin

Lenin was born Vladimir Ilyich Ulyanov in 1870, but later changed his name to avoid arrest by the Tsarist police. Lenin's background was not working class, but he was attracted to radical politics from a young age, and was expelled from university for taking part in student protests. His brother was executed for his part in a plot to assassinate Tsar Alexander III.

Lenin spent some time in internal **exile** in Siberia then left Russia for Western Europe, where he developed the revolutionary ideas that were later known as Marxism-Leninism. Karl Marx had taught that once industrial capitalism had developed, workers would be exploited by their bosses and would rise up in a class struggle against them. But Lenin believed that a party of determined revolutionaries could seize power and introduce communism.

After the split of the Social Democrats in 1903, Lenin was one of the most important leaders of the Bolsheviks. He returned to Russia too late to take part in the revolution of 1905 and was forced back into exile in Switzerland, where he remained until 1917. Then, after the March revolution of 1917, the Germans helped him to return home. They hoped he would weaken Russia's war effort. Lenin was smuggled across Germany on a train, reaching Petrograd in April.

Lenin's great contributions to the Bolsheviks before 1917 were his intellectual leadership and his determination. He was a tireless propagandist, churning out dozens of books and articles, and founding *Pravda*, the Bolshevik Party newspaper. He was difficult and prickly towards those who disagreed with him, but nobody doubted his ability. His insistence on discipline and his refusal to compromise made the Bolsheviks the most formidable force in Russian revolutionary politics.

The growing power of the revolutionary groups

Some groups wanted to work with the Provisional Government; the Mensheviks even had members who served as ministers. However, the Bolsheviks were more hostile towards the government, especially after the return of Lenin from exile in April.

Lenin's April Theses

According to Lenin's **April Theses**, the Bolsheviks had to overthrow the government as soon as possible and seize power for themselves. They could then set up a socialist dictatorship. To bring this about, it was essential to gain control of the Petrograd Soviet. Some Bolsheviks disliked the idea of destroying the results of a revolution that had only just occurred, but they fell into line with Lenin's policy. The Bolsheviks' propaganda machine swung into action in support of the slogans 'All Power to the Soviets!' and 'Peace! Bread! Land!'

At first, the Bolsheviks were only a minority in the soviet. When an All-Russian Congress of Soviets was held in June, the Bolsheviks had fewer than half as many delegates as the Mensheviks and the Social Revolutionaries. However, the Bolsheviks were not tainted by co-operation with the Provisional Government, and as the weakness of the government became clearer, the Bolsheviks grew bolder.

ACTIVITIES

Work with a partner to think about the sort of characteristics a revolutionary leader would need to have, then identify how many of them Lenin had.

VOICE YOUR OPINION!

Look at the Bolshevik slogans. Think back to the problems facing the Provisional Government which you identified in the 'Getting started' activity. How successful do you think the Bolsheviks would be with these slogans?

The July Days

In July, demonstrations organised by the Bolsheviks turned into an uprising against the government. This took the Bolshevik leaders by surprise. Lenin was on holiday when the disturbances started, and could not make up his mind whether to try and seize power or not. Petrograd was entirely in the hands of rioting mobs, but without leadership they could achieve nothing. Lenin's hesitation gave the government time to move loyal troops into the city, and the 'July Days' came to a rapid end.

Hundreds of Bolsheviks were arrested; Lenin was accused of being a German spy and fled to Finland. However, the Provisional Government's fortunes continued to decline. In an attempt to restore discipline in the army, in July Kerensky appointed **General Kornilov** as commander-in-chief.

The Kornilov Affair

Kerensky promised Kornilov support in restoring the authority of officers over the ordinary soldiers. However, Kerensky soon began to have second thoughts, as this was bound to bring him into conflict with the soviets. On the other hand, Kornilov had powerful support among the middle and upper classes, who expected him to restore some control in Russia. On 8 September, Kornilov, assuming he had Kerensky's support, ordered his troops to occupy Petrograd, as a first step to breaking the power of the soviet. Kerensky had to choose whether to back this move or not. He lost his nerve and dismissed Kornilov from his command.

Kornilov decided to revolt against Kerensky's government, but he had no chance of success. His troops had no enthusiasm for overthrowing the soviet, and were easily persuaded by the Bolsheviks to abandon the attempt. The revolt collapsed with no fighting, but it revealed how totally the Provisional Government depended on the soviet for its survival. During the revolt, many Bolshevik leaders were released from gaol as part of the soviet's preparation to resist an attack by Kornilov's men. It was clear that the Bolsheviks had the most influence over the soldiers and workers who would have done the fighting. These 'Red Guards' were practically the Bolsheviks' private army.

By late September, the soviets in most major cities, including Petrograd and Moscow, were in Bolshevik hands. Now it was just a matter of selecting the most favourable moment for a takeover of government. Under Trotsky, one of Lenin's closest colleagues, the Military Revolutionary Committee of the Petrograd Soviet was actively planning to seize power.

GradeStudio

Which had the biggest effect on the Bolsheviks' seizure of power: the July Days or the Kornilov Affair? **[10 marks]**

Examiner's tip

In order to answer this question successfully you must know about both events, otherwise your argument will be incomplete; revision is all important.

Once you are happy that you can recall all the relevant knowledge then it is a matter of attributing significance to the two events: which one had the most effect? Look at the end result of each event and decide for yourself which one had the biggest effect. Finally, ensure you can prove your point by backing up your answer with relevant arguments.

KEY WORDS

Exile – *banishment from one's country or to a remote part of the country.*

KEY PEOPLE

General Kornilov – *an army general who fell out with Kerensky and tried unsuccessfully to overthrow his government.*

KEY CONCEPTS

April Theses – *document written by Lenin in April 1917 calling for uncompromising opposition to the Provisional Government.*

Why were the Bolsheviks able to seize power in November 1917?

LEARNING OBJECTIVES

In this lesson you will:

- examine how the Bolsheviks were able to seize power
- analyse the strengths of Lenin as a leader and decide how effective the actions of the Bolsheviks were once in power.

KEY PEOPLE

Leon Trotsky – *one of the most important leaders of the revolution.*

Lenin returns from hiding

By mid-October 1917, Lenin's main concern was to ensure that, when Kerensky's government collapsed, the Bolsheviks would be able to seize power. Moderate groups like the Mensheviks still had influence in the Petrograd Soviet. However, Lenin believed that if the Bolsheviks could seize power by force, the other groups would not have the courage to fight them. Lenin returned from hiding in Finland, and took control of the Bolsheviks' preparations. The decision was taken to stage an armed uprising, but no date was fixed.

The Bolshevik seizure of power

Meanwhile, Kerensky seemed as out of touch with reality as the Tsar in his last days. He ordered the Petrograd garrison to the front to take part in the fighting against the Germans. The soldiers had no desire to sacrifice themselves, so they mutinied and declared themselves loyal to the Bolsheviks. On 3 November, **Trotsky**'s Military Revolutionary Committee announced that it had taken command of the garrison. Lenin was still worried that the working classes of Petrograd would not support a Bolshevik takeover.

During 6–7 November 1917, Red Guards occupied government buildings throughout the city. Most citizens of Petrograd did not even notice that a revolution was taking place. Kerensky fled the city and the rest of the Provisional Government barricaded themselves in the Winter Palace. The palace was guarded by a few thousand soldiers, including young cadets and around 200 women soldiers from the 1st Petrograd Women's Battalion, but they gradually slipped away. Late in the evening of the 6th, guns opened fire on the palace. Finally, around 2 am on 7 November, Bolsheviks entered the palace and arrested the ministers inside. This event was later transformed by Bolshevik propaganda into an epic assault against determined defenders.

VOICE YOUR OPINION!

Why do you think the Provisional Government was protected by the Women's Battalion?

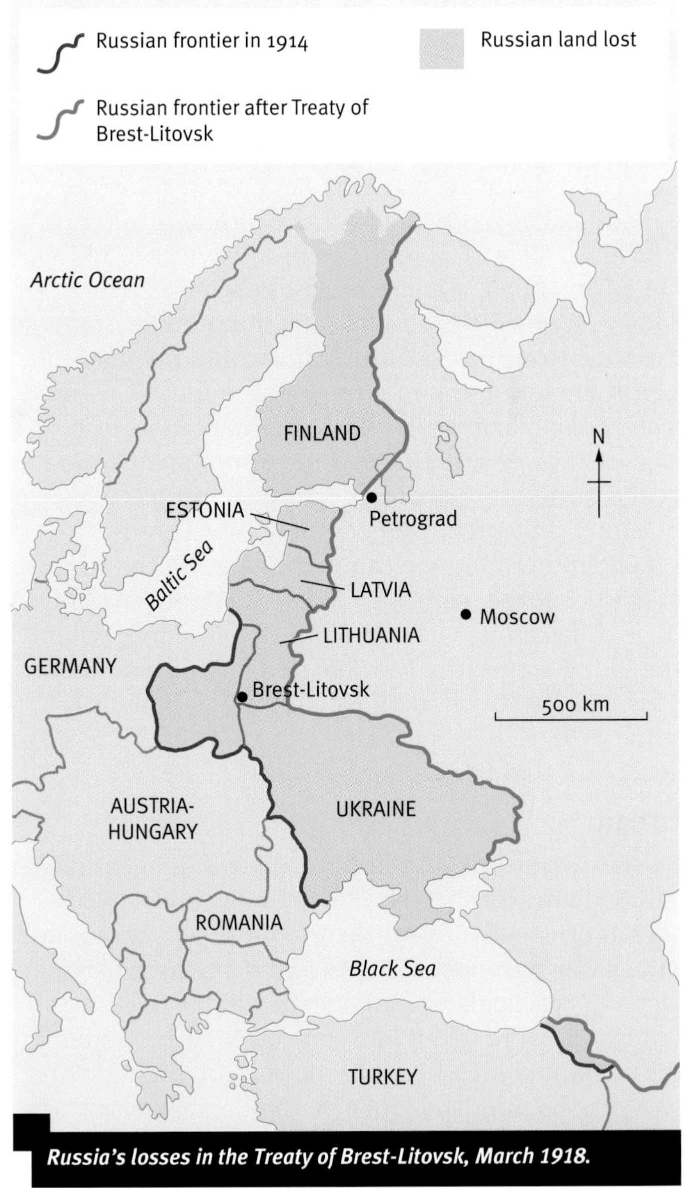

Russia's losses in the Treaty of Brest-Litovsk, March 1918.

Bolshevik success?

Their determination and the weakness of the Provisional Government had enabled the Bolsheviks to seize power. On hearing of the Bolsheviks' takeover, the Mensheviks and SRs in the Petrograd Soviet reacted just as Lenin had hoped. They walked out in disgust, leaving the Bolsheviks in total control. The way was clear for Lenin to form a Bolshevik government. However, although the Bolsheviks controlled the capital, their authority was minimal in the rest of the country. In Moscow, loyalist troops fiercely resisted the takeover, and the city was not in Bolshevik hands for another ten days. Before long the Bolsheviks' enemies would begin to fight back, and then the true level of their support would become clear.

GradeStudio

Russia faced three main problems in 1917: how well did Lenin deal with them? **[10 marks]**

Examiner's tip

Your first task is to recall what the three problems were; if you cannot do this then you cannot answer the question.

Secondly you must explain how Lenin tried to deal with each problem, including the outcome of Lenin's actions in each area.

Finally, you should make a judgement on how well Lenin fared when dealing with each of the problems. It would be suitable to say he succeeded in some areas and not others.

Bolshevik rule

Working people supported the Bolsheviks because of their promise to do something about the three major problems facing most Russians – Peace, Bread and Land.

Peace

On 8 November, the Decree on Peace was issued. This decree called for a fair and honourable end to the war. However, the Germans would not give Lenin the fair and honourable peace that he wanted. The Russian armies had disintegrated; most of the soldiers had deserted and gone home. The Germans' peace terms were so harsh that most of the Bolsheviks wanted to reject them, but Lenin accepted them to save the revolution. By the Treaty of Brest-Litovsk, signed in March 1918, Russia lost huge areas on its western frontier – Finland, Poland, the Baltic States, the Ukraine and half of Belorussia. This was half of its territory in Europe, including some of its richest agricultural land. Half of Russia's grain and coal production was lost.

Bread

Bolshevik power over the economy was increased. Although the Bolsheviks allowed small businesses to stay in private hands, workers' control of factories and mines was introduced. Banks and many of the larger factories, particularly in the textile and metal industries, were taken into state ownership. Under the combined pressures of state control, inflation and lack of consumer spending, production collapsed. The peasants also refused to release their grain for sale. The Bolsheviks quickly faced an economic crisis.

Land

Another decree was issued on 8 November: the Decree on Land. This announced that all landowners' estates would be confiscated and the land made available to the peasants. Private ownership of land would be abolished. A huge redistribution of land to the poorer peasants began immediately.

Dealing with opposition

Lenin took the necessary steps to deal with his opponents. He closed down all opposition newspapers, and in December 1917 he set up a secret police force called the Cheka. At first, the Cheka concentrated on criminals and **saboteurs**, but before long any opponent of the Bolsheviks was at risk of murder, torture or imprisonment.

Lenin allowed the long-promised elections for a new parliament to go ahead, and the Constituent Assembly finally met on 5 January 1918. The vast majority of Russians voted for socialist parties, the Bolsheviks gained only 24 per cent of the vote, against the SR's 38 per cent. The Assembly met for only one day. When it would not accept Bolshevik control, it was dispersed by Bolshevik troops, and demonstrations in favour of the Assembly were met with bullets. From now on, Russia was ruled by the Bolshevik Party (renamed the Communist Party in March 1918). Whoever controlled the party controlled Russia.

KEY WORDS

Saboteurs – *people who deliberately destroy something for a political purpose.*

Why did the Bolsheviks win the Civil War?

LEARNING OBJECTIVES

In this lesson you will:

- examine the events of the Civil War
- investigate the level of opposition and the reasons for the communist success.

Opposition to the Bolsheviks

As the communist dictatorship emerged, its enemies began to organise resistance. The opposition included many different groups – monarchists, middle-class liberals, landowners, industrialists, army officers, Mensheviks and Social Revolutionaries, not to mention foreign powers hostile to the existence of a communist state. By comparison, the communists were a small group. They had strong support among industrial workers, but little or no party organisation in rural areas.

GETTING STARTED

Look at Source A below. Without knowing anything about the Civil War which ravaged Russia, what guesses can you make about it from the cartoon?

The Whites

Before long, anti-communist armies, known as the Whites, were put together under the command of Tsarist generals: Yudenich in the north-west, Kolchak in Siberia, and Denikin, Alexeev and Kornilov in the south. Czech prisoners of war being transported out of the country on the Trans-Siberian Railway formed the Czech Legion and joined the Whites. The British landed troops in the far north at Archangel and Murmansk, and the French at Odessa in the south. The communists seemed to be surrounded.

ACTIVITIES

How do you know that this cartoon is drawn from a communist point of view? As you read on, think whether you would portray the leaders of the Whites as snarling dogs.

SOURCE A

A communist cartoon of 1919. The three dogs are labelled Denikin, Kolchak and Yudenich.

VOICE YOUR OPINION!

Are there any similarities between Trotsky and Lenin's personalities?

However, the opponents of the communists had many different aims and ambitions. By contrast, the communists were united and single-minded. The Whites were also geographically split, unable to help each other or co-ordinate their efforts. The communists held a central position, which included Russia's two greatest cities – Moscow (the Bolsheviks moved the capital back to Moscow in March 1918) and Petrograd. They were also under a single command.

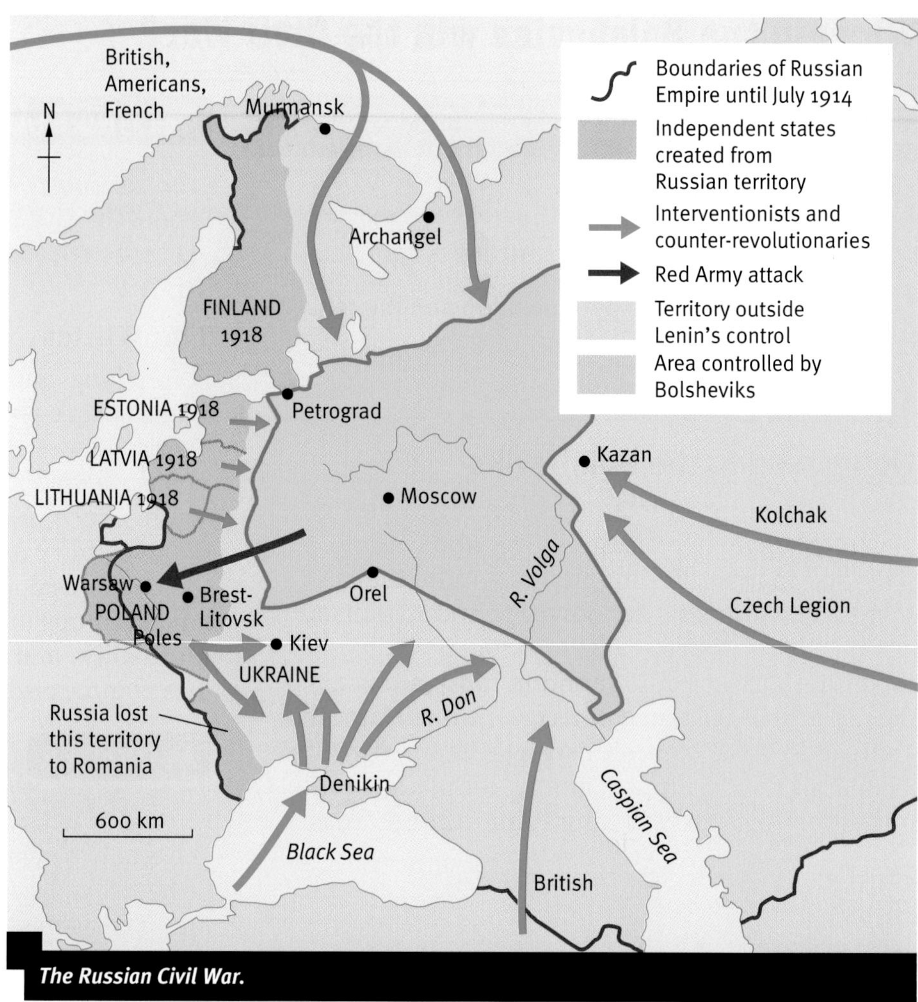

The Russian Civil War.

Trotsky's Red Army

At first, the communist forces were weak. Then Trotsky created a Red Army that was capable of defeating the Whites. His ruthlessness, determination and charisma made him ideal for the task.

Although Trotsky had joined the Bolsheviks only in 1917, he had quickly established himself as Lenin's second-in-command and had organised the November revolution. Now he used his talents to ensure that the revolution would survive. Trotsky encouraged officers from the Tsar's old army to join the Reds, and took their families hostage to make sure they stayed loyal. He established fierce discipline, including summary executions for deserters. He travelled around by train to meet the troops and spur them to ever-greater efforts. By 1920 the Red Army comprised around five million men.

War Communism

The Russian economy had to provide the army with the supplies it needed. To achieve this, the communist government introduced a new policy known as War Communism. The state took over all aspects of the economy, nationalising more industry and controlling the production and distribution of all goods. Normal economic life came to an end. Once the army's needs were catered for, there was little spare for anyone else. Food supplies were so poor that Lenin sent Cheka units (the Bolshevik secret police) into the countryside to seize peasants' grain stores.

The Red Terror

Then, following an assassination attempt on Lenin in August 1918, a 'Red Terror' was launched. The Cheka was unleashed on the regime's opponents. Mass executions were used to intimidate any possible opposition. Members of the middle and upper classes were automatically suspected of being disloyal to the communists. As many as three-quarters of a million people may have been murdered by the Cheka during the three years of civil war.

The execution of the Romanov family

Among the victims of the Red Terror were the ex-Tsar and his family. Exiled to Ekaterinburg in the Ural Mountains, the royal family posed an obvious threat to the communists, particularly if they fell into the hands of the Whites. When the Whites' advance brought them near to where the Tsar was held, it was decided to kill the whole family. On the night of 16–17 July 1918, the Tsar, his wife, their son and four daughters, with some of their servants, were taken into the cellar of the house where they were staying and shot. Their bodies were buried in a nearby forest, where they remained undiscovered until the fall of communism in 1991.

SOURCE B

Nicholas II and his family. The entire family was executed by the communists in July 1918.

SOURCE 

My next visit to Moscow took place after the fall of Ekaterinburg to the Whites. Talking to a colleague, I asked in passing, 'Oh yes, and where is the Tsar?'

'It's all over,' he answered. 'He has been shot.'

'And where is the family?'

'And the family along with him.'

'All of them?' I asked, apparently with a touch of surprise.

'All of them,' he replied. 'What about it?' He was waiting to see my reaction. I made no reply.

'And who made the decision?' I asked.

'We decided it here. Lenin believed we shouldn't leave the Whites a live banner to rally around, especially under the present difficult circumstances.'

I did not ask any further questions and considered the matter closed. Actually the decision was not only convenient but necessary. The execution of the Tsar's family was needed not only in order to frighten, horrify and dishearten the enemy, but also in order to shake up our own ranks to show there was no turning back.

In 1935, Trotsky published his diaries. Here he describes how he heard of the Tsar's death.

GradeStudio

The Civil War brought nothing but misery to the Russian people. How far do you agree with this statement? Explain your answer. **[10 marks]**

Examiner's tip

Clearly there were a lot of negative events that happened and they cannot be ignored, but you must not forget that in 1921 people in Russia were no longer ruled by an autocratic Tsar. However, this small gain may be heavily outweighed by the extreme violence that characterised the Civil War. Don't forget the Russian people had no knowledge of what Stalin would unleash on them either, so you cannot mention that in your answer.

VOICE YOUR OPINION!

Do you agree with Trotsky that the Tsar and his family had to be shot? How effective was this level of terror?

KEY WORDS

Labour camps – *prison camps in which the prisoners are forced to do hard labour.*

The end of the Civil War

The fighting in the civil war was exceptionally bloody and vicious, with countless atrocities committed by both sides. The Whites enjoyed early successes, but were never able to co-ordinate their attacks or agree on a single commander. After Germany's defeat in November 1918, the Allies lost one of the main reasons for intervening in the civil war. Within a year, most of their troops had left Russia. Their intervention had allowed the Reds to portray the Whites as unpatriotic.

In addition, the fear that a White victory would mean losing the gains of the revolution helped to keep the peasants on the communists' side. The Reds gradually took the upper hand and were finally victorious in 1920. Around half a million people had been killed.

Conclusion

The Russian people suffered terribly in the civil war. The economy collapsed, money became almost worthless, and people had to rely on the black market for food. In 1920, industrial production was less than 20 per cent of the 1913 level, and the harvest produced only 60 per cent of the normal amount of grain. During the civil war, famine and disease claimed eight million lives and the communist regime became a cruel dictatorship. Even many of the communists' supporters were beginning to wonder if the ideals of the revolution were being forgotten.

Aftermath: The Kronstadt Rising

In March 1921 the sailors at Kronstadt, the naval base near Petrograd, mutinied. They demanded an end to the communist dictatorship and to the forced seizures of grain. The Kronstadt sailors had previously been supporters of the communists. Trotsky had called them 'the pride and glory of the Russian Revolution'. If they were prepared to mutiny, anyone could. On 16–17 March, 50,000 Red Army troops were sent to storm the Kronstadt fortress. Some 10,000 of them died in the attack, but finally the sailors were defeated. More than 2000 of those captured were executed without trial. A further 8000 of them fled to Finland. Thousands more were sent to **labour camps**. That spring, peasant revolts were crushed with similar ruthlessness, although the famine spreading through Russia's countryside did as much to break the peasants' resistance.

How far was the New Economic Policy a success?

LEARNING OBJECTIVES

In this lesson you will:

- examine the reasons for and the success of the New Economic Policy (NEP)
- assess the reasons for a rise in production in Russia.

GETTING STARTED

The NEP was introduced to promote an increase in production; it affected industry as much as agriculture. Look at Source A. How is the poster getting its message across?

The New Economic Policy

Against a background of economic crisis and political opposition, in 1921 Lenin introduced the New Economic Policy (NEP). He realised that a real change of policy was needed if disaster was to be avoided. The peasants had to be given an incentive to produce more food and to release their produce for sale. This could be done only if state control was relaxed and the peasants were allowed to make a profit on what they produced. In other words, capitalism and a free market had to be brought back. For many communists this was a bitter humiliation, but they realised that their survival depended on it.

SOURCE A

The poster says, 'From the NEP Russia will come the Socialist Russia.'

Successes of the NEP

Once peasants and shopkeepers could work for a profit, goods appeared for sale. New small businesses and market stalls sprang up in the towns. A whole new class of profiteers emerged, who did well out of the new freedom to trade. They were known as 'NEP men'. The government kept control of the country's largest industries, but elsewhere capitalism made a comeback. Many workers who had supported the revolution thought the NEP was a betrayal of socialism. Lenin saw it as the only way to get the country back on its feet. Communism would have to wait a little longer.

By 1926–27 production had returned to pre-1914 levels. The recovery happened as much in heavy industry as in agriculture, so it probably owed much to the years of stability and peace. But the introduction of the NEP was particularly significant in the countryside, where peasant disturbances became a thing of the past. Even so, progress was not quick enough for those of Lenin's colleagues who wanted to transform Russia into a modern, industrialised state.

Lenin's death

In May 1922 Lenin suffered a stroke, which was followed by two further strokes in December 1922 and March 1923. After these, he was no longer able to play an active role in political life. A struggle for the leadership began, which would not be finally resolved for several years. On 21 January 1924, Lenin died. The first phase of the communist transformation of Russia was over.

ACTIVITIES

Look at the graph of increased production under the NEP. Clearly production rose between 1921 and 1926, but what would you say was the main cause of the rise?

Fact file

Russia became known as the Soviet Union (a shortened version of Union of Soviet Socialist Republics – USSR) in 1922.

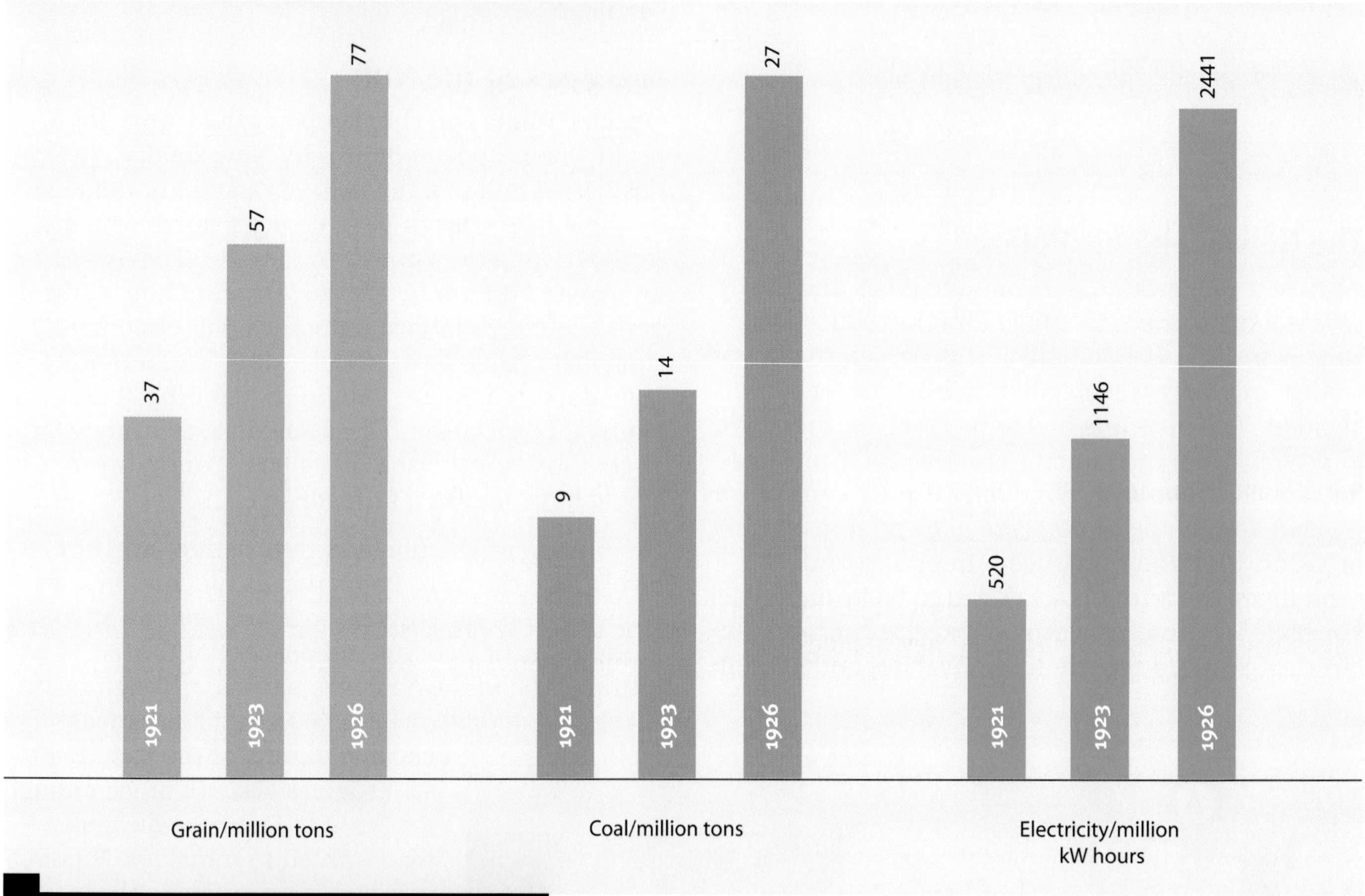

	1921	1923	1926
Grain/million tons	37	57	77
Coal/million tons	9	14	27
Electricity/million kW hours	520	1146	2441

The increase of production under the NEP.

GradeStudio

How did the Bolsheviks gain power and consolidate their rule? **[6 marks]**

Examiner's tip

This question needs careful thought and planning. Clearly there are two parts to it: firstly, you must explain how the Bolsheviks came to power (taking in the effect of the war, the Tsar's inability to make the correct decisions, the Provisional Government and its failures – the Kornilov Affair – as well as Lenin's actions).

Secondly, you should look to explain the Bolshevik consolidation of power which will include the Civil War and how they dealt with any uprisings.

Planning is key here: you do not want to start writing without thinking about what you are going to say. The question is asking for explanations, so make sure that you provide three or four reasons. Your reasons should include some examples that explain how power was gained and some that explain consolidation.

How did Stalin gain and hold on to power?

Why did Stalin, and not Trotsky, emerge as Lenin's successor?

LEARNING OBJECTIVES

In this lesson you will:

- analyse the qualities of the contenders for leadership and make judgements between them
- explain the reasons for the choice of Stalin as leader.

GETTING STARTED

What qualities would the Russian people be looking for in a new leader? Do these qualities vary from those that the Communist Party would want? Did either the people or the party get the leader they wanted?

The struggle for power between Trotsky and Stalin

After Lenin's death, Stalin eventually emerged as the dominant figure in the Communist Party. This did not happen immediately. A struggle for power between Stalin and Trotsky went on for several years before Stalin was finally able to triumph in the late 1920s.

Trotsky as contender

Trotsky was the best known of the communist leaders after Lenin. He was extremely able and could claim both to have organised the Bolshevik takeover in 1917 and to have saved the Bolshevik government by organising the Red Army during the Russian Civil War. He also had a reputation outside the Soviet Union, having been Commissar for Foreign Affairs. However, he never really had much chance of taking over because the other communist leaders disliked him and found him arrogant. They also mistrusted him for not joining the Bolsheviks until 1917. He had lost support by wanting to persist with War Communism when the NEP was introduced. Finally, in a country with a long and deep tradition of anti-Semitism, it was Trotsky's disadvantage to be Jewish.

ACTIVITIES

For both Trotsky and Stalin, note down their positive and negative points as potential leaders. Discuss with a partner which of the two men you think would have been a better leader for the Soviet Union, and why.

Stalin as contender

Stalin was almost the complete opposite of Trotsky. Although he had been a prominent Bolshevik for many years, he had no outstanding achievements to his name. He came from a working-class background and had none of Trotsky's brilliance. He was an organiser and a loyal supporter of Lenin, who after 1917 rose steadily into positions of influence in both the Communist Party and the government. In 1924 Stalin was little known outside the Soviet Union, but during his time as Commissar for Nationalities, and then as General Secretary of the Communist Party, he had taken the chance to appoint his supporters into positions of influence.

Lenin's opinion

In Lenin's political testament (or will), he had warned that Stalin had concentrated enormous power in his hands and should be removed as General Secretary. Yet the other communist leaders were worried by Trotsky's radicalism and his belief in 'permanent revolution', which they saw as opposition to the NEP. They preferred Stalin's belief in 'socialism in one country', which seemed to mean allowing the Soviet Union to move towards socialism more slowly.

ACTIVITIES

Summarise the reasons that Stalin was preferred to Trotsky.

The emergence of Stalin

In the aftermath of Lenin's death, Stalin, together with **Zinoviev** and **Kamenev** – two other communist leaders who had ambitions of their own – emerged and took power. Trotsky was accused of trying to split the Communist Party and take power for himself. Because he was so unpopular, few were willing to defend him against these charges.

Stalin consolidates his position

One by one, Trotsky was stripped of his positions of power. He ceased to be Commissar for War in January 1925, lost his place on the Politburo (the Soviet Union's cabinet) in 1926, and was removed from the Central Committee of the Communist Party in October 1927. Shortly afterwards he was expelled from the party and sent into internal exile. Finally, in 1929 he was forced out of the country and eventually into exile in Mexico.

No sooner had Stalin manoeuvred Trotsky out of power than he turned on Kamenev and Zinoviev. Both were sacked from their party and government posts, and although Stalin allowed them back into the party in 1928, their power was broken. By 1928 Stalin had emerged as the sole leader of the Soviet Union. However, the struggle for power had left him deeply suspicious of his colleagues.

VOICE YOUR OPINION!

Look back at your work on Lenin as a leader and compare him to Stalin. Which of the two men has the best qualities to act as leader?

SOURCE A

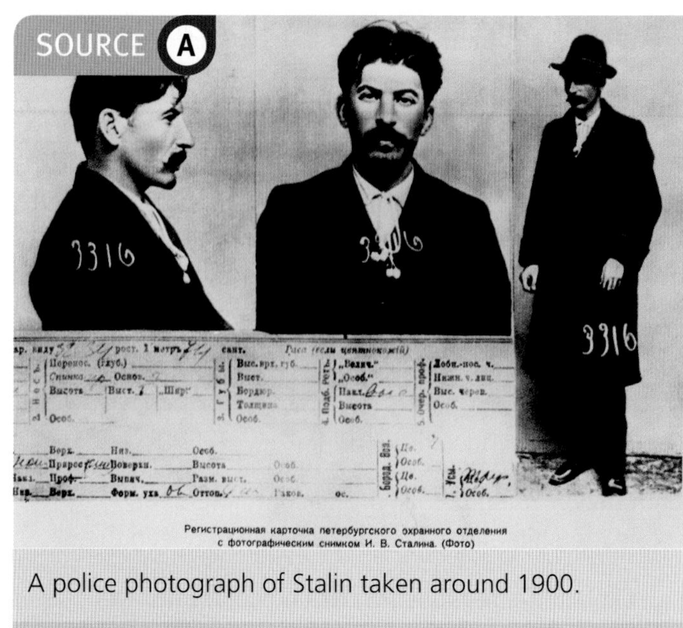
3316
3316
3316
Регистрационная карточка петербургского охранного отделения с фотографическим снимком И. В. Сталина. (Фото)

A police photograph of Stalin taken around 1900.

KEY PEOPLE

Lev Kamenev – *Bolshevik revolutionary arrested by Stalin in 1934, accused of spying and eventually shot after a show trial.*

Gregory Zinoviev – *Bolshevik revolutionary arrested by Stalin in 1934, accused of spying and eventually shot after a show trial.*

KEY WORDS

Subterfuge – *a trick or deception used in order to achieve your goal.*

Fact file

Stalin

Stalin was born in Georgia, in the far south of the Russian Empire. He was one of the few Bolshevik leaders from a working-class background. His father was a shoemaker. Stalin was born Josif Dzhugashvili, but used false names once he became a professional revolutionary. He finally settled on Stalin ('man of steel') in 1913.

As a young man, Stalin trained as a priest at the seminary in Tbilisi, but he was expelled when he became involved with local revolutionaries. In his late teens he joined the Social Democratic Party and devoted himself to revolutionary activities, including bank raids to raise party funds. He was arrested several times and exiled to Siberia. When not in prison, he was constantly being sought by the secret police. It was a hard and secretive way of life, and it left Stalin with a taste for conspiracy and **subterfuge**.

Although Stalin played little part in the 1905 revolution, he gradually became well known in the Bolshevik Party. Lenin trusted him and made him editor of the party newspaper, *Pravda*. He was imprisoned during the First World War and was only able to return to Petrograd from Siberia in February 1917. By then he was one of the leaders of the party, and he was prominent in organising the Bolsheviks during 1917. Once they took power, he held a succession of posts that enabled him to build a strong position. By the time of Lenin's death, he was well placed to deal with his rivals in the struggle for leadership.

Why did Stalin launch the purges?

LEARNING OBJECTIVES

In this lesson you will:

- investigate aspects of the purges and their outcome
- assess the importance of the NKVD to the purges through the use of source material.

GETTING STARTED

The period of the purges is sometimes called 'the Russian Holocaust' by historians. Think back to when you studied the Jewish Holocaust and briefly write down what constituted that particular atrocity. As you go through the next chapter see if there are any similarities between the two.

Background

The struggle for power after Lenin's death demonstrated that the leaders of the Communist Party disagreed strongly with each other on a variety of issues. By the end of the 1920s, Stalin had got the better of Trotsky and his other rivals, but he was still concerned that sooner or later his enemies would attempt to overthrow him.

The purges

Since it had come to power, the Communist Party had periodically 'purged' its membership, getting rid of those who were suspected of being disloyal. Now Stalin began to plan a purge of the top levels of the party, to deal with his rivals once and for all.

By 1934 Stalin believed that his opponents were planning to replace him with Kirov, the young and popular boss of the Leningrad section of the party. He secretly ordered Yagoda, head of the **NKVD** (the secret police), to have Kirov murdered. When this was done, Stalin used it as an excuse to turn on his enemies. Zinoviev, Kamenev and others were accused of being involved in the murder. They were arrested, put on trial and in January 1935 sentenced to long gaol terms.

The Great Terror

This was not enough for Stalin. Later that year he accused Zinoviev and Kamenev – along with Trotsky, who was now living in exile – of being spies for foreign countries. When in 1936 the NKVD provided evidence that their supporters had been in contact with Trotsky, they were put on public trial on charges of terrorism. Despite being promised their lives if they confessed, when they did so they were shot. This trial, in August 1936, marked the start of the 'Great Terror'. For two years the people of the Soviet Union were subjected to a campaign of state terror in which the secret police hunted Stalin's enemies, real and imagined, in all sectors of Soviet society. Literally nobody was safe.

Stalin launched the terror by sacking Yagoda, whom he thought had shown insufficient enthusiasm for rooting out traitors among the 'Old Bolsheviks' – the other leading communists who had played a part in the struggles that brought the Communist Party to power. He replaced him with Yezhov, who showed none of Yagoda's restraint. Two further show trials of Old Bolsheviks followed during 1937–38, with a procession of senior party figures admitting a variety of imaginary crimes against the state. Those who were unwilling to confess were persuaded by torture and threats against their families. Almost all were found guilty and shot, although a few cheated Stalin's plans by committing suicide.

KEY CONCEPTS

NKVD – *the secret police under Stalin's regime.*

SOURCE A

One day, Stalin lost his pipe. Stalin phoned the NKVD and demanded that they find his pipe immediately. Two hours later, Stalin finds his pipe behind the sofa. When Stalin phoned the NKVD the second time they told him that they had arrested ten people in attempting to find the pipe. When Stalin told him to release the men as he had found the pipe, the NKVD officer replied: 'But, Comrade Stalin, seven of them have already confessed.'

Soviet joke from the 1930s, described in *Stalin*, by John Simpkin.

ACTIVITIES

Complete the table below.

Action	Outcome
Murder of Kirov	
Trial of Zinoviev and Kamenev	
Purge of the Communist Party	
Purge of the military	
Crushing of potential opposition	
Purge of the NKVD	
Assassination of Trotsky	

During 1937 Stalin turned against the generals of the Red Army. According to the confessions forced out of them, they were plotting to overthrow Stalin. So many senior officers were shot during the purges that when Germany attacked the Soviet Union in 1941, the Red Army was seriously short of competent leaders. This was a major factor in the initial success of the German invasion.

The Secret police

Yezhov's NKVD was the instrument that Stalin used to crush any potential opposition. They arrested and shot hundreds of thousands of people in all walks of life. Even the official Soviet records admit that nearly 700,000 people were executed during the Great Terror of 1937–38. Stalin took a personal role in many of these murders. The NKVD prepared lists of victims for Stalin to authorise. He approved nearly 400 of these lists, containing around 40,000 names.

Damage to the economy

By 1938 the terror was beginning to have severe effects on the economy. The sheer numbers of managers, officials, supervisors, foremen, officers, scientists and engineers who had disappeared meant that many organisations were close to collapse. Stalin decided to end the Great Terror. As a final twist, however, he first turned against the NKVD. Many of its senior officers were shot and Yezhov was replaced by another of Stalin's cronies, Beria. At a party meeting the following year, Stalin personally denounced Yezhov. He was arrested and finally shot in 1940.

In 1940 Stalin's agents finally caught up with Trotsky, whom they had been hunting for years. In exile in Mexico, Trotsky was murdered with an ice pick by an NKVD agent. The death of Stalin's greatest enemy marked the true end of the Great Terror. Every one of Stalin's rivals was now dead.

GradeStudio

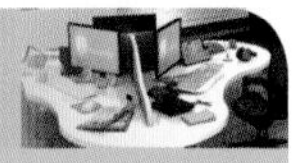

Study Source A. What is the message of the joke? Use the source and your own knowledge to explain your answer. **[6 marks]**

Examiner's tip

The first thing you need to do when answering this question is to explain the message of the source. To develop your answer, you also need to support it with specific evidence from the source as well as your own knowledge. Make sure you use some real examples of NKVD terror to reinforce what the joke is telling you.

What methods did Stalin use to control the Soviet Union?

LEARNING OBJECTIVES

In this lesson you will:

- examine the methods of control used by Stalin
- investigate and make judgements on the impact of Stalin's methods of control.

GETTING STARTED

When we talk about 'control' we usually mean how someone gets other people to do what they want. Before learning about how Stalin controlled the Soviet people, make a list of all the ways people can be controlled. (If you are struggling for ideas use your school as an example: how do the teachers control their pupils?)

Stalin's totalitarian state

The Soviet Union under Stalin was a **totalitarian** police state. No opposition was tolerated and any sign of independence or individualism was crushed. All Soviet people lived in fear of arrest by the secret police, the NKVD. There was no rule of law, no human rights. Once arrested, prisoners could be beaten, tortured or murdered. Many of those arrested simply disappeared and nobody knew what had happened to them. Often people had no idea why they had been arrested. It was not necessary to have committed a crime – being suspected of disloyalty to Stalin's state was enough. In these circumstances, few dared to oppose him. The terror was at its worst towards the end of the 1930s, but it was a feature of Soviet life throughout Stalin's years as dictator.

There were four main methods used by Stalin to control the Soviet Union: informers, prison camps, propaganda and the cult of personality.

Informers

The NKVD used an army of informers in schools, factories and farms – children were even encouraged to inform on their parents. A young peasant boy, Pavlik Morozov, who informed on his father for hoarding grain, was held up as an example to others. Russians ceased to talk freely with anyone they did not know well, and even then it was a risk. The poet Osip Mandelstam read his friends a poem in which he criticised Stalin. One of them informed on him, and he was sent into internal exile for three years.

ACTIVITIES

Make sure you take notes as you read through the information on each of the methods (a spider diagram would work well here).

Labour camps

Victims of the police state who were not executed for their 'crimes' were usually sent to labour camps. These were located in some of the most inhospitable and remote areas of the Soviet Union. The prisoners were used as slave labour on many of the prestige projects of the Five-Year Plans. Up to a quarter of a million convicts worked on the White Sea Canal, of whom nearly two-thirds did not survive the appallingly harsh conditions. When the canal was finished, it was too shallow to take the large ships for which it had been intended.

Inside the camps, conditions were brutal. Prisoners were expected to work in all weathers, even in the icy conditions of the Soviet winter. They were never given enough food. Camp guards had complete power over the inmates and routinely used violence against them. It has been estimated that around three million people were imprisoned in the camps by 1939. During Stalin's time in power, several million convicts probably died in the camps from hunger, cold and exhaustion.

Propaganda

In the Soviet Union under Stalin, people were not allowed to think for themselves. They were told what to think by the state. Education served the purposes of the Communist Party. Pupils were taught the communist version of history and even communist theories about science. Propaganda influenced almost every aspect of life. The mass media – radio, films, newspapers – were all controlled by the state and could only produce approved material. The state's messages were everywhere, at work, at school, on posters in the streets. Even artists were brought under state control. They were only allowed to produce work that reflected the glorious achievements of communism.

The cult of personality

The most important propaganda message of all was that Stalin was the greatest genius of his time. The Soviet people were taught to believe that Stalin was all-powerful and all-knowing. They came to look upon him as a god. His image was everywhere – in photographs and paintings, and on statues – and writers competed to produce the most glowing tribute to his achievements. In a set of eight records made of one of his speeches, the last record consisted solely of applause! In a single speech, one local party leader managed to call Stalin 'Leader of Genius of the **Proletarian** Revolution', 'Supreme Genius of Humanity', 'Leader of Genius of the Toilers of the Whole World' and 'Inspirer and Organiser of the Victory of Socialism'.

The flood of pro-Stalin propaganda, never balanced by a single word of criticism, created a kind of hero worship known as the **cult of personality**. It helps to explain why one of the most evil dictators the world has known was revered by many of the Soviet people.

SOURCE A

We receive our sun from Stalin,
We receive our prosperous life from Stalin
Even the good life in the tundras filled with snow-storms
We made together with him,
With the son of Lenin,
With Stalin the wise.
Thou, bright sun of the nations, The unsinking sun of our times,
And more than the sun, for the sun has no wisdom.

Song about Stalin by Alexis Tolstoy, 1937.

KEY WORDS

Proletarian – *relating to working-class people.*

Totalitarian – *a system in which the government controls every aspect of its citizens' lives.*

KEY CONCEPTS

Cult of personality – *a system which encourages devotion to a political leader.*

VOICE YOUR OPINION!

With a partner, discuss which of the methods used by Stalin to control the Soviet Union would be the worst; for instance is it worse to have the threat of a prison camp hanging over you or to have everything you read censored? Make sure you can justify your reasons.

GradeStudio

Describe the main features of Stalin's purges. **[4 marks]**

Student's response

Stalin's purges are generally agreed by historians to have taken place between 1936 and 1938. The purges were a series of campaigns orchestrated by Joseph Stalin and designed to remove anyone who opposed him (1). One of the main features (2) of the purges was the use of the NKVD to extract confessions of possible opponents and place them on trial (3). Although the trials of Kamanev and Zinoviev took place in 1934 they are a good example of the work of the NKVD under the label of the 'purges' (4). A further feature of the purges were the show trials themselves; political opponents were tortured to extract a confession then put on trial where they publicly confessed to whatever it was they were supposed to have done. In this way Stalin was able to rid himself of an estimated 2 million opponents (5). The result of the purges was that nobody in any position of power could feel safe, therefore giving Stalin complete control over the Soviet Union (6).

Examiner's comment

1 These opening statements are very general and not completely specific to the question. In this example they serve to give the reader a small background to the subject of the purges. If the student's answer stopped now they are likely to receive one mark only for a 'general' comment.
2 A good introduction to the main part of the answer. It shows the student is now about to address the question.
3 On its own, this is a relevant point to make and would get one mark.
4 This is 'supporting detail' and would secure a further mark.
5 A relevant point with supporting detail: two marks.
6 Full marks for this particular question and nicely concluded.

How complete was Stalin's control over the Soviet Union by 1941?

LEARNING OBJECTIVES

In this lesson you will:

- examine Stalin's methods of control and their success
- investigate the important people in Russian history, 1905–41.

GETTING STARTED

You must ensure that you understand fully the methods Stalin used to control the Soviet people. The following paragraph contains a lot of good information on how Stalin kept control. Read through it and separate the different factors of control into the headings given below:

- The cult of Stalin
- Culture and censorship
- Education
- Religion
- National identity.

Stalin used a variety of methods to ensure he dominated Russian life for instance he made writers, artists and musicians follow strict government rules if their work was to be allowed, Stalin also had pictures of himself put up everywhere. Furthermore, he named places after himself (Stalingrad) and destroyed books which did not adhere to the party line. In schools Stalin insisted that children were taught that he was a great leader. Christian leaders were also imprisoned and Muslim mosques and schools were closed down as well as making people clap whenever his name was mentioned. In addition to all this, Stalin had school textbooks rewritten to fit his version of Russian history and pictures of people he did not like were removed or altered. Stalin also imposed Russian culture on everybody and the Russian language was made compulsory for all to learn. Finally all books which did not follow the party line were destroyed.

The extent of Stalin's power

The events of the 1930s left Stalin as the unchallenged ruler of the Soviet Union. He had destroyed all opponents or potential opponents. He was the only member of Lenin's Politburo (cabinet) left alive by 1941. All the others had died, been killed or committed suicide. The Communist Party had been repeatedly purged at all levels. The armed forces had lost almost their entire officer class. The secret police itself had been purged. The combined effects of terror, propaganda and official perks for the privileged few ensured that the Soviet people stayed subservient. Rarely in history has one person held such absolute power over the lives of the people he ruled.

SOURCE A

This cartoon about Stalin's Russia was published in France during the 1930s. The banner reads, 'We are quite happy'.

VOICE YOUR OPINION!

You have investigated the methods Stalin used to control his country. Consider the information above. Do you think that Stalin found it difficult to control the lives of millions of ordinary people?

ACTIVITIES

One of the most difficult aspects of studying Russian history is that there are so many unfamiliar names to remember. Take this opportunity to go back over the past sections and write down every name you come to and a brief 'pen portrait' of that person. Ensure that you do this for the last section as well.

The reality of control

Nonetheless, there were limits even to Stalin's power. In a huge country like the Soviet Union, it was impossible for the government to control everything. Open opposition was rare, but local officials and managers would often fail to co-operate with orders that they did not like. This is part of the reason why Stalin tried to purge these groups so thoroughly in 1937–38.

The scale of the social and economic changes in the Soviet Union during the 1930s also made it difficult for the government to control all aspects of people's lives. Petty crime and hooliganism were common in the cities; divorce and abortions were also rising fast. There were plenty of signs that, in their private lives, people behaved as they wanted rather than as the government wished.

Stalin's state was totalitarian at an official level, dealing ruthlessly with any signs of opposition and murdering opponents of the regime. However, in practice, Stalin found it much harder to control the lives of millions of ordinary people.

SOURCE B

Реальность нашей программы
—это живые люди, это мы с вами,
наша воля к труду, наша готовность
работать по-новому,
наша решимость выполнить план.

The caption reads: 'Under the leadership of great Stalin – forward to Communism.'

GradeStudio

Study the poster in Source B. Why did Stalin publish this? Use the source and your own knowledge to explain your answer. **[7 marks]**

Examiner's tip

This question is asking you why it was published, NOT 'what does it tell you about Stalin's control over the Russian people?' You will at some point explain what the picture contains, but do not make that the first thing you do. Instead start with a direct answer to the question 'why did he publish this poster?' then answer through reference to details in the poster and your own knowledge of relevant content.

What was the impact of Stalin's economic policies?

Why did Stalin introduce the Five-Year Plans?

LEARNING OBJECTIVES

In this lesson you will:

- assess the need for the three Five-Year Plans
- investigate the success of the Five-Year Plans.

Stalin's ambitions for the Soviet Union

Stalin was determined to modernise the Soviet Union. He worried that if the country did not build up its economic strength, then sooner or later the capitalist powers would invade and destroy the achievements of communism. He believed the New Economic Policy was working too slowly. It would take decades to transform the Soviet Union into a modern economy. Instead he felt that something much quicker was needed.

GETTING STARTED

Stalin did not confine his reign of terror to the years 1936–38: his Five-Year Plans also persecuted groups he could blame for the country's economic failures. Listed below are the eight groups represented in the above source. Match the group to the picture and see if you can think of one reason why each group would be persecuted.

- Mensheviks
- Drunkards
- Landlords
- Capitalists
- White Russians
- Priests
- Kulaks
- Journalists

Agriculture

Starting in 1928, Stalin forced profound changes on agriculture and industry. **Collectivisation** was introduced in agriculture. The state took over agricultural production, forcing peasants to work together on huge collective farms. This change was fiercely resisted by the peasants, who wanted to farm their own land. It took much violence to force collectivisation through, and agriculture was left permanently weakened.

Industry

Industry was modernised through a series of Five-Year Plans. The state set targets and priorities for industry. With massive investment and superhuman efforts from the Soviet Union's workers, within a decade the Soviet Union had become a major industrial power.

VOICE YOUR OPINION!

How do you think Stalin 'encouraged' the peasants to accept his changes to the way they worked?

ACTIVITIES

Complete the following table while reading about three Five-Year Plans.

Five-Year Plan	Target area	How achieved?	Overall outcome
First: 1928–33			
Second: 1933–37			
Third: 1938–41			

The Five-Year Plans

Stalin saw his plan to industrialise the Soviet Union as a matter of life or death. If his plans failed, he believed the Soviet Union's enemies would crush it. The Soviet Union was still a rural, backward country. Stalin was determined that within ten years it would be transformed into one of the world's great industrial powers. To do this he used Five-Year Plans. Gosplan, the state planning bureau, was given the task of devising the plans. The idea was that the state would decide targets for industrial production, and would use central planning and direction of the nation's resources to achieve the priorities set out in each plan.

The first Five-Year Plan, 1928–32

The first Five-Year Plan was launched in 1928. It focused on building up heavy industries like coal and steel. To encourage Soviet workers, a propaganda campaign urged them to complete the plan in just four years. The targets set were tough, but enormous increases in production were achieved. However, the successes of the first plan also brought social and economic problems. The Soviet Union's transport system could not cope with all the extra goods produced. Towns and cities had to grow rapidly to house the expanding industrial workforce. The demand for housing, food, clothing and transport was so great that the system came close to collapse. The increase in production was being paid for by a decline in living conditions. Rationing was introduced to make sure that industrial workers had enough to eat, and towards the end of the plan targets had to be cut as the frantic growth of industry slowed down.

The second Five-Year Plan, 1933–37

The second Five-Year Plan concentrated on improvements in transport and in the production of machinery. More investment was allocated to consumer goods. However, this does not mean that heavy industry was neglected. By the time of the second plan, many of the big projects of the first plan were in operation, and this enabled three times as many new enterprises to be set up during the second plan as in the first. It was a time for consolidation and building on the gains of the first plan.

The third Five-Year Plan, 1938–41

The third Five-Year Plan ran for only three and a half years before it was interrupted by war. More and more resources were transferred into defence-related industries. The success of the plan was also undermined by the purges, in which many of the Soviet Union's most important planners and managers became victims. Nonetheless, when war broke out in 1941, Germany was attacking the world's second greatest industrial power, rather than the backward, agricultural nation the Soviet Union had been only 15 years earlier. This transformation had been brought about by the Five-Year Plans.

KEY CONCEPTS

Collectivisation – *process whereby the state organises all land and labour into collective farms, sets targets and takes all the produce.*

SOURCE A

The Dnieper Dam, built during the Five-Year Plans.

Why did Stalin introduce collectivisation?

LEARNING OBJECTIVES

In this lesson you will:

- examine the reasons for collectivisation
- consider the main reasons why Stalin introduced collectivisation.

GETTING STARTED

Source A shows people demonstrating. Without reading the translation of the banner, what do you think they are demonstrating about? Think about how they look. What is their likely profession?

A revolution in agriculture

By the end of the 1920s it was clear to Stalin that the NEP would not transform the Soviet Union into a modern industrial state. The biggest problem was agriculture. The land was farmed by peasants who used traditional, inefficient methods and were reluctant to change. The NEP had encouraged the peasants to produce more, but it was the peasants who profited from this, and not the state.

Stalin had four reasons for wanting change in the countryside:

- He needed to get his hands on the peasants' grain so that he could sell it for export. Using the foreign currency this would raise, he could buy vital equipment for industry.
- The industrial workers needed cheap food. If the peasants controlled grain sales, they would try to keep the price high. This meant that industrial workers would need to be paid more.
- Soviet agriculture needed to be modernised.
- The growing towns needed more workers; collectivisation might lead to fewer farmers and more industrial workers.

Stalin planned to set up collective farms, on which peasants would work together under government control. The collectives would be large, modern and efficient. The government would be able to keep as much of the produce as it needed, and pay the peasants for their labour.

Blaming the kulaks

Throughout the Soviet Union, the peasants rebelled against collectivisation. Stalin responded by sending the army and the secret police into the countryside to terrorise the peasants. Stalin claimed that it was only the richer peasants (called kulaks) who were resisting, for their own selfish reasons. This was an attempt to stir up class hatred between different groups of peasants, but it showed Stalin's ignorance of peasant life. By the end of the 1920s there were few true kulaks left – most had already perished during the civil war. Most peasants in Soviet villages were now very similar in wealth and status.

Enforced famine

The truth was that the great majority of peasants hated Stalin's collectivisation policy, and would never willingly have co-operated with it. In the end, they were forced to. The soldiers simply seized all stocks of grain. If the peasants handed these over voluntarily, they starved. If they did not, and attempted to hide their stocks, they were shot. Rather than lose all they had, most peasants killed all their animals and ate them while they could. In no time at all, famine loomed.

VOICE YOUR OPINION!

Does Source A show support for Stalin's actions? Explain your answer.

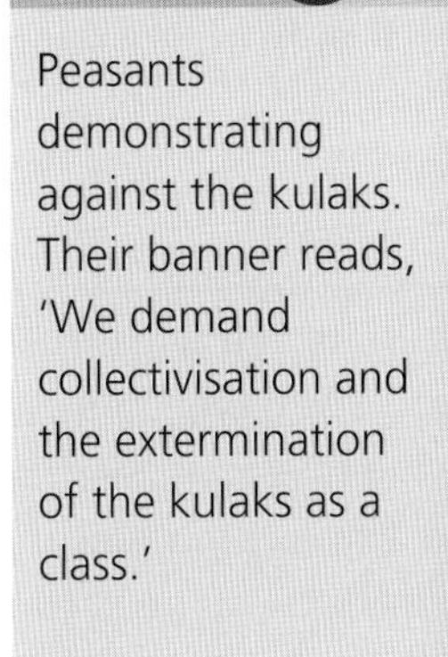

SOURCE A

Peasants demonstrating against the kulaks. Their banner reads, 'We demand collectivisation and the extermination of the kulaks as a class.'

Fact file

Collectivisation timeline 1927–39

1927
Collectivisation begins. Peasants asked to take part voluntarily; they refuse.

1928
Stocks of grain and produce seized and sent to the towns and cities.

1929
Compulsory collectivisation enforced by the army. Peasants burn crops and barns, and kill and eat their livestock.

1930
Stalin halts collectivisation because of famine. Peasants are allowed to own a small plot of land.

1931
Collectivisation restarts.

1932–33
Famine, especially in Ukraine (where five million die). Stalin blames the kulaks and a process of 'elimination' begins – their land is taken and whole villages are executed or sent to Siberian labour camps.

1934
Stalin orders the deaths of seven million kulaks.

1939
99 per cent of land is collectivised; 90 per cent of peasants live on one of 4000 state farms (kolkhoz) run by government officials.

Faced by these terror tactics, about 14 million households had joined collectives by the beginning of 1930. Unknown millions of peasants were forced off the land and went to swell the ranks of industrial workers in the cities. The more unfortunate peasants were labelled as kulaks and sent off to labour camps. In the atmosphere of terror which gripped the countryside, many were prepared to accuse their neighbours of being kulaks to save their own skins.

When collectivisation was complete, Stalin could treat the peasants as slave labour. In the Ukraine during 1932–33, Stalin demanded targets higher than the total amount of grain produced. The targets were rigorously enforced, and the peasants left to die of starvation. Those who tried to save themselves or their families by stealing some food from the collective were executed. Nowadays it is accepted that Stalin deliberately caused this famine to crush the resistance of the peasants. Probably around five million died as a result.

ACTIVITIES

Working in pairs or small groups, allocate the following tasks:

- Some of you will look for evidence to support the view that the introduction of collectivisation reflected the need to produce more food and modernise agriculture.
- The remainder will look for evidence to support the view that the reason for collectivisation was Stalin's need to crush the peasants in the same way that he crushed all other opposition.

Once the evidence has been found, both sides should debate and make notes on the others' arguments.

GradeStudio

'The most important reason why Stalin introduced collectivisation was to improve the agricultural sector.' Explain how far you agree with this statement. **[10 marks]**

Examiner's tip

You are being asked to argue whether improvements in agriculture were the real reason for collectivisation. This means you must have an alternative. Look carefully at this section again and come up with an alternative reason why collectivisation was introduced and then find the evidence to prove it. It is important to reach and support a final conclusion about how far improvements in agriculture were the most important reason for collectivisation. When you plan your answer, make sure you consider what information you need to save for your conclusion.

How successful were Stalin's economic changes?

LEARNING OBJECTIVES

In this lesson you will:

- learn about the results of collectivisation.
- examine the results of collectivisation from a communist perspective and make a decision on whether it was a good idea.

GETTING STARTED

Make a bar chart using the information from the table below. Try to get all four products on one chart. Make four comments about the chart.

The modernisation of Soviet industry

During the 1930s the Soviet Union became an industrialised nation. New factories were built, enormous dams and canals were constructed (often using the inmates of prison camps as slave labour), whole new towns sprang up, and the mineral resources of new areas were developed. An endless barrage of propaganda urged workers to make ever-greater efforts. Workers who produced more than the targets set for them were praised and given rewards. A whole movement was started urging workers to follow the example of Alexei Stakhanov, a coal miner, who was claimed to have exceeded his work quota by 1400 per cent in cutting 102 tons of coal in six hours.

This frenzied atmosphere produced problems as well as successes. The emphasis on targets meant that factory managers were much more concerned with quantity than quality. There was also a great shortage of skilled workers, so managers had great trouble keeping essential staff. They had to resort to giving higher wages and other incentives to certain workers. However, most workers were treated much less well. There was tough discipline, with fines for those who were late or absent without permission. Often, in the rush to boost production, safety standards were ignored, and accidents were common.

VOICE YOUR OPINION!

Did the modernisation of Soviet industry improve the lives of the workforce?

How successful were the Five-Year Plans?

It is impossible to be precise about the Soviet Union's achievements during the Five-Year Plans. Statistics released by the Soviet government, both at the time and later in the communist era, were completely unreliable. Not only did the government lie for propaganda purposes, but it was also being lied to by thousands of its own party bureaucrats and industrial managers with an interest in boosting their production figures.

To confuse matters more, even Western historians who have tried to estimate the Soviet Union's progress during the 1930s have reached differing conclusions. Nobody disputes that the Soviet Union was rapidly modernising and industrialising during these years, but the real questions are exactly how much was achieved, and whether similar progress could have been made without using the enormous power of the state.

The figures in Source A show the difficulty of agreeing over exact figures for the Five-Year Plans. The success of the first Five-Year Plan led Stalin to increase targets to the 'optimal' plan which was, of course, met so the targets were 'amended' even higher. Western historians suggest the 'actual' figures were those in column four.

SOURCE A

Product (in million tons)	1927–28 1st plan	1932–33 Optimal	1932 Amended	1932 Actual
Coal	35	75	95–105	64
Oil	11.7	21.7	40–55	21.4
Iron Ore	6.7	20.2	24–32	12.1
Pig Iron	3.2	10	15–16	6.2

Taken from Michael Lynch, *Stalin and Khrushchev: The USSR, 1924–64.*

Collectivisation

Stalin always claimed that it would have been impossible to modernise agriculture without collectivisation. Some modernisation occurred. Machine tractor stations were set up to help mechanise agriculture. Farms began to specialise in certain products, which made it easier for new ideas and techniques to be adopted. Collectivisation also served Stalin's purpose. He was able to gain control of the Soviet Union's agricultural produce, and sell it for the hard currency he desperately needed.

However, collectivisation dealt agriculture a devastating blow, and it did not quickly recover. Production remained low. Not until the mid-1950s did production reach the levels that had been achieved before the First World War.

Some historians have even begun to question whether collectivisation brought the benefits Stalin wanted. The direct costs of introducing machinery and the slump in production meant that the Soviet Union was on balance worse off because of Stalin's collectivisation policy. The appalling human cost may have been completely pointless.

By 1936 collectivisation was almost complete. However, Stalin's aim of treating the peasants like agricultural wage labourers had not quite been achieved. Even under collectivisation peasants needed an incentive to work. Most peasants now worked together on co-operative farms known as **kolkhoz**. These handed over to the state whatever produce was demanded, but if there was any profit left over, the peasants could share it. In addition, they were allowed small private plots of land for their own use, and could sell what they produced in the kolkhoz market. The number of peasants working on state farms (**sovkhoz**) for wages was much smaller.

GradeStudio

How successful were Stalin's economic policies? **[10 marks]**

Examiner's tip

The answer must include both collectivisation and the Five-Year Plans. Was one more successful than the other? Do the figures suggest that the five-years plans were successful? How do you define success? Also, note that there was a human cost, and even though the question does not explicitly ask you to take this into account you should mention it to give a rounded and complete answer. When you have explained the successes and failures of Stalin's economic policies, it is important to reach and support a final conclusion about whether or not they were successful. When you plan your answer, make sure you consider what information you need to save for your conclusion.

ACTIVITIES

In pairs decide whether the successes of collectivisation outweigh the failures. From a communist perspective what do you think the answer would be? Explain you answer.

KEY WORDS

Kolkhoz – *a collective farm where all produce was handed over to the government.*

Sovkhoz – *a state-run farm where produce was handed over to the government in return for wages.*

Successes of collectivisation	Failures of collectivisation
99% of Russian agriculture had been collectivised into a quarter of a million kolkhoz.	The numbers of cattle/sheep and goats fell dramatically during the period.
Grain produce had risen to 97 million tones by 1937 and there were cash crops for export.	Millions of kulaks were killed.
Over 17 million peasants left the countryside to work in the towns and cities.	Terrible famines caused the deaths of further millions.
Agriculture was forced to implement new ways of working (fertilisers/tractors/new attitudes and ideas).	
The communists now had complete control of farming either through fear or enthusiasm; the kulaks had been eliminated.	

How were the Soviet people affected by the changes?

LEARNING OBJECTIVES

In this lesson you will:

- examine the effect of the changes to Soviet life on three different groups of people
- decide whether any group benefited from the changes.

Background

By concentrating on three main areas it is possible to build a picture of how the Soviet people were affected by the changes taking place in industry and agriculture and by the purges. Ethnic minorities, women and different social groups all had varying experiences under Stalin.

Ethnic minorities

Under Stalin the non-Russian nationalities of the Soviet Union were at first allowed to preserve their own cultural traditions and identities. However, this tolerant approach was replaced after 1934 with a policy of Russification. Ethnic minority groups were now encouraged to see themselves as Soviet citizens rather than as separate nationalities. The Russian language was made a compulsory subject in the school curriculum. Russian was also made the official language of state organisations like the army. Russians were encouraged to migrate into non-Russian areas, and non-Russian graduates were deliberately found jobs inside Russia itself. In this way the concentration of national groups in their own regions was diminished.

During the purges, the leaders of ethnic minority groups were a particular target for persecution. In addition, the Soviet government's disapproval of religion had harmful effects on the Muslim central Asian nationalities of the Soviet Union. The government pressurised them to close Islamic schools and hospitals, and thousands of mosques were forced to close.

It seems ironic that Stalin, a Georgian himself, should have been so willing to undermine the cultures of the Soviet Union's national groups. However, his suspicion of anything different or individual made the nationalities an obvious target. His purpose was to make them forget their own traditions, language and culture, and to turn them into loyal Soviet citizens.

SOURCE A

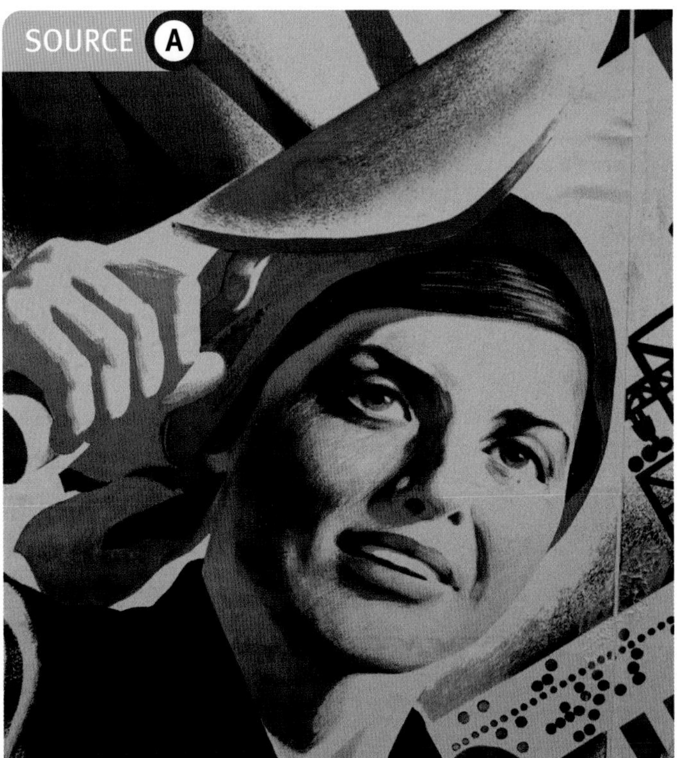

A Soviet propaganda poster from 1927 encouraging women to work.

Women

The socialist revolution in the Soviet Union was supposed to give women the same freedoms as men. Soviet propaganda always showed women as equal partners in the struggle to build the communist state. In the early years after the revolution, abortion and divorce were made easy to obtain, but under Stalin more conservative social values were re-established. The state encouraged marriage and parenthood, and awarded medals to women who had more than ten children. Sexual promiscuity was frowned upon, and the automatic right to abortion was abolished.

In the world of work, Soviet women were given equality with men, and the distinctions between men's and women's work were much less marked in the Soviet Union than in other countries. The problem for Soviet women was that while they were given opportunities to work – indeed, were expected to work – traditional male attitudes in social and home life still held sway, with domestic chores regarded as the women's responsibility. Soviet society remained male-dominated, and it is noteworthy that not a single woman held high office during Stalin's years in power.

Social groups

Soviet society in the 1930s consisted of three major groups.

- *Peasants*. All of them were now working on socialist-style farms, typically on a kolkhoz. In general, they were resentful of what had been done to them and would have found it hard to survive without the private plots of land they were allocated. Agriculture remained in deep depression, and life in the countryside was grim.
- *Industrial workers*. By the end of the 1930s, life was beginning to improve. Wages were still lower than in 1928, but more people were working, so most families had a little more to spend. The chaos and disruption of the first Five-Year Plan gave way to a few years of greater stability. Housing was poor, but rationing came to an end, and a few more consumer goods became available. Free education and medicine were made available to more and more of the population.
- *The social elite*. The managers, scientists and party bosses had a much higher standard of living than the workers. In fact, under Stalin, society became more traditional again, with no pretence of equality between the social groups. The elite was given privilege and status. Not only did they earn more, but they enjoyed all kinds of perks, like special shops and holidays in state-run resorts. Nowhere was this trend more obvious than in the armed forces, which went back to the use of traditional ranks and titles, and ornate uniforms for officers.

However, being a member of a social elite was no guarantee of safety – these were the groups so viciously purged in 1937–38. Indeed, class jealousy between the workers and the elites made it easier for Stalin to purge the bosses and officials without losing the support of the ordinary people, who often enjoyed the downfall and humiliation of those previously in authority over them.

ACTIVITIES

In groups of three choose one of the social groups each. Using the information here and looking back through this section, work out whether your group benefited from the changes affecting them. Be ready to compare with the other two members of your group and decide whether any of them benefited from Stalin's changes.

GradeStudio

The following brought misery to the Soviet people during the 1930s:

i The Five-Year Plans
ii Collectivisation
iii The purges

Which of these do you think brought the greatest misery? Explain your answer referring only to i, ii and iii. **[10 marks]**

Examiner's tip

This is a major question and requires planning if it is to be answered successfully. The good thing is that you know what to write about, so jot down what you know about each of the three bullet points. Next attribute an order to them: which brought the most and the least misery. You must reinforce your argument with cast-iron examples from the text and your notes. To give a really good answer you could add some of the good points about the three points (but that doesn't mean saying something like 'the purges weren't all bad because at least people did what they were told.' (You should aim to include some statistics of production rises instead.)

Get your sources sorted

The overall message is that the workers of Petrograd should give their support to the Bolsheviks if there is to be a fair and just redistribution of the country's resources.

1 Trotsky is second in command of the Bolsheviks and knows what is going on. He is making direct promises to the poor by saying what they will do when in power.

2 'The Soviet Government' does not exist yet but this meeting's purpose is to drum up support for the Bolsheviks.

3 The date is important. The Provisional Government is on its way out although it does not know it, therefore Trotsky does not know that the Bolsheviks will be victorious in a matter of days. This gives us an insight into the hopeful rhetoric of this political speaker.

SOURCE A

ЦАРЬ, ПОП И БОГАЧ
НА ПЛЕЧАХ У ТРУДОВОГО НАРОДА

There is no doubt who is in control of the action in this cartoon. The rich man is driving the stretcher whilst all around him are dying, he is making progress at the expense of the poor man.

The artist is showing the Tsar sitting on a throne on the shoulders of the peasants. There is no mistake that he is doing nothing while all around him are starving and dying because of him.

The priest is snivelling behind the Tsar as if he is afraid to come out. This shows the church as the Tsar's lackey: a comment on the relationship between the two institutions.

All are starving and bewildered. Another comment on the state of the peasants in Russia at this time. Despite the peasants farming the land it is always they who starve.

What is the message of this source?

SOURCE 

The Soviet Government will give everything that is in the country to the poor and to the people in the trenches. You well-to-do folk have two coats – hand one over to the soldiers who are cold in the trenches. You have warm boots? Sit at home – the workers need your boots.

22 October 1917 Leon Trotsky speaking at a meeting in Petrograd.
From Donald W. Mack, *Lenin and the Russian Revolution*.

Russia, 1905-41

Grade Studio

On your chosen Depth Study you will have to answer a compulsory source-based question, and one structured question from a choice of two. The source-based question will be based on three sources and will consist of three sub-questions. These sub-questions will test your source-handling skills (AO3) but you will also have to use your knowledge and understanding of the topic (AO1 and AO2) to help you answer effectively. Here is an example of the source-based question.

Study the sources carefully, and then answer the questions which follow.

Source A

A French poster of Stalin from the 1930s.

Source B

I was in love with that man and I love him still. The day he died I wept like a baby. I loved him for his mind, his logic, his manliness and especially his courage. He was the one person great enough to keep the Soviet Union together after Lenin's death. It was for him that we worked and sacrificed and died. He was a genius of his time.

A former manager of a collective farm remembering Stalin in 1967.

Source C

A cartoon published in France in 1936 by Russian exiles, commenting on proceedings in the Soviet parliament.

a Study Source A. What is the message of this cartoon? Use the source and your knowledge to explain your answer. **[6 marks]**

b Study Source B. How far does this source prove that the Soviet people loved Stalin? Use the source and your knowledge to explain your answer. **[7 marks]**

c Study Source C. Why do you think this cartoon was published in France in 1936? Use the source and your knowledge to explain your answer. **[7 marks]**

You might wish to have a go at parts **a** and **c**. We are going to have a look here at part **b**.

Answering the question

STEP 1: What claims are made in the source that are relevant to the issue of whether or not the Soviet people loved Stalin? This manager says he loves him still, gives several reasons for loving him, and calls him a genius. So the source indicates that people loved Stalin.

STEP 2: However, just because the source says people loved Stalin, it doesn't have to be true. If all Soviet people felt the same then this would be proof – but did they? From your own knowledge, judge how other Soviet people would have felt.

STEP 3: In any case, is this man a credible witness? Using your own knowledge, you need to consider whether a man who was a manager of a collective farm during the 1930s is likely to give a balanced view, or whether he is more likely to be a supporter of Stalin whose views will be one-sided.

STEP 4: The question asks 'How far' the source proves that people loved Stalin. This should make you consider the possibility that some did, and some did not. The best answers will always reach a balanced conclusion that deals directly with the issue of 'How far?'

Examiner's tip

The question is asking about proof. There is a difference between a source, on the one hand, saying or suggesting something – in this case whether or not the Soviet people loved Stalin – and on the other hand actually proving that it was true. You will have two ways of deciding about proof. First, you can consider whether or not the source – here a former manager of a collective farm – is likely to be a reliable witness. Second, you can compare what he says with what you actually know about the topic. Only by using your knowledge to test the claims made in the source will you be able to reach a reasoned judgement about the issue of proof

Student's response

Read the following answer. Does it test the claims made in the source in order to reach a balanced conclusion?

I think this source is valid as proof that the Soviet people loved Stalin. The man says he cried when Stalin died, and you would not do this unless you felt something for him. Although it seems strange because we know Stalin was so cruel, it is true that Russians thought Stalin was a genius. They were encouraged to think this because of the 'cult of personality', which was propaganda claiming that Stalin was a great leader, but they thought it was true because of all the changes Stalin brought about to build up industry and modernise Russia.

Examiner's comment

This answer does test the claims made in the source. Using knowledge of Stalin's achievements and the propaganda he used, the student reaches the conclusion that the source is proof. Answers like this don't simply accept what the source says, and therefore they earn a good mark. The weakness in this response is that it is unbalanced, looking at one side of the argument only, and it cannot therefore reach the top level. To achieve the top mark, it would have to demonstrate that many Russians, for example the kulaks, would have hated Stalin. By showing that some loved him but some did not, it would be possible to make some final judgement about 'how far' the source was proof.

THE BROXBOURNE SCHOOL
LIBRARY RESOURCE CENTRE

The USA, 1919–41

Introduction

The USA emerged from the First World War as the richest country in the world. During the 1920s it experienced a consumer boom as its industries poured out more and more products for Americans to buy. Goods like motor cars, radios and washing machines became available to many ordinary people. Americans had more money to spend, and more leisure time in which to spend it. This was the 'Jazz Age' or the 'Roaring Twenties', a time to party and have fun.

However, many Americans did not share in the growing prosperity. It has been estimated that as much as half of the population actually lived below the poverty line. It was also true that American society had a nasty, intolerant side, and blacks and immigrants faced discrimination in housing, education and employment. Many people in rural areas, particularly agricultural workers, lived in poverty, as agriculture faced a crisis of over-production and falling prices. This was a period when Prohibition, the banning of the sale of alcohol, brought about a rapid growth in organised crime.

In any case, over production and the Wall Street Crash of October 1929 brought the party to an end. There was simply a limit to how much people could buy. The collapse of the stock market led to widespread unemployment, and thousands of businesses went bust. President Hoover hoped that his policy of 'rugged individualism' would help deal with the effects of the Depression. He was wrong and lost the 1932 presidential election to Franklin Roosevelt, who promised a 'New Deal' to the American people. The New Deal involved spending huge amounts of government money in an attempt to create jobs. It partly worked. After 1933 unemployment did come down, but even Roosevelt found it impossible to get all Americans back to work until the Second World War broke out and production was stepped up to supply war goods.

ACTIVITIES

1 Draw a table with three columns:
   - a Knowledge
   - b Want to know
   - c Learning

This is a KWL grid; fill in two columns now and the last one when you have completed your studies of the chapter.

- The first column is what you already know. Here you should include anything at all about the period – events, people, significant dates, etc.
- The second column is for you to write questions, what are you not sure about and would like to know.

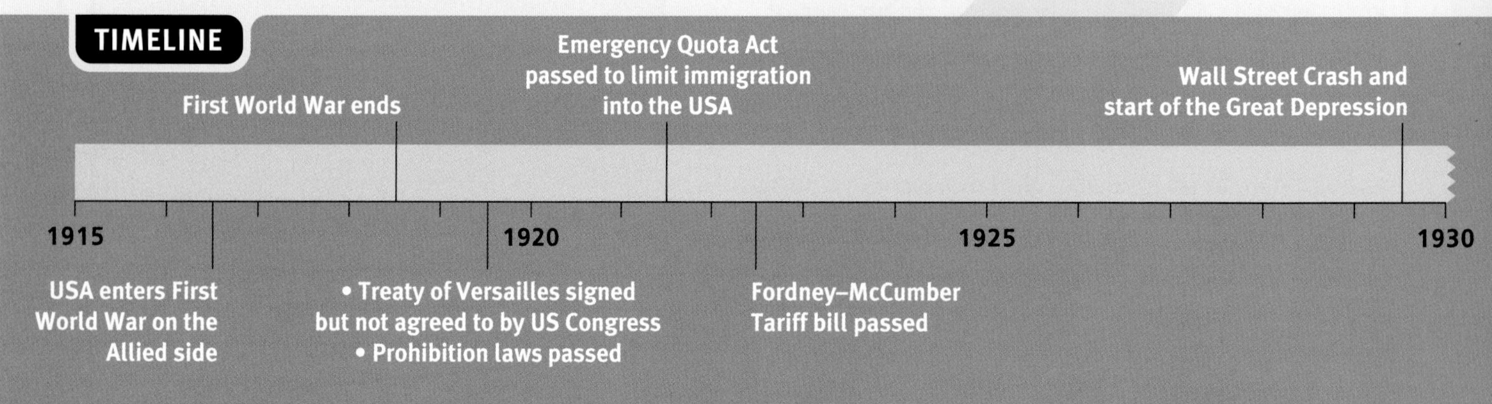
TIMELINE
Emergency Quota Act passed to limit immigration into the USA
First World War ends
Wall Street Crash and start of the Great Depression
1915
1920
1925
1930
USA enters First World War on the Allied side
• Treaty of Versailles signed but not agreed to by US Congress
• Prohibition laws passed
Fordney–McCumber Tariff bill passed

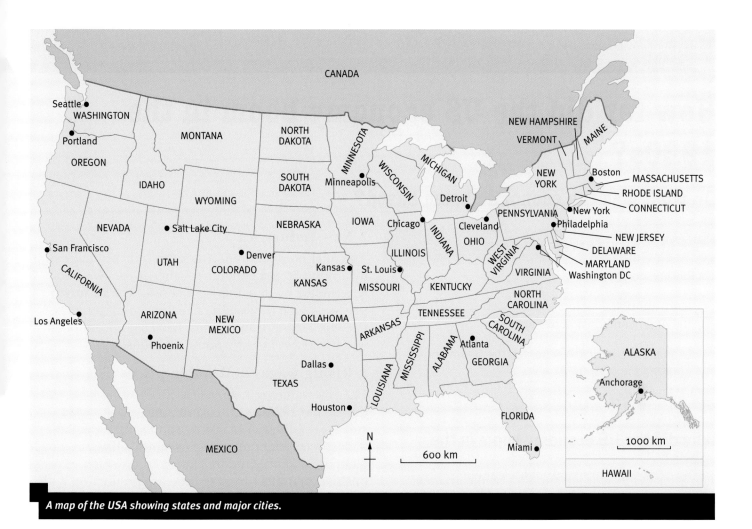

A map of the USA showing states and major cities.

HISTORY DETECTIVE

Work with a partner to investigate the two decades covered by this chapter – the 1920s and 1930s.

You are going to complete a research task for a brief section in an encyclopaedia. You must describe the decade in no more than 300 words; the layout and presentation style is up to you but you should aim to cover as many of the key events as possible. This task encourages you to be both brief and selective in the detail you include to allow you to cover more ground, but you may have to read a little deeper anyway to discover what to include or miss out.

Present your findings to the class and vote on which decade was the most turbulent for American society.

1935
1940
1945
New Deal starts
• Second World War begins in Europe
• Roosevelt re-elected for historic third term
• Japanese attack Pearl Harbor, USA enters Second World War

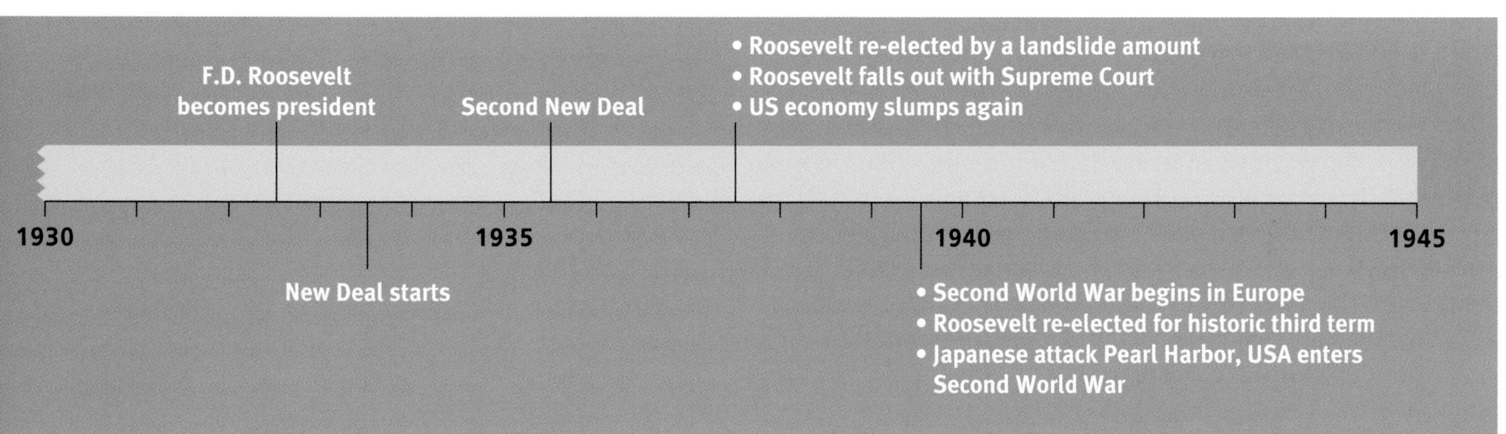

F.D. Roosevelt becomes president
Second New Deal
• Roosevelt re-elected by a landslide amount
• Roosevelt falls out with Supreme Court
• US economy slumps again

How far did the US economy boom in the 1920s?

On what was the economic boom based?

LEARNING OBJECTIVES

In this lesson you will:

- learn about the factors that created and sustained the American boom in the 1920s
- examine the industries that led the boom and benefited most from it.

Why did the US economy boom in the 1920s?

The First World War left the USA as the greatest economic power in the world. It had not suffered the financial and physical damage that affected the European nations. Its industries had been boosted by wartime production and it was owed enormous sums by its Allies, to which it had made war loans. The **Republicans** were in power throughout the 1920s, and followed policies that stimulated the economy still more. The 1920s were **boom** years in the USA. Yet this was not a boom in which everyone shared. Agriculture was depressed, and some groups, notably many blacks, continued to suffer in poverty. By the end of the decade, there were clear signs that the boom was coming to an end.

On what factors was the economic boom based?

1 The USA's wealth

By the start of the twentieth century, the USA was the world's leading industrial nation. It was rich in raw materials such as coal, iron ore and oil, and had much fertile land. Its population, made up mainly of immigrants, was hard working and ambitious. The First World War marked the moment at which the USA changed from being rural and agricultural to urban and industrial. By 1920 more than half of the population lived in towns and cities.

2 New industries

The total production of American industry increased by around 50 per cent during the 1920s. This boom was fuelled by demand from consumers for new products such as washing machines, refrigerators, vacuum cleaners and radios. Most significant of all was the growth of the motor car industry.

3 Rising wages and stable prices

The real value of incomes rose by around a quarter during the 1920s. At the same time, prices were steady or falling. A major reason for this was the widespread adoption of the **assembly-line** techniques pioneered by Henry Ford, which enabled manufacturers to increase production and make goods cheaply.

4 Government policies

Throughout the 1920s control of the American economy was in the hands of **Andrew Mellon**, Secretary of the Treasury. He believed that government should play as little part in economic life as possible, and he gave big business what it wanted. Businessmen believed that, if taxes were low, people and companies would have more money to invest. These investments would help industry expand still more. Throughout the 1920s, Mellon cut taxes.

The other main demand of business was for protection against cheap foreign imports. The government responded by increasing **tariffs**. The Fordney–McCumber Tariff Act of 1922 raised tariffs higher than ever before. However, by the end of the decade, home demand was beginning to fall, and other nations had imposed their own tariffs against American goods, so industry found it hard to export its surplus production.

5 Hire purchase

The consumer boom was encouraged by the easy availability of **credit**. Hire purchase enabled consumers to buy the goods they wanted with a small deposit and then pay off the rest in weekly or monthly instalments. Mail-order catalogues gave people in every part of country the chance to benefit from the consumer boom because the latest fashions were available to them by post.

6 Weak unions

The Republican governments, like businessmen, were hostile towards trade unions. Employers were allowed to use violence to break strikes and to refuse to employ union members. Unions were excluded altogether from the car industry until the 1930s. This allowed employers to hold down wages and to keep hours of work long, at a time when profits were rising fast.

The role of the US government

The US government had helped create the right conditions for this period of prosperity. They had relaxed regulations – with low taxes and a laissez faire approach, which meant competition could be positive. The freedom offered by the government's refusal to get involved allowed rapid expansion of successful businesses. Perhaps most importantly, people bought American goods because the government made foreign goods so expensive. Furthermore, the population of the USA grew rapidly in the 1920s, through immigration and rising birth rates.

SOURCE A

The front cover of the Sears, Roebuck and Co. catalogue, spring and summer 1927.

KEY WORDS

Assembly-line – *an arrangement of workers, machines and equipment in which the product being assembled passes consecutively from operation to operation until complete.*

Boom – *a period of time during which sales or business activity increases rapidly.*

Credit – *a contractural agreement in which a borrower receives something of value now, with the agreement to repay the lender at some date in the future. Also the borrowing capacity of an individual or company.*

Tariffs – *a list or system of duties imposed by a government on imported or exported goods.*

KEY PEOPLE

Andrew Mellon – *American banker, industrialist, philanthropist, art collector and Secretary of the Treasury from 4 March 1921 until 12 February 1932. His controversial theory was that by lowering the tax rates across the board, he could increase the overall tax regime.*

The impact of the boom

The cycle of prosperity meant that increased prosperity in turn increased prosperity.

- Advertising billboards and radio commercials put new products directly into the mind of the consumer.

KEY CONCEPTS

Republican – *a member of the Republican Party of the United States.*

- Sophisticated sales methods developed as companies aimed to sell people things that they never realised they needed.
- Hire purchase meant that people for the first time didn't need to have the cash to buy something – they could take it on credit and pay in instalments.
- People felt the need 'to keep up' with their neighbours' new purchases, and this drove consumption.

CASE STUDY

The rise of the car manufacturing industry

As early as 1920 car manufacturing was the USA's most valuable industry, and by 1929 it employed more workers than any other – half a million. It is impossible to guess how many jobs were created by 'spin-offs' from the motor industry, not just in firms making components, but also in the oil industry, in road construction and in services such as hotels and restaurants, which developed across the country to serve the newly mobile population. In 1929, nearly 4.5 million cars were manufactured, mostly by the three great firms that dominated the industry – Ford, General Motors and Chrysler. By this time, around 27 million motor vehicles were registered in the USA.

The social consequences of the motor car

Mass ownership of cars had many social effects: some obvious – traffic jams and road accidents became a part of life; some less predictable but just as important, such as the growth of suburbs. The USA is a huge country; to move around it people had previously been dependent on public transport such as railways or on horse-drawn wagons and coaches. Now they could go where they wanted.

Isolated rural communities were brought into contact with the outside world. Farmers could drive to the nearest town for their supplies, and young people could drive into town for entertainment. City dwellers could now escape into the country or drive further afield for holidays. Many people in the USA were able to move anywhere to look for work, and were no longer tied to their home area.

Fact file

The 1920s US economy

Between 1920 and 1929, **Gross National Product** rose 40 per cent and income per person rose by 27 per cent, leading to mass production (e.g. Ford motor cars), a consumer boom (including buying things on hire purchase) and a **stock market** boom.

- Between 1920 and 1929, sales of automobiles rose from 8 m to 23 m; by 1925, one Ford car was built every 10 seconds.
- The entertainment industry flourished, with people flocking to cinemas, jazz clubs and **speakeasies.**
- Consumer durables such as fridges and electrical goods such as telephones and radios became popular. Plastic, cellophane and nylon were produced for the first time.
- Farmers were encouraged to produce too much (over-production) and much of it was wasted, but this meant that prices were low.
- Banks and the stock exchange provided opportunities for **speculation** that offered low risk for even the poorest person **'buying on the margin'**.

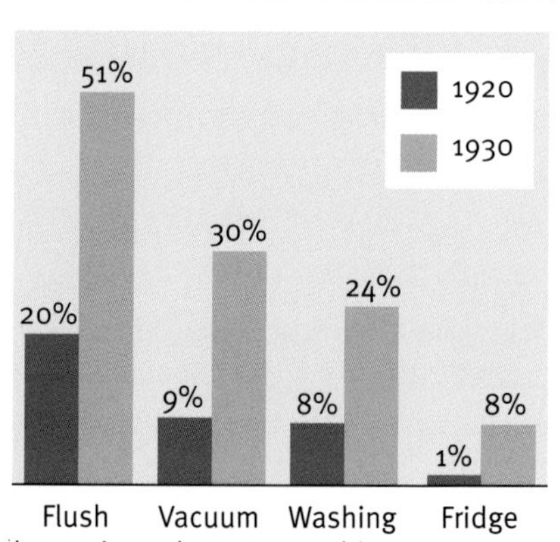

a) Percentage of households with goods

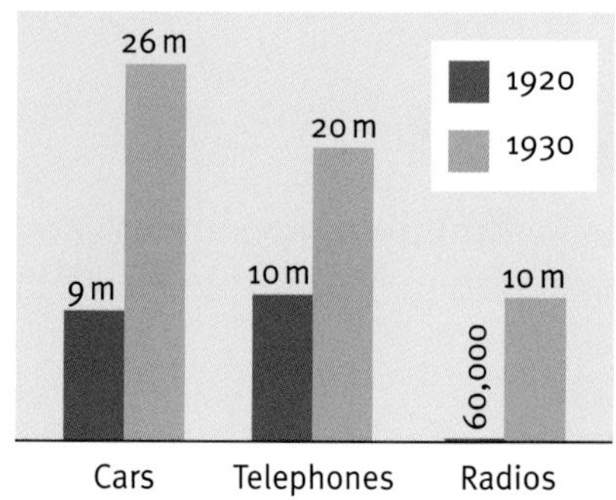

b) Increase in sales

Percentage of households with goods and increase in sales in America, 1920 and 1930.

ACTIVITIES

1 Two key ideas were central to American government policy in the 1920s:
   - rugged individualism – the belief that eventually everyone will help themselves if left to their own devices
   - isolationism – America protected her own interests by ignoring events elsewhere in the world.

   Which factor do you think was more influential in providing the climate for prosperity? Explain your answer with examples.

2 Conclude the true role of rugged individualism in the boom.

3 Study the causes of the boom. How far do you agree with the following statement:

   'The main cause of the boom was the rise in mass production which created an environment in which businesses could survive on a much larger scale than before. With little competition for global trade after the First World War, America found it easy to create and sustain demand, with advertising funding a cycle of prosperity.'

   Again, use evidence to support your ideas and offer a conclusion to illustrate your overall argument.

KEY WORDS

'Buying on the margin' – *buying securities with credit available through a relationship with a broker, called a Margin Account. Ownership on goods and shares is supported through this account.*

Gross National Product – *the total market value of all the goods and services produced by a nation during a specified period.*

Speakeasies – *illicit or unlicensed establishments selling alcoholic beverages in secret.*

Speculation – *the process of selecting investments with a higher risk in order to profit from an anticipated price movement.*

Stock market – *the market in which shares are issued and traded through exchanges. It is one of the most vital areas of a market economy as it provides companies with access to capital and investors with a slice of ownership in the company and the potential of gains based on the company's future performance.*

Explain how mass production worked. **[6 marks]**

LEARNING OBJECTIVES

In this lesson you will:

- learn about the areas the boom did and did not reach
- consider what this reveals about America's success.

Winners of the boom

The boom of the 1920s was created by the development and growth of the new industries – most importantly, cars, electrical goods and chemicals. The growth of national wealth meant that people had money to spend on goods that were new or that would previously have been seen as luxuries. Increasing wealth was visible in other ways. The construction industry boomed, with government money poured into road building. Skyscrapers changed the face of cities.

Henry Ford and the automobile industry

One industry symbolises the 1920s boom more than any other – automobile manufacture. The industry had begun in the early years of the century, but it was in the 1920s that the price of cars dropped to the point at which ordinary people could hope to own one. The greatest figure in the car industry was Henry Ford. The Ford Motor Company was started in 1903. By 1908 Ford had developed the first version of the 'Model T' – the 'universal car', as Ford called it – specifically intended to be a car for the masses and not just for the privileged few. From 1913 Ford's factory was organised on assembly-line principles. Unlike traditional manufacture, in which a worker would carry out a whole range of tasks in making a product, the assembly line brought the work to the worker, who would carry out just one task – say, bolting in a seat – before the line moved the work on to the next man. This was the first use of the assembly line in modern manufacturing, and it produced a revolution in industry. Huge numbers of identical, standardised cars could be built more quickly and cheaply than ever before. Ford could cut the price of the Model T, so more people could afford one. The original price of $850 fell to just $260 by 1924 – not surprising when the man-hours needed to assemble one fell from 12½ to 1½ in the same period. Up to 1926 the Model T was the USA's bestselling car. By the time production finished in 1927, 15 million had been made.

Those unaffected by the boom

However, traditional industries, such as textiles, coalmining and shipbuilding, either grew less quickly or even declined. These were already mature industries with developed markets, in which consumer demand could grow only to a limited degree. They had less scope for expansion than the new industries.

- The textile industry of the north-east faced competition from factories in other parts of the country, such as the south, where labour was much cheaper, and from artificial fibres, and many factories had to close.
- Coal was another industry under pressure. Greater use of electricity and oil for heating meant that demand for coal fell. The least profitable mines were forced to shut down.

However, these were the exceptions. In general, American industry prospered throughout the 1920s.

SOURCE A

An advertisement for an early Model T Ford.

Why did agriculture not share in the prosperity?

LEARNING OBJECTIVES

In this lesson you will:

- learn about the importance of farming for American society and the reasons why farmers were not able to maintain productivity
- prepare a report that evaluates the issues facing farmers in 1920s America and outlines the changes necessary for government policy.

The decline in agriculture during the 1920s

Not everyone prospered during the boom years. For the USA's farmers the 1920s were years of hardship and falling prices. Having benefitted from high prices paid for their produce during wartime, farmers were ill-prepared to cope with the basic problem affecting agriculture – over-production. American agriculture was simply too successful: it produced more than the country could eat or use, and because of international competition and tariffs, it proved impossible to deal with the surplus by

SOURCE A

A cartoon showing problems faced by American farmers in the 1920s.

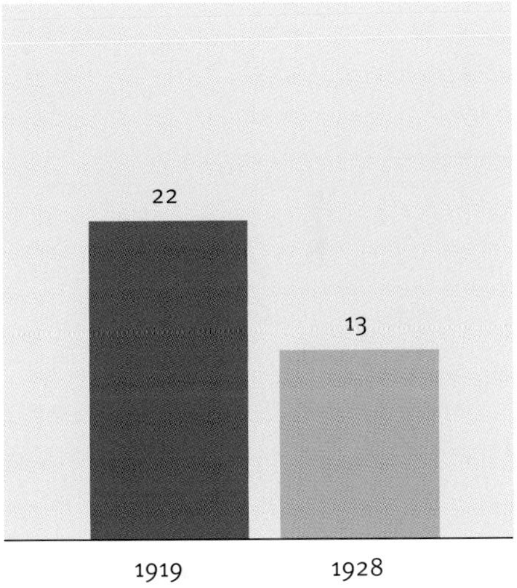

	1919	1928
Farmers' income in billions of dollars	22	13

a) Farmers' income in billions of dollars

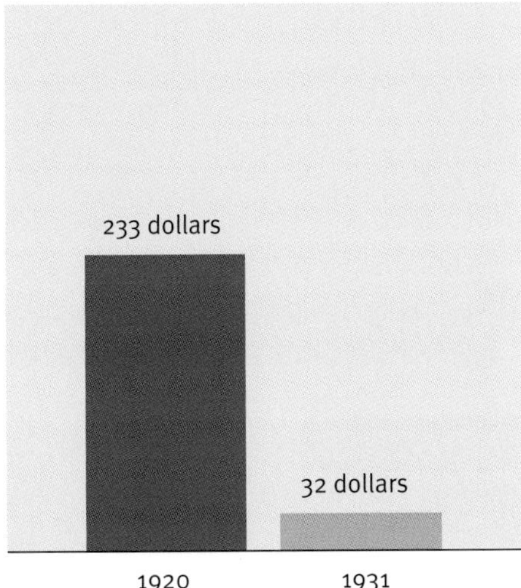

b) Price of a bushel of wheat

The decline in American agriculture, 1919–31.

exporting it. Prices collapsed and, with them, farmers' incomes. In a poor state like South Carolina, farmers were earning only a third of the average wage of all other workers. Many farmers borrowed money in the hope that prices would recover. They never did, so sooner or later these farmers had to leave the land and forfeit their farms to the bank. In 1920 one-third of the USA's population was in farming families, but by 1929 this proportion had fallen to one-quarter.

Rural America saw little sign, then, of increasing prosperity. Farms enjoyed few of the basic amenities that were becoming standard in the rest of the USA. Less than 10 per cent had electric light or mains water supplies. The situation was especially bad in the south, where farms had traditionally been dependent on single crops, usually cotton or tobacco. Not only was the price of these at rock bottom, but the crops were regularly decimated by pests such as the boll-weevil. Agricultural workers in the south, who were generally black people, were either paid starvation wages or employed as sharecroppers – a system in which they were paid no cash at all, but instead received a proportion of the crop to sell. In practice, this made them almost entirely dependent on their employer, who provided housing and made loans to the workers against their share of the crop.

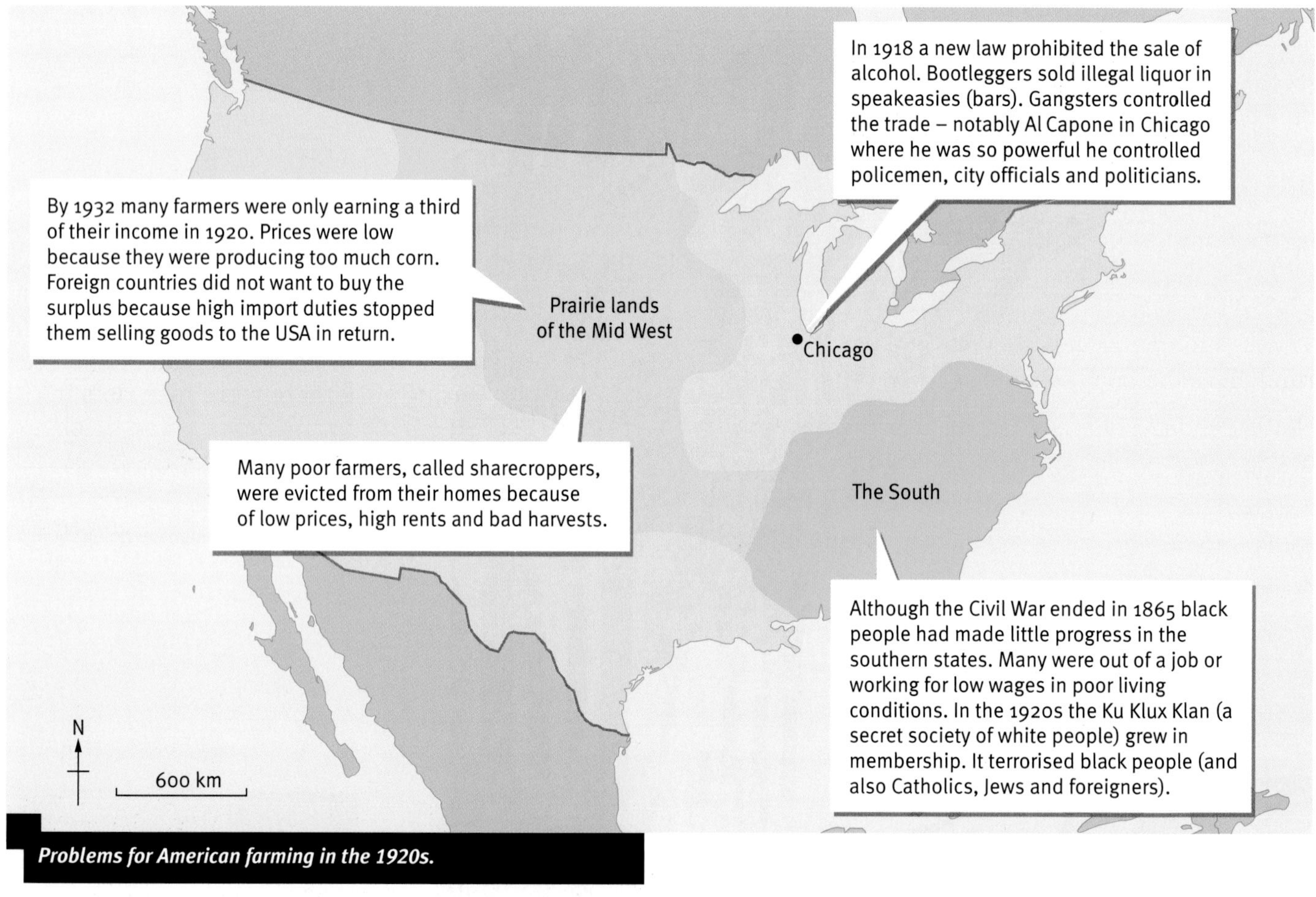

In 1918 a new law prohibited the sale of alcohol. Bootleggers sold illegal liquor in speakeasies (bars). Gangsters controlled the trade – notably Al Capone in Chicago where he was so powerful he controlled policemen, city officials and politicians.
By 1932 many farmers were only earning a third of their income in 1920. Prices were low because they were producing too much corn. Foreign countries did not want to buy the surplus because high import duties stopped them selling goods to the USA in return.
Prairie lands of the Mid West
Chicago
Many poor farmers, called sharecroppers, were evicted from their homes because of low prices, high rents and bad harvests.
The South
Although the Civil War ended in 1865 black people had made little progress in the southern states. Many were out of a job or working for low wages in poor living conditions. In the 1920s the Ku Klux Klan (a secret society of white people) grew in membership. It terrorised black people (and also Catholics, Jews and foreigners).
N
600 km

Problems for American farming in the 1920s.

ACTIVITIES

1. Study the graph and the cartoon in Source A and list five things that explain the problems farmers experienced in the 1920s.
2. Using the map and the information in this lesson, compile a report to be presented to the government that documents the difficulties facing American farmers. Your report should cover:
   - the debt that farmers were forced to take on
   - the fruitless surplus of food that was encouraged by the Republican government
   - the fact that farmers are a proud group in society and should be cherished above all
   - the impact of prohibition
   - the contrast between life on a farm and life in a city.

Did all Americans benefit from the boom?

LEARNING OBJECTIVES

In this lesson you will:

- find out about the groups who did not benefit from the boom
- assess the responsibility of the government and the importance of broader social trends.

GETTING STARTED

'The government is responsible for the happiness and prosperity of its people.'

Hold a class debate to discuss this statement.

Which Americans did not benefit from the boom?

The USA became much richer during the 1920s, but it would be wrong to think that this wealth was shared out equally. It has been estimated that, in 1929, 60 per cent of all American families lived below the **poverty line**. Many of these were in rural areas, but the poor were numerous in the big cities too. Those who benefited from the boom were the rich and the middle classes. In 1929, one third of all income was earned by only 5 per cent of the workforce. Throughout the decade the poor remained poor; in rural areas the poor became even poorer.

Neither did the boom affect all areas of the country equally. The west and the north-east, where most of the country's industries were located, felt the most benefit; the south, which was almost entirely agricultural, did the worst. However, even some agricultural areas did better than others. Fruit farmers, for instance, were able to benefit from growing demand for fresh produce and were among the best-paid groups in the country. Wheat farmers of the Great Plains, by contrast, suffered a decade of low prices caused by falling demand and stiff international competition.

The USA's black population suffered discrimination of all kinds, not least in employment. Historically, most black people had lived in the south, but during the First World War many families had moved to cities in the north, attracted by jobs available in the factories. Once the war finished, competition for jobs increased, and many whites resented the black newcomers. During 1919 there were race riots in many cities. But whatever problems urban black people in the north had to cope with, those who stayed in the south faced more, working as agricultural labourers and living in conditions of extreme poverty. Even their situation was marginally superior to that of the Native Americans, who, as a government report of 1928 admitted, were on reservations where the land was generally so poor that it was impossible to scrape a living from it.

So, despite the boom and the undoubted benefits that it brought to many people, by the end of the 1920s the USA was still a deeply divided society, with enormous differences between rich and poor, white and black, city and country.

SOURCE A

Child workers in the cotton fields in the 1920s.

SOURCE B

A black family and their home in Virginia in the 1920s.

ACTIVITIES

1 Investigate the following groups who were unable to share in the prosperity of the economic boom in 1920s America:
- textile workers
- poor farmers
- black sharecropper family
- miners
- new immigrants.

a What were their lives like? Take each group in turn and aim to find four things that define the difficulties they experienced, then rank them in order of significance.

b Explain why the government was not helping these groups and what this says about the American dream.

2 **a** Pick the two groups that you are most comfortable with and write a paragraph to explain why they did not share in the boom. Use the following quote as a reference point: 'The 1920s was a time of unprecedented prosperity for all Americans.'

b Share your paragraph with a partner and get them to identify areas where you were successful/unsuccessful.

BRAIN BOOST Poverty [FLOP]

Farming – 1929 farmers' wages 40 per cent of national average, 500,000 farmers go bankrupt

Low wages: top 5 per cent of the population earned a third of the income, but 40 per cent were below the **poverty line**

Old industries (textiles and coal) – a coal miners' wages were one third of the national average. There were two million employed throughout the 1920s

Poor black Americans – one million black farm workers lost their jobs in the 1920s. Black people stuck in low-paid, **menial jobs**.

VOICE YOUR OPINION!

How does poverty affect your judgement of a person's character?

Do you think that groups like those discussed in this lesson experienced more than just financial hardship?

KEY WORDS

Menial jobs – *jobs of low status that require a low level of skills. Can be of little social significance and secure little respect.*

Poverty line – *the lowest income level recognised as an acceptable amount of money to live off; below it, you would be officially poor.*

GradeStudio

How far did the US economy boom in the 1920s? **[10 marks]**

Examiner's tip

Remember that in a question which asks you 'how far' you need to explain both sides of the argument, giving specific evidence to support your arguments. At the end of your answer, you must reach and support a conclusion in which you make a final judgement about 'how far' you agree with the statement. However, don't simply sum up what you have already said.

How far did US society change in the 1920s?

What were the 'Roaring Twenties'?

LEARNING OBJECTIVES

In this lesson you will:

- investigate how America changed socially and culturally during the 1920s
- evaluate how far the changes in this area supported and encouraged the boom and how far they offered distractions from its failures.

GETTING STARTED

You will need five sticky notes.

1 List all the things that you like to do with your spare time.
2 Write down your top five and pass them to your class teacher to create a whole-class list of the most popular pastimes.
3 With the help of your teacher and your classmates, identify which pastimes originated in America and take them away from your list.

You should find that a great deal of what we deem cultural in the modern era comes from America and, more specifically, from the 1920s.

The fun side of 1920s America

The popular image of the USA in the 1920s is of life as one long, crazy party, with jazz music playing on the radio, young, fashionable women known as **flappers** wildly dancing the Charleston, large quantities of illegal alcohol being consumed and everyone behaving in as scandalous a manner as possible. These were the 'Roaring Twenties', and there is an element of truth in the image. In the aftermath of the First World War, people were determined to have fun. They had more money and the leisure time in which to spend it. Women were freer than ever before to live their own lives; the flappers drank, smoked, dated and wore outrageous new fashions. The older generation could scarcely believe what was happening. The entertainment industry boomed. The 1920s were golden years for Hollywood films, with the first 'talkie' released in 1927. This was also the 'Jazz Age', with its crazes for new music and new dances.

SOURCE A

A Chicago nightclub in the 1920s.

But American society had another, much less permissive side to it. Throughout the 1920s, Prohibition, which made the making and selling of alcohol illegal, was in force. Not everyone wanted to join the party, and neither was everyone allowed to. These were also years of violent **racism** and intolerance, with minorities excluded from any chance of sharing in the good times.

The movies

The movie industry had begun before the First World War, but its popularity soared during the 1920s. Audiences more than doubled during the decade, and 95 million people a week were going to the cinema in 1929.

KEY CONCEPTS

Racism – *the belief that race accounts for differences in human character or ability, and that a particular race is superior to others.*

However, many people were worried by the impact of the movies, particularly on the morals of the young. As early as 1922 the Hollywood studios established a code which set strict rules about what could be shown on screen. These rules, which were expanded in 1930 to create the Hays Code, were particularly tight on how relationships between the sexes were portrayed.

Sport

Sport was another form of mass entertainment that flourished as workers began to enjoy greater prosperity and to have more leisure time. Baseball was the most popular sport of the urban working classes, with great players like 'Babe' Ruth of the New York Yankees becoming national heroes. In 1927 he set a record for hitting home runs – 60 in a season – which lasted until 1961. By 1930 he was earning $80,000 a year – an immense amount for the time.

The most famous boxer of the time was Jack Dempsey, world heavyweight champion from 1919 to 1926. His courage and punching made him a tremendous favourite with the fans.

One of the true sporting heroes of the time was the golfer Bobby Jones. He was the greatest golfer in the world, but he also set the highest standards of sportsmanship. On one occasion, he hit his ball into some trees, and accidentally trod on it while looking for it. Nobody else saw this happen, but he immediately told his playing partner and accepted a penalty of one shot. Later, someone tried to congratulate him for his honesty. 'You might as well praise a man for not robbing a bank' was Jones's reply.

ACTIVITIES

1 Write a short answer to explain why you think that the 1920s was called the 'Roaring Twenties'.

2 a Create a spider diagram with the term 'cultural expansion' in the centre. Use the information from this lesson to aform the branches of your diagram.

  b Plot your research onto the diagram, but aim only for the essential information. Use the following format:
  - topic area
  - key example
  - explanation.

  c Return to your completed spider diagram and rate the influence of each section in order of importance. Which change do you think was the most/least exciting?

Music

Another name for the 1920s is the 'Jazz Age'. Jazz was a new form of music that evolved from earlier forms of black music, such as the blues and ragtime. Its spread was assisted by the migration during the war of southern black people into northern cities. Famous night clubs like the Cotton Club in Harlem, New York, provided opportunities for some of the greatest performers, such as Duke Ellington, Louis Armstrong and Bessie Smith, to perform and achieve national reputations. The craze for jazz music was further encouraged by the development of radio as a form of mass entertainment.

One spin-off from the popularity of jazz was the dance crazes. The drinkers and party-goers were always on the watch for a new dance to try. The most famous of these crazes was for the Charleston, the dance that will always be associated with the flappers, but there were others too, such as the Black Bottom. These dances were linked by their sexual suggestiveness and their ability to scandalise the older generation.

Radio

The music of the 1920s was, more often than not, played on the radio. Sales of records actually fell as the popularity of the radio increased. At the start of the decade, few people possessed a radio, but by the end they were everywhere. In 1920, $2 million worth of radios were purchased, but in 1929 the figure was $600 million.

KEY WORDS

Flapper – *a young, independent woman who showed disdain for conventional dress and behaviour.*

HISTORY DETECTIVE

This is an area too vast to investigate properly in a textbook. At home do the following:

- Research an area you have covered that interests you.
- Find a figure from the era who was famous in that field.
- Compile a factfile of this person's life, e.g. when they were born, where they lived, what they did, etc.
- Bring your completed factfile back to class and create a display to show the key characters of the cultural boom.
- Perhaps you could return to your class work and add a few more examples so you are armed for the examination!

How widespread was intolerance in US society?

LEARNING OBJECTIVES

In this lesson you will:

- learn about the level of intolerance in US society and who it was directed against
- explore why Americans did not recognise and react to the threats and violence made towards its own citizens.

GETTING STARTED

1 a Discuss with a partner the definition of the following words.
   - Discrimination • Prejudice • Persecution.

  b Rank them in order of how damaging they are.

  c Report your discussions to the class and work together with your teacher to produce a set of class definitions.

Immigration

Most of the USA's population was descended from immigrants – unless, of course, they were immigrants themselves. During the 19th century, as the interior of the USA was opened up for settlement, people from Europe poured in. However, by the early 20th century, Americans were beginning to feel that their country was full up, and that there was little room left for new immigrants. The First World War heightened this feeling, as well as stirring up fear and hatred of foreigners, and of Germans in particular. Many Americans looked at the crowded slums of the big cities, teeming with immigrants from dozens of countries, many of whom spoke little if any English, and decided that enough was enough. Mass immigration had to be ended. This duly happened when Congress passed the Johnson–Reid Act of 1924, which fixed a **quota** of 150,000 immigrants a year – almost all of whom would be from Europe, because Asian immigration was halted entirely.

The Red Scare

There was another motive for limiting immigration – the fear that immigrants might be bringing **socialist** ideas with them. The Russian Revolution of 1917 convinced many Americans that communism was about to take over the world. Serious strikes in a number of major industries during 1919 were taken as evidence that communist agitators were already at work in the USA. Attorney-General Palmer responded by ordering a round-up of several thousand suspected socialists, and deporting those who were recent immigrants. A wave of anti-communist hysteria – known as the 'Red Scare' – swept the country. This reached its height when prominent politicians began to receive bombs in their mail, and finally Palmer's house in Washington was blown up. The most famous victims of the Red Scare, however, were not politicians, but two Italian immigrant **anarchists**, Sacco and Vanzetti.

The Sacco and Vanzetti case

In April 1920 a robbery took place at a shoe factory in the state of Massachusetts. The robbers stole $16,000 and shot two of the staff dead. A month later, two poorly educated Italians, Sacco and Vanzetti, were arrested and charged with the murders. There was little firm evidence against them, although when arrested they were both carrying firearms. From the start it was clear that the police had suspected them as much for their radical political beliefs, and for the fact that they were immigrants, as for the likelihood of them being guilty of the crime. Their trial was a farce. A biased judge made it clear that he wanted them found guilty. Evidence was tampered with by both the prosecution and the defence. Throughout the trial the pair maintained their innocence, but it made no difference. They were convicted and sentenced to death. The American public, whipped up by the Red Scare, demanded a scapegoat for the bomb outrages that had culminated in September 1920 with an explosion in New York which killed 30 people. For the next six years, Sacco and Vanzetti struggled to prove their innocence and gain a retrial. An international campaign was fought for their release. Another man was found who confessed to the murders. But the authorities refused to budge. Sacco and Vanzetti died in the electric chair in August 1927.

KEY WORDS

Anarchist – *a person who encourages a lack of civil order or peace.*

Quota – *a number or percentage, especially of people, constituting or designated as an upper limit.*

Socialist – *a person who supports a system of social organisation in which the means of producing and distributing goods is owned and shared collectively.*

Segregation and discrimination against black people

In the south, black people were kept in a permanent state of poverty and disadvantage by a range of official restrictions known as the 'Jim Crow' laws. These ensured that black people were segregated (kept apart) from white people. They lived in separate areas, went to separate schools, and were not allowed to use facilities reserved for white people. Most black people in the south were dependent on agriculture and suffered badly from the farming depression of the 1920s. Their misery was made worse by the violence that many suffered at the hands of white people, who were determined to demonstrate their social dominance. They lived in permanent fear of white **lynch** mobs, who could murder black people for no reason and with little chance of anyone being arrested. The politicians, police and judges were all white, and could be relied upon to turn a blind eye to violence against black people.

In the early 1920s there were around 50 lynchings a year, and few perpetrators were ever brought to justice. Black people in the northern cities did not face this kind of official discrimination and violence, but were still affected badly by the racism of American society.

They lived in the poorest housing, found it hardest to get jobs, were paid the lowest wages, and were most dependent on government relief. White people regarded them as inferior, and from time to time the antagonism between white people and black people blew up into race riots. Ten per cent of the USA's population was black, but to a great extent they were excluded from the opportunities and freedoms that other Americans took for granted.

The Ku Klux Klan

In the mid-19th century, after the American Civil War, a terrorist organisation was started in the south to try to preserve white supremacy over the newly freed black slaves. The members of this organisation dressed in white robes and wore pointed hoods to conceal their identity. They struck terror into the black community with their night-time raids and crosses of fire. The organisation was the Ku Klux Klan. In time it died out, although persecution of black people continued in other ways.

In 1915 the Klan was started again in Georgia by William Simmons. He kept the original Klan's ideas and costume, but added a whole new list of targets for the Klan's hatred: Catholics, Jews, foreigners, homosexuals and anyone of liberal views. In Simmons' eyes, the Klan stood for the preservation of 'true American values' – the values of white, Protestant, rural America. Most other Americans simply regarded the Klan as violent bigots.

SOURCE A

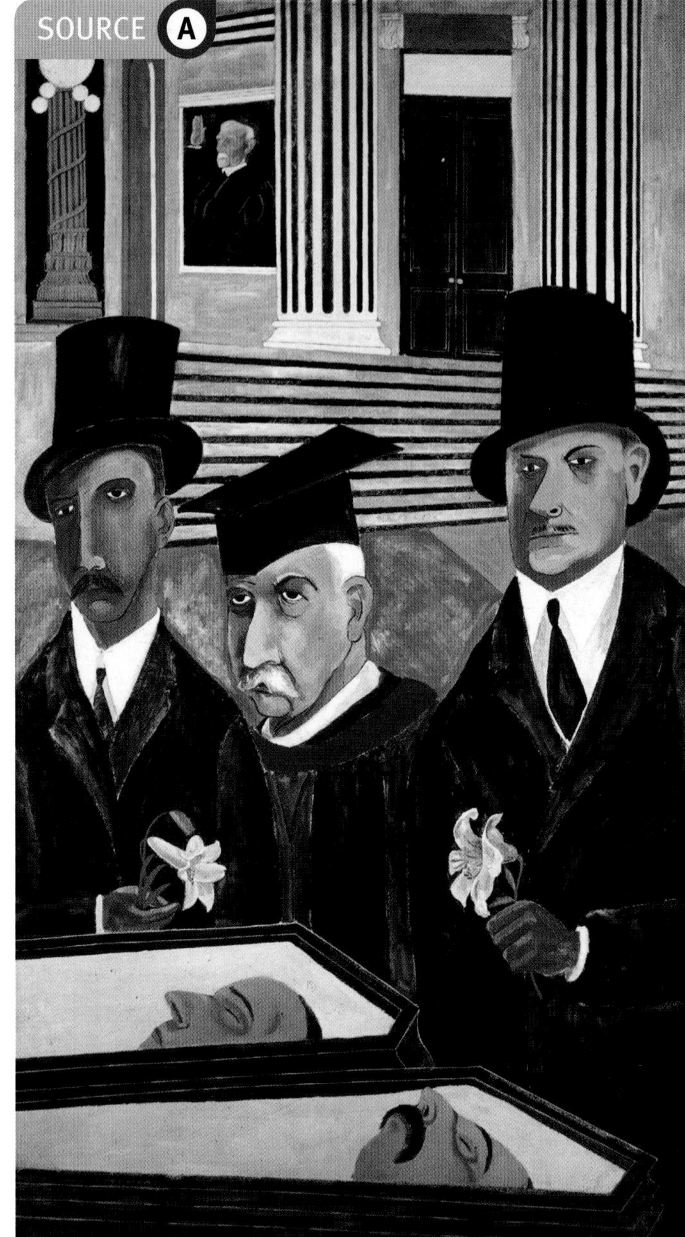

A painting of Sacco and Vanzetti by Ben Shahn (1931–32).

The new Klan grew slowly at first, but benefitting from the anti-foreigner atmosphere generated by the First World War, it began to recruit members from outside its traditional homeland of the Deep South. By 1925 it had reached a peak of five million members, which brought it considerable influence in national and state politics. Although it was a secretive organisation, its members became

KEY WORDS

Lynch – *to execute (especially by hanging) without due process of law, as by a mob.*

SOURCE B

Members of the Ku Klux Klan, 1925.

confident enough to parade openly through many cities, including Washington. The Klan had a strong appeal to white people who felt threatened and left behind by the social and economic changes of the 1920s. Its extreme, racist, conservative views were not dissimilar to those later put forward by European parties like the Fascists and the Nazis, which also thrived in the uncertainty and insecurity created by the First World War. Although the amount of racist violence actually declined during the 1920s, the threat posed by the Klan was very real, and a number of appalling murders were carried out by its members.

By the end of the 1920s, membership of the Klan had gone into decline. Its reputation was undermined by a number of scandals, notably the conviction of the Klan leader in the state of Indiana for the rape and murder of a woman on a train. Its influence rapidly waned, although it continued to pose a threat to black people in small towns in the south.

The Scopes Trial, 1925

This sensational case illustrated how wide a gulf existed by the mid-1920s between traditional small-town American and the modern values and outlook of the big cities. A biology teacher in the town of Dayton, Tennessee, had been giving lessons on **Charles Darwin**'s theory of evolution. Although Darwin's ideas were not as widely accepted then as they are now, this event would not normally have grabbed the attention of the world's press. However, in 1925, the state of Tennessee had passed a law forbidding the teaching of evolution, which it condemned as contrary to the account of creation given in the Bible. The teacher, Johnny Scopes, was arrested and put on trial.

It was obvious that the real issue was not whether Scopes was guilty (because he had been teaching evolution), but whether the religious beliefs and social values of rural America could be maintained against the advance of science. Two renowned lawyers were brought in to argue the case – Clarence Darrow for the defence, and William Jennings Bryan for the prosecution.

The world's press flocked to the small courtroom in which the case was tried. They called it the 'Monkey Trial' because of Darwin's assertion that human beings had evolved from apes. Scopes was bound to lose; Darrow's purpose was not to win the case, but rather to demonstrate the threat that such laws posed to freedom of thought and speech. In the turning point of the trial, Darrow called Bryan as a witness. He destroyed Bryan's case by questioning him in detail about the story of creation in the Bible, and forcing him to admit that he did not believe every word as literal truth.

The strain of giving evidence in the hot courtroom, under Darrow's relentless questioning, proved too much for Bryan. He was taken ill and died five days later. The judge duly found Scopes guilty and fined him $100. However, the Tennessee Supreme Court overturned the verdict a year later, and the law was never used again.

VOICE YOUR OPINION!

For which groups in American society was life least free?

Discuss as a class, citing examples to support your arguments.

KEY PEOPLE

Charles Darwin – *demonstrated that all living things evolved from earlier forms of life by the process of natural selection. This related to animals, but became a swiftly manipulated way of assessing human society to support existing religious and racial stereotypes.*

Explain the impact of the KKK on American society.

[6 marks]

Why was prohibition introduced, and then later repealed?

LEARNING OBJECTIVES

In this lesson you will:

- learn about the reasons for and the impact of prohibition
- assess the effects of prohibition and consider the issues involved in enforcing the law.

GETTING STARTED

Think of a time when you were told explicitly not to do something. What do you think the most popular human reaction to that is?

SOURCE A

An Anti-Saloon League poster (1927).

Why was prohibition introduced?

Many people in the USA thought alcohol was harmful and wanted it banned, or prohibited. After the First World War they got their way. In 1919 Congress (the US parliament) passed the 18th Amendment to the Constitution, which introduced prohibition on the manufacture, sale and transport of alcohol (although, interestingly, it was not made illegal to drink it). The Volstead Act, passed the same year, gave the federal government the power to enforce prohibition, and with effect from January 1920, the USA became 'dry'. What was known as the 'Noble Experiment' had begun. But why had it been introduced?

1 It already existed

Many individual states already had their own prohibition laws. There were 13 totally 'dry' states by 1919, but a majority of other states had also introduced some kind of control on the sale and manufacture of alcohol. The 18th Amendment simply made prohibition nationwide.

2 Moral reasons

Those who opposed alcohol argued that it caused a variety of social problems, such as violence, poverty, crime and sexual promiscuity. If alcohol were banned, they believed that the USA would be a better, healthier, more moral place in which to live.

3 Campaigners

Many organisations led campaigns against alcohol. The most famous was the Anti-Saloon League of America, which was founded in 1893. These organisations launched an effective propaganda campaign and put pressure on politicians to support their cause. As they had the support of many of the churches, they were very effective in making it seem that any politician who failed to support them was in favour of crime and immorality. Not many politicians were brave enough to put votes at risk in this way. The pressure was greatest in rural areas. In many ways, prohibition was another indication of the struggle between traditional and modern values, and between the country areas and the cities, which affected the USA in the 1920s. As one prohibition campaigner put it: 'Our nation can only be saved by turning the pure stream of country sentiment and township morals to flush out the cesspools of cities and so save civilisation from pollution.'

4 First World War

Many of the USA's brewers were of German descent. When the USA joined the war in 1917, there was a lot of anti-German feeling, and campaigners were able to argue that it would be patriotic to close the brewers down. After all, they were using up grain that could otherwise have been sent to Europe to help feed the USA's allies.

What were the effects of prohibition?

Prohibition had almost exactly the opposite effect from that intended. Once it was banned, alcohol became more attractive and consumption increased. In many cities, the law was ignored. Illegal bars, known as 'speakeasies', opened in their thousands. But if the manufacture of alcohol was illegal, where was it all coming from?

1 Moonshine

The first reaction of those determined to beat prohibition was to make their own alcohol. These concoctions were known as 'moonshine', but unfortunately the end result could be poisonous. Several hundred people a year died from this during the 1920s. Despite the efforts of government prohibition agents, it was impossible to stop this illegal production.

ACTIVITIES

1 **a** Using the evidence of this lesson, create a table with the following headings:
- Impossible to police
- Damaging to society
- Damaging politically

Organise the material from this lesson under the three headings.

b Using your table, explain why prohibition had a negative influence on American society.

2 Smuggling

It proved impossible for the USA to seal its thousands of miles of frontiers, let alone its coastline, to prevent alcohol coming into the country. Famous 'rum-runners' like William McCoy made fortunes by smuggling alcohol from the West Indies and Canada. In four years, McCoy is thought to have smuggled $70 million worth of whiskey.

3 Organised crime

The enormous profits to be made from alcohol inevitably attracted the attention of gangsters, who were able to take control of many cities by bribing local policemen, judges and politicians. This meant the criminals could operate with little fear of arrest. The most notorious city was Chicago, where Mayor 'Big Bill' Thompson was known to be a close associate of the gangster Al Capone. Competition between gangs led to constant violence. In Chicago alone, between 1927 and 1931, over 200 gang members were murdered, with nobody convicted for these crimes. The boost to organised crime was easily the most significant long-term consequence of prohibition. The profits made during the prohibition period were so vast that the Mafia was able to extend its power, first into other areas of criminal activity, such as prostitution, labour rackets and illegal gambling, and then into a whole range of what appeared to be legitimate businesses.

Fact file

AL CAPONE

In 1925, Al Capone became the boss of the Mafia in Chicago. He took over from his friend, Johnny Torrio, who had been injured during an attack. Capone soon showed an unparalleled talent for ruthless violence against all his competitors. He was implicated in dozens of murders. The violence reached its peak in 1929 with the St Valentine's Day Massacre, in which seven members of a rival gang were machine-gunned to death. At the end of the 1920s, Capone was earning $100 million a year. The web of corruption and bribery that he used to protect himself worked well in Chicago, but was not effective against federal government agents who, in 1931, were able to have him arrested and imprisoned for 11 years on tax-dodging charges. This was enough to put an end to his career as the USA's most feared criminal.

SOURCE B

Cartoon against prohibition laws.

	1921	1925	1929
Illegal distilleries seized	9746	12,023	15,794
Gallons of distilled spirits seized	414,000	1,103,000	1,186,000
Number of arrests	34,175	62,747	66,878

The fight against alcohol production in the USA, 1921–29.

Why was prohibition repealed?

As time passed, it became obvious to almost everyone that prohibition was not working and was doing enormous damage. However, it took a long time before politicians were able to admit this openly. Al Smith, Democratic candidate in the presidential election of 1928, was a well-known 'wet' (that is, he wanted prohibition repealed), yet he lost the election heavily to the 'dry' Republican, **Herbert Hoover**. Nonetheless, some states went ahead and repealed their own prohibition laws, leaving it up to the federal government to enforce prohibition if it could. The Depression made an important difference. With millions out of work, it seemed nonsense that the government was spending large amounts of money on enforcing an unpopular and ineffective law. The money could surely be spent more wisely on helping the poor. Opponents of prohibition were also able to argue that, by making alcohol legal again, an enormous number of jobs would be created, and tax revenues could again be raised on its sale.

Hoover was the one president who made a serious effort to enforce prohibition. In the presidential election campaign of 1932 he faced an opponent, **Franklin D. Roosevelt**, who promised a repeal of the 18th Amendment. By this time, public opinion was firmly in favour of repeal. Roosevelt won, and one of his earliest actions was to introduce the 21st Amendment to the Constitution, repealing prohibition. On 5 December 1933 this was approved, and the 'Noble Experiment' came to an end.

What is the message of Source B?

Use the source and your own knowledge to explain your answer. **[6 marks]**

Examiner's tip

First, write down what the cartoon means, then support your ideas with evidence from the source. Finally, explain the meaning of the cartoon using what you know about prohibition.

KEY PEOPLE

Herbert Hoover – *the 31st American president, serving from 1929–33. A Republican and successful politician, he was held accountable for the Wall Street Crash and resulting Depression, paying the price for his predecessor's actions.*

Franklin D. Roosevelt – *the Democratic successor to Hoover. A hugely popular president who worked tirelessly to revive the American economy with hands on policies from an active federal government.*

How far did the roles of women change during the 1920s?

LEARNING OBJECTIVES

In this lesson you will:

- find out about the changes in the roles and responsibilities of American women in the 1920s
- explore the idea that not all women were liberated to the same extent.

GETTING STARTED

Priority pyramid

Arrange the statements below into order of importance for independence:

Ability to choose who to marry

Ability to vote

Ability to choose and follow a career

Ability to choose your own fashion style

Ability to socialise where you like

Which do you think is more controversial? More achievable?

Discuss with your class what the opportunities are for women today? Clearly things have dramatically improved, but could you argue that opportunities are equal?

Changing times

There is little doubt that the First World War brought about important changes in behaviour and social attitudes.

- In 1920 women gained the right to vote.
- During the 1920s, more and more women went out to work. They became financially independent to a degree unknown in previous generations. They no longer had to live at home.
- Contraception became generally available.

Being less dependent on men, women could make their own decisions about how to live. The divorce rate rose quickly. Certainly, there were changes that anyone could see. Women looked different. They cut their hair short in the new 'bobbed' style; they wore make-up; they went out on their own without a **chaperone**; they smoked in public. The new fashions were much simpler and freer than before the war, and skirts became much shorter.

SOURCE A

Think of the modern young American girl in every town and city of this great country. She is the loveliest physical creature since the age of the Greeks, and has the brightest mentality – if it were only used.

Do they ever think, these beautiful young girls? Do they ever ask whence they have come, whither they are going? It would seem not. Their aim appears to be to allure men, and to secure money. What can a man with a mind find to hold him in one of these lovely, brainless, unbalanced, cigarette-smoking morsels of undisciplined sex whom he meets continually? Has the American girl no modesty, no self-respect, no reserve, no dignity?

An extract from an article in *Cosmopolitan* magazine, written by a female English journalist in 1921.

SOURCE B

Flappers dancing in the 1920s.

KEY WORDS

Chaperone – *a person, especially an older or married woman, who accompanies a young unmarried woman in public.*

Fact file

Flappers:

- wore short, bobbed hair
- wore daring skirts and dresses that were often low-cut and short
- smoked cigarettes in public
- were bare-legged or wore knee-length stockings
- owned and drove cars and motorbikes
- went out on their own without a chaperone
- danced with men and chose not to wear gloves.

Older people found flappers threatening and improper. However, it is important not to make too much of these changes; most women were not flappers. They were too busy at work, or raising families, to go out to parties. More important than fashion in changing their lives was the greater availability of labour-saving devices like washing machines and vacuum cleaners, which began to free them from domestic chores. As ever, change had a greater impact on city life than it did on those who lived in the country. There, traditional values of decency and respectability still acted as a powerful restraint on how people behaved.

The flapper phenomenon, while recognised in history books as a bold change, should not be seen as a universal example of how women's lives were changed. In reality the social revolution and the consumer boom were restricted to urban areas where women had slowly found a more independent atmosphere and values. For most women across America, little changed; they were still primary carers and home makers, often not earning a living or living independently. Their freedom was still restricted by the traditional structure of society, and they still suffered from economic inequality.

ACTIVITIES

1 Look at Source B and read the information in this lesson, then discuss the following questions with a partner.
   - a Do you think that the images of flappers are evidence that some women took the freer atmosphere of the 1920s too far?
   - b Do you think that this interpretation is mere sensationalism?
   - c Is it fair to say that all women changed their attitudes to clothes, hair and social expectations in the 1920s?

2 a Looking at the evidence in this lesson, apply your knowledge to evaluate the level of change in women's lives during the 1920s.
   - b Share your answers with a partner and explain your evidence, challenging them to explain their answers. See if you can both agree.

SOURCE 

Clara Bow, one of the most successful film stars of the 1920s.

GradeStudio

'Outside the cities of the north many American women felt little change in their daily lives.'

How far do you agree with this statement?

[10 marks]

Study Source C, which shows a successful film star, Clara Bow, in 1929. Does the source prove that the position of all women in the USA had improved by the end of the 1920s? Use the source and your own knowledge to explain your answer. **[6 marks]**

Examiner's tip

Each key question you study in your depth study could be assessed in different ways in your examination. Look at these questions. They assess the same topic, but different skills. What are the main differences in how you would approach each question?

What were the causes and consequences of the Wall Street Crash?

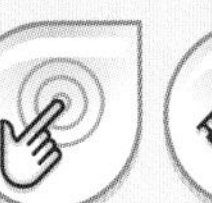

How far was speculation responsible for the Wall Street Crash?

LEARNING OBJECTIVES

In this lesson you will:

- find out about the key causes of the Wall Street Crash
- consider the impact of America's false prosperity.

GETTING STARTED

Match up the words with the statements:

- Over-production
- Weaknesses in the banking system
- Uneven distribution of income
- Problems with the international economy.

In 1920 there were 30,000 independent banks in the USA. They were small and vulnerable if people were to withdraw all their money at once. There were regular problems with these banks. Between 1923 and 1930, 5000 banks collapsed.

Wealth was unevenly divided; in 1929 33 per cent of the nation's wealth belonged to just 5 per cent of its population. 70 per cent of the population lived below the poverty line of $2500 a year. Therefore only a few people could benefit from the consumer boom.

Consumer goods and automobiles were some of the most popular new products to appear in the 1920s. However, the encouragement of mass production led to eventual over-production when everyone who wanted a certain product had bought one. People could not simply keep buying forever.

The tariff system made trade with Europe difficult; as the American involvement in Europe grew in the forms of loans and investment, so did the need to trade. This was an increasingly difficult issue.

Background

In 1928, when Herbert Hoover was elected president, the USA was still enjoying the benefits of the economic boom. During the election campaign, Hoover praised the economic achievements of the Republican governments of the 1920s and predicted an end to poverty in the USA. This was one of the worst predictions in history.

In October 1929 the Wall Street stock market in New York crashed. Panic selling of shares ruined hundreds of thousands of investors as prices slumped. The effect on the American economy was profound. The wave of bankruptcies that followed the crash destroyed all confidence in American business. In the Great Depression that followed, up to 13 million people were made unemployed. The desperation of the people, and the failure of the government to do anything effective to help them, led directly to the victory of Franklin Delano Roosevelt in the 1932 presidential election.

Wall Street – America's financial centre

Wall Street is in New York, at the heart of the financial district of the city. It is the home of the American stock market, where people can buy and sell shares in businesses. Companies issue shares to raise money. Investors buy the shares, hoping to make money. Owning shares means you own part of the company. The more shares you have, the more of the company you own. If the company does well, it shares its profits out among its shareholders by giving them a dividend, and the price of its shares rises. Investors can then sell their shares at a profit. Of course, the opposite can happen too. The price of the shares will fall if the company does badly, and the investors might lose some or all of their money.

During the 1920s, the Wall Street stock market was a good place for investors to put their money. $100 invested in typical shares in 1920 would have been worth around $325 by 1929. This rise in value reflected the general prosperity and industrial growth of the 1920s boom. Investors had become used to the idea that speculation in shares was a safe bet, and that prices would almost always go up. Like Hoover, they assumed that the good years would go on forever.

The role of speculators

Nowadays, tight rules govern the way stock markets are run, but in 1929 this was not the case. Wall Street attracted all kinds of shady financiers, who were looking for ways of making quick money. New corporations with imaginary assets could be set up, and misleading information issued to gullible investors. Nobody thought it mattered – the price of shares, even in dubious enterprises, always went up, so nobody lost money. A practice known as 'buying on the margin' pushed prices still higher. Here, for a small fraction of the price (generally around 10 per cent), a speculator could buy shares, wait until the price rose, then sell the shares, pay off what was owed and pocket the profit! It was a perfect way to make money with little effort or expense – as long as prices rose.

The banks were as much taken in by the lure of the stock market as were small investors. Indeed, the banks were only too ready to lend money for stocks to be bought 'on the margin'. As prices were forced ever upwards, few people stopped to ask whether the shares were actually worth the money. Shares are a stake in a real business, and the price of the shares should reflect the value of the business. But investors were ignoring this. The stock market was like a giant, speculative bubble, gently floating away from the reality of the American economy.

The state of the American economy

Although the economy did well during the 1920s, it did not grow at the same rate as the price of shares. By 1928 the growth of the economy was showing signs of slowing down. Foreign trade was declining, agriculture remained depressed, and home markets for consumer goods were becoming saturated. Above all, a slow realisation was dawning that the boom had been fuelled by debt. Banks had lent money too easily. Investors and businesses had been all too willing to take the money. But eventually debts have to be repaid. Everything depended on the economy continuing to prosper and, just as importantly, on everyone believing that it would continue to prosper.

Fact file

What triggered the Wall Street Crash?

- For companies, falling demand and falling prices meant lower profits.
- Lower profits eventually had to mean a lower share price.
- Share prices had risen higher than was justified – once investors realised this, they would have to sell.
- Many people who did not have the cash to buy shares bought them 'on the margin'.
- When investors realised that their shares were overpriced they began to sell to ensure they got their money back.
- Those who bought on the margin soon realised as share prices started to fall that the loans they had taken out to buy them were more expensive than their supposedly profitable shares.
- The rush to sell caused shareholders to panic, and the spiral of depression struck fast.

ACTIVITIES

Discuss the following statements with a partner and complete the tasks below:

- For companies, falling demand and falling prices meant lower profits.
- Between 1924 and 1929 the value of shares rose by five times.
- Lower profits eventually had to mean a lower share price.
- Share prices were driven up by the number of people wishing to invest in order to make what appeared to be a guaranteed profit.
- Share prices rose to unrealistic levels – once investors realised this, they would have to sell.
- Over-production was encouraged by the government.
- Under-consumption was an inevitable consequence of a capitalist society.
- Many people who did not have the cash to buy shares bought them 'on the margin'.

a Select the three main causes and then select the three least important.

b Now try to place them in chronological order to help you understand why the crash happened.

What impact did the Crash have on the economy?

LEARNING OBJECTIVES

In this lesson you will:

- learn about the economic impact of the Wall Street Crash and how far it reached across the continent
- evaluate the role of the US government and the effectiveness of its response.

GETTING STARTED

1 Discuss the concept of 'rugged individualism' with a partner. What was it about the concept that was good? And where did it fail?
2 How far is it possible to argue that it helped create the boom?

KEY WORDS

Bankrupt – *unable to pay debts; financially ruined; impoverished.*

Black Thursday

As the New York stock market opened on Thursday, 24 October 1929, dealers were nervous. The previous day had seen a lot of investors selling shares and prices dropping sharply. For a week or so, the market had been unstable. Now, on 'Black Thursday', it was about to collapse. Almost from the start of trading, prices moved downwards. Frustratingly, the 'ticker-tape' that transmitted current prices around the country was running almost an hour late, so it was impossible for investors to be sure of how prices were moving. During the morning, the market was engulfed by panic selling. Even with prices in free fall, nobody wanted to buy. With every passing minute, fortunes were being lost. More and more investors, desperate to cut their losses, gave orders to sell their stock. Complete panic was avoided only when representatives of the USA's biggest banks started to buy shares, thus bolstering the market. Temporarily, investors recovered their nerve – surely the banks would not throw their money away if anything was seriously wrong? By the end of the day, prices had recovered somewhat – but that was little consolation to the thousands who had been ruined during the day by selling at a loss. Over the weekend, a kind of nervous calm was restored. Everyone was praying that 'Black Thursday' would not be repeated.

In fact, the Crash had barely started. On Monday the 28th, prices fell sharply again. This time, ominously, the big banks made no move to support the market. Tuesday the 29th was the worst day of all. Over 16 million shares were traded during the day as prices slid downwards, out of control. The value of some of the USA's greatest companies was being slashed. $10,000 million was lost in a single day's trading. Thousands were **bankrupted** – small investors who had bought 'on the margin', firms that had bought and sold shares, banks that had lent money against the value of shares. Their money had simply disappeared. October 1929 did not see the end of the collapse in share prices. The market continued to fall, bit by bit, until 1932, at which time the average value of shares was only one-fifth of what it had been after the October 1929 crash. The bubble of speculation had burst, with terrible consequences for both the USA and the rest of the world.

The financial and economic effects of the Wall Street Crash

It would be too simple to say that the Wall Street Crash caused the Great Depression. What cannot be doubted is that it sparked the Depression off. The American economy went into a vicious downward spiral of bankruptcy, in which production and unemployment slumped, and which devastated normal economic life, first in the USA and then, by the destruction of international trade, throughout the world.

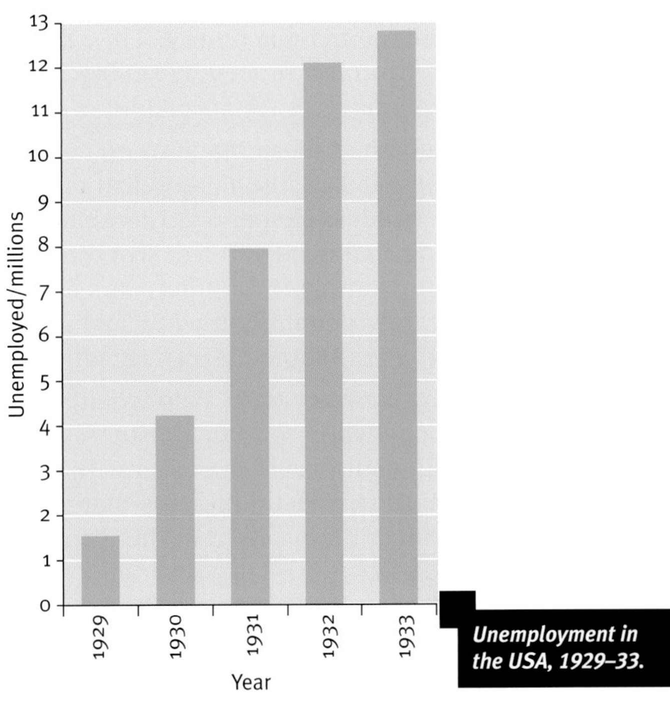

Unemployment in the USA, 1929–33.

SOURCE A

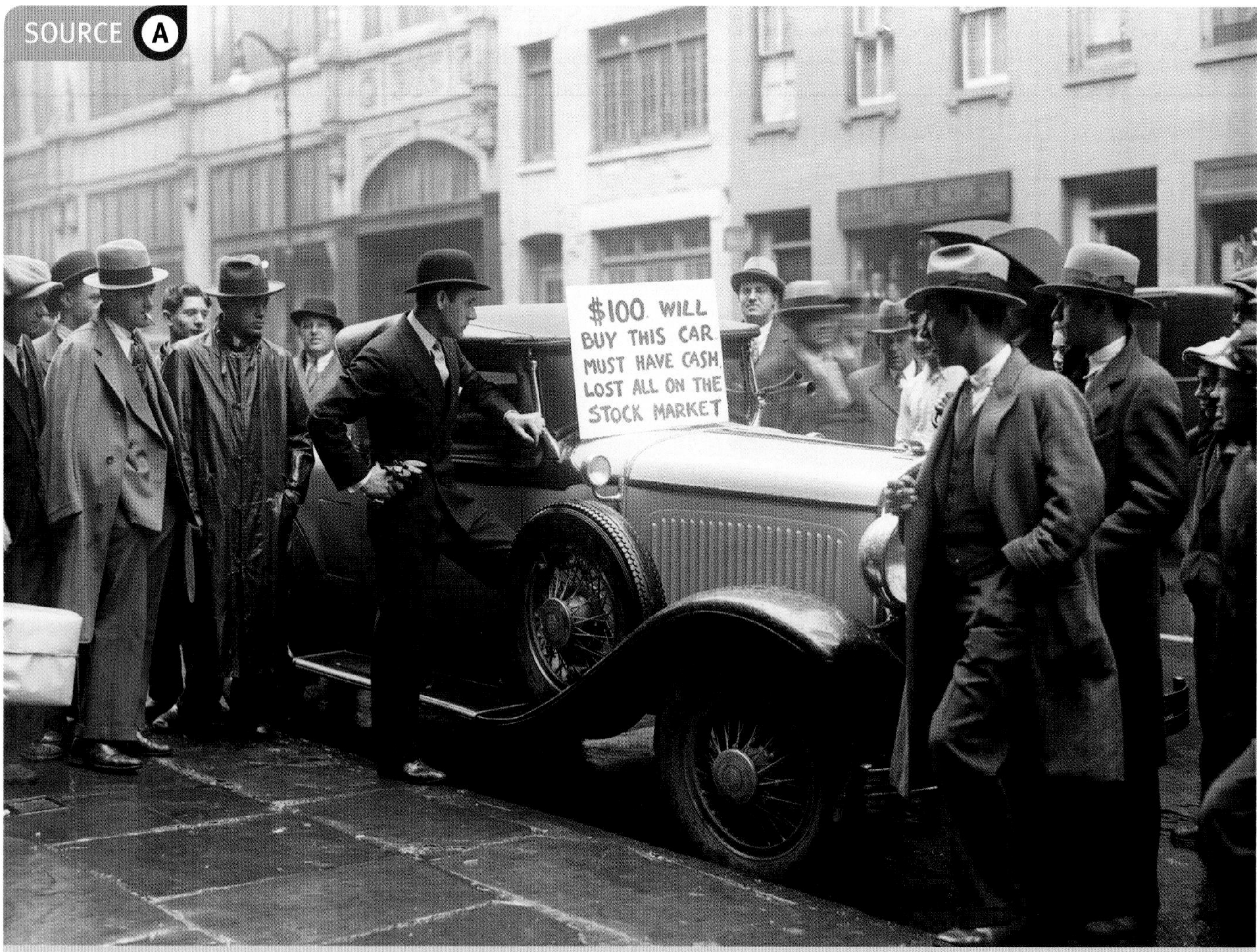

A car for sale after the Wall Street Crash, October 1929.

How did this occur?

- Businesses need money. They have to buy raw materials, equipment and machinery. They must pay wages. They can raise money by selling goods or by borrowing.
- The Crash made both of these much more difficult. Many people had lost a great deal of money and now had less to spend. So companies made fewer goods, and needed fewer workers and factories. For example, 4.5 million cars were sold in 1929, but only one million were sold in 1932. As a result, unemployment rose rapidly.
- Borrowing money was no easier. Who would want to lend money when so many businesses were failing? You would never get it back. In any case, it was often the banks themselves that were going broke – 5000 of them closed in the three years after the Crash.
- As money disappeared, industry shut down.

By 1932, a quarter of the working population was unemployed. As many as a third of the population were members of families in which the breadwinner was out of work. By 1933 production of manufactured goods was barely 20 per cent of its 1929 level. The economy was ceasing to function.

SOURCE B

We seem to have stepped Alice-like through an economic looking glass into a world where everything shrivels. Bond prices, stock prices, commodity prices, employment – they all dwindle.

One writer sums up the plight of the USA after the stock market crash.

Aspect of economy	1929 (percentage)	1932 (percentage)
Share prices	100	17
Overall production	100	60
Wages	100	40
Share dividends	100	43
Foreign trade	100	40
Unemployment	100	600

Economic statistics showing percentage change between 1929 and 1932.

The reaction of President Hoover

Hoover was notably unsuccessful in dealing with the effects of the Crash, and this failure saw him voted out of office in 1932. As a Republican, he believed that governments should stay out of business matters. Like most businessmen, when the Crash first occurred, Hoover assumed that all he needed to do was wait, and that eventually things would return to normal. But it soon became obvious that doing nothing would not be enough. The USA was in the grip of a Depression far more serious than any experienced before. Even Hoover eventually realised that government might have to play a role in dealing with it. He pleaded with employers to keep their nerve, and not to sack workers or cut their pay. He realised that this would just make matters worse. When this did not work, he set up the Reconstruction Finance Commission to make loans to businesses which were in trouble. He encouraged states and cities to launch public works programmes to make jobs for the unemployed. The Federal Farm Board purchased surplus crops in an attempt to hold up prices.

These were all good ideas, but Hoover did not really believe in them, and the programmes were not big enough to make a difference. Some of Hoover's measures actually made things worse. Under pressure from farmers and manufacturers, in 1930 he agreed the Hawley–Smoot tariff, which placed even higher taxes on imports. Naturally enough, other nations retaliated by doing the same, which made it even harder for the USA to export its surplus production. The damage done to world trade began to push the rest of the world into Depression.

SOURCE C

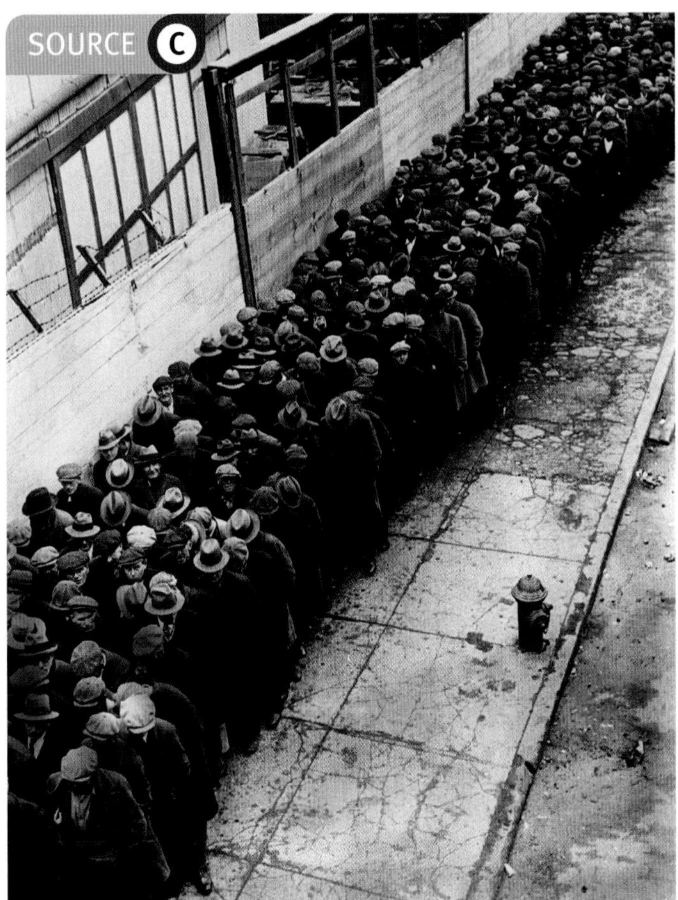

Hungry unemployed people in New York queue for food on Christmas Day, 1931.

Unfairly, Hoover's name came to be associated with the effects of the Depression. The name 'Hoovervilles' were given to the shanty towns built by the homeless unemployed, and 'Hoover blankets' were the newspapers that the destitute huddled under for warmth. Hoover's image was of being heartless and uncaring. It was not true, but he was undoubtedly the wrong man for the task of bringing about the USA's recovery.

SOURCE D

1100 men standing in a Salvation Army breadline on March 10, 1930 near the Bowey Hotel in Manhattan, New York, descended upon two trucks delivering baked goods to the hotel ... Cookies, rolls and bread were flung onto the street with the hungry jobless chasing after them.

Irving Bernstein, *The Lean Years: A History of the American Worker, 1920–1933.*

SOURCE E

Eleven children in that house. They've got no shoes, no pants. In the house, no chairs. My God, you go in there, you cry, that's all.

A Philadelphia shopkeeper reported in *The Nation*, 1932.

Fact file

Effects of the Depression

Trade fell – both internal and overseas.

Unemployment – widespread unemployment put whole towns out of work; Tennessee was particularly badly hit.

Farmers abandoned homes – with nothing to grow and no money to make, they left in their thousands, creating the southern 'dustbowl'.

Faith in system lost – e.g. 'Bonus Army' workers began to unite in their frustration 'in Hoover we trusted, now we're busted'.

Rugged Individualism failed – the policy that built the boom was also the reason for its failure.

Indiscriminate in terms of class – money was short for all, in fact those who had the most lost the most. Suicides skyrocketed alongside deaths.

Destitution – hobos and Hoovervilles were clear and unavoidable signs of America's widespread poverty.

Effects visible – production ground to a halt, factories closed, the entertainment industry declined.

GradeStudio

Describe the social consequences of the Wall Street Crash. **[4 marks]**

Examiner's tip

In questions like this you get one mark for each valid point you make and an extra one for any supporting detail.

ACTIVITIES

1 **a** Look at Sources A–E and the table and graph. What do these reveal about the impact of the Depression? Do you think that they are a fair reflection of what really happened?

b Look at the date of each source. How does it affect the source's reliability?

2 Working in pairs, list the biggest impact of the crash. Your aim is to compose a caption for a newspaper article that summarises the key issues. Your work should be catchy and memorable; it could be in the form of a rhyme or a pun but should show your understanding.

What were the social consequences of the Crash?

LEARNING OBJECTIVES

In this lesson you will:

- learn about the consequences of the Depression for the American people
- examine the effects of the Depression on people's lives and assess its impact in different parts of the country.

GETTING STARTED

Look at the photos in Sources A and B. Discuss with a partner what you think these pictures reveal about the impact of the Depression on people's daily lives.

Life during the Great Depression

The USA was supposed to be the land of opportunity, where a good life was available for all those willing to work hard. Now just finding work was a problem. The numbers of unemployed increased by the day. Countless families lost their homes, or were split up, when parents lost their jobs. The USA was not a welfare state, and the unemployed were dependent on charity. Soon breadlines – queues of unemployed people lining up for handouts of food – became a feature of city life. Hundreds of thousands of destitute people wandered the streets looking for food, work or somewhere to stay. Shanty towns constructed from scrap metal and tents sprang up on waste ground in the cities. By 1932 money to help the poor was running out. In June the city of Philadelphia had to cut off all relief funds to 50,000 families. The situation seemed hopeless.

The Bonus Marchers

A crisis point was reached in the summer of 1932. Since May, destitute veterans (ex-First World War servicemen) and their families had been arriving in Washington DC and demonstrating for the 'bonus' payment that had been promised to them by an Act passed in 1924. The bonus, around $500, was not payable until 1945, but the veterans wanted it now. In camps around the city, about 25,000 veterans gathered. The government was worried by their presence. In the desperate atmosphere of the time, it was possible to see the veterans as a revolutionary threat. Hoover refused to meet the veterans, and by the summer the situation had reached a stalemate. The veterans showed no sign of moving or taking any

SOURCE A

'Hoovervilles' just outside Seattle, 1932.

SOURCE B

This shot, entitled 'Migrant Mother', by Dorothea Lange (1936), came to typify the individual struggle caused by the Depression.

other action, and the government was not going to give them the bonus. Hoover decided that the veterans would have to be evicted. He called in the army, which launched attacks on the marchers' camps, driving the veterans and their families out of the city.

Any remaining sympathy the American people might have had for Hoover was lost as he tried to explain away the action by claiming that most of the marchers were communists and criminals, and that more than half of them had never been in the armed forces (around 65 per cent had been, of whom nearly 70 per cent had served overseas).

SOURCE C

They used to tell me I was building a dream, and so I followed the mob,
When there was earth to plow, or guns to bear, I was always there right on the job.
They used to tell me I was building a dream, with peace and glory ahead,
Why should I be standing in line, just waiting for bread?

Once I built a railroad, I made it run, made it race against time.
Once I built a railroad; now it's done. Brother, can you spare a dime?
Once I built a tower, up to the sun, brick, and rivet, and lime;
Once I built a tower, now it's done. Brother, can you spare a dime?

***Brother, Can You Spare a Dime?*, lyrics by Yip Harburg (1931).**

SOURCE D

They came with their gas bombs and their bayonets. The troops fired the shacks on the edge of the camp. Tanks and soldiers guarded the bridge back into the city so that no refugees could get into Washington. They might disturb the sleep of a few of the government officials.The jeers and cries of the evicted men and women rose over the crackling of the flames. The flames were mirrored in the drawn bayonets of the infantry as they advanced through the camp. There is no way of knowing whether, in the debacle, a few homeless men perished or not.

An eyewitness account of the attack on the Bonus Marchers.

ACTIVITIES

Like many crises, the Depression forced America to look at itself. The stories that came out of the Depression inspired both artists and musicians.

1 a Consider the song lyrics (Source C) inspired by the Wall Street Crash and the subsequent Depression.

b Now come up with your own rhyme, poem or short story to plot the impact of the Depression. It must include:

- a focus on the emotional outbreak of this crisis
- the spread of the Depression, geographically and socially
- the role of the government and what people thought of it
- the impact of the event on the American Dream
- the possibility of recovery.

However you decide to structure your work, your focus should be what happened to American society, given that before 1929 America was one of the most developed and thriving nations.

c Once completed, record your response or share it with the class.

2 As a class, create an emotive word bank for the impact of the Depression. This could be referred to in later lessons when you consider how America recovered from the Depression, and it would be useful in examinations.

Why did Roosevelt win the election of 1932?

LEARNING OBJECTIVES

In this lesson you will:

- learn about the policies of President Roosevelt and understand why he offered new hope to many Americans
- explore the difficulty the Democrats had in breaking the mould of the established ways of government in America.

GETTING STARTED

Look at Source A.

Discuss with a partner how Roosevelt's speech would have been received by:

- The business community
- Regular workers
- Government officials.

The presidential campaign, 1932

The Democrats' choice as candidate in the 1932 presidential election stood before the delegates at the nominating convention in Chicago to make his acceptance speech. He could not stand unaided – 11 years earlier he had been paralysed by polio, and now his legs were locked in place by metal braces. He was not the Democrats' first choice, but was a compromise when none of the other candidates could win enough support. He was, though, to become one of the great men of the twentieth century, as the USA was about to find out. The candidate was Franklin Delano Roosevelt.

Roosevelt's early life

Franklin D. Roosevelt came from a privileged background, the only son in a wealthy old Dutch family from New York state. He was a fairly aimless student, both at school and at Harvard University. He worked for a law firm, but he was not much good at that either. He was the typical indulged rich boy, looking for a purpose in life. He found it in politics. A distant relative of ex-president Theodore Roosevelt, he had the social contacts that enabled him to make rapid progress in his chosen career. He also found that in politics his friendly, open and optimistic personality was a great asset in winning votes.

Elected first as a state senator in New York in 1910, by 1913 he was Assistant Secretary to the Navy in Wilson's government, and in 1920 he ran as the Democrats' vice-presidential candidate. Unfortunately for him, 1920 was the year of the Republican landslide, which saw Harding elected president. Then, in 1921, Roosevelt caught polio, which left his legs paralysed. At that time, physical disability was an almost impossible barrier to a career in politics, but Roosevelt showed the steely determination that lay beneath his apparently easy-going character. He was fortunate to be wealthy enough not to have to worry about making a living, and he could afford the best care available. But he refused to allow his illness to force him out of politics.

In 1928 Roosevelt felt strong enough to stand for governor of New York state, and won by a narrow margin. This was the office he held when the Depression struck the USA. As governor, he took vigorous action to help the unemployed in his state, setting up the Temporary Relief Administration, which used public money on schemes to create employment – a forerunner of the ideas he would later implement as president. To many people, it seemed clear that Roosevelt's lengthy illness had given him a sympathy for the problems of ordinary people, which would make him act to relieve the suffering caused by the Depression. He had critics, who complained that he was inconsistent, or that his ideas were woolly and vague, but even they could not ignore his sheer energy and willingness to experiment.

SOURCE A

The country needs ... and demands bold, persistent experimentation ... above all, try something.

Extract from Franklin Roosevelt's campaign speech, 1932.

SOURCE B

Cartoon comparing F.D. Roosevelt with President Hoover, during the American presidential campaign of 1932.

The presidential election, 1932

Roosevelt's opponent in the election was President Hoover, who by this time was extremely unpopular. Everyone knew what Hoover stood for. His policies to deal with the Depression were not working, and he seemed to believe that the only solution was to wait for the economy to cure itself. Even in the depths of the Depression, Hoover did not regard business as the responsibility of the government. So a vote for Hoover would be a vote for doing nothing. When Hoover went out campaigning, he often received a hostile reception. His train was frequently pelted with eggs and tomatoes, and demonstrators carried placards reading 'Hang Hoover'.

The contrast between Hoover and Roosevelt was striking. Although it was not clear exactly what Roosevelt intended to do about the Depression, voters were clear that he would do something. Although Roosevelt's and Hoover's ideas were not all that different, their personalities and image were almost opposites. Roosevelt ran an energetic, optimistic campaign which, above all, offered the USA hope. At a time when millions of unemployed Americans were dependent on soup kitchens for their next meal, his words made them feel that at last someone was on their side. Even the middle classes who were still in work responded to Roosevelt, as they saw in him the only hope to save the USA from revolution.

When the results of the election were announced, Roosevelt had won a remarkable victory. He received 22.8 million votes against Hoover's 15.8 million. In 1932 there were 48 states in the USA, and 42 of them chose Roosevelt. However, although he had been elected, he would not be president until his inauguration in four months' time. Meanwhile, Hoover would be a 'lame duck' president, still in office, but with no power or authority, and with the economic crisis becoming worse by the day.

ACTIVITIES

1. Study Sources A and B.
   a. Is it fair to say that for the American population Roosevelt offered a 'breath of fresh air' approach to politics?
   b. How far was Hoover simply in the wrong place at the wrong time?
   c. Were Roosevelt's policies simply aiming to placate (please) the population, or do you think they had more substance?
2. Work in pairs. You are both part of the presidential campaign groups; one is Republican supporting the re-election of President Hoover, and the other is a Democrat looking to install Roosevelt as president. Use the information in this lesson to write a speech for each candidate to explain why people should vote for him. Complete your speeches in consultation. They should be no more than 200 words.

Explain why Roosevelt won the election of 1932.
[6 marks]

How successful was the New Deal?

What was the New Deal which was introduced in 1933?

LEARNING OBJECTIVES

In this lesson you will:

- examine the methods and promises of the New Deal introduced by Roosevelt and the Democrats
- consider the success of the policies in achieving their aim of reversing the spiral of depression.

GETTING STARTED

Read Source A. What might the phrase 'New Deal' make people think? What does that phrase imply about government involvement and the rights of the people?

Introduction

Roosevelt had promised the American people a 'New Deal'. The moment he came into office, he launched a programme of legislation that gave the government a central role in dealing with the effects of the Depression. By spending public money on a huge scale, Roosevelt attempted to create jobs and put the USA back to work. Most Americans supported these efforts – Roosevelt remained president until his death in 1945. However, many were worried that he had given government a role that went against American traditions. The Supreme Court declared some of his New Deal measures to be unconstitutional, and business bitterly resented government controls. The New Deal did not solve the problem of unemployment, although the numbers of unemployed did fall significantly.

SOURCE A

I pledge you, I pledge myself, a New Deal for the American people.

From Roosevelt's acceptance speech to the Democratic Party, Chicago, 1932.

SOURCE B

The only thing we have to fear is fear itself. Our greatest primary task is to put people back to work. This is no unsolvable problem if we face it wisely and courageously. It can be accomplished in part by direct recruiting by the government itself, treating the task as we would treat the emergency of a war, but at the same time, through this employment, accomplishing greatly needed projects to stimulate and reorganise the use of our natural resources.

From Roosevelt's inauguration speech.

Instead, it was the impact of the Second World War that finally revived the American economy.

Roosevelt becomes president

Roosevelt's inauguration as president took place on 4 March 1933. The USA was poised on the brink of economic disaster. That day, banks throughout the country had failed to open. Nobody trusted the banks any more, because so many had gone bust. Had they opened, they would have collapsed because of the thousands of panicking depositors who wanted to withdraw their money. Millions of Americans gathered around their radios to listen to Roosevelt's inauguration speech. His calm, confident voice immediately gave them reassurance.

ACTIVITIES

1. Look carefully at Source B and discuss with a partner what you think Roosevelt's key aims were.
2. How do you think the following people would react to Roosevelt's plans?
   - **a** A farm worker in the south
   - **b** A northern banker
   - **c** A single mother in a northern city
   - **d** An unskilled labourer in the mid-west.

The inauguration speech was a summary of the 'New Deal', which would be brought into being in Roosevelt's first 'Hundred Days' in power. Between the inauguration and 16 June, when the session of Congress came to an end, a whole series of laws designed to deal with the impact of the Depression had been passed.

The 'fireside chats'

Roosevelt was one of the first politicians to realise the potential of radio as a means of communication. During the banking crisis, he started his 'fireside chats', broadcasting to the nation as if he were talking to a group of friends in his own living room. These fireside chats were extremely important both for keeping Americans in touch with what the government was doing, and for creating a sense that the whole nation was united in facing its problems together.

Helping the banks

If the banks stayed closed, the economy would cease to function. Very quickly, nobody would have any money to spend. If the banks opened, they might collapse. Roosevelt solved the immediate crisis by passing the Emergency Banking Act. It forced all banks to stay closed for four days. Those whose finances were completely hopeless were ordered to close permanently. The rest were promised the backing of government grants so that the public could regain confidence in them. Roosevelt broadcast to the nation, appealing for the panic to end and for people with money to take it back to the banks. It worked, and the banks were saved.

Roosevelt was also determined to bring Wall Street under control. The Securities Act forced companies issuing new shares to provide full information about the company to the public. This was followed up in 1934 with the establishment of a Securities and Exchange Commission, which was given sweeping powers to control the activities of the stock market.

SOURCE C

An American cartoon about the Agricultural Adjustment Administration (AAA), 1933.

Helping the farmers

Agriculture's most serious problem was over-production. While this continued, prices would remain low and farmers would be unable to make a decent living. Roosevelt's solution was to pay farmers for not producing! The Agricultural Adjustment Act allowed the government to influence prices by destroying surplus produce, and giving farmers compensation for lost production.

Helping the unemployed

Within three weeks of the inauguration, Roosevelt took an important first step in helping the unemployed. By setting up the Civilian Conservation Corps (CCC), the government provided work for unemployed young men on a whole range of environmental projects in the countryside. As pay rates were very low, the work could be criticised as forced labour. But the CCC carried out many useful projects, such as strengthening river banks, fish farming, fighting forest fires and controlling mosquitoes to prevent malaria.

Next, in an attempt to help the destitute, the Federal Emergency Relief Administration (FERA) was set up. This could make grants of federal money to state and local governments to help them give relief to the unemployed.

Helping industry

The National Industrial Recovery Act set up two important agencies. The National Recovery Administration (NRA) tried to create a partnership between the government and industry. The idea was that each industry would agree an employment code with the government. The code would guarantee workers fair wages and conditions in return for fair prices that could be charged for the goods. The government rewarded firms that agreed a code by favouring them when contracts were awarded.

The Act also created an agency called the Public Works Administration (PWA). This aimed to use unemployed skilled industrial workers on large-scale public construction projects. Over the next few years, PWA workers would construct many of the USA's public buildings. Another feature of the Act was that workers were given the right to collective bargaining of wages. This gave an enormous boost to trade unions, which could now organise in industries where previously they had been excluded.

Helping home-owners

Many home-owners who had been affected by the Depression faced the threat of losing their homes if they could not keep up their mortgage repayments. This would be bad both for the family evicted from their home, and for the bank which would not recover its money. To prevent this happening the government set up the Home-Owners' Loan Corporation (HOLC), which gave low-interest loans to home-owners. Such loans would enable home-owners to adjust mortgage repayments to cope with temporary unemployment.

Help to the depressed areas

The valley of the Tennessee River was a particularly depressed region, where half the population of the area was dependent on government relief for survival. The Tennessee Valley Authority (TVA) was set up to regenerate the area by encouraging industry and helping agriculture.

The 'alphabet agencies'

During the Hundred Days the government created many organisations, set up to carry out the work of the New Deal, with acronyms like AAA, TVA, CCC and so on. In the years to come, the New Deal would create even more of what soon became known as the 'alphabet agencies'.

The end of prohibition

Another of the measures taken during the Hundred Days was the ending of prohibition. This process was started by the Beer Act of March 1933, which legalised the manufacture and sale of beer and light wines again. The process was completed when the 21st Amendment to the Constitution was ratified at the end of the year.

How far did the character of the New Deal change after 1933?

LEARNING OBJECTIVES

In this lesson you will:

- learn about the similarities and differences between the first and second New Deals
- examine the level of government intervention and the consequences of the government's activities.

GETTING STARTED

1 Consider the following statement: 'Any work is good work if it helps to avoid economic stagnation.' How far do you think the statement applies to America in the Depression era?

2 Why might some people be critical of this concept? (Consider the idea of 'boondoggling' – a scheme that wastes time and money.)

SOURCE A

An American cartoon of 1937, commenting on Roosevelt's clash with the Supreme Court.

The Second New Deal

By 1935 the first phase of the New Deal had been carried out. However, with a presidential election to face in 1936, Roosevelt had several problems. The Supreme Court was beginning to challenge some of the New Deal laws, and radical opponents of the New Deal were criticising him for not taking enough action to help the poor. Roosevelt's response was to introduce another phase of reform, which some historians have called the 'Second New Deal'.

To continue providing work for the unemployed, a new agency, the Works Progress Administration (WPA), was set up. Its aim was to find emergency short-term employment for unskilled workers, mainly in construction projects. However, it also sponsored community arts projects. In its eight years of existence, the WPA found work for around eight million people.

One of the casualties of the Supreme Court's hostility to the New Deal was the Public Works Administration, whose codes were found to be an infringement of the rights of individual states, and therefore unlawful. However the Wagner Act of 1935 tried to restore some protection to workers by confirming their right to join trade unions and forbidding employers from preventing the organisation of unions.

Under pressure from critics, in 1935 Roosevelt introduced the Social Security Act. This set up a national insurance scheme, which provided old age pensions, unemployment benefits and financial support for the handicapped. It was funded by contributions paid by workers, employers and government.

The AAA also had to close because of the Supreme Court. However, the government continued to find ways of helping the farmers. The Resettlement Administration (RA) helped poor farmers by purchasing equipment for them, and even resettled some of the poorest on land purchased by the RA. Grants were also given to farmers for soil conservation schemes.

The presidential election, 1936

Roosevelt's enormous popularity guaranteed him victory in the 1936 election. The Republicans' unfortunate candidate, Alf

Landon, never had a chance and went down to an even heavier defeat than Hoover had suffered in 1932. It seemed as if Roosevelt had overwhelming support for continuing with the New Deal. Instead, he was drawn into a quarrel with the Supreme Court, after which the spirit of reform never really recovered. By 1936 almost all of the great achievements of the New Deal were in place. From now on, a combination of determined opposition, misjudgements by Roosevelt, a return to Depression and the approach of world war meant that no more significant reforms would be made.

Fact file

Impact of the Second New Deal

- The Wagner Act replaced the NRA/the National Labour Relations Board (NLRB); it protected workers' right to join a trade union and protected them from victimisation.
- An anti-socialist attitude was prevalent among certain sections of the government, which disliked the new role government played in people's lives; it was considered as too much like the system in Germany and Russia.
- Social Security was America's first system of social welfare. It provided unemployment insurance and old-age pensions, and gave help to the disabled and children in need.
- Support for homeowners was provided via loans to buy houses and to reduce excessive rents.
- Farming subsidies were given via the Soil Conservation Act. This replaced the banned AAA.
- Fair Labour Standards set hours and conditions of work and set a minimum wage.
- The Second New Deal did not deliver on all its promises; expectations had not been met and Americans still experienced difficulties.
- However, the Second New Deal didn't go far enough for Roosevelt. He was saddened at the lack of faith in him after he had become America's longest-serving president.

ACTIVITIES

1 **a** Discuss with a partner how you think the First and Second New Deals differed in the following areas:
- focus of intervention
- level of government involvement
- scale of the projects
- popular support.

b Write down your ideas in a new spider diagram, using the four points as branches and any others you think might be useful. Add analysis and judgement wherever possible to clarify your interpretation of events.

2 How far do you agree with the following statement?
- 'The Second New Deal was built firmly on the foundations set by the First. It would not have been possible without the faith shown in Roosevelt by the people, and without exception their faith in him was justified.'

'The Second New Deal threatened American civil liberties.'

How far do you agree with this statement?

[10 marks]

Examiner's tip

Your first argument will agree with the statement. Your second argument will discuss the counter-argument: that the Second New Deal was beneficial to Americans.

Then write a conclusion explaining your overall judgement.

Why did the New Deal encounter opposition?

LEARNING OBJECTIVES

In this lesson you will:

- learn about the level of opposition that the New Deal faced and the role of individuals in directing the opposition
- research the background and evaluate the legitimacy of the various criticisms of Roosevelt.

GETTING STARTED

AAA – Agricultural Adjustment Act
CCC – Civilian Conservation Corps
EHS – Emergency Housing Section
FLSA – Fair Labour Standards Act
HOLC – Home Owners Loan Corporation
NRA – National Recovery Administration
SSA – Social Security Act
TVA – Tennessee Valley Authority
WPA – Works Progress Administration

Look carefully at the different agencies introduced by President Roosevelt in the New Deal era. Which ones were the most controversial? Discuss with a partner and prioritise the organisations into an order ranging from the most to the least controversial. Explain your decisions and note down your conclusions for future reference.

Opponents of the New Deal

Roosevelt's political opponents were, naturally enough, consistent critics of the New Deal. Their most basic objection was that Roosevelt had allowed government to become involved in economic life in an unprecedented manner. New Deal laws tried to create jobs, fix prices, dictate working conditions and control levels of production – all activities that opponents felt were none of the government's business. They also saw these measures as a threat to the traditional freedom of Americans to live without interference from government. It was also true that Roosevelt's measures cost a good deal of money, and some Americans resented paying higher taxes to fund employment schemes which they thought were a waste of time. Most ordinary Americans were simply too grateful to Roosevelt for trying to cope with the country's problems to worry about whether the freedom of the rich to make money was being limited. However, the aims of the New Deal were clearly sympathetic towards the poor, the unemployed, the exploited and the working class, so Roosevelt's opponents found it easy to criticise him for steering the USA along the road to socialism.

SOURCE A

American cartoon of November 1937 commenting on Roosevelt's plans to reform the Supreme Court.

Opposition from the Supreme Court

The Supreme Court is the highest court of law in the USA. One of its functions is to judge whether laws passed by Congress are consistent with the terms of the American Constitution. If the court finds them unconstitutional, the laws cannot stand. From the start of the New Deal, it was clear that Roosevelt would have problems with the court. As the nine judges were mainly conservative by nature and politics, there was always the chance that they would declare against a piece of New Deal legislation. This eventually happened in 1935 when the court found the National Industrial Recovery Act unconstitutional. Subsequently, it also found against the Agricultural Adjustment Act. The possibility of the court dismantling the whole New Deal appalled Roosevelt. To him it seemed as if the court was prepared to put legal quibbles before the wishes of the country.

After his re-election in 1936, Roosevelt determined to reform the Supreme Court so that it could no longer block his plans. His idea was to increase the number of judges from nine to 15. Under normal circumstances, he would have had to wait for one of the judges to die or retire before getting the chance to appoint a replacement. Naturally enough, presidents always nominate judges who are sympathetic to their own political views. Now Roosevelt planned to appoint six at once! It was clear to everyone that this would give him control over the court. Even many of his friends were very uneasy about this. In fact, the plan was one of Roosevelt's biggest mistakes. Americans believe that one of the ways their constitution protects their freedom is by ensuring that politicians cannot interfere in the work of judges. Roosevelt's plan to 'pack' the court with his own allies produced a storm of criticism, and made him look like a dictator. It was obvious that Congress would never approve, and eventually he was forced to back down and withdraw the plan.

However, in a way, Roosevelt still won his battle with the court. He had made the judges realise that they could not use their power just to impose their own political views on the country. From then on, they were much more cautious in the way they interpreted their duties.

SOURCE B

First of all let me assert my firm belief that the only thing we have to fear is fear itself. Our greatest primary task is to put people to work. It can be accomplished in part by direct recruiting by the government itself, treating the task as we would the emergency of a war, but at the same time ... accomplishing greatly needed projects.'

President Roosevelt speaking in his inaugural address, 1933.

SOURCE C

In other periods of depression it has always been possible to see some things which were solid and on which you could base hope, but as I look about, I now see nothing to give ground for hope.

Former President Coolidge speaking in 1933.

ACTIVITIES

Study Sources B and C, then discuss the following questions with a partner.

1. Is it fair to say that Roosevelt faced clear opposition from the outset?
2. What does the attitude of Coolidge towards the Depression say about some of Roosevelt's fellow politicians?

Radical critics of the New Deal

Ironically, Roosevelt was also criticised for not doing enough to help the poor and oppressed. These radical critics claimed that the effect of the New Deal was not to change American society, but to enable capitalism to survive.

Father Coughlin

Coughlin was known as the 'radio priest'. Based in Detroit, he built up an enormous national audience for his broadcasts. At first he supported the New Deal, but he rapidly became disillusioned with Roosevelt. Coughlin formed the National Union for Social Justice, which at its peak had over seven million members. His ideas were confused and incoherent, but his basic message was that the New Deal was not providing social justice. To people whose lives had been shattered by the effects of the Depression his simplistic and extreme ideas had much appeal, although as the years went by it became ever clearer that Coughlin had much in common with the European fascists. For him the New Deal was the 'Jew Deal', and he did not hesitate to preach a gospel of hate to his gullible listeners.

Dr Francis Townsend

Townsend and Coughlin were two of the founders of the Union Party, which opposed Roosevelt in the 1936 election. Townsend achieved fame as the author of the 'Townsend Plan' – a scheme by which all those over 60 years old would receive a monthly pension of $200 in return for a promise to retire from work and to spend all the pension each month. 'Townsend Clubs' were organised to campaign for the plan. These were influential in pushing the

BRAIN BOOST **WHO OPPOSED THE NEW DEAL?**

Businessmen – because it interfered with their businesses and gave workers rights

Republicans – after 1938, Republicans took over the Senate, and Roosevelt was unable to get any more New Deal legislation through

Activists – like Huey Long (Senator for Louisiana and organiser of the 'Share the Wealth' campaign to confiscate fortunes over $3 m)

State governments said that the federal government was taking their powers

Supreme Court ruled the NRA and the AAA illegal because they took away the states' powers. (In 1937, Roosevelt threatened to force the Supreme Court judges to retire and to create new ones, leading to a constitutional crisis.)

Extremists – used scaremongering tactics to undo the faith in the New Deal and in Roosevelt's reputation

Declining health of Roosevelt – how long could he continue to lead the USA?

Old Establishment – sympathetic at first but ultimately a bulwark to reform

Fear of communism/socialism – particularly given the rise of Hitler and Stalin

Francis Townsend (who campaigned for a pension of $200 a month) said it did not go far enough

ACTIVITIES

1 Complete the table below to better understand how the new role of the government was viewed by the different sectors of American society.

Opposition	What did they think FDR was doing wrong?	Supporters	FDR's response
Republicans			
The rich			
Huey Long			
Charles Coughlin			
Francis Townsend			

2 Write a paragraph that aims to categorise not only the type of opposition but also how effective it would be in frustrating Roosevelt's aims.

government into passing the Social Security Act of 1935 which, among other measures, introduced old age pensions.

Huey Long

Unlike Townsend and Coughlin, Huey Long was a professional politician who, for a short while, posed a real threat to Roosevelt. Elected Governor of Louisiana in 1928 as spokesman for the poor and underprivileged of the state, he used every trick in the political book, as well as some criminal ones, to boost his personal power. He became a virtual dictator in Louisiana, intimidating and bribing his opponents into silence. Yet however disreputable his methods, nobody could doubt his effectiveness. Public services in the state improved rapidly and his popularity soared.

Long became a fierce critic of Roosevelt, whom he blamed for being too cautious and not doing enough to help those in need. Long's 'Share Our Wealth' scheme promised to confiscate the fortunes of millionaires and to hand out the proceeds so that all American families could buy a home, a car and a radio. The government would buy up all agricultural surpluses and sell them as cheap food. The state would provide a range of benefits such as free education and old age pensions. Once Long became a senator for Louisiana in 1930 he became a national figure, and by 1934 he was clearly preparing himself to be a rival to Roosevelt for the presidency. Had he not been assassinated in September 1935, he might well have stood against Roosevelt in the 1936 election.

SOURCE D

Dear Mr President,

This is just to tell you that everything is all right now. The man you sent found our house all right and we went down to the bank with him and the mortgage can go on for a while longer ... I never heard of a president like you, Mr Roosevelt ... God Bless you.

Letter sent to President Roosevelt in 1936.

SOURCE E

They missed the way the President used to talk to them. They'd say, 'He used to talk to me about my government'. There was a real dialogue between Franklin and the people.

Reaction of the people to Roosevelt's death, described by Mrs Roosevelt in *When FDR died* by Bernard Asbell (1961).

VOICE YOUR OPINION!

Is it fair to say that Roosevelt's actions were un-American?

THE SHADOW IS THERE - - - - By Jerry Costello

An American cartoon of January 1937.

GradeStudio

How far does Source F explain why there was opposition to the New Deal? **[7 marks]**

Examiner's tip

Remember to use the evidence in the source to explain why there was opposition to the New Deal, and then use your own knowledge to explain other reasons. Finish your answer with a supported conclusion about 'how far'.

Did all Americans benefit from the New Deal?

LEARNING OBJECTIVES

In this lesson you will:

- learn about the benefits of the New Deal in context
- use statistical analysis to evaluate the impact of the New Deal's policies on unemployment and on the Gross National Product.

GETTING STARTED

'First of all let me assert my firm belief that the only thing we have to fear is fear itself ... Our greatest primary task is to put people to work ... It can be accomplished in part by direct recruiting by the government itself, treating the task as we would the emergency of war but at the same time ... accomplishing greatly needed projects'

- Discuss with a partner the language that Roosevelt uses here.
- Compose a list of assessment criteria that Roosevelt's success could be judged from this inaugural speech.
- How far is the success of the New Deal dependent on your point of view?

The New Deal and farmers

The New Deal did much to improve the lives of American farmers. Measures were taken to restrict production, raise prices, encourage soil conservation, provide loans to purchase equipment and to help indebted farmers to save themselves from eviction. These were all effective, but they benefitted large-scale farmers the most. By the mid-1930s, farmers' incomes were rising, but small farmers, farm labourers and sharecroppers saw little of the benefit. There was still much poverty in rural America, and particularly in the south.

In 1934–35 a long-term drought hit the prairie states, and in many areas the soil was turning to dust. With no rain, previously fertile areas were becoming deserts. Parts of Kansas, Oklahoma, Texas and Colorado became known as the 'Dustbowl'. The farmers in these areas had little choice but to pack up their belongings and leave the land. Many of them, known as 'Okies' (after the state of Oklahoma), made their way west to look for work in California.

The plight of the Okies was famously described by John Steinbeck in his novel *The Grapes of Wrath*, and illustrated in pictures taken by photographers commissioned by the Farm Security Administration, a New Deal agency. They suffered great hardship, and were often treated with suspicion and contempt in the areas through which they passed.

The New Deal and the poor

One of the most valid criticisms of the New Deal is that it did not go far enough in dealing with poverty, or in helping the poorest people to improve their position in American society. Emergency relief prevented people from starving, jobs were provided for as many of the unemployed as possible, and the Social Security Act of 1935 began to set up a system of national insurance. However, although around 30 per cent of all black families were dependent on emergency relief for survival, no New Deal laws specifically attempted to assist black people. Roosevelt felt dependent on the support of Democrats from the south, who were determined that no concessions should be made to improve the status of black Americans. Reluctance to deal with the race issue gave ammunition to Roosevelt's critics, who claimed that he was less interested in social justice than in preserving the USA's existing social structure.

The New Deal and workers

Roosevelt believed that it was important to create a new relationship of trust and co-operation between workers and employers. He was sympathetic to the cause of workers' rights, and tried to improve working conditions. The National Recovery Administration codes did a lot to regulate conditions in many industries, and when the Supreme Court declared these unconstitutional, the Wagner Act recovered some of the lost ground, establishing workers' rights to join unions and to bargain collectively for their wages. During the 1930s, union membership rose steadily.

Nonetheless, the USA's employers deeply resented this aspect of the New Deal, and many did all they could to deny workers their rights. Many large companies hired thugs to beat up union activists and to intimidate workers who went on strike.

This cartoon is celebrating one of the most successful and controversial organisations initiated by President Roosevelt.

During 1937 there were many violent strikes in the steel and automobile industries. During a strike by steelworkers in Chicago, ten demonstrators were shot dead by police, and 90 wounded, in what became known as the 'Memorial Day Massacre'. Workers used 'sit-down strikes' – occupying their factories to make sure the machinery could not be kept running. However, without the backing of the New Deal laws, these workers would almost certainly have been defeated by the employers. As it was, during 1937 there were around 4700 strikes, about 80 per cent of which were settled in favour of the workers.

ACTIVITIES

1 Consider Source A then answer the following questions.
   - **a** 'The NRA was a propaganda machine. It was largely ineffective in comparison to the government's portrayal of it.' Is this a fair interpretation?
   - **b** While the NRA brought new rights for employees, there were still too many operating out of the reach of the states' new welfare programme. Why did the New Deal not reach as far as the government pretended?
   - **c** Should the above issues be classed as failures or as reasonable exceptions in the context of the New Deal's successes?

2 Plot the following information onto a graph. Trace a line through your points and then complete the questions below.

Year	**1927**	**1928**	**1929**	**1930**	**1931**	**1932**	**1933**	**1934**	**1935**	**1936**	**1937**	**1938**	**1939**	**1940**	**1941**
Billions of US dollars	97	99	106	92	76	59	55	61	73	82	90	85	92	101	128

   - **a** Mark the Depression years, 1929–33.
   - **b** Mark the New Deal years, 1933–38.
   - **c** Mark the start of the Second World War.
   - **d** Write a paragraph that outlines the key issues statistically within these periods. Look for the trends, the biggest area of growth or decline, and the average output in dollars.

Did the fact that the New Deal did not solve unemployment mean that it was a failure?

LEARNING OBJECTIVES

In this lesson you will:

- evaluate the overall impact of the New Deal
- present clear arguments to justify or criticise the policy given the prevailing economic conditions.

GETTING STARTED

Roosevelt's task was far too great. He had to cope with a situation never before faced by a president: an unprecedented failure of confidence in both the economic system and the role of the government. To accuse him of failing to overcome the problems he faced is unreasonable. Restoration, not reinvention, was Roosevelt's primary objective.

- How far is this a fair statement on which to base assessments of Roosevelt?
- What would be another way of judging his success?

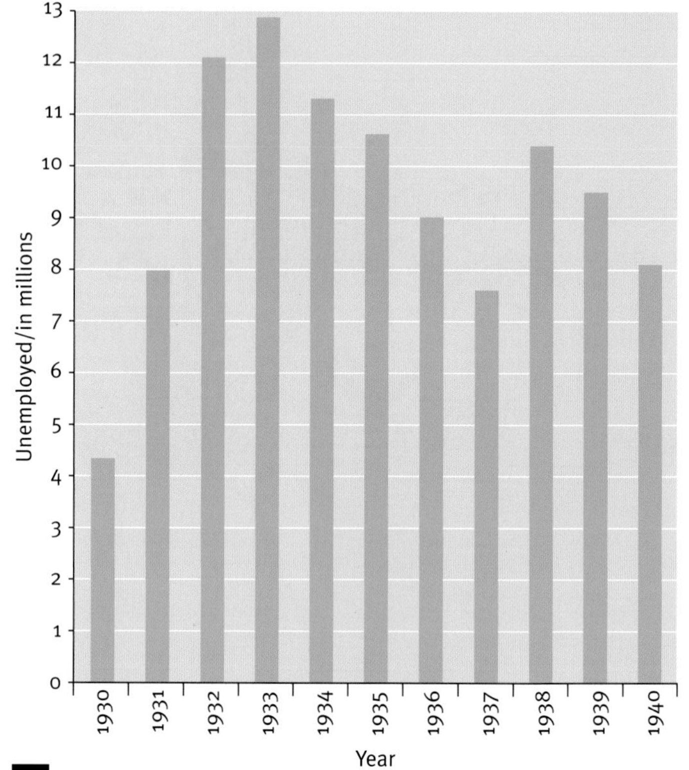

USA unemployment figures, 1930–40.

The slump of 1937–38

The limitations of the New Deal were exposed by events in 1937. Although conservative critics always tried to portray Roosevelt as a socialist spendthrift, in reality he believed just as strongly as the Republicans in balancing the budget. In early 1937 it seemed that the economy was recovering well. Roosevelt decided to take the opportunity of cutting the amount spent on New Deal programmes. Without the stimulus of government spending, the economy promptly plunged back into depression. Industrial production fell by a third, and unemployment jumped by nearly three million. By early 1938, Roosevelt had acknowledged his mistake and increased spending again, but even by 1940 employment had not recovered to the level of early 1937.

The New Deal – success or failure?

Judgements on the New Deal have been remarkably varied, although no one denies its importance.
It did not solve unemployment, but it did reduce it. It did not solve the problems of the Depression, but it did much to protect Americans from its worst effects. On the next page you can read the opinions of several modern historians on why the New Deal was important. Once you have read them, decide whether you think the New Deal was a failure or not.

As you have seen, one of the main aims of the New Deal was to put the USA back to work. Various agencies took part, such as the PWA, the CCC and the WPA. Literally millions of Americans were found work on government-sponsored projects.

However, there was a limit to the effectiveness of these schemes. Critics suggested that they did not provide 'real jobs' – the moment government ceased to pay, the jobs would disappear. And although the USA benefitted enormously from much of the work carried out – new roads, schools, hospitals, conservation schemes and so on – there was also a concern that many of the tasks were just making work for the sake of it. The greatest worry, though, was that unemployment would not go away. The government could reduce it, but they could not solve it. True, the numbers of unemployed fell year by year (at least until the return of the Depression in 1937–38), but by 1936 there were still nine million people out of work. The effort that the government was making was huge, but it was not enough.

SOURCE A

WORLD'S HIGHEST STANDARD OF LIVING
There's no way like the American Way

Black people queuing for food handouts, 1937 (Margaret Bourke-White).

SOURCE B

Important advances had been made in working conditions, relief of poverty, and the running of business, but there had been no economic miracle. To have achieved such an economic miracle would have required policies of government spending on a scale beyond Roosevelt's dreams or nightmares. Instead, his policies were often hesitant or contradictory, perhaps due to his lack of interest in, and understanding of, economics.

A historian commenting on Roosevelt's policies.

SOURCE C

If the New Deal is to be judged by economic success alone, then the verdict must be a mixed one. But, generally speaking, the economy had by 1937 recovered to the level reached before the Depression started in 1929. [However,] the New Deal established a far more important role for the Federal government in a whole range of areas previously considered to be outside its scope. Roosevelt quite deliberately extended the powers of central government in order to achieve a fairer society that offered its citizens greater security.

A historian commenting on the role of the New Deal in Federal government.

SOURCE D

Unquestionably the most important [achievement] was the preservation of American democracy, the American constitution, and American capitalism. By his gallantry, energy, eloquence and warmth of heart, Roosevelt not only transformed the prestige of his office but galvanised an entire generation with faith in their country, their leader and their political system.

A historian commenting on Roosevelt's achievements in preserving the American way of life.

VOICE YOUR OPINION!

If it was the war that proved truly significant, does this change your opinion of Roosevelt's policies?

Is it fairer to argue that it was the New Deal that allowed America, and subsequently Europe, to survive the threat of Hitler?

GradeStudio

'The New Deal solved the problems of America's Depression.' How far do you agree with this statement? Explain your answer. **[10 marks]**

Examiner's tip

Your answer might include:

- reference to the Alphabet Agencies
- the impact of government intervention and the responsibilities that followed
- the restrictions on success caused by opposition
- the impact of the Second World War
- the galvanising effect of Roosevelt
- the danger of short-term successes and the negative impact of such high-level government intervention.

Make sure you explain both successes and failures of the New Deal. A good way to structure your paragraphs is Point, Evidence, Explanation, Link (back to the question). Then write a conclusion explaining your overall judgement.

Get your sources sorted

SOURCE A

'Instead of offering new policies in the election campaign, Hoover concentrated on claiming that things would become far worse if the Democrats gained power . . . this compared badly with the confidence that Roosevelt showed. The Democratic candidate's smile and optimism proved far more popular with the electorate than Hoover's grim looks.

This difference of presentation was important because, in some ways, the two candidates seemed to have similar policies; for example, government support for ailing businesses and job-creation schemes featured in the programmes of both candidates'.

Roger Smalley, *Depression and the New Deal*.

Hoover's election focus was on attacking the other side; this was perceived as a weakness.

Roosevelt's optimism was a positive feature of his campaign and helped people to focus on what he was saying. It established a trust that was a very effective tool and a powerful weapon to combat Hoover.

The ideas were in many ways immaterial because in a country like America elections are often about personality rather than policies.

SOURCE B

'This is pre-eminently the time to speak the truth, the whole truth, frankly and boldly. Nor need we shrink from honestly facing conditions in our country today. This great nation will endure as it has endured, will revive and will prosper.

So first of all let me assert my firm belief that the only thing we have to fear is fear itself – nameless, unreasoning, unjustified terror which paralyses needed efforts to convert retreat into advance. . .

Our greatest primary task is to put people to work. This is no unsolvable problem if we face it wisely and courageously.'

Franklin D. Roosevelt, inaugural speech, March 1933.

Such declarations of honesty are very well received by the population.

Linking to the past ensures faith in the fact that Roosevelt can overcome present problems and sets them in an appropriate context.

The statement about not fearing fear is beautifully poetic, at once true and also perfectly summarising the problems of the Depression; it became one of the best known quotations of the 20th century.

This line summarises the Democratic principles that Roosevelt would use. Employment was empowerment and it would be the actions of every individual that would bring America out of Depression.

3Cs & 1J

Look at the following questions and fill your answer into this frame:

- **Comment** – What is the meaning of the cartoon?
- **Content** – What is happening in the cartoon?
- **Context** – What was happening at the time?
- **Judgement** – What is your verdict on the reliability and usefulness of the cartoon?

Essential Knowledge

- The Depression hit America hard after 1929.
- The Wall Street Crash uncovered elements of the economy that had not been so successful during the boom of the 1920s (e.g. farming) as well as exposing new weaknesses.
- The effect of this, together with a lack of confidence within the business and banking sectors, sent the country into a spiral of Depression – it would require great change to save the economy.
- It is important to reflect on the ideals of the Democratic Party and its tendency to be much more involved with shaping the economy than the Republicans.

What is the message of the source?

Before you begin to answer this question, remember what is meant by the 'message' of the source. It is not simply a quote from a source nor a description of what it shows but rather the overall impression that the source conveys about one or more things.

For example if you can understand the difference between the two political parties in the American government and the difference between intervention and rugged individualism, then you can set the efforts of Roosevelt in context. It is best to begin your answer with 'The message of this source is …' Once you have worked out the message, ensure that you support your argument using information from both the source and your own knowledge. If you do this, you can get the full seven marks.

The establishment of jobs was a crucial element on which Roosevelt's plans would be measured. The Alphabet Agencies played a vital role in this.

This was perhaps the most important area that needed support. Farmers were struggling even before the crash and there had to be significant financial support offered to ensure they could recover.

By showing Roosevelt pulling all the boats together, the cartoon is suggesting that by pulling the different strands of the economy together, Roosevelt can achieve success. Roosevelt is the only man who can complete the task.

America after the Wall Street Crash was lost at sea and the boats were drifting further away from the security of the port. They needed to be brought back together to ensure safety.

SOURCE C

What a Man!

This source reflects the artist's recognition of both the ability of Roosevelt and the 'superhuman' nature of the task ahead of him.

The shoal of doubt is the dangerous place towards which the ships were drifting under the leadership of Hoover. The ships had to be pulled away towards security. Doubt is one of the most destructive things about a depression, because without confidence the capitalist system cannot function.

Roosevelt is shown as a strong and athletic giant; this is intended to demonstrate his influence and the power of his 'big' ideas rather than his size or physical presence.

Bank confidence was important because without it the government could not ensure that the system fed businesses and individuals with enough money in the form of loans.

The irony of prohibition was its damaging effects on the economy. Roosevelt wasted no time in restoring the industry to its former strength, creating new jobs across the country.

The economy is included in the boats because it needed to be pump primed and started again.

The USA, 1919-41

Here is an example of a question that requires you to consider two sides of an argument. This is a common type of question in Unit A971. The skill you require is to use your knowledge of the topic to give evidence in supporting a two-sided argument.

To what extent was America 'fair and free' during the 1920s? Explain your answer. **[10 marks]**

Mark scheme

Level 1: General and vague assertions
Level 2: Identifies or describes factors from at least one side of the argument
Level 3: Explains evidence supporting one side of the argument
Level 4: Explains evidence supporting both sides of the argument
Level 5: As level four, but also reaches and supports a final judgement in answer to the question.

Examiner's tip

Think about everything you have learnt about America in the 1920s and decide which parts are relevant to this question. It's always a good idea to plan what specific evidence you are going to use to support each side of the argument. Look at this mark scheme before thinking about what you would need to do to answer the question:

[1] Americans pride themselves on being a 'fair and free' nation and many historians would agree that in 1920s it was. [2] An example of this freedom is the liberty that people experienced through owning a car such as Henry Ford's Tin Lizzy. [3] This provided people with a greater degree of freedom because it meant that they could travel to different places. In turn this meant that they were free to enjoy their lives by going to the cinema or visiting clubs where they could dance the Charleston.

Examiner's comment

[1] This is a good start. The candidate is using the principle of a three-part paragraph: They have made a clear point, supported it with specific evidence and then linked the evidence to the question in order to explain their ideas.
[2] By giving examples of how America was free and fair the candidate has achieved level two: identification.
[3] In the example above the candidate explains their evidence and so the answer moves up to a level three. This will earn approximately half marks.
To go up to level four you need to explain the other side of the argument. Now look at this example:

Examiner's comment

Americans pride themselves on being a 'fair and free' nation and many historians would agree that in 1920s it was. An example of this freedom is the liberty that people experienced through owning a car such as Henry Ford's Tin Lizzy. This provided people with a greater degree of freedom because it meant that they could travel to different places. In turn this meant that they were free to enjoy their lives by going to the cinema or visiting clubs where they could dance the Charleston.

However, for some people living in America in the 1920s life was far from 'fair and free'. Evidence to prove this can be found in the treatment of black people, who were often treated as inferior. In the Southern states of America life for black people was especially unfair. A group called the Ku Klux Klan (KKK) terrorised black people. They would often attack and even kill innocent victims just because of the colour of their skin. Many policemen and judges were members of the KKK so very little was done to protect black people, and so life for black people often failed to be 'fair or free'.

By explaining evidence from both sides of the argument the candidate moves up to level four. To strengthen this still further the candidate could explain more than one piece of evidence for each argument.

To attain level five the candidate needs to reach an overall judgement about the original question: was America 'fair and free'? It is important to save something new for this conclusion, rather than just summarising what has already been said. Have a go at writing your own conclusion in which you reach and explain a clear judgement in answer to this question.

How was British society changed, 1890–1918?

Introduction

This unit involves historical enquiry into a period of British history. It gives you opportunities to:

- investigate specific historical questions, problems and issues
- use a range of historical sources and reach reasoned conclusions
- analyse and evaluate how the past has been interpreted and represented in different ways.

This unit is very different from the other units. The main target is the use of source material – interpreting, evaluating and using it. The contextual knowledge is not required in great detail and is never required for its own sake. It is to enable the sources to be understood and used in their historical context so that you can investigate the way the past has been interpreted and represented.

The specified content is defined through key questions and focus points. The key questions encourage an issues-based and investigative approach to the content. Focus points indicate the issues that need to be addressed in each key question. You will be expected to demonstrate understanding of the key questions and focus points using knowledge of relevant historical examples.

SOURCE A

West Front, or Principal Entrance of the London Workhouse, Bishopsgate Street.

A workhouse in London in the nineteenth century.

Fact file

This Depth Study is examined on Unit A972 of the final examination. The examination consists of a number of sources and between five and seven questions. It lasts for 1 hour 30 minutes and is worth 30 per cent of the final result. In the Grade Studio that follows, you can see the kinds of questions you might have to answer and the skills you will require to do well. Here is a full list of all the focus points:

1. What were working and living conditions for the poor like in the 1890s?
2. How were social reformers reacting to the social problems of the 1890s?
3. Why did the Liberal government introduce reforms to help the young, old and unemployed?
4. How effective were these reforms?
5. What was the social, political and legal position of women in the 1890s?
6. What were the arguments for and against female suffrage?
7. How effective were the activities of the suffragists and the suffragettes?
8. How did women contribute to the war effort?
9. How were civilians affected by the war?
10. How effective was government propaganda during the war?
11. Why were some women given the vote in 1918?
12. What was the attitude of the British people at the end of the war towards Germany and the Paris Peace Conference?

What skills do you need if you are going to do well on the final exam paper?

SOURCE B

We found the condition of things in the House almost revolting. The place was dirty. The stores were empty. The inmates had not sufficient clothes, and many were without boots to their feet. The food was so bad that the wash-tubs overflowed with what the poor people could not eat. It was almost heart-breaking to go round the place and hear the complaints and see the tears of the aged men and women. Not one of them had a change of clothing. Their under-clothes were worn to rags. If they washed them they had to borrow from each other in the interval. The inmates' clothes were not only scanty, they were filthy. On one occasion the whole of the workhouse linen was returned by the laundry people because it was so over-run with vermin that they would not wash it.

A description of Poplar Workhouse, by Will Crooks, 1906.

GradeStudio

Study Sources A and B and the question that follows. Read the sample answer and then the examiner's comments.

Question: Which of these two sources is of most value to the historian studying workhouses in the 19th century?

[8 marks]

Student answer 1

These sources are very useful. The workhouses were terrible places. A Royal Commission on the Poor Law in 1832 collected evidence that demonstrated that the Poor Law was ineffective. The purpose of the resulting Poor Law Amendment Act of 1834 was to do away with the waste and inefficiency of the old system. The Act abolished direct payments to the poor, and revived the austere workhouse as a way to prevent people becoming dependent on poor relief. No one ever resolved the dilemma that the only way to make workhouse conditions significantly worse than the outside world was to starve the inmates.

Examiner's comment

What is wrong with this answer? You might be impressed with the detailed knowledge that this candidate shows. There is certainly plenty of factual material which suggests that this candidate has learned a lot about the Poor Law. But does the answer address the question? In a question like this, you need to compare the two sources and decide which one would help the historian best understand what workhouses were like. Any knowledge you have should be used to help demonstrate the advantages and disadvantages of each source. This is called using knowledge to put the sources into context, or using contextual knowledge.

Now look at Student answer 2. The contextual knowledge has been highlighted. Look at the way the candidate uses this knowledge to answer the question. This is a much better answer. Notice that you don't have to use lots of knowledge and facts to produce a good answer.

Student answer 2

Both of these sources are useful. Source A gives us a good idea of what a workhouse looked like. This is only one workhouse, but if it was typical of other workhouses, then they must have been grim places. It looks a bit like a prison. However, it does not show us what the workhouses were like on the inside. Source B tells us a lot about how the people in the workhouse must have felt. It tells us about their food and clothing, and it also tells us how dirty these places were. I think this source is more useful to the historian. However, there are lots of things about workhouses that you can't find out from either of these sources. **I know, for example, that the people who ran the workhouses were cruel. They handed out harsh punishments. They also separated families when they arrived at the workhouse.** This must have been very hard for families. The two sources are useful, and the second one is better, but the historian would still want to look at more evidence.

What were working and living conditions like for the poor in the 1890s?

LEARNING OBJECTIVES

In this lesson you will:

- learn about the nature of poverty, the need for change and the reasons why it occurred
- gather a range of evidence for an enquiry into the reasons why reform was needed and make a judgement on the decisive factor which led to change.

Social and economic changes

Due to the **industrial revolution**, Britain was transformed during the 19th century. Factories and towns developed where previously there had only been countryside. This change brought many problems. Conditions in the new industrial towns were often terrible. Housing for the workers was poor, cramped and dirty, often with no proper sanitation. **Epidemic** diseases, such as **cholera**, spread easily. Working conditions in the factories were dangerous and unhealthy. Eventually governments were forced to deal with these problems, and Factory Acts, Education Acts and Public Health Acts followed.

At the start of the 19th century, governments interfered very little in most people's lives, but by 1900 the idea that only the government was powerful enough to deal with society's most serious problems was well established. The Liberals after 1906 took this idea an important step further by accepting that governments should not only protect the population from harm, but that they should also try to guarantee a good, basic minimum standard of living for everyone, even if the only way to do this was to take money from the rich to help the poor.

Many people in the 19th century thought that it was the poor who were responsible for their own poverty; that they were lazy or wasted money on alcohol, tobacco and other non-essential goods. Although there was help for the poor, this help was very limited and based on principles set down in the Poor Law of 1834. The most important feature of this law was that any able-bodied person wanting help would have to agree to go into a **workhouse**. These were set up all over the country and paid for out of the rates (money collected from householders by the parish). Conditions in workhouses were deliberately made so harsh that only the most desperate would want to enter. The food and clothing provided were very basic. Men, women and children were separated and were forced to work for long hours at hard and boring tasks. Above all, there was a great sense of shame at having to depend on the workhouse for charity.

In fact, the 1834 Poor Law never worked totally as intended. In some industrial areas in times of economic hardship, so many people needed help that they could not possibly all be found places in workhouses. In these cases, the authorities gave outdoor relief – in other words they gave handouts of money or food, which is exactly what the law was supposed to avoid. The most serious problem, however, was that the Poor Law was not really intended to solve the problem of poverty, but rather to reduce the amount spent on the poor. It was reasonably effective in achieving this, and Poor Law Unions in many parts of the country worked well in providing not just poor relief but also some basic education and medical care for the poor. However, by the end of the 19th century it was becoming ever clearer that poverty remained one of society's greatest problems.

KEY WORDS

Cholera – *infectious and often fatal disease caused by bacteria in the water.*

Epidemic – *widespread disease in a community.*

KEY CONCEPTS

Industrial revolution – *a period of intense growth generated by the use of fossil fuels and a concept of large-scale production.*

Welfare state – *system of measures designed to ensure a basic minimum standard of living for all.*

How were the social reformers reacting to the social problems of the 1890s?

SOURCE A

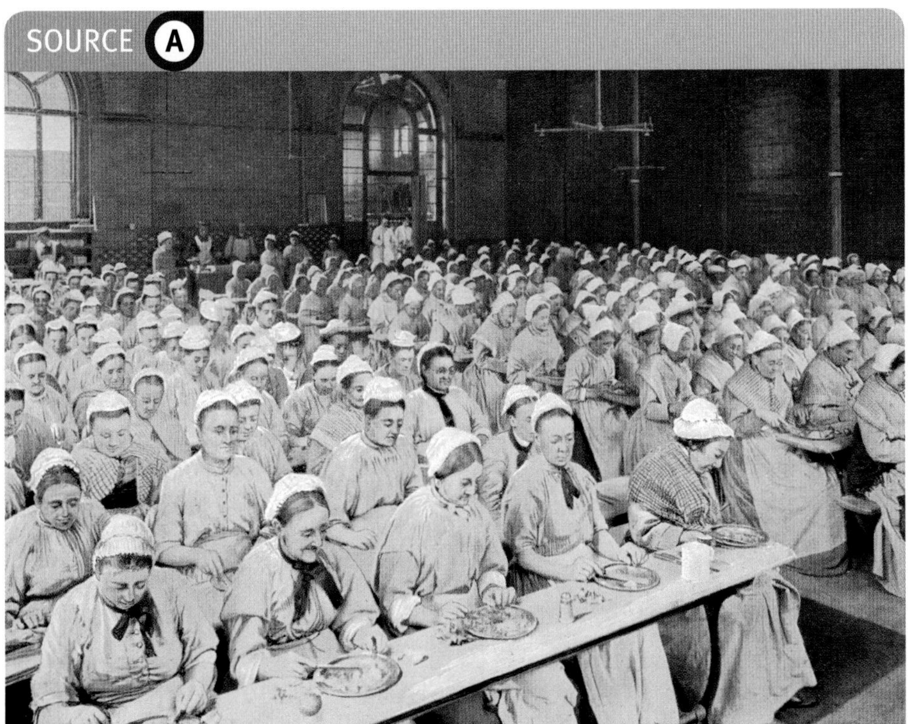

Women in the St Pancras workhouse, London, eating a meal, 1901.

LEARNING OBJECTIVES

In this lesson you will:

- learn about the help available to sick, unemployed, old and young people at the end of the 19th century
- investigate how social reformers reacted to the social problems of the 1890s.

ACTIVITY

Look back to the two sources in the introduction to this chapter. Compare Sources A and B on these pages. How similar is this source to the new sources in the introduction? Explain your answer fully, using details from all three sources.

Helping the sick

Those who were sick could not work. Even in the 19th century the link between illness and poverty was recognised, and outdoor relief was available to those in need. By the end of the century Poor Law hospitals offering free treatment had been built throughout the country, providing the basis for a national hospital system.

Helping the unemployed

By the end of the 19th century the attitude of the Poor Law authorities to the unemployed had softened a little. From 1886 local authorities were allowed to provide work for the unemployed, and the Unemployed Workmen Act of 1905 allowed them to raise money specifically for this purpose.

Helping the old

The old were also entitled to outdoor relief, but many had to be admitted to workhouses in order to be looked after. Old age was probably the single most important cause of poverty. Estimates put the proportion of old people receiving relief at around 30–40 per cent. Their treatment in the workhouse improved as the century progressed. Eventually couples were not split up, they were allowed visitors and given allowances for 'luxuries' like tea and tobacco.

KEY WORDS

Chancellor of the Exchequer – *the person responsible for raising government funds through taxation or borrowing and controlling overall government spending.*

Workhouse – *a place where people who were unable to support themselves could go to work and live. Conditions were designed to be worse than those of the lowest paid person outside.*

KEY PEOPLE

David Lloyd George – *a government minister who became Chancellor of the Exchequer in this period; he led reforms in National Insurance, Social Services and Pensions.*

Winston Churchill – *a popular politician who became President of the Board of Trade in 1906. He supported the Liberal Reforms, and introduced the Trade Boards Bill, the first minimum wages in Britain, Labour Exchanges, and helped to draft the National Insurance Act of 1911.*

Helping the young

Pauper (poor) children had to be admitted to the workhouse along with their parents, but attitudes towards them tended to be slightly kinder since they could not really be blamed for being poor. Many Poor Law Unions attempted to remove children from the workhouses by sending them to live with local families. Schooling was also provided. Thus although the working of the Poor Law became more flexible towards the end of the 19th century, it was only concerned with coping with the worst effects, rather than dealing with the causes, of poverty. Before the causes could be tackled, detailed studies of the lives of the poor would be needed, so that the nature, extent and causes of poverty could be identified.

Studies in poverty: Charles Booth and Seebohm Rowntree

Towards the end of the 19th century, many books were published about poverty. These did much to make the general public more sympathetic towards the poor. Two of the most influential studies were carried out by **Charles Booth** and **Seebohm Rowntree**. Booth studied the lives of the poor in London, and Rowntree concentrated on York.

Booth's study

Between 1886 and 1903 Booth published a series of volumes called *Life and Labour of the People in London*. Using evidence from house-to-house enquiries, school records, **census returns** and interviews with doctors and clergy who worked in these areas, he described in great detail what it was like to be poor. He defined poverty as an income of less than £1 a week for a family of five, and calculated that around 30 per cent of the population of these areas lived below this 'poverty line'. He demonstrated the link between poverty and a high death rate. He identified the main

KEY WORDS

Census returns – *a record of confirmation for all citizens. Information includes occupation, address and family arrangements.*

Philanthropy – *the act of donating money, goods, services or time to support a socially beneficial cause, with a defined objective and with no financial or material reward to the donor.*

Royal Commission – *a committee of inquiry established by royal charter or warrant by the government to look into issues of considerable public importance. The process is designed to be independent.*

KEY PEOPLE

Charles Booth – *English social investigator and pioneer in developing the social survey method, who made an exhaustive study of poverty in London that was published as* Life and Labour of the People in London.

Seebohm Rowntree – *a sociologist and philanthropist known for his studies of poverty and welfare, who conducted a survey of working-class homes in York in 1897–98 and published his findings in* Poverty: a Study of Town Life *(1901).*

SOURCE 

A family living on [the poverty line] must never spend a penny on railway fares or the omnibus. They must never go into the country unless they walk ... They must never contribute anything to their church or chapel, or give any help to a neighbour which costs them money. They cannot save. The children have no pocket money. The father must smoke no tobacco. The mother must never buy any pretty clothes. Finally, the wage earner must never be absent from work for a single day.

Extract from B. Seebohm Rowntree's *Poverty: A Study of Town Life*, 1901.

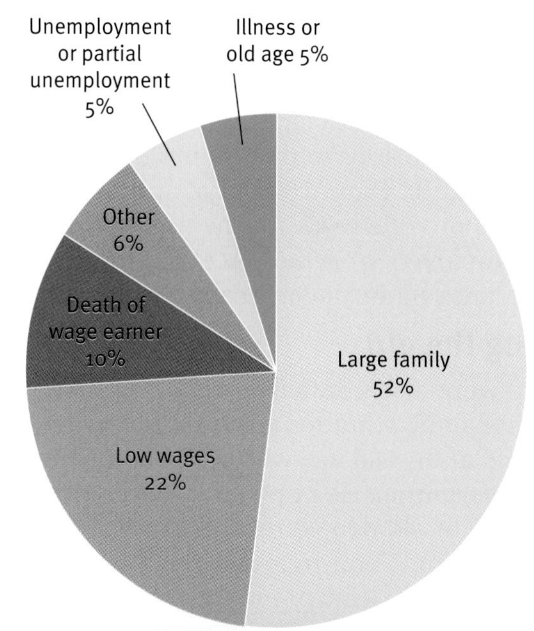

The most common causes of poverty as identified by Seebohm Rowntree in his report of 1901.

causes of poverty: sickness, old age, unemployment, large families, low wages. Above all, he demonstrated that the great majority of the poor were not responsible for their own poverty, and that they were forced into poverty by factors beyond their control.

Rowntree's findings

In case anyone should imagine that these conditions were only to be found in London, the publication of Rowntree's *Poverty: a Study of Town Life in 1901* demonstrated that the situation was just as bad even in a medium-sized provincial city like York. Rowntree's findings were similar to those of Booth. He, too, found around 30 per cent of the population living in poverty, with an income of around £1 a week or less. Above all, both studies demonstrated that the existing Poor Law was totally inadequate for dealing with the problem of poverty.

After the publication of these studies there was no longer any excuse for a lack of action. When the Boer War broke out in 1899, 40 per cent of all recruits were found to be unfit for military service because of the effects of poverty, and the government had to set up a committee to enquire into the 'Physical Deterioration of the People'. This was followed in 1905 by the appointment of a **Royal Commission** to review the Poor Law. Although this Commission did not report until 1909, and its members disagreed over what improvements to recommend, its appointment showed that the problem of poverty had become one of the major issues of the time.

GradeStudio

Study Source B, and the pie chart from Rowntree's report. How useful do you think they are for showing us what it was like to be poor in the early years of the 20th century? Use the source and your own knowledge to explain your answer. **[8 marks]**

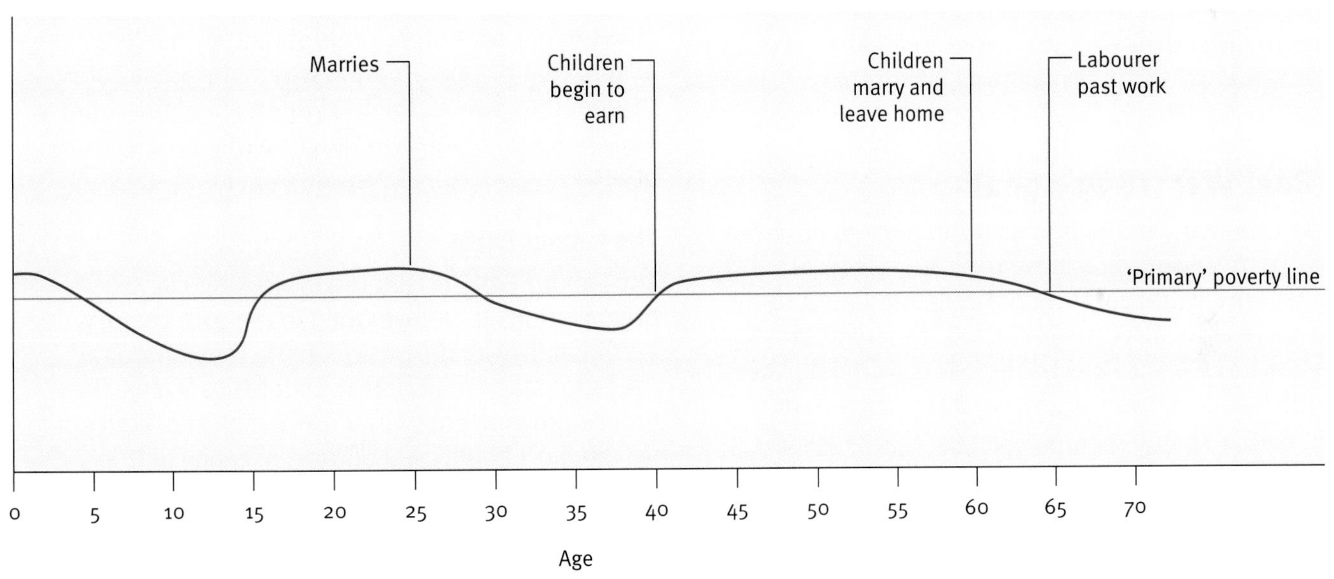

Rowntree's poverty line, from his report of 1901. The poverty line represented an income of around £1 a week or less (equivalent to £77.84 in today's money).

ACTIVITIES

Work in groups of four to prepare a party political broadcast that aims to convince the population that the Liberals are the right party to address the nation's problems. The broadcast should include:

- a discussion of the investigations of the social reformers Rowntree and Booth
- consideration of the good work done for the poor by the Labour Party
- a recognition of the need to maintain Britain's industrial presence and compete with other nations
- consideration of the need to maintain the power of Britain's Empire by having a strong, healthy population
- a new-found **philanthropy** in the richer classes.

Why did the Liberal government introduce reforms to help the young, old and unemployed?

LEARNING OBJECTIVES

In this lesson you will:

- identify the various factors and motives for the reforms of 1906–14.

Historians have identified various factors and motives for the reforms of 1906–14.

National efficiency

By this time, Britain was in decline as a world power. This led politicians to believe that Britain had to improve its national efficiency by improving the health and efficiency of the workforce. If Britain was to compete and reassert its position as a world power, then it had to be run efficiently and a strong, healthy and well-educated workforce would go some way towards sharpening Britain's competitive edge.

The Boer War (1899–1902)

During this war, the British army experienced great difficulty in finding fit young men to recruit as soldiers. One in three potential recruits failed to reach the medical requirements. This shocked politicians and led to questions being asked about the physical condition of the working-class male. There was real concern that Britain's chances of winning future wars would be seriously harmed unless something was done to ensure basic health levels among the population.

Popular socialism

The Labour Party had just been established and it was winning popularity for its campaigns for social welfare policies, such as old-age pensions and unemployment benefits. The ruling Liberal Party realised that its traditional support in many working-class areas would decline if voters turned to the Labour Party instead. To counter this threat, the Liberals came to believe that they had to introduce social reforms or risk losing political support from the working classes.

Fact file

The Conservative Party

Traditionally the Conservative Party was the party of the landed classes and the aristocracy. In general Conservatives felt that the government should be responsible for the operation of government but not necessarily required to help each and every citizen.

They believed in a policy of laissez faire, which meant non-interference in the workings of the free market.

The Liberal Party

The Liberal Party was traditionally more inclusive and was often seen as the party of new wealth and industrialists. Liberals believed firmly in central government control; reforms should be made to ensure that the government was managed according to what they saw as the best interests of the country. They believed in intervention to protect the existing order.

The Labour Party

The Labour Party originated in working-class organisations that developed in the 19th century. Traditionally Labour was the party that supported the interests of the poorest people in society. The party's growing popularity was a matter of concern for the more traditional parties, as many of their ideas were seen as revolutionary.

A new Liberalism

A new type of Liberalism had emerged by 1906, and it was this 'new liberalism' that provided the inspiration for the reforms. New Liberals, such as Lloyd George, Winston Churchill and Herbert

Asquith, argued that there were circumstances in which it was right for the state to intervene in people's lives. David Lloyd George, who was Chancellor of the Exchequer from 1908, came from a humble Welsh background. He was well known for his fiery speeches and his willingness to whip up the feelings of the poor against the rich and privileged.

The German model

The German Chancellor, Otto von Bismarck, passed a series of progressive social measures in the 1880s and 1890s. This, coupled with Germany's economic and military strength, impressed both Lloyd George and Churchill. Amongst Bismarck's measures was an early form of sickness insurance for German workers. This inspired Lloyd George and Churchill to introduce similar reforms in Britain.

'Gas and water socialism'

Public works schemes to improve living conditions and public health had been established in the late 19th century, often set up and run by Liberals. Joseph Chamberlain, a Liberal councillor, had transformed the public health of the people of Birmingham with a series of impressive reforms. These local schemes provided the inspiration to introduce similar schemes on a national scale.

SOURCE A

RICH FARE.

THE GIANT LLOYD-GORGIBUSTER: "FEE, FI, FO, FAT,
I SMELL THE BLOOD OF A PLUTOCRAT;
BE HE ALIVE OR BE HE DEAD,
I'LL GRIND HIS BONES TO MAKE MY BREAD."

A cartoon showing Lloyd George and commenting on the People's Budget of 1909.

GradeStudio

Look at Source A. It shows David Lloyd George, and it was drawn in 1909. By this time, the Liberals had passed a number of measures, and to pay for them, Lloyd George introduced a budget that increased taxes in order to raise more money for the government. (Note that a plutocrat was a wealthy person.)

See if you can answer the following question.

Do you think this cartoonist supported or opposed the measures introduced by David Lloyd George? Give reasons for your answer. **[9 marks]**

Examiner's tip

Try to work out the main message of the cartoon. Which popular children's story is the cartoon based on? Which character from that story is Lloyd George portrayed as? What word is written on the club that Lloyd George is holding? What do you think the cartoonist is trying to say here? What does the caption say? What does this tell us about who the cartoonist sympathises with?

How effective were these reforms?

LEARNING OBJECTIVES

In this lesson you will:

- examine the changes brought in by the Liberal government after 1906 and learn about their effectiveness
- identify patterns in policy and evaluate the government's response within its historical context.

GETTING STARTED

As you read through this lesson, you should note the order in which the Liberal Party introduced help; first the children, then the old and then the workers. Discuss with a partner why you think this was the chosen approach.

Reforming the nation

The Liberal Party had long planned to reform the way in which the country was run, but pressure from other parties and a fear of doing too much too soon stopped Lloyd George and his supporters from achieving all their goals.

Reforms for children

- The School Meals Act of 1906 allowed local authorities to provide free school meals for the poor. By 1914 around 150,000 free meals a day were being served.
- Free school medical inspections were introduced in 1907. All children were to be inspected by a doctor or nurse at least once a year. At first, any necessary treatment was not free, but this too was provided from 1912.

The Children's Charter

A collection of measures in 1908 became known as the 'Children's Charter'. These dealt with a wide range of issues affecting children. Child care committees were set up to try to support families where children were obviously suffering from the effects of poverty or **neglect**. Young offenders were dealt with in special courts, and the **probation** system was set up, whereby offenders were released on condition that they behaved and were placed under the supervision of a probation officer. For those cases where it was necessary to keep young people in custody, borstals (reforming houses for young people) were established so that they would not have to be sent to the same jails as adults. It was made illegal to sell tobacco, alcohol or fireworks to young people under the age of 16. Working hours for children were strictly limited, and it was made illegal for children to do certain types of unsuitable work.

Old age pensions

The Old Age Pensions Act was passed in 1908. This established a system to give the poorest people over the age of 70 (those with an income of less than £21 a year), a pension of 5s a week which they could collect at their local Post Office. Smaller pensions were paid to those who were slightly better off. The fact that the pension was paid outright as a 'present', with no contribution to it from the old themselves, was a complete novelty, and was much criticised by opponents of the government. They claimed it would discourage old people in future from saving for their own retirement, and would rob them of their independence by making them dependent on government handouts.

KEY WORDS

Bill – *a draft of a proposed law presented for approval to a legislative body.*

Neglect – *to fail to complete a duty through carelessness or oversight.*

Probation – *a period of time in which a new idea is trialled to evaluate how successful it will be.*

SOURCE A

A cartoon about the introduction of old age pensions, first paid in 1909.

Pensions were paid for out of taxes collected from richer people. The government felt that the national finances would be able to pay for them, although they seriously underestimated the numbers of old people who would qualify for pensions. It was expected that the scheme would cover about half a million people, but by 1913 nearly double this number were receiving pensions. In some areas of the country as many as four out of every five old people qualified for the pension.

Labour exchanges

The idea of labour exchanges was put forward in an important report on unemployment published in 1909 by the economist, **William Beveridge**. He saw the problem of unemployment as being caused largely by inefficiency. Too many men were employed in casual work, from which they would be frequently laid off. Then they would face the problem of finding more work. Beveridge felt they should be given help to find good, permanent employment. The Labour Exchanges Act of 1909 was intended to help them do this.

Labour exchanges were set up throughout the country, and the unemployed were expected to register with them. Local employers looking for workers would notify the labour exchange of vacancies, and unemployed workers would then be put in touch with these employers. This was a convenient arrangement which was efficient and meant that the unemployed no longer had to go around looking for work. The first labour exchanges were set up in 1910, and by 1914 there was a national network of around 400 exchanges, filling a million vacancies a year.

Low pay was also an important cause of poverty. The Trade Boards Act of 1909 tried to do something about problems of low pay and poor conditions in what were known as the 'sweated industries', small-scale industries not covered by the rules of the various Factory Acts. The Act meant that minimum rates of pay could be established for these trades.

National Insurance

Even reasonably well off workers could be plunged into poverty if they lost their jobs. Many already paid into private insurance schemes, and some unions also arranged benefits for their members. Roughly 50 per cent of the working population had taken out some kind of insurance against sickness, but a much lower proportion, around 10 per cent, were covered against the effects of unemployment. Lloyd George was aware of health insurance schemes already operating nationally in other countries, and he chose the German system as the one to copy.

KEY PEOPLE

William Beveridge – *a British economist and social reformer.*

The National Insurance Act of 1911 was in two parts. The first dealt with health insurance, and the second with unemployment insurance.

Health insurance

This scheme was compulsory, and covered all workers earning £160 a year or less. In 1911, £160 a year was a good wage, and the insurance therefore covered much of the working population – around

SOURCE B

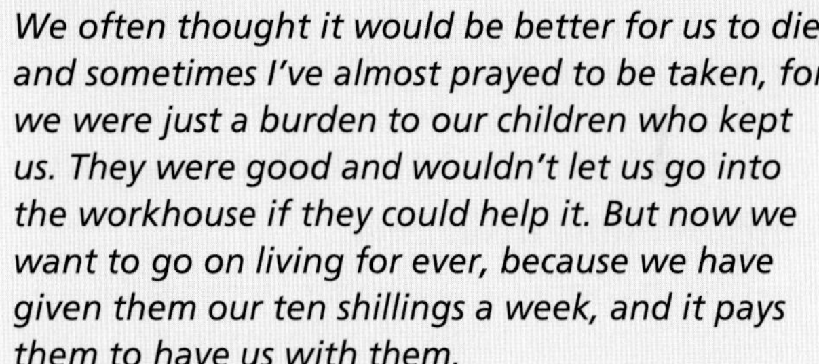

We often thought it would be better for us to die, and sometimes I've almost prayed to be taken, for we were just a burden to our children who kept us. They were good and wouldn't let us go into the workhouse if they could help it. But now we want to go on living for ever, because we have given them our ten shillings a week, and it pays them to have us with them.

A man over 90 years old talks to a journalist about the introduction of old age pensions.

SOURCE C

How can any sensible man regard the situation [the introduction of pensions] without dismay? The strength of this nation has been its great reserve of wealth and the sturdy independent character of its people ... They money from unjust taxation will be distributed in small hand outs and will weaken the character of the people by teaching them to rely, not on their own hard work and savings, but on the state.

A letter to *The Times* in 1908 about the Old Age Pensions Bill.

ACTIVITIES

What was the popular reaction to the introduction of pensions?

Which source do you feel is most reliable as a piece of evidence? Explain your answer with reference to the sources.

16 million people in total. Out of their wages, people had to pay 4d a week (17s a year) into an insurance fund. Employers had to add 3d to this, and the government 2d, making a total of 9d a week (nearly £2 a year) for each worker.

Employers were responsible for running the scheme; they collected contributions from their workers' wages, and stamped each worker's national insurance card as evidence that payments had been received. The insurance cover itself was not provided by the government, but instead was in the hands of large insurance companies and 'Friendly Societies'. The scheme gave workers free medical care from a doctor, although workers still had to pay for their own medicines. After at first opposing the plan, doctors soon changed their minds when they realised that it would guarantee them much more work than they had ever had before. When ill, or unable to work, workers could claim payment of 10s a week for 26 weeks. The scheme also included a maternity benefit payment of 30s on the birth of a child, but apart from this families of insured workers were not covered.

Unemployment insurance

This part of the National Insurance Act was the work of Winston Churchill. Unlike health insurance, which was provided in several countries before Britain, unemployment insurance was available nowhere else.

This scheme did not include all workers. It was intended to protect men in industries particularly affected by seasonal unemployment, such as building, shipbuilding and engineering. It covered about two and a half million workers. Contributions to the fund were 2.5d a week from the worker and 2.5d from the employer. When unemployed, workers in the scheme could claim 7s a week for up to 15 weeks, not enough to live on, but enough to help them cope until they found another job. Benefits were paid out at a labour exchange, and to receive the money unemployed men had therefore to be registered with the labour exchange to be looking for alternative work.

The significance of the Liberal reforms

The legacy of the Liberal reforms has played a huge part in the lives of your family already. In these laws, for the first time, there was a defined period in every British person's life where they were deemed a child, a period where they played their part for society as a worker, and a distinct period at the end of their life where the state could support them. This was a revolutionary idea across the world at the time and formed the foundations of modern Britain. Over a century later, many of these ideas are still ignored across the world.

SOURCE D

The years between 1906 and 1914 saw the building of the foundations of the welfare state of today. The Liberals were prepared to go further than the Victorians by allowing the state to take an active part in people's lives. By 1914 they had improved on the work of their predecessors, enlarged the field of direct state aid, and pointed the way to the future. They had not produced a social revolution as their opponents predicted ... Their proposals were not very extreme; for all the fuss, there was virtually no redistribution of income [when money is taken from the rich to be distributed to others].

From a British history book published in 1971.

SOURCE E

By this Act [the National Insurance Act of 1911], Lloyd George introduced into Great Britain the scheme of paying for social reform mainly out of the pockets of the poor. Instead of taxation falling chiefly on the richer classes, he successfully introduced a different sort of 'sideways' redistribution, whereby the healthy and employed workers were made to contribute towards the needs of the sick and the workless.

From *A History of The Common People* published in 1938.

GradeStudio

Read Sources A to E. Do these sources prove that the Liberal welfare reforms were successful? Explain fully whether you agree or disagree with this statement.

[12 marks]

Examiner's tip

Some of these sources suggest that the reforms were successful, but some do not. The trick is to use sources from both sides of the argument as well as your own knowledge in order to reach a judgement about whether these sources provide sufficient evidence to prove the statement.

Get your sources sorted

Essential knowledge

- Lloyd George increased taxation in his budget of 1908; this was an essential move to cover the new financial commitments of the government.
- The money helped provide much-needed funds for the poorest groups in the country.
- To many people this seemed like a blatant attack on the rich.
- Lloyd George was something of a radical figure in the government anyway, and many traditional politicians on both sides felt his ideas were not good for Britain and certainly not good for them.
- His actions increased support for the Conservative Party in certain sections of society.

SOURCE A

INCOME TAX PAYER
CRESCENDO;
OR, THE TUNE THE OLD COW'S LIKELY TO DIE OF.
THE COW. "STOP! STOP! THIS ISN'T MILKING; IT'S MURDER!"

A British cartoon of 1914 showing Lloyd George, then Chancellor of the Exchequer.

Now that you have had a go at analysing sources, look at Source B. What can you learn from this source about the Liberal welfare reforms of 1906–14?

SOURCE B

A cartoon designed to show the concerns held by some sections of the government of giving too much to the people.

GradeStudio

What impression does Source A give of Lloyd George as Chancellor of the Exchequer? **[6 marks]**

Examiner's tip

- Why do you think Lloyd George is smiling?
- What do you think the cow and its milk are meant to represent?
- Is the source in favour of or against the changes made by Lloyd George? How can you tell?

What was the social, political and legal position of women in the 1890s?

LEARNING OBJECTIVES

In this lesson you will:

- learn about the inequality of the sexes in 19th-century Britain
- assess the changing social, political and legal position of women in the 1890s.

The inequality of the sexes in 19th-century Britain

In 19th-century Britain, men and women were not equal. Economically, women were dependent on men; socially, they were expected to be obedient to men; legally, they had fewer rights than men. The range of employment open to them was very limited, and in any case, married women were not expected to work. As late as 1911, barely 10 per cent of married women were in paid employment.

Despite this position, attitudes towards women were slowly starting to change. Even before 1890 some marriages were coming to be seen as more of a partnership of equals. By 1882 laws had been passed to allow women to keep their own incomes and property when they married. An increasing number of middle-class couples began to use contraception, which reduced the size of middle-class families and brought an improvement to their quality of health and life. Many doctors were against the use of contraception however, arguing that it would cause women to suffer 'a mania leading to suicide'. Contraceptives were too expensive for most working-class families. Despite these changes, until 1891, a man could legally imprison his wife in her own home. Until 1925, children automatically belonged to their mother's husband. Legally then, little significant progress had been made.

GETTING STARTED

Historically, women have always been treated as second-class citizens. Examine the statements below and discuss with a partner why you think these beliefs a) originated and b) continued into the modern age?

- Women are the weaker sex, both physically and emotionally.
- A woman must have a man to protect her throughout her life. She should never be left alone.
- Women should never be educated in schools or attend university.
- Women cannot be professionals such as doctors or politicians.
- A woman should not own property; all rights and privileges should pass from father to son.

SOURCE A

Cartoon showing inequality experienced by women in British society at the beginning of the 20th century.

SOURCE B

The inclusion of women in politics would harm the number, character and strength of our future race. It would limit women's ability and inclination for motherhood, and would lead to their unwillingness to manage the home, and home is the first and lasting strength of social life in all countries.

From a speech given in February 1912 by Charles Hobhouse, a member of the Liberal government.

From the 1870s onwards greater educational opportunities led to a number of women entering professional occupations. Many girls' high schools were founded and women were beginning to be allowed to study at some universities. The London Medical School opened its doors to women in 1878. Elizabeth Garrett Anderson was the first woman to qualify as a doctor, although she faced a great deal of opposition. Some men claimed that studying hard would damage women's brains, but Anderson's success proved such ideas wrong. After 1870, with the expansion of education, there was a large increase in the number of women teachers to go with the increasing number of women entering the medical profession. These jobs were mainly taken up by middle-class women. However, more jobs were also becoming available for working-class women. The growth of shops and department stores in the second half of the 19th century created jobs as shop assistants. Although the hours were long, working conditions were better than for those employed in domestic service. The invention of the telephone and the typewriter led to the availability of good jobs in offices. The number of women office workers increased by 400 per cent from 1861 to 1911.

If this was the legal and social position of women, what about the political position? Women's involvement in local government had been increasing during the 19th century. At this level of politics, the major gain of the 1890s was the 1894 Local Government Act, pressed for by women's groups. By 1900, there were about one million women eligible to vote at council and parish elections. In 1907 women were given the right to stand as candidates at county council elections. Such advances in local government had come increasingly to be regarded as a means of furthering the campaign for the parliamentary vote.

ACTIVITIES

1 Study Source A. Given what you can see in this image, are you surprised by what Charles Hobhouse says in 1912 (Source B)?
2 Find out more about the social, political and legal position of women in the 1890s.

Fact file

Until 1870, any money a woman earned belonged to her husband.

Until 1882, once a couple were married, the woman's property belonged to her husband.

Until 1891, a man could legally imprison his wife in her own home.

Until 1925, children automatically belonged to their mother's husband.

HISTORY DETECTIVE

Investigate the social expectations of women at the beginning of the 20th century. Compile your research into a short fact file and present your findings to the class.

What were the arguments for and against female suffrage?

LEARNING OBJECTIVES

In this lesson you will:

- learn about the arguments for and against female suffrage
- evaluate the evidence in its historical context.

ACTIVITIES

Carefully study the arguments for and against female suffrage and the source evidence, and complete the following tasks.

1 Write a short letter to the government explaining what women could do for the country. Aim to consider at least two or three points for each side and include a final paragraph that is persuasive.

2 Share your completed letter with a partner and read theirs in return. You will now take on the role of the MP or government official receiving the letter. Bear in mind that, in an utterly male-dominated environment, even the most liberal and supportive of politicians would have found it difficult to publicly support the women's suffrage movement. You must therefore write a reply letter that rejects the arguments put forward.

Changing attitudes

However, by 1900 attitudes were beginning to change. It was becoming easier for women to gain a proper education, and to train for certain professions, mainly teaching. Indeed, by 1914 more girls were staying in education after the age of 16 than boys. Inventions such as the telephone and typewriter brought women into offices, and the development of shops and department stores opened up new job opportunities for women as shop assistants. Young, unmarried, middle-class women in particular benefitted from these opportunities, and as a result could lead more independent lives. It was just as well that they could: Britain's population was unbalanced, with well over one million more women than men. Out of these social changes, a women's movement, campaigning for women's rights, began to develop. By the turn of the century, this movement focused on one issue in particular – women's suffrage (the right to vote).

Arguments for and against women's suffrage

Arguments for	Arguments against
• Women had as much right to the vote as men. • Votes for women had already been introduced in other parts of the world, such as New Zealand, and parts of the USA and Australia. • Some women (since 1888) already had the right to vote in local elections. Why not in parliamentary elections too? • Modern women were more independent and educated than in previous generations. • It would be democratic to give women the vote. Through the 19th century the right to vote had been given to more and more men – now was the time to include women.	• It was claimed by some men that politics was an unsuitable activity for women. They said that women had no interest in politics, and would not understand difficult political issues. • Many women, including Queen Victoria, were against the idea of giving women the vote. • There were many more important social issues to be fighting for which would affect the lives of large numbers of women, rather than the vote, which was only really of interest to a small number of middle-class women. • Not all men had the vote at this time, so why should women have it? • Almost nobody, not even male supporters of women's suffrage, thought you could give the vote to all women. But giving the vote to some women (the wealthiest or the most educated) might give an advantage to one political party (probably the Conservatives) over the other (the Liberals). • Opponents of women's suffrage claimed that the violent tactics of some of the campaigners proved women did not deserve the vote. • Women should not be able to vote because they would take no part in protecting the country in time of war (an argument used more and more as war approached).

How effective were the activities of the Suffragists and Suffragettes?

LEARNING OBJECTIVES

In this lesson you will:

- learn about the public response to the issue of women's suffrage
- assess the successes of the WSPU and NUWSS and consider the wider argument of what is the best way of bringing about political change.

GETTING STARTED

As you read through this lesson, plot the events of the women's suffrage movement on a timeline, noting down the key stages of the campaigns of both the Suffragists and Suffragettes.

The Suffragists

By the end of the 19th century, the campaign for women's rights was well under way. In 1897 **Millicent Fawcett** formed the NUWSS (National Union of Women's Suffrage Societies), which united most of the existing campaign groups into a single national organisation. The NUWSS was orderly, moderate and believed in using peaceful, persuasive tactics. It was quite an impressive organisation. Its members were known as Suffragists. Their campaign was quite successful in getting the issue of votes for women into the public eye, and they won a good deal of support for their cause. Even those who were strongly opposed to the idea of female suffrage could not deny their admiration for the suffragists' devotion to their cause. Their slow but sure approach would probably have succeeded eventually, but some women did not want to wait that long.

The suffragists wrote thousands of letters to the government and they did much to raise the profile of women as serious candidates for the vote. In short, between 1897 and 1914 they worked tirelessly to abolish the myths and negative stereotypes surrounding women in British society. They were pioneering on an international level as one of the first groups of the modern age to champion female suffrage. Inevitably, however, Fawcett and her followers had to show great patience in the face of the male-dominated establishment, who were quite content to let the women protest but had no intention of letting their desires bear fruit.

The Women's Social and Political Union (WSPU) – the Suffragettes

In 1903 a group of Suffragists, frustrated by the lack of progress made by the NUWSS, broke away and formed their own organisation, the WSPU (Women's Social and Political Union). This group was led by **Emmeline Pankhurst**, and her daughter, Christabel.

SOURCE A

Millicent Fawcett formed the NUWSS, which campaigned tirelessly for women's suffrage. They used peaceful, law-abiding methods to persuade people to support their cause.

SOURCE B

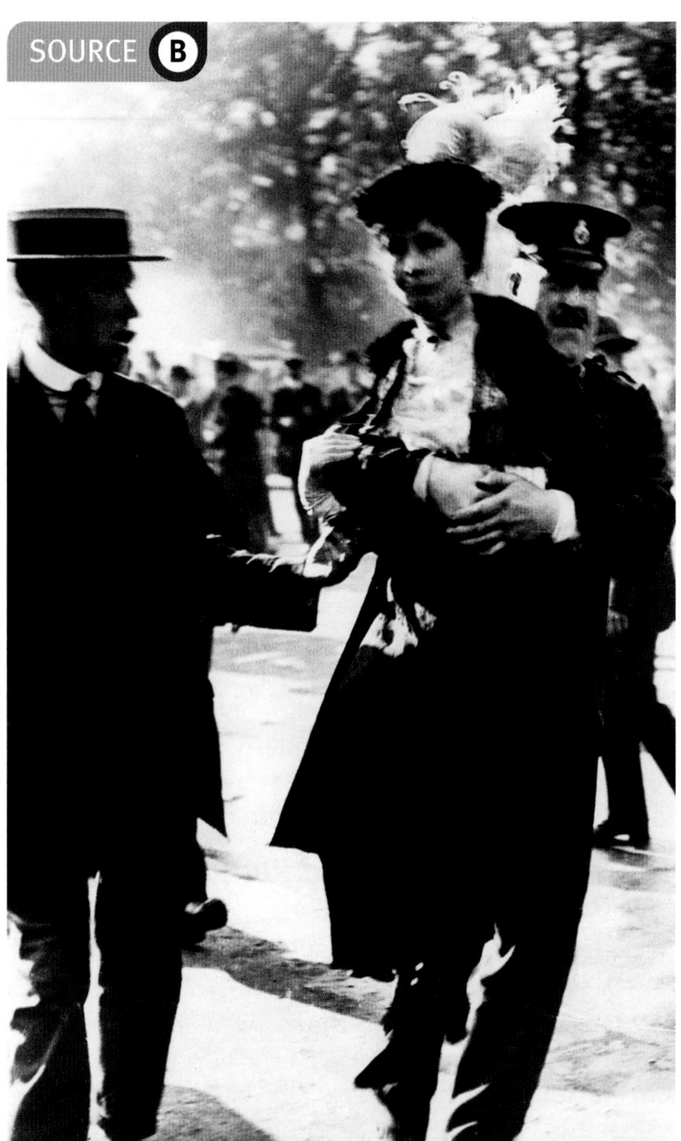

Arrests were a common occurrence among the Suffragettes. They brought attention to the movement but were not always desirable.

SOURCE C

Our heckling campaign made women's suffrage a matter of news – it had never been that before. Now the newspapers were full of us. We woke up the old suffrage associations. We had defied the police, we were awake at last. We were prepared to do something that women had never done before – to fight for themselves, for their own human rights.

From Emmeline Pankhurst's autobiography, *My Own Story*, published in 1914.

Another Pankhurst daughter, Sylvia, was also a leading figure in the movement, but her priorities were rather different. She worked in the East End of London, trying to help improve conditions for poor women in that area. This led to quarrels with her mother and sister, and eventually Sylvia formed her own organisation, the Women's Suffrage Federation, in protest against her mother's support for the First World War.

What action did the Suffragettes take?

Members of the WSPU were determined to use direct, and if necessary violent, actions to achieve their aims. The organisation was largely middle-class in nature, which made their noisy, awkward and 'unladylike' behaviour totally mystifying to their opponents. They soon became known as the 'Suffragettes'. At first their campaign consisted of demonstrations and minor acts of public disorder, such as chaining themselves to the railings outside Buckingham Palace or disturbing the meetings of political opponents. However, their frustration increased as, time and again, Parliament discussed but refused to agree proposals for women's suffrage. They turned to violent, illegal methods, such as smashing windows, arson and assaults on leading politicians.

SOURCE D

Be very careful not to open suspicious parcels arriving by post. On the other hand do not leave them lying unopened in the house. They should be dealt with carefully and promptly. These harpies [the Suffragettes] are quite capable of trying to burn us out.

A letter from Winston Churchill to his wife, written in February 1913.

KEY PEOPLE

Millicent Fawcett – *a prominent suffragist and early feminist who became president of the NUWSS. She distanced herself from the violent activities of others and focused on improving women's educational opportunities.*

Emmeline Pankhurst – *a leading British women's rights activist who helped to found the more militant Women's Social and Political Union (WSPU) (the suffragettes) – an organisation that became notorious for its militant activities.*

The Suffragette campaign reached a new peak of violence in 1913 when yet again Parliament failed to grant women the vote. There was a renewed outburst of window smashing, cutting telegraph wires and burning empty buildings. Politicians lived in dread of receiving letter bombs. Charles Hobhouse, the well-known Liberal opponent of women's suffrage, frequently received letters full of grass seed and pepper from local suffragettes who knew he suffered from hay fever. More seriously, there was an arson attack on his home which, fortunately, only succeeded in setting his back door on fire.

SOURCE E

THE CAT AND MOUSE ACT
PASSED BY THE LIBERAL GOVERNMENT
WSPU
BUY AND READ 'THE SUFFRAGETTE' PRICE 1D
WOMEN'S SOCIAL & POLITICAL UNION - LINCOLN'S INN HOUSE - KINGSWAY W.C.

Poster commenting on the 'Cat and Mouse Act' of 1913.

The 1913 Derby

Events at the famous horse race, the Derby, brought the situation to a climax. During the race, a suffragette, Emily Davison, walked out in front of the horses. She tried to grab hold of one of them, which happened to be the king's horse, Anmer, but in the collision she was knocked to the ground and fatally injured. She died in hospital four days later. It is clear that her actions were a deliberate protest, probably an attempt to draw attention to the Suffragette cause by stopping or disrupting the race. Many people have assumed that she committed suicide in order to be a martyr to the women's cause; certainly her death was treated that way by the Suffragettes. However, a return ticket was found in her handbag, suggesting that she only intended to upset the race.

The reactions of the authorities

At first many men did not take the Suffragettes seriously. Then they became exasperated as they realised that the Suffragettes were serious and were not going to give up. But above all, the authorities were rather confused about how to deal with them. The problem was that decent, well brought up young ladies were not supposed to behave like the Suffragettes. The fact that most Suffragettes came from middle-class backgrounds, were educated and apparently had quite comfortable lives, made it even harder for men to understand what they were complaining about. The frustration and hostility this caused led to many Suffragettes being very roughly treated by men, who objected to their activities, and tried to break up their demonstrations.

The tactics of the Suffragettes forced the authorities to take action against them. More and more were sent to jail as punishment for their protests. The Suffragettes responded by going on hunger strike. Scared of the consequences of women starving themselves to death, the prison authorities felt they had no choice but to force-feed the hunger strikers, which caused a public outcry and led to widespread criticism. Finally, in 1913, parliament passed what was known as the 'Cat and Mouse Act'. This allowed prisons to release hunger-strikers whose health was deteriorating, but once the women had recovered they could be arrested again and taken back to prison to continue their sentence. After her arrest in February 1913, Emmeline Pankhurst went on hunger strike. During the rest of the year she was released and re-arrested on six occasions as she repeatedly went back on hunger strike.

How effective were the campaigns of the Suffragists and Suffragettes?

The Suffragists were the earliest movement to form, and the largest, but in many respects their work, although admired, was overshadowed by the more direct, headline-grabbing activities of the Suffragettes. What they did provide was a structure for political reform and a unifying principle of women's rights that was echoed across the world. Despite their proficient and persistent campaigning their influence was not the driving force in the campaign for female suffrage.

Historians are undecided whether or not the Suffragettes' campaign was effective. They certainly caught the public's attention. The problem was that their violent tactics lost them much of the support which they might otherwise have gained through the justice of their cause. Despite several votes in parliament on the issue, by the time the First World War broke out in the summer of 1914 women's suffrage had still not been achieved. The Suffragettes abandoned their campaign and supported the war effort. As matters turned out, this was the most effective way of achieving their aims. In the end it was not violent protests and demonstrations that won women the vote, but the contribution they made to winning the war.

The work of the Suffragists and Suffragettes proved ultimately futile in the period up until 1914. Their shared objective but wildly opposing methods acted against each other and had a neutralising effect that meant both groups could simply be dismissed by the government. The women's suffrage movement in Britain at the turn of the 20th century would have been much more successful if it could have found a way to unite in the face of adversity, but each side was left to offer only bitter commentary on the other's tactics.

GradeStudio

Study Source E. What could a historian studying the Suffragettes learn from this source? Use the source and your own knowledge to explain your answer.

[6 marks]

VOICE YOUR OPINION!

How far do you think that the methods of the two groups were counter-productive?

ACTIVITIES

1 By now you should have completed your timeline of the Suffragists' and Suffragettes' campaigns for votes for women. Look over the timeline and see if you can identify any patterns. For example:

- Can you see any reasons for the increasing popularity of the Suffragettes?
- Is there a reason why the Suffragettes might have become more aggressive in their tactics?

2 Complete the three pie charts opposite by deciding on the significance of the Suffragists and Suffragettes in answers to each question. You can be as mathematical as you like and even outline the evidence that explains why you made your choices, but the most important thing is that the charts should have no blank sections and that they reflect your opinion.

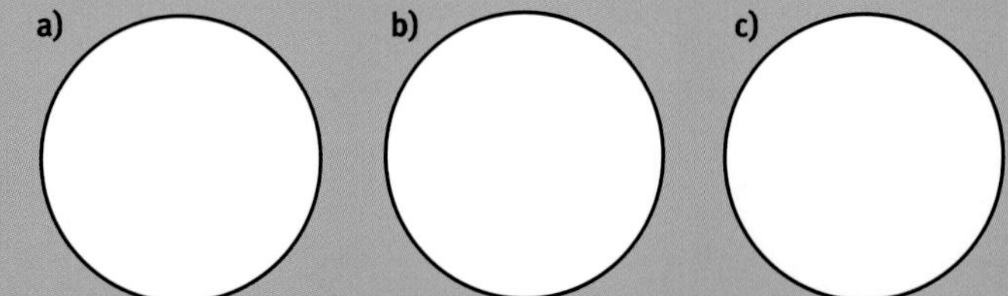

a Which movement – the Suffragists or the Suffragettes – do you think women would be more likely to support?

b Which group posed the biggest threat to the government?

c Which group do you think had the most effective tactics?

How did women contribute to the war effort?

LEARNING OBJECTIVES

In this lesson you will:

- learn about the considerable changes in the role of women in British society brought about by the First World War
- categorise and evaluate the range of roles taken on by women and their effectiveness in those roles.

GETTING STARTED

In pairs, discuss the following points:

- If the suffrage groups could not unite before the war, what do you think would have to change when war broke out?
- What benefits if any would a 'united front' bring?
- How long do you think that the two groups could work alongside one another?

Women in employment during the First World War

When the war broke out in August 1914, the women's movement immediately abandoned the struggle for the vote, and leading Suffragists and Suffragettes promised that their followers would devote themselves to the struggle of winning the war. In the first rush of enthusiasm which greeted the outbreak of war, as men flocked to join the armed forces, women prepared to take the places at work that men had left behind. However, to start with, things did not work out quite that way. Only in March 1915 did the government get round to creating a register of women willing to do war work, but even then it failed to find enough work for all the volunteers to do.

However, by this time individual women had begun to find work for themselves as drivers, bus conductors, police, railway staff – all traditionally men's work – but there was no official blessing for their efforts. In July 1915, as a result of growing frustration at how little was being done, the

SOURCE A

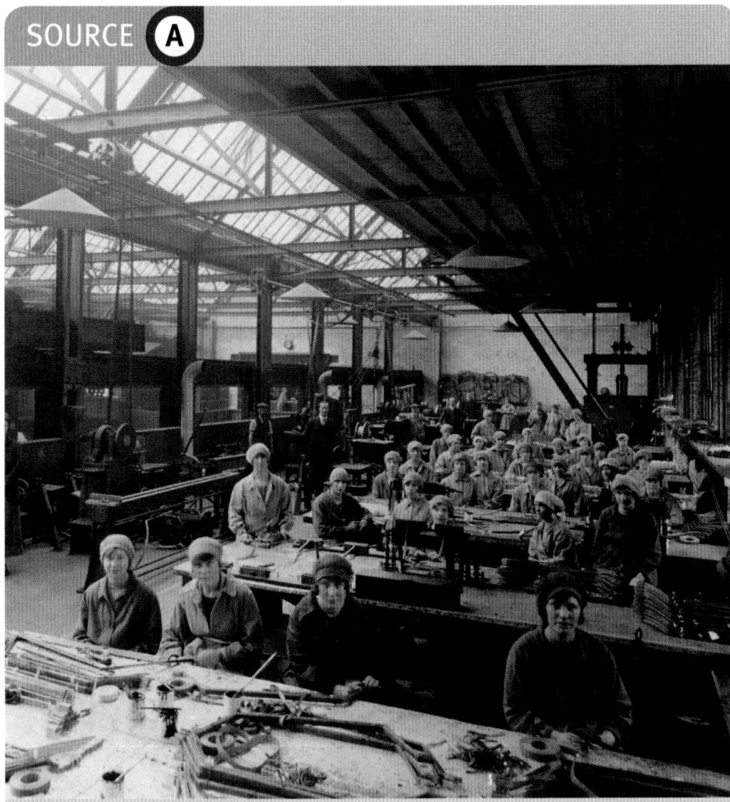

Women working in a munitions factory during the First World War, c.1915.

SOURCE B

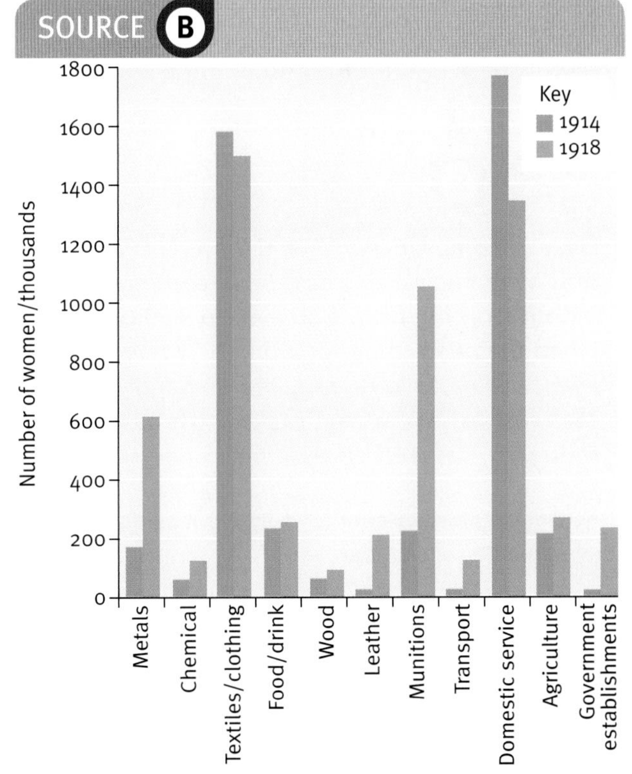

The employment of women in industry, 1914 and 1918.

Suffragettes organised a huge demonstration in London demanding the 'Right to Serve'. It seemed to do the trick; from this point on, numbers of women entering vital war work of various kinds increased rapidly.

The demand for female labour increased even more after the introduction of **conscription** in 1916. During the war a total of around five million men joined the armed forces. To keep British industry going, it was vital that their places at work were filled. Women worked in factories, steel mills, driving buses, building ships, or working in agriculture in the 'Land Army'. Perhaps most importantly, they worked in huge numbers in the munitions factories, making bullets and shells. Some women went to the war zones to help out, and did valuable work in the Voluntary Aid Detachment, Women's Auxiliary Army Corps, and Women's Royal Naval Service.

For large numbers of middle-class women, employment during the war was the first time they had received their own wage packet and been financially independent from their husbands. For many working-class women, of course, working was nothing new, but the war gave all women a much greater sense of their value to society. Although many women lost their jobs once the war was over and the men returned home, attitudes had changed permanently, and there were never again such clear divisions between men's and women's work.

SOURCE C

I was in domestic service and 'hated every minute of it' when war broke out. I was earning £2 a month working from 6.00 a.m. to 9.00 p.m. So when the need came for women 'war workers' my chance came to 'out.' I started on hand-cutting shell fuses … We worked 12 hours a day … I thought I was well off earning £5 per week.

One woman's memories of working in a munitions factory during the First World War.

KEY WORDS

Conscription – *compulsory military service.*

SOURCE D

They appear more alert, more critical of the conditions under which they work, more ready to make a stand against injustice than their pre-war selves. They have a keener appetite for experience and pleasure, and a tendency quite new to their class to protest against wrongs even before they become intolerable.

Comments about women workers from the Report of the Chief Factory Inspector, 1916.

GradeStudio

Study Sources A to D. Which source is most useful to the historian studying the role of women in the First World War? **[8 marks]**

Examiner's tip

In your answer, avoid the temptation to talk about the value of different types of sources just because they are different types. For example, if you said '*Source B is best. It is a graph and it contains facts. The photograph is just a snapshot*' you would score only 1–2 marks. Remember that the answer to this question all depends on what the historian wants to know. For example, Source A is good for showing what the inside of a munitions factory was like. However, Source B gives us information about how many women worked in munitions factories, compared to women workers in other sectors. Source C describes the feelings of women about working in wartime and Source D tells us one person's opinion of the effects on women of working in wartime. The trick is to demonstrate that, together, the sources can give us a rounded picture of different aspects of women at work in wartime Britain.

HISTORY DETECTIVE

During the First World War, what roles did women take on in your local area? Carry out research using your local library or via the internet.

How were civilians affected by the war?

LEARNING OBJECTIVES

In this lesson you will:

- learn about the government policy of DORA and how it helped the Home Front
- contextualise the impact of the war at home with regard to events on the Western Front and make an informed judgement on the effectiveness of the domestic war effort.

Recruiting

At the start of the First World War, volunteers rushed to join the armed forces. **Lord Kitchener**, the Minister for War, was in charge of raising an army. There was a genuine surge of patriotism, encouraged by the belief that Britain was right to go to war against the brutal aggression of Germany. There was also a widespread misunderstanding of what the war would be like. People had a romantic idea of war as an exciting adventure that would, in any case, be over before Christmas. Over half a million men joined up in the first six weeks of the war, many of them worried that if they waited, they might miss the 'fun'. By the end of November 1914, Parliament had authorised the recruitment of two million men.

It took some time for the early enthusiasm to fade and for an awareness of the reality of war to sink in. By 1915 casualties were mounting fast, and a massive propaganda effort was made to try to maintain the numbers prepared to enlist. There were posters everywhere urging men to join up.

SOURCE A

'Name, please.'

'Austin J. Heraty, 15 Bailey Street, Newcastle.'

'Age?'

'18, sir.'

The sergeant looked at me and said 'Did you say 18, Mr Heraty? I am very sorry, but I'll tell you what you can do. You can walk around the town, but if you come back into this room tonight, you must be 19 years of age.'

Only then did the penny drop. I walked around the town and in 60 seconds was back in the room. Soon I had signed up.

A soldier describes how he signed up for the war.

SOURCE B

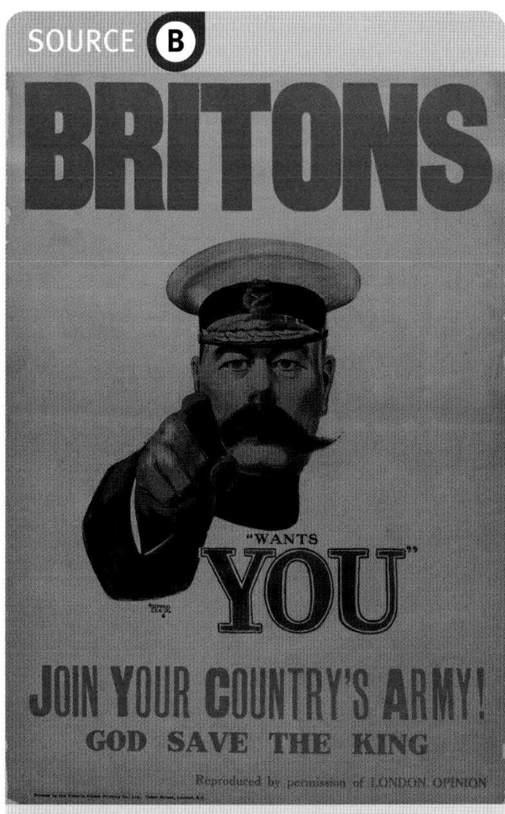

This 1914 recruitment poster depicting Secretary of State for War **Lord Kitchener** was the most famous image used in the British Army recruitment campaign of World War I. It is estimated that over three million men signed up as a result of it.

The Defence of the Realm Acts (DORA) and their impact on civilian life

The First World War had a greater impact on civilian life than any previous war. This was clearly shown by the passing of the Defence of the Realm Acts in 1914. These acts, known as 'DORA', gave the government powers to intervene in people's lives to a degree that had never been known before. This even included the introduction of British Summer Time (to allow more daylight hours to work in) and the right to water down beer in pubs (to reduce drunkenness and improve productivity).

DORA gave the government control over the newspapers and other mass communications like the radio. All news had to be approved by the government's press office, and newspapers were not

KEY PEOPLE

Lord Kitchener – *the Secretary of State for War. The first member of the military establishment to have such a role.*

allowed to tell people the truth about the casualties on the Western Front. Instead they told stories about heroic deeds and victories.

The government also had the power to force workers to stay in jobs that were considered vital, and to take over control of mines and railways. This became particularly important in 1916 when a 'munitions crisis' left soldiers short of equipment.

Conscription

Many of the soldiers who joined up at the start of the war were soon killed or wounded. Long periods of **stalemate** in the fighting were interrupted by attacks on the enemy's **trenches** in which thousands of casualties occurred in a single day. The longer it went on, the more men were needed to fight. By the spring of 1915, it was becoming clear that the number of men enlisting voluntarily would not be enough. The British government began to consider conscription. This had never been used before, and the government was worried about how controversial it might be.

National Registration Act, July 1915

As a first step towards conscription, a National Register was made of all men and women between the ages of 15 and 65 years, giving details such as age and occupation. Now at least it was possible to identify all those who might be eligible for national service.

The Derby Scheme

The National Register was followed by the 'Derby Scheme' in October 1915. This invited men to promise that they would join up if they were asked to do so. They were told that those who had a good reason not to join up would not be called up, and that no married men would be taken before all the unmarried ones had gone. Needless to say, the scheme did not work well, with less than half of those of military age being prepared to make the promise. From the government's point of view, however, it was not a waste of time, because it had now demonstrated that a voluntary approach would not work. It was now in a much stronger position to introduce conscription.

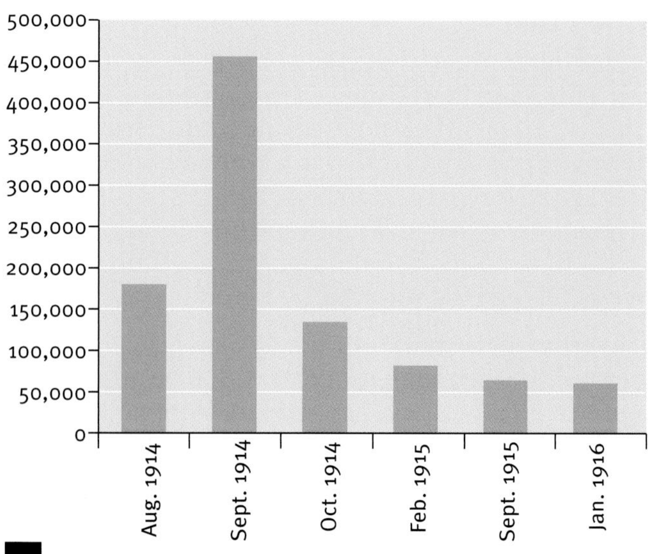

Volunteers for the army, 1914–16.

VOICE YOUR OPINION!

DORA gave the government the power to act without debate, but on some occasions it could be said that they went too far in the changes they made. For example, they reserved the right to cut the opening hours of pubs and water down beer. They also adapted the clock by introducing British Summer Time as an energy-saving measure.

Discuss with a partner whether or not you think these changes were necessary.

The Military Service Acts

In 1916, two Acts brought in conscription, first for unmarried men, and then, in May, for all men of military age (between 18 and 41 years). This did not, of course, mean that all men had to join up. Those in 'reserved occupations' doing vital war work, such as miners, could be exempted. There was also a small number, who, because of their anti-war beliefs, refused to fight. These were known as **conscientious objectors**. In all there were about 16,000 'conchies', most of whom were prepared to accept other kinds of war work, such as driving ambulances. However, about 1500 refused to co-operate in any way, and were imprisoned.

The introduction of conscription ensured that there was a hardly a family in the country which was not affected by the war. Of the five million who served in the British armed forces during the war, around 750,000 were killed and two million injured. Families at home lived in constant fear of hearing that a husband, brother or son had been killed. Everyone knew someone who had lost a loved one.

Rationing

DORA allowed the government to take over land in order to grow crops for food. It also set up the 'Land

KEY WORDS

Stalemate – *a deadlock in a battle situation where neither side makes any progress.*

Trenches – *a wartime construction intended to offer protection from destructive new weapons by placing soldiers below ground level.*

Army'. In 1914 much of Britain's food came from abroad, but German submarines, or **U-boats**, had begun sinking the ships that carried the food. This meant that more food had to be grown in Britain – and less eaten.

By 1917, under the pressure of an intensified German U-boat campaign, food was certainly in much shorter supply. In some areas of the country it became necessary to queue for coal, sugar, potatoes and margarine. The royal family announced that it would cut its food consumption by a quarter. The government tried a scheme of voluntary rationing, and when this did not work, a system of 'meatless days', which was equally useless. Eventually, individual shopkeepers and local councils began to introduce their own rationing schemes to make sure that available goods were shared around fairly. By the end of the year a national system of sugar rationing had been set up, with each household sent a rationing card which entitled the holder to half a pound of sugar a week.

As goods became scarcer, so prices rose. The government began to subsidise the price of bread and potatoes. During 1918 rationing was extended to other goods: meat in April, with the ration fixed at three quarters of a pound per week. Tea and butter followed. Ration cards, from which shopkeepers would clip 'coupons' as they were used, were issued by the government.

These measures were enough to ensure that the British people did not suffer too much during the war. In fact, for many, and particularly for the less well-off, rising wages during the war actually meant they were able to afford an improved diet.

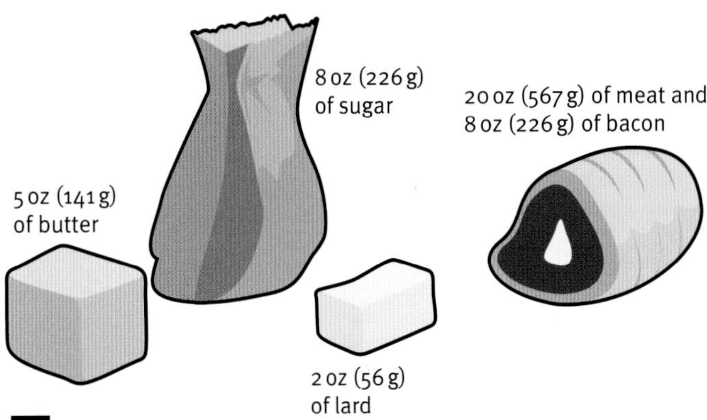

The amount of meat, bacon, butter, sugar and lard people were entitled to per week under the rationing system adopted by the government in 1918.

KEY WORDS

Conscientious objectors – *men who refused to fight because of their anti-war beliefs.*

U-boat – *a warship of German origin, later known as a submarine, that could travel entirely underwater.*

GradeStudio

Study all the sources in this chapter.

'The government's response to the war was undeniably British; when reform was needed they asked first, enforced later.'

How far do the sources in this chapter support this statement? Use details of the sources and your knowledge to explain your answer. **[10 marks]**

ACTIVITIES

Some of the changes made as a result of the Defence of the Realm Act were unpopular, and the government faced complaints of 'interfering' throughout the war.

1 Complete the table below. In the final column, aim to gauge the level of support using the following scale:

- 5 = very positively received; very popular
- 0 = had no effect on people's opinion
- minus 5 = very negatively received; very unpopular.

What had to be done?	What was achieved?	How was it introduced?	What effect did it have on the war effort?	Feeling of support?

2 Using your completed table as a reference point, do you think the British government was sensitive to the needs of all its citizens during 1914–18?

How effective was government propaganda during the war?

LEARNING OBJECTIVES

In this lesson you will:

- learn about the impact of propaganda on the British public and the methods employed by the British government
- consider the process of creating a piece of propaganda and assess the effectiveness of the British government's propaganda.

GETTING STARTED

- In pairs, list the emotions involved in persuading someone to do something for you.
- From the list you have made, evaluate which emotion would be the most effective.
- Which groups in society do you think would be the easiest to control in this way?

The use of propaganda during the war

During the First World War, the government used propaganda to try to ensure that the attitudes of the people remained positive towards the war effort. In order to win a major war, a nation needs the unswerving support of its people. Without such support it cannot rely on its workers to make extra efforts to produce vital war equipment. Nor can it rely on its citizens to go without everyday necessities which can no longer be provided. So it was essential that the British people felt that they were fighting a 'just war', that the Germans were evil and had to be stopped. It was for this reason that the government encouraged people to think that they were fighting a war to help 'brave little Belgium'. They also did nothing to stop the extraordinary stories that German soldiers were carrying out acts of atrocity such as bayoneting babies.

As the war went on, soldiers saw the realities of war. At home people realised that it was not some glorious game that 'would be all over by Christmas'. But even though disillusionment increased as losses mounted, and there seemed no prospect of an end to the fighting, there is no evidence that the British people ever lost their basic determination to see the war through to a successful end. In fact, in the early stages of the war, the general population was so positive in its attitudes that an official propaganda effort was hardly needed – the media were in any case full of pro-war messages. Almost everyone shared the same patriotic anti-German feelings, whipped up by a flood of stories about the terrible behaviour of the Germans during the invasion of Belgium. Some of the most famous propaganda stories developed by exaggeration as they passed, almost like Chinese whispers, from one newspaper to the next (see Source E on page 317).

SOURCE A

A propaganda poster by Hopps, successful in both Britain and America in confirming hatred and distrust of Germany.

SOURCE B

A First World War poster by Robert Baden-Powell depicting the shared responsibility of society in the war.

DORA made sure that what the press printed was approved by the government, but most newspaper editors were only too happy to print what the government wanted. Even private companies, notably the London Electric Railways Company, joined in the recruitment drive, printing and displaying their own propaganda posters. The government's propaganda efforts, then, could afford to concentrate on specific campaigns like saving food, buying savings bonds or recruitment into certain industries.

War Propaganda Bureau

However, early in the war, the government established a secret War Propaganda Bureau. One of its first efforts was to appoint a committee to see whether some of the German atrocities had happened. A report published in 1915 concluded (on remarkably little evidence) that many of the atrocities had indeed occurred.

Department of Information

Later in the war, Lloyd George set up a Department of Information, which co-ordinated propaganda efforts. It had four main functions:

- providing propaganda material to shape opinion at home and abroad
- supervising propaganda material for use in cinemas
- gathering political intelligence from abroad
- controlling war news released to the newspapers.

In March 1918 it became the Ministry of Information under the leadership of Lord Beaverbrook, owner of the *Daily Express* newspaper.

It is impossible to judge how effective the government's propaganda efforts were. The anti-German propaganda, however widely believed, could not have done any more than reinforce existing opinions held by the British people. The stories may, however, have been more important in persuading neutral countries, particularly the USA, to support the Allied side in the war. Most propaganda, though, does not consist of outright lies and distortions. British society came under unprecedented government control during the war, and most propaganda was simply information that the government wanted presented in the most favourable way.

ACTIVITIES

The propaganda in the First World War had to be instantly noticeable and memorable at the same time. The British public also had to be left to feel that the decision to support the war was not only theirs but in their interests.

Examine Source B.

1 Assess its effectiveness on an emotional level.
2 Now consider its effectiveness given the target audience.

Explain the effectiveness of British propaganda in the First World War. **[6 marks]**

Why were some women given the vote in 1918?

LEARNING OBJECTIVES

In this lesson you will:

- identify the key reasons for the extension of the female franchise
- explore the impact of over two decades of consistent campaigning by women for the right to vote.

GETTING STARTED

The women's rights movement in the early 20th century was arguably essential to Britain's victory in the First World War

- Write three reasons why the Suffragist and Suffragette movement was of benefit to the home front
- Share your answers with a partner
- Discuss with the rest of your class how far women had an influence in the First World War.

SOURCE A

How could we have carried on the War without women? Short of actually bearing arms in the field, there is hardly a service in which women have not been at least as active and efficient as men. But what I confess moves me still more is the problem of reconstruction when the War is over. The questions which will then necessarily arise with regard to women's labour and women's functions in the new order of things are questions in which I find it impossible to withhold from women the power and the right of making their voices heard.

H. H. Asquith, the former prime minister, speaking in 1917.

The impact of the First World War

It was women's contribution to the war effort by working on the land, in factories, in all sorts of jobs at home and with the troops that made certain they would be granted the vote. Although the majority of British women before the war had not actively supported the campaign for the vote, the experience of war work changed attitudes in many important ways. Women felt more independent, and aware that they were capable of making a much more important contribution to society than men had previously allowed. They were beginning to feel equal to men.

Women had shared the burdens and dangers of winning the war – why should they not have the same rights as men? But men's attitudes began to change as well. The sight of women doing all kinds of 'men's work' had challenged traditional ideas and stereotypes about women. This made it much harder for the opponents of women's suffrage to argue that they were not capable of voting responsibly.

The fact that the wartime government became a coalition of all the political parties also helped the women's cause. The arguments which had been used to deny them the vote before the war were now put to one side, especially once Lloyd George, a prominent supporter of women's rights, became Prime Minister in December 1916. At last there was recognition that, when the time came to deal again with the issue of the franchise, women would have to be included.

The 1918 Representation of the People Act

As the war continued, it became obvious that the franchise would, as a matter of urgency, have to be reviewed. Under the 1867 and 1884 Reform Acts, the vote was given to male householders who could prove they had lived in the same place for 12 months at the time the electoral register was drawn up. Technically, then, all the soldiers serving overseas had, by 1916, lost the right to vote. The second problem was that not all men possessed the vote, yet it was widely accepted that, since all soldiers had faced the slaughter and sacrifice of the war together, they should all have the vote after the war.

If, then, Parliament would have to review the male franchise, there would also be an opportunity to introduce votes for women. This is exactly what happened. Proposals for extending the franchise were agreed, though Parliament still could not bring itself to grant women the vote on the same basis as men. By the terms of the Representation of the People Act (1918) all adult males over the age of 21 were given the vote. However, only those women over the age of 30 who were householders or the wives of householders were allowed to vote.

Though the Act still discriminated against women, most supporters of the campaign for women's rights were prepared to accept it, on the grounds that it was obvious that votes for all women could not be long delayed. In fact, it took ten years; universal suffrage for women was achieved in 1928.

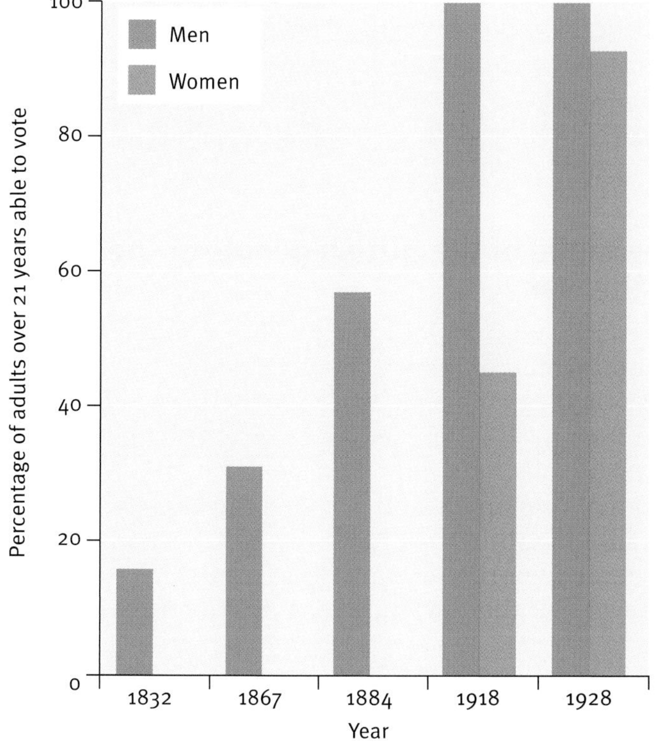

The extension of the suffrage in Britain, 1832–1928.

ACTIVITIES

'It was the war that forced change for women's rights; without it there would have been no justification for extending the franchise.'

1 Make a list of the reasons why this is a plausible argument. What is the alternative argument?
2 If this was the view of the government in 1918, what does it reveal about the opinions of two decades of consistent campaigning for female suffrage?
3 Why did the government only extend the vote to women over 30 years in 1918?
4 Write a short account of the importance of the suffrage campaign and victory in 1918. You should aim to at least provide a counter balance for the above quotation.

SOURCE B

"WHAT'S THE DISTURBANCE IN THE MARKET-PLACE?"
"IT'S A MASS MEETING OF THE WOMEN WHO'VE CHANGED THEIR MINDS SINCE THE MORNING AND WANT TO ALTER THEIR VOTING-PAPERS."

A cartoon for *Punch* by Henry Matthew Brock, published on 18 December 1918, which depicts the residual sexism undermining government reforms.

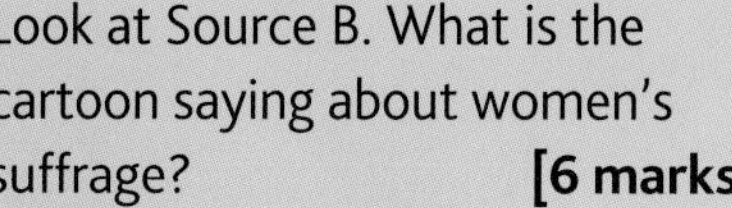

Look at Source B. What is the cartoon saying about women's suffrage? **[6 marks]**

Examiner's tip

Remember it is important to write objectively wherever possible to ensure that you give enough credibility to each argument.

What was the attitude of the British people at the end of the war towards Germany and the Paris Peace Conference?

LEARNING OBJECTIVES

In this lesson you will:

- understand the impact of the propaganda and the effects of the war on the mood of the nation
- evaluate the driving force behind people's anger and use your contextual knowledge to investigate the impacts of making impassioned judgements.

SOURCE A

British poster of 1919.

GETTING STARTED

In both Britain and France at the end of the war, political elections were looming to form the new government. Both leaders, Lloyd George and Georges Clemenceau, were anxious to be re-elected. Do you think Germany would be a big factor in their campaigns? Why?

The mood of the British people at the end of the war

Having spent over four years fighting the Germans, when the end of the war finally came in November 1918 the British people were not inclined to forgive and forget. Although, unlike France, Britain had suffered relatively little damage during the war, the casualty rate amongst the armed forces was horrifying. Almost every family had been touched by bereavement. Germany was blamed for starting the war and there was a strong desire for revenge.

Much of the propaganda of the war had portrayed the Germans as brutes and barbarians. There was little pity or sympathy in Britain for the Germans, even though there had been far more German than British casualties, and civilians in Germany had suffered much more than in Britain from shortages of food and other vital supplies. There was an almost universal desire, stirred up by the popular press, to make Germany pay. Headlines like 'Hang the Kaiser!' summed up the popular mood.

SOURCE B

The Prime Minister and his principal colleagues were astonished by the passions they encountered in the constituencies. The brave people whom nothing had daunted had suffered too much. Their feelings were lashed by the popular press into a fury. The crippled and mutilated soldiers darkened the streets. Every cottage had its empty chair. Hatred of the beaten foe, thirst for his just punishment, rushed up from the heart of deeply injured millions.

Winston Churchill, then Minister of Munitions, writing about the 1918 election campaign.

The fact that there was a General Election in Britain at the end of 1918 made matters worse, as politicians vied with each other to promise ever harsher treatment for Germany. Even Lloyd George, the Prime Minister, who well understood the dangers of treating Germany too harshly, was swept along on the wave of anti-German feeling and promised at a meeting in Bristol that 'Germany must pay to the uttermost farthing, and we shall search their pockets for it'. After the election, as preparations for the Paris Peace Conference began, he would come to regret having encouraged the British public's thirst for revenge.

Different attitudes about the treatment of Germany at the Paris Peace Conference

Lloyd George was one of the outstanding personalities of the Conference of the Paris Peace Conference of 1919. However, he had a difficult task in balancing his own personal views about how to treat Germany with those of the British people he was representing. He was under a lot of pressure to insist on a harsh peace, even though he knew that this would be disastrous in leaving Germany resentful and more likely to cause trouble in future. In fact, by the time the conference assembled in January 1919, Lloyd George was not alone in realising that the more extreme demands of the British public could never be met.

VOICE YOUR OPINION!

Was Lloyd George responsible for manipulating public opinion or do you think the reverse is true – that the public hatred of Germany developed during the war forced him to be more forceful with the peace settlement?

ACTIVITIES

1 Study Sources A and B. What do these suggest that Britain would do to the defeated German nation as the armistice was signed?

2 'Squeeze them until the pips squeak' was the phrase used by Lloyd George before the 1919 conference held in the Palace of Versailles. Look at the diagram below and try to explain the sources of anger for a) the government and b) the people.

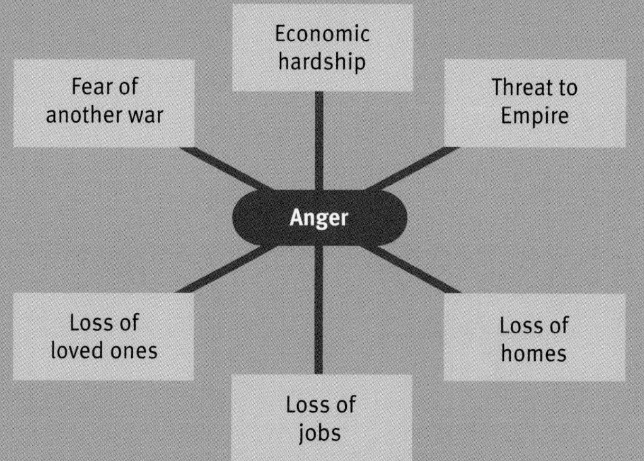

3 Return to the party political broadcast you created at the start of this chapter (page 309). How far had the social and economic situation changed for the people of Britain by 1918? Were people still worried about the same issues?

GradeStudio

Study Source A. 'This source is clearly biased against the Germans so is of no value to the historian studying the Paris Peace Conference.' Explain whether you agree or disagree with this view using details from the source and your own knowledge. **[8 marks]**

Unit A972 assessment: British Depth Study, 1890-1918

Your chosen British Depth Study will be the focus of the second of the written question papers you will take. The paper will be a source-based exercise, with the main focus on AO3 (analysis and evaluation of sources), but, as you will also have to use your knowledge and understanding of the period to help you answer the questions, AO1 and AO2 (recall and explanation) will also be important.

The paper will consist of a set of sources on an issue taken from the Depth Study, along with no fewer than five and no more than seven compulsory questions. These questions will all be about the sources, but will be of many different types. Below you will find examples of some of these question types. The first deals with the issue of reliability – whether or not you can believe what a source tells you.

Unit A972 assessment: Britain and the First World War

The use of propaganda

Study the sources carefully. Then answer **all** the questions.

Source A

Even for those who were not keen to join the army, there were enormous pressures to sign up. The government carried out a skilful propaganda campaign which portrayed the Germans as evil beasts. It was said that they had bayonetted babies and murdered nuns on their march through Belgium. Recruitment posters emphasised the need to help the country and to protect women and children from the horrors of war. Men who did not join up were made to feel like cowards.

An extract from a recent history book describing attitudes at the beginning of the war.

Source B

RED CROSS OR IRON CROSS?

WOUNDED AND A PRISONER
OUR SOLDIER CRIES FOR WATER.
THE GERMAN "SISTER"
POURS IT ON THE GROUND BEFORE HIS EYES.
THERE IS NO WOMAN IN BRITAIN
WHO WOULD DO IT.
THERE IS NO WOMAN IN BRITAIN
WHO WILL FORGET IT.

A British poster issued early in the war.

Source C

A Call
from
the Trenches.

(Extract from a letter from the trenches.)

"I SAW a recruiting advertisement in a paper the other day. I wonder if the men are responding properly – they would if they could see what the Germans have done in Belgium. And after all, it's not so bad out here – cold sometimes, and the waiting gets on our nerves a bit, but we are happy and as fit as fiddles. I wonder if .... has joined, he certainly ought to."

Does '...........................' refer to you?

If so

ENLIST TO-DAY.
God Save the King.

A recruiting advertisement in* The Times, *15 April 1915.

Source D

TIME FOR
ONE MORE
MITCHELL'S
GOLDEN DAWN
CIGARETTES.

A British advertisement for cigarettes in 1915.

Source E

According to what the British newspaper, The Times, *has heard from Cologne, via Paris, the unfortunate Belgian priests who refused to ring the church bells when Antwerp was taken were sentenced to hard labour.*

***Written in the Italian newspaper,* Corriere della Sera.**

Source F

According to information which has reached Corriere della Sera, from Cologne, via London, it is confirmed that the barbaric conquerors of Antwerp punished the unfortunate Belgian priests for their heroic refusal to ring the church bells by hanging them as living clappers to the bells, with their heads down.

***Written in* Le Matin.**

QUESTIONS

1. Study Source A.
   How much could a historian studying the use of propaganda in the First World War learn from this source? Use details of the source and your knowledge to explain your answer. (6 marks)
2. Study Source B.
   What is the message of this source? (8 marks)
3. Study Sources B and C.
   Which of these two sources do you think would have had the greater impact on the British people? Use details of the sources and your knowledge to explain your answer. (8 marks)
4. Study Source D.
   In what ways could this source be useful to a historian studying the First World War? (8 marks)
5. Having read Source E, are you surprised by what is said in Source F? Use the sources and your knowledge to explain your answer. (8 marks)
6. Study all the sources.
   'The use of propaganda in the First World War was subtle and extremely clever'.

   How far do the sources in this exercise agree with this interpretation? Use details of the sources and your knowledge to explain your answer. Remember to identify the sources you use. (12 marks)

Unit A972 assessment: The Liberal Reforms

Old Age Pensions and National Insurance

Study the sources carefully. Then answer all the questions.

Source A

A photograph showing living conditions for a London East End family in the early years of the 20th century.

Source B

David Lloyd George became Chancellor of the Exchequer in 1908. In his first budget speech he said that the government was going to introduce old age pensions. Old people would no longer be dependent on the Poor Law or the kindness of their friends and relatives. 'We are', he said 'lifting the shadow of the workhouse from the homes of the poor'.

An account of the work of Lloyd George, from a school textbook written in 1999.

Source C

When the Old Age Pensions began, life was transformed for the aged. They were relieved of anxiety. They were suddenly rich. Independent for life! At first when they went to the Post Office to get their pension tears of gratitude would run down the cheeks of some – and there were flowers from gardens and apples from trees for the girl who merely handed them the money.

An extract from a novel by Flora Thompson. She had once been a Post Office worker handing out the benefits.

Source D

Darby is 72, with a cataract in one eye and very little sight in the other. His wife Joan was 71 last October. They have lived on money given to them by their son and the meagre earnings from Joan's cleaning work.

Interviewed by a reporter Darby chuckled and said 'It isn't wealth. No you couldn't call it wealth. But it's something for sure. The pension is not a charity. It's a right,' Darby said proudly.

An article in the Daily Express on 2 January 1909.

Source E

Dear Sir,

The strength of this kingdom, in all its past struggles, has been its great wealth and the sturdy independent character of its people.

The measure will destroy both.

It will take the wealth from its possessors by unjust taxation and will sap the character of the people by teaching them to rely, not on their own efforts, but on the State.

A letter written to The Times newspaper in 1908 complaining about the decision to introduce pensions.

Source F

THE PHILANTHROPIC HIGHWAYMAN.
"I'LL MAKE 'EM PITY THE AGED POOR!"

A cartoon from Punch in 1909. It shows Lloyd George as a highwayman carrying out a robbery to pay for old age pensions.

Source G

THE DAWN OF HOPE.

Mr. LLOYD GEORGE'S National Health Insurance Bill provides for the insurance of the Worker in case of Sickness.

Support the Liberal Government in their policy of SOCIAL REFORM.

A government poster advertising National Health Insurance. The doctor sitting by the bed is Lloyd George.

QUESTIONS

1 Study Source A.
What can you tell from this source about what it was like to be poor in the early years of the twentieth century? Use details of the source and your knowledge to explain your answer. (6 marks)

2 Study Sources B and C.
Which of these sources gives a more reliable account of the importance of old age pensions? Explain your answer fully, using details from the sources and your own knowledge. (8 marks)

3 Study Sources C and D.
Which of these sources do you think gives the better impression of the impact of old age pensions? Use details of the sources and your knowledge to explain your answer. (8 marks)

4 Study Sources E and F.
How similar are these two sources? Use details of the sources and your knowledge to explain your answer. (8 marks)

5 Study Source G.
'This source is particularly important to a historian studying the impact of the Liberal reforms because it was issued by the government.' How far do you agree with this statement? Use details of the source and your knowledge to explain your answer. (8 marks)

6 Study all the sources.
'The Liberal reforms were a huge benefit to the British people.'
How far do the sources in this exercise support this statement? Use details of the sources and your knowledge to explain your answer. Remember to identify the sources you use. (12 marks)

Unit A972 assessment: The Suffragettes

Grade Studio

How important were the Suffragettes in helping win the vote for women?

Study the sources carefully. Then answer all the questions.

Source A

We believe that if we get the vote it will mean better conditions for our unfortunate sisters. We believe that only through new laws can any improvements be made and that new laws will not be passed until women have the same power as men to put pressure on governments.

We have tried every way. We have presented larger petitions than were ever presented before and succeeded in holding greater public meetings than men ever held. But we have been criticised and had contempt poured upon us.

Violence is the only way that we have to get the power which every citizen should have – the same kind of power that the worst of men have. The same kind of power that the wife-beater has, the same power that the drunkard has.

Emmeline Pankhurst speaking in her defence in court in 1912.

Source C

Hasn't Mrs Pankhurst the sense to see that the very worst kind of campaigning for the vote is to try to intimidate or blackmail a man into giving her what he would gladly give her otherwise.

David Lloyd George, a member of the government, speaking in 1913 after his house had been bombed by Suffragettes.

Source D

By 1913 the activities of the militant Suffragettes had reached the stage at which nothing was safe from their attacks. Churches were burnt, public buildings and private residences destroyed, bombs were exploded, the police and individuals were assaulted and meetings broken up. The feeling amongst MPs, caused by the extravagant and lawless action of the militants, hardened their opposition to the women's demands. So on 6 May the House of Commons voted against giving women the vote by a majority of 47.

Viscount Ullswater, a senior official in the House of Commons in 1913, writing in 1925 about the campaign for votes for women.

Source B

A poster issued in 1912 by a group of woman artists supporting votes for women.

Source E

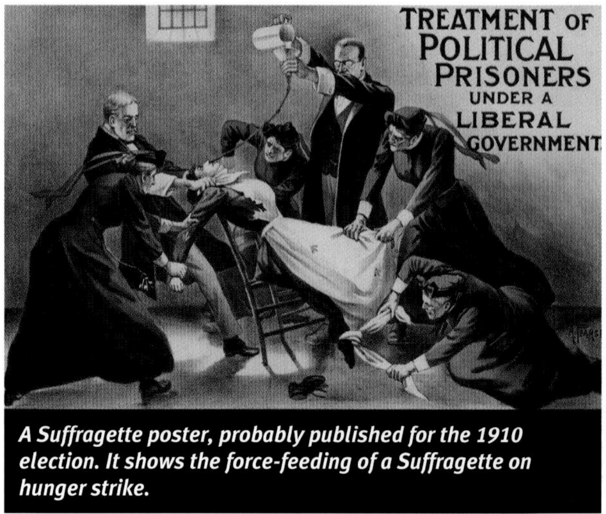

A Suffragette poster, probably published for the 1910 election. It shows the force-feeding of a Suffragette on hunger strike.

Source F

It must be remembered that the behaviour of the Suffragettes served a very important purpose. Without it the government could have (and did before 1913) stated that there was no real 'evidence' that women even wanted the vote. The militants destroyed this theory. By destroying property, staging demonstrations and creating riots, the militants kept 'the cause' constantly in the public eye.

The effects of World War are important because they raised women in the eyes of Parliament and all men who remained in Britain – and they also raised many women's estimation of themselves. But the militancy of the Suffragettes is the main reason why women gained the vote in 1918.

An extract from an article written by a male member of the British Suffrage Society in 1996.

Source G

It was in the year 1918 that disaster took place. A member of the House of Commons stood up and said, 'If you are extending the vote to our brave soldiers, how about our brave munitions workers?' That argument was difficult to resist. Then ... 'How about our brave women munitions workers?' And having agreed to the first argument it was impossible to resist the second.

An extract from the memoirs of Lord Birkenhead, a Conservative politician.

QUESTIONS

1 Study Source A.

What could a historian studying the Suffragettes learn from this source? Use details of the source and your knowledge to explain your answer. (6 marks)

2 Study Source B.

'This source is obviously biased, so it is of no value to a historian studying attempts by women to win the vote.' How far do you agree? Use details of the source and your knowledge to explain your answer. (8 marks)

3 Study Sources C and D.

How far do you agree that these two sources show the Suffragettes did not have the support of men in the country? Use details of the sources and your knowledge to explain your answer. (8 marks)

4 Study Source E.

Why do you think this picture was produced? Use details of the source and your knowledge to explain your answer. (8 marks)

5 Study Sources F and G.

How similar are these two sources? Use details of the sources and your knowledge to explain your answer. (8 marks)

6 Study all the sources.

'The Suffragettes were vital in helping women win the vote.'

How far do the sources in this exercise support this statement? Use details of the sources and your knowledge to explain your answer. Remember to identify the sources you use. (12 marks)

GradeStudio

Study the source and then answer the question which follows.

Source A

WE WANT WORK
TAX THE FOREIGNER NOT US
BRITISH WORKERS UNEMPLOYED
UNEMPLOYED
"THE PEOPLE'S" BUDGET!
GENIAL FOREIGNER: — HOW THEY MUST WISH THAT MR LLOYD GEORGE HAD TAXED US INSTEAD OF THEM

A Conservative Party election poster of 1910. The Conservatives wanted to tax foreign trade rather than raise income tax to pay for social reforms.

1 Study Source A.
Do you think this gives a reliable impression of the impact of the 'People's Budget'? Use details of the poster and your own knowledge to explain your answer. **[8 marks]**

Examiner's tip

Many questions will deal with the issue of reliability, though not all will ask about it as directly as this one. Avoid the temptation of answering on the basis of the type of source you are given. Weak students will look at Source A and say that it is not reliable because it is a cartoon, and cartoons are supposed to make people laugh. Such answers ignore the content of the source – what it actually says or shows. Without judging the reliability of the content, you will not get anywhere.
Look at the detail of the source – is it over-emotional or using loaded language? Does it make fun of someone, or show them in an unflattering way? These kinds of details can reveal the bias or one-sidedness of a source. One of the best ways of working out whether you can trust a source is to check its details against other information available to you. This may be other sources on the paper, or your own knowledge. This kind of checking is called cross-referencing. Lastly, you can get clues about reliability by considering the purpose of the person who created the source. What impact did the artist who drew this cartoon want to have on his/her audience? Given its purpose, is it likely that this poster would give a fair impression of events?

Answering the question

STEP 1: Identify the claims that the cartoon is making. Its message is that the 'People's Budget' has made people unemployed, and that if the Conservative plan of taxing foreign trade had been followed instead, this would not have happened.

STEP 2: Are these claims fair and accurate? You should know from your own knowledge that the Liberals' reforms were strongly resisted by the rich, and that the People's Budget was at first rejected by the House of Lords. The Conservatives were behind this opposition, so their views in this cartoon are likely to be one-sided.

STEP 3: Would the Conservatives have any particular purpose for publishing this poster? We know that it was an election poster, so obviously they were trying to persuade people to vote for them. Is this likely to make what they say about the People's Budget reliable?

Student's response

Read the following answer. Does it evaluate the reliability of the cartoon both by checking its content (cross-reference) and analysing its purpose?

Source A is saying that British workers would have preferred the Conservatives to put up taxes on trade rather than pay for the Liberals' reforms through income tax. This is not true, though. The amount of extra tax people had to pay was very small because most of the reforms were paid for through insurance schemes. This poster was not printed to tell the truth because it is an election poster, so it is unreliable.

Examiner's comment

This is a strong answer. It shows detailed contextual knowledge in what it says about the impact of the People's Budget, and uses this effectively to undermine the reliability of the poster's claims. What it fails to do is move on from this to consider the purpose of the poster, limiting itself to undeveloped comment about source type (it's an election poster so it will be unreliable). If it had gone on to say, for example, that its purpose was to scare people with the threat of unemployment so that they would vote against the Liberals, then it would have reached the highest level.

Study the source and then answer the question which follows.

Source B

FEMALE SUFFRAGE
GREAT LIBERAL MEETING
TO-DAY AT 3
THE SHRIEKING SISTER.
The Sensible Woman. "YOU HELP OUR CAUSE? WHY, YOU'RE ITS WORST ENEMY!"

A cartoon of 1906 from a British magazine.

2 Study Source B.

Why do you think this cartoon was published in 1906? Use details of the cartoon and your own knowledge to explain your answer. **[7 marks]**

Answering the Question

STEP 1: Identify what the cartoonist was saying, the message he was trying to get across to his audience. As with all cartoons there are several sub-messages; for example that the Suffragettes are extremists. However, it is the main message of the cartoon that you should base your answer upon. This is the idea that the Suffragettes are harming their own cause by using extreme methods.

STEP 2: Why was this message particularly relevant in 1906? The WSPU had been started in 1903 and by 1906 the Suffragettes were coming increasingly to the public's attention, disrupting public meetings and using tactics like chaining themselves to railings as a protest. Many people, including more moderate women, were alarmed by these developments.

STEP 3: Given the message and the context, why did the cartoonist draw this cartoon? We can presume his sympathies were with the 'sensible woman' in the cartoon, and that he wanted to warn potential Suffragettes of the harm they could do to the cause of Votes for Women, or alternatively to remind men that there were many non-violent women who were working quietly for the vote so that they would not be put off supporting women because of the acts of the Suffragettes.

Examiner's tip

There's a question within a question here, and the best answers will succeed in dealing with both aspects. First, why was the cartoon published, and second, why in 1906? It would be possible to answer by dealing with only one of these aspects, but if you do this you will not score highly. Good answers will be based on a sound interpretation of the cartoon. This means identifying the cartoonist's message and, as the question demands, using details of the cartoon to support your interpretation. Once you have done this you will have to address why this message had particular relevance in 1906, which means using your knowledge of what was happening at the time to explain the cartoonist's purpose in representing events in this way.

Student's response

Read the following answer. Does it successfully explain why the cartoon was published, using analysis of its context, message and purpose?

The cartoonist is probably quite in favour of votes for women because he seems to be saying that he is worried that the violence of the Suffragettes will do more harm than good. You can see this because the sensible woman talks about 'our cause', meaning that she too wants the vote but knows the Suffragettes might put people off. The cartoonist wants to get this message across and is using the sensible woman to do it. He would only do this if he wanted votes for women too, so his purpose is to try to persuade people not to lose sympathy with the more moderate women who are fighting for the vote.

Examiner's comment

This is a methodical and clear answer. It successfully interprets the cartoon and gives a plausible purpose that the cartoonist might have had in drawing it. It would certainly earn a good mark, but to reach the top level it would have to show some contextual knowledge of why this cartoon was published at that particular time, that is, in 1906. The cartoon itself holds a clue that could be used. It shows the women outside the venue for a 'Great Liberal Meeting'. In 1906 the Liberal government had just won an election and come to power. The Suffragettes had disrupted many of the election meetings, but there was hope that the Liberals would be more sympathetic towards the women's cause than the previous government. The cartoonist obviously did not want the Suffragettes' violence to spoil this opportunity.

This final question deals with women working during the First World War.

Study the source and then answer the question which follows

Source C

A painting from 1917 showing women munitions workers. It was painted by an official government artist whose task it was to paint pictures of various aspects of life during the First World War.

3 Study Source C.
How useful is this picture as evidence about the role of women during the First World War? Use details of the source and your own knowledge to explain your answer. **[8 marks]**

Answering the question

STEP 1: What does the source show? You can see women working in a munitions factory. What impressions are you given about this work, and the women doing it? Do you get a positive or a negative impression from the picture? Let's hope we can all agree that the artist has made the women look well organised, purposeful and happy in their work.

STEP 2: Is the impression given by the picture accurate? If not, we cannot say that the picture is useful as information. Use your knowledge of what it was like for women to work in munitions factories to judge the reliability of the picture.

STEP 3: If you decide that the picture is not factually accurate, then ask yourself why the artist might have wanted to represent events in this way. In 1917 the war was still going on – what possible purposes would the government have had for wanting to give a positive impression of women's role in the war? The utility of this source as evidence about women's role in the war is perhaps more a matter of what the government wanted people to think than as a factual record of what women did.

Examiner's tip

Questions that deal with the usefulness, or utility, of sources will often be asked on the British Depth Study paper. Basic answers to such questions simply state that the source is useful for the information it provides. Not much better than this are answers that deny a source's usefulness because of what it does not tell you. What these answers miss is any evaluation of the source – any sense of doubting whether it can be trusted or not. If you cannot believe a source, you have to question its usefulness. It cannot be factual information, but perhaps it might still be evidence of something else – maybe as evidence of why or how someone might wish to mislead or misrepresent events. The fact that Source C was painted by an official artist might make a difference to how you could use the source as evidence. You should consider that the government might want women's work to be portrayed in a certain way, to give a particular message to the viewer. This is where your knowledge of the topic can come in, to help you judge whether or not the picture is consistent with this. The highest marks in utility questions will always go to answers which do not simply accept the source at face value, but which use source evaluation to judge its usefulness.

Student's response

Read the following answer. Does it successfully explain the utility of the source?

The source is useful about women and the war but you have to be a bit careful about it. Because it's an official picture, the artist sets out to represent the women in a certain way. The artist wants the viewer to sympathise with the women, and to admire them. You can tell by the way the artist focuses on the girl in the middle. She's a typical, hardworking person, and she's putting her life in danger by carrying round the explosives. The artist makes her a symbol of women's war effort. This doesn't make the picture totally unreliable, because women did work in munitions factories, and it was dangerous, but it does mean you need to be careful about the evidence you get from it.

Examiner's comment

This answer is based on a real understanding of the nature of the source. Its evaluation of the content of the source is very effective, and it would certainly earn a high mark. However, one element is still missing. To get into the top level the answer needs to make it clear what exactly the source is useful for, despite the doubts about its reliability. A sentence concluding that the real utility of the source is as evidence about the impression the government wanted people to have of women's war work, rather than as evidence about the work itself, would have done the trick.

How far did British society change between 1939 and the mid-1970s?

This chapter deals with the extent to which British society changed in the three decades following the end of the Second World War. After confronting military challenges on the Continent, Britain now faced the unexpected challenge of dealing with social changes closer to home. This chapter deals with the effects of three such changes on British society:

1 The arrival of different immigrant groups to Britain.
2 The growth of feminism.
3 The birth of the teenager.

The first part of the chapter will explore the different reasons which contributed to immigration to Britain during this period. It will then look at the different experiences which immigrants encountered and explain the contribution they made to British society. One question to explore is the extent to which their contribution to British society came in spite of, rather than because of, their experiences.

The second change in British society will be explored by looking at the different ways in which women were discriminated against in British society. It will then look at the extent to which meaningful change had taken place for women by the end of this historical period. Finally, it will analyse the causes of some of these changes. One question to explore is whether or not the growth of the feminist movement was the pivotal factor in securing some of these changes.

Finally, the phenomenon of the teenager will be introduced, with a study of the different factors which greatly changed the lives of young people in Britain. Following on from this, it will look at features of their behaviour throughout the 1960s. Lastly, it will look at the extent to which life had really changed for teenagers during this period. It will also analyse the degree to which these changes affected all, as opposed to just a few, young people in Britain at this time.

By the end of this chapter, students should be more aware of the type of changes which took place, the causes of those changes, and the effect they had on British society. Arguably, the main challenge is to investigate the links and connections between these three different social changes. It is important to establish which of these social changes had the most effect on British society during this time. A further question to ask is whether these changes reinforced each other, rather than it just being a coincidence that there were three movements for change occurring concurrently.

Another key theme in this chapter is the role of politicians in bringing about these social changes, for example by government legislation and Private Members' Bills. It is also worth considering the role of foreign affairs, such as the decline of the Empire and the creation of the European Economic Community. Finally, the significance of individuals throughout this period cannot be underestimated, for example Bob Marley, Enoch Powell, Germaine Greer and Elvis Presley.

One of the most important aspects of any period of change is that there will always be a mixture of those who have and have not approved of it along the way. In the case of this period, another key question to answer is whether or not there appeared to be any consensus within British society towards the changes that took place.

Overall, the story of these changes, and the reaction to them, did not end in the 1970s. The issues surrounding multiculturalism, gender discrimination and the lives of young people prove that these social changes are still very much a part of our lives today. However, this chapter puts some of those modern-day issues into context and, therefore, the past is once again a vital tool with which to explain the present.

What impact did the Second World War have on the British people?

LEARNING OBJECTIVES

In this lesson you will:

- learn to understand the impact of the Second World War on the British people
- be able to analyse the message of a source concerning this issue.

Fact file

Second World War in Britain 1939 – Britain declares war on Germany on 3 September; **evacuation** of civilians from major cities.
1940 – **Rationing** begins; Germany begin **Blitzkrieg** (The Blitz)
1941 – The Blitz ends
1942 – **Beveridge** Report published
1945 – Germany surrenders

Impact of the Second World War on British People

The Second World War had a far more significant impact on the British population than the First World War (1914–18). This was mainly due to the threat of German bombers (**Luftwaffe**) and the consequent effect it had on the population. Overall, there were five main areas in which this impact was most acutely felt.

1 German Blitzkrieg – this was a continuous bombing campaign by the German Luftwaffe across many towns and cities in Britain until May 1941. The goal of the Blitz was to break the morale of the British but despite the heavy loss of life and property, Britain arguably became more resolved to defeat Hitler. However, it caused a great deal of destruction in Britain: 40,000 **civilians** lost their lives and more than a million houses were destroyed or damaged in London alone.

2 Rationing – rationing was introduced in Britain so that the population did not starve because of the restrictions in food imports and the shortage of workers in the countryside. During the war, many foods, furniture and petrol were rationed. The government issued everyone with an identity card and ration book. The books contained **coupons** that were signed by the shopkeeper every time rationed goods were bought, which meant that people could only buy the amount they were allowed.

3 Evacuations – because of the blitzkreig, large numbers of people in Britain, mainly children, were evacuated to safer areas of the country. Some children were even sent abroad (e.g. to Canada, the USA and Australia). One consequence of this was that many people in the countryside discovered the poor health and hygiene of British children. This helped to pave the way for the Beveridge Plan.

4 Women – women made an enormous contribution to the war effort during 1939–45. The Women's Land Army and the Women's Voluntary Service worked on farms and helped to clear up after the Blitz. All parts of the military were open for women to join, with some even used as secret agents in occupied France. More than 350,000 women worked in civil defence (air raid precautions, fire fighting and nursing) as well as the munitions factories, construction and manufacturing. They also looked after families in the absence of fathers.

5 Beveridge Report – in 1942 **Winston Churchill**'s Conservative government commissioned Sir William Beveridge to conduct a report into the state of Britain and to assess the effectiveness of existing schemes of social insurance. Beveridge identified five 'Giant Evils' in British society (want, disease, ignorance, squalor and idleness) that needed to be overcome. In 1945, after a **landslide** election victory, the new Labour government, led by **Clement Atlee**, set out to solve these problems with a series of Welfare Reforms that would care for people from the 'cradle to the grave'. These included the Family Allowances Act (1945), the National Insurance Act (1946) and the National Health Service Act (1946).

KEY WORDS

Blitzkrieg – *a swift and violent military offensive with intensive aerial bombardment.*

Luftwaffe – *German term for an airforce.*

KEY PEOPLE

William Beveridge – *produced a report in 1942 that served as the basis for the post-war welfare state.*

Winston Churchill – *Prime Minister of the United Kingdom, 1940–45.*

Clement Atlee – *Prime Minister of the United Kingdom, 1945–51.*

SOURCE A

A cartoon first published in the *Daily Express* on 14 October 1940.

The impact of the evacuations

The first official evacuations took place two days before the Second World War began but within a few months, the majority of the evacuees were returned to their homes. However, once the Germans had completed a swift conquest of France, many children were evacuated and this was intensified as the Blitz began, continuing right up until the end of the war. It was a scary experience for children since they had no idea where they were going to and unsure about whether or not they would see their family again. However, it was also exciting as many of them would never have experienced life outside their home town.

The impact on class relations

The war caused the middle classes to be increasingly aware of the condition of working-class children. The evacuees' move to the countryside caused many working-class and middle-class people to live together and they therefore learned a great deal about each other. The clearest expression of this shift in attitude was seen in the Beveridge Report of 1942 which aimed to provide a welfare state that would substantially improve the lives of working-class people in Britain.

The impact of war on family life

There were other, more negative, effects of the war on children stemming from the high number of absent fathers. Some have attempted to link this to rising crime and delinquency, although it is important to avoid stereotyping.

SOURCE B

Dear Mother,

I had a very adventerous jorney. I did enjoy the train ride.My school teacher is fantastic.What kind of clothes are you making?I hope you are safe from the raids.You told me that fires started last night. I would absolutely love to see the barrage balloons. Where I am is wonderful. My new school is very fine. My new teacher Caroline is superb. I hope the war will end soon.

Love from Margeret.

Letter written by a modern-day child from the perspective of a child evacuee.

ACTIVITIES

1 Look at Source B. What does this source suggest about the experiences of children as evacuees?

What is the message of the cartoon in Source A?

[6 marks]

What immigrants were living in Britain in 1945?

LEARNING OBJECTIVES

In this lesson you will:

- learn about immigration to Britain before, during and after the Second World War.

Immigration before the Second World War

Immigration essentially means the one-way movement of individuals from one territory to another. In a sense, Britain is a nation of immigrants, as ever since prehistoric times the British Isles have witnessed the arrival of successive groups of newcomers (see the table below).

Era	Newcomers	Cause
Pre-1066	Romans, Saxons, Vikings	Invasion force
1066	Normans	Invasion force
1500s	Dutch Protestants	Religious persecution
1680s	French Protestants	Religious persecution
1840s	Irish	Potato Famine in Ireland
1880s	Jews	**Pogroms** in Russia
1914–18	Refugees	To escape the fighting in mainland Europe
1939–45	Refugees	To escape Nazi rule
1946	Eastern Europeans	To escape from **Communism**

The First World War witnessed a significant number of Afro-Caribbean immigrants arriving in Britain to fight. Due to their experience back home, many were able to work in the war industries and the merchant navy. There was therefore a substantial black population in Britain before the Second World War, especially around the ports. The First World War also saw many wounded Belgian soldiers arrive in Britain, with around 10,000 being recorded as living in this country in the census of 1921.

Throughout the 1930s, some 10,000 Jewish children arrived in Great Britain as refugees. Many would later continue their journey to the USA and Canada, though a significant number would remain in this country after the war.

Before the Second World War, the 1931 census showed that around 45,000 people living in Britain claimed Poland as their birthplace.

The data from censuses reveal that Britain could arguably claim to be a **multicultural** society prior to 1939.

Immigration during the Second World War

During the war, the Allies captured thousands of German and Italian troops in Europe. Consequently, over 300,000 German and Italian Prisoners of War (POWs) were brought to Britain. Once the war had ended, many of these prisoners did not want to return to their homeland and decided to stay in Britain, where they became known as displaced persons. In addition, there were many work-permit schemes which recruited Italians, Ukrainians, Austrians and Poles. The total number of **aliens** recruited under the Attlee government (1945–51) was around 345,000.

Furthermore, the contribution of both the GIs and Commonwealth soldiers were hugely significant to the Allied victory in Europe, and many of these soldiers continued their lives in Britain after the war.

Immigration after 1948

Therefore, there were significant numbers of immigrants already living in Britain by 1945. They came as a result of problems in their own countries and the need to help Britain during wartime. However, it was after the war, particularly from 1948, that large numbers of immigrants began to arrive in Britain.

ACTIVITY

Think about why the census is such a reliable source of information for historians.

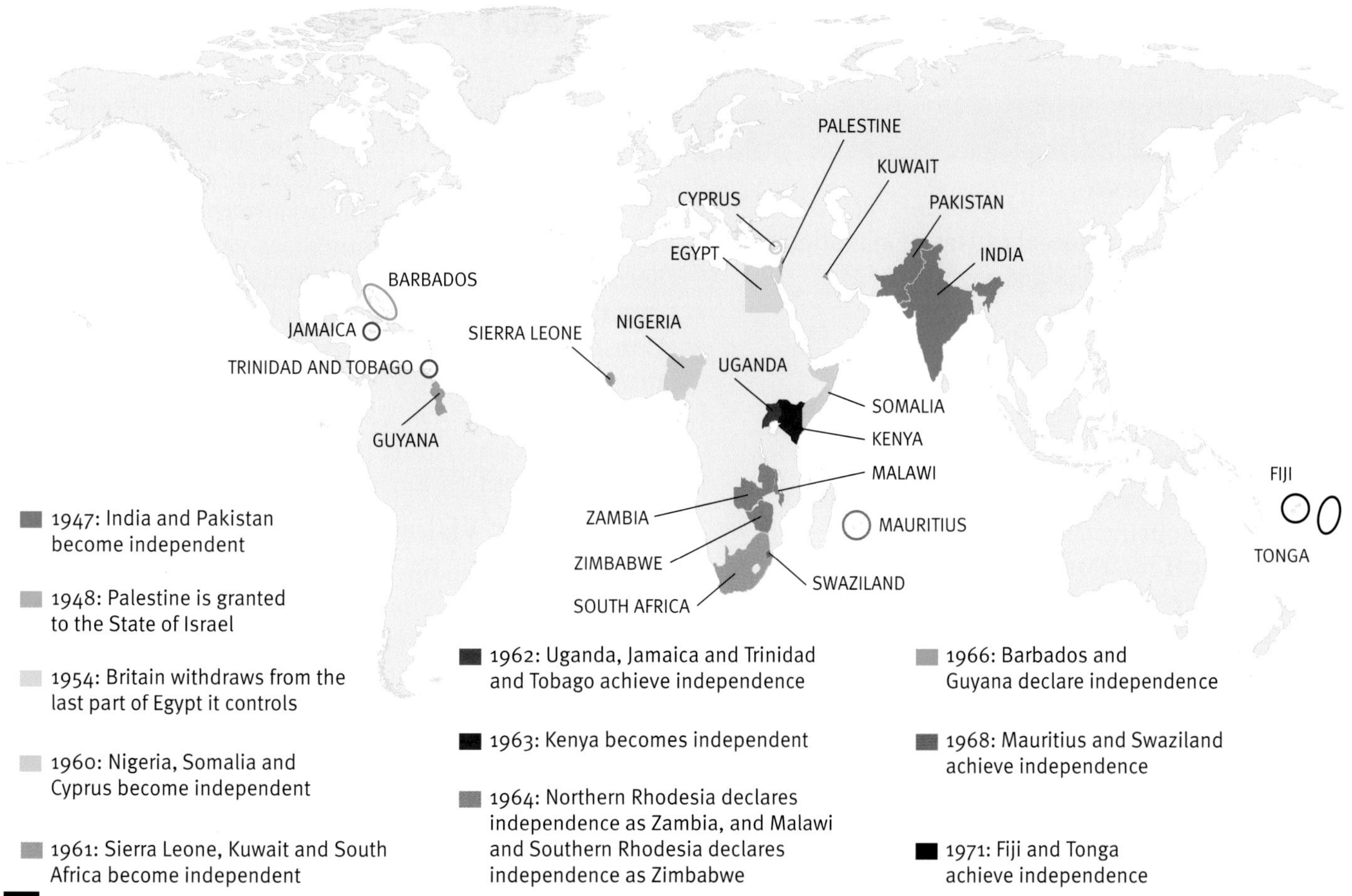

PALESTINE
KUWAIT
CYPRUS
PAKISTAN
EGYPT
INDIA
BARBADOS
JAMAICA
SIERRA LEONE
NIGERIA
TRINIDAD AND TOBAGO
UGANDA
SOMALIA
GUYANA
KENYA
MALAWI
FIJI
ZAMBIA
MAURITIUS
TONGA
ZIMBABWE
SWAZILAND
SOUTH AFRICA

- 1947: India and Pakistan become independent
- 1948: Palestine is granted to the State of Israel
- 1954: Britain withdraws from the last part of Egypt it controls
- 1960: Nigeria, Somalia and Cyprus become independent
- 1961: Sierra Leone, Kuwait and South Africa become independent
- 1962: Uganda, Jamaica and Trinidad and Tobago achieve independence
- 1963: Kenya becomes independent
- 1964: Northern Rhodesia declares independence as Zambia, and Malawi and Southern Rhodesia declares independence as Zimbabwe
- 1966: Barbados and Guyana declare independence
- 1968: Mauritius and Swaziland achieve independence
- 1971: Fiji and Tonga achieve independence

Decolonisation of the British Empire (1948–72). Almost all of these countries joined the Commonwealth of Nations once they had left the British Empire.

Arrival on the *Empire Windrush*

It was in 1948 that large numbers of West Indians began to arrive. The *Empire Windrush* arrived at Tilbury in Essex on 22 June 1948, carrying 492 passengers from the Caribbean wishing to start a new life in the United Kingdom. The passengers were the first large group of West Indian immigrants to the UK after the Second World War.

SOURCE A

A photograph of the *Empire Windrush*, taken in the 1950s, after it had been used to transport families to Britain.

ACTIVITY

Why is it not surprising that there was more immigration from the Caribbean than from Asia during the 1950s?

KEY WORDS

Commonwealth of Nations – *a voluntary association of independent states, most of which are former colonies of the British Empire.*

Kindertransport – *name of the mission which saw the United Kingdom rescue thousands of children (mostly Jewish) from Nazi-occupied territory.*

KEY CONCEPTS

Alien – *a legal term for a person in a country who is not a national citizen.*

Communism – *a theory which argues for an equal and classless society where there is common ownership of all the means of production and property.*

Multicultural – *a state of racial, cultural and ethnic diversity within a specified place.*

Pogrom – *extensive violence directed against a particular ethnic or religious group.*

Why did different groups migrate to Britain between 1948 and 1972?

LEARNING OBJECTIVES

In this lesson you will:

- learn about the different causes of migration to Britain between 1948 and 1972
- analyse the usefulness of different sources concerning this issue.

The arrival of the passengers has become an important landmark in the history of modern Britain, symbolising the beginning of modern **multicultural** relations which were to change British society significantly over the following years. Later in 1948, another ship, the *Orbita*, brought 180 to Liverpool; and the following year another 253 came on the *Georgic*. In addition to the Caribbean, the 1950s saw immigrants begin to arrive from India and Pakistan. In total, there were perhaps 350,000 non-whites in Britain by the start of 1962, around 0.7 per cent of the population.

Causes of immigration (1948–72)

Throughout this period, the extent of immigration increased dramatically from places such as the Caribbean, India, Pakistan and Uganda. Overall, the causes of this trend can be organised into five main factors.

1 The 1948 British Nationality Act

This confirmed the right of Commonwealth citizens to come and settle in Britain. This meant that all citizens within the majority of the countries listed above could freely come to Britain regardless of their race, religion or colour. As an example, a large number of Ugandan immigrants came to Britain whilst it was still part of the British Empire. Equally, however, a large number of immigrants from India came to Britain because it was still a member of the **Commonwealth of Nations** although it was no longer part of the Empire.

India and Pakistan joined the Commonwealth of Nations in 1947. Jamaica and Trinidad and Tobago joined in 1962.

2 Likelihood of finding work

There were severe labour shortages in Britain after the war, which meant that jobs became readily available. Recruiting campaigns were run in the West Indies to attract workers to take up employment with expanding organisations such as London Transport and the National Health Service. It is important to realise that the prospect of working in England meant that immigrants from countries such as India and Pakistan (where there was a great deal of poverty in the immediate years after the Second World War) could earn up to 30 times as much as they could earn in their country of origin. Consequently, Indians began arriving in large numbers shortly after their country gained independence in 1947. Many drove buses or worked in textile factories, and by the 1960s many had started to open corner shops and run post offices.

3 Romantic vision of Britain

In addition to the obvious material benefits of immigration, many potential immigrant groups had a romantic and glamorised image of Britain. They had been taught at school to regard Britain as the 'Mother Country' and to regard the British monarch as their monarch. In their schools, they learned about English literature and history, which sparked a natural curiosity to come here.

4 Economic problems at home

Immigrants did not come from wealthy countries. Often, there were significant economic problems including poverty, unemployment and a high birth rate. For example, many immigrants came from Pakistan after the construction of the Mangla Dam in the early 1960s had submerged some 250 villages in the Mirpur district and displaced 100,000 people. Many of the residents of some villages moved to Britain. However, although economic factors were a big cause of immigration, typical migrants were not unemployed and had above-average skills.

SOURCE A

Those arriving in London for the first time from 1948 onwards had high expectations. This was often based on faulty information. The source of this wrong information was largely the formal education given by the established churches in the colonies. The churches gave too rosy a view of the British way of life. The popular media reinforced these impressions, England, the West Indian population had been taught, was the land of opportunity. Merit, knowledge and skills, it was believed, were the keys for colonial peoples to great opportunities.

From *Longest Journey: A History of Black Lewisham* by J. Anim-Addo.

5 Violence at home

Fear was another reason why immigrants came to Britain in the 1950s. For instance, many left India because they wanted to escape the disruption and violence between communities that coincided with the division of British-controlled India into Pakistan and India. During the Partition, as many as two million people died in communal violence. Many Hungarians chose to migrate to Britain in the wake of their bitter experiences of Soviet aggression during the Hungarian Revolution in 1956.

6 Other factors

There were certain other causes of immigration to the UK, such as the fact that certain groups were sometimes forced to leave their countries, as was the case in 1972 when President **Idi Amin** expelled 60,000 Asian Ugandans, blaming them for controlling the economy for their own purposes. Another factor was that while many immigrants might have preferred to go to the USA as their first choice, restrictions imposed on entry made many travel to Britain instead.

SOURCE B

Period	West Indians	Asians	Total (including others)
1948–53	14,000	4000	28,000
1954	11,000	1300	18,000
1955	27,500	7600	42,700
1956	29,800	7600	46,850
1957	23,000	11,800	42,400
1958	15,000	10,900	29,850
1959	16,400	3800	21,600
1960	49,650	8400	58,050
1961	66,300	48,850	115,150
Jan–June 1962	27,000	43,000	83,700

UK immigration statistics.

GradeStudio

Study Sources A and B. Which is more useful to a historian studying immigration into Britain between 1948 and 1972? **[8 marks]**

ACTIVITIES

1. Analyse the data in Source B to find the most significant year of migration for Britain, along with any other noticeable trends in the patterns of migration, particularly in the relationship between West Indian and Asian immigration.
2. Identify three things that Sources C and D do not tell us about why Ugandans migrated to Britain. Which source is the most useful to historians in relation to why the Ugandans migrated to Britain?

SOURCE D

Ugandan-Asians arriving in the UK in 1972.

KEY PEOPLE

Idi Amin – *military dictator who was President of Uganda, 1971–79.*

SOURCE C

'When he [Amin] expelled Asians, it was politically one of the most astute moves he could have made.'

Yasmin Alibhai-Brown, a Ugandan-Asian journalist who lives in Britain, told BBC news.

What were the experiences of immigrants in Britain?

LEARNING OBJECTIVES

In this lesson you will:

- learn about the different experiences of immigrants in Britain after the Second World War
- analyse the reliability of one source concerning this issue.

GETTING STARTED

Work in pairs. Imagine you have just disembarked from the *Empire Windrush*. One of you must write a list of three things which you would be excited about. The other must write three things which you would be apprehensive about. After this has been completed, compare your thoughts and think about what you would be the most excited and the most apprehensive about. Explain your thoughts to the class.

Experience of immigrants in Britain

There was no one single description that can adequately describe or summarise the hugely varied experiences of immigrants in Britain after the Second World War. However, general patterns can be identified and the experiences can loosely be ordered into six main stages after the initial welcome and positive experiences of many immigrants on arrival.

Stage 1 – A gradual uneasy welcome

On arrival, immigrants usually settled in a relatively small number of towns and cities because they were **discriminated** against in housing. At this time, it was perfectly lawful for landlords to stipulate 'No Coloureds' or 'No Blacks'. Some landlords, like the notorious Peter Rachman, took advantage of the situation by charging overly expensive rents for overcrowded accommodation, which particularly harmed the Afro-Caribbean immigrants who formed the bulk of his tenants.

Stage 2 – Increased tension (riots in 1958)

In 1958, white youths attacked West Indians. On the night of Saturday 30 August in Notting Hill, a mob of 300 to 400 white people, many of them **Teddy Boys**, were seen on Bramley Road attacking the houses of West Indian residents. The disturbances, rioting and attacks continued every night until they finally petered out by 5 September. The Metropolitan Police arrested over 140 people during the two weeks of the disturbance, mostly white youths, but also many black people found carrying weapons. Although the Notting Hill Carnival was started as a positive response to the riots, the overall effect was that tension increased between the black community and the Metropolitan Police, which was accused by members of the black community of not taking their reports of racial attacks seriously.

SOURCE A

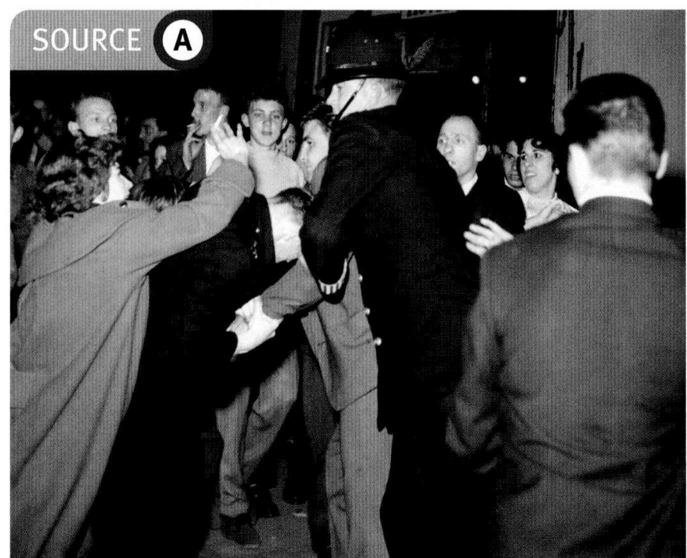

The Notting Hill race riots.

SOURCE B

The thing about the so called Notting Hill race riots is that they were not real race riots at all. People are always fighting in an area like the ghetto; clubs are always being invaded and broken up … the general opinion was that a few Teddy boys had simply been making a nuisance of themselves.

Taken from the autobiography of Michael De Freitas, a Black Power activist, in 1968.

ACTIVITIES

- How do these two sources differ about what happened in Notting Hill in 1958?
- Why might these two sources disagree?

SOURCE C

The whole thing exploded in 1958. It just became part of your life. I don't think it was a case of you try to forget it, blank it out of your mind, in a way you became immune to it, immune is the wrong word, it just became part and parcel of life, if you were to target all the incidents and racism that you encountered one could go on for weeks.

An interview with Loftus Burton after the Notting Hill riots. He was born in Dominica in 1950 and arrived in Britain in 1958 just before the riots.

Stage 3 – Conservative government gets tougher on immigration laws (Commonwealth Immigrants Act 1962)

In 1962, the Commonwealth Immigrants Act imposed restrictions on immigration into Britain from the Commonwealth for the first time. Whereas previously, citizens of the Commonwealth of Nations had extensive rights to migrate to the UK, the government now only permitted those with government-issued employment vouchers to settle. The era of unrestricted entry for Commonwealth citizens from countries such as India and Pakistan was now over.

The Act was a response from **Harold Macmillan**'s Conservative government to the many complaints made against the new arrivals, such as the fact that they were considered lazy and would not work, or that they would work for smaller wages which undercut other workers, or that they were responsible for crime, and finally that they were unwilling to mix with local communities. This trend of restricting immigration increased as time went on and, by 1972, only holders of **work permits** or people with parents or grandparents born in the UK could gain entry.

HISTORY DETECTIVE

What were the main criteria by which potential immigrants could get a voucher after the 1962 Act?

Stage 4 – Labour government attempts to protect immigrants (Race Relations Act 1965 and 1968)

Many politicians, though by no means all, were appalled by the level of **prejudice** which the immigrants had to endure. In 1965 the Labour government introduced the Race Relations Act which made it illegal to discriminate on grounds of race in public places (such as cafes, dance halls, hotels and cinemas). As well as this, the Race Relations Board and the National Committee for Commonwealth Immigrants were set up to handle racial complaints and to promote contacts between the different races in Britain. The 1968 Race Relations Act went further than the 1965 Act, as it outlawed discrimination in housing, employment, the provision of goods and services, in trade unions and in advertising. However, despite the best intentions on the part of the government, the legislation did not fully succeed in changing attitudes.

KEY CONCEPTS

Discrimination – *giving prejudicial treatment to either a person or a group.*

Prejudice – *a pre-determined feeling, either favourable or unfavourable.*

Work permit – *legal authorisation which allows a person to take employment.*

KEY PEOPLE

Harold Macmillan – *Conservative politician who was British Prime Minister 1957–63.*

Enoch Powell – *a British right-wing politician who held particularly outspoken views on immigration.*

KEY WORDS

Teddy boys – *a subculture of young men who wore clothes inspired by the styles of the Edwardian period.*

SOURCE D

It almost passes belief that at this moment twenty or thirty additional immigrant children are arriving from overseas in Wolverhampton alone every week – and that means 15 or 20 additional families in a decade or two hence ... We must be mad, literally mad, as a nation to be permitting the annual inflow of some 50,000 dependents, who are for the most part the material of the future growth of the immigrant-descended population. It is like watching a nation busily engaged in heaping up its own funeral pyre. So insane are we that we actually permit unmarried persons to immigrate for the purpose of founding a family with spouses and fiancées whom they have never seen.

Extract from Enoch Powell's 'Rivers of Blood' speech, 1968.

ACTIVITIES

The following statements about Source E are concerned with either its reliability or usefulness. Sort them out into the appropriate category.

- A photo taken before the age of technology is almost certainly going to be an unaltered image.
- The date of the photo shows that it was taken soon after Enoch Powell's 'Rivers of Blood' speech (20 April 1968) and is therefore representative of some views at the time.
- The source only shows one street and does not mention the other reactions taking place in London.
- The source shows that many dock workers were hostile to immigration.

Stage 5 – Enoch Powell exploits racial tensions ('Rivers of Blood' speech, 1968)

Enoch Powell was a Conservative MP who held strong views about immigration and used speeches to warn Britain of its dangers. On 20 April 1968 in Birmingham, Powell said that he could see storm clouds brewing for Britain because of the admission of immigrants. He pointed to the growing numbers of immigrants and their unwillingness to integrate and famously said, refering to a quotation from the time of ancient Rome, 'I seem to see the River Tiber foaming with much blood'.

SOURCE E

23 April 1968: Demonstrating dock workers, holding banners in support of the Conservative politician Enoch Powell, march past Monument in the City of London on their way to the House of Commons.

Powell's speech produced intense interest and anger. Many immigrants felt insulted and believed that their time here might be limited. The Conservative leader at this time, **Edward Heath**, sacked Powell from the shadow cabinet for the inflammatory tone of his remarks. Although the press condemned it, Powell received thousands of letters of support from immigration officers at Heathrow and London dock workers. It showed that anti-immigration feeling certainly existed in Britain.

Stage 6 – Anti-immigrant political party (establishment of the National Front in 1967)

The **National Front** was an extreme **right-wing** group set up in 1967. Its purpose was to oppose immigration and multicultural policies in Britain. Although it placed a ban on **Nazi** members, it had many links with far-right organisations. It became well-known for its noisy demonstrations, particularly in London, and made some significant

HISTORY DETECTIVE

Why might dock workers be a group which is opposed to immigration?

gains in local elections in the 1970s. It is important to remember, however, that there was never a National Front MP in Britain, and so their attitude did not have widespread support. However, their loud and aggressive posturing, particularly in London where they clashed with anti-fascist protesters, served to make many immigrant groups feel extremely uncomfortable.

Conclusion

Overall, the experience of immigrants throughout this period was fairly negative and included riots, anti-immigration legislation and finally the emergence of an anti-immigration political party. In spite of all this, the 1970s did see the emergence of a multicultural society in Britain.

It is important to bear in mind, however, that what happened to one particular group of migrants did not necessarily happen for all the other groups, and the experience of South African, Irish and Indian immigrants varied to a great extent. As such, a source that recounts a particular experience of one migrant or group of migrants does not necessarily represent the experiences of all the other thousands of migrants. Therefore, it is important when handling sources to be aware of the dangers of generalising.

ACTIVITIES

Working in groups, organise and then deliver a presentation about the changing experiences of immigrants in the UK from the 1950s to the 1970s. Each slide must represent a different stage and should include a photo relevant to the information in that slide.

SOURCE F

'I have three children, all of them married now, with family. I shan't be satisfied till I have seen them all settled overseas. In this country in 15 or 20 years' time the black man will have the whip-hand over the white man.' As I look ahead, I am filled with foreboding. Like the Roman, I seem to see the River Tiber foaming with much blood.

Extract from Enoch Powell's 'Rivers of Blood' speech, 1968.

KEY WORDS

National Front – *a British political party mostly active during the 1970s and 1980s, which was widely considered to be racist.*

ACTIVITIES

- The first three sentences of Source F show Powell describing what someone had allegedly said to him. Is this an effective way of delivering a speech? Explain your answer.
- What was the aim of Powell's Rivers of Blood speech? (Look at Source D also.)
- Why might it have been called the Rivers of Blood speech? (Look at Source D also.)
- Several months later, the Labour government passed the Race Relations Act (November 1968). How might this have been connected to this speech?

KEY CONCEPTS

Right-wing – *a political viewpoint which generally seeks to retain traditional values.*

Nazi – *a term to denote someone who believes in the policies adopted by the Hitler government in Nazi Germany, 1933–45.*

KEY PEOPLE

Edward Heath – *Conservative politician, British Prime Minister, 1970–74.*

GradeStudio

How far do you trust Source E as evidence of the reaction to Enoch Powell's speech? **[7 marks]**

What contribution had immigrants made to British society by the early 1970s?

LEARNING OBJECTIVES

In this lesson you will:

- learn about the contribution which immigrants had made in Britain by the early 1970s
- analyse the way in which sources provide an accurate view of the impact of immigrants.

GETTING STARTED

Think of at least three ways in which immigrants have made a significant contribution to British society today?

SOURCE A

The Great London Mosque on Brick Lane.

Overall contribution of immigrants to British society

By the early 1970s, many immigrants had become sporting heroes and founders of well-known businesses. Even today, health and transport services continue to be supported by nurses, doctors and managers from overseas. In addition, across Britain's towns and cities, there are not only churches but also synagogues, mosques, Hindu, Sikh and Buddhist temples. The overall contribution of immigrants to British society can be divided into four categories.

1 Establishment of permanent communities

The flow of refugees has been continuous since the end of the Second World War. Many of those who arrived in the 1950s, 1960s and 1970s have established permanent communities in a particular part of the United Kingdom. Places such as Spitalfields, the Leylands in Leeds (Jews), and Limehouse in London (Chinese) have come to be closely identified with concentrated immigrant settlement. In the case of Spitalfields in East London, this area has been dominated by several different immigrant communities over recent decades. Over the course of the 20th century, the Jewish presence diminished in that part of London and was replaced by a large number of Bangladeshi immigrants.

2 Economic impact

There are many examples of where immigrants have added huge value to the British economy. The garment business, for instance, was and still is dominated by migrant communities. Ethnic forms of dress, fabrics and accessories are all popular influences in fashion, running through the work of fashion designers and street styles. This serves as a clear example of how immigrants could use their knowledge of fashion in their own countries to good effect in a new market. In addition, South Asian immigrants have been particularly influential in textile production. One of the reasons for this was that in order to bear the costs of mechanisation, textile factories had to maintain production around the clock and needed a large workforce.

3 Festivals and celebrations

The carnival tradition was a notable contribution of West Indian immigrants to British society. A fully fledged Caribbean carnival didn't emerge onto the streets in London, where most migrants lived, until the early 1960s. The first carnival began in 1959 in St Pancras Town and was a response to the depressing state of race relations at the time, as was shown by the Notting Hill riots and the appalling events such as the brutal murder in Notting Hill of a Jamaican, **Kelso Cochrane**, by a gang of white youths. In 1965, **Claudia Jones** organised the moving of the carnival to Notting Hill, and by 1976 150,000 people were attending this annual event. It was in effect a demonstration by which migrants asserted their right to be in the UK, and a gesture of solidarity by some local residents.

4 Music

Throughout the 1960s, migrants' music attracted and inspired a generation of white working-class youth, partly because of its distinctive and rebellious sounds and associations. In particular, the arrival in England of reggae music's international superstar, **Bob Marley**, in 1976 had a particularly dramatic effect. Marley's success helped to spawn a Black British music industry based on reggae. His connection with the **Rastafarian** movement and the language of his lyrics gave his music an authenticity and depth which inspired and influenced waves of young Caribbean people, who, having been raised in Britain, were beginning to want to discover their Caribbean roots. Marley's album *Exodus* stayed in the British album charts for 56 consecutive weeks. It included four UK hit singles: *Exodus, Waiting In Vain, Jamming,* and *One Love.*

Other examples

There are many other examples of the way in which immigrants left a lasting impression on British society during this period. For instance, by the late 1960s South Asians had bought up to 2000 cinema houses that were being closed down or demolished in places like Manchester and Glasgow, in order to show imported films from their own countries. As well as this, immigrants have made a lasting impression on the British national diet. This includes the **Huguenots** who brought oxtail soup; the Jews who brought smoked salmon bagels, chicken soup and fried fish; Indians who pioneered Chicken Tikka Masala; and the Chinese who introduced Sweet and Sour Pork. Some of these meals were even slight alterations of native dishes created specially for Western tastes.

HISTORY DETECTIVE

Using the internet for research, answer the following question: How did Claudia Jones pioneer the Notting Hill Carnival?

VOICE YOUR OPINION!

In which area out of those listed above do you think immigrants have made the most significant impact?

ACTIVITIES

1 Prepare and then deliver a presentation about the wide-ranging impact of immigrants in the UK.

2 In groups, discuss the role of immigrants in bringing about change to British society. How did this happen? Should the government take any of the credit?

Conclusion

It is clear, therefore, that by the mid-1970s immigrants had made a varied and telling impression on British society. However, arguably the true test of whether a multicultural society had emerged by the mid-1970s is determined by whether or not there is genuine economic equality between the cultures. Certainly the Race Relations Act 1976, which prevented discrimination on the grounds of race in fields such as employment and education, would suggest that the UK government intended there to be a multicultural society. This was definitely a step towards a multicultural society but by this time migrants were far less likely to receive as good an education or as good a job as the white population.

KEY PEOPLE

Kelso Cochrane – *an Antiguan immigrant whose murder in Britain in 1959 sparked racial tensions in London.*

Claudia Jones – *a black nationalist and feminist who is remembered for starting the Notting Hill Carnival.*

Bob Marley – *a Jamaican musician and song-writer who was most famous for his performance of reggae music.*

KEY WORDS

Rastafarian – *a belief in a monotheistic religion that accepts both Jesus Christ and Haile Selassie I, the former emperor of Ethiopia, as incarnations of God.*

Huguenots – *members of the Protestant reformed church of France who left France in the 16th century to escape from religious persecution.*

GradeStudio

How far do Sources A and B give an accurate view about the way in which immigrants have established themselves in the UK? **[9 marks]**

Get your sources sorted

1 **Study Source A.** What is the message of this source? Use details of the source and your knowledge to explain your answer. **[6 marks]**

To answer this question, you need to consider three main things:

a What topic is being considered? *The discrimination faced by black people in employment.*

b What impression am I left with after looking at this source? *Black people are severely discriminated against in Britain when it comes to finding employment.*

c What is in the source that gives me this impression? (i) *Most black applicants were told that there was no vacancy and only one out of 40 was actually offered the job.* (ii) *This was not due to a shortage of jobs as White and Hungarian applicants had little trouble in securing employment.*

SOURCE A

Three applicants (a black Briton, a white Briton and a Hungarian) applied for the same 40 jobs. The black Briton always applied first.

	White Briton	Hungarian	Black Briton
Offered job or told vacancy existed and advised to apply	15	10	1
Told 'No vacancy at present' but details taken for future reference; or asked to call back; or told 'there should be a vacancy shortly'	15	7	2
Told 'no vacancy'	10	23	37
Total	40	40	40

From *Racial Discrimination in Britain*, a report published in 1968.

SOURCE B

The latest dose of well meaning foolishness from the Home Office would extend the Act to deal with discrimination on grounds of colour, race or ethnic origins in employment, housing, insurance and credit facilities. Discrimination on any of these grounds is wicked and uncivilised. We doubt it happens as much as people think it does. The trouble is that immigrants are being encouraged to believe that if they are asked to leave a first-class railway seat, when they have only a second-class ticket, it is because of their colour.

From an article about the Race Relations Act of 1965, published in the *Yorkshire Post* in 1967.

SOURCE C

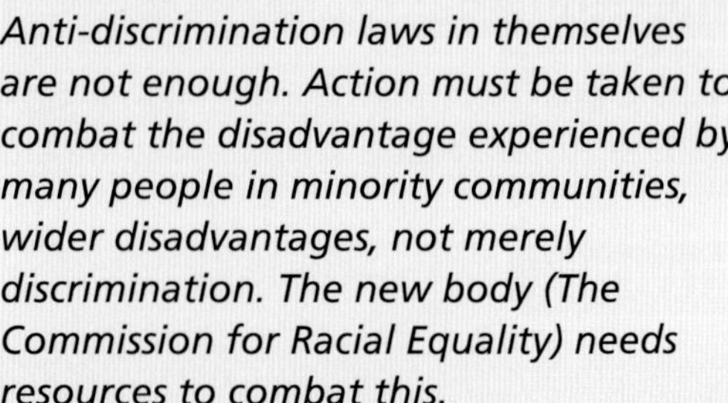

Anti-discrimination laws in themselves are not enough. Action must be taken to combat the disadvantage experienced by many people in minority communities, wider disadvantages, not merely discrimination. The new body (The Commission for Racial Equality) needs resources to combat this.

From a speech by Alan Beith, a Liberal MP, 1976.

2 Study Sources B and C. Which source is more useful in telling you about the success of the government in improving race relations? Use details of the sources and your own knowledge to explain your answer. **[8 marks]**

To answer this question, you need to consider four main things:

a What is the topic I need to use this source for? *Whether or not the government has been successful in improving race relations.*

b Which source is more useful in terms of the information it provides? *Source B represents the opinion that it is unlikely that discrimination 'happens as much as people (or the government) think it does'. This is useful as it is clearly a different opinion to Source C, which argues that 'Anti-discrimination laws in themselves are not enough'. Source B criticises the government for doing too much, which implies that it is not successful. It shows that there was more than one response to the Race Relations Act of 1965.*

c What source is more useful in terms of who provides that information? *It is likely that Alan Beith's account is more useful since as an MP he might be better informed than the journalist in Source B. However, as a Liberal MP, he was not in government and might therefore feel obliged to criticise the government regardless of the truth.*

d What is the overall judgement? *They are both fairly useful in terms of the information they provide, but the fact that Source B was written closer to the Race Relations Act and not by a rival MP perhaps makes it slightly more useful.*

3 Study Source D. How far do you trust this source? Use details of the photo and your knowledge to explain your answer. **[7 marks]**

To answer this question, you need to consider four main things:

a Is the content of the source believable? As a photograph, it represents an accurate picture, which is not surprising given the fact the Enoch Powell certainly had his supporters, particularly from dock workers.

b Do I trust the person who took it? A newspaper, however, is produced to sell and it is possible that this graffiti could have been deliberately planted in order to cause even greater controversy.

c Do I trust when it was written? The date of May 1968 makes sense since that it is just a couple of months after Powell's 'Rivers of Blood' speech in March, which provoked a great deal of anger as well as some support.

d Do I trust it bearing in mind why it was taken? Ultimately, despite the fact that it represents a realistic message, the fact that a black man is walking in front of this graffiti whilst the photographer is watching suggests that it might have been staged. As such, it might not be *totally trustworthy*.

4 Study Sources E and F. Which source do you think gives a more accurate view about the attitude of the government towards immigrants? Use details of the sources and your knowledge to explain your answer. **[9 marks]**

A straightforward way to answer a comparative question like this is to divide your answer into three parts:

a How accurate is the first source in showing the attitude of the government towards immigrants? *George Dixon argues that the government's attitude was that immigrants were 'Coloured Britons', which crucially means that they are considered British. He laments the lack of progress which black people have made in Britain but it is clear his view is that the government has a positive view of immigrants. This is a realistic viewpoint as Roy Jenkins was a member of the Labour government, which was altogether more receptive to the needs of immigrants, as was shown by the passing of the Race Relations Act in 1965 and 1968.*

b How accurate is the other source in relation to this? *In one way, Source F confirms the argument of Source E. The former shows Hugh Gaitskell, who in 1961 was the Labour Party leader, welcoming immigrants. This implies that, like Roy Jenkins, he encouraged immigration. The man on the right represents the Conservative minister, R.A. Butler, who takes the opposite view to Jenkins, namely the need to restrict immigration. This is again a believable view given that during the following year in 1962, the Conservative government passed the Commonwealth Immigrants Act, which restricted the right of people who lived in the Commonwealth of Nations countries to migrate freely to the UK.*

c What is my overall judgement on this issue? *It appears that Source E is a slightly more accurate view about what the government of the time felt about immigration but it is hard to compare given that they are referring to different governments.*

SOURCE D

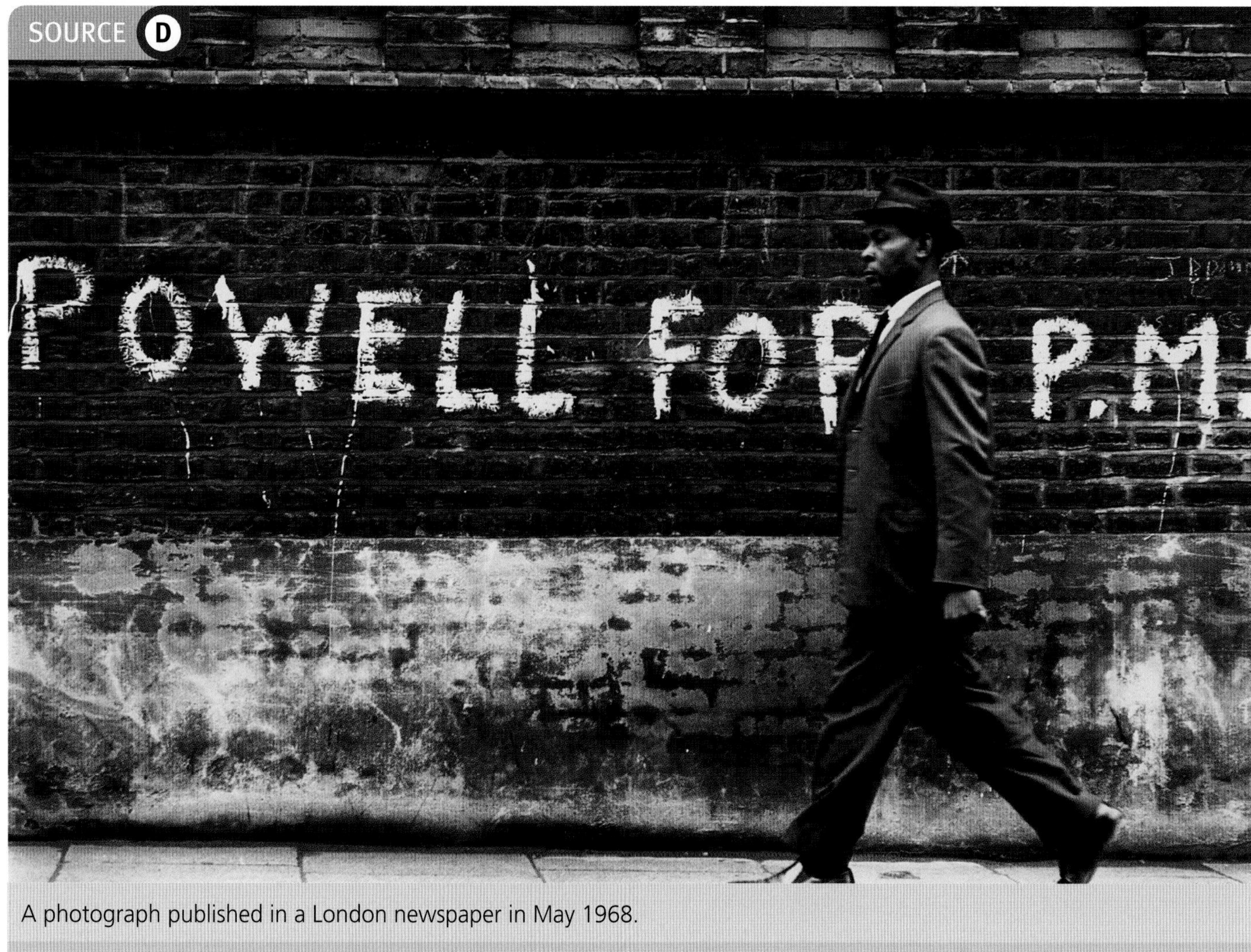

A photograph published in a London newspaper in May 1968.

5 Study Source A. Are you surprised that this was published in 1968? Use details of the table and your knowledge to explain your answer. **[8 marks]**

There are three steps involved in answering this question:

a What is significant about that date? *The two main reasons why the year 1968 is significant in the history of immigrants to Britain was because it was the year of Enoch Powell's River of Blood speech and the passing of the Race Relations Act in 1968 by the Labour government.*

b How does the source highlight this? *The source shows that 37 out of 40 black applicants for a job were told 'no vacancy', while only 1 out of 40 received an offer of a job. This source could therefore have been published as a way of applying pressure on the government to pass the Race Relations Act. Alternatively, it might be a reaction to the furore created by Enoch Powell's speech.*

c What was the motive for this source? *It is arguably the case that 1968 was the most intense year in the history of immigration to Britain during the first three decades after the Second World War. Therefore it is not surprising that a source such as this, with a strong and powerful message, was published at that time.*

SOURCE E

In some cases it is obvious that black teenagers don't get a fair deal compared with white teenagers. The only reason being that we are black: we think black, we act black and most of all, we're proud to be black. When we leave school we have no sense of belonging anywhere. We are what integration is all about. A few years ago Mr Roy Jenkins MP, called us 'Coloured Britons'. He said that we dress and speak much as whites do and we look for the same opportunities. Few of us have found them.

From an article by George Dixon, a West Indian writer, 1976.

6 Study *all* the sources. 'Immigrants were treated well in the 1950s and 1960s'. How far do the sources in this paper support this statement? Use details of the sources and your knowledge to explain your answer. Remember to identify the sources you use. **[12 marks]**

There are three main approaches in any answer to a question such as this:

a Which sources agree with the statement? *On the one hand, immigrants had a positive experience in the 1950s and 1960s. Source F, for instance, shows a leader of a political party, Hugh Gaitskell, welcoming them. Source B also backs this up as it says that 'we doubt it (discrimination) happens as much as people think it does'. This is backed up by my own knowledge, as black people were able to make a significant contribution to popular culture and the arts, among many other things.*

b Which sources disagree with the statement? *On the other hand, immigrants did not have a pleasant experience during this time, as is shown by Source A, because they were not able to find work very easily. This is backed up by Source C, which says that 'anti-discrimination laws in themselves are not enough' and Source E, which states that 'black teenagers don't get a fair deal'. Source D shows that there was a great amount of resentment which was targeted at immigrants. This is backed up by my own knowledge, as there were frequent race riots, such as those in Notting Hill in 1958.*

c What is my overall judgement about this issue? *Overall, it is clear that the sources in this paper both agree and disagree with the statement. It is also clear that part of the reason for the lack of common ground amongst the sources is that immigrants themselves had very different experiences.*

SOURCE F

Cartoon published by the *Daily Express* on 6 December 1961.

What was the impact of the National Health Service on people's lives?

LEARNING OBJECTIVES

In this lesson you will:

- learn to understand the impact of the National Health Service on people's lives
- analyse the message of a cartoon on this issue.

Fact file

British governments: 1945–79

- 1945–51: Labour (Prime Minister – Clement Attlee)
- 1951–64: Conservative (Winston Churchill until 1955, **Anthony Eden** until 1957, Harold Macmillan until 1963, **Lord Alec Douglas-Home** until 1964)
- 1964–70: Labour (**Harold Wilson**)
- 1970–74: Conservative (Edward Heath)
- 1974–79: Labour (Wilson until 1976, **James Callaghan** until 1979)

What type of health service existed before the war?

Before the war, healthcare was provided as a result of an insurance system. In 1911, this National Health **Insurance System** provided medical care for around 21 million people. It became clear to both Beveridge and the Labour Party that people were being denied medical help simply because they could not afford to pay.

What was the National Health Service?

In 1946 the National Health Service Act provided medical treatment, in hospital and from a General Practitioner (GP), free at the point of need. Dental and optical treatment was also included as part of this service. Under this Act, Britain's hospitals were **nationalised**, which meant that they were taken over by the government. In addition, GPs were encouraged to move from 'over doctored' areas to regions with a shortage, thus ensuring equal provision for all. Incidentally, private practice was allowed to continue. The new service (the National Health Service, NHS) came into operation in July 1948. **Aneurin Bevan**, the health minister in Attlee's government, was the person responsible for the Act though it stemmed to a large degree from the Beveridge Report which was published during the war.

Problems with the National Health Service

Once the NHS was introduced, it proved to be extremely popular with most people. Ninety-five per cent of all of the medical profession joined the NHS. The demand for its services in its first year (with 187 million **prescriptions** being written and 8 million pairs of spectacles dispensed) showed the pent-up demand for decent healthcare that had not been catered for by the previous arrangements. As a result of this popularity, resources began to be used up and spending on the NHS became much higher than predicted. From its earliest days, therefore, the NHS seemed to be short of money. For example, the £2 million put aside to pay for free spectacles over the first nine months of the NHS went in six weeks. The government had initially estimated that the NHS would cost £140 million a year by 1950. In fact, by 1950 the NHS was costing £358 million.

Bevan's resignation from the Labour government

It was only a matter of time before the cost of the NHS had to be weighed up against its popularity. In April 1951, when defence expenditure was rising steeply, because of the Korean War which Britain was involved with, the new Chancellor of the Exchequer, **Hugh Gaitskell**, decided to introduce charges for false teeth and spectacles. Bevan believed that the socialist principle of a free health service was being compromised. He threatened to

CITIZENSHIP TASK

In groups, through the use of hot-seating, justify and defend your views on whether or not Bevan was right to resign over Hugh Gaitskell's budget.

resign and, when neither Gaitskell nor the cabinet would budge, he duly did, along with two other ministers (**John Freeman** and **Harold Wilson**). After all his work, Bevan wanted a free health service and nothing else. However, in spite of these charges, including for prescriptions which was to be added later, the NHS has made a remarkable difference to people's lives despite not being a perfect system. It allowed the whole population the right to see a doctor or have an operation without the need to pay. As such, it is a fairly unique system in comparison to many other countries and no doubt played a large part in attracting many immigrants to Britain throughout this period.

SOURCE A

'SOCIALISTS!'

A cartoon showing Harold Wilson, Aneurin Bevan, Michael Foot and Ian Mikardo attacking Herbert Morrison, Clement Attlee and Hugh Gaitskell (July 1951).

KEY WORDS

Prescription – *medicine prescribed by a doctor.*

HISTORY DETECTIVE

The majority of the National Health Service is still under the control of the government today. What other organisations does the government today still control?

ACTIVITY

Sort these comments below into either those concerned with the detail of the source or those concerned with its message.

- The Labour government was divided over the issue of charging for spectacles and dentures.
- There are two groups of people on either side of the road.
- Two wealthy-looking people are showing off their spectacles and teeth.
- The Labour government of Attlee, Gaitskell and Morrison are siding with the wealthy in favour of the needy.

GradeStudio

What is the message of the cartoon in Source A?
[6 marks]

KEY CONCEPTS

Insurance System – *a system where people derive a benefit as a result of paying into a fund along with others such as government and an employer.*

Nationalised – *taken over by the government.*

KEY PEOPLE

Anthony Eden – *Prime Minister of the United Kingdom, 1955–57.*

Alec Douglas-Home – *Prime Minister of the United Kingdom, 1963–64.*

James Callaghan – *Prime Minister of the United Kingdom, 1976–79.*

Aneurin Bevan – *Labour Minister of Health, 1945–51, responsible for the passing of the National Health Service Act.*

Hugh Gaitskell – *Labour Chancellor of the Exchequer, 1950–51.*

John Freeman – *resigned with Aneurin Bevan and Harold Wilson over National Health Service charges.*

What was life like for most women in the 1950s, 1960s and early 1970s, and how were they discriminated against?

LEARNING OBJECTIVES

In this lesson you will:

- learn about what life was like for women after the Second World War and how they were discriminated against
- analyse the usefulness of a source concerning this issue.

The contribution of women during the Second World War

Women worked in planning, secretarial work, support, administration and maintenance. They also took over the jobs of men by working in munitions factories, agriculture and transport. In 1939 women were encouraged to volunteer to work and, by 1941, all single women (aged 19–30) were conscripted, which was later extended to married women without children. Overall, women played a vital role in the war effort. The number of women working doubled to more than seven million, with around half a million women joining the armed forces.

What changed for women?

Women saw some positive changes in their lives as a result of developments during the war. School meals became available for all children, which allowed women to work all day, and new convenience foods were developed. Many women found that they could cope with children, housework and new jobs. However, at the end of the war there were campaigns to encourage women to give up their jobs.

Women were the recipients of some government legislation which had differing effects. There seemed to be the beginnings of equality with the passing of the 1943 Equal Pay Commission, but it proved ineffective. A more positive step was the 1945 Butler Education Act which guaranteed all females the right to a secondary education.

What was life like for most women in the 1950s?

Cult of domesticity

Unlike the First World War, which was responsible for giving women the vote, the Second World War did not produce any significant changes in the lives of women. Ultimately, women were still seen as belonging in the home and very few people believed that a woman could possibly be the family's main breadwinner. The **Beveridge Report**, which was published during the war, was based on the assumption that the average family unit consisted of an employed father and a non-employed mother.

SOURCE A

Mother and future Prime Minister: **Margaret Thatcher** with her children Carol and Mark in 1959.

ACTIVITIES

Below are several claims which could be made as a result of Source A. Which of these claims might you need a second opinion for?

- Some women were involved in politics.
- Many adult women were mothers at a young age.
- Women could combine their domestic and professional lives.
- Women enjoyed their role in domestic life.

This meant that the 1950s, like the 1930s, saw a pervasive cult of **domesticity** with the traditional view of women as home-makers proving remarkably resilient, a view encouraged by much commercial advertising.

Changes in education

The 1944 Education Act was responsible for significant change in the lives of women. It outlawed the sacking of women teachers who were married, while the provision of good-quality education, especially in the grammar schools, widened women's horizons. By the early 1960s, nearly a third of **undergraduates** were female, and the professions saw a steady increase in the number of women entrants. However, girls attending modern schools still had a curriculum biased towards domestic duties. Such schools often provided furnished rooms wherein girls might learn the essential skills of housewifery.

Wage comparisons with men

The growth of part-time work for women offered material gains for women, but in other spheres, female workers consistently lagged behind their male counterparts. This is particularly true in terms of the wage differential between men and women, with a particularly large gap coming in 1940, when women earned 42 per cent of men's wages. The average wage differential during the 1920s to 1970s was fairly consistent at approximately 50 per cent.

The feminist movement of the 1960s and 1970s

The slow pace of change in women's lives after the Second World War added to the frustration on the part of many women. As a result, a **feminist** movement, which called for equality for women and campaigned for women's rights and interests, became more active in Britain during this time. During the 1960s, its main areas of concern were not necessarily legal equality but more unofficial inequality in, for example, educational opportunities and employment. They also felt that women were treated as second-class citizens and did not receive adequate support from the state over important issues like contraception and divorce.

SOURCE B

Is it too much to ask that women be spared the daily struggle for superhuman beauty in order to offer it to the caresses of a subhumanly ugly mate?

From *The Female Eunuch*, 1970, written by Germaine Greer, a leading feminist.

SOURCE C

One point to be clear about at the outset is that the UK started from a very low baseline in relation to equal pay. In the 1960s earnings of full-time women as a proportion of full-time men's earnings were only just over 60% and separate (and lower) women's rates of pay were common in the private sector. So, for example, at Ford UK, there were four rates of pay for production workers – skilled male; semi-skilled male; unskilled male; female. The only group of female production workers were sewing machinists. They were paid less than the (unskilled) men who swept the floors.

From a recent report about Gender Pay Gaps in the United Kingdom.

KEY CONCEPTS

Domesticity – *home and family life.*

Feminist – *someone who believes in equality for women and campaigns for women's rights.*

Heavy industry – *the manufacture of large, heavy items.*

Light industry – *the manufacture of small, light items, such as clothes and furniture.*

KEY PEOPLE

Margaret Thatcher – *Conservative politician who was British Prime Minister, 1979–90.*

KEY WORDS

Undergraduate – *a student in post-secondary education, usually a university.*

Beveridge Report – *a report written in 1942 containing a series of recommendations for social reform.*

How useful is Source A in telling the historian about the role of women during this period? **[8 marks]**

How much change had taken place for women by 1975?

LEARNING OBJECTIVES

In this report you will:

- learn about how the lives of women had changed by 1975
- analyse a source and assess whether it provides an accurate view about this issue.

GETTING STARTED

Following on from the previous activity, put these five demands of the feminist movement in order of importance. Explain the reasons for your choice to the person next to you.

- Right to have an abortion
- Availability of the contraceptive pill
- More opportunities for women to get a divorce
- End to all sexual discrimination
- Equal pay.

Change in the lives of women by 1975

By 1975, the lives of women were almost unrecognisable from what they had been at the end of the Second World War. A great deal of government legislation had led to enormous changes in women's lives compared with 20 years earlier. Overall, there were five main areas in which the lives of women changed.

1 Contraceptive pill (1961)

On 4 December 1961, Enoch Powell, then Conservative Minister of Health, announced that the oral contraceptive pill *Conovid* could be prescribed through the NHS at a subsidised price. These new rights of birth control had a hugely important effect on women, in that it gave them more control over their lives, and it also meant that they married and started families at a later date. As a result, it increased women's opportunities in education and employment, and also their income levels.

2 Abortion Act (1967)

This was introduced by David Steel as a **Private Member's Bill**, but was backed by the Labour government, It passed in October 1967 after a heated debate and a **free vote**, and came into effect in April 1968. The Act made abortion legal in the UK. As with the introduction of the contraceptive pill six years earlier, the Act gave women a great deal more control over their lives. Abortion is, however, an extremely controversial measure which is vehemently opposed, particularly by certain religious groups.

HISTORY DETECTIVE

Before abortion was legalised by the 1967 Act, many women still had abortions. How did they manage to do this?

SOURCE A

Cartoon by Michael Cummings, published by the *Daily Express*, 23 March 1973.

ACTIVITIES

1 Prepare a talk about which piece of legislation you think is the most significant. In addition, consider how far women's lives had changed by 1975 compared with 1945.

2 a Consider Source A. Which of the following statements are points of view and which are pieces of evidence that can back up points of view?
- Source A does not reflect all women's lives during this period.
- Many women disapproved of measures such as the teaching of Sex Education to infants.
- The introduction of the contraceptive pill and the Abortion Act were hugely controversial measures.
- Source A shows big books that are both for and against the contraceptive pill and abortion.
- Women's lives changed during a short space of time.
- The source shows how all the books at once are too heavy to carry.

b Now see if you can link the point of view with its corresponding piece of evidence from Source A.

3 In groups, consider whether you think the situation in 1975 represents satisfactory progress for women. Think about any areas that were not covered by the government legislation.

3 Divorce Reform Act (1969)

This Act was passed by Parliament in 1969 and came into effect in 1971. As with the Abortion Act two years earlier, it came about as a result of a private member's bill with a free vote. However, it was clearly the case that the large Labour majority in Parliament after 1966 was more open to such changes than previous parliaments had been. The Divorce Reform Act allowed a couple to divorce on the grounds of adultery, cruelty, desertion for at least two years, or by mutual consent (after two years) – or after five years if only one person wanted a divorce.

4 Equal Pay Act (1970)

This was established by Parliament to prevent discrimination as regards to terms and conditions of employment between men and women. It came into force many years later, in December 1975. One of the problems which women had encountered as they found jobs throughout the 1950s and 1960s was that they were often exploited by employers who paid them lower wages than men. This went some way to redressing the imbalance and gave women more of a chance of supporting themselves and not being so dependent on a man.

VOICE YOUR OPINION!

In your groups, discuss the differences between government legislation and Private Member's Bills. Think also about whether or not Private Member's Bills are a good thing.

5 Sex Discrimination Act (1975)

This Act protected both men and women from discrimination on the grounds of gender. The Act mainly applied to employment, training, education, harassment and the provision of goods and services. This was the final element of a very rewarding period for women, during which time their lives were made considerably better and they acquired a greater degree of freedom from discrimination and a greater control over their lives.

KEY CONCEPTS

Free vote – *a vote where Members of Parliament vote according to their own beliefs rather than following party policy.*

Private Member's Bill – *a proposed law which is introduced by a Member of Parliament who is not a government minister.*

Does Source A give an accurate view about how women's lives had changed by 1975? **[9 marks]**

What factors led to changes in the roles of women?

LEARNING OBJECTIVES

In this lesson you will:

- learn about the different causes of the changes in women's lives
- evaluate the reliability of a source as evidence about this issue.

GETTING STARTED

Do you remember the five changes which improved women's lives? Summarise the key facts about each change.

- Contraceptive pill
- Abortion Act
- Divorce Reform Act
- Equal Pay Act
- Sex Discrimination Act.

BRAIN BOOST

Contraception
Abortion
Divorce
Equality
Sex discrimination

Why did women's lives change?

Change seldom happens on a big scale unless there are a number of forces that work together in bringing it about. In the case of the changes to the lives of women, there were four main causes of this change.

1 The Women's Liberation Movement

The women's liberation movement became particularly strong in Britain towards the end of the 1960s, and in 1970 **Germaine Greer**, an influential member, published her seminal text *The Female Eunuch*. The women's liberation movement, or 'women's lib', was an influential movement which brought publicity to the feminist cause. It is important to remember that politicians tend to be very susceptible to pressure from organisations such as these, knowing that they have a wide influence and can therefore be very useful in terms of votes at election time.

2 European influence

Throughout this period, Britain was gradually becoming closer to the **European Economic Community** (EEC, later renamed the European Union), which it finally joined in January 1973. As a member, Britain had to comply with the original EEC Treaty (Source B). Unsurprisingly, other powerful European countries such as France soon followed Britain's example of the Equal Pay Act (1970) by passing a similar Act two years later.

3 Attitude of the Labour government

It is no coincidence that many of these changes to women's lives, such as the Abortion Act and the Divorce Reform Act, happened under a Labour government. Wilson's first period in office witnessed a range of social reforms, including the abolition of capital punishment, legalisation of male homosexual acts between consenting adults in private, and the abolition of theatre censorship. Although many of them originated as a result of private members' bills or free votes, they still had to be passed by Parliament, which had a majority of Labour MPs. It is clear, therefore, that the large Labour majority after 1966 meant that the government was more open to such changes than previous governments. However, not all Labour MPs backed the reforms, while some of the reforms received support from other parties.

SOURCE A

What other pressure groups would a government be likely to listen to?

4 Private Members' Bills

Although the Labour government was quite receptive to the idea of changing the lives of women, it did not initiate most of the legislation. For instance, the 1967 Abortion Act was introduced by David Steel as a Private Member's Bill. These bills were a convenient way for Parliament to tackle controversial issues, because any government support might have split the Cabinet.

SOURCE 

Each Member State shall in the course of the first stage ensure and subsequently maintain the application of the principle of equal remuneration for equal work as between men and women workers.

Extract from the original EEC Treaty, Signed in Rome 25 March 1957.

ACTIVITIES

1. You learned in the previous lesson about five important changes. Who was most responsible for them? A pressure group, the EEC, the Labour government, or Members of Parliament? Prepare a case to present to the rest of the class to explain which one deserves to get the most credit. You must also explain why your choice deserves more credit than the other three.
2. The following statements are either concerned with the reliability or message of Source C. Arrange them into the appropriate category.
   - Men were very sarcastic to the idea of gender equality.
   - This source is taken from a newspaper which, at the time, was known to be critical of the feminist movement.
   - This source was written a day after a large feminist march, which shows that it was a direct response.
   - Sex discrimination was rife, even within the family.

KEY PEOPLE

Germaine Greer – *an Australian journalist and academic who championed the cause of feminism in the later part of the 20th century.*

KEY WORDS

European Economic Community (EEC) – *an organisation founded in 1957 which aimed to bring about economic integration between European countries.*

GradeStudio

How far do you trust Source C as evidence of public opinion about women? **[7 marks]**

SOURCE C

"There's certainly no discrimination between the sexes in this house. I let the women graduate from menial kitchen duties to concrete mixing and so forth."

Cartoon by Carl Giles, first published by the *Sunday Express* on 4 February 1973. The previous day, 300 women marched to the House of Commons in support of William Hamilton's Anti-Discrimination Bill. The Bill proposed setting up a board to hear complaints about discrimination on the ground of gender.

Why were there changes in the lives of teenagers in the 1960s?

LEARNING OBJECTIVES

In this lesson you will:

- learn about the different reasons why the lives of teenagers changed in the 1960s
- analyse the usefulness of a source concerning this issue.

ACTIVITIES

It is clear that the internet has allowed the youth of today to do many things which the previous generation could not. Consider what new things teenagers in the 1960s had available to them (e.g. televisions) during their youth which their parents did not. Afterwards, think about the likely effect of these items on teenagers' lives.

GETTING STARTED

In pairs, think about the historical events which your parents or grandparents might have witnessed which you have not. Following on from this, think about how that might affect their outlook on life in contrast to yours.

Teenagers in the 1950s

Until 1950, the term 'teenagers' had never been used before. Children were known as girls and boys and became known as youths once they displayed signs of growing up. Often, many young people would get married and move out to a place of their own by the time they were around 21. Getting married was a way of the youth joining the adult world. However, teenagers began to come to public notice during this period, and they did not approach life in such a predictable way. They began to reject the seemingly dull, timid, old-fashioned and uninspired British culture around them and sought new pleasures and activities that were often totally at odds with what their parents considered acceptable.

Influences on teenagers in the 1960s

There were three main causes in bringing about this change in the lives of teenagers.

1 Cultural influences

During the 1950s a range of influences including film, television, magazines and the rock music scene were perfectly designed for the new market grouping of teenagers. In particular, the American influence on European teenagers was huge, such as Rock and Roll idols like **Elvis Presley** and film stars such as **James Dean** and **Marlon Brando**. They set fashions almost unwittingly and had a mesmerising effect on British teenagers in terms of the way they dressed, spoke and spent their free time.

2 Consumer goods

As mentioned earlier, the 1950s and 1960s saw a sudden flurry of activity as consumer goods denied to war-torn Europe become available, and a consumer **boom** was actively encouraged. This provided teenagers with the tools to cultivate their own styles in clothes, haircuts and even travel abroad. This spearheaded a generation gap between parents and their offspring.

SOURCE A

British teenagers dancing to rock 'n' roll music in the 1950s.

VOICE YOUR OPINION!

Why would these influences have more of an effect on youth than any other social grouping?

3 Financial power

Teenagers soon became the market's dream, as they had comparatively huge spending power compared to previous generations. These single young people with cash from paid work made self-indulgent purchases, sometimes with even more freedom than adults. For instance, they soon had their own fashions, music, cafes, and by the end of the decade even their own transport in the form of scooters. Consumer goods and media influences became targeted at the teenage market, which caused them to develop an even more unique type of identity.

SOURCE B

A 'youth culture' was created, due to the fact that school-leavers found it easy to get jobs. It has been calculated that in 1959 teenagers had £830 million to spend; and most of this went on buying records and record-players.

Robert Pearce, *Contemporary Britain: 1914–1979*, 1997.

SOURCE C

" God bless Paul, John, George and Ringo—and Lord help Cassius Clay ! "

Cartoon first published by the *Daily Mail* on 25 February 1964. Paul, John, George and Ringo were The Beatles; Cassius Clay was the boxer later known as Mohammad Ali.

KEY WORDS

Boom – *a time of rapid growth in wealth.*

GradeStudio

How useful is Source C in telling the historian about the lives of teenagers? **[8 marks]**

ACTIVITIES

1 Organise and deliver a presentation about the reasons why teenagers' lives changed in the 1960s. You will need to explain how each of the three factors mentioned in this lesson played a part. In addition, come to a conclusion about which one was the most important factor. In terms of organisation, try to introduce your presentation by talking about teenagers' lives in the 1950s. Afterwards, produce three short sections about each of the three factors. Conclude with your overall opinion on the most important factor.

2 Consider Source C. Separate the following statements which are concerned with message from those concerned with usefulness.
- This is a drawing of only one teenager's room and is not necessarily reflective of all teenagers in Britain.
- As it is a cartoon, it is not totally realistic and perhaps reflects an exaggerated opinion of teenagers.
- Teenagers are heavily influenced by popular culture.
- The heroes of teenagers were very different to the heroes of their parents.

KEY PEOPLE

Elvis Presley – *an American singer and cultural icon, known as the 'King of Rock and Roll'.*

James Dean – *an American actor who became a cultural icon despite his premature death at the age of 24.*

Marlon Brando – *Academy-Award winning American actor who starred in films such as* The Godfather *and* Apocalypse Now.

The Beatles – *enormously successful pop and rock band from Liverpool that formed in the 1960s.*

How did teenagers and students behave in the 1960s and early 1970s?

LEARNING OBJECTIVES

In this lesson you will:

- learn about the different ways in which teenagers and students behaved in the 1960s
- analyse the reliability of one source concerning this issue.

GETTING STARTED

Can you think of any trends that have been started by teenagers?

Teenagers' changing behaviour

It is clear from the information already mentioned that teenagers no longer wanted to act or dress like their parents, and by the late 1950s they could afford not to. Their behaviour during the 1960s and early 1970s can be divided into five separate areas.

1 They worshipped their idols

Music, in particular pop and rock music, became a dominant form of expression for the young. As such, bands like The Beatles and The Rolling Stones came to be seen as leaders of youth culture and were worshipped almost as gods by teenagers. What was so attractive about these bands was that their message to the young was taken to mean that they should not accept tamely what they were told by any authority but rather find things out for themselves.

HISTORY DETECTIVE

Find out three songs by The Beatles that you think would have been enjoyed by teenagers at this time. Make sure you write down an explanation for your choices.

2 They became more daring when it came to expressing themselves

Teenagers became absorbed by the latest fashion trends, and increasingly had the confidence to experiment with previously untested things. For instance, London girls became especially willing to try the new mini skirt. The fashion trend took off because it was so different and because you usually had to be youthful to get away with an outfit that was so controversial, particularly among adults. What it shows, however, is that teenagers adopted trend-setting behaviour during this period whereas previously the trends were set for them.

3 Emergence of a youth subculture

During this period, youth-based subcultures such as the **Mods** and **Rockers** became more visible. Mods were associated with sophistication on scooters while rockers developed a more macho image on motorcycles. Mods sometimes clashed with Rockers, although fights between rival Mod gangs were also very common. In 1964, there were several well-publicised battles at seaside resorts such as Brighton, Margate and Hastings. The Mods and Rockers conflict led to a moral panic about violence and drug-use among young people in Britain. Later on in the 1960s, many other subcultures would emerge such as hippies, skinheads and punk rockers.

SOURCE A

Fights broke out yesterday between gangs of youths at three coast resorts. After a promenade skirmish at Brighton involving more than 1000, five girls were taken to hospital. At Margate two youths were taken to hospital with knife wounds and at Bournemouth between 40 and 50 youths were arrested after a fight between local gangs.

Margate magistrates imposed fines totalling £1900 on 36 people involved in Sunday's disturbances at the resort. They also gaoled three offenders for three months each and sent another five to detention centres for periods of up to six months. At Brighton two youths were sentenced to three months' imprisonment and others were fined.

Article from *The Times* published on 19 May 1964.

'I hear you've joined the Mods and Rockers, sergeant . .'

Cartoon by Franklin first published by the *Daily Mirror* on 9 June 1964.

5 Public protest

As part of their new-found identity, teenagers became more willing to challenge decision-makers. In 1958 the **Campaign for Nuclear Disarmament** was formed, organising well-publicised protest marches. In the 1960s there were political demonstrations, which sometimes led to violence, especially against the Vietnam War. People also voiced extensive criticisms of authority, including politicians, the church and parents. It appeared that although teenagers seemed to be uncertain about the best way to improve society, they were perfectly clear about the current problems with society in the 1960s and 1970s.

4 More violent and criminal behaviour

In addition to the presence of a youth subculture, there was also an increasing tendency for teenagers to behave violently and commit crimes. There were several violent youth gangs, including the Teddy Boys who played a part in attacking black people during the Notting Hill riots. Teenagers also used drugs, especially cannabis, to a greater degree, which in part was influenced by the culture of groups such as hippies and the lyrics of bands such as the Beatles, particularly evident in their *Sgt Pepper* album.

KEY WORDS

Campaign for Nuclear Disarmament (CND) – *a movement which calls for all countries to dismantle their nuclear weapons.*

Mods – *subculture that originated in London during the 1950s whose interests included pop music and tailor-made suits.*

Rockers – *a subculture that originated in Britain in the 1960s among motorcycle-riding youths.*

ACTIVITIES

Find out about the behaviour of teenagers during this period using a range of sources from the internet. You should then select and synthesise information which sheds light on teenager behaviour and make a note of the website you retrieved it from.

GradeStudio

How far do you trust Source A as evidence of teenage and student behaviour during the 1960s and early 1970s? **[7 marks]**

VOICE YOUR OPINION!

How important is the right of citizens to protest?

How did the lives of all teenagers change in the 1960s and early 1970s?

LEARNING OBJECTIVES

In this lesson you will:

- learn about the effect of education on the lives of teenagers
- assess whether a source provides an accurate view of this issue.

GETTING STARTED

Try to think of at least three major changes that have taken place in education during your lifetime.

Changes in education

Many factors have already been discussed concerning the different influences on teenagers during this period. However, perhaps the biggest change to have had an impact on their lives was in education. In the years after the Second World War, there had been significant changes in this area, in both secondary education and higher education.

Comprehensive education

By the end of the Second World War, the Education Act (1944) had ensured that secondary education in England, Wales and Northern Ireland was free to all pupils at least up until the age of 14 years. It was managed under the **Tripartite System**, which consisted of **grammar schools**, secondary technical schools (very few were ever built) and secondary modern schools. Pupils were sent to these schools on the basis of an 11-plus examination in the last year of their primary education. Due to the lack of many technical schools, there ended up being fierce competition for the available grammar school places, which put considerable pressure on young people at an early age. However, there was a great uproar at the perceived low standards in the secondary modern schools which, from the late 1940s onwards, paved the way for the introduction of the comprehensive school. This provided free education from 11 to 16 years and did not select children on the basis of academic ability.

Following the 1964 general election, the new Labour government instructed all local authorities to prepare plans for the creation of comprehensive schools. The main consequence of this was that it has allowed many children to gain access to further and higher education and prevented children who failed the 11-plus from feeling like second-class citizens.

ACTIVITIES

Working in groups, prepare arguments both in favour and against the introduction of comprehensive schools in the United Kingdom.

Expansion of university education

In the years following the Second World War, both Labour and Conservative governments oversaw and supported the expansion of higher education. During this period many new universities were founded, such as Warwick, Norwich, Lancaster, Sussex, Kent, Stirling, Essex and York, as well as 30 new **polytechnics**. As a result, the 1960s and early 1970s witnessed an enormous expansion in the number of full-time university students in the UK, with even more of an increase to come in future years. Moreover, local education authorities (LEAs) now paid student fees and provided non-mature students with maintenance grants. This gave young people from poorer backgrounds the opportunity to go to university.

Increasing opportunities

Overall, teenagers born in the 1950s enjoyed far greater opportunities than their parents had enjoyed. It is important to recognise that teenagers would endure very different educational experiences, but there is little doubt that the more education they received, the less likely it was that they would be influenced by anything resembling authority.

VOICE YOUR OPINION!

Is the fact that more people went to university a good thing? Explain your answer.

HISTORY DETECTIVE

Use the internet to find out how the number of people who went to university in the UK increased each year throughout the 1960s and 1970s. Put this information into a spreadsheet and see what patterns you can deduce.

SOURCE A

Cartoon by Franklin, first published by the *Daily Mirror* on 26 July 1963.

KEY WORDS

Tripartite System – *education system which divided secondary schools into grammar schools, technical schools, and modern schools.*

Grammar school – *schools that select their pupils on the basis of their intellectual ability.*

Polytechnic – *a higher education institution that aimed to teach both academic and vocational subjects.*

ACTIVITIES

1 Which one of the following points of view best reflects Source A?
- Young people were staying at school for longer and longer.
- The government was determined for pupils to stay at school longer, but young people were unsure why.
- Not everyone agreed with the government's agenda to get more people in education.
- Pensioners were going back to school.

2 Does Source A give an accurate view about the lives of teenagers during the 1960s and the early 1970s?

Unit A972: British Depth Study, 1939-75

Your chosen British Depth Study will be the focus of the second of the written question papers you will take. The paper will be a source-based exercise, with the main focus on AO3 (analysis and evaluation of sources), but, as you will also have to use your knowledge and understanding of the period to help you answer the questions, AO1 and AO2 (recall and explanation) will also be important. The paper will consist of a set of sources on an issue taken from the Depth Study, along with no fewer than five and no more than seven compulsory questions. These questions will all be about the sources, but will be of many different types. Below you will find examples of some of these question types. The first deals with the issue of reliability – whether or not you can believe what a source tells you.

Study the source and then answer the question which follows.

Source A

"Punish me?!! But I'm only a poor, suffering victim of an acute attack of boredom..."
Cummings
OSTEND
CLACTON

A cartoon from 1964 commenting on violence which took place at Clacton between Mods and Rockers.

a Study Source A. Do you think this gives a reliable impression of young people during the 1960s? Use details of the cartoon and your knowledge to explain your answer. **[8 marks]**

Examiner's tip

Many questions will deal with the issue of reliability, though not all will ask about it as directly as this one. Avoid the temptation of answering on the basis of the type of source you are given. Weak students will look at Source A and say that it is not reliable because it is a cartoon, and cartoons are supposed to make people laugh. Such answers ignore the content of the source – what it actually says or shows. Without judging the reliability of the content, you will not get anywhere. Look at the detail of the source – is it over-emotional or using loaded language? Does it make fun of someone, or show them in an unflattering way? These kinds of details can reveal the bias or one-sidedness of a source. One of the best ways of working out whether you can trust a source is to check its details against other information available to you. This may be other sources on the paper, or your own knowledge. This kind of checking is called cross-referencing. Lastly, you can get clues about reliability by considering the purpose of the person who created the source. What impact did the artist who drew this cartoon want to have on his/her audience? Given its purpose, is it likely that this cartoon would give a fair impression of events?

Answering the question

STEP 1 – Identify what it is that the source says about youth in the 1960s. It depicts young people as violent, bored troublemakers.

STEP 2 – Is this a fair and accurate picture of young people in the 1960s? You should know that there were repeated outbreaks of trouble between Mods and Rockers. But was this typical behaviour? And does the cartoon betray bias in its use of irony – does the cartoonist really mean that the person in the cartoon is a poor, suffering victim?

STEP 3 – Would the newspaper have any particular purpose in publishing this cartoon? We know that the development of youth culture during the 1950s and 1960s led to a 'generation gap' between young and old. Perhaps the newspaper would have been happy to appeal to the hostility its readers would have felt towards the young.

Read the following answer. Does it evaluate the reliability of the cartoon both by checking its content (cross-reference) and analysing its audience/purpose?

Student's response

Source A is portraying young people in a negative way. It makes them look ignorant and violent. Obviously there were some who got involved in trouble. The Mods and Rockers got into fights on most Bank Holidays, so the cartoon has some truth. But most young people weren't like that. Another youth movement of the 1960s was all about peace and loving everybody, so those young people would not have caused violence. You can also tell the cartoonist is biased about young people because of the way he makes fun of the Mods and Rockers by claiming they are to be pitied because they are suffering from boredom. By mocking them he shows that his view about young people is unreliable.

Examiner's comment

This is a good answer. It shows detailed contextual knowledge in what it says about the young people in the 1960s, and uses this effectively to undermine the reliability of the cartoon's claims. What it fails to do is move on from this to consider the audience/purpose of the cartoon, although it does detect the use of irony by the cartoonist, which is another indication of bias/unreliability. If it had gone on to say, for example, that a newspaper would probably not publish cartoons that its readers disagreed with, and would therefore have made sure that this cartoon had an anti-youth message, so as both to confirm and to shape the opinions of its readers, then it would have reached the highest level.

Here is another question, this time on immigration.

Study the source and then answer the question which follows.

Source B

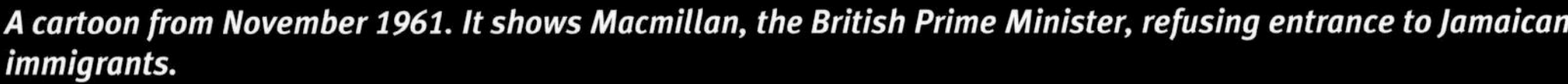

A cartoon from November 1961. It shows Macmillan, the British Prime Minister, refusing entrance to Jamaican immigrants.

b Study Source B. Why do you think this cartoon was published in 1961? Use details of the cartoon and your knowledge to explain your answer. **[7 marks]**

Answering the question

STEP 1 – Identify what the cartoonist was saying, the message he was trying to get across to his audience. As with all cartoons there are several sub-messages; for example, that immigrants are coming to Britain from the Commonwealth. However, it is the main message of the cartoon that you should base your answer upon. This is the idea that Macmillan wishes to restrict non-white immigration.

STEP 2 – Why was this message particularly relevant in 1961? By this time immigration had become a major issue in British politics and the government was under pressure to introduce restrictions. This would lead to the Commonwealth Immigrants Act of 1962.

STEP 3 – Given the message and the context, why did the cartoonist draw this cartoon? By depicting Macmillan as he does, the cartoonist indicates disapproval of the government's policy. The intention of the cartoon is clearly to persuade the reader that the government's policy is wrong, and thus to increase opposition to its plans.

Examiner's tip

There's a question within a question here, and the best answers will succeed in dealing with both aspects. First, why was the cartoon published, and second, why in 1961? It would be possible to answer by dealing with only one of these aspects, but if you do this you will not score highly. Good answers will be based on a sound interpretation of the cartoon. This means identifying the cartoonist's message and, as the question demands, using details of the cartoon to support your interpretation. Once you have done this you will have to address why this message had particular relevance in 1961, which means using your knowledge of what was happening at the time to explain the cartoonist's purpose in representing events in this way.

Student's response

Read the following answer. Does it successfully explain why the cartoon was published, using analysis of its context, message and purpose?

The cartoonist seems to be saying that the government's policy on immigration is unfair. White immigrants are being allowed into Britain but black immigrants are not. This was particularly significant at this time as the government was considering placing legal restrictions on Commonwealth immigration. This cartoon is a comment on the Commonwealth Immigrants Bill which Parliament was considering at this time, so the reason why the cartoon was published at this time was to say that the bill was wrong.

Examiner's comment

This is a methodical and clear answer. It successfully interprets the cartoon and gives a good explanation for why the cartoon was published at that particular time. It would certainly earn a good mark, but to reach the top level it would have to show some awareness of the cartoonist's purpose, such as persuading people that the government was being unfair, and thereby increasing opposition to the Immigration Bill.

This final question deals with the 'Women's Lib' movement.

Study the source and then answer the question which follows

Source C

'..then do the dishes, put the children to bed, and don't let us come home to find you watching Miss World!'

A newspaper cartoon of November 1971, on the day when police searched the headquarters of the Women's Lib movement in London after threats to disrupt the broadcast of the Miss World competition.

c Study Source C. How useful is this picture as evidence about the 'women's lib' movement? Use details of the source and your knowledge to explain your answer. **[8 marks]**

Answering the question

STEP 1 – What does the source show? You can see two women leaving the house with placards, perhaps to take part in a demonstration. They are giving orders to the two men they are leaving in the house. What impressions are you given of the women and the men? Do you get a positive or a negative impression from the cartoon? Let's hope we can all agree that the artist has tried to make the scene humorous, and therefore make fun of attempts by the Women's Lib movement to disrupt the Miss World competition.

STEP 2 – Is the impression of the Women's Lib movement given by the cartoon accurate? If not, we cannot say that the picture is useful as information. Use your knowledge of what the Women's Lib movement involved, and what it was trying to achieve, to judge the reliability of the picture.

Examiner's tip

Questions that deal with the usefulness, or utility, of sources will often be asked on the British Depth Study paper. Basic answers to such questions simply state that the source is useful for the information it provides. Not much better than this are answers that deny a source's usefulness because of what it does not tell you. What these answers miss is any evaluation of the source – any sense of doubting whether it can be trusted or not. If you cannot believe a source, you have to question its usefulness. It cannot be factual information, but perhaps it might still be evidence of something else – maybe as evidence of why or how someone might wish to mislead or misrepresent events. The way in which the characters in the cartoon are represented might well make a difference to how you could use the source as evidence. You should consider the possibility that the humorous nature of the cartoon is a way of trivialising the issues, and that this could indicate the bias of the cartoonist. This is where your knowledge of the topic can come in, to help you judge whether or not the picture is consistent with what you know about the topic. The highest marks in utility questions will always go to answers which do not simply accept the source at face value, but which use source evaluation to judge its usefulness.

STEP 3 – If you decide that the picture is not factually accurate, then ask yourself why the artist might have wanted to represent events in this way. In 1971 the Women's Lib movement was still fairly young, and its ideas were often mocked by men. What possible purposes would the artist have had for wanting to give a negative impression of women's attempts to achieve equality with men? The utility of this source as evidence about the Women's Lib movement is perhaps as evidence of what its opponents thought about it, and the ways in which they fought against it rather than as a factual record of the movement itself.

Student's response

Read the following answer. Does it successfully explain the utility of the source?

The source is not useful about the Women's Lib movement. The reason is that it does not give you any accurate information about the movement. It is just a cartoon drawn by someone who wanted to make fun of women, and to do this it just makes the characters in the cartoon the reverse of what they would be in real life, as if they would be really funny. The cartoonist does not care that women were objecting to the Miss World contest because of the way it treated women and made them appear as sex objects. Instead of taking the issues seriously, the cartoon just makes a cheap joke, so it cannot be useful as evidence.

Examiner's comment

This answer is based on a real understanding of the nature of the source. Its evaluation of the content of the source is very effective, and it would certainly earn a high mark. However, one element is still missing. To get into the top level the answer needs to make it clear what exactly the source is useful for, despite the doubts about its reliability. A sentence concluding that the real utility of the source is as evidence of the way men reacted to the ideas of the Women's Lib movement, rather than as evidence about the movement itself, would have done the trick.

Exam**Café**

Tools and Tips

Right, now you are ready for the exam. Or are you?

What do you need to do to prepare?

Exam Café will help you focus on the skills that you will need to display in order to do well in the exam. There is also a CD-ROM with specific advice for each of the units you will have studied. If you have used Grade Studio and Brain Boost throughout the course, you will already have practised some of the key skills that are vital in revision and the final exam.

Getting started

Remember the purpose of revision is to help you understand content and be able to present it in the right way in the exam.

Revision may seem like a daunting task but if you follow these hints and tips it will seem much more simple.

- Organise your notes before you start; make sure that you have everything that you need.
- Know what you will be tested on in each exam. There are check lists on the CD-ROM which will help you work out what you need for each paper.

- Plan a realistic revision timetable. Remember that history is not the only subject you will need to revise, and you are still allowed to have a social life as well! On the CD-ROM there are examples of how to organise a revision timetable.

- When revising make sure you are in a calm and organised environment. If your desk is messy, you won't be as focused!
- Set yourself realistic targets and divide your time into small sections of about half an hour at a time with lots of breaks and rewards.
- Some people find it helps to revise with a friend and test each other.
- Try not to cram too much in. Pick out key points and summarise the main ideas and events. See your CD-ROM for useful hints on how to summarise.

- Find a revision style that suits you. Everyone is different so don't worry if your friends are revising in a different way to you. If your way works, then stick to it.
- Don't leave everything until the last minute!

There are lots of ways to revise and it is important that you find one that suits you.

On the next page there are some examples of techniques that you might find useful.

Revision

Revision techniques

Mind maps

A mind map is a diagram used to represent key topic ideas branching from a central key word.

Try to use colour, images and short snappy phrases (rather than lots of writing) on your mind map. If you make it look good, you are more likely to remember what's on it.

Flash Cards

Flash cards are good for helping you remember key facts and figures.

Have a question or a clue on one side and all the information you need to remember on the other.

Try to use images, bullet points and mnemonics on your flash cards as these will help you remember things.

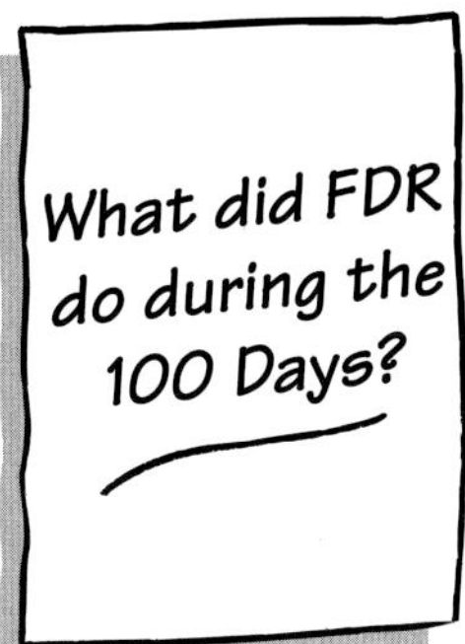

- Fireside chats
- Closed banks
- Reopened trustworthy banks
- Given emergency powers by congress
- Repealed prohibition
- Started alphabet agencies (The New Deal)

Mnemonics

A mnemonic is where you take the first letter of each word you are trying to remember and turn it into a different phrase.

For example:
*P*irate
*V*alery
*H*ates
*J*elly

helps you remember some of the key individuals you will need to know about (Pare, Vesalius, Harvey, Jenner).

You could also add images to help visualise ideas in the exam.

Timelines

A timeline will help you see the 'big picture' in history. By putting all your ideas together chronologically you will be able to see how events link to each other.

Treaty of Versailles — 1919
Failed Uprising, Hitler jailed. Hitler writes *Mein Kampf* — 1923
Wall Street Crash — 1929
Hitler comes to power — 1933

On timelines you can mark turning points and measure progress or change.

You could also colour code topics and key ideas and add images to help you memorise the content.

Exam Preparation

Lesson 1: Unit A971: International Relations

LEARNING OBJECTIVES:

In this lesson, you will:

- familiarise yourself with the types of questions that you will be asked on the International Relations section of Unit A971
- use mark schemes to help you understand what skills the examiner is looking for.

GETTING STARTED

Symbolism is often used in political cartoons. What are the following images symbolic of?

1	2	3	4
A lion	A dove	A swastika	Uncle Sam

In Unit A971 you will be assessed on International Relations. You will have studied two of the following:

- The inter-war years 1919–39
- The Cold War 1945–75
- A new world? 1948–2005

In the section you choose you will have to answer all of question one and then either question two or question three. You must answer all parts of each question you attempt.

Question One

In question one there are two sections. The first is usually a question about the meaning of a source; the second is usually asking you to explain an aspect of a topic you have studied.

There are examples of these questions for every topic on the CD-ROM.

ACTIVITIES

Choose one of the following cartoons and then answer the question below.

A) A cartoon entitled 'Peace and future cannon fodder'.

Clemenceau is saying 'Curious! I seem to hear a child weeping.'

B) A cartoon entitled 'Peep under the Iron Curtain'.

On the wall is written 'No admittance, by order Joe'.
The signpost reads 'Russia'.

C) The caption reads 'Excuse me sir, is this little lady bothering you?'

The lady is labelled 'solidarity' and the mugger is named 'Polish government'.

What is the message of this cartoon? Use the source and your own knowledge to explain your answer. **[7 marks]**

Use the mark scheme below to help you answer this question.

Level	Description	Marks
1	Uses surface features only.	1
2	Says what the cartoon means without supporting ideas.	2–3
3	Says what the cartoon means with supporting detail from either the cartoon or own knowledge.	4–5
4	Says what the cartoon means with supporting detail from the cartoon and own knowledge.	6–7

ExamCafé

Questions Two and Three

These questions tend to have three parts to them.

There are examples of these questions for every topic on the CD-ROM.

Part a

This type of question asks you to describe a key feature or event. These questions tend to be worth four marks, so remember four facts.

You might also get marks for developing or explaining an idea more fully.

Choose one of the following questions to have a go at:		
In what ways did the Treaty of Versailles punish Germany? **[4 marks]**	What happened at the Bay of Pigs invasion of 1961? **[4 marks]**	What were the main aims of the Provisional IRA? **[4 marks]**

Ask someone else to mark your answer. You will get one mark for each relevant point and an additional mark for supporting detail.

Part b

This type of question asks you to explain an aspect of the topic. The skills required in this question are the same as those for question one, part **b**.

Choose one of the following questions to have a go at:		
Explain why the League of Nations failed to deal with Mussolini's invasion of Abyssinia. **[6 marks]**	Explain why Khrushchev sent missiles to Cuba in 1962. **[6 marks]**	Explain how Gorbachev's policies led to the collapse of Soviet control in Eastern Europe. **[6 marks]**

Use the mark scheme below to help you answer this question.

Level	Description	Marks
1	General answer, lacking specific knowledge.	1
2	Identifies and/or describes reasons for the factor or event in question.	2–3
3	Explains reasons for the factor or event. One explained reason. **[3–4 marks]** Two or more explained reasons. **[5–6 marks]**	3–6

Part c

This type of question is a two-sided argument, usually worth ten marks.

You will also be assessed with this type of question in the section on your chosen depth study. There are examples of two-sided argumentative questions on the next two pages.

Lesson 2: Unit A971: Depth Study

There are examples of these questions for every topic on the CD-ROM.

Exam Café

LEARNING OBJECTIVES

In this lesson you will:

- familiarise yourself with the types of questions that you will be asked on the Depth Study section of Unit A971
- use mark schemes to help you understand what skills the examiner is looking for.

GETTING STARTED

Copy and complete the table below to make sure you understand which topics you will be assessed on in Unit A971.

International Relations	1 2
Depth Study	3

The other part of Unit A971 assesses you on your chosen depth study. You will have learnt about one of the following:

- Germany, 1918–45
- Russia, 1905–41
- The USA, 1919–41
- Mao's China, c.1930–76
- Causes and events of the First World War, 1890–1918
- End of Empire, c.1919–69
- The USA, 1945–75: Land of freedom?

In your depth study (section D of the exam) you will be required to answer two complete questions.

You must answer the first question in the depth study section, which is normally based on sources. But the sources are only to prompt your answer and so you should not rely on them too much. You must show off your own knowledge too.

In the first question there are usually three parts. These are some of the types of questions you might get.

Type of question:	How to answer:
You might be referred to a source and asked whether it fully explains the situation.	Use detail from the source and your own knowledge to explain what the source shows. However, you must also use your own knowledge to **explain** any relevant detail that the source does not include.
You might be asked to explain the message of a source. In these questions the source will often be a political cartoon.	**Explain** what the meaning of the cartoon is, supporting your ideas with detail from the cartoon and also your own knowledge of the topic.
You might be asked whether or not a source proves a statement or point of view.	Use detail from the source and your own knowledge to explain what the source shows. However, you must also use your own knowledge to **explain** any relevant detail that the source does not include.

These are just a few examples of the types of questions you might be asked in this section. For specific examples from your depth study have a look at the CD-ROM or the Grade Studio sections included throughout this book.

In the final section of your depth study you will choose between two questions. You must attempt all parts of whichever question you choose.

Part (a) is usually a four-mark description question.

Part (b) is usually a question asking you to explain an aspect of the topic. You have already looked at the skills required for these types of questions in the Exam Café section on International Relations.

Part (c) tends to be a mini argumentative essay and is usually worth ten marks.

ACTIVITIES

Choose one of the following questions to have a go at:

Depth study:	Question:
Germany, 1918–45	'The Weimar Republic was doomed to fail.' To what extent do you agree with this question.
Russia, 1905–41	'Rasputin's involvement with the Russian royal family was the main cause of their downfall.' To what extent do you agree with this statement?
The USA, 1919–41	How successful was the New Deal?
Mao's China, c.1930–76	The following were reasons why China had become a great world power by the time Mao died in 1976: (i) its growing military strength; (ii) its entry into the United Nations Organisation in 1971; (iii) Its increased economic strength. Which of these reasons do you think was the most important? Explain your answer, referring to (i), (ii) and (iii) only.
Causes and events of the First World War, 1890–1918	'Haig mismanaged the Battle of the Somme.' To what extent do you agree with this statement?
End of Empire, c.1919–69	'After the Second World War the most important reason for the growth in nationalism in Kenya was the grievances of Africans regarding land ownership.' To what extent do you agree with this statement?
The USA, 1945–75: Land of freedom?	'Martin Luther King did more for civil rights in America than Malcolm X.' To what extent do you agree with this statement?

HOW TO ANSWER THIS TYPE OF QUESTION

- You need to explain each side of the argument, giving specific evidence from your own knowledge to support your ideas.
- When you have examined all sides of the argument you need to make a judgement. Do you agree with the statement?
- Make sure that when you make your judgement you don't simply repeat what you have already said. Save something new for this paragraph.

Lesson 3: Unit A972: British Depth Study

LEARNING OBJECTIVES

In this lesson you will:

- familiarise yourself with the types of questions that you may be asked on Unit A972
- practise evaluating sources by asking questions about them.

GETTING STARTED

Choose one of the sources below. For each source work out what is happening by asking the following questions:

- When was the source made?
- Who is the source about?
- Where is the source about?
- What is the source about?
- Why was the source made?

Source D

How was British society changed, 1890–1918?

Source E

How far did British society change between 1939 and the mid-1970s?

Remember that Unit A972 is a source-based paper; however, it is also important that you are able to place the sources you are given into historical context, and so you also need to know the topic that you have studied. This will be either:

How was British society changed, 1890–1918?

Or

How far did British society change between 1939 and the mid-1970s?

WHAT TYPE OF QUESTIONS WILL YOU BE ASKED?

The exam will include some background information and a range of sources on a particular topic. You will be asked questions about the sources and what they tell you about the topic you are studying. The exam will mainly test your understanding of the uses and limitations of sources as evidence.

You will often be asked the following types of questions about the sources:

1 What **impression** do they give of a person or event?
2 Whether (and how far) a source is **useful** for an enquiry.
3 Whether a source is **reliable** for an enquiry.
4 Why different sources can say different things about a person or event.
5 What the **purpose** of a source is.
6 How far the sources **support** a particular viewpoint or opinion.

Examiner's tips

Many candidates presume that they will be able to rely on the sources in Unit A972. **Do not make this mistake!** While you may want to prioritise revising for Unit A971, it is still important to know your stuff for Unit A972!

ACTIVITIES

1 Copy out the types of questions listed above.
2 In the boxes below there is advice on how to answer each of the types of source-based question. Can you match them to the types of question?

You will need to say what you can and cannot learn from the source. Use your own knowledge to explain what the source does not show.	You will need to say whether you can trust the source to be giving an accurate or truthful representation of events and explain why you think this.	You will need to use all the sources and say whether they support or do not support the view. Remember to use evidence from the sources to support your ideas and make your own judgement regarding whether or not you agree with the statement in your last paragraph.
You will need to say why a source was made at that particular time. What is it trying to achieve?	You will need to compare what the sources say and explain why you think the authors of the source say these things.	You will need to make inferences about the content in the source, which you must support with evidence.

HOW TO HANDLE SOURCES

Do not be afraid to make notes on the exam paper. You should annotate the sources you are asked about; highlighting any important information either in the source or the contextual information you are given.

Lesson 4: Unit A972: British Depth Study

LEARNING OBJECTIVES

In this lesson you will:

- practise a unit A972-style question
- understand how to structure your responses, using the **P**oint, **E**vidence, **E**xplanation technique.

GETTING STARTED

Copy and complete the following chart to show what topics you will need to know. Remember, you will have only studied one of the time periods, so you only need to copy out one of the columns.

How was British society changed, 1906–18?	How far did British society change between the 1950s and the 1970s?
1	1
2	2
3	3

ACTIVITIES

Read through the following examples of Unit A972-style questions and the answers that the candidate has given.

Think about the how the examiner suggests the candidate could improve their answer and then choose one of the examples to have a go at yourself.

How was British society changed, 1890–1918?

Source F

A photograph showing women working in a munitions factory during the First World War.

How useful is this source to a historian studying why women were given the vote in 1918?

Candidate's answer

This source shows women working in a munitions factory during the First World War. It is useful to a historian studying why women were given the vote as it shows one of the ways that women gained the government's respect enough for them to be given the vote. The picture shows women supporting the war effort by working in factories making supplies for the soldiers on the front line such as the bullets that you can see these women making. When the war broke out the suffragettes halted their campaigns and encouraged women to support the war effort. They held the 'Right to Serve March' which was a large protest in which they aimed to persuade the government that they should be allowed to work in factories (like the one in the photo) in order to support the war effort. By filling vital roles such as this women demonstrated that they were as dedicated to their country as men and so they persuaded the government to let them vote too.

Examiner's comment

This is a good answer with a clear point, evidence (from the source and from the candidate's own knowledge) and explanation. The candidate uses the source for evidence but also places the source into its historical context using their own knowledge.

To improve this answer, the candidate should try to consider what the source does not show, by explaining what other factors helped women to gain the vote.

How far did British society change between 1939 and the mid-1970s?

Source G

A photograph of feminists protesting in London, 1971.

How useful is this source to a historian studying the nature of women's grievances during the 1960s and 1970s?

Candidate's answer

This source is useful to a historian studying the nature of women's grievances during the 1960s and 1970s because it tells us that women were paid less then men. In the photograph one woman is carrying a banner that reads 'Equal pay, no delay' and the women seem to be on a protest march demanding this which shows that they must have been getting paid less then men. From my own knowledge I know that women's salaries were often around half of what a man would get paid for doing exactly the same work. The source is therefore useful in explaining that women felt aggrieved about being paid less than men as this gave them a lower economic standing in society and made it difficult for them to independent.

Examiner's comment

This is a good answer with a clear point, evidence (from the source and from the candidate's own knowledge) and explanation. The candidate uses the source for evidence but also places the source into its historical context using their own knowledge. To improve this answer, candidate should try to consider what the source does not show, by explaining some of the other grievances women had at this time.

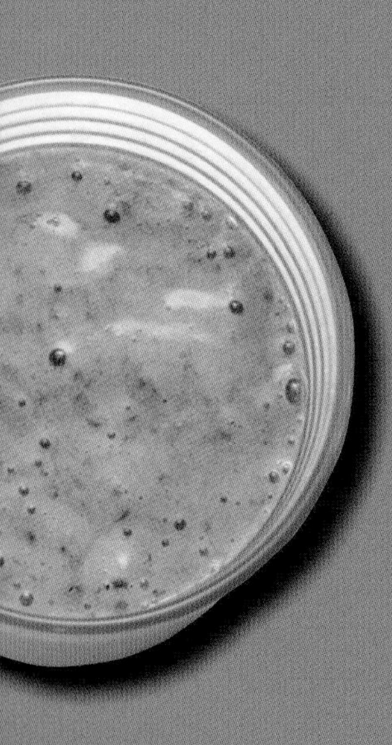

Glossary

Al-Qaeda – an international terrorist organisation which aims for an end to foreign influence in Muslim countries.
Anarchy – a state of chaos and disorder due to lack of government control.
Anti-Semitism – hostility to Jewish people.
Apartheid – a policy of racial segregation.
Armistice – a temporary suspension of hostilities by those at war.
Aryan race – according to Nazi racial theorists, Germans and other 'Nordic' types – tall, lean, athletic, blond and blue-eyed – belonged to a separate and superior race known as the Aryan race.

Bolsheviks – a party led by Lenin which took its name from the Russian word for 'majority'. They believed in seizing power at the first opportunity.
Brezhnev Doctrine – Soviet foreign policy, practised by Leonid Brezhnev, which believed that if one socialist country should fall to capitalism, it is a problem for all socialist countries.
Buffer zone – an area of land between two hostile countries.

Caliphs – heads of state of Islamic communities which are ruled by Islamic religious law.
Capitalism – an economic system in which the means of producing wealth are privately owned and controlled rather than publicly.
Chicano – an American of Mexican descent.
Coalition – two or more parties that share power in government.
Collectivisation – process whereby the state organises all land and labour into collective farms, sets targets and takes all the produce.
Conscientious objectors – men who refused to fight because of their anti-war beliefs.
Conscription – compulsory military service.

Defoliate – strip all foliage from trees.
Democracy – a political system in which the people exercise power through elected representatives.
Diktat – the peace imposed on the Germans by the Allies at the end of the First World War.
Disarmament – the act of reducing, limiting, or abolishing weapons.
Discrimination – giving prejudicial treatment to either a person or a group.

Eastern bloc – A term used during the Cold War to describe the Soviet Union and the countries it controlled.
Egalitarianism – political belief that all people should be treated as equals.
Espionage – the use of spies by governments to discover the secrets of other nations.

Fedayeen – a term used to describe militant groups formed from within the Palestinian refugee population.
Freikorps – (free corps) volunteer soldiers who bitterly opposed communism.
Friendly fire – fire during wartime from one's own side or allied forces.

Gaza – the largest city in the Gaza Strip and the Palestinian territories.
Ghetto – part of a town or city, usually very poor, occupied by a minority group such as the Jews.
Glasnost – Russian term for greater openness and transparency in Soviet government.
Grassroots – ordinary people who are the main body of an organisation's membership.
Guomindang/Kuomindang – Chinese Nationalist Party, which was the main political rival to the Chinese Communist Party.
Guru – a Hindu or Sikh religious teacher.

Hamas – created in 1987 as an Islamic paramilitary organisation and political party.
Hyperinflation – a very extreme increase in prices.
Hypocrisy – being insincere by pretending to have qualities or beliefs not really held.

Ideology – a set of ideas that people agree with.
Imperialism – extending the rule of an empire over foreign countries, or belief in the importance of your empire.
Indigenous – belonging to an ethnic group which is native to a particular area.
Insurgent – someone who is involved in a violent uprising, lacking the organisation of a revolution, against a sovereign government.
Iron curtain – a metaphor used by Churchill to describe the post-war division of Europe.

Jim Crow Laws – laws enforcing racial segregation, named after a character in an old song popularised by the comedian 'Daddy' Rice. Rice ridiculed black people and the way they spoke.

Kibbutzim – collective communities in Israel that were traditionally based on agriculture.
Kindertransport – rescue mission in which the United Kingdom took in nearly 10,000 predominantly Jewish children from Nazi Germany and Nazi-occupied territories.
Kolkhoz – a collective farm where all produce was handed over to the government.
Ku Klux Klan – secretive white supremacist organisation that terrorised and murdered black people, Jews and people from other minority groups.
Kurd – An Iranian-speaker who lives in Kurdistan. Most Kurds are officially Muslim.

Legitimate – legally allowed.
Leprosy – a disease characterised by patches of altered skin and nerve tissue (lesions) that gradually spread to cause muscle weakness, deformaties and paralysis.

Maoist – belief in the thoughts of Mao Zedong.
Marshall Plan – American aid that was aimed at ending hunger and poverty.
Martial law – a system of rules during times when the military is in charge.
Marxists – followers of Karl Marx's theory that social change could only happen after a violent struggle between the ruling capitalist class and the workers.

Mensheviks – a party that took its name from the Russian word for 'majority', although its support increased in later years. The Mensheviks believed in co-operating with other groups to improve the lives of working people.
Militarism – the principle of maintaining a large and aggressive fighting force.
Missionary – someone who travels to another country in order to spread the word of God.
Monopoly – exclusive control of trade in a commodity, such as grain, or a service.
Mujahideen – Muslims who are fighting in a holy war.

Napalm – a jelly-like substance consisting of petrol thickened by special soaps.
Nationalism – strong belief in the power of your own country.
National Front – a British political party mostly active during the 1970s and 1980s, which was widely considered to be racist.
NKVD – the secret police under Stalin's regime.

Oath of allegiance – the German army swore this to Hitler in 1934: they will do what he wants.
Okhrana – the Tsar's secret police.

Partition – an attempt to resolve political disputes through the drawing of territorial boundaries.
Perestroika – Russian term for the restructuring of the Soviet economy.
Plebiscite – a referendum, when all electors can vote on an important issue.
Prague Spring – period between January and August 1968 where the Czechoslovak government tried to give its citizens more political rights.
Prejudice – a pre-determined feeling, either favourable or unfavourable.
Proletarian – relating to working-class people.
Propaganda – production of material to strongly promote one opinion.
Putsch – an attempt to overthrow the government.

Quota – a number or percentage, especially of people, constituting or designated as an upper limit.
Qur'an – central religious text of Islam.

Racism – the belief that race accounts for differences in human character or ability, and that a particular race is superior to others.
Radical – someone who holds an extreme viewpoint.
Reconnaissance – military observation to discover useful information.
Red Army – Communist Army (especially in Civil War).
Referendum – direct vote in which the people are asked to either accept or reject a particular proposal.
Reichstag – the German lower house of representatives (similar to our House of Commons).
Reparations – compensation for war damage paid by a defeated state.
Republic – a country without monarchy.

Sanctions – limits placed by one country on another.
Satellite states – smaller countries that look to a bigger one for protection and trade.
Segregation – the practice of separating people on the grounds of race, sex or religion, for example in schools and public or commercial facilities.
Sharecropper – a tenant farmer who gives a share of each crop to the landowner as rent.
Solidarity – a non-communist Polish trade union federation.
Soviet – an elected workers' council.
Sovkhoz – a state-run farm where produce was handed over to the government in return for wages.
Sparticists – communist group led by Luxemburg and Liebknecht, which took part in a failed uprising in 1919.
Speakeasies – illicit or unlicensed establishments selling alcoholic beverages in secret.
Stalemate – a situation in which neither side can make progress.

Taliban – the organisation which ruled most of Afghanistan during 1996–2001.
Totalitarian – a system in which the government controls every aspect of its citizens' lives.
Transvaal – a republic in the north of South Africa which was colonised by Boer settlers in the 1830s and 1840s.
Tripartite System – education system which divided secondary schools into grammar schools, technical schools, and modern schools.

Ultimatum – a final, uncompromising demand or set of terms, which if rejected could lead to the use of force.

Vietcong – Vietnamese guerilla army.
Vietnamisation – policy of letting Vietnamese fight their own war (Nixon).
Vigilante – a person who takes the law into their own hands.

Warlord – a military commander exercising civil power in a region, whether in nominal allegiance to the national government or in defiance of it.
Welfare State – system of measures designed to ensure a basic minimum standard of living for all.
West Bank – a landlocked territory on the west bank of the Jordan River in the Middle East.

Zemstvo – local council.

THE BROXBOURNE SCHOOL
LIBRARY RESOURCE CENTRE

Single User Licence Agreement: OCR GCSE History B Modern World History ActiveBook CD-ROM

Warning:

This is a legally binding agreement between You (the user or purchasing institution) and Pearson Education Limited of Edinburgh Gate, Harlow, Essex, CM20 2JE, United Kingdom ('PEL').

By retaining this Licence, any software media or accompanying written materials or carrying out any of the permitted activities You are agreeing to be bound by the terms and conditions of this Licence. If You do not agree to the terms and conditions of this Licence, do not continue to use the OCR GCSE History B Modern World History ActiveBook CD-ROM and promptly return the entire publication (this Licence and all software, written materials, packaging and any other component received with it) with Your sales receipt to Your supplier for a full refund.

Intellectual Property Rights:

This **OCR GCSE History B Modern World History ActiveBook CD-ROM** consists of copyright software and data. All intellectual property rights, including the copyright is owned by PEL or its licensors and shall remain vested in them at all times. You only own the disk on which the software is supplied. If You do not continue to do only what You are allowed to do as contained in this Licence you will be in breach of the Licence and PEL shall have the right to terminate this Licence by written notice and take action to recover from you any damages suffered by PEL as a result of your breach.

The PEL name, PEL logo and all other trademarks appearing on the software and OCR GCSE History B Modern World History ActiveBook CD-ROM are trademarks of PEL. You shall not utilise any such trademarks for any purpose whatsoever other than as they appear on the software and OCR GCSE History B Modern World History ActiveBook CD-ROM.

Yes, You can:

1 use this OCR GCSE History B Modern World History ActiveBook CD-ROM on Your own personal computer as a single individual user. You may make a copy of the OCR GCSE History B Modern World History ActiveBook CD-ROM in machine readable form for backup purposes only. The backup copy must include all copyright information contained in the original.

No, You cannot:

1 copy this OCR GCSE History B Modern World History ActiveBook CD-ROM (other than making one copy for back-up purposes as set out in the Yes, You can table above);
2 alter, disassemble, or modify this OCR GCSE History B Modern World History ActiveBook CD-ROM, or in any way reverse engineer, decompile or create a derivative product from the contents of the database or any software included in it;
3 include any materials or software data from the OCR GCSE History B Modern World History ActiveBook CD-ROM in any other product or software materials;
4 rent, hire, lend, sub-licence or sell the OCR GCSE History B Modern World History ActiveBook CD-ROM;
5 copy any part of the documentation except where specifically indicated otherwise;
6 use the software in any way not specified above without the prior written consent of PEL;
7 subject the software, OCR GCSE History B Modern World History ActiveBook CD-ROM or any PEL content to any derogatory treatment or use them in such a way that would bring PEL into disrepute or cause PEL to incur liability to any third party.

Grant of Licence:

PEL grants You, provided You only do what is allowed under the 'Yes, You can' table above, and do nothing under the 'No, You cannot' table above, a non-exclusive, non-transferable Licence to use this OCR GCSE History B Modern World History ActiveBook CD-ROM.

The terms and conditions of this Licence become operative when using this OCR GCSE History B Modern World History ActiveBook CD-ROM.

Limited Warranty:

PEL warrants that the disk or CD-ROM on which the software is supplied is free from defects in material and workmanship in normal use for ninety (90) days from the date You receive it. This warranty is limited to You and is not transferable.

This limited warranty is void if any damage has resulted from accident, abuse, misapplication, service or modification by someone other than PEL. In no event shall PEL be liable for any damages whatsoever arising out of installation of the software, even if advised of the possibility of such damages. PEL will not be liable for any loss or damage of any nature suffered by any party as a result of reliance upon or reproduction of any errors in the content of the publication.

PEL does not warrant that the functions of the software meet Your requirements or that the media is compatible with any computer system on which it is used or that the operation of the software will be unlimited or error free. You assume responsibility for selecting the software to achieve Your intended results and for the installation of, the use of and the results obtained from the software.

PEL shall not be liable for any loss or damage of any kind (except for personal injury or death) arising from the use of this OCR GCSE History B Modern World History ActiveBook CD-ROM or from errors, deficiencies or faults therein, whether such loss or damage is caused by negligence or otherwise.

The entire liability of PEL and your only remedy shall be replacement free of charge of the components that do not meet this warranty.

No information or advice (oral, written or otherwise) given by PEL or PEL's agents shall create a warranty or in any way increase the scope of this warranty.

To the extent the law permits, PEL disclaims all other warranties, either express or implied, including by way of example and not limitation, warranties of merchantability and fitness for a particular purpose in respect of this OCR GCSE History B Modern World History ActiveBook CD-ROM.

Termination:

This Licence shall automatically terminate without notice from PEL if You fail to comply with any of its provisions or the purchasing institution becomes insolvent or subject to receivership, liquidation or similar external administration. PEL may also terminate this Licence by notice in writing. Upon termination for whatever reason You agree to destroy the OCR GCSE History B Modern World History ActiveBook CD-ROM and any back-up copies and delete any part of the OCR GCSE History B Modern World History ActiveBook CD-ROM stored on your computer.

Governing Law:

This Licence will be governed by and construed in accordance with English law.

© Pearson Education Limited 2009